Sufism in an Age of Transition

Islamic History and Civilization

VOLUME 71

Sufism in an Age of Transition

ʿUmar al-Suhrawardī and the Rise of the Islamic Mystical Brotherhoods

By

Erik S. Ohlander

BRILL

LEIDEN • BOSTON
2008

On the cover: Anonymous, *Ṣāḥib silsila al-Suhrawardī*. MS. in private collection (Lahore), fol. 97.

This book is printed on acid-free paper.

Library of Congress Cataloging-in-Publication Data

A C.I.P. record for this book is available from the Library of Congress.

ISSN 0929-2403
ISBN 978 90 04 16355 3

PRINTED IN THE NETHERLANDS

For my family

CONTENTS

LIST OF ILLUSTRATIONS

Charts

Tables

ACKNOWLEDGMENTS

This book could not have been written without the generous support of numerous individuals and institutions. First, I would like to thank my teachers at the University of Michigan, Ann Arbor, who helped me conceive the initial work on which this study is based: Kathryn Babayan, Michael Bonner, Juan R.I. Cole and, especially, Alexander Knysh, whom I am certain could have easily written another book of his own in the time he chose to spend preparing me to write my own. The initial research for this project was made possible through the financial support of the Department of Near Eastern Studies, the Horace H. Rackham School of Graduate Studies, and the Center for Middle Eastern and North African Studies at the University of Michigan. Similarly, I would like to thank the American Research Institute in Turkey, Istanbul, and my friends in the İlâhiyat Fakültesi of Marmara University for their hospitality, as well as the Süleymaniye, Köprülü, and Beyazıt Devlet Libraries for providing me with access to their collections. The same goes for the many libraries at home and abroad whose collections I utilized in preparing this work. I would also like to thank my colleagues and students at Indiana University—Purdue University, Fort Wayne, for creating a pleasant environment in which to write this book, the Purdue Research Foundation for a Summer Faculty Grant which allowed me to finish it, Trudy Kamperveen at Brill for her efforts in helping to actualize it, and a certain anonymous reviewer for helping me to polish it. A special debt of gratitude is owed to the many colleagues and friends who have aided or encouraged in various ways over the long course of this project; you know who you are. All faults, of course, remain mine and mine alone. Finally, I would like to thank my wife Tara, whose extraordinary patience borders on the sublime.

A NOTE ON TRANSLITERATION AND DATING

In keeping with recent English-language scholarship in Islamic studies, the transliteration of Arabic, Persian, Turkish, and Urdu words generally follows the simplified scheme derived from the *Encyclopaedia of Islam* used in the *International Journal of Middle Eastern Studies* with two main exceptions. First, names, titles, and words of Turco-Mongol origin are rendered in modern Turkish orthography whenever possible. Second, although the vast majority of the sources employed in this study were written in Arabic, I have not let that eclipse the presence of the other languages in which al-Suhrawardī, his teachers, students, disciples, and later biographers wrote or spoke, and thus have made some allowances for the orthography and pronunciation of Persian and Urdu. For those words, place names, and titles which have become significantly anglicized, deference has been made to *The Unabridged Oxford English Dictionary*. Naturally, such words are not italicized. In the case of Arabic personal names, the definite article *al-* is not alphabetized. As pre-modern (and most modern) Muslim historiographers use only the Islamic lunar calendar for dating, dates are given first according to the *hijrī* calendar and then in Common Era (Gregorian calendar), separated by a slash. Thus, the 1st of Muḥarram, 632—which corresponds to the 26th of September, 1234—would be given as 1 Muḥarram, 632/26 September, 1234. Bibliographic references to materials published in Iran note the Iranian-Islamic *shamsī* year with the abbreviation sh. followed by the corresponding Gregorian year in brackets.

ABBREVIATIONS

Primary Sources

AdM	Abū ʾl-Najīb al-Suhrawardī, *Kitāb ādāb al-murīdīn*
AH	ʿUmar al-Suhrawardī, *Aʿlām al-hudā wa-ʿaqīdat arbāb al-tuqā*
ʿAM	ʿUmar al-Suhrawardī, *ʿAwārif al-maʿārif*
AMKh	ʿUmar al-Suhrawardī, *Ajwibat ʿan masāʾil baʿḍ aʾimmat Khurāsān*
BN	Ibn Kathīr, *al-Bidāya wa-l-nihāya fī ʾl-taʾrīkh*
DhR	Abū Shāma al-Maqdisī, *Dhayl ʿalā ʾl-rawḍatayn*
DhTB	Ibn al-Najjār, *Dhayl Taʾrīkh Baghdād*
GE	R. Gramlich (trans.), *Die Gaben der Erkenntnisse des ʿUmar as-Suhrawardī*
GhṬ	ʿAbd al-Qādir al-Jīlānī, *al-Ghunya li-ṭālibī ṭarīq al-ḥaqq*
HT	ʿUmar al-Suhrawardī, *Hudā al-ṭālibīn wa-miṣbāḥ al-sālikīn*
IrM	ʿUmar al-Suhrawardī, *Irshād al-murīdīn wa-injād al-ṭālibīn*
JM	Ibn al-Sāʿī, *al-Jāmiʿ al-mukhtaṣar fī ʿunwān al-tawārīkh wa-ʿuyūn al-siyar*
JQb	ʿUmar al-Suhrawardī, *Jadhdhāb al-qulūb ilā mawāṣilat al-maḥbūb*
KF	ʿUmar al-Suhrawardī, *Kashf al-faḍāʾiḥ al-yūnāniyya wa-rashf al-naṣāʾiḥ al-īmāniyya*
KḤ	(pseudo-)Ibn al-Fuwaṭī, *Kitāb al-ḥawādith*
KM	Hujwīrī, *Kashf al-maḥjūb*
KT	Ibn al-Athīr, *al-Kāmil fī ʾl-taʾrīkh*
KW	al-Ṣafadī, *Kitāb al-wāfī bi-l-wafayāt*
LTA	Ibn al-Athīr, *al-Lubāb fī tahdhīb al-ansāb*
MA	N. Pūrjavādī, ed. *Majmūʿa-yi āthār-i Abū ʿAbd al-Raḥmān al-Sulamī*
MJ	al-Yāfiʿī, *Mirʾāt al-jinān wa-ʿibrat al-yaqẓān*
MS	Tashköpruzāde, *Miftāḥ al-saʿāda wa-maṣābiḥ al-siyāda*
MT	Ibn al-Jawzī, *al-Muntaẓam fī taʾrīkh al-mulūk wa-l-umam*
MZ	Sibṭ Ibn al-Jawzī, *Mirʾāt al-zamān fī taʾrīkh al-aʿyān*
NZ	Ibn Taghrībirdī, *al-Nujūm al-ẓāhira fī mulūk miṣr wa-l-qāhira*
PGB	Najm al-Dīn Rāzī Dāya, *Mirṣād*; H. Algar (trans.), *The Path of God's Bondsmen*
ShDh	Ibn al-ʿImād, *Shadharāt al-dhahab fī akhbār man dhahab*

SL	Abū Naṣr al-Sarrāj, *K. al-luma'*; R. Gramlich (trans.), *Schlaglichter über das Sufitum*
SN	al-Dhahabī, *Siyar a'lām al-nubalā'*
SQ	al-Qusharyī, *Risāla*; R. Gramlich (trans.), *Das Sendschreiben al-Qušayris über das Sufitum*
ṬFSh	Ibn Kathīr, *Ṭabaqāt al-fuqahā' al-shāfi'iyīn*
ṬFSh²	Ibn Qāḍī Shuhba, *Ṭabaqāt al-fuqahā' al-shāfi'iyya*
TIbW	Ibn al-Wardī, *Ta'rīkh Ibn al-Wardī*
TIr	Ibn al-Mustawfī, *Ta'rīkh Irbil*
TIsl	al-Dhahabī, *Ta'rīkh al-islām wa-wafayāt al-mashāhīr wa-l-a'lām*
TMA	Ibn al-Fuwaṭī, *Talkhīṣ majma' al-ādāb fī mu'jam al-alqāb*
ṬSh	al-Isnawī, *Ṭabaqāt al-shāfi'iyya*
ṬShK	al-Subkī, *Ṭabaqāt al-shāfi'iyya al-kubrā*
TW	al-Mundhirī, *al-Takmila li-wafayāt al-naqala*
WA	Ibn Khallikān, *Wafayāt al-a'yān wa-abnā' al-zamān*

Secondary Sources

BSOAS	*Bulletin of the School of Oriental and African Studies*
EI¹	*Encyclopaedia of Islam*, First Edition
EI²	*Encyclopaedia of Islam*, Second Edition
EIr	*Encyclopaedia Iranica*
GAL	C. Brockelmann, *Geschichte der Arabischen Litteratur*
IJMES	*International Journal of Middle East Studies*
JAOS	*Journal of the American Oriental Society*
JIS	*Journal of Islamic Studies*
JMIAS	*Journal of the Muhyiddin Ibn 'Arabī Society*
JRAS	*Journal of the Royal Asiatic Society*
JSAI	*Jerusalem Studies in Arabic and Islam*
JSS	*Journal of Semitic Studies*
MIDEO	*Mélanges de l'Institut Dominicain d'Études Orientales du Caire*
Naṣ.	A. Hartmann, *An-Naṣir li-Dīn Allah. Politik, Religion, Kultur in der späten 'Abbāsidenzeit*
REI	*Revue des Études Islamiques*
RSO	*Rivista degli Studi Orientali*
StI	*Studia Islamica*
Suh.	'Ā'isha Yūsuf al-Manā'ī, *Abū Ḥafṣ 'Umar al-Suhrawardī: ḥayātuhu wa-taṣawwufuhu*
TDVİA	*Türkiye Diyanet Vakfi İslâm Ansiklopedisi*

WZKM	*Wiener Zeitschrift für die Kunde des Morgenlandes*
ZDMG	*Zeitschrift der Deutschen Morgenländischen Gesellschaft*

Manuscript Collections

C.B.	The Chester Beatty Library, Dublin
Köp.	Köprülü Library, Istanbul
Süley.	Süleymaniye Library, Istanbul
Tüb.	Universitätsbibliothek, Tübingen

Miscellaneous Abbreviations

fol.	folio/folios (a = recto; b = verso)
Ijz.	*ijāza* ('license')
K.	*kitāb* ('book')
MS.	manuscript
R.	*risāla* ('epistle')
W.	*waṣiyya* ('testament')

INTRODUCTION

Over the course of the 6th/12th and early-7th/13th centuries, a not entirely disparate group of charismatic Sufi masters began to emerge across the Abode of Islam: ʿAbd al-Qādir al-Jīlānī (d. 561/1166) and Aḥmad al-Rifāʿī (d. 578/1182) in Iraq, Najm al-Dīn Kubrā in Transoxiana (d. 617/1220), Muʿīn al-Dīn Chishtī (d. 633/1236) in India, Abū ʾl-Ḥasan ʿAlī al-Shādhilī (d. 656/1258) in North Africa, and, in the heart of the old imperial capital of Baghdad, Shihāb al-Dīn Abū Ḥafṣ ʿUmar b. Muḥammad al-Suhrawardī (539–632/1144 or 1145–1234). Although each of these Sufis had much in common, their most significant affinity lay in their names being ever thereafter inextricably linked with a complex of social, religious, and cultural trends subsumed under the rubric of what is generally identified as a fundamental institution of Islamic mysticism following the Mongol invasions of the 7th/13th century: the Sufi order, or *ṭarīqa* (pl. *ṭuruq*), particular 'initiatory ways' associated with the teachings of an eponymous Sufi master reflexively 'passed down' by his spiritual, and in no small number of cases blood, heirs to their own confraternity of disciples and, in an oftentimes divaricating fashion, they to theirs in a manner strikingly similar to the Zen Buddhist lineages of pre- and early-modern Japan or the *shoshalot* of the Hasidim.

Although a good deal has been written on the history of Sufism as a system of thought, its teachers and theorists, major personalities, literary productions, and general presence in Islamic social, cultural and intellectual history over time and space, the processes which contributed to the emergence of the earliest *ṭarīqa* lineages, however, are still not well understood. Simply put, our collective understanding of the nature, scope, and factors behind the institutionalizing drive in medieval Sufism—and the eventual fraternalization of formerly decentralized Sufi *ṭarīqa*s into transnational fraternities over the course of the late 9th/15th to the 12th/18th centuries—is, to put it mildly, defective and uneven. In large part, this can be attributed to the simple fact that many of the key personalities involved in the process have not yet been thoroughly examined, partially as a result of the (now largely abandoned) paradigm of classicism and decline, and partially as a result of the (still quite vigorous) tendency to privilege Sufism's mystico-philosophic content over and against reading it as part and parcel of the broader historical patterns informing pre-modern Islamic societies. It is of course a platitude to fault either the personal predilections of previous generations of Orientalists or the ideological and institutional biases which promoted such neglect,[1] but this is certainly a curious state of affairs considering that it is the Sufi brotherhoods and not Sufism's 'classical' theoretical and literary heritage which come to mind when the word '*taṣawwuf*' is evoked in contemporary Islamic contexts.

When it is mentioned, in large part accounts of the genesis and development of *ṭarīqa*-based Sufism between the 6th/12th–9th/15th centuries as we find them in the standard textbooks on the history of Sufism generally are less than satisfactory. In her now classic *Mystical Dimensions of Islam*, for instance, the late Annemarie Schimmel offered a cursory reading of the development of *ṭarīqa*-based Sufism, saying that: "it must have been a response to an inner need of the community that was not being met spiritually by the scholasticism of orthodox theologians; people craved a more intimate and personal relationship with God and with the Prophet", the Sufi brotherhoods literally "converting Sufism into a mass movement—a movement in which the high ambitions of the classical Sufis were considerably watered down."[2] Similar appraisals were offered earlier by A.J. Arberry in a chapter of his introduction to Sufism entitled "The Decay of Sufism", and by G.C. Anawati and Louis Gardet, Marjian Molé, and Fazlur Rahman just to cite the most representative.[3]

---

[1] On the construction of 'Oriental mysticism' generally, see: Richard King, *Orientalism and Religion: Postcolonial Theory, India and the 'Mystic East'* (London: Routledge, 1999), esp. 7–35. James Morris makes a similar appraisal in his "Situating Islamic 'Mysticism': Between Written Traditions and Popular Spirituality," in *Mystics of the Book: Themes, Topics, and Typologies*, ed. Robert A. Herrera (New York: Peter Lang Publishing, Inc., 1993), 293–333 (esp. 308–310). On the colonial construction of Sufism as an object of study and its modern repercussions, the comments of Carl Ernst are insightful (*The Shambhala Guide to Sufism* [Boston & London: Shambhala, 1997], 1–18; and, idem, "Between Orientalism and Fundamentalism: Problematizing the Teaching of Sufism," in *Teaching Islam*, ed. Brannon Wheeler [New York: Oxford University Press, 2003]: 108–123).

[2] Annemarie Schimmel, *Mystical Dimensions of Islam* (Chapel Hill, NC: University of North Carolina Press, 1975), 231, 239.

[3] A.J. Arberry, *Sufism: An Account of the Mystics of Islam* (London: George Allen & Unwin, Ltd., 1950), 119–133; Georges Anawati and Louis Gardet, *Mystique musulmane*, 4th ed. (Paris: J. Vrin, 1986), 66–73; Marjian Molé, *Les mystiques musulmans* (Paris: Presses Universitaires de France, 1965), 119–122; and, Fazlur Rahman, *Islam*, 2nd ed. (Chicago: The University of Chicago Press, 1979), 150–166.

In recent years, an ambitious group of French scholars have set out to reevaluate the phenomenon of *ṭarīqa*-based Sufism, most notably the history of the Sufi orders in their diverse regional and sectarian contexts.[4] In large part, however, the focus of this body of work concerns the articulation of *ṭarīqa*-based Sufism following the age in which the eponyms of the major *ṭarīqa* lineages lived and worked, and makes no comprehensive historiographical or theoretical revisions to older paradigms concerning the development, rise, and diffusion of the early *ṭarīqa* lineages. For this, scholars of Sufism must still seek recourse with the standard, and still very influential, models of J. Spencer Trimingham and Marshall G.S. Hodgson, two accounts which despite their age still play a significant role in informing scholarship relating to the rise, development, spread, and social and political significance of *ṭarīqa*-based Sufism from the 6th/12th century forward.

Predicated on a three-tiered model, Trimingham's reading of this development posits that the history of the Sufi orders should be seen as occurring in three distinct stages, namely: 1) the '*khānaqāh* stage' which came to prominence in the 4th/10th century and which was characterized by an individualistic and elitist master and a circle of pupils, frequently itinerant and having little or no communal regulation; 2) the '*ṭarīqa* stage', or formative period, of the 6th/12th–9th/15th century, a largely bourgeois movement characterized by the appearance of *silsila-ṭarīqa*s and the conforming of the original mystical spirit to a new organized standard of tradition and legalism; and, 3) the '*ṭā'ifa* stage' which began in the 9th/15th century with the consolidation of Ottoman hegemony and was characterized by the transmission of an allegiance alongside the proliferation of new sub-orders within existing *ṭarīqa* lines.[5] Trimingham qualified his typology, however, positing that it gives the impression of a precision which did not exist and is no more than a generalization of trends, for as he quite rightly points out in the final stage the three in one way or another continued to exist contemporaneously. Although his typology had been much criticized

[4] Most notably the collective volumes edited by Alexandre Popovic and Gilles Veinstein: *Les ordres mystiques dans l'islam: cheminements et situation actuelle* (Paris: Éditions de l'École des Hautes Études en Sciences Sociales, 1986); and, *Les voies d'Allah: Les ordres mystiques dans le monde musulman des origines à aujourd'hui* (Paris: Librairie Arthème Fayard, 1996).

[5] J. Spencer Trimingham, *The Sufi Orders in Islam* (Oxford: Oxford University Press, 1971).

due to its inescapable reliance on a theory of classicism and decline,[6] no comprehensive alternative has yet been proposed, and when applied to the question of the formative period, especially to the particular geographical boundaries framing the activities of early eponymic Sufi masters such as Suhrawardī, still serves as useful a purpose.

Similarly, the model of Hodgson. Set within the broader world-historical vision structuring his masterful *The Venture of Islam*, he saw the rise and development the Sufi orders and their associated institutions as a natural synthesis between the community-oriented, legalist, world-affirming *jamāʿī-sunnī* communalism and world-denying modes of religiosity characteristic of the High Caliphal Period (692–945 CE), coming, during the first centuries of the Earlier Middle Period (945–1258 CE), to "dominate religious life not only within the Jamâʿî-Sunnî fold, but to a lesser extent even among Shîʿîs."[7] In his reading, Hodgson identifies a number of psycho-social causes which allowed for *ṭarīqa*-based Sufism to attain such a position: 1) the mystical orientation is able to sanction elements of religious life downgraded by a strong kerygmatic moralism; 2) mysticism in general, once socially validated as an acceptable life-orientational mode, is able to accommodate the ordinary sphere of human activity; and, 3) in articulating a socially conscious activism, the populist outlook which the Sufis inherited from the Ḥadīth Folk fulfilled the old Irano-Semitic dream of "a pure life over and against the injustice that seemed built into city life on the agrarianate level."

According to Hodgson, the 'human outreach' we find in Sufi masters such as Suhrawardī, predicated as it was on a generally tolerant attitude towards diversity and a comprehensive humanity, gave the Sufi tradition a decisive advantage over other forms of religiosity within the Abode of Islam and when combined with the institutional forms which it took, constituted an ideal vehicle for a ranging public outreach. The 'keynote' of the whole system was the master-disciple relationship and it was the Sufi master who constituted the center of gravity around which *ṭarīqa*-based Sufism was organized. In their capacity to reach out to the masses, Sufi shaykhs and the institutions which housed them were able

[6] See especially Frederick de Jong's review in *JSS* 12.2 (1972): 279–285, as well as the comments of Carl Ernst and Bruce Lawrence in *Sufi Martyrs of Love: The Chishti Order in South Asia and Beyond* (New York: Palgrave Macmillan, 2002), 11–13.

[7] The following synopsis is drawn from Marshall G.S. Hodgson, *The Venture of Islam: Conscience and History in a World Civilization* (Chicago: University of Chicago Press, 1974), 2:201–254.

to bring a whole new audience within the Sufi fold, the result being that an even larger "clientèle than those interested in either preaching or dhikr was sooner or later brought into the Sufi orbit", finding in the figure of the holy Sufi *pīr*, especially after his death, both an intercessor and source of blessing. As Hodgson puts it, this tradition of "intensive interiorization re-exteriorized its results and was finally able to provide an important basis for social order", allowing for an increased expression of popular piety such as, to take a typical example, the acceptable Islamicization of local pre-Islamic shrines.

As to the success of *ṭarīqa*-based Sufism vis-à-vis Sunni *sharīʿa*-mindedness, Hodgson points towards the prominent trend of positing a close relationship between *sharʿī* and Sufi modes of religiosity, saying that in representing the inner side (*bāṭin*) of Islam as a natural complement to its outer form (*ẓāhir*), Sufism was allowed a measure of autonomy. In turn, the spread of *ṭarīqa*-based Sufism, predicated as it was on an increasingly international network of interconnected institutions, is explained by Hodgson as being rooted in: 1) the Sufis' natural tolerance of local differences and their sensitivity to the *Sitz im Leben* of socio-cultural diversity; 2) the manner in which Sufism was able to provide for the maintenance of local forms of authority and legitimacy; and, 3) the supplementation and/or replacement of older forms of unity and order (such as the old caliphal bureaucracy) with a "comprehensive spiritual hierarchy of pîrs". Embracing all levels of society, the popularization of *ṭarīqa*-based Sufism during this period thus secured its continued existence as a mainstay of the Islamicate social order during the Later Middle Period (1258–1503 CE).

As with his reading of other trends in the development of Islamicate societies during the Middle Periods, however, Hodgson's conclusions are subject to refinement and correction. While it is clear, for instance, that in certain settings formalized networks of Sufi masters came to provide for the maintenance of local forms of authority and legitimacy, and that in their capacity to reach out to the masses, Sufi shaykhs such as Suhrawardī and the institutions which housed them came to accommodate an increasingly diverse population of affiliates and, as centers of social integration, came to provide a basis for social order, Hodgson's reading of those processes which led to the rise of the early *ṭarīqa* lineages and the increasing institutionalization of Sufism does not adequately account for the (perhaps not overtly apparent) socio-political, cultural, and religious trends which informed and ultimately sustained it. This, of course, cannot be attributed to a lack of historical insight on

Hodgson's part, but rather the lack of adequate sources at his disposal. It is here where studies such as this one intervene.

As evinced in the very *raison d'être* of this book, ultimately it is only through the systematic production of detailed, contextualized historical studies of the main actors who participated in the rise of institutionalized *ṭarīqa*-based Sufism, and then their comparison as case studies, which will allow us to advance broader synthetic conclusions on the nature and scope of the topic. In turn, if they are to serve as the sources upon which a comprehensive picture of the blossoming of *ṭarīqa*-based Sufism during Hodgson's Later Middle Period are to be built, then such studies must also take into account both the broader sweep of the historical moments in which they transpired as well as the social, political, institutional, religious, and textual genealogies informing them. As will be shown over the course of this book, in the case of the moment which gave birth to the project of Suhrawardī and his disciples, there were certain forces at play which both Trimingham and Hodgson ultimately overlooked, among others the systematic patronage of the ruling class which both encouraged and allowed for the construction, maintenance, and perpetuation of such a system and, in particular, the close ties which obtained between the culture of the ulama, the transmission of religious learning, and the praxis of the Sufi *ribāṭ*s and *khānaqāh*s in major urban centers such as Suhrawardī's Baghdad.

* * *

As the eponym of one of the oldest *ṭarīqa* lineages and author of an extremely influential Sufi manual, the *'Awārif al-ma'ārif*, the figure of Suhrawardī looms large in the annals of Sufi history, his vision of an institutionalized, *ribāṭ*-based, hierarchically arranged and rule-governed system of Sufi religiosity exerting a measurable influence on the development of *ṭarīqa*-based Sufism in the eastern—and to a lesser extent central and western—Islamic lands during the period of the reconstitution of urban polities following the Mongol invasions of the 7th/13th century. Born into a family of religious scholars in the predominantly Kurdish and Persian-speaking town of Suhraward in 539/1144–45, Suhrawardī came to Baghdad as a youth, studied the religious sciences and heard *ḥadīth*, inherited his uncle's position as a local Sufi shaykh, and after finding a powerful patron in the person of the Abbasid caliph al-Nāṣir li-Dīn Allāh, established himself as one of the premier personalities of the city's vibrant Sufi landscape during the first quarter of the 7th/13th century. Secure in his urban Sufi cloisters, he wrote numerous books and treatises in both Arabic and Persian, served the caliph as an ambassador, trained disciples, and invested interested 'lay folk' with the Sufi habit, all the while gathering around himself a group of men who would later give form and shape to what would come to be known as the *ṭarīqat al-suhrawardiyya*, the 'Suhrawardī way'. After the Mongol sack of Baghdad in 656/1258, his numerous disciples took it as their task to establish his 'way' in Greater Syria, Egypt, Iran, and North India, joining a larger movement of other such disciples of particularly charismatic Sufi masters which was to have a profound and lasting influence on the religious landscape of the pre-modern Islamic East. Through the efforts of his disciples, foremost among them Najīb al-Dīn ʿAlī b. Buzghush (d. 678/1280) in Iran and Bahāʾ al-Dīn Zakariyyā Multānī (d. 661/1262) in India, both his Sufi manual, the *ʿAwārif al-maʿārif*, and the particular initiatic way associated with it and its teachings enjoyed a widespread dissemination, coming to flourish most visibly in the Indian Subcontinent where a self-reflexive *ṭarīqat al-suhrawardiyya* would eventually become among the most factionalized and sub-divided Sufi brotherhoods in the entirety of the Abode of Islam.

Despite his importance and in contrast to the relative wealth of primary source material, however, critical scholarship on Suhrawardī is scarce, and for the most part accounts of his life and teachings in modern scholarship have usually been presented in a rather cursory manner.[8] Among the few works which focus specifically on Suhrawardī, the research of Angelika Hartmann on Suhrawardī's relationship with the Abbasid caliph al-Nāṣir li-Dīn Allāh and the shaykh's polemical treatises is foundational, but limited in its focus.[9] On the biography of

[8] e.g., Gustav Flügel, *Die arabischen, persischen und türkischen Handschriften der Kaiserlich-Königlichen Hofbibliothek zu Wien* (Vienna: K.K. Hof- und Staatsdruckerei, 1865–1867), 3:329–332 (no. 1896); Carra de Vaux, *Les penseurs de l'islam* (Paris: Librairie Paul Geuthner, 1923), 4:199–207; Otto Spies, *Muʾnīs al-ʿushshāq* (Stuttgart: Kohlhammer, 1935), 4–7; C. van den Bergh, "as-Suhrawardī," *EI*[1], 4:547; Helmut Ritter, "Philologika IX. Die vier Suhrawardī. Ihre Werke in Stambuler Handschriften," *Der Islam* 24 (1938): 36–46; GAL I, 569–571, S I, 788–791; Richard Gramlich, *Die schiitischen Derwischorden Persiens* (Wiesbaden: Franz Steiner Verlag, 1965); 1:8–15; Trimingham, *The Sufi Orders in Islam*, 33–37; Schimmel, *Mystical Dimensions of Islam*, 245–246; and, Alexander Knysh, *Islamic Mysticism: A Short History* (Leiden: Brill, 1999): 195–203.

[9] Angelika Hartmann, "La conception governementale du calife an-Nāṣir li-Dīn Allāh," *Orientalia Suecana* 22 (1973): 52–61; idem, *An-Nāṣir li-Dīn Allāh (1180–1225). Politik, Religion, Kultur in der späten ʿAbbāsidenzeit* (Berlin: Walter de Gruyter, 1975), 233–254; idem, "Bemerkugen zu Handschriften ʿUmar as-Suhrawardīs, echten und vermeintlichen Autographen," *Der Islam* 60 (1983): 112–142; idem, "Sur l'édition d'un texte arabe médiéval: Le Rašf an-naṣāʾiḥ al-īmānīya wa-kašf al-faḍāʾiḥ al-yūnānīya de

Suhrawardī in particular, Richard Gramlich has provided a very useful checklist of his main teachers, associates, and disciples in his excellent German translation of the *ʿAwārif al-maʿārif*,[10] and H. Kâmil Yılmaz has neatly summarized the primary data on Suhrawardī's life, main works, and principle teachers and disciples in the introduction to a Turkish translation of the text co-authored with İrfan Gündüz.[11] Neither of these works, however, are comprehensive. In addition, the Iranian scholar Qāsim Anṣārī wrote a well-documented introduction to Suhrawardī's life, works, and teachings in the introduction to his edition of an early Persian translation of the *ʿAwārif al-maʿārif* as did the late Jalāl al-Dīn Humāʾī in his introduction to ʿIzz al-Dīn Kāshānī's *Miṣbāḥ al-hidāya*.[12] As with the works of Gramlich and Yılmaz, both of these serve as excellent starting points for the construction of a comprehensive biography of Suhrawardī and are equally important for the information which they contain on the authors of their respective texts, both heirs to the teachings of Suhrawardī through the line of one of his premiere disciples in Iran, ʿAlī b. Buzghush. Likewise, in the introduction to his doctoral thesis—a partial edition and study of Suhrawardī's *Nughbat al-bayān fī tafsīr al-qurʾān*—the Turkish scholar Yaşar Düzenli has also provided a summary of Suhrawardī's life, teachers, works, and disciples based on the standard Arabic historiography.[13] Beyond this, a few other editors and translators of some of Suhrawardī's minor works have provided biographical overviews, but mostly of a limited nature.[14]

ʿUmar as-Suhrawardī," *Der Islam* 62 (1985): 71–97; idem, "Cosmogonie et doctrine de l'âme dans l'oeuvre tardive de ʿUmar as-Suhrawardi," *Quaderni di Studi Arabi* 11 (1993): 1–16; idem, "Kosmogonie und Seelenlehre bei ʿUmar as-Suhrawardi (st. 632/1234)," in *Gedenkschrift Wolfgang Reuschel: Akten des III. Arabistischen Kolloquiums, Leipzig 21.–22. November 1991* (Stuttgart: Franz Steiner Verlag, 1994), 135–156; and, idem, "al-Suhrawardī, Shihāb al-Dīn Abū Ḥafṣ ʿUmar," *EI*², 9:778–782.

[10] *GE*, 1–15.

[11] H. Kâmil Yılmaz, "Giriş: Sühreverdi, Hayatı ve Eserleri," in *Tasavvufun esasları* (Istanbul: Erkam Yayınları, 1993), ix–xxxii.

[12] Ismāʿīl Māshāda Iṣfahānī, *ʿAwārif al-maʿārif*, ed. Qāsim Anṣārī (Tehran: Shirkat-i Intishārāt-i ʿIlmī va Farhangī, 1364 sh. [1985]), xii–xviii; reviewed by Najīb Māyel Heravī, "Tarjama-yi ʿAwārif al-maʿārif-i Suhravardī," *Nashr-i Dānish* 6 (1364 sh. [1985–1986]): 114–120; and, ʿIzz al-Dīn Kāshānī, *Miṣbāḥ al-hidāya wa-miftāḥ al-kifāya*, ed. Jalāl al-Dīn Humāʾī (Tehran: Chāpkhānah-yi Majlis, 1367 sh. [1988], 19–23).

[13] Yaşar Düzenli, "Şihâbuddin Sühreverdî ve Nuğbetü'l-Beyân fî Tefsîri'l-Kurân: Adlı Eserinin Tevbe Sûresine kadar Tahkîki" (Ph.D. diss., Marmara Üniversitesi, Sosyal Bilimler Enstitütsü [Istanbul], 1994), 1–31.

[14] Namely, Morteza Sarraf in his edition of Suhrawardī's two *Futuvvat-nāmas* (*Traites des compagnons-chevaliers, Rasaʾil-e Javanmardan: recueil de sept Fotowwat-Nâmeh* [Tehran &

In addition to these works, two recent monographs on Suhrawardī shed light on his life, works, and thought, although both are somewhat limited in their scope, coverage, and scholarly rigor. The first is a lengthy, but uncritical, sketch of Suhrawardī's 'life, character, and teachings' written by the Qatari scholar ʿĀʾisha Yūsuf al-Manāʿī as her M.A. thesis at al-Azhar University in Cairo.[15] This work, which is based on a good portion of Suhrawardī's extant Arabic writings and a carefully selected body of pre-modern Arabic historiography, is a synchronic study of Suhrawardī as an *ʿālim* and Sufi, describing the contours of his thought with little regard to either the historical context in which he operated or to the broader discursive milieux informing and constraining his activities. Despite such critical shortcomings and the absence of key Persian and Turkish sources, al-Manāʿī did a through job in marshalling the data preserved in the Arabic historiography and most of Suhrawardī's Arabic works, and along with the work of Hartmann, her monograph represents an important foundational study whose many gaps are filled in here. Unfortunately, the same cannot be said for the recent work of Qamar ul-Huda on Suhrawardī and the establishment and diffusion of the Suhrawardiyya in the Indian Subcontinent.[16] Based almost solely on Suhrawardī's influential Sufi handbook, the *ʿAwārif al-maʿārif*, a very selective reading of the secondary literature, and a small selection of South Asian sources, his work presents a reading of what

---

Paris: Departement d'Iranologie de l'Institut Franco-Iranien de Recherche & Librairie d'Amerique et d'Orient, 1973], 22–24 (Persian text) the content of the texts being the object of a lengthy commentary by Henri Corbin (37–58 [French text]); Muḥammad Shīrvānī in his edition and Persian translation of two of Suhrawardī's testaments ("Vaṣiyyat-nāma-yi Shihāb al-Dīn Abū Ḥafṣ ʿUmar b. Muḥammad-i Suhravardī," *Sophia Perennis/Jāvidān-i khirād* 2.2 [1976]: 31); Nasīm Aḥmad Farīdī Amravhī in his Urdu translation of some of Suhrawardī's testaments and *futūḥāt* (*Vaṣāyā Shaykh Shihāb al-Dīn Suhravardī* [Lahore: al-Maʿārif, 1983], 4–8); Aḥmad Ṭāhirī ʿIrāqī in his edition of Suhrawardī's *Ajwibat ʿan masāʾil baʿḍ aʾimmat Khurāsān* ("Pāsukhhāʾi Shihāb al-Dīn ʿUmar-i Suhravardī," *Maqalāt u Barrasīhā* 49–50 [1369/1411/1991]: 45); and, ʿAbd al-ʿAzīz al-Sayrawān in his edition of Suhrawardī's *Aʿlām al-hudā wa-ʿaqīdat arbāb al-tuqā* (Damascus: Dār al-Anwār, 1996), 11–22.

15 al-Manāʿī, *Abū Ḥafṣ ʿUmar al-Suhrawardī: ḥayātuhu wa-taṣawwufuhu* (Doha: Dār al-Thaqāfa, 1991).

16 Qamar ul-Huda, "The Ṣūfī Order of Shaikh ʿAbu Hafs ʿUmar al-Suhrawardī and the Transfer of Suhrawardîyya Religious Ideology to Multan" (Ph.D. diss., University of California, Los Angeles, 1998); idem, "The Remembrance of the Prophet in Suhrawardī's *ʿAwārif al-maʿārif*," *JIS* 12.2 (2001): 129–150; and, idem, *Striving for Divine Union: Spiritual Exercises for Suhrawardī Ṣūfīs* (London & New York: RoutledgeCurzon, 2003).

he calls Suhrawardī's "religious ideology". While the relative merits of the author's interpretive conclusions can be debated, the same cannot be said for its historiographical content. Egregiously careless in its use of what little primary sources it actually refers to, the work suffers from a host of simply inexcusable factual errors, including identifying Suhrawardī as a Ḥanbalī!

The state of the primary sources bearing upon Suhrawardī, his teachers, students, disciples and the *ṭarīqa* lineage which bears his name is much better. We are fortunate that as a visible player in the politics of his day, a fairly active transmitter of *ḥadīth*, and befitting the status and importance of his teachings to the later Sufi tradition, biographical information on Suhrawardī and his associates is extensive in pre- and early-modern Islamic historiography. Be this as it may, as is with many figures from this period, such material is widely dispersed throughout a host of biographical dictionaries, annalistic histories, court and regional chronicles, and various Sufi hagiographies. Most of these sources are in Arabic, a good number in Persian, a few in Turkish, and a smattering in Urdu. Chronologically, these sources span a period of over seven-hundred years, although the heaviest concentration of materials centers around the two centuries following Suhrawardī's death (i.e., 7th/13th–9th/15th centuries). Given the agglutinative nature of pre-modern Islamic historiography in general, however, later authors tend to simply repeat earlier accounts, although the different ways in which they do so shed light on larger issues of narration, representation, and the writing of history among particular groups in pre-modern Islamic society. Overall, however, the standard prosopographical and other works which mention Suhrawardī, his teachers, students, and disciples is more or less normative for the people and period under consideration and as such represent, in most cases, the same body of one would consult when researching any number of largely Shāfiʿī ulama who lived and worked in the central and eastern lands of Islamdom between the 6th/12th–8th/14th centuries. If one were to exclude the Sufi hagiographies, in fact, there is little to differentiate Suhrawardī from any number of Shāfiʿī scholars of a similar stature living, teaching, and plying their religious expertise in cities such as Baghdad, Damascus, Cairo, or Isfahan, and it is perhaps no accident that the first mention of any member of his family, in fact, comes in a biographical handbook of *ḥadīth* transmitters, in this case one composed by the celebrated Shāfiʿī *muḥaddith* ʿAbd al-Karīm b. Muḥammad al-Samʿānī (d. 562/1166).[17] In addition to this body of sources, various types of materials preserved in the Suhrawardiyya corpus itself, in particular manuscript copies of Suhrawardī's works, are invaluable, most notably in their marginalia, addenda, and certificates of transmission (*ijāzāt*) or audition (*samāʿ*), materials largely ignored or only cursorily treated up until now.

It is, however, one thing to compose a history of a certain individual and quite another to produce something which looks beyond the boundaries of that individual's life and times. Self-contained and largely abstract exposés of the theories, ideas, and teachings of various Sufis are, in fact, all-too-well represented in the body of academic literature on Sufism, and as I have commented elsewhere, such an approach does little to advance our understanding of the subject in any meaningful way.[18] At the same time, there are a number of recent studies which have broken away from this paradigm, analyzing their subjects along philological, historical, and discursive lines with a view towards constructing a reading which both explicates ideas and teachings while at the same time situating those ideas within their broader socio-political, economic, and religious contexts.[19] When all is said and done, nowadays the rather shopworn genre of the traditional analytic biography (i.e., life—times—works) can at best hope to meet with any real measure of success only if it is tempered with a keen sense of historical context and is attentive to the broader concerns of current discourse within the humanities and social sciences, something which the present work firmly envisions itself as doing, in particular through reading textual production as a history of discourse necessarily rooted

---

[17] al-Samʿānī, *K. al-ansāb*, ed. ʿAbdullāh ʿUmar al-Bārūdī (Beirut: Dār al-Jinān, 1988), 3:341 (s.v., al-Suhrawardī).

[18] See my review of Binyamin Abrahamov's *Divine Love in Islamic Mysticism* in *JRAS, series 3*, 13.3 (2003): 383–385.

[19] The works of R.S. O'Fahey (*Enigmatic Saint: Ahmad Ibn Idris and the Idrisi Tradition* [Evanston, IL: Northwestern University Press, 1990]) and Knut Vikør (*Sufi and Scholar on the Desert Edge: Muhammad b. ʿAlī al-Sanūsī* [London: Hurst & Co., 1995]) are particularly excellent examples as are, in a different way, that of Vincent Cornell (*Realm of the Saint: Power and Authority in Moroccan Sufism* [Austin: University of Texas Press, 1998]) on the institution of the Sufi master and saint in North African landscapes and that of Dina Le Gall (*A Culture of Sufism: Naqshbandīs in the Ottoman World, 1450–1700* [Albany: State University of New York Press, 2005]) on the rise, dissemination, and transformations of the Naqshbandiyya order from Central Asia westward.

in a context simultaneously shaped and constrained by both the inertia of the past and the exigencies of the present. Guided by the principle that a carefully structured narrative of Suhrawardī's career alongside a close reading of his textual legacy will help to furnish a better understanding of the broader social, cultural, and religious contexts framing this important moment in the history of Sufism, this book not only endeavors to uncover the dynamics operating in the life and career of such a key figure but strives to illuminate just how such a figure was able to go about successfully negotiating the complex and interrelated social, political, and religious milieux which constituted the setting of his activities in the first place.

This negotiation was not innocent, and as shown over the course of this study, Suhrawardī programmatically appropriated and utilized a variety of discursive strategies as part of a broader program aimed at consolidating and formalizing a system of mystical praxis to which he considered himself an heir, attempting to recast and reinterpret it along lines more-or-less dictated by immediate socio-political realities. Understanding the scope of such a project, however, requires that one first come to terms with the historical subtext which framed it. Chapter One is devoted to mapping this subtext, identifying and discussing the contours of the social, political, and religious spaces within which Suhrawardī and his associates moved. Here, three primary, but interrelated, clusters of 'before' and 'after' which converged in Suhrawardī's historical moment are analyzed: the dominance of political program, the structures and practices of certain 'educational' institutions, and, third, the discourse and authority of the text.

Chapter Two takes up the issue of Suhrawardī's biography. Here, questions of time, place, and identity are central: what did it mean to inhabit a space where one was called upon to play simultaneously the roles of Sufi shaykh, *ʿālim*, popular preacher, diplomat, and apologist, and in turn, how were such roles represented by both contemporary narrators and those looking back from the vantage point of later historical moments? In turn, Chapter Three moves from the narratives of prosopographers and historiographers to Suhrawardī's own representation of himself. Interrogating a particularly important cluster of his written works which deal with the 'sciences of the Sufis' (*ʿulūm al-ṣūfiyya/al-qawm*), their genealogy, content, and authority, this chapter fleshes out the ways in which this particular actor represented himself both within and across multiple centers of affiliation and identity. Arguing that Suhrawardī envisioned himself and the self-identified group (*ṭāʾifa*) for whom he spoke as the only legitimate 'heirs to the Prophet', this chapter maps out the details of Suhrawardī's project of co-opting the spiritual and exegetical authority of any number of competing groups (*ṭawāʾif*) populating the Islamic body politic. As shown in this chapter, Suhrawardī accomplished this task through delineating a universalizing vision of theory and praxis which attempted to systematically re-center the totality of Islamic revelatory, cosmologic, and soteriological traditions in the hands of the particular Junaydī-Sufi tradition for which he spoke.

Moving from the theoretical to the practical, Chapter Four investigates how Suhrawardī projected this vision onto the actual physical and social landscapes in which he moved. Drawing upon a host of practical writings, correspondence, and testaments written for disciples and others, this chapter explores the organizational, social, and religious dimensions of the Sufi *ribāṭ* and the types of activities pursued, and relationships forged, within it. Showing how Suhrawardī set out to propagate a socially-open and accommodationist *ribāṭ*-based Sufi system, this chapter argues that Suhrawardī was successful in systematizing and consolidating the particular form of institutionalized mysticism which he championed precisely because it legitimized and maintained itself by attending to a wider body of reproducible social acts and cultural codes which extended far beyond the Sufi *ribāṭ*s themselves.

Positing that the world in which Suhrawardī moved is one best read in terms of its intersections, Chapter Five closes the circle opened in Chapter One, asking how we might understand the 'official roles' which Suhrawardī may have played in his capacity as a public figure attached to the court of the caliph al-Nāṣir li-Dīn Allāh. Examining three instances where Suhrawardī's own program intersected with that of his patron: his publication of a prescriptive creed written for a general audience, his composition of two manuals on the *futuwwa* intended for dissemination in Anatolia, and, near the end of his life, the composition of two polemics directed against the *falāsifa*, this chapter argues that Suhrawardī pursued what amounted to a 'dual strategy' of defending al-Nāṣir's conception of the caliphate while at the same time systematically de-centering contesting claims to religious and spiritual authority and repositioning it squarely in the hands of his own self-identified *ṭāʾifa*.

CHAPTER ONE

SITUATING AL-SUHRAWARDĪ IN TIME, SPACE, AND TEXT

Despite the magnitude of his presence in the annals of Sufi history, Abū Ḥafṣ ʿUmar al-Suhrawardī was at one and the same time much more and much less than the sum of his parts. He was neither an innovator nor a consolidator, but something in between; his ideas were certainly not radical, but neither were they conventional; the trajectory of his life and career was not unusual, but neither was it ordinary. He appears a man of contradictions, an individual who while a vigorous proponent of worldly withdrawal, did not limit himself to the concerns and debates of a relatively small, although admittedly quite powerful, group of religious scholars or world-renouncing Sufis. In fact, he embraced the role of being a public figure in a world where enunciating and maintaining such authority was a delicate and dangerous art. Through all of this, he engaged in an ambitious project which aimed to consolidate and perpetuate certain replicable, institutionalized forms of mystical theory and praxis, a system whose very structure would come to indelibly mark *ṭarīqa*-based Sufism throughout the central and eastern lands of Islamdom in the centuries following his death.

At the same time, Suhrawardī's engagement with the particular institutionalizing strand of the Sufi tradition which he championed was itself not entirely new, being the outcome of a long process of historical development, a process which converged in both his person and in the complex and intersecting social, religious, and political landscapes of Baghdad during the late 6th/12th and early 7th/13th centuries. Indeed, to write a history of an individual like Suhrawardī is to simultaneously write a history of a broader subtext, to uncover a genealogy of historical agents, events, ideas, and practices which came to converge in the specificities of his particular historical moment. In short, it is difficult if not impossible to make meaningful interpretive statements regarding Suhrawardī's career, teachings, contributions and legacy without reference to the forces which inevitably shaped them, in particular those political, institutional, and textual forces which figured so prominently in shaping the world in which Suhrawardī, his teachers, disciples and associates moved.

The Political Setting

To understand Suhrawardī is to also understand the spatial and temporal contexts in which he lived, and in large part the moment of this particular actor was intimately tied with the moment of another, the 34th Abbasid caliph, al-Nāṣir li-Dīn Allāh (r. 575–622/1180–1225). For Suhrawardī, al-Nāṣir loomed large, for it was largely under his auspices that he was placed in the rather precarious position of negotiating a space where he was called upon to play simultaneously the roles of Sufi shaykh, Shāfiʿī *ʿālim*, public preacher, diplomat, and polemicist, a combination of roles which, although certainly configured in the frame of the moment, were themselves the outcome of certain trends converging in the figure of Suhrawardī, roles which a Shāfiʿī Sufi master living and working within an urban nexus such as Baghdad could not but help to have thrust upon him. At the same time, however, as much as his person was important for al-Nāṣir, Suhrawardī was but a small piece of a much larger program of reform and centralization, a program which drew upon individuals and institutions who, in the grand scheme of things, were much more important and influential than this particular Sufi shaykh and his urban cloisters. In much the same way, al-Nāṣir himself was but a piece of a much larger complex of historical processes which came to converge in his own historical moment and who in that moment was an agent who was more often than not overshadowed by others.

Although by all accounts an important figure in the political history of Islamdom in the latter 6th/12th through the first quarter of the 7th/13th centuries, in the end the role which this particular caliph played in the events leading up to the profound social, political, and geographical changes which Islamdom was to undergo following the Mongol invasions, the continued Turkification of Anatolia, and the rise of the Ayyubid-Mamluk hegemony in the west, was comparably much less important than those played by his contemporaries. By all accounts, for the events which eventually led to the establishment of the 'Age of Empires' in the 10th/16th century, it is neither to the last Abbasid caliphs nor al-Nāṣir in particular where one needs to look, but rather to his contemporaries, the Ayyubids to his west, the Khwārazm Shāhs and Mongols to his east, and the Seljuk sultanate of Rūm to his north. At the same time, however, the fortunes of each of these dynasties, al-Nāṣir included, were intimately tied to an historical process beginning many centuries earlier.

As Hodgson pointed out almost forty years ago, the Earlier Middle Period (945–1258 CE) "faced problems of totally reconstructing political life in Islamdom...seeing great political inventiveness, making use, in state building, of a variety of elements of Muslim idealism."[1] Beginning in the 3rd/9th century the patterns of governance characteristic of the High Caliphal Period (692–945 CE) began to give way to new forms of military and administrative practice which came into being as centrifugal forces in the provinces progressively led to more and more regional autonomy and, consequently, the need for alternative configurations of administrative practice. The ascendancy of the Buyids (320–447/932–1055) in southern Persia and Iraq and of the Sāmānids (204–395/819–999) and later Ghaznavids (351–431/962–1040) in the east set the tenor of this new configuration of power, drawing the outlines of a type of regime which would reach its apogee under the monumental success of the Great Seljuks (431–590/1040–1194).

Under the early Abbasids, the Abode of Islam can more or less be characterized as enjoying the benefits of a strong, unified, central state. Run by a wealthy, culturally self-assured elite—the Abbasid caliphs, their court, and their regional governors—such stability contributed to the development of a new, syncretic, cosmopolitan Islamic civilization which in many ways derived its vitality from administrative and institutional patterns of governance centralized in the caliphal government of Baghdad. With the dissolution of this pattern, however, the Abbasid caliphs became what amounted to figureheads retaining only symbolic, *de jure* authority, real *de facto* authority being vested in provincial governors, who in cultivating regional courts, competed with both the Abbasids and their own provincial rivals to secure a place as ruling political and cultural elites.

Beginning with the Buyids, the regimes which engaged in such competitions employed a number of institutions, policies, and practices through which they consolidated and centralized power, and in building upon the practices of the High Caliphal Period, as well as upon the Persian and Turkic patterns of governance to which they were heirs, instituted various religious, military, economic, and administrative institutions and practices which would indelibly change the very character of Islamdom itself. Institutions such as the *iqṭāʿ* and appanage systems, alternative enunciations of power and authority, new forms of military

[1] Hodgson, *The Venture of Islam*, 2:12.

organization, and the patronage of various religious institutions each served as vehicles by which such regimes attempted to centralize and consolidate power and authority. For individuals such as Suhrawardī, it was primarily in the realm of the patronage of religious institutions, and to a lesser extent in the ideological dimensions of the enunciation of power and authority, where what might be called the political and what might be called the spiritual or religious overlapped.

Living at the cusp of a transformational moment in the history Islamdom at the end of the Earlier Middle Period, Suhrawardī and his patron al-Nāṣir were heirs to certain institutions, practices, and configurations of political power which had developed over the previous two centuries. Such configurations were both ideological and administrative. In the figure of the Buyid amir ʿAḍuḍ al-Dawla (r. 367–372/978–983) we witness, for instance, the enunciation of an alternative configuration of power and authority which drew upon older Iranian ideals of kingship. This configuration of power would later be challenged by al-Nāṣir while at the same time being replicated by his opponents, most notably the Khwārazm Shāh Jalāl al-Dīn Mangübirdī (r. 617–628/1220–1231).

Although a slow process, the dissipation of Abbasid absolutism found a certain culmination in the movement of new peoples into the Near Eastern heartlands, movements which resulted in sweeping socio-cultural and political changes and the establishment (after 656/1258) of a wholly new, non-Arab, ruling elite in the region. It was the movement of one such group, the Seljuks, which most visibly shaped the patterns of political, ideological, and administrative practice which would come to characterize the Islamic Near East in the time of al-Nāṣir and Suhrawardī. In defeating both the Buyids and the Ghaznavids, the Seljuks were able to reunify these provinces under centralized control while at the same time justifying their usurpation of authority in terms of their publicly enunciated role as champions of Sunni Islam against the Shiite Fāṭimids in Egypt (297–567/909–1171), an enunciation which certainly secured them a place in historical memory as one of the driving forces behind the so-called Sunni revival of the 5th/11th–6th/12th centuries.

The role of the vizier *par excellence* Niẓām al-Mulk (d. 485/1092) in the spread of the *madrasa* system and his vigorous patronage of Shāfiʿī scholars is usually singled out as one of the most important components of this program. The extent of the general picture which emerges out of this phenomenon, its ultimate rationale, character and impact has certainly been questioned,[2] but the fact that Niẓām al-Mulk was vigorous in his promotion of Shāfiʿī learning cannot be denied. Part of his reasoning behind supporting such activities was undoubtedly to help bring a measure of stability to the intense sectarian conflicts which existed among the various Sunni legal schools (and by extension whatever social tensions they may have masked), by all accounts also one of the driving forces behind al-Nāṣir's policies. At the same time, however, it was clear that the Niẓām al-Mulk also hoped to capitalize upon the authority wielded by the ulama, tying them to the government by programmatically cultivating their support. The same can be said for the caliph al-Nāṣir.

In addition to patronizing such centers of Sunni learning, Niẓām al-Mulk also actively engaged in encouraging the spread of Sufi cloisters (*khānaqāhs*). Narratives preserved in the Sufi literature of the period present a host of anecdotes in which we find Niẓām al-Mulk patronizing Sufis and founding *khānaqāhs*, a practice which not only allowed the Seljuk state to keep both the Sufis and the jurists in check, but also to capitalize upon the legitimizing power wielded by both.[3] Such policies would be replicated by later powerful political and military figures such as Nūr al-Dīn Zangī (d. 607/1211) in Syria and, much to the benefit of Suhrawardī himself, by al-Nāṣir in Baghdad.

The Nāṣirian Project

It was on the eve of the Mongol invasions that the old Seljuk ideal of the unity of Islamdom was given a fresh impetus by the 34th

[2] The older scholarly reading of positing that the establishment of the *madrasa* was due in part to a desire to train 'administrators' and 'bureaucrats' to serve the Seljuk state has been shown to be largely false. This critique was first voiced by Hodgson in *The Venture of Islam* (2:47–48) and subsequently developed by Makdisi, among elsewhere, in his oft cited *The Rise of Colleges: Institutions of Learning in Islam and the West* (Edinburgh: Edinburgh University Press, 1981), and has been taken up again by Jonathan Berkey in *The Transmission of Knowledge in Medieval Cairo: A Social History of Islamic Education* (Princeton: Princeton University Press, 1992), by Michael Chamberlain in his *Knowledge and Social Practice in Medieval Damascus, 1190–1350* (Cambridge: Cambridge University Press, 1994), and, with a shift in emphasis, by Daphna Ephrat in her *A Learned Society in a Period of Transition: The Sunni "Ulama" of Eleventh Century Baghdad* (Albany, NY: State University of New York Press, 2000).

[3] Nicely accounted for by Hamid Dabashi in *Truth and Narrative: The Untimely Thoughts of ʿAyn al-Quḍāt al-Hamadhānī* (Surrey, UK: Curzon Press, 1999), 110–154; and Omid Safi in *The Politics of Knowledge in Premodern Islam: Negotiating Ideology and Religious Inquiry* (Chapel Hill: The Unversity of North Carolina Press, 2006).

Abbasid caliph, al-Nāṣir li-Dīn Allāh (r. 575–622/1180–1225). The son of the rather lackluster caliph al-Mustaḍīʾ bi-Amr Allāh (r. 566–575/1170–1180), from the start al-Nāṣir li-Dīn Allāh proved himself to be a shrewd politician. Quickly doing away with much of the old guard who had enjoyed a virtual stranglehold over his father's office, he initiated a far-reaching and sophisticated military and ideological program aimed at rehabilitating and reestablishing the caliphate to its former prestige through centralizing all types of power and authority in his own person. Through a series of strategic alliances with various political powers, the cultivation of certain circles of ulama and Sufis, the patronage of religious institutions and specific types of religious learning, the reorganization of the *futuwwa*, forging mutually beneficial relationships with the Shia, and a systematic program of religious propaganda, al-Nāṣir succeeded in redefining and, in some measure, reestablishing the caliphate as a real and effective power and the person of the caliph as its pivot.

Upon the assumption of his rule, the provinces to both the east and west of the caliphal heartlands of central Iraq were under the control of powerful and competing dynasties. In the east, Transoxiana with its great cities of Samarqand and Bukhara were held by the Qarakhānids (to 609/1212) who at that time were under the shadow of the non-Muslim Qara Khiṭay to their north (Turkistan) and the Khwārazm Shāhs (to 628/1231) to the north and west. To the south, the region from Afghanistan down to Sijistān was under the control of the successors to the Ghaznavids, the Ghūrids (to 612/1215) who, like the Qarakhānids in Transoxiana, would soon succumb to the powerful Khwārazm Shāhs who at the time controlled the entire region south of the Aral Sea and most of Khurāsān. As for the southern Iranian provinces, Kirmān was under the control of a branch of the Seljuks who, in 584/1188, would succumb to occupation by the Ghuzz (Oghuz) Turks, while to their west Fārs remained under the control of Seljuk *atabegs*, the Salghūrids, until 681/1282. Closer to home, the Jibāl (Persian Iraq) was under the control of the Great Seljuks and their last sultan, Ṭoghrıl III (r. 571–590/1176–1194) while the province of Khūzistān remained disputed. North of the Jibāl, the area southwest of the Caspian Sea (Jīlān and Azerbaijan) was under the control of the İldigüzids, another Seljuk *atabeg* dynasty whose fortunes dwindled considerably under the rule of Ṭoghrıl III while much of west-central Anatolia was firmly in control of the Seljuks of Rūm who, from Konya, would remain more or less independent until falling under Il Khānid suzerainty in the middle of the 7th/13th century. To the northwest of Iraq, the important province of the Jazīra was under the control of the Zangids, who however, would soon succumb to the expansionist policies of the Ayyubids who under the celebrated Saladin (d. 589/1193) were at the time firmly in control of Egypt and quickly gaining ground in Syria and Palestine. Upon taking the throne, al-Nāṣir sent missions led by figures such as Baghdad's *shaykh al-shuyūkh* Ṣadr al-Dīn al-Nīsābūrī and the rector of the Baghdad Niẓāmiyya Raḍī al-Dīn al-Ṭālqānī to each of these dynasties asking for their pledge of fidelity (*bayʿa*) to the new caliph.[4]

It was against this backdrop from which al-Nāṣir began to pursue an ambitious program of reasserting the primacy of the caliphate. Employing a dual strategy which oscillated between calculated military advances and a systematic program of politico-religious propaganda, he brought a measure of centralization and renewed power to the caliphate which had been lacking since the time of the Buyids. His first order of business was to strengthen the territorial integrity of the caliphate, reasserting control over key provinces lost first to the Buyids and then to the Seljuks. This was accomplished primarily through a series of alliances. The first object of reclamation were those provinces still under control of the Seljuks. In 583/1187, al-Nāṣir rejected a request made by sultan Ṭoghrıl III to restore the old Seljuk Palace (Dār al-Salṭana) in Baghdad and instead ordered its demolition,[5] shortly thereafter forming a short-lived alliance with the İldigüzid *atabeg* Qızıl Arslān and, upon his death, with the Khwārazm Shāh ʿAlāʾ al-Dīn Tekish (r. 567–596/1172–1200) against Ṭoghrıl III. Although the first attempt at direct military engagement was a spectacular failure and Qızıl Arslān proved to be of little help, al-Nāṣir's alliance with Tekish eventually paid off, for in 590/1194 Ṭoghrıl III was put to the sword, al-Nāṣir victoriously displaying his head in Baghdad.[6] As to be expected, however, after this victory Tekish began to assert his own claims to power over the old Seljuk domains, demanding control of the Jibāl in the same manner in which the Seljuks had ruled it before him. Having

[4] *KT*, 9:443; Ibn Wāṣil, *Mufarrij al-kurūb fī akhbār Banī Ayyūb*, ed. Jamāl al-Dīn al-Shayyāl (Cairo: al-Idārat al-ʿAmmāt li-Thiqāfa, 1954–1961), 2:92.

[5] *KT*, 10:44; *SN*, 22:215; and, *TIsl*, 47:18 (*ḥawādith, anno* 583).

[6] al-Ḥusaynī, *Akhbār al-dawlat al-saljūqiyya*, ed. Muḥammad Iqbal (Lahore: University of Punjab Press, 1933), 193; *TIsl*, 47:93–94 (*ḥawādith, anno* 590); and, Juvaynī, *The History of the World-Conqueror*, trans. J.A. Boyle (Manchester: Manchester University Press, 1958), 1:303.

no desire to grant Tekish free rein over the province, a military confrontation ensued, but in the end al-Nāṣir was left only with a portion of Khūzistān under his control.[7]

The end of Seljuk rule brought with it another challenge, namely the rising power of the Ayyubids who at the time were complaining that the caliph, and other Muslim rulers, were not doing enough to support the jihad against the Crusaders.[8] For his part, al-Nāṣir capitalized upon Saladin's preoccupation with the jihad, extending his suzerainty northward exactly at the time when Saladin was most embroiled in Palestine, during the siege of Acre (585/1189) taking his hometown of Tikrit, the city of Irbil, and other strategic locations along the Euphrates which had only recently come under Ayyubid control, thus curtailing Saladin's project of expansion in the Jazīra.[9] After Saladin's death, al-Nāṣir's relationship with his successors obtained something of a more cordial tone. Saladin's successor in Damascus, his son al-Malik al-Afḍal (r. 582–592/1186–1196), forged good relations with Baghdad, and under him complaints against al-Nāṣir's apparent lack of interest in the jihad became much softer, and premature requests for diplomas of investiture or excessive demands for military assistance more or less stopped altogether.

Following the death of the Khwārazm Shāh Tekish in 596/1200, al-Nāṣir was confronted with another dangerous threat to his expansionist program. Upon assuming the throne, the son of Tekish, ʿAlāʾ al-Dīn Muḥammad b. Tekish (r. 596–617/1200–1220), demanded that his name be mentioned in the *khuṭba* in Baghdad, a request which al-Nāṣir was not about to grant.[10] What followed was a long series of mutual provocations between the caliph and the Khwārazm Shāh, the Ghūrids fighting on behalf of al-Nāṣir and the non-Muslim Qara Khiṭāy siding with ʿAlāʾ al-Dīn Muḥammad, the whole culminating with the Khwārazm Shāh declaring al-Nāṣir deposed, nominating as anti-caliph a *sayyid* from Tirmidh, and finally, in 614/1217–1218 threatening to

---

[7] Juvaynī, *World-Conqueror*, 1:303–304; and, *Nṣr.*, 75–78.

[8] On which, see Herbert Mason, *Two Statesmen of Mediaeval Islam: Vizir Ibn Hubayra (499–560 AH/1105–1165 AD) and caliph an-Nâṣir li Dîn Allâh (553–622 AH/1158–1225 AD)* (The Hague: Mouton, 1972), 89–90; *Nāṣ.*, 86–87; H.A.R. Gibb, *The Life of Saladin* (Oxford: Oxford University Press, 1973), 16, 62; and, Andrew Ehrenkreutz, *Saladin* (Albany, NY: State University of New York Press, 1972), 209–210, 215–216.

[9] *SN*, 22:208–213; and, *Nṣr.*, 87–88; idem, "Al-Nāṣir," *EI²*, 7:998.

[10] *SN*, 22:139–143.

march on Baghdad itself.[11] It was to dissuade the Khwārazm Shāh from invading the city that al-Nāṣir sent Suhrawardī as an emissary to his camp, a mission which although ultimately unsuccessful, was followed by the withdrawal of his forces due to inclement weather.[12]

Although the details are sketchy, it seems that at some point al-Nāṣir may have entered into negotiations with the Mongols in an effort to forge some sort of alliance with them against the Khwārazm Shāh, Jalāl al-Dīn Mangübirdī, who upon the death of ʿAlāʾ al-Dīn Muḥammad in 617/1220 had vigorously continued his father's claim against al-Nāṣir.[13] If there was ever any alliance between al-Nāṣir and the Mongols, however, it came to naught for in 621/1224 al-Nāṣir made an urgent appeal to the Ayyubid prince al-Malik al-Ashraf for assistance in fending off the Khwārazm Shāh, ostensibly sending Suhrawardī on a second mission to the Ayyubid court in order to secure a military commitment. This mission, however, yielded little in the way of results, and Nāṣir died shortly thereafter, his office falling first to his son Muḥammad b. al-Nāṣir (r. 622/1125) and then to al-Mustanṣir (r. 623–640/1226–1242) who continued some of al-Nāṣir's policies although not to much effect. Aged and suffering from debilitating illness, Suhrawardī seems to have played little to no role under al-Mustanṣir, dying in Baghdad some ten years after al-Nāṣir in 632/1234.

The second dimension of al-Nāṣir's program was ideological. Capitalizing upon sources of authority and legitimacy which appealed to a broad spectrum of Islamicate urban populations, al-Nāṣir envisioned both a revitalized caliphate returned to its former glory, the whole of the Abode of Islam turning towards it as the sole spiritual center and axis of political power and legitimacy. In pursuing this program, al-Nāṣir systematically tapped into both real and symbolic repositories of authority, fusing daring notions of spiritual authority and the ideals of the chivalric *futuwwa* into a newly configured caliphal office which looked beyond the standard legal formulations of *khilāfa/imāma* and

[11] *KT*, 10:300; *MZ*, 8.2:582–583; and, Juvaynī, *World-Conqueror*, 2:363–365.

[12] *KT*, 10:300; *MZ*, 2:583; and, Juvaynī, *World-Conqueror*, 2:366–367. On Suhrawardī's mission and the events which followed, see Chapter Two.

[13] Although accusations of al-Nāṣir contributing to the Mongol invasions are rife within pre-modern Muslim historiography (e.g., *BN*, 13:107–108), there has been much debate over the exact nature of his relationship—if any—with them. On this, see: W. Barthold, *Four Studies on Central Asia*, trans. V. Minorsky (Leyden: E.J. Brill, 1956), 1:37; Mason, *Two Statesmen*, 111–112; *Nṣr.*, 83–85; idem, "Al-Nāṣir," *EI*[2], 7:998; and, Hodgson, *The Venture of Islam*, 2:285.

the discourse of the *siyāsat sharʿiyya* theorists. At the same time, al-Nāṣir entered, certainly with more vigor than his immediate predecessors, into the world of the ulama, presenting himself as a *mujtahid* recognized by all four Sunni *madhhab*s, a trustworthy transmitter of *ḥadīth*, and a vicarious participant in the largely Ḥanbalī-led polemic against dialectical theology (*ʿilm al-kalām*) and Peripatetic philosophy (*falsafa*). It was scholars and Sufis such as Suhrawardī and his associates whom al-Nāṣir drew in as the main participants in such endeavors, systematically co-opting the religious, social, and spiritual authority which they held and then deploying it, in quite public and far-reaching ways, as a vehicle through which his claims to primary politico-religious authority were enunciated.

At the beginning of his rule, al-Nāṣir initiated a program of religio-political propaganda called '*al-daʿwa al-hādiya*' ('the guiding call'), sending out designated and specially empowered propagandists (*dāʿī*s) such as the *shaykh al-shuyūkh* Ṣadr al-Dīn al-Nīsābūrī to Persia, Khurāsān, Azerbaijan, Syria, and Egypt in order to spread it.[14] Quite different from the *daʿwa* of either his father or that of Nūr al-Dīn b. Zangī or Saladin, al-Nāṣir's propaganda took into account the new political and religious realities of his day. Since the Fāṭimid threat had already been dealt with by Saladin and, in contradistinction to Seljuk-era propaganda, the Bāṭiniyya were no longer considered much of a challenge to the integrity of Sunni Islam, al-Nāṣir's *daʿwa* widened the aperture through which prospective converts to the cause were addressed, calling above all for a rapprochement between the various sectarian communities and dogmatic trends which contributed, as al-Nāṣir saw it, to the disunity of Islamdom. In addition to merely calling for such a reconciliation, al-Nāṣir actively pursued such a détente by cultivating the Shia, defending the conversion of his political ally the Grand Master of the Assassins of Alamūt, Rukn al-Dīn Ḥasan III, to Sunni Islam as genuine as well as keeping in close contact with the ʿAlid *nuqabāʾ* of Baghdad and surrounding himself with Imāmī viziers and other high officials and counselors.[15]

Taking this *daʿwa* as the guiding ideology of his broader program, one of the first and perhaps most consequential components of

[14] *KT*, 9:443; Ibn Wāṣil, *Mufarrij*, 2:92; *Nṣr.*, 72, 120; idem, "Al-Nāṣir," *EI*[2], 7:1000. On Ṣadr al-Dīn al-Nīsābūrī, see Chapter Two.

[15] Mason, *Two Statesmen*, 99–101, 104–106; *Nṣr.*, 119–121, 137–162; idem, "Al-Nāṣir," *EI*[2], 7:1000; and, Hodgson, *The Venture of Islam*, 2:281, 283–284.

this project was al-Nāṣir's wide-ranging attempts to bring the socio-religious influence of the ulama under his direct control. He did this in a number of ways. First, he systematically tried to both curtail and capitalize upon the power of the Ḥanbalites, cultivating the support of powerful Ḥanbalī scholars and officials, both within and outside of his administration, while at the same time reversing his father's policy of more or less blind-support for the most vocal Ḥanbalī scholars such as the celebrated Ibn al-Jawzī (d. 597/1200), whom he exiled to Wāsiṭ in 590/1194.[16] Second, in an attempt to bring some measure of personal control over those institutions and public spaces populated by the ulama and Sufis, al-Nāṣir actively patronized *madrasas*, Sufi *ribāṭs*, and associated institutions. In 589/1193, for instance, he enlarged the Niẓāmiyya Madrasa, calling the new portion al-Nāṣiriyya,[17] while at the same time initiating a program which would lead to the foundation of at least six new Sufi *ribāṭs* whose directors he would personally appoint. Again, Suhrawardī and his associates played an important part in this process, gaining important positions within the increasingly formalized networks of these institutions through the direct involvement of al-Nāṣir himself. Third, in order to further buttress his own claim to religious authority, al-Nāṣir actively cultivated the image of an *ʿālim*. On his own authority, he declared himself a *mujtahid*, transmitting *ḥadīth* from Aḥmad b. Ḥanbal's *Musnad* as well as compiling a collection of seventy *ḥadīth*, the *Rūḥ al-ʿārifīn*, which he personally transmitted to representatives of each of the four Sunni *madhhabs* as well as systematically sponsoring its dissemination throughout the Muslim heartlands.[18] Alongside such moves, in his desire to effect a certain rapprochement between mutually hostile dogmatic trends prevalent among urban ulama, he also supported what amounted to an inquisition against the *falāsifa*, actively supporting the destruction of philosophical literature as well as the composition of polemics against its practitioners.

Alongside this program, al-Nāṣir pursued a sweeping project which aimed at the unification and reorganization of the urban *futuwwa* clubs under the aegis of the caliph himself. Forging contacts with the *futuwwa*

---

[16] H. Laoust, "Ibn al-D̲jawzī," *EI*², 3:751.

[17] *KT*, 10:124–125.

[18] Mentioned both by Ibn Ṭiqṭaqā in *al-Fakhrī* (Beirut: Dār Ṣādir, 1380 [1970]), 322, and by al-Dhahabī in *SN*, 22:193, 197–198 (where both Suhrawardī and his student Ibn al-Najjār are mentioned among those who transmitted the book outside of Baghdad). On this, see *Nṣr.*, 207–232.

shortly after his accession, al-Nāṣir was initiated into a branch of the order in 578/1182–1183, thereafter slowly promulgating a series of moral and legal injunctions which concentrated absolute authority for its rites and regulations in his own person. Although he had personally initiated individuals into the *futuwwa* earlier, in the same year in which al-Nāṣir installed Suhrawardī in his new Sufi *ribāṭ* (599/1203), the Ribāṭ al-Marzubāniyya, he began to sponsor more vigorously the initiation of princes and governors into the order, thus tying them, in his position as their superior in the hierarchy of the *futuwwa*, ever more closely to the axis of spiritual power in Baghdad.[19] The caliph's relationship with the *futuwwa* was a life-long one, and some twenty-five years after having become an initiate himself, in 604/1207 al-Nāṣir issued a decree in which he proclaimed himself, in no uncertain terms, the *qibla* of the *futuwwa* and the apex of its hierarchy, outlining a series of dogmatic principles and norms with which non-compliance was punishable by death.[20] An important part of this reform was genealogical, for in addition to concentrating absolute authority for the *futuwwa* in his own person on the basis of prophetic *ḥadīth*, al-Nāṣir promulgated a new initiatic chain for the *futuwwa* which brought it, from Adam down through the Prophet Muḥammad and ʿAlī b. Abī Ṭālib, down to his own person.[21] As with his systematic forays into the world of the ulama, al-Nāṣir's involvement with the *futuwwa* was personal, and as with the former both he and those involved in his program enunciated their affiliations publicly, concretizing their claims to such repositories of authority in real terms.

As Hodgson perceptively pointed out many years ago, much of the genius of al-Nāṣir's program lay in the manner in which he skillfully demonstrated his own 'membership' in those spheres of authority which served as vehicles for consolidating the power of the caliphate, being a full member of the class of amirs by way of his military control over the Mesopotamian plains and his effective web of political alliances, a full member of upper class and courtly circles through his participation in a revitalized courtly *futuwwa*, and a full and 'certified' member of the ulama through his activities in jurisprudence and the transmission

[19] *MZ*, 8.2: 513; Ibn Ṭiqṭaqā, *Fakhrī*, 322; *SN*, 22:194, 204; *Nṣr.*, 107; and, idem, "Al-Nāṣir," *EI*², 7:998.
[20] *JM*, 221–222 (decree cited on 223–225).
[21] *Nṣr.*, 101–102; and, idem, "Al-Nāṣir," *EI*², 7:999.

of *ḥadīth*.[22] Although remaining something of a personal effort and certainly being cut short by the Mongol invasions, al-Nāṣir's ambitious program was, for the time, a particularly appropriate response to the political and religious disunity which he set out to ameliorate. In paying close attention to the exigencies of the decentralized political organization of the time and the complex networks of personal patronage and social contract by which they were sustained, as well as making full use of the multiple—yet as we will see ultimately overlapping—locations of socio-religious authority entrenched within Islamicate urban landscapes, al-Nāṣir's project certainly provided an ingenious solution to the actualities of his historical moment.

The Institutional Setting

Given the tenor of al-Nāṣir's policies as well as those pursued by various rulers throughout the central Islamic lands during the period, it is hardly surprising that we find in Suhrawardī an individual who himself championed a clear program of centralization and institutionalization. Much like al-Nāṣir's attempts to relocate absolute temporal and spiritual authority in his own person through co-opting or capitalizing upon institutions and locations of authority available to him, so too did Suhrawardī engage in a project which attempted to secure, centralize, and maintain authority through the medium of institutions. Throughout his writings, Suhrawardī characterizes the society in which he lived as being comprised of definable '*Personengruppen*' (*ṭawāʾif*, sing. *ṭāʾifa*), individual group commonalities tied together by common concerns, shared ideas, or similar existential locations. In defining his own *ṭāʾifa*—which he identifies variously as the 'world-renouncing religious scholars' (*al-ʿulamāʾ al-zāhidīn fī ʾl-dunyā*) or simply as the Sufis (*al-ṣūfiyya*/*al-qawm*)—Suhrawardī clearly delineates a number of core characteristics which mark them out from others, the most visible being comprised of a shared body of disciplinary practices which, in the urban milieu of late 6th/12th-early 7th/13th-century Baghdad, were most often constructed institutionally.

Such institutions did not necessarily need to be physical, although they could be, nor did they have to be permanent, although in their

[22] Hodgson, *The Venture of Islam*, 2:284.

self-perpetuation they often were. On the one hand, we have incorporeal, social institutions such as the master-disciple relationship (*ṣuḥba*), a pattern of behavior which informed activities spanning a broad spectrum of personal avocations and professional occupations: from the transmission of religious knowledge and learning in the form of texts (*ḥadīth, fiqh, qirāʾāt*, etc.), to religious practices such as preaching (*waʿẓ/tadhkīr*) and specialized juridical skills such as disputation (*jadal/munāẓara*), and from the transmission of crafts or trades (*ṣināʿāt*) to the spiritual training (*tarbiya*) which a Sufi master (*shaykh/pīr*) gave to his disciples (*murīdūn*). Such institutions were both transitory and permanent: transitory and ephemeral in that they came into being whenever two people met to engage in *ṣuḥba* and then dissolved when the relationship ended, and permanent and enduring in that they embodied a set of generally accepted practices which could be replicated at any one time or place when two individuals purposefully came together to attain a predetermined goal. Such 'institutions of process' were important enough to the collective identity of Suhrawardī's *ṭāʾifa* to be codified in texts, in particular as prescriptions on the proper behaviors (*adab*) which one was excepted to observe while engaging in such disciplines.

On the other hand, there were physical institutions, tangible and often intentionally designed and designated 'institutions of place' such as the *madrasa* or its specialized derivatives such as the *dār al-ḥadīth* and *dār al-qurʾān*, the public pulpit where both regularly scheduled and impromptu preaching sessions (*majlis al-waʿẓ*) were held, and the Sufi cloister (*ribāṭ/khānaqāh*), among others. More often then not, such institutions were intentionally constructed—or in the case of the *majlis al-waʿẓ* regularly scheduled—designed to exist in perpetuity through the apparatus of pious endowment (*waqf*). For Suhrawardī, his teachers, students, and disciples, two of these physical institutions in particular, the Sufi cloister (*ribāṭ/khānaqāh*) and the *madrasa*, served as the physical spaces within which the 'institutions of process' defining their collective identity as a *ṭāʾifa* were pursued. Suhrawardī's program systematically drew upon the possibilities which such institutions offered, being deeply informed by the social practices which sustained them. A key feature of the institutionalized *ribāṭ*-based Sufi system which Suhrawardī describes in his writings lays in the interplay between the social practices (or 'institutions of process') associated with 'institutionalized learning' among ulama scholars and those associated with life in the Sufi *ribāṭ*, each space overlapping and merging in a broader complex of authoritating practices surrounding the transmission of religious learning or mystical knowledge. For Suhrawardī and his disciples, in fact, the very structures which shaped the production, transmission, and replication of religious knowledge in the *madrasas* was replicated in the complex of practices informing the Sufi *ribāṭ* and institutionalized, *ṭarīqa*-based Sufism more generally. As important as they were, however, both have yet to be well accounted for.

As to the former, its genesis as an institution is not well understood, and as quite rightly pointed out by Fritz Meier it is impossible to identify exactly when the *ribāṭ* or *khānaqāh* first appeared or to delineate its precise history as an institutional form associated strictly with Sufism.[23] When speaking of such institutions, the usual starting place is the 2nd/8th-century Sufi *duwayra* (the diminutive of *dār*, 'house') or *ribāṭ* on the island of ʿAbbādān said to be founded by ʿAbd al-Wāḥid b. Zayd (d. c. 133/750), which became a chief training ground for Iraqi ascetics and which was manned mostly by *ghāzīs* who along with their military service engaged in acts of worship and supererogatory piety.[24] As discussed in Chapter Four, these earlier military connotations of the *ribāṭ* were not lost on the Sufis of later generations, Suhrawardī in fact positing that the urban Sufi *ribāṭ* is first and foremost a space for the greater jihad against the *nafs* just as it used to be a space for the lesser jihad against the infidels. Institutionally, such *ribāṭ*-linked activity played an important role in the development of *ṭarīqa*-based Sufism in the Maghrib, serving as one of the primary instruments in the spread Sufi modes of religiosity in the region.[25]

In the central and eastern lands of Islamdom, overt and sustained connections between Sufism and such spaces begin to proliferate in the historiography and prosopography only in the 5th/11th century when (especially in works dealing with or composed within the Seljuk domains)

---

[23] *Abū Saʿīd b. Abī'l-Ḫayr (357–440/967–1049): Wirklichkeit und Legende* (Leiden-Tehran-Liège: E.J. Brill, 1976), 302–303. More recently, Jacqueline Chabbi has emphasized the same, saying that: "It is not known at exactly what point in history the term *ribāṭ* and parallel terms, in particular *khānḳāh* in the East, *zāwiya* in the West, were first effectively and regularly applied to groups of mystics devoting themselves to practice of piety, *ʿibāda*, in a building to which they had rights of ownership." ("Ribāṭ," *EI*², 8:495)

[24] Knysh, *Islamic Mysticism*, 17. As demonstrated by Michael Bonner, the *ribāṭs* of the Arabo-Byzantine frontier were well known as locations of asceticism during this period, serving as places where the likes of the future paragons of pious asceticism Ibrāhīm b. Adham (d. 160/777) and Ibn al-Mubārak (d. 181/797) made their names (*Aristocratic Violence and Holy War* [New Haven, CT: American Oriental Society, 1996], esp. 107ff.).

[25] On this, see: Cornell, *Realm of the Saint*, 39–62.

the connection between Sufi masters, disciples, and the *khānaqāhs* which they populated begins to appear as a stock image. Despite this, its genesis as an institution and, more importantly, the kinds of associations it might have held for those who first mention it are unclear. A word of disputed etymology,[26] the institution of the *khānaqāh* is first recorded in the 4th/10th century in the *Ḥudūd al-ʿālam* whose anonymous author (writing in 372/982) mentions that in Samarqand there stands the "monastery of the Manicheans (*khānagāh-i mānaviyān*) who are called *nighūshāk* ('auditores')"[27] and by al-Muqaddasī (d. c. 380/990) in his *Aḥsan al-taqāsīm*, where he states that these institutions were associated solely with the Karrāmiyya.[28] Present in Khurāsān, Jurjān, Ṭabaristān, and in Jerusalem (where Ibn Karrām's [d. 255/869] tomb was located), the ascetic and theological movement of the Karrāmiyya represent, along with the Malāmatiyya, two distinctive strains of Persian religiosity which although subsumed by the *ṣūfiyya*, left important marks on the theoretical and practical vocabulary of nascent *ṭarīqa*-based Sufism.

According to the standard reading, the *khānaqāh* system, and to a lesser extent the 'missionary' and polemical tradition, of the Karrāmiyya was quickly taken over by the Khurāsānī *ṣūfiyya* and became an integral part of the broader Sufi landscape of Khurāsān and Iraq.[29] One such example of this is the career of the enigmatic shaykh Abū Isḥāq Kāzarūnī (d. 426/1033) whose *khānaqāh* in his native Kāzarūn (a town located near Shiraz) provided food and lodging for itinerant travelers as well as distributing charity to the poor; his order, which came to be known as the Isḥāqiyya or Murshidiyya (after Kāzarūnī's appellation '*shaykh-i murshid*'), spread throughout Fars and in the 8th/14th century, into Anatolia where Kāzarūnī *khānaqāhs* became landmarks. As has been noted, the Kāzarūniyya and their *khānaqāhs* did not seem, however, to

---

[26] According to Chabbi the word is a compound of the Persian *khān(eh)-*, in its usual sense as 'house', and the locative suffix *-gāh*, although medieval writers put forth other etymologies, deriving it from *khwān* ('feast table') or from the verb *khwāndan*, in its usual meaning as 'to read/recite'. ("Khānḳāh," *EI²*, 4:1025). In Persian, it is vocalized either *khānagāh* or *khāngah* (Muḥsin Kiyānī, *Taʾrīkh-i khānaqāh dar Īrān* [Tehran: Kitābkhāna-yi Ṭahūrī, 1369 sh. (1991)], 55). The Arabized forms are '*khānqāh*' and '*khāniqa*' (pl. *khawāniq*).

[27] As quoted in Chabbi (op. cit.); see *Ḥudūd al-ʿĀlam: "The Regions of the World"*, trans. V. Minorsky (London: Luzac, 1970), 113.

[28] al-Muqaddasī, *The Best Divisions for Knowledge of the Regions*, trans. Basil Collins (Reading, UK: Garnet Publishing Ltd., 1994), e.g., 285.

[29] C.E. Bosworth, "The Rise of the Karrāmiyya in Khurāsān," *Muslim World* (1960): 8.

represent anything approaching an organized Sufi *ṭarīqa* as such, forming rather a network of disciples whose main purpose was charity.[30]

Despite the mention of such spaces in the literature, the sources shed little light on how they were actually used by those who populated them. Similar to the case of the *madrasa*, in fact, it is not until a bit later that we are presented with consistent information on this point. As Nicholson noted some eighty years ago, it is with the celebrated Sufi of Mayhana Abū Saʿīd b. Abī ʾl-Khayr (d. 440/1049) that we are confronted with the first 'rule' of the Sufi *khānaqāh*, a development in which he saw "a model in the outline of the fraternities that were established during the 12th century; and in the ten rules…the first Mohammedan example of a *regula ad monachos*."[31] As quoted in the *Asrār al-tawḥīd fī maqāmāt al-Shaykh Abī Saʿīd* of Muḥammad b. Munawwar, this ten-point rule (which came to be called the *rusūm-i Bū Saʿīdī*) lays out a number of general principles which the denizens of the *khānaqāh* are enjoined to follow, but by no means is it comprehensive.[32]

According to the 6th/12th-century historian ʿAbd al-Ghāfir b. Ismāʿīl al-Fārisī (d. 529/1134) it was Abū Saʿīd who was "the first to sit within a *khānaqāh* and to introduce the observance of the rules of conduct (*adab*) and the path (*ṭarīqa*) as well as the fulfillment of entering in a commitment to the way, up until today as is the usual custom",[33] and as such serves as an important representative of this trend. Although Meier objects to this statement as such, saying that Abū Saʿīd was not the founder of the *khānaqāh* as an institution (for there were others before his) he does posit that Abū Saʿīd was the first to lay the ground

---

[30] Meier, *Abū Saʿīd*, 306–307; Hamid Algar, "Kāzarūnī," *EI*², 4:851; and, Julian Baldick, *Mystical Islam: An Introduction to Sufism* (London: Tauris, 1989), 59–60.

[31] R.A. Nicholson, *Studies in Islamic Mysticism* (Cambridge: Cambridge University Press, 1921), 76.

[32] Because of the richness of primary documentation, we are more informed about the details of the career and teachings of Abū Saʿīd b. Abī ʾl-Khayr than virtually any other Sufi of his time. Along with the *Ḥālāt u sukhanān-i Shaykh Abū Saʿīd Abū ʾl-Khayr Mayhanī* complied by Abū Saʿīd's great-great-grandson Jamāl al-Dīn Abū Rawḥ Luṭfullāh b. Abī Saʿīd (d. 541/1147), the *Asrār al-tawḥīd* of Luṭfullāh's cousin, Muḥammad b. Nūr al-Dīn Munawwar b. Abī Saʿd Asʿad, constitutes one of the major source for Abū Saʿīd's biography and teachings. John O'Kane has published a translation of this important text as *The Secrets of God's Mystical Oneness* (Costa Mesa, CA & New York: Mazda Publishers in association with Bibliotheca Persica, 1992). These ten rules, dictated to his secretary Abū Bakr Aḥmad b. ʿAlī al-Ustuwāʾī (d. c. 477/1085), are said to have been given along with a set of ten other 'oral' rules specifically directed at the shaykh and a set of ten more for the novice (Meier, *Abū Saʿīd*, 310–311).

[33] *K. al-siyāq li-taʾrīkh Nayshābūr*, as quoted by Meier, *Abū Saʿīd*, 309.

rules for the regulation of the residents of a specifically Sufi *khānaqāh*. This was certainly an important development, and as Terry Graham has pointed out represents the merging of a number of trends in the Khurāsānī socio-religious landscape, especially the coalescence of intentional Sufi communities infused with the ethos of the *javānmardī* (*futuwwa*) tradition.[34] In the figure of Abū Saʿīd b. Abī ʾl-Khayr, the role of the spiritual director within the context of an intentional Sufi community during this period is highlighted, and he is presented (perhaps anachronistically) as an authoritative master who gives guidance to groups of disciples, directing and guiding them along a path whose *raison d'être* and ultimate aim seem well defined. From this point forward, references to such *khānaqāh*s and the teachers and students who inhabited them steadily proliferate in the sources and as a recognizable image comes to witness a certain measure of both rhetorical and documentable stabilization.

As noted earlier, it was under the Great Seljuks (429–590/1038–1194) in particular where we witness the most visible consolidation of the tradition of patronage which seems to be tied to the stabilization of this image, a mutually beneficial relationship in which Sufis, scholars, and holy men populating both the *madrasa*s and Sufi *khānaqāh*s come to be closely tied with the various imperial projects of their patrons, providing them with the religious and spiritual legitimacy which they sought and in return receiving physical, and in certain cases ideological, capital which allowed for the expansion of the modes of religiosity which they championed. If Khurāsān was the crucible in which the lines of this process were forged, it is in Baghdad where they come to be subjected to a certain measure of refinement. The vigor of Baghdad's religious and cultural life certainly had an effect on this process, and although not *sui generis* by any measure of the imagination, it was there where the transformation of Sufi communities from more or less sporadic and loosely organized groups of disciples and masters into increasingly corporate and hierarchical entities took place. In the key eponymic figure and near contemporary of Suhrawardī, ʿAbd al-Qādir al-Jīlānī, for instance, we find a charismatic Ḥanbalī preacher (*wāʿiẓ*) and teacher of law (*mudarris*) who also served as director of a Sufi *ribāṭ*, a tradition

[34] "Abū Saʿīd Abīʾl-Khayr and the School of Khurāsān," in *The Heritage of Sufism*, vol. 1, ed. Leonard Lewisohn (Oxford: Oneworld, 1999), 83–135; cf. ʿAbd al-Ḥusayn Zarrīnkūb, *Justujū dar taṣawwuf-i Īrān* (Tehran: Amīr Kabīr, 1357 sh. [1978]), 192–205.

which his immediate descendents would carry on in Baghdad after him as well as spread outside of Iraq following his death, his legacy being appropriated and recast by later, mostly Shāfiʿī, Sufis who saw in him the model of the ideal Sufi shaykh.[35] Although an eponym, al-Jīlānī should not be considered as having exerted no influence on the development of *ṭarīqa*-based Sufism, and André Demeerseman has shown the extent to which his system depended on the classical Sufi tradition, noting particularly his familiarity with the standard modes of Sufi discourse, its technical terminology, practices, and devotional framework. As he shows, ʿAbd al-Qādir al-Jīlānī promoted an organized method of Sufism predicated on the division of participants into four principal grades—namely the *murīdīn*, the *fuqahāʾ*, the Sufis (*al-qawm*), and the masters (*shuyūkh*)—and as rector of a Sufi *ribāṭ*, he both initiated disciples into his system by way of investiture with the *khirqa* as well as subjected his disciples to a set of rules which they followed while under his direction.[36]

More decisive in the development of *ṭarīqa*-based Sufism than ʿAbd al-Qādir al-Jīlānī, however, is the tradition associated with the eponyms of the Suhrawardiyya brotherhood, Abū Ḥafṣ ʿUmar al-Suhrawardī and his uncle Abū ʾl-Najīb. In the latter's Sufi manual, the *Ādāb al-murīdīn*, we find a thoroughly practical work which deals in large part with the 'institutions of process' comprising the social relationships which obtained in the 'institution of place' of the Sufi *ribāṭ*. Of particular importance is the final section of the work, which focuses on the institution of *rukhaṣ* (sing. *rukhṣa*), or 'dispensations' from various difficult practices or requirements of the Sufi path designed for the *ribāṭ*'s expanding 'lay' constituency. The fact that Abū ʾl-Najīb includes a section on dispensations in such a work evinces the continued penetration of *ṭarīqa*-based Sufism into the wider social arenas of late 6th/12th-century Baghdad. Such modes of what Hodgson called the 'human outreach of the mystics' were an important part of the program pursued by such individuals, forming one of the main channels through which *ribāṭ*-based systems of Sufism were able to secure a presence as an easily replicable (and sustainable) socio-religious space alongside the mosque, *madrasa*, and public pulpit as ubiquitous features of urban neighborhoods throughout

---

[35] Jacqueline Chabbi, "ʿAbd al-Kâdir al-Djilânî, personnage historique," *StI* 38 (1973): 75–106.

[36] *Nouveau regard sur la voie spirituelle d'ʿAbd al-Qadir al-Jilani et sa tradition* (Paris: J. Vrin, 1988), 26–52.

the central and eastern lands of Islamdom during the 6th/12th and 7th/13th centuries.

The Madrasa *and the Culture of Religious Learning*

Among the works attributed to the Baghdadi historian, and student of Suhrawardī, Ibn al-Sāʿī[37] (d. 674/1276), is a book entitled *Akhbār al-rubuṭ wa-l-madāris*, a treatise which by its very title evinces the importance of a second space within which Sufis such as Suhrawardī moved; a space which like the *ribāṭ* was defined as much by the practices and activities which occurred within it as by its actual physical and institutional characteristics. As discussed over the course of this book, the culture of religious learning which existed within the *madrasas* of major urban centers such as Baghdad, Cairo, Damascus, and Isfahan, was intimately linked with the culture of the Sufi *ribāṭs* and *khānaqāhs*. Individuals such as Suhrawardī, in fact, moved effortlessly between such venues, and in the case of him, his teachers, students and disciples, not only does the historiography preserve detailed information on their activities in both arenas, but hints at how the core practices which sustained the culture of the *madrasa* were replicated in the Sufi *ribāṭ*.

As with the Sufi *ribāṭ*, however, the provenance this institution and how it may have functioned in its initial stages remains a matter of debate. Some have looked for a derivation outside of the Abode of Islam proper, such as the great Russian Iranist and Turcologist W. Barthold who proposed a solution which traced the genealogy of the *madrasa* much earlier than any others, speculating that it was inspired by Central Asian Buddhist monasteries (*vihāra*), the presence (or at least memory) of which in Transoxiana posed an institutional challenge to an

---

[37] A Shāfiʿī historian, biographer, *muḥaddith*, *adīb*, and Sufi, Ibn al-Sāʿī seems to have spent his entire life in Baghdad, working for a time as a librarian (*khāzin al-kutub*) at both the Niẓāmiyya and Mustanṣiriyya *madrasas*. A prolific compiler and author, he wrote widely, although his primary forte was historiography. He also authored a number of treatises on Sufism, among them a *K. al-zuhhād* and a *K. akhbār al-Ḥallāj*. Most of the one-hundred or so works attributed to him, however, are no longer extant, and even fewer have been edited. Known for associating with various shaykhs and ascetics of Baghdad, Ibn al-Sāʿī was invested with the *khirqa* by Suhrawardī in 608/1211–1212 (al-Dhahabī, *Tadhkirat*, 4:1469, and, Ibn Rāfiʿ, *Muntakhab*, 138), although what he took was probably the *khirqat al-tabarruk* as he does not seem to have associated with Suhrawardī as a formal disciple. On him, see: *KḤ*, 422 (*anno* 674); *TIsl*, 56:161–163 (*anno* 674, no. 176); *ṬSh*, 2:70–71; *BN*, 13:270 (*anno* 674); *ṬFSh*[2], 1:461–462 (no. 441); and, Rosenthal, "Ibn al-Sāʿī," *EI*[2], 3:925–926.

increasingly self-conscious Muslim polity.[38] Others have placed its genesis in that period of transition between the disintegration of Abbasid sovereignty under the Buyids and coming to power of the Seljuks, the hypothesis of the late George Makdisi being the most widely accepted and often quoted.

Makdisi envisioned the *madrasa* proper as a product of three main stages,[39] finding its precursor in a series of mosque-caravansary complexes which—based on a single reference given by Ibn al-Jawzī—were popularized by Badr b. Ḥasanawayh (d. 450/1014), a Kurdish vassal of the Buyids who is said to have founded a string of such 'complexes' over the course of his thirty-two year reign.[40] As with the Sufi *ribāṭ* and *khānaqāh*, by the time of Suhrawardī the *madrasa* was a prominent feature of urban landscapes across the Abode of Islam, patronized by rulers, endowed in perpetuity via *waqf*, and serving as important spaces within which the transmission of religious learning took place. At the same time, as with the Sufi *ribāṭ*s the nature of how such institutions were organized, why they became objects of patronage, and how the ulama and others actually used them has remained a matter of debate. Beginning—as with many key debates in the field of Islamic Studies—with Ignaz Goldziher's thesis, the standard reading posits that during the 5th/11th century, the Seljuks 'founded Sunni colleges' in order to promote the advanced study of the Sunni religious sciences in

[38] Barthold, *Four Studies*, 1:79.

[39] In his entry on the subject in *EI*², Makdisi both restates (and prudently revises) some of the details of the narrative given in *The Rise of Colleges*. His three stages model sees the origins of the *madrasa* proper in the *masjid* which functioned as an informal instructional center where individual scholars would hold teaching sessions (*majālis*)—both ad hoc and organized—on the Qur'ān and Ḥadīth; a second *masjid-khān* complex stage, an extension of the former in which foreign students who came to attend the *majlis* of a particularly illustrious scholar (usually to collect *ḥadīth* but increasingly for the purposes of legal study) would find housing in the caravansary (*khān*) attached to the mosque; and, finally, the *madrasa* proper which grew out of the *masjid-khān* complex, stimulated by the vigorous patronage of Niẓām al-Mulk. ("Madrasa," *EI*², 5:1126).

[40] Makdisi, *Rise of Colleges*, 29–30; cf. *MT*, 7:272. Makdisi also cites a variant found in Ibn Kathīr (*BN*, 11:354). Based on both the obscurity of the reference and the use of the term in local Khurāsāni histories of earlier provenance, Roy Mottahedeh has proposed that we should look elsewhere for a model, Khurāsān ("The Transmission of Learning: The Role of the Islamic Northeast," in *Madrasa: la transmission du savior dans le monde musulman*, ed. Nicole Grandin and Marc Gaborieau [Paris: Éditions Arguments, 1997], 65), and indeed in his study of medieval Nīshāpūr, Richard Bulliet has given a list of buildings called *madrasa*s in which legal studies were pursued, four of which antedate the time of Badr b. Ḥasanawayh (*The Patricians of Nishapur: A Study in Medieval Islamic Social History* [Cambridge, MA: Harvard University Press, 1972]).

an attempt to counter the influence of Shiism, this program of institutionalized learning being aimed at producing a class of well-trained Sunni religious professionals who would serve the state by assuming positions within the bureaucracy and the officially sanctioned 'religious establishment'.[41] In this reading, the institutionalization of the *madrasa* system was to provide for yet another institution, namely that of an organized cadre of Sunni intellectual warriors who would serve what came to be called the 'Sunni revival'.[42] From this moment forward, so the story goes, the *madrasa* system would be disseminated throughout Islamdom and would come to serve as the primary forum for the teaching and dissemination of an organized, monolithic, Ashʿarite-Sunni orthodoxy.[43] Research on the *madrasa* in the next generation did not do much to change this picture, and while Orientalists such as J. Pederson[44] attempted to deepen our knowledge of this feature of Muslim

[41] The classic statement is to be found in the *Vorlesungen*: "For a long time the Ashʿarites could not venture to teach their theology in public. It was not taught as a formally acknowledged part of the system of orthodox theology until the middle of the eleventh century, when the famous vizier of the Seljuqs, Niẓām al-Mulk, established in the great schools he had founded in Nishapur and Baghdad positions for the public teaching of the new theological ideas." (Goldziher, *Introduction to Islamic Theology and Law*, trans. A. & R. Hamori [Princeton: Princeton University Press, 1981], 104).

[42] George Makdisi has offered what is perhaps the standard critique of this notion of a 5th/11th-century Sunni revival under the Seljuks. In short, he argues that this 'revival' is wrongly attributed to factors which had almost nothing to do with it and that what occurred under the Seljuks was simply the outcome of a process initiated at the beginning of the century ("The Sunnī Revival," in D.S. Richards ed. *Islamic Civilisation, 950–1150: A Colloquium Published under the Auspices of the Near Eastern History Group, Oxford—The Near East Center, University of Pennsylvania*, Papers on Islamic History, no. 3. [Oxford: Bruno Cassirer Ltd., 1973], 155–168). One particular episode which is worthy of note in this regard is the proclamation of the Q̱ādirī Creed by the caliph al-Q̱ādir (r. 381–422/991–1031); again Makdisi provides the most coherent reading (*Ibn ʿAqīl: Religion and Culture in Classical Islam* [Edinburgh: Edinburgh University Press, 1997], 301, 304–308).

[43] The classic statement is to be found in the *Vorlesungen*: "For a long time the Ashʿarites could not venture to teach their theology in public. It was not taught as a formally acknowledged part of the system of orthodox theology until the middle of the eleventh century, when the famous vizier of the Seljuqs, Niẓām al-Mulk, established in the great schools he had founded in Nishapur and Baghdad positions for the public teaching of the new theological ideas." (*Introduction to Islamic Theology and Law*, trans. A. & R. Hamori. [Princeton: Princeton University Press, 1981], 104).

[44] "Masdjid," rpt. in *E.J. Brill's First Encyclopaedia of Islam (1913–1936)* (Leiden: E.J. Brill, 1987), 5:350–376. Peterson asserted that there was no substantial difference between the *madrasa*, mosque, and congregational mosque (*jāmiʿ*), the distinction being purely linguistic. Makdisi provided a through critique of his reading (see his "Muslim Institutions of Learning in Eleventh-century Baghdad," *BSOAS* 24 [1961]: 48–50; and, idem, *The Rise of Colleges*, 304–305).

intellectual life, old notions retained their prominence. Indeed, some twenty years ago, George Makdisi perceptively remarked: "many works have been written on Muslim education. Their number, however, has not been commensurate with the amount of light they shed on the origin, nature and development of Muslim institutions of learning".[45]

In a lengthy series of truly erudite studies, Makdisi took it as his task to provide this light. For him, the *madrasa* was first and foremost a place where the study of law (*fiqh*) was pursued: "A *fiqh* lesson was referred to by the term *dars*; the professor of *fiqh* was a *mudarris*; and *darrasa*, used in the absolute, meant to teach *fiqh*."[46] Accordingly, the 'post' of the *mudarris* as well as 'the teaching of law' were both subsumed under the term *tadrīs*. The *madrasa* was a privately endowed institution founded and maintained through the law of *waqf*. Through this device the founder (*wāqif*) of such an institution was able to stipulate, within set legal limits, the scope and nature of the institution which he endowed. Thus, in the *waqfiyya* ('endowment document') of his celebrated *madrasa* opened in Baghdad a year before Suhrawardī's death, the Abbasid caliph al-Mustanṣir (r. 623–640/1226–1242) stipulated that the transmission of *ḥadīth* was to take place on Monday, Thursday and Saturday of every week and that each of the four *mudarrisūn* who taught *fiqh* in the *madrasa* were only to transmit the established books of their respective *madhhab*s and not those of their own authorship.[47] The nature of the stipulations contained in the *waqfiyya*s, at least as far as can be gathered for this early period, varied considerably, but in the case of large institutions such as the Mustanṣiriyya legislated down to the last detail what could and could not happen therein, the number of students who were to be admitted, and the nature of the stipends which were to be provided for students, teachers, and 'support staff'.

According to Makdisi, the manner in which the 'faculty' of the *madrasa* were organized did not always assume a strict difference between those who were 'students' and those who were 'professors'. Because the *madrasa* was at its core a place where individual texts were transmitted by individual scholars, it was not uncommon for a more advanced scholar to assume the role of 'professor' one day and that of 'student' the next. Those giving lessons, either dictating texts (*imlā'*) or engaging

---

[45] Makdisi, *The Rise of Colleges*, 292.
[46] Idem, "Muslim Institutions of Learning," 10.
[47] *KḤ*, 85–86.

in disputations, would be assigned a particular spot within the structure, usually beside a pillar, from where he would execute his teaching duties to a group of students gathered around him in a circle (*ḥalqa*). This was his *majlis* and in this respect, the *mudarris* seems to have differed little from his counterparts in the mosque, the public pulpit, or the Sufi *ribāṭ*. In turn, the *mudarris* was entitled to engage the services of a variety of assistants—who were almost always advanced students themselves and whose positions were provided for by the *madrasa*'s endowment—most notably a *nā'ib mudarris* ('deputy') who would assume his teaching duties in case of absence or when the *mudarris* held several separate posts (*tadārīs*), a *mu'īd* ('*repetitor*') who would both repeat the lesson as well as explain difficult portions to the students, and a *mufīd* who imparted 'useful information' (*fawā'id*) to students after the day's lesson had been given.[48] In addition to the transmission of texts, a ubiquitous feature of all types of learning in any case, the *mudarris* would rehearse the proper method of disputation (*munāẓara*) with those students who were aiming to acquire what Makdisi calls 'a license to teach law and issue legal opinions' (*ijāzat al-tadrīs wa-l-fatwā*). Under the guidance of his *mudarris*, the potential *muftī/faqīh* would study this method of disputation (*ṭarīqat al-naẓar*) which, put briefly, consisted of a thorough knowledge of the agreed upon and divergent legal opinions of the jurisconsults (*khilāf*) and the 'disputed questions' (*al-masā'il al-khilāfiyya*), a mastery of dialectic (*jadal*), and the ability to utilize all three to 'win' organized contests of disputation and thus attain 'leadership' (*riyāsa*) in his particular locale.[49]

According to the schema provided by Makdisi, students—at least those pursuing a course of legal education—were usually spoken of in three broad categories, namely: 1) *mubtadi'* ('beginner'); 2) *mutawassiṭ* ('intermediate'); and, 3) *muntahī* ('terminal'), the same terms which Suhrawardī uses in his description of the various levels of the Sufi aspirant. Within these categories, students were also ranked according to whether or not they received stipends; in the former case there were the *mutafaqqih* ('he who is applying himself to the acquisition of *fiqh*') and the *faqīh*, a term which could either designate the jurisconsult proper or an advanced student of law; in the latter case the *faqīh* would most usually be attached to a master-jurisconsult, or *maṣḥūb* ('mentor'), as a

[48] Makdisi, *The Rise of Colleges*, 188–196.
[49] Ibid., 108–111; 128–140.

ṣāḥib ('protégé'). It was during his period of 'fellowship' (*ṣuḥba*)—which of course was the same term used for the training of a novice (*murīd*) under a Sufi master (*shaykh*)—when the potential *faqīh/mudarris/muftī* would compile a *taʿlīqa*, an original composition culled from the 'notes' he took from his master's lectures (*ʿallaqa ʿanhu*) and which would come to serve as his own 'syllabus' (*ṭarīqa*) or compendium of disputed legal questions and their answers once he established himself as a teacher or legal professional.

For all its intricacies and philological detail, Makdisi's 'reconstruction' of the *madrasa* (at least as it came to exist in the central Islamic lands during the Later Middle Period) has been criticized by a number of scholars. None too surprisingly, the bulk of this criticism revolves around the rather prescriptive picture which Makdisi painted of the *madrasa*s as 'curricular institutions', as places defined by some type of top-down organizational structure and not by the people who inhabited them. For Makdisi, in fact, the end product of the *madrasa* system and its *raison d'être* was the professional jurisconsult, nothing more and nothing less. The *madrasa* ostensibly achieved this goal through a relatively organized faculty and student body pursuing a pre-determined and specialized curriculum, the upshot of the whole enterprise being focused solely on 'determining orthodoxy' in Islam. Having emerged triumphant following the *miḥna* of the 3rd/9th century the traditionalists, as Makdisi characterizes them, set about actively constructing an organizational and institutional structure so conceived as to protect them from their two main adversaries, namely the governing power upon whom they preferred not to depend and their ideological adversaries, the rationalists, whom they desired to exclude from the process of determining orthodoxy.[50] In their efforts to assert hegemony over this process, the traditionalists organized themselves into 'legal guilds' and pursued their agenda within the context of what amounted to 'guild colleges',[51] which in being based on *waqf* were essentially private and as such beyond the reach of competing hegemonies, both political and ideological.

[50] Idem, "Baghdad, Bologna, and Scholasticism," in *Centers of Learning: Learning and Location in pre-Modern Europe and the Near East*, ed. J.W. Drijvers & A. MacDonald. (Leiden: Brill, 1995), 143–144.

[51] Idem, *The Rise of Humanism in Classical Islam and the Christian West, with Special Reference to Scholasticism* [Edinburgh: Edinburgh University Press, 1990], 16–38; and, idem, *Ibn ʿAqīl*, 57–65.

A number of recent studies have challenged this picture, arguing that the *madrasa*s and the culture of learning which filled them was more informal and fluid than Makdisi claimed and that as an institution the *madrasa*s were largely tangential to the formation of scholarly groupings and the crystallization of the *madhhab*s/legal guilds, including the Ḥanbalites/traditionists. The previously cited study of Daphna Ephrat on the ulama of 5th/11th-century Baghdad, argues for the primacy of *adab* and personal social networks over and against any type of institutional hegemony, positing that the *madrasa* was merely a new and more institutionalized form of organization into which the essential cultural and social practices of a diffuse and highly individualized culture of religious learning were poured. Calling for a reevaluation of Makdisi's thesis that the *madrasa*s played a major role in the consolidation of the *madhhab*s and their evolution into religious factions, she posits that in the early 5th/11th century no professional religious establishment had yet been consolidated, and that the essential informality of Islamic religious learning effectively prohibited the formation an institutionalized learned elite along the lines which it would emerge in later Mamluk and Ottoman contexts.

Seeing no evidence for a state-supported curriculum or agenda to use such institutions as training grounds for future bureaucrats and civil officials, Ephrat emphasizes that appointments were made largely along personal lines rather than on ties of patronage binding a scholar to political rulers, suggesting that the Seljuk sultans and viziers founded *madrasa*s not so much for members of a certain school, as for a particular scholar with whom they were probably closely associated. The upshot of Ephrat's reading in terms of its relationship to the issue of the *madrasa* is that it was not primarily the institutional setting which allowed for a measure of coherency to obtain among the Sunni ulama, but rather the manner in which such spaces reinforced the social practices through which such a body came to constitute itself.

Taking up the following period—this time in Damascus—Michael Chamberlain has argued that Makdisi mistook what were actually social practices for institutional structures. Concerning himself with these practices, Chamberlain attempts to show that many of the activities and structures which Makdisi took as being 'educational' in nature were in fact reflective of a more widespread culture of competition played out, in a context of *fitna*, among the Damascene elites (*aʿyān*) in order to secure and reproduce social status. In fact, Chamberlain sees the struggle of city notables for 'stipendiary posts' (*manṣab*s) in the *madrasa*s as analogous to that of military elites for *iqṭāʿ*s. In essence, he attempts to show that the principle consequence of the *madrasa*s of medieval Damascus was "to provide a package of prizes that changed the nature of aʿyān social competition…the madrasas were important religious and social institutions with many purposes which had nothing to do with education."[52] Dismantling the picture of the internal organization of the *madrasa* which Makdisi built up in the *Rise of Colleges*, Chamberlain also reads the functional categories of students and teachers which Makdisi laid out as being essentially descriptive, arguing that the *muʿīd, mufīd*, and so forth were but stipendiary categories, having nothing whatsoever to do with function. Finally, Chamberlain brings into question the primacy of the legal curriculum as well as the notion that the *madrasa*, and indeed the pursuit of religious knowledge in general, aimed at producing certified legal experts. What he shows instead, is that what was stipulated in the *waqfiyya*s and what actually transpired in the *madrasa*s were often two very different things and that the study of law was actually just a part of a much larger whole. The upshot of Chamberlain's study, as far as it concerns us here, is that the *madrasa*s of medieval Damascus certainly did not seem to exercise any kind of hegemony over the transmission, (re)production, and deployment of knowledge nor did they function solely to train a cadre of legal professionals. Individuals interested in religious learning, for whatever reason, could participate in the culture of the *madrasa* in a variety of ways and at a number of levels.

As it concerns the activities of Suhrawardī, his teachers, students, associates and disciples, the upshot of these re-readings of Makdisi are two. First, there is the issue of the place and status of the *madrasa* vis-à-vis both the powers who patronized them and the elite scholarly groupings of ulama who constituted their most visible, although not sole, constituency. As shown in the following chapter, not only did three generations of the Suhrawardī family (not to mention a host of their associates) benefit greatly from the patronage of officials and the *ribāṭ*s which they built and the *madrasa*s which they endowed, but that for al-Nāṣir in particular both the *madrasa*s and Sufi *ribāṭ*s served as important repositories of human capital, places from which authoritative scholars and ideologues could be drawn to support the ideological dimensions of his program. Second, although the transmission of both religious

[52] Chamberlain, *Knowledge and Social Practice*, 91.

and mystical learning most certainly demanded personal relationships and not institutional affiliations, as Shahab Ahmad has argued this does not mean that as an institution, the *madrasa* was not possessed of a measure of social, political, or cultural importance for certain learned groups nor was it marginal to the culture of learning, but rather that it served—like Suhrawardī's Sufi *ribāṭ*s—as a space in which established forms of social organization and practice were reconceptualized in new institutionalized forms.[53] For individuals such as Suhrawardī and his associates, such institutions *were* important, important enough that an entire complex of proper behaviors (*ādāb*), hierarchies of organization, and rules regarding social interactions among its constituents were codified in writing, both by Sufis such as Suhrawardī (most notably in his *ʿAwārif al-maʿārif*) and by ulama such as the late 6th/12th-century Ḥanafī scholar Burhān al-Dīn al-Zarnūjī in his *Taʿlīm al-mutaʿallim.*[54]

The Textual Setting

In addition with the political and institutional forces which converged in Suhrawardī's historical moment, there was a third cluster which provided another space within which Suhrawardī, his teachers, students and disciples moved. This space was the discourse and authority of the text, a space which in Suhrawardī's Baghdad informed both political program, the programmatic perpetuation of a particular Sufi tradition to which he considered himself an heir, and the very patterns of social behavior which sustained the Sufi *ribāṭ*s and Sunni *madrasa*s. Like the first two clusters, the discourse and authority of the text was possessed of a genealogy as well, a genealogy which much like the other two can be traced to the collective endeavor of successive generations of Muslims to the problem of working out the dictates and prescriptions of the original revelation in time and space. At the same time, however, the genealogy of the discourse and authority of the text as it came to express itself in Suhrawardī's time and space served to be a deeper and more immediate presence in the world within which he

[53] "Review of *A Learned Society in a Period of Transition*, by Daphna Ephrat," *JAOS* 123.1 (2003): 179–182.

[54] Al-Zarnūjī, *Taʿlīm al-Mutaʿallim—Ṭarīq al-Taʿallum (Instruction of the Student: The Method of Learning)*, trans. G.E. von Grunebaum and Theodora Abel (New York: King's Crown Press, 1947).

moved than the others, for at its core it was a practice vested with soteriological significance.

As Talal Asad has argued, in writing an anthropology of Islam "one should begin, as Muslims do, from the concept of a discursive tradition that includes and relates itself to the founding texts",[55] and for individuals such as Suhrawardī, these founding texts were understood as existing in a hierarchy, a gradation which although articulated in time in space was, at its core, numinous and transhistorical. At the apex of this hierarchy was the primary reference point to which all other texts refer, the Qurʾān, the central repository of symbols, values, and narratives which served as both the collective patrimony of the Muslim community and the conclusive, unchangeable revelation to humankind prior to the Day of Judgment. After this came the Ḥadīth, the record of the words and deeds of Muḥammad and his companions which when taken together provide the pattern of exemplary behavior (*sunna*) by which the original dictates of the Qurʾānic message are articulated in time and space. Following this, are the collective mass of reports and anecdotes (*akhbār/āthār*) of the three generation succeeding the Prophet: 1) his immediate companions (*ṣahāba*); 2) their successors (*tābiʿūn*); and, 3) the 'successors to the successors' (*atbāʿ al-tābiʿīn*); who together comprise the 'pious forebears' (*al-salaf al-ṣāliḥ*). It is this last group in particular which was of particular importance for Suhrawardī and the particular strand of the Sufi tradition which he inherited, for it was the *salaf al-ṣāliḥ* who provided the genealogies of specific collective endeavors of Muslim scholars. Simply put, over the course of its development each religious science searched for a paragon from among the *salaf al-ṣāliḥ*, an individual who could be appropriated as its founding father and thus become the guarantor of its legitimacy as a religious science, and for Suhrawardī and the particular Junaydī-tradition to which he considered himself an heir, the Sufis were no different.[56] It was to the *exempla*, doctrines, interpretations, and prescriptions of this hierarchy of texts and individuals in which ulama and Sufis such as Suhrawardī and his associates vested their soteriological hopes and ambitions, projecting

[55] Talal Asad, *The Idea of an Anthropology of Islam* (Washington, D.C.: Center for Contemporary Arab Studies, Georgetown University, 1986), 14.

[56] On this, see E. Chaumont, "al-Salaf waʾl-Khalaf," *EI*², 13:900; and, Richard Gramlich, "Vom islamischen Glauben an die 'gute alte Zeit,'" in idem (ed.), *Islamwissenschaftliche Abhandlungen Fritz Meier zum 60. Geburtstag* (Wiesbaden: Steinwi, 1974), 110–117.

the authority of the past into the present in an attempt to ascertain what is valid and correct.

At the same time, although to participate in such an endeavor was to personally confront the Qur'ānic message and its articulation in the *exempla* of the authorities of the past, it was also a way to secure a place within a broader collective endeavor which conferred status and authority upon its practitioners. As has already been noted, even the caliph al-Nāṣir li-Dīn Allāh himself engaged in the production and transmission of texts as an instrument through which he attempted to enunciate and legitimize authority. Similarly, among the ulama and other interested parties, both in and outside of the *madrasas* and Sufi *ribāṭs*, the transmission of texts, especially *ḥadīth*, served as one of the most public and widely-accepted means through which membership in that particular group could be secured, the status of which inevitably spilled over into wider social arenas. For individuals such as Suhrawardī, actively participating in this and other patterns of behavior characterizing a shared culture of religious learning served as a particularly powerful instrument through which status was achieved, conserved, and perpetuated.

In the circles within which Suhrawardī moved, the discourse and authority of the text not only served as an instrument of authority and status, but as an instrument of memory as well. As an instrument of memory, texts served as loci of self-identification, a means through which an individual was able to situate himself within a tradition by affiliating with an either real or imagined genealogy. Here, texts both constrained and shaped the trajectory of Suhrawardī's own textual production, for in providing him with a set of authoritative conventions and rhetorical strategies which had already been established as the apparatus through which the particular strand of the Sufi tradition to which he saw himself as an heir had expressed itself, he was simultaneously able to capitalize upon the authority of that tradition while at the same time make calculated choices on how to configure and deploy that authority to serve his own programmatic vision. Similar processes occurred within other arenas of learning as well. The jurists self-consciously affiliated with the genealogies of their respective *madhhabs* and forged links with the past through the composition, perpetuation, and study of biographies/hagiographies of their eponymous founders while at the same time constructing a living record of what they saw to be a communal jurisprudential enterprise, preserving the collective weight of each generation of jurists in collections of juridical opinions (*fatāwā*) and theoretical works on jurisprudential theory associated with particular schools (*madhāhib*, sing. *madhhab*). In a similar manner, philosophers, physicians, and hermeticists cultivated and constructed an entire body of instruments through which links with a past, antedating that of the jurists to be sure, were made through the construction of genealogies and the cultivation of a view of history which linked them to Hellenic and Late Antique traditions while at the same time forging communal identities through the production of biographical dictionaries devoted to *ḥukamā'*. The same was done by administrative officials who, in addition to writing manuals on their crafts, produced biographical dictionaries of viziers and secretaries specifically aimed at providing a model of past practice which could be reproduced in the present.

Texts and the Writing of Identity

In his capacity as both a theorist and author, Suhrawardī presented himself as heir to a particular tradition of Sufism, the school of al-Junayd al-Baghdādī[57] (d. 298/910). An individual who already by the time of Suhrawardī had come to be configured as a paragon of the sober (*ṣaḥw*) trend of Sufism, the figure of al-Junayd al-Baghdādī came to serve as a foil against which opposing trends in Sufism were set into relief, most notably in opposition to the drunken (*sukr*) trend which found its own paragon in the person of Abū Yazīd (or, Bāyazīd) al-Bisṭāmī[58] (d. 234/848 or 261/875), his older contemporary and polar

[57] A native of Baghdad, al-Junayd is undeniably one of the most important representatives of that particular strand of the Sufi tradition to which Suhrawardī saw himself as an heir. Nephew and disciple of the Baghdadi spiritual master Sarī al-Saqaṭī (d. 251/867), he was born into an urban mercantile family, his father trading in glassware and al-Junayd himself trading in tussah silk. According to his biographers he received a through education in the religious sciences and studied with, among others, Shāfiʿī ulama such as Abū Thawr (d. 240/855) and Ibn Kullāb (d. c. 240/855) and was a close associated of al-Ḥārith al-Muḥāsibī (d. 243/857). On his life and thought, see: A.H. Abdel-Kader, *The Life, Personality and Writings of al-Junayd* (London: Luzac & Co., 1962), 1–63; Arberry, "al-Djunayd," *EI²*, 2:598; and, Knysh, *Islamic Mysticism*, 52–56 *passim*.

[58] Born in the city of Bisṭām (or Basṭām) in the province of Qūmis, he spent the majority of his life there save for the few times he was obliged to leave due to the hostility of the ulama (Gerhard Böwering, "Besṭāmī (Basṭāmī)," *EIr*, 4:183). He is reported to have met or corresponded with many illustrious Sufis and about five-hundred of his *aqwāl* are preserved in early sources such as Sarrāj's *K. al-lumaʿ*, and somewhat later in the *K. al-nūr min kalimāt Abī Yazīd Ṭayfūr* compiled by al-Sahlajī (d. 476/1084), there also being reports of a no longer extant Persian *Manāqib-i Bāyazīd Bisṭāmī* upon which Sahlajī may have drawn. (ibid.) Much of Bisṭāmī's fame rests with his *shaṭaḥāt*, for which see: Carl Ernst, *Words of Ecstasy in Sufism*, (Albany: State University of New York Press,

opposite. The way in which Suhrawardī engaged this genealogy was through later textual figurations of the Junaydī tradition, a discrete corpus of texts which by the time of Suhrawardī had come to constitute something of a canon existing alongside a much larger body of texts in the religious sciences. Included among this corpus are those works which Suhrawardī quotes directly in his own writings, beginning with the key Sufi handbook of the 4th/10th century, the *K. al-luma*ʿ *fī ʾl-taṣawwuf* of Abū Naṣr al-Sarrāj[59] (d. 378/988) which Suhrawardī presents as constituting an authoritative statement on the Sufi way of al-Junayd (*ṭarīq al-qawm*) and the *K. al-taʿarruf li-madhhab ahl al-taṣawwuf* of Abū Bakr al-Kalābādhī, a popular text about which Suhrawardī is reported to have said: "if it were not for the *Taʿarruf*, we would know nothing about Sufism".[60]

Following these two texts, Suhrawardī relied heavily on the mass of Sufi *akhbār* and *aqwāl* preserved in the biographical dictionaries (hagiographies) of ʿAbd al-Raḥmān al-Sulamī (d. 412/1021), the *Ṭabaqāt al-ṣūfiyya*,[61] and the *Ḥilyat al-awliyāʾ* of Abū Nuʿaym al-Iṣfahānī[62] (d. 430/1038). By the time of Suhrawardī, both of these works had achieved some measure of popularity as standards, and it was from this fecund repository of Sufi hagio-historiography in particular which Suhrawardī draws upon throughout his own writings, quoting *khabar* after *khabar* as the proof texts upon which a particular prescriptive state-

1985), 15, 26–27, 29–30, 43–45; and, Joseph van Ess, *Theologie und Gesellschaft im 2. und 3. Jahrhundert Hidschra* (Berlin: Walter de Gruyter, 1991–1997), 4:387–395.

[59] *K. al-lumaʿ fī ʾl-taṣawwuf*, ed. R.A. Nicholson. G.M.S, no. 22. (Leiden: E.J. Brill; London: Luzac & Co., 1914); addenda in: A.J. Arberry, *Pages from the Kitāb al-Lumaʿ of Abū Naṣr al-Sarrāj* (London: 1947); German translation by Richard Gramlich as *Schlaglichter über das Sufitum* (Stuttgart: Franz Steiner Verlag, 1990). In addition to the introductions of Nicholson, Arberry, and Gramlich, on al-Sarrāj see: P. Lory, "al-Sarrādj," *EI*², 9:65–66; Baldick, *Mystical Islam*, 55; and, Knysh, *Islamic Mysticism*, 118–120.

[60] A note prefacing a copy of the *K. al-taʿarrūf* in MS. Süley., Süleymaniye 731$_{\text{mü.}}$, fol. 251b.

[61] *Ṭabaqāt al-ṣūfiyya* [+*Dhikr al-niswat al-mutaʿabbidāt al-ṣūfiyyāt*], ed. Muṣṭafā ʿAbd al-Qādir ʿAṭāʾ (Beirut: Dār al-Kutub al-ʿIlmiyya, 1998); updated edition of the Arabic text of *Dhikr al-niswa* and translation by Rkia E. Cornell as *Early Sufi Women* (Louisville, KY: Fons Vitae, 1999). On Sulamī, see: Gerhard Böwering, "al-Sulamī," *EI*², 9:811–812, which gives a most extensive bibliography of the sources on his life and works.

[62] *Ḥilyat al-awliyāʾ wa-ṭabaqāt al-aṣfiyāʾ*, 10 vols. in 5 (Beirut: Dār al-Kitāb al-ʿArabī, 1967–1968). On him and his work, see J. Pedersen, "Abū Nuʿaym al-Iṣfahānī," *EI*², 1:142–143; Raif Khouri, "Importance et authenticité des textes de Ḥilyat al-awliyāʾ," *StI* 26 (1977):73–113; Knysh, *Islamic Mysticism*, 128–130; and, Jawid Mojaddedi, *The Biographical Tradition in Sufism: The Ṭabaqāt Genre from al-Sulamī to Jāmī* (Richmond, Surrey: Curzon Press, 2001), 41–67.

ment or interpretation rests. After this body of material, Suhrawardī made equally heavy use of the celebrated Sufi manual and biographical dictionary of Abū ʾl-Qāsim al-Qushayrī (d. 465/1072), the *R. al-qushayriyya*,[63] which alongside his uncle Abū ʾl-Najīb al-Suhrawardī's *Ādāb al-murīdīn* is presented as a key authority in Suhrawardī's writings, the text in fact serving as a template for one of his own Sufi handbooks, the *Irshād al-murīdīn* as well as being liberally quoted in numerous others works, most notably the *ʿAwārif al-maʿārif*. In addition, the *Qūt al-qulūb* of the enigmatic Abū Ṭālib al-Makkī[64] (d. 386/996) is also presented by Suhrawardī as an authority. He does not quote al-Ghazālī's *Iḥyāʾ ʿulūm al-dīn*[65] as a source, although its ethos does permeate his works.

Taken together, the texts in this corpus share a number of things. First, and this is best evinced in the hagiographical literature, is a vision of doctrine and praxis which is predicated upon the authority of the past, a past which is not as important in terms of its historicity than a past which is worth preserving because of its ability to provide a pattern of exemplary behavior, a habitus, in the present. In his aforementioned *Ṭabaqāt al-ṣūfiyya*, Sulamī explains:

> The prophets—peace be upon them—are followed by the saints (*awliyāʾ*) who succeed them in their model behavior, prompting their communities to follow their path (*ṭarīqa*) and their way (*samt*). There was never a moment when they were not calling people onto the Truth or proving it by explanations and decisive proofs. In every age they are set in generations (*ṭabaqāt*), saint succeeding saint through adhering to his predecessor's exempla (*āthār*) and emulating his [method of] wayfaring (*sulūk*). By them, aspirants (*murīdūn*) are educated in proper manners and unifiers (*muwaḥḥidūn*) find consolation in their examples... the Prophet—may God bless and greet him—said: "My community is like the rain, it is not known whether its

[63] 2 vols. ed. ʿAbd al-Ḥalīm Maḥmūd and Maḥmūd b. al-Sharīf (Cairo: Dār al-Kutub al-Ḥadītha, 1972–1974); German translation as by Richard Gramlich as *Das Sendschreiben al-Qušayris über das Sufitum* (Wiesbaden: Franz Steiner Verlag, 1989). On his life and works see: Gramlich, op. cit., 11–19; Knysh, *Islamic Mysticism*, 130–132; and, Mojaddedi, *The Biographical Tradition*, 99–124.

[64] Abū Ṭālib al-Makkī, *Qūt al-qulūb*, 2 vols. (Cairo: Muṣṭafā al-Bābī al-Ḥalabī, 1381 [1961]); German translation by Richard Gramlich as *Die Nahrung der Herzen*, 4 vols. (Wiesbaden: Franz Steiner Verlag, 1995). Turkish translation and partial study by Muharrem Tan as *Kalplerin Azığı*, 4 vols. (Istanbul: İz Yayıncılık, 1999). Biographical material on him is slim, for which see my entry "Abū Ṭālib al-Makkī," *Encyclopaedia of Islam Three* (Leiden: Brill, forthcoming).

[65] Abū Ḥāmid al-Ghazālī, *Iḥyāʾ ʿulūm al-dīn*, 5 vols. (Beirut: Dār al-Kutub al-ʿIlmiyya, 1996). Still not properly edited, most of the work has already been translated into European languages, with more volumes forthcoming under the auspices of the Islamic Texts Society's al-Ghazālī project.

> beginning or its end is the best", and what the Prophet—may God bless and greet him—was alluding to is that up until the end, his community would not be devoid of the saints and the substitutes (*budalāʾ*) who explain to the community the externals of his religious laws and the internals of his divine truths, prompting them to adhere to its manners (*ādāb*) and religious obligations in word and deed. Among every community, they are the successors (*khulafāʾ*) to the prophets and messengers—may God bless them—and the masters of the divine realities of *tawḥīd*, the transmitters, the possessors of veridical insights (*firāsāt ṣādiqa*) and beautiful manners (*ādāb*), the successors to the model customs of the messengers—may God bless all of them—up until the coming of the Final Hour.[66]

As Gibb perceptively observed some forty years ago, such biographical forms of writing have deep roots in Islamic civilization itself, for the enduring social and intellectual trend which informed so much of its production was the idea that "...the history of the Islamic Community is essentially the contribution of individual men and women to the building up and *transmission* of its specific culture; that it is these persons (rather than the political governors) who represent or reflect the active forces in Muslim society in their respective spheres; and that their individual contributions are worthy of being recorded for future generations."[67] Although I would replace Gibb's use of 'individual' with 'individual groups of', his reading is an important one, for as a genre, Sufis biographical dictionaries such as those of Sulamī and Iṣfahānī were not unique creations, far from it. Part of a much larger genre of biographical literature which had much of the same goal, namely to capture and configure the past in such a way as to address the needs of the present either by securing a genealogy by which one might enunciate the virtues of a particular group or by providing a pattern of exemplary behavior which could be replicated in the present, there is little difference in the form, function, and intent of texts apparently as different in subject and content as Ibn Abī Yaʿlā's (d. 458/1066) *Ṭabaqāt al-ḥanābila* and Sulamī's *Ṭabaqāt al-ṣūfiyya*, each of which utilized not only the same form (genre) but in many ways the same rhetorical strategies to meet their ends. At the same time, as with any shared form of writing about the past, biographical literature was contested, Ibn al-Jawzī for instance objecting to the classificatory scheme of Abū

[66] al-Sulamī, *Ṭabaqāt al-ṣūfiyya*, 20–21.

[67] "Islamic Biographical Literature," in *Historians of the Middle East*, Bernard Lewis and P.M. Holt, eds. (London: Oxford University Press, 1962), 54 (italics mine).

Nuʿaym's *Ḥilyat al-awliyā'* and producing his own work, the *Ṣifat al-ṣafwa*, as a corrective.[68]

Concomitant with the biographical literature, Suhrawardī also inherited the use of a special technical language and system of praxis which, like the former, served to define Sufism as a science and tradition with its own genealogy and jargon which, in its very uniqueness, simultaneously shared a space with a much larger body of juridical, theological, and exegetical literature. It is certainly no accident that the period in which that particular strand of the Sufi tradition to which Suhrawardī considered himself an heir came to systematize such a literature occurred at the same time when the other religious sciences (*fiqh, kalām, tafsīr, ḥadīth*) were consolidating their own, each striving to delineate the rules and norms by which they could regulate themselves internally while at the same time secure a place for their endeavors as a communally practiced science (*ʿilm*). Like many ulama of his day, Suhrawardī participated in many of these fields, and as shown in the next chapter accepted the rules and norms which governed each as natural and self-evident.

The body of theoretical and systematic Sufi texts which Suhrawardī quotes in his works is a small one, consisting mainly of the standards of the Junaydī tradition which by the 6th/12th century, along with the Sufi biographical dictionaries of Sulamī and Iṣfahānī, had come to form something of a canon for champions of the Junaydī tradition, such as Suhrawardī. Here, Qushayrī's aforementioned *Epistle* is of paramount importance, followed to a lesser extent by the *K. al-lumaʿ fī 'l-taṣawwuf* of Sarrāj, Kalābādhī's *K. al-taʿarruf*, and Abū Ṭālib al-Makkī's *Qūt al-qulūb* among others. Much like the biographical dictionaries, these works also served as instruments of authority and memory, looking back to the paragons of the past for both authoritative patterns of behavior as well as for a way to describe the actual experiences generated through such behavior.

In such works, the experiential content and spiritual geography of the Sufi path is lain out in a special technical language, one which carefully differentiates between transitory spiritual states (*aḥwāl*) and abiding spiritual stations (*maqāmāt*), modes of cognition and epistemological experience (*mushāhada, kashf, maʿrifa*, etc.), the psycho-spiritual constitution of the human being (*nafs, qalb, sirr*, etc.), ontological verities

[68] Ibn al-Jawzī, *Ṣifat al-ṣafwa* (Cairo: Dār al-Ṣafā, 1411 [1990–1991]), 1:17–21.

(*ḥaqāʾiq*), and above all the complex of practices and behaviors which allow one to successfully navigate all of the above. At the same time, however, the way in which this special technical language (*iṣṭilāḥāt*) is deployed in such texts is not 'innocent'. As with the writing of biography, its enunciation in the written word also served as part of a broader program of asserting the identity of a specific *ṭāʾifa* vis-à-vis other group commonalities which were doing the same, often utilizing the same instruments. As Qushayrī himself lays out in the beginning of the second part of his famous *Epistle*:

> Know that it is common knowledge that every group (*ṭāʾifa*) among the corporate body of religious scholars (*ʿulamāʾ*) employ certain expressions amongst themselves which distinguish them from others. They have agreed upon such usage in the interest of precise mutual understanding and so that others interested in their art might find it easier to grasp what they mean. The members of this group (*ṭāʾifa*), however, employ certain expressions amongst themselves which only carry meaning in summary form, thus veiling them from those whose ways differ from their own and making them ambiguous to outsiders. They do this out of earnest concern of such secrets being divulged to those to whom they do not belong, for such verities (*ḥaqāʾiq*) are not amassed through assiduous effort or acquired by personal initiative. Rather, they are spiritual significances (*maʿānin*) that God Most High has entrusted to the hearts of certain folk for whose verities He has selected the innermost secrets of certain people.[69]

Here we witness both a clarification and an obscuring, a very important enunciation of identity and solidarity which evinces both the contested nature of the very genealogy which Qushayrī so carefully lays out in the biographical section preceding this introduction to the *iṣṭilāḥāt* section of his epistle while at the same time prefiguring or predetermining the field of discourse which is allowed to obtain after it. Unlike the very clear Ashʿarite creed which is presented at the beginning of his *Epistle*, to acquire the 'significances' hinted at in this section of the work, one must accept uncertainty, willingly yield to the non-discourse and ultimately non-rational character upon which the science of this particular *ṭāʾifa* is predicated. At the same time, and this is something well attested to in Sarrāj, the manner in which this, and the following section on the mystical stations and states (*maqāmāt wa-aḥwāl*) and the Sufi *adab* of travel, discipleship, and mystical audition (*samāʿ*) is supported is through proof-texts, first the Qurʾān, the Ḥadīth, *āthār* of the *salaf al-ṣāliḥ*, and

---

[69] *SQ*, 106.

the *akhbār/aqwāl* of the paragons of the Junaydī tradition. Here, then, we have a science (*ʿilm*) of a particular *ṭāʾifa* which is unlike the other religious sciences, such as those of the jurisprudents and theologians, in its character (e.g., non-discursive, intentionally obfuscatory) yet at the same moment deeply attuned to the authoritating and legitimating practices of those very same groups. In Qushayrī—a Shāfiʿī scholar, *ḥadīth* transmitter, and preacher—in fact, we find a figure who, much like Suhrawardī, was deeply involved in the politics of his day, coming to serve in various capacities as a player in both political and sectarian conflicts. In his adopted town of Nīshāpūr, Qushayrī was a visible participant in the well known Ḥanafī-Shāfiʿī struggle which reached its climax under the powerful Seljuk vizier al-Kundurī, while in Baghdad—which he visited in 448/1056—he is said to have forged a particularly cordial relationship with the Abbasid caliph al-Qāʾim.[70] At the same time, as with Iṣfahānī, Sarrāj, and Sulamī we find in Qushayrī an individual who was deeply concerned with the enunciation and perpetuation of a specific, genealogically-supported tradition of learning and praxis which rooted its claims in the authority of the past while at the same time predicating them on their reproducibility in the present. For him, the codification of a specific technical language was but part of a larger program of consolidating a particular self-contained, and largely self-reflexive, solidarity which simultaneously encompassed a genealogy, a language, and a praxis.

Alongside this technical language was the actual praxis which constituted the core of the Junaydī tradition as it had developed up to Suhrawardī's time, a complex of practices which in a certain measure were systematically codified in a body of texts. Constituting a set of normative and replicable practices which in the end provide the real content of Suhrawardī's *ribāṭ*-based Sufi system, in such works we find a privileging of a practical and highly detailed method presented, both conceptually and rhetorically, in a manner which replicates contemporary manuals of *fiqh*, laying out the correct methods of both personal devotions (*ʿibādāt*) and interpersonal relations (*muʿāmalāt*) to which the member of this particular *ṭāʾifa* was bound. As with the *fiqh* texts, such manuals are prescriptive, providing each and every required, recommended, or prohibited act, supererogatory or otherwise, with

---

[70] On this, see Heinz Halm, "Der Wesir al-Kunduri und die Fitna von Nishapur," *Welt des Orients* 6.2 (1971): 205–233.

the appropriate textual support, namely the Qurʾān, Ḥadīth, and the *aqwāl/akhbār* of past Sufi masters. It is not unusual that such literature appropriates such forms, for like the contemporary *fiqh* works, such texts embody a mode of religiosity firmly situated in a *jamāʿī-sunnī* vision of *sharīʿī*-revivalism, a practical and somewhat activist ideological orientation which looks back to an idealized past when the unity of the entire Muslim community was maintained through a strict adherence to the Prophet's Sunna and a self-conscious obedience to the divine law.

Works such as Abū Ṭālib al-Makkī's *Qūt al-qulūb* and its later incarnation in Ghazālī's *Iḥyāʾ ʿulūm al-dīn* as well as, to a certain extent at least, ʿAbd al-Qādir al-Jīlānī's *al-Ghunya li-ṭālibī ṭarīq al-ḥaqq*, all operate on a strategy which attempts to demonstrate that Sufi doctrines and practices are derived from the Qurʾān and Ḥadīth and are exemplified in the practice of the *salaf al-ṣāliḥ* and the paragons of the early Sufi tradition. This vision is programmatically taken up by Suhrawardī in his own works, most notably his *ʿAwārif al-maʿārif*. As a middle of the road, conservative *jamāʿī-sunnī* piety, the authors of each of these texts support their assertions by a careful selection of authoritating texts which reinforce that vision, the general mode of exposition being to cite and then elaborate on a particular Qurʾānic verse or, more often, a *ḥadīth*, showing at the same time how the body of Sufi authorities support such interpretations. Here, there is little difference between the textual practices of either the jurists or theologians, both of whom deployed similar rhetorical strategies in articulating their own doctrines and practices, an approach consistent with what obtained in the biographical dictionaries.

Much like the works of Abū Ṭālib al-Makkī, what we find in the writings of Suhrawardī is a programmatic appropriation and referencing of a set body of literature. Simultaneously looking back to two distinct pasts, the first that of the Prophet and the *salaf al-ṣāliḥ* and the second that of the paragons of the Junaydī tradition, his works can be seen as being situated at the convergence of a trend which begins in the writings of Sarrāj and Sulamī, was passed through the systematizing filter of Shāfiʿī scholars such as Qushayrī, and ended up articulating itself within the idiom of *jamāʿī-sunnī sharīʿī*-revivalism which informed so much of the production of the Muslim religious sciences in the central Islamic lands between the 5th/11th and early-7th/13th centuries. In his capacity as an heir to this past Suhrawardī played the role of both collator and consolidator, participating in a process which although certainly not culminating in him did, in particularly visible ways, shape the trajectory which *ṭarīqa*-based Sufism was to take in the lives and works of those who in turn saw themselves as his direct heirs.

Texts as Objects

Alongside the way in which such texts served as instruments of authority and repositories of memory in terms of their content, the text as an object also served as an instrument of authority and legitimacy, for as a hypostatized repository of learning, a text linked its possessor to both a physical object (the transmitted text) as well as to a process taking place in time and space (the event of its transmission). As such, the text could come to serve as an instrument of affiliation and status, a thing sought out and asked for, procured and conserved, exchanged, reproduced, and deployed. Here, the actual content of the text was subordinate to its material presence and the event of its transmission, for the very manner in which individuals such as Suhrawardī engaged the text as a transmittable object was more or less normative across all fields of learning and all learned textual traditions, from the fields of *ḥadīth* and jurisprudence to belles-lettres and Peripatetic philosophy. The core of this process centered upon the text as an object with an authoritative genealogy, an object literally embodied in the personhood of its chain of transmitters (*isnād*) existing, for the person receiving the text, at the junction between the authority of the past and its enunciation in the present. The meeting point for the individual was the 'institution of process' of the master-disciple relationship, an institution surrounded by a complex of normative practices and behaviors existing within a shared culture of formal behaviors (*adab*).

Alongside this *adab*, there were the actual 'institutions of process' through which the transmission of a text from a master to a student could occur. Developed largely within the discipline of the transmission of *ḥadīth*, by Suhrawardī's time this model had come to be considered normative, informing the transmission of texts across the religious sciences. The primary and most authoritative instrument was through the process of *samāʿ* ('audition'), meaning that the recipient would actually hear the text recited aloud by its transmitter (*musmiʿ*) either from memory or read from a written text. Secondly, a recipient could receive a text by way of reading it (*qirāʾa*) back to its transmitter which he would then compare with his own version of the text and correct any mistakes which the recipient might have in his version. These two modalities of transmission were generally designated as being *riwāya*

ʿalā ʾl-wajh ('face-to-face transmission'), and were understood to be the best methods of transmitting texts, although there were other modalities which did not rely upon direct contact between the transmitter and the recipient.[71]

Having received a particular text, the transmitter could then authorize a recipient to transmit it on his authority, confirming that he had received an accurate and authorized copy by conferring upon him an *ijāza* ('license') of transmission. This instrument was used in two forms: the *ijāzat al-qirāʾa* and the *ijāzat al-samāʿ*. The most important of these was the *samāʿ*, the certificate of audition, which was actually attested to in writing somewhere in the manuscript itself such as before or after the title, after the colophon, or in the margins, orienting the text in time and space through recording key elements of the transmission even such as the name of the transmitter (*musmiʿ*), a list of those present at the audition of the text, its date and location, and the transmitter's signature confirming the soundness of the copy. The transmission of texts in such a manner is well represented in both the collective manuscript record of Suhrawardī's written legacy as well as in his biography and those of his disciples and students. In fact, much of the information which is preserved on the lives and activities of Suhrawardī is centered upon their participation in the transmission of texts, most notably *ḥadīth*. For his part, as we shall see, Suhrawardī took such activities very seriously, programmatically situating himself within a larger culture of *ḥadīth* transmission through the production and dissemination of a 'list of authorities' (*mashyakha*) as well as formally transmitting *ḥadīth* to a host of well-known and respected ulama to whom he granted licenses to transmit on his authority.

At the same time, as well as with many of the same individuals, Suhrawardī also transmitted an 'unwritten text', namely a particular knowledge (*ʿilm*) which although unlike the content of a *ḥadīth* or the text of a Sufi manual in form mirrored its signification and underlying structure. As made clear in the Chapter Four, in Suhrawardī's system the inculcation of a particular mystical formula (*talqīn al-dhikr*) or the bestowal the Sufi 'habit of discipleship' (*khirqat al-irāda*) can be understood as being equivalent to the text (*matn*) of a *ḥadīth*, the initiatic

[71] Detailed descriptions of each of these modalities can be found in: Georges Vajda, "De la transmission du savoir dans l'islam traditionnel," *L'Arabisant (Association Français des Arabisants, Paris)* 4 (1975): 1–9; and, Jacqueline Sublet, "Le modèle arabe: éléments de vocabulaire," in *Madrasa*, 13–27.

genealogy (*nisba*) by which each are supported being equivalent to the *isnād* which supports the *matn*. In the same way, Suhrawardī granted both licenses of transmission (*ijāzāt*) to individuals empowering them to transmit texts while at the same time granting special licenses to certain individuals empowering them to transmit the *ʿilm* constituting his Sufi system, both, of course, being predicated upon the authoritating instrument of the *isnād/silsila*. All of this occurred within the same complex of normative patterns of behavior (*adab*) surrounding the social activity of transmitting texts.

* * *

Whether it be effected through physical objects such as texts and written *ijāzas*, textual configurations of the past as represented in Sufi biographical dictionaries and mystical manuals, or the transmission of *ḥadīth*, for *sharīʿa*-minded Sufis such as Suhrawardī, his teachers, students and disciples, the discourse and authority of the text served as one of the primary instruments through which an individual was able to secure identity and forge relationships with his contemporaries. It is the interplay between this cluster of practices and objects, the institutional forms of organization and praxis associated with the *madrasa* and Sufi *ribāṭ*, and al-Nāṣir's program of reform and centralization which furnishes both the subtext and setting for the activities of an individual who came to confront them in an energetic and, ultimately, quite consequential way. To understand what this confrontation might have meant for the historical development of *ṭarīqa*-based Sufism, we must first uncover the ways in which this particular actor went about navigating this moment of convergence, a task which in the case of a 7th/13th-century *ʿālim* and Sufi master such as Suhrawardī must begin with the traces which he left behind in the works of those who took it as their task to narrate the lives of such individuals in their own texts. It is to these narratives which we now turn.

CHAPTER TWO

THE MAKINGS OF A SUFI MASTER

Sometime near the end of the first quarter of the 7th/13th century, the celebrated traveler, scholar, and geographer Yāqūt al-Rūmī (d. 626/1229) composed an entry for his geographical dictionary, the *Muʿjam al-buldān*, on a small town in northwestern Iran called Suhraward.[1] Like so many entries in this famous work, his description of the town is terse: "it is a town situated near Zanjān in the province of Jibāl from which have come a group of righteous individuals (*ṣulaḥāʾ*) and religious scholars (*ʿulamāʾ*)".[2] In his entry, Yāqūt singles out two individuals as particularly noteworthy representatives of this group, two Sufis from the same family who emigrated to Baghdad during the 6th/12th century and subsequently made something of a name for themselves in the imperial capital:

> Among them are Abū ʾl-Najīb... al-Bakrī al-Suhrawardī, a jurist, Sufi, and preacher who came to Baghdad as a young man, heard *ḥadīth* from ʿAlī b. Nabhān and pursued the study of jurisprudence with Asʿad al-Mīhanī and others, and—as it is claimed—heard [*ḥadīth*] from Abū ʿAlī al-Ḥaddād in Isfahan. He engaged in asceticism and spiritual exertion to such a degree that he sold water in Baghdad and ate from what it gave him. He then occupied himself with preaching (*tadhkīr*) and became

---

[1] A town said to be situated on the road between Hamadhān and Zanjān to the south-west of Sulṭāniyya in the far north of the Jibāl region, but whose actual location is the matter of some debate. According to Nöldeke, the name Suhraward may be connected to the name Suhrāb, a Persian governor of al-Ḥīra (cited in "Suhraward," *EI²*, 9:777) although Plessner has argued that dating the foundation of the town to such an early period is unfounded (ibid.). Based on the report given by the 4th/10th-century Arab geographer Ibn Ḥawqal and later that of Ḥamd Allāh Mustawfī (who visited Suhraward in the 8th/14th century) Guy Le Strange locates it as a neighbor of the town of Sujās (or, Sijās), along the Hamadhān-Zanjān road which linked Jibāl to Azerbaijan, both of the towns being possessed of substantial Kurdish populations. According to Ibn al-Mustawfī Suhraward fell into ruin after the Mongol invasions, being reduced to the status of a large village. (Le Strange, *The Lands of the Eastern caliphate*, 2nd ed. [Cambridge: Cambridge University Press, 1930], 223; W. Barthold, *An Historical Geography of Iran*, trans. Svat Soucek, ed. C.E. Bosworth [Princeton: Princeton University Press, 1984], 208).

[2] Yāqūt, *Muʿjam al-buldān*, ed. Ferdinand Wüstenfeld (1866–1873; reprint, Beirut: Dār Ṣādir, 1955–1957), 3:289.

> famous for it. In Baghdad, he built *ribāṭs* for the Sufis among his companions and was appointed as a teacher in the Niẓāmiyya where he dictated *ḥadīth*. In 558 [1163] he came to Damascus intending to visit Jerusalem, although he was prohibited from doing so on account of the hostilities between the Muslims and their enemies [i.e., the Crusaders]. Upon his arrival, a most honorable reception was granted to him by Nūr al-Dīn Maḥmūd b. Zangī. There, he held regular assemblies at which he preached, but after only a short stay returned to Baghdad... [and among them is]...his paternal nephew, al-Shihāb...al-Suhrawardī, the Imām of his age in eloquence and in spiritual station...He came to Baghdad and there found a ready market for his wares. He preached to the people and came to the attention of the Commander of the Faithful al-Nāṣir li-Dīn Allāh who made him a *muqaddam* over the shaykhs of Baghdad and sent him on important ambassadorial missions. He wrote a book entitled the *ʿAwārif al-maʿārif*.[3]

While neither of these two individuals were as controversial as the city's most celebrated son, the *doctor illuminatus*, Shihāb al-Dīn Yaḥyā al-Suhrawardī (d. 587/1191),[4] both attained a certain measure of fame and prominence during their lifetimes and, for Yāqūt at least, represented a certain type of individual whose life, career, and character allowed them to encapsulate the claim to fame of an entire city. Although he was most certainly aware of the scandalous life and work of Yaḥyā al-Suhrawardī, for he writes an entry on him in another work,[5] the controversial philosopher does not fit the pattern of the type of

[3] Ibid., 3:289–290.

[4] Shihāb al-Dīn Yaḥyā b. Ḥabash b. Amīrak al-Suhrawardī (549/1154–587/1191), founder of the 'Illuminationst philosophy' (*ḥikmat al-ishrāq*), a non-Aristotelian and anti-Peripatetic school of philosophy and metaphysics which exerted a sustained influence on a long line of Persian thinkers. In many ways, this school reached its apogee in so-called 'school of Isfahan' whose key representatives such as Mīr Damād (d. 1040/1631) and Mullā Ṣadrā (d. 1050/1640) commented and expounded upon al-Suhrawardī's illuminationst system. Much like ʿUmar al-Suhrawardī, Yaḥyā al-Suhrawardī was actively engaged in the politics of his day, cultivating relationships with powerful rulers such as the Rūm Seljuk ʿAlāʾ al-Dīn Kayqubād (d. 634/1237), the Seljuk ruler Sulaymān Shāh (d. 556/1161), and even the son of Saladin, and governor of Aleppo, the amir al-Malik al-Ẓāhir Ghāzī (r. 582–613/1186–1216). Due to some political miscalculations on the philosopher's part, Saladin ordered him executed and, after some hesitation, he suffered an ignominious death in Aleppo in 587/1191, thus earning him the popular sobriquet *al-maqtūl*, or 'the murdered'. An excellent overview of Yaḥyā al-Suhrawardī's philosophical system and a detailed bibliography are provided by Hossein Ziai in "al-Suhrawardī, Shihāb al-Dīn Yaḥyā," *EI*², 9:782–784.

[5] Yāqūt, *Irshād al-arīb ilā maʿrifat al-adīb*, Gibb Memorial Series, vol. 6.1–3/5–6, ed. D.S. Margolioth (E.J. Brill: Leiden-London, 1907–1927), 4:269; not to mention the fact of Yāqūt's intimate knowledge of Aleppo and its surrounding districts (Claude Gilliot, "Yāḳūt," *EI*², 11:265).

individual which Yāqūt had in mind when characterizing Suhraward as a place which gave birth to a group of 'righteous individuals and religious scholars'. His contemporaries, Abū 'l-Najīb and ʿUmar al-Suhrawardī did.

It would come as little surprise in fact if Yāqūt had made mention of the spectacular, the surprising, or the contentious in his entry on Suhraward, for as with most medieval historians, chroniclers, prosopographers, and geographers, he was certainly not adverse to reporting upon the 'wonders' (*ʿajāʾib*) of a particular place or time, and mentioning Yaḥyā al-Suhrawardī in this entry would not have been unusual.[6] At the same time, however, it would not have been *representative*, for what seems to have made Abū 'l-Najīb and ʿUmar al-Suhrawardī more worthy of mention then their compatriot, in Yāqūt's view at least, was that both embodied certain characteristics worthy of mention, namely being upright and pious religious scholars and serious men of religious. Strangely enough, however, this estimable thing was at the same time thoroughly commonplace, and as a ubiquitous feature of urban landscapes across medieval Islamdom was not a reference which would have been lost on Yāqūt's readers, for undoubtedly anyone who had an interest in reading such a dictionary would have most certainly been familiar with any number of *ṣulahāʾ* and ulama, but probably not with the master of the Philosophy of Illumination.

After Yāqūt, many other individuals wrote encapsulated biographies of these two men, each shaping their particular representation of Abū 'l-Najīb and ʿUmar al-Suhrawardī in a manner confirming and corroborating the particular vision framing their work. Almost a century later, for example, someone like the great Shāfiʿī scholar, judge, and biographer Tāj al-Dīn al-Subkī (d. 771/1370) wrote about an ʿUmar al-Suhrawardī who was not merely a exemplary representative of a town known for giving birth to righteous individuals and religious scholars, but rather an ʿUmar who exemplified the figure of a laudable Shāfiʿī jurist, energetic and well-respected *ḥadīth* transmitter, and pious Sufi

[6] al-Dhahabī does just this, in his lengthy entry on al-Nāṣir li-Dīn Allāh mentioning (among other wonders such as a lamb who was born with the face of a man and the Tigris overflowing its banks) the wonder of this particular year (587/1191) being that: "al-Suhrawardī the magician, and professed alchemist and philosopher, appeared in Aleppo, and that the jurists issued a fatwa condemning him to death by starvation, ordering his body to be burnt." (*SN*, 22:214; cf. *TIsl*, 47:74–75 [*ḥawādith*, *anno* 587]).

shaykh—a combination, which perhaps not so incidentally, was very well represented in the population of al-Subkī's Cairo:

> ...The shaykh Shihāb al-Dīn al-Suhrawardī, author of the *ʿAwārif al-maʿārif*, was born in Rajab in the year 539 [1144–1145] in Suhraward, came to Baghdad, and became a disciple of his paternal uncle the shaykh Abū Najīb ʿAbd al-Qāhir, learning Sufism and preaching from him. He was also a disciple of the shaykh ʿAbd al-Qādir [al-Jīlānī] and in Basra of shaykh Abū Muḥammad b. ʿAbd. He heard *ḥadīth* from his paternal uncle and from Abū ʾl-Muẓaffar Hibatullāh b. al-Shiblī[7]...and others. Ibn al-Dubaythī narrated [*ḥadīth*] from him as well as Ibn Nuqṭa...Ibn Najjār...and many other people. He was a distinguished jurist, an upstanding and observant Sufi, a knowledgeable ascetic, and the master of his age in the science of divine realities. He was the final word in the training of disciples, summoning people to the Creator and to wayfaring on the path of devotions and pious solitude...and here are some juridical questions and opinions related on his authority...[8]

For other pre-modern authors and compliers, Abū ʾl-Najīb and ʿUmar al-Suhrawardī came to mean something else entirely. For the celebrated 9th/15th-century Sufi littérateur ʿAbd al-Raḥmān Jāmī (d. 898/1492), for example, these two individuals were worthy of mention not because of their status as representatives of legal and religious learning or their facility in public preaching, but rather because they exemplified the qualities of a saintly Sufi shaykh, a complex of characteristics which includes things unmentionable to an individual such as al-Subkī, not the least of was saintly miracles (*karāmāt*). On the former, he says:

> Shaykh Ḍiyāʾ al-Dīn Abū ʾl-Najīb ʿAbd al-Qāhir al-Suhrawardī—may God sanctify his secret—was perfect in both the esoteric and exoteric

[7] Number two in Suhrawardī's *Mashyakha*, the Shāfiʿī *muḥaddith* and *muʾadhdhin* Abū ʾl-Muẓaffar Hibatullāh b. Aḥmad b. Muḥammad al-Shiblī (d. 557/1162) was a disciple of Abū ʾl-Najīb Suhrawardī who transmitted six *ḥadīth* to him—in his uncle's *majlis* in Baghdad—during Ramadan, 556/September, 1161 (*Mashyakha*, C.B. MS. Arab 465_9, fols. 85b–86b). According to the *Mashyakha*, he was the last surviving transmitter from the important *muḥaddith* and member of the famous family of Ḥanafī ulama and Abbasid officials, Abū Naṣr al-Zaynabī (d. 479/1086), son of the *naqīb al-nuqabāʾ* of Baghdad Abū ʿAlī al-Zaynabī (d. 450/1058) and brother of the equally famous Baghdadi *muḥaddith* Abū ʾl-Fawāris Ṭirāḍ b. Muḥammad al-Baghdādī (d. 491/1098). On him, see: *TIr*, 1:138 (s.v. Abū al-Faraj al-Wāsiṭī), 1:194 (s.v. al-Suhrawardī), and, 2:220 (*ḥawāshī*, no. 3); *TW*, 1:127 (s.v. no. 32); *SN*, 20:393–394 (no. 267), and, *TIsl*, 44:242–243 (*anno* 557, no. 267).

[8] *ṬShK*, 8:339–340. In a similar manner the great Ottoman scholar and *ʿālim* Tashköpruzāde (d. 968/1561) included Suhrawardī's biography in his sizable encyclopedia of the religious sciences in a section entitled: "on the seventh discipline of *sharīʿa* sciences: the science of jurisprudence (*ʿilm al-fiqh*)". (*MS*, 2:355–356)

> sciences and composed many works and treatises. His familial genealogy reaches back to Abū Bakr-i Ṣiddīq—may God be pleased with him—through twelve links, whereas his initiatic genealogy goes back to shaykh Aḥmad-i Ghazālī... In the *Tāʾrīkh* of Imām-i Yāfiʿī it is said that: "one of the companions of shaykh Abū ʾl-Najīb-i Suhrawardī—may God have mercy on him—said: "one day I was passing through the bazaar of Baghdad with the shaykh and we came upon a butcher's stall. There was a sheep suspended there, and the shaykh stood up and said, 'this sheep is saying: "I was killed, but not ritually slaughtered".' The butcher lost his senses and when he returned to himself confirmed the words of the shaykh and repented.[9]

In a similar manner, Jāmī's entry on ʿUmar al-Suhrawardī privileges the same qualities and characteristics which embody the figure of his paternal uncle:

> As to his agnomens Imām-i Yāfiʿī wrote that he was: 'the peerless teacher of his age and time, the dawn of lights and the spring of divine secrets, the guiding proof of the Sufi path and the interpreter of the divine reality, the teacher of the greatest shaykhs and one who unites esoteric and exoteric knowledge, the paragon of gnostics and support of wayfarers, the scholar-divine Shihāb al-Dīn Abū Ḥafṣ ʿUmar b. Muḥammad al-Bakrī al-Suhrawardī—may God Almighty sanctify his secret.' He was from the descendents of Abū Bakr-i Ṣiddīq—may God be pleased with him—whose affiliation with Sufism came from his paternal uncle Abū ʾl-Najīb al-Suhrawardī. He kept company with shaykh ʿAbd al-Qādir-i Gīlānī and associated with many others from among the great shaykhs. They say that for a while he had been with some of the *abdāl* on the island of ʿAbbādān and that he associated with Khiḍr—peace be upon him. Shaykh ʿAbd al-Qādir told him: "You are the last of the famous men of Iraq." He composed many works such as the *ʿAwārif*, the *Rashf al-naṣāʾiḥ*, and the *Aʿlām al-tuqā*, among others. The *ʿAwārif* was composed in Mecca (sic!), and every time a problem would occur to him he would turn to God and circumambulate the House [i.e., the Kaʿba], asking for divine assistance in lifting the problem and for knowledge of the truth of the matter.[10] He was the shaykh of the shaykhs of his age in Baghdad and masters of the path from countries near and far would write to him with questions. One of them wrote to him: 'O' my master, if I refrain from

---

[9] Jāmī, *Nafaḥāt al-uns min ḥaḍarāt al-quds*, ed. Maḥmūd ʿĀbidī (Tehran: Intishārāt Iṭalāʿāt, 1380 sh. [1991]), 420–421.

[10] Actually, Jāmī, following al-Yāfiʿī (*MJ*, 4:79–90), is confusing the *ʿAwārif al-maʿārif* with the *Aʿlām al-hudā*, the latter of which was written in Mecca in accordance with the above method as Suhrawardī himself explains in his introduction to work (*AHu*, 46).

> action I incline toward idleness but if I act, I become prideful,' to which he responded, 'act and seek God's forgiveness for being prideful'.[11]

As with many pre-modern Sufis, Jāmī's account came to be the standard upon which many later representations of Suhrawardī were based (especially in the Persian and Turkish hagiographical traditions), although at the same time, the kernel of the biographical representation narrated by authors with an 'ulamalogical' bent such as Yāqūt, Subkī, or Dhahabī continued to be replicated by later authors. In the early pre-modern period, for example, the figure of Suhrawardī continued to be narrated in a wide variety of such texts, each retelling adding something of a distinctive mark to its own positioning of such an individual vis-à-vis an ever increasing mass of available biographical sources. Much unlike Jāmī, for instance, for the great 11th/17th-century Ḥanbalī compiler Ibn al-ʿImad, who relied heavily on the collective weight of some five centuries of Islamic prosopography, the figure of ʿUmar al-Suhrawardī is presented as blending the qualities of a Shāfiʿī jurist, Sufi master, and author, without the preaching or miracles:

> The shaykh Shihāb al-Dīn al-Suhrawardī, the paragon of the folk of divine unity and the shaykh of the gnostics; Abū Ḥafṣ and Abū ʿAbdullāh ʿUmar b. Muḥammad b. ʿAbdullāh b. Muḥammad al-Taymī al-Bakrī, the Sufi and Shāfiʿī, was born in the year 539 [1144–1145] in Suhraward and came to Baghdad where he attached himself to Hibatullāh b. al-Shiblī, from whom he heard *ḥadīth*, and became a disciple of his paternal uncle Abū ʾl-Najīb. He studied jurisprudence and the [religious] arts and composed treatises, among them the *ʿAwārif al-maʿārif* which explains the 'Sufi path of al-Junayd' (*ṭarīqat al-qawm*). He reached the utmost limit in the training of disciples, wayfaring, and scholarly preeminence in Iraq.[12]

Whereas for authors such as Yāqūt, Subkī, Jāmī or Ibn al-ʿImād, ʿUmar al-Suhrawardī fits a pre-determined pattern of a preacher, laudable Shāfiʿī jurist, Sufi shaykh, or all-around *ʿālim*-cum-Sufi, in other tellings he also appears as a symbol of authority and legitimization, especially in connection, imagined or otherwise, with the celebrated figures of his day. In the middle of the 11th/17th century in India, for instance, the Mughal prince Dārā Shukūh penned an entry on ʿUmar al-Suhrawardī in his compendium of the shaykhs of the major Sufi brotherhoods, the *Safīnat al-awliyāʾ*. Although this entry belongs to the

[11] Jāmī, *Nafaḥāt*, 473–474.
[12] *ShDh*, 7:268–270.

section devoted to the shaykhs of the Suhrawardiyya order, as a devotee of the Qādirī order, Dārā Shukūh chooses to focus on the 'relationship' between Suhrawardī and the eponym of his own brotherhood, ʿAbd al-Qādir al-Jīlānī (d. 561/1166). Here, the figure of Suhrawardī is completely overshadowed by that of Jīlānī, the former serving as a vehicle to exemplify the miraculous qualities and saintly miracles of ʿAbd al-Qādir, a very common trope, in fact, in hagiographies of this particular member of the *awliyā*ʾ:[13]

> His *kunya* is Abū Ḥafṣ, his agnomen *shaykh al-shuyūkh*, his name ʿUmar b. Muḥammad, al-Bakrī-i Suhrawardī and he is from the decedents of Abū Bakr-i Ṣiddīq—may God be pleased with him—shaykh of the shaykhs, the pole and succor of the age, religious scholar and man of praxis, virtuous and perfect—the leader of his age. His juridical rite was that of Imām-i Shāfiʿī and his spiritual path that of complete obedience to the divine law and the custom of the Prophet of the Muslims. In Baghdad he was the most famous of his contemporaries and was a disciple of his uncle shaykh Abū ʾl-Najīb-i Suhrawardī (the same shaykh Abū ʾl-Najīb who is mentioned in the initiatic lineage of the Kubrawiyya). He was acquainted with his presence, the pole of the divines and the succor of the folk, shaykh Muḥyī ʾl-Dīn ʿAbd al-Qādir-i Gīlānī—may God be pleased with him!—and through the blessings of attachment to his noble presence acquired great benefits and spiritual favor and both the elect and the commoners of Baghdad flocked to serve him [as disciples]. It is reported that shaykh Shihāb al-Dīn said: "in my youth I wished to take up the study of dialectical theology and desired to study a few books on the subject, but my paternal uncle prohibited me from doing so. One day my uncle took me with him to visit his presence, shaykh ʿAbd al-Qāḍir—may God be pleased with him. He said to me, 'wait, we will go to a man whose heart is given knowledge by God Almighty.' I waited and when I finally sat down before his blessed countenance, shaykh Abū ʾl-Najīb said, 'O' master, this nephew of mine is occupied with the science of dialectical theology and every time I prohibit him from that he returns to it.' The succor of the Muslims said, 'O' ʿUmar what are the chief books which you have memorized?' I said, 'such and such a book and such and such a book', and he brought down his blessed hand upon my chest and, by God, not one word from those books remained in my memory and I

[13] This is perhaps best represented in al-Shaṭṭanawfī's (d. 713/1314) *Bahjat al-asrār* (Cairo: Muṣṭafā al-Bābī al-Ḥalabī, 1330 [1912]) and, in a more precise fashion, in the *Qalāʾid al-jawāhir fī manāqib ʿAbd al-Qādir* of Yaḥyā al-Tādifī (d. 963/1555), recently translated by Muhtar Holland as *Necklaces of Gems: A Biography of the Crown of the Saints, ʿAbd al-Qadir al-Jilani* (Fort Lauderdale, FL: Al-Baz Publishing, 1998). In fact, Dārā Shukūh loosely quotes a tradition preserved by al-Tādifī in this account of the exploits of ʿAbd al-Qādir (*Necklaces of Gems*, 122).

> completely forgot every single question from them, and by that had my fill of the science of divinity." He said, 'whatever I have obtained was from the blessing of his presence, shaykh ʿAbd al-Qādir-i Gīlānī'.[14]

Biographical extracts such as these certainly do not provide a very complete picture of the life, works, and influence of ʿUmar al-Suhrawardī, for although uniformly included within both the standard biographical dictionaries of prominent ulama and universal Sufi hagiographies, the compilers of such works inevitably remember and position Abū Ḥafṣ ʿUmar al-Suhrawardī by way of privileging this or that denominative befitting the multiple learned and professional roles, avocations, and pious personas which a 7th/13th-century Sunni ulama with connections to Sufism invariably takes on in such retellings. Individually, such sources provide less of a complete and reliable statement of what Suhrawardī said or did at any one time than a window into the particular concerns of those who were doing the writing *about* Suhrawardī. When taken together such sources exemplify the ways in which a particular narrative kernel can be manipulated to articulate a particular vision of what an individual like ʿUmar al-Suhrawardī meant to a particular author in a particular time and place. The point is that, while the intertextual and agglutinative nature of such materials inevitably leads to much repetition, their lacunas, additions, and rhetorical (re)configurations are oftentimes just as telling as the initial appearance of a particular narrative or anecdote.

The question is, then, once this is recognized what does one do with such sources? Although such materials tend to inscribe upon their subjects what oftentimes amount to seemingly arbitrary and artificial boundaries, in fact, tightening the circle of possibility in terms of who may or may not be included and who can or cannot be excluded lies at the heart of the practice of prosopography in general. One cannot fault such sources for what they are nor at the same time force them to be something which they are not; one must endeavor to discover the possibilities which they offer *as they are*. For the writing of a biography of an individual such as Suhrawardī, whose biographical horizon is constrained as much by the inevitable horizon of life possibilities available to him as an actor in a specific time and place as by the nar-

[14] Dārā Shukūh, *Safīnat al-awliyāʾ*, lithograph (Cawnpore: Munshī Nūlkishvār, 1301 [1884]), 112–113; cf. idem, *Sakīnat al-awliyāʾ* (Tehran: Muʾassasa-yi Maṭbūʿātī-yi ʿIlmī, 1965), 19–20; and, al-Tādifī, *Necklaces of Gems*, 122.

rative structures and forms available to those who wrote about him, one such possibility is representational. In the context of the materials we are dealing with here, representation entails a number of things. First, it presupposes that such sources can be read as literature. In a literary discourse of any type, individual content is inevitably shaped and constrained by established conventions, rules, norms and patterns. Such elements serve to secure and position any one work as a member of a class (genre) while at the same time providing the author with an accepted practice through which he can conceive, compose, and transmit a work. The Sufi biographical enterprise detailed in the previous chapter is one such example of how this process worked for a particular group, for as was discussed, writing to and from a genre, whether it be a biographical dictionary of prominent Shāfiʿī ulama or a universal Sufi hagiography, gave an author such as Subkī or Jāmī access to a shared repository of forms, symbols, tropes, and structures whose particulars were not used haphazardly. In such a context, genre was a powerful thing, and as we have seen in the case of the initial constructions of a particular Sufi tradition through the medium of biographical writing, in many ways the manner in which later authors wrote the lives of individuals such as Suhrawardī was just as much a part of a larger project of legitimization and canonization pursued within a space of contested identities than a pious effort to preserve traditions and teachings.

Second, when taken together, the various ways in which Suhrawardī is represented in these sources tells us a great deal about 'the making of' a 7th/13th-century Sufi shaykh who himself was intimately involved in a project of legitimization and canonization and whose own written production paid close attention to genre as a instrument of power. As we will see, Suhrawardī played multiple roles—from *ḥadīth* transmitter (*muḥaddith*) to preacher (*wāʿiẓ*), from Sufi master of training and instruction (*shaykh al-tarbiya wa-l-taʿlīm*) to master of benediction (*shaykh al-tabarruk*), from Qurʾānic exegete (*mufassir*) to jurist (*faqīh*), from caliphal ambassador and ideologue to a director of five Sufi cloisters in Baghdad, and from pious resident of Mecca (*mujāwir*) to one of the 'forty cosmic substitutes' (*abdāl*)—each role carefully presented in a rhetoric underscoring its particular significance. While neither his biographers nor Suhrawardī himself comments upon all of these roles simultaneously, they are nonetheless *simultaneously present* in the collective memory of nearly seven centuries of Islamicate biographical and historiographical literature. Paying close attention to the specific structural, stylistic, rhetorical, and ideological constraints of a particular moment of representation allows us to fashion, as it were, a reconstituted narrative which captures both discrete historical data while at the same time contextualizing its specificities in a broader cultural tradition of narrating the past.

Third, even in near-contemporary biographical accounts, individuals such as Suhrawardī are often represented in terms of their 'paragonic' value, that is: as a special class of individuals who embody the virtues which supply the real or imagined prestige by which members of the ulama or hierarchy of Sufi masters and saints (*awliyā'*) secure their position in society. As in the broader literary discourse which frames much of the prosopographical writing constituting our sources, paragons serve as a mirror of the broader networks of values, ideologies, and discursive arenas within which those representing them moved, in the process enshrining the identities, aspirations, and self-image of a particular discursive community in that supreme artifact of 'ulamaology', the biographical text. While the inherent flexibility of the various prosopographical and historiographical genres provided our learned authors with many options in representing an individual such as Suhrawardī, most notably the possibility of programmatically using biography to support the dissemination and communication of particular agendas, the figure of the paragon as a conventional trope guided much of the representation in which they engaged. Paragon or not, it is more than a biographical curiosity that Suhrawardī's early life in many ways is represented as having mirrored that of his forebears, for the particular strand of the Sufi tradition to which he was heir was an affair very much rooted in the conservation and reproduction of family allegiances to particular sectarian and juridical affiliations, a fact not lost on the prosopographers.

The Banū ʿAmmūya

Allegedly a descendent of the first caliph Abū Bakr (d. 12/634), Suhrawardī hailed from a family who traced their juridical credentials back to late 2nd/8th-century Medina and who seem to have flourished as Shāfiʿī jurisprudents for at least two generations preceding his birth. The first mention of any positive Sufi affiliations within the family outside of the Suhrawardiyya corpus come with Suhrawardī's paternal great-uncle, Wajīh al-Dīn Abū Ḥafṣ ʿUmar al-Suhrawardī (455–532/1063–1137), who in addition to playing the role of a Shāfiʿī jurist also directed a Sufi *ribāṭ* in Baghdad. According to the early Suhrawardiyya *nisbat al-khirqa*, however, the family's affiliation with Sufism went back one generation further, namely with ʿUmar al-Suhrawardī's great-grandfather, the son of ʿAbdullāh ʿAmmūya (the paternal namesake of the family) and father of Wajīh al-Dīn, Muḥammad b. ʿAbdullāh (c. 348–468/959–1076). According to this tradition, he was the first member of the family to be invested with the *khirqa* (by Aḥmad al-Aswad al-Dīnawarī) which he then passed on to his son Wajīh al-Dīn in a simultaneous investiture ceremony which he conducted alongside the patron saint of Anatolian *ahilik*, Akhī Faraj al-Zanjānī (d. 457/1065). Just as his father had invested him, so too would Wajīh al-Dīn invest his paternal nephew Abū ʾl-Najīb, and Abū ʾl-Najīb his paternal nephew ʿUmar, and he his own son, ʿImād al-Dīn, and so on for at least three more generations.[15]

Like most families of Sunni religious scholars, the Banū ʿAmmūya took pride in a genealogy which linked them back to a companion of the Prophet Muhammad, in their case the first caliph Abū Bakr. Leading back through the eponymous patriarch of the family, ʿAbdullāh ʿAmmūya, the importance of this genealogy lay in its connection with the great-grandson of Abū Bakr, the *faqīh* of Medina ʿAbd al-Raḥmān, one of the primary lines of Bakrī descent claimed by numerous *fuqahā*ʾ during the era of Suhrawardī, including the vituperative critic of Baghdad's Sufis, Ibn al-Jawzī himself. Such genealogies were often contested, and in fact a later critic, Muḥammad al-Qābisī, is reported to have said of Abū ʾl-Najīb: "he was actually from the house of the amir Ḥasanawayh al-Kurdī and was not of Bakrī descent"[16] (see Chart 1).

According to his own admission, ʿUmar al-Suhrawardī was born into this noble linage either near the end of Rajab or the beginning of Shaʿbān, 539 (December, 1144 or January, 1145).[17] Born as he was into

---

[15] As discussed in Chapter Five, although sublimated in later articulations of the Suhrawardiyya initiatic lineage the merging of two separate *silsila*s through the modality of simultaneous investiture may have proved to be of service in Suhrawardī's program of co-opting the initiatic genealogy of the *futuwwa*.

[16] al-Tādifī, *Necklaces*, 421.

[17] According to Ibn al-Mustawfī (d. 637/1239), Ibn al-Dubaythī told him that he asked Suhrawardī himself about this and that the shaykh replied thusly (*TIr*, 1:193). Same in *TW*, 6:122; *WA*, 3:448; and, al-ʿUmarī, *Masālik al-abṣār fī mamālik al-amṣār*, vol. 8, *al-Sifr al-thāmin fī tawāʾif al-fuqahāʾ wa-l-ṣūfiyya*, ed. Basām Muḥammad Bārūd (Abu Dhabi: al-Majmaʿ al-Thaqāfī, 2001), 227. For his part, al-Dhahabī cites Rajab, 539 as the correct date (*SN*, 22:374, and, *TIsl*, 52:112; cf. Ibn al-Dimyāṭī, *al-Mustafād*

Chart 1.

The Bakrī Genealogy of the Banū ʿAmmūya

Abū Bakr al-Ṣiddīq
Muḥammad b. Abī Bakr
al-Qāsim
ʿAbd al-Raḥmān
ʿAbdullāh[1]
Muḥammad
al-Qāsim
al-Naḍr
al-Qāsim[2]
al-Ḥusayn
Saʿd
ʿAbdullāh ʿAmmūya
Muḥammad b. ʿAbdullāh (d. 468/1076)

ʿAbdullāh b. Muḥammad al-Suhrawardī (d. c. early 6th/12th cen.)
Wajīh al-Dīn Abū Ḥafṣ ʿUmar al-Suhrawardī (d. 532/1137)

Abū ʾl-Najīb ʿAbd al-Qāhir al-Suhrawardī (d. 563/1168)
Abū Jaʿfar Muḥammad al-Suhrawardī (d. 539/1144)
Abī ʾl-Ḥārith Aʿazz b. ʿUmar al-Suhrawardī (d. 557/1162)

Shihāb al-Dīn Abū Ḥafṣ [and: Abū ʿAbdullāh, Abū Naṣr, Abū ʾl-Qāsim] ʿUmar b. Muḥammad al-Qurashī, al-Taymī, al-Bakrī, al-Suhrawardī[3] (d. 632/1234)

---

1 al-Dhahabī adds: "*wa-huwa ibn faqīh al-madīna wa-ibn faqīhihā*". (*SN*, 12:374)

2 From this point in his lineage al-Suhrawardī shared a common *nasab* with the famous Ḥanbalī scholar Ibn al-Jawzī (d. 597/1200).

3 al-Dhahabī adds: al-Ṣūfī *thumma* al-Baghdādī. (*SN*, 12:374)

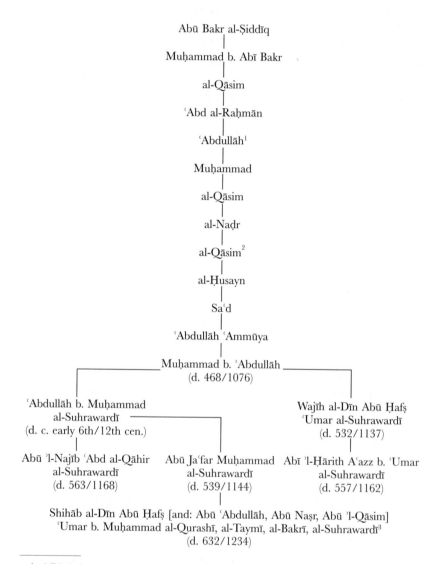

a family of Shāfiʿī ulama with a history of judicial service, Suhrawardī's initial career path seems to have been determined from the start by that of his relatives, namely his paternal great-uncle, Wajīh al-Dīn, his father, Abū Jaʿfar, and Abū Jaʿfar's brother Abū ʾl-Najīb. Like ʿUmar al-Suhrawardī would do later, each of these three men left their hometown of Suhraward and journeyed to Baghdad in order to pursue the study of jurisprudence, his great-uncle Wajīh al-Dīn and his paternal uncle Abū ʾl-Najīb both being buried in the city, while his father returned to Suhraward in order to take up the city's judgeship.

Muḥammad b. ʿAmmūya al-Suhrawardī (d. 468/1076)

With the exception of the aforementioned Abū ʾl-Najīb, what can be gleaned from the sources about Suhrawardī's paternal relatives is quite limited. Nothing is known about the paternal eponym of the family, ʿAbdullāh ʿAmmūya, save he transmitted *ḥadīth* to his son and grandson and that it was through him from which the Banū ʿAmmūya's claims to Bakrī descent were traced. Similarly, next to nothing is known about Suhrawardī's paternal great-grandfather Muḥammad b. ʿAbdullāh al-Suhrawardī[18] (d. 468/1076) save that he was a jurist who also engaged in the transmission of *ḥadīth* and who, according to the Suhrawardiyya initiatic tradition, was invested with the *khirqa* by Aḥmad al-Aswad al-Dīnawarī through a secondary Junaydī line. Abū ʾl-Najīb passed down a tradition to his son ʿAbd al-Laṭīf that his grandfather was something of an ascetic, eating only once every forty days,[19] and according to a report transmitted by Abū Ṭāhir al-Silafī and quoted by Dhahabī, Suhrawardī's great-uncle Wajīh al-Dīn said that he died in 468/1076 at the ripe old age of 120 lunar years.

min dhayl taʾrīkh baghdād, ed. Bashshār ʿAwwād Maʿrūf [Beirut: Muʾassasat al-Risāla, 1986], 327; *TFSh*, 2:835; and, *NZ*, 6:283 [*anno* 631]). Sibṭ Ibn al-Jawzī simply gives 539 (*MZ*, 8.2:679).

[18] On him, see: *TIsl*, 34–35:268–269 (*anno* 468, no. 266); and, Ibn al-Mulaqqin, *al-ʿIqd al-mudhhab fī ṭabaqāt ḥamalat al-madhhab*, ed. Ayman Naṣr al-Azharī (Beirut: Dār al-Kutub al-ʿIlmiyya, 1997), 282 (no. 1023).

[19] *TIr*, 1:111–112, adding that one of his contemporaries, the ascetic Ibrāhīm Bārān, told Abū ʾl-Najīb: "I was a companion/disciple (*ṣaḥibtu jiddaka*) of your grandfather Muḥammad b. ʿAbdullāh al-Bakrī and it was his custom to eat just once every forty days. After that he would isolate himself from people and sit by a spring, taking no one with him. One time, I happened to see him there from a distance and lo and behold there was a group of people around him discoursing, but when I approached I saw only him and there was no one else there!" (ibid., 112)

Wajīh al-Dīn al-Suhrawardī (d. 532/1137)

In comparison to his father, the biographers present us with more information on ʿUmar al-Suhrawardī's paternal great-uncle, the *qāḍī* Wajīh al-Dīn Abū Ḥafṣ ʿUmar b. Muḥammad al-Suhrawardī[20] (455–532/1063–1137). He seems to have been the first member of the family to leave Suhraward, going to Baghdad where he studied jurisprudence under Abū ʾl-Qāsim ʿAlī b. Abī Yaʿlā al-Dabūsī, a Shāfiʿī jurist who taught at the city's Niẓāmiyya from 479/1086 until his death in 482/1089[21] as well as (according to Ibn al-Najjār) studying with the celebrated Abū Ḥāmid al-Ghazālī himself.[22] Even though almost everyone of note who was in Baghdad during this time is said to have attended the lectures of al-Ghazālī, Ibn al-Najjār's report is important in that it evinces another possible link between the Banū ʿAmmūya and the two Ghazālīs, Abū ʾl-Najīb having been a disciple of Aḥmad-i Ghazālī who also serves as a node in his, and his nephew's, *nisbat talqīn al-dhikr* (see Chart 2). In addition, during this period Wajīh al-Dīn also heard *ḥadīth* from a number of the city's *muḥaddithīn*[23] just as he had done earlier from his grandfather ʿAbdullāh ʿAmmūya, sometime thereafter also engaging in the transmission of *ḥadīth* himself as well as composing a commissioned history of the two *Sunan*s entitled *al-Mujāhidī*.[24]

Despite his inclusion in the *silsila* of the later Suhrawardiyya, not much else has been preserved about Wajīh al-Dīn's life save that he was a man of affairs who after a brief stint as an *ʿālim*-in-training left his studies to pursue a life of asceticism and renunciation. Although his biographers call him a *qāḍī*, it is not stated exactly where he served as such, although it was probably in his home town of Suhraward. According to Ibn al-Jawzī—who personally laid eyes on Wajīh al-Dīn

[20] On him, see: al-Samʿānī, *K. al-ansāb*, 3:341 (s.v., al-Suhrawardī); *MT*, 10:75 (*anno* 532, no. 94); *DhTB*, 5:188–189 (no. 465); Ibn Mulaqqin, *ʿIqd*, 282 (no. 1023)—whom he conflates with Muḥammad b. ʿAmmūya al-Suhrawardī; *TIsl*, 41–42:289–290 (*anno* 532, no. 99); and, *GE*, 1–2, fn. 3.

[21] *LTA*, 1:410.

[22] *DhTB*, 5:189.

[23] Most notably from the famous Ḥanbalī jurist, *muḥaddith*, and preacher Abū Muḥammad Rizqullāh al-Tamīmī (d. 488/1095) and the rather obscure poet and littérateur Abū ʾl-Ḥusayn ʿĀṣim al-Karkhī (d. 482/1089); see *KT*, 10:180–81; and, *MT*, 9:51–52.

[24] The printed edition of Ibn al-Najjār's text is fragmentary, but this work sounds to have been quite interesting: "...he composed a history on the two *Sunan*s entitled *al-Mujāhidī* commissioned by Mujāhid al-Dīn [...] in Baghdad, and he mentions in it that since the beginning of the world to the year 514 [...]." (*DhTB*, 5:188)

Chart 2.

al-Suhrawardī's *nisbat talqīn al-dhikr**

The Prophet Muḥammad

↓

ʿAlī b. Abī Ṭālib
(d. 40/661)

↓

al-Ḥasan al-Baṣrī
(d. 110/728)

↓

[recognized but unspecified]

↓

Abū ʾl-Qāsim al-Junayd
(d. 298/910)

↓

Abū ʿAlī al-Rūdhbārī
(d. 322/934)

↓

Abū ʿAlī al-Kātib
(d. c. 340/951)

↓

Abū ʿUthmān al-Maghribī
(d. 373/983–84)

↓

Abū ʾl-Qāsim Jūrjānī
(d. 469/1076–77)

↓

Abū Bakr al-Nassāj
(d. 487/1094)

↓

Aḥmad-i Ghazālī
(d. 520/1126)

↓

Abū ʾl-Najīb al-Suhrawardī
(d. 563/1168)

↓

ʿUmar al-Suhrawardī
(d. 632/1234)

* al-Suhrawardī, *R. fī ʾl-dhikr*, fol. 20a (cited in *Suh.*, 137—following the *nisbat al-khirqa*, perhaps the unspecified links were: Ḥabīb al-ʿAjamī → Dāwūd al-Ṭāʾī → Maʿrūf al-Karkhī → Sarī al-Saqaṭī); Ibn Rāfiʿ, *Muntakhab*, 147–148 (no. 122—only from al-Junayd with differences in the *isnād*); Jāmī, *Nafaḥāt*, 559 (no. 546—only from al-Junayd); and, Maʿṣūmʿalīshāh, *Ṭarāʾiq*, 2:310, 332 (only from al-Junayd and less Abū ʿAlī al-Kātib).

but admits that he never heard *ḥadīth* from him (apparently despite their shared genealogy)—he was the director of one of Baghdad's Sufi *ribāṭ*s called Ribāṭ Saʿādat al-Khādim.[25] This *ribāṭ*, located on the Tigris near the Bāb al-Ghurba, was actually a house built by the *khādim al-rasāʾil* of the caliph al-Mustaẓhir (r. 487–512/1094–1118), a *mamlūk* by the name of ʿIzz al-Dīn Abū ʾl-Ḥasan al-Rūmī al-Mustaẓhirī (d. 500/1106), who stipulated through pious endowment (*waqf*) that it was to go to the Sufis, and that Wajīh al-Dīn al-Suhrawardī and his descendents were to be its directors.[26] In the time of Ibn al-Fuwaṭī (d. 723/1323), members of the family still lived there, most likely the direct descendents of Wajīh al-Dīn's son Aʿazz b. ʿUmar al-Suhrawardī.[27] In addition to transmitting *ḥadīth* to him, it was Wajīh al-Dīn who first invested his nephew Abū ʾl-Najīb with the Sufi *khirqa* upon the latter's arrival in Baghdad, the same thing which Abū ʾl-Najīb would do for his own nephew upon his arrival in city some forty years later. Wajīh al-Dīn died in Rabīʿ I, 532/September or October, 1137 and was buried in Baghdad's Shūnīziyya cemetery, the resting place of al-Junayd.[28]

Abū ʾl-Jaʿfar al-Suhrawardī (d. 539/1145)

As for Suhrawardī's father, Abū ʾl-Jaʿfar[29] much less is known. Like both Wajīh al-Dīn and Abū ʾl-Najīb, he is said to have come to Baghdad where he studied Shāfiʿī jurisprudence and preaching (*waʿẓ*) under the tutelage of Asʿad al-Mīhanī[30] as well as—according to an eyewitness report—preaching in the Jāmiʿ al-Qaṣr and the Baghdad Niẓāmiyya,[31] after which he returned to Suhraward and assumed the position of judge (*qāḍī*), perhaps taking over the position from his uncle Wajīh al-Dīn upon his death in 532/1137. His brother Abū ʾl-Najīb was also a student of Asʿad al-Mīhānī and it is possible that the two studied under him

[25] *MT*, 10:75; cf. *DhTB*, 5:188–189.

[26] *TMA*, 1:158–159 (s.v. ʿIzz al-Dīn al-Rūmī, no. 187); Muṣṭafā Jawād, "al-Rubuṭ al-baghdādiyya," *Sumer* 10 (1954): 249; cf. *TIsl*, 41–42:289.

[27] *TMA*, op. cit.; also, *DhTB*, 5:188.

[28] Located on the west bank of the city (Gaston Wiet, *Baghdad: Metropolis of the Abbasid caliphate*, trans. Seymour Feiler [Norman, Oklahoma: University of Oklahoma Press, 1971], 116, 170).

[29] On him see *SN*, 22:376, and, *TIsl*, 53:114 (s.v. Abū Ḥafṣ ʿUmar al-Suhrawardī); and, *ṬShK*, 6:122 (no. 643).

[30] On him, see Bayhaqī, *Taʾrīkh ḥukamāʾ al-islām*, ed. Mamdūḥ Ḥasan Muḥammad (Cairo: Maktabat al-Thaqāfat al-Dīniyya, 1996), 160; and, Makdisi, "Muslim Institutions of Learning," 41–43.

[31] The witness being Yūsuf al-Dimashqī. (*SN*, 22:376, and, *TIsl*, 53:114)

at the same time. According to Subkī, who quotes a first-hand report of Yūsuf al-Dimashqī, Abū Jaʿfar "abounded in knowledge and was an eloquent preacher who assumed the chief judgeship of Suhraward where he was murdered in 539 [1145]".[32] According to a report which ʿUmar al-Suhrawardī personally related to his student Ibn al-Najjār[33] (d. 642/1245), this occurred while he was still an infant:

> My father was killed in Suhraward when I was six months old. At the time, our city was possessed of an oppressive chief of police (*shiḥna*) who was murdered by a gang of townsfolk who later claimed that my father was their leader. The servant boys (*ghilmān*) of the victim came and assaulted my father whereupon the townsfolk fell upon them and murdered them. Civil unrest was so stirred up that the sultan crucified four of the townsfolk. This weighed heavy on my uncle Abū ʾl-Najīb and he donned the *qabāʾ*[34] saying, 'I want nothing to do with Sufism until I am conciliated with regard to this twist of fate!'.[35]

Abū Jaʿfar left no surviving works nor seems to have done much which the prosopographers and chroniclers would have been interested in, most likely due to his choosing to return to Suhraward for which—in contrast to Baghdad—we have no local histories, a desideratum for many medieval Muslim cities. Unlike his brother Abū ʾl-Najīb and

---

[32] *ṬShK*, 6:122. The date 537 is also attested in the manuscripts but is obviously a scribal error resulting from the similarity between the orthography of the words 'seven' (سبع) and 'nine' (تسع); 537 cannot be correct in any case because Suhrawardī's own admission of having been born in Rajab or Shaʿbān 539 and that he left Suhraward at age sixteen, that is in 555. This, then, would place the death of his father in Dhū ʾl-Ḥijja, 539/May or June, 1145.

[33] A celebrated Shāfiʿī *muḥaddith* from Baghdad, Ibn al-Najjār left his hometown and traveled for some twenty-eight years throughout the lands of Islam in search of religious, medical, and literary learning, eventually returning to Baghdad where he received an appointment as director of the newly built Mustanṣiriyya Madrasa, a position which he occupied until his death. Author of some twenty works spanning numerous topics and genres, his most famous work, a continuation al-Baghdādī's *Taʾrīkh Baghdād*, was further continued by his disciple, and another associate of Suhrawardī, Ibn al-Sāʿī. Like him, Ibn al-Najjār is reported to have been invested with the *khirqat al-tabarruk* by Suhrawardī, even though early in his career he had declined to make a donation to the shaykh's *ribāṭ* (*SN*, 23:133). He was also one of those whom the caliph al-Nāṣir licensed to narrate from his *Rūḥ al-ʿārifīn*, a task which he accomplished in Mecca and Media, Damascus, Jerusalem, Aleppo, Baghdad, Nīshāpūr, Marv, and Hamadhān. On him, see: Yāqūt, *Muʿjam al-uddabāʾ*, 19:49–51 (no. 13); Ibn al-Dubaythī, *Mukhtaṣar*, 1:137 (no. 268); *TIr*, 1:360–261 (no. 255); *KḤ*, 245–246 (*anno* 643); *SN* 23:131–134 (no. 98); *TIsl*, 53:217–220 (*anno* 643, no. 260); and, *KW*, 5:9–11 (no. 1963).

[34] That is, to his regular (non-Sufi) clothing. On the *qabāʾ* see: R. Dozy, *Dictionnaire détaillé des noms des vêtements chez les arabes* (1845; reprint, Beirut: Librairie du Liban, n.d.), 352–362.

[35] *SN*, 22:375; and, *TIsl*, 52:113 (cf. *ṬFSh*, 2:835).

his uncle Wajīh al-Dīn, he is not included in any later *salāsil* of the Suhrawardiyya, although Suhrawardī's son, ʿImād al-Dīn (d. 655/1257) was known, perhaps in memory of his grandfather, by the filionymic Abū Jaʿfar.

Aʿazz b. ʿUmar al-Suhrawardī (d. 557/1162) and Sons

In addition to his immediate relatives, other sections of the family are also reported to have been members of the ulama, in particular the son of Wajīh al-Dīn al-Suhrawardī, Aʿazz al-Suhrawardī[36] (d. 557/1162), a *muḥaddith* of little standing who is reported as having transmitted *ḥadīth* from Abū ʿAlī b. Nabhān[37] (d. 511/1117). His two sons, who were cousins of ʿUmar al-Suhrawardī and also residents of Baghdad, seem to have emulated their father's rather lackluster career, perhaps living in their grandfather's *ribāṭ*, the Saʿādat al-Khādim (Ribāṭ al-Sharṭ), as stipulated in the terms of its *waqf*. The first of them, Muḥammad b. Aʿazz al-Suhrawardī[38] (527–606/1131–1209), heard *ḥadīth* from his grandfather and others in Baghdad as well as narrating to a number of important individuals such as the historian Ibn al-Dubaythī[39] (d. 636/1239) and the famous *muḥaddith* Najīb al-Dīn ʿAbd al-Laṭīf (d. 672/1273–1274). The second, ʿUmar b. Aʿazz al-Suhrawardī[40] (542–624/1147–1227), also engaged in the transmission of *ḥadīth*. In addition to these three, two grandsons of Aʿazz al-Suhrawardī also engaged in transmitting *ḥadīth* at the same time when Abū ʾl-Najīb and Abū Ḥafṣ ʿUmar al-Suhrawardī

---

[36] On him see Ibn Ḥajar al-ʿAsqalānī, *Tabṣīr al-muntabih bi-taḥrīr al-mushtabih* (Delhi: al-Dār al-ʿIlmiyya, 1986), 1:21 (s.v. Aʿazz).

[37] A Baghdadi *muḥaddith* of the late 5th/11th–early 6th/12th century. On him see *MT*, 9:195; Ibn al-Dubaythī, *al-Mukhtaṣar al-muḥtāj ilayhi*, ed. Muṣṭafā Jawād (Baghdad: Maṭābiʿ Dār al-Zamān, 1963), 1:12; *TMA*, 3:570; and, al-Dhahabī, *al-ʿIbar fī khabar man ghabar*, ed. Ṣalāḥ al-Dīn al-Munajjid and Fuʾād Sayyid (Kuwait: Dāʾirat al-Maṭbūʿat wa-l-Nashr, 1960–1963), 4:25.

[38] Who was known to Ibn al-Najjār who interviewed him about his grandfather Wajīh al-Dīn (*DhTB*, 5:188–189). On him see Ibn al-Dubaythī, *Mukhtaṣar*, 1:26 (no. 47); *TMA*, 3:341 (no. 2376); and, *TIsl*, 49:209–210 (no. 306).

[39] Ibn al-Dubaythī was a respected Shāfiʿī *muḥaddith* and expert in *ʿilm al-rijāl* who composed, among other works, a continuation to al-Samʿānī's continuation of al-Baghdādī's *Taʾrīkh Baghdād*. One of the teachers of Ibn al-Najjār, he heard *ḥadīth* from Suhrawardī as well as taking the *khirqat al-tabarruk* from him. A very active transmitter, Ibn al-Mustawfī reports hearing *ḥadīth* from him when he visited Irbil in 611/1215, and his biographers provide a long list of others who did the same, including Suhrawardī's students Ḍiyāʾ al-Dīn al-Maqdisī and ʿIzz al-Dīn al-Fārūthī. On him, see: *TIr*, 1:194–195 (no. 97), 2:324–326 (*ḥawāshī*, nos. 1–5); *WA*, 4:28; *KW*, 3:102; *ṬShK*, 8:61–62 (no. 1074); GAL I, 402 ff., S I 565; and, Franz Rosenthal, "Ibn al-Dubaythī", *EI*^{2}, 3:755–756.

[40] *TW*, 5:303–304 (no. 2152); and, *TIsl*, 51:202–203 (no. 256).

were active in Baghdad. In addition to transmitting on the authority of the prolific Sufi *muḥaddith* Abū ʾl-Waqt al-Sijzī[41] (d. 553/1158), the first of them, Asʿad al-Suhrawardī[42] (547–614/1152–1217), is identified as a Sufi while the second, Abū Zakariyyā al-Suhrawardī[43] (d. 616/1219), is only mentioned has having transmitted *ḥadīth* from his father on the authority of Abū ʾl-Waqt. Members of the family were active in Baghdad and Syria as *ḥadīth* transmitters well into the 8th/14th century. They are never mentioned in the Suhrawardiyya sources.

Abū ʾl-Najīb ʿAbd al-Qāhir al-Suhrawardī (d. 563/1168)

Due to his prominence in the culture of religious learning of 6th/12th-century Baghdad as well as his importance to the later Suhrawardiyya tradition, we are much better informed about Abū ʾl-Najīb ʿAbd al-Qāhir al-Suhrawardī[44] (c. 490–563/1097–1168) than any other member of the family with the possible exception of ʿUmar al-Suhrawardī himself. The sheer number of students and disciples who are recorded as having associated with him, numbering well over fifty in the prosopography of the following two centuries, evince his prominence as a *ḥadīth* transmitter and *shaykh al-tarbiya* in the Baghdad of his day. Born around 490/1097

[41] A disciple of the famous Sufi master ʿAbdullāh-i Anṣārī, Abū ʾl-Waqt (ʿAbd al-Awwal b. ʿĪsā b. Shuʿayb b. Ibrāhīm b. Isḥāq al-Sijzī, al-Harawī, al-Mālīnī) is an important figure who deserves further study, on him, see Ibn Nuqṭa, *K. al-taqyīd li-maʿrifat al-ruwāt wa-l-sunan wa-l-masānīd* (Hyderabad: Maṭbaʿat Dāʾirat al-Maʿārif, 1983) 2:163–164; and, *TIsl*, 44:112–121 (no. 93).

[42] On him see *TIsl*, 50 (*anno* 614, no. 202).

[43] On him see ibid., 50:327 (*anno* 616, no. 429).

[44] On him, see: al-Samʿānī, *K. al-ansāb*, 7:197 (s.v., al-Suhrawardī); *MT*, 10:225 (*anno* 563, no. 318); Yāqūt, *Muʿjam*, 3:289–290 (s.v., Suhraward); *KT*, 11:254 (*anno* 563); *LTA*, 1:589–590 (s.v., al-Suhrawardī); *TIr*, 1:107–112 (no. 39) and 2:143–160 (*ḥawāshī*, nos. 1–52); Ḥamd Allāh Mustawfī, *Tārīkh-i guzīda*, ed. ʿAbd al-Ḥusayn Navāʾī (Tehran: Intishārāt-i Amīr-i Kabīr, 1364 sh. [1985]), 666; *SN*, 20:475–478 (no. 302); *TIsl*, 45:163–167; *TIbW*, 2:233–234 (*anno* 632, s.v. Shihāb al-Dīn al-Suhrawardī); *KW*, 19:48–49 (no. 42); *MJ*, 3:382–383 (*anno* 563); *ṬShK*, 7:173–175 (no. 881); *ṬSh*, 2:64–65; *BN*, 12:204; Ibn al-Mulaqqin, *ʿIqd*, 134 (no. 347); *ṬFSh²*, 1:325 (no. 309); *NZ*, 5:380; Jāmī, *Nafaḥāt*, 420–241; al-Munāwī, *al-Kawākib al-durriyat fī tarājim al-sāda al-ṣūfiyya*, ed. Muḥyī ʾl-Dīn Dīb Mistū (Damascus: Dār Ibn Kathīr, 1993), 2:250–253; al-Shaʿrānī, *al-Ṭabaqāt al-kubrā*, ed. ʿAbd al-Raḥmān Ḥasan Maḥmūd (Cairo: Maktabat al-Ādāb, 1993–2001), 2:312–313; Ḥājjī Khalīfa, *Kashf al-ẓunūn*, ed. S. Yaltakaya and K.R. Bilge (Istanbul: Maarıf Matbaası, 1941–1943), 43; *ShDh*, 6:346–347 (*anno* 563); al-Nabhānī, *Jāmiʿ karāmāt al-awliyāʾ*, ed. Ibrāhīm ʿAṭwah ʿAwaḍ (Cairo: Muṣṭafā al-Bābī al-Ḥalabī, 1962), 2:220–221; GAL I, 436, S I, 780; Kaḥḥāla, *Muʿjam al-muʾallifīn* (Damascus: al-Maktabat al-ʿArabiyya, 1957–1961), 5:311; Milson, *Rule*, 10–16, and, idem, "al-Muqaddima," in *AdM*, 1–16 (Arabic text); *GE*, 2–3 (no. 4); and, Florian Sobieroj, "al-Suhrawardī, Abu ʾl-Nadjīb," *EI²*, 9:778.

in Suhraward, Abū ʾl-Najīb heard *ḥadīth* in Isfahan before coming to Baghdad as a young man sometime around 507/1113.[45] According to his biographers, for two years he lived a humble life, selling water in the streets from a jug which he carried upon his back, but eventually he took up studying at the Niẓāmiyya where he pursued, under the direction of Asʿad al-Mīhanī and al-Faṣīḥī,[46] the study of Shāfiʿī jurisprudence, *ḥadīth*, Arabic grammar, and belles-lettres, somewhere along the line taking the *khirqa* from his paternal uncle Wajīh al-Dīn.

At the age of twenty-five, perhaps in imitation of Wajīh al-Dīn, Abū ʾl-Najīb broke with his studies, cut himself off from public life, and left Baghdad. At some point, he returned to Isfahan where he joined the circle of the celebrated Aḥmad-i Ghazālī (d. 520/1126), after which he came back to Baghdad and attached himself to the controversial Sufi preacher Ḥammād al-Dabbāṣ (d. 525/1130–1131). After the death of al-Dabbāṣ, Abū ʾl-Najīb began to preach publicly and shortly thereafter is reported to have founded a Sufi *ribāṭ* and Shāfiʿī *madrasa* on the western bank of the Tigris. According to his younger contemporary Ibn al-Najjār, before this time Abū ʾl-Najīb and his meager group of companions were in possession of a ruined building (*khariba*) on the Tigris, but his growing fame attracted the attention of the sultan (Masʿūd) who visited him, he being followed by his amirs who did the same.

Thereafter, the ruined building was turned into a *ribāṭ* and a *madrasa* was built next to it, the complex "becoming a place of sanctuary for those who took refuge in it out of fear of persecution by the caliph and the sultan."[47] Although not mentioned specifically in the sources, one can deduce that from the perspective of the Seljuk sultan Masʿūd, his *shiḥna* Masʿūd al-Bilālī, and the Seljuk amirs, patronizing such a Shāfiʿī Sufi as Abū ʾl-Najīb was good policy and there is little reason to doubt that a substantial donation was made for the construction of this new *ribāṭ* and *madrasa*. Just as with Wajīh al-Dīn and Abū Ḥafṣ ʿUmar later, for Abū ʾl-Najīb the Sufi *ribāṭ* was a space where politics, Sufism, and religious learning intertwined.

---

[45] Ibn al-Mustawfī reports that he heard *ḥadīth* from Abū ʿAlī b. Nabhān in 508/1114–1115 (*TIr*, 1:110); also, *TIsl*, 45:165; and, Milson, *Rule*, 11.

[46] Abū ʾl-Ḥasan ʿAlī b. Muḥammad al-Faṣīḥī (d. 516/1122) taught Arabic at the Baghdad Niẓāmiyya, eventually being dismissed on charges of Shiite sympathies (Milson, op. cit., 12).

[47] *TIsl*, 45:164; and, *ṬShK*, 7:175.

It was here where Abū ʾl-Najīb made a name for himself as a *shaykh al-tarbiya* and Shāfiʿī scholar, initiating, investing, and training disciples—including men of note such as the famous Shāfiʿī historian and *muḥaddith* Ibn ʿAsākir (d. 571/1175), the influential Sufi author and later teacher of Najm al-Dīn Kubrā, ʿAmmār al-Bidlīsī (d. between 590 and 604/1194 and 1207), the well-known *muḥaddith* and biographer al-Samʿānī, and the *shaykh al-shuyūkh* of Baghdad Ibn Sukayna—as well as teaching Shāfiʿī jurisprudence, preaching to the public, transmitting *ḥadīth*, and issuing fatwas. Given both the number of individuals who are reported to have associated with him during this period as well as his inclusion in the initiatic lineages of numerous early Sufi lines (see Chart 3), it is apparent that he was by all accounts a popular and important teacher, mentioned in connection with a mixed lot of Sufis, *ḥadīth* transmitters, jurists, and others, most of whom were clearly affiliated with the Shāfiʿī *madhhab*. According to Ibn al-Mustawfī his *ribāṭ*-cum-*madrasa* was home to both students of jurisprudence (*mutafaqqiha*) and Sufis (*ṣūfiyya*), individuals from each group staying as residents there in order to study with him or place themselves under his direction.[48] Although the reliability of the report is questionable, according to Ibn Athīr, Abū ʾl-Najīb was present at the inauguration of the caliph al-Muqtafī (r. 530–555/1136–1160) in 530/1136, in addition to taking the oath of loyalty (*bayʿa*) to him, exhorting the new caliph with a particularly eloquent sermon.[49]

[48] *TIr*, 1:107; cf. al-Nuʿaymī, *al-Dāris fī taʾrīkh al-madāris*, ed. Jaʿfar al-Ḥusaynī (Damascus: ʿUḍw al-Majmaʿ al-ʿIlmī al-ʿArabī, 1948–1951), 1:226 (s.v. al-Mujīr al-Wāsiṭī).

[49] Ibn al-Athīr, *al-Taʾrīkh al-bāhir fī-l-dawlat al-atābikiyya*, ed. ʿAbd al-Qādir Aḥmad Ṭulaymāt (Cairo: Dār al-Kutub al-Ḥadītha, 1963), 53. He mentions Abū ʾl-Najīb in the same way in his account of the inauguration of the caliph al-Mustarshid (r. 512–529/1118–1135), saying: "after the prayers were finished and he had been buried (i.e., al-Mustaẓhir), the children of the caliph, the amirs, jurists, judges, and Sufi shaykh (*mashāyikh al-ṣūfiyya*) took the oath of loyalty to him. The chief judge (*qāḍī al-quḍāt*) ʿAlī b. Muḥammad al-Damaghānī presided over the oath taking and among those who took the oath of allegiance was the shaykh Abū ʾl-Najīb al-Suhrawardī who then exhorted him with a particularly eloquent sermon (*wa-waʿaẓahu mawʿiẓat*^{an} *balīghat*^{an})." (ibid., 22) The historicity of this account is questionable for a number of reasons. First, there is no evidence that Abū ʾl-Najīb was this type of public figure at such an early date, having only arrived in the city some five years earlier and then leaving for Isfahan some three years later. Second, the accounts of the inaugurations of both al-Mustarshid and al-Muqtafī given by the other historiographers do not mention his presence nor does Ibn al-Athīr mention Abū ʾl-Najīb in his other accounts of the events (*KT*, 8:629, 9:77–79). Third, the exact same construction is used in both accounts (*wa-waʿaẓahu mawʿiẓat*^{an} *balīghat*^{an}), something which could point to any number of things such as a conflation of the two inaugurations, a difference in Ibn

Chart 3.

Early Initiatic Lineages Associated with Abū ʾl-Najīb al-Suhrawardī*

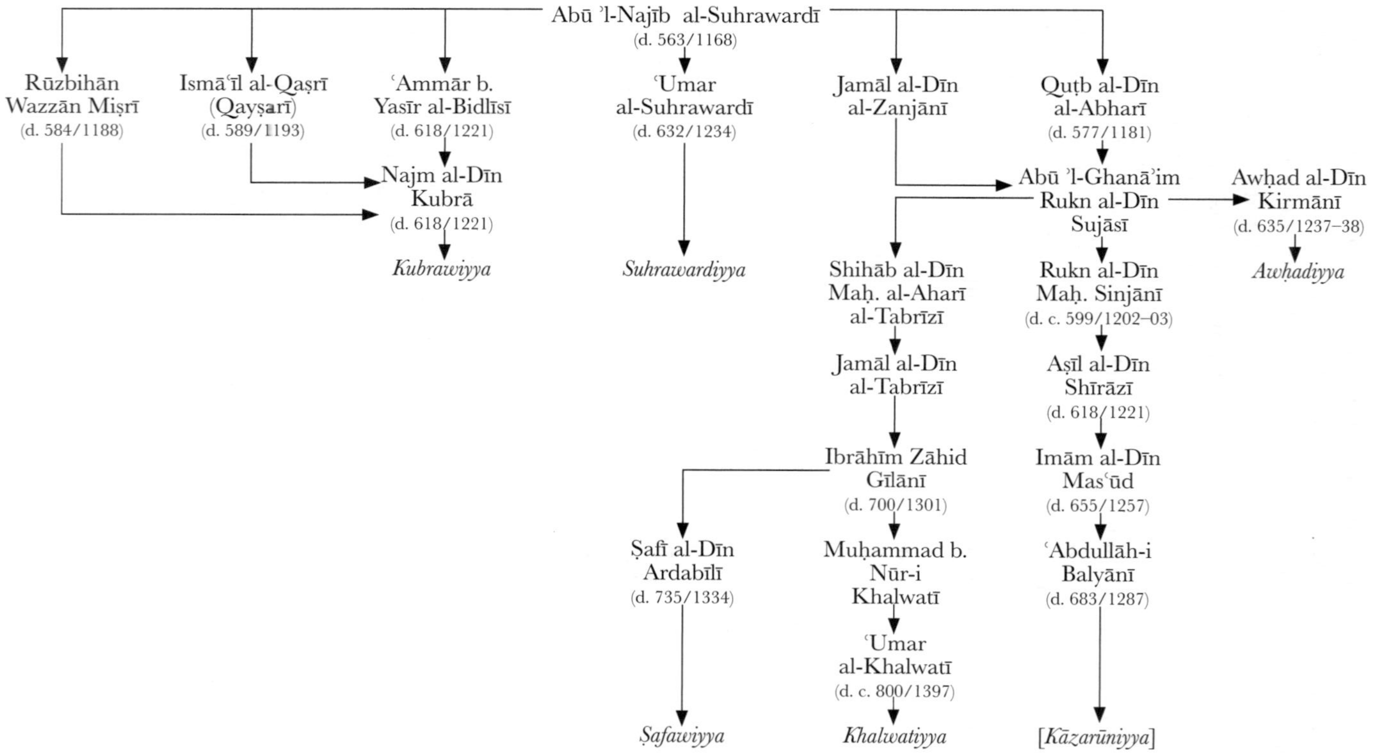

* Ibn Rāfiʿ, *Muntakhab*, 147–148 (no. 122); *MJ*, 3:40–41 (s.v. Najm al-Dīn Kubrā); Jāmī, *Nafaḥāt*, 264 (no. 325), 421–427 (nos. 465–467), 586 (no. 570); Maʿṣūmʿalīshāh, *Ṭarāʾiq*, 2:108, 311–312, 335; Kissling, "Aus der Geschichte des Chalvetijje Ordens," table 1; Qazvīnī (ed.), *Shadd al-izār*, 311–314 (fn. 1); Gramlich, *Derwischorden*, 1:8–10; Mojaddedi, *Biographical Tradition*, appendices 3–5; and, Steinfels, "Travels and Teachings", 80.

Some years later, on Tuesday, the 17th of Muḥarram 545 (16 May, 1150), after a series of disturbances at the institution, Abū ʾl-Najīb was appointed to the office of teacher (*tadrīs*) of the Niẓāmiyya, the caliph al-Muqtafī being forced against his will to grant his formal permission to the appointment at the hands of Seljuk interests in the city,[50] and for two years he stayed there teaching Shāfiʿī *fiqh* and transmitting *ḥadīth*. In 547/1152, however, the Seljuk sultan Masʿūd died and in the power vacuum which resulted, the caliph al-Muqtafī and his vizier Ibn Hubayra began to assert control over Baghdad, among other things ordering the dismissal of Abū ʾl-Najīb from the Niẓāmiyya. Although benefiting from the public protest of the Shāfiʿī *fuqahāʾ* attached to the institution and, for a few days at least, the protection of the Seljuk *shiḥna* of Baghdad Masʿūd al-Bilālī—who fled to Tikrit shortly thereafter—Abū ʾl-Najīb was dismissed from the office on the caliph's order.[51] In his account of the events of his dismissal Ibn al-Jawzī—certainly no fan of Baghdad's powerful Shāfiʿī *fuqahāʾ* and their close associations with the Seljuk *shiḥna* of the city—censures Abū ʾl-Najīb for defying the caliph's orders to stop preaching there by holding his lectures and lessons in Persian.[52]

After this debacle, we hear little about Abū ʾl-Najīb until 557/1161–1162 when his cousin, and director of the Ribāṭ Saʿādat al-Khādim, Abī ʾl-Ḥārith Aʿazz al-Suhrawardī died. After this, Abū ʾl-Najīb left Baghdad with the intention of traveling to Jerusalem, most likely taking his young ward ʿUmar al-Suhrawardī with him.[53] His biographers give no clue as to why he decided to leave at this time, but it is possible that the death of his cousin raised questions over the directorship of Wajīh al-Dīn's *ribāṭ*. If there was any struggle over succession, however, it is not accounted for, and in that same year we find Abū ʾl-Najīb in Mosul, preaching to much acclaim in the city's congregational mosque. From there, he traveled on to Damascus where he is said to have been honorably received by Nūr al-Dīn Zangī, once again gaining fame for

al-Athīr's sources, a problem in the manuscripts, or perhaps a partiality (Ibn al-Athīr's or another's) which valued Abū ʾl-Najīb being inserted into these accounts, either as an assertion of his importance (or of the constituency he represented) or of his later tergiversation in siding with the Seljuks against al-Muqtafī.

50 *MT*, 10:142.

51 Milson, *Rule*, 13–15.

52 *MT*, 10:148; and, Makdisi, "Muslim Institutions of Learning," 43.

53 In the *ʿAwārif* Suhrawardī refers to traveling with his uncle in Syria (*ʿAM*, 2:66/ *GE*, 30.5).

his fiery public preaching. Due to the continuing hostilities between Nūr al-Dīn Zangī and the Crusaders, however, he was prohibited from traveling further than Damascus and was forced to return to Baghdad where he died a few years later on the 17th of Jumādā II, 563/28 February, 1168. He was buried in his *madrasa*.[54]

*Compared to his illustrious nephew, Ab*ū ʾl-Najīb's literary output was not vast, and he seems to have spent most of his time engaged in other pursuits. Beyond his important Sufi handbook, the *K. ādāb al-murīdīn*, his biographers credit him with one other work, the *Gharīb al-maṣābīḥ*,[55] a commentary on al-Baghawī's (d. 516/1122) *Maṣābīh al-sunna*, a popular collection of *ḥadīth* later made famous in the recension of Walī al-Dīn (d. 732/1342) entitled *Mishkāt al-maṣābīḥ*. Although not as productive as his nephew, his influence, however, was vast and far-reaching. ʿUmar al-Suhrawardī, for instance, quotes him extensively in his own Sufi handbook, the *ʿAwārif al-maʿārif*, and the *K. ādāb al-murīdīn* heavily influenced his as well as later generations of Sufis, which in addition to numerous commentaries was also translated into Persian.

ʿUmar, Son of Muḥammad: 550–563/1155–1168

Despite his grief over Abū Jaʿfar's murder in 539/1144, Abū ʾl-Najīb was conspicuously absent from his nephew's life during his childhood in Suhraward. Having left the city some thirty years prior to ʿUmar's birth, he seems to have had little to do with his nephew before the teenage boy's departure from Suhraward in 555/1160. None too surprisingly, the sources at our disposal present no details as to Suhrawardī's upbringing or education prior to arrival at the threshold of his uncle's Baghdadi *ribāṭ*-cum-*madrasa* eight years before the aged shaykh's death in 563/1168.

[54] Referred to by most of his biographers. In *TMA*, 102, fn. 4, the editor (quoting Maḥmūd Shukrī al-Ālūsī's *Masājid al-Baghdād wa-āthārihā* [Baghdad: Maṭbaʿat Dār al-Salām, 1924], 89) says that Abū ʾl-Najīb is reported to have been buried in his *madrasa*, which later became a mosque known as the Mosque of Najīb al-Dīn which (at least in the 1920's when al-Ālūsī was writing) was located near the Tigris, separated from the river by an officer's club. At that time, the mosque still had a *madrasa* attached to it.

[55] MS. Süley., Şehid Ali Paşa 453, fol. 1a–52b with the title *Sharḥ baʿḍ al-alfāẓ al-mushkilāt fī ʾl-maṣābīḥ*. Another work, entitled simply *R. fī ʾl-iʿtiqād*, attributed to Abū ʾl-Najīb in Süley., Hâlet Ef. İlavesi 3_{10}, fol. 206b–210b is simply an extract (*muntakhab*) from his *K. ādāb al-murīdīn*, but its early copy date (Ram. 694/July–Aug., 1295) and location (Simnān) are of importance.

It is easy to speculate that befitting his station as the son of a *qāḍī*, the young ʿUmar would have received the usual *kuttāb* education normally given to boys like him.[56] This would have most certainly included instruction in the Qurʾān, penmanship, some study of mathematics, and perhaps the memorization of certain *ḥadīth*. We can also assume that he would have received some extra lessons, learning to speak and write Arabic at a young age, most certainly his second language, perhaps in preparation for his eventual journey westwards to take up the family business, although he did apparently require some 'tutoring' in the finer points of Arabic grammar and belles-lettres upon arriving in the imperial capital. Be this as it may, we are informed by one of his disciples (Ibn Bāṭīsh) that Suhrawardī left his home town for Baghdad when he was sixteen years of age,[57] a report confirmed by an anonymous biographical note contained in an important anthology of Suhrawardī texts which places his arrival in Baghdad in the year, perhaps prior to Shawwāl, 555/1160.[58]

The details of his journey are unknown, but according to his earliest biographers upon arriving in the city ʿUmar immediately attached himself to Abū ʾl-Najīb and as with his father before him took to the study—under his uncle's careful tutelage—of jurisprudence (*fiqh*) and preaching (*waʿẓ*) as well as hearing *ḥadīth* from him and his associates in his uncle's teaching circle (*ḥalqa*) held in his Tigris *ribāṭ*-cum-*madrasa*. Although the biographers differ as to the amount of detail they provide, during this period Suhrawardī also engaged in the study of the ancillary sciences one would expect a budding Shāfiʿī *ʿālim* to achieve mastery in such as the sciences of juridical divergence (*khilāf*) and jurisprudential questions (*masāʾil*), and Arabic grammar and literature (*adab*).[59] In addition to this, it was Abū ʾl-Najīb who both initiated and directed Suhrawardī in the science of Sufism, investing him with the

[56] On which, see my entry "Primary Schools, or Kuttab," in Josef W. Meri, ed., *Medieval Islamic Civilization: An Encyclopedia* (New York: Routledge, Taylor & Francis Group, 2006), 2:641.

[57] al-Subkī, *Ṭabaqāt al-shāfiʿiyya al-wusṭā*, as cited in *ṬShK*, 8:339, fn. 4.

[58] *Nasab al-Suhrawardī*, MS. Tüb. Ma VI 90_2, fol. 52b. Same in *Wafāt al-Suhrawardī*, MS. Süley., Fatih 2742_2, fol. 322b; and, Faṣīḥ al-Dīn Aḥmad b. Muḥammad Khwāfī, *Mujmal-i faṣīḥī*, 3 vols. ed. Maḥmūd-i Farrūkh (Mashhad: Kitābkhāna-yi Bāstān, 1960), 1.2:252.

[59] *TW*, 6:122; *WA*, 3:446; *SN*, 22:375; *TIbW*, 2:232; Ibn al-Dimyāṭī, *Mustafād*, 327; *ṬFSh*, 2:835; and, *NZ*, 6:283–284 (*anno* 631).

khirqa just as Wajīh al-Dīn had done with him upon his arrival in the city many years earlier.

Although the details are sketchy, during his student days it is usually claimed that in addition to Abū ʾl-Najīb, Abū Ḥafṣ ʿUmar al-Suhrawardī also associated with the popular Ḥanbalī preacher, Sufi moralist, and eponym of the Qādirī brotherhood ʿAbd al-Qādir al-Jīlānī.[60] As with other such episodes which link Suhrawardī to the paragons of the Sufi tradition, however, the exact nature of their relationship is open to debate. Although it is quite possible that the two may have met during the five of so years after Suhrawardī's arrival in Baghdad, there is no evidence that Suhrawardī's uncle Abū ʾl-Najīb was a close associate of Jīlānī nor that he allowed his young ward to attach himself to other teachers during the period of his novitiate. As discussed below, the rather scant evidence which places a still very young Suhrawardī together with a quite aged Jīlānī points in another direction entirely.

What is certain, however, is that during this time Suhrawardī busied himself in the collection of *ḥadīth*, an activity which would prove of immense consequence in his latter life. As evinced in both his *Mashyakha* and the *rijāl* works, Suhrawardī began hearing *ḥadīth* almost immediately upon his arrival in Baghdad in 555/1160 and seems to have continued to do so for some time following his uncle's death in 563/1168. This was an important phase of his training, and many of the *ḥadīth* which he collected during this period appear in the works he composed after establishing himself as a respectable *ʿālim* and Sufi shaykh some years later. Although we will return to the role which the transmission of *ḥadīth* played in Suhrawardī's political career in Chapter Five, it is important to remember that like his forebears, Abū Ḥafṣ ʿUmar al-Suhrawardī was first and foremost a member of the ulama, and as such he moved within a world which regulated itself through the conservation and maintenance of certain replicable practices as well as through an ever persistent process of self-scrutiny and internal policing. Although for many, the boundaries and borders of this world were most certainly vague and ill-defined, for individuals like Suhrawardī, the world of a late 6th/12th-century Sunni *ʿālim* was a world of elites, one where

[60] *TW*, 6:122; *WA*, 3:446 (cf. *Wafāt al-Suhrawardī*, fol. 322b); *SN*, 22:374; *TIsl*, 52:112; *TIbW*, 2:232; *ṬFSh*, 2:835; Ibn Duqmāq, *Nuzhat al-anām fī taʾrīkh al-islām*, ed. Samīr Ṭabbārah (Beirut: al-Maktabat al-ʿAṣriyya, 1999), 60; *ṬFSh*[2], 1:400; and, *ShDh*, 7:268.

membership meant literally everything: the rules of the game were known by all and if one chose not to play by them, then one could expect to be excluded from membership in the group, both in this world and in its aftertext.

In late 6th/12th-century Baghdad, Damascus, Cairo, Isfahan, or Bukhara an *ʿālim* of this type was entitled to 'belong' precisely because he acted as an *ʿālim* should act. If he did not transmit *ḥadīth*, for instance, than he would most certainly not be mentioned in the *rijāl* works; if he did not give fatwas or transmit licensed legal learning, it would be highly unlikely for him to find a place as either an *imām* or *khaṭīb* in his place of residence, and he might risk not being mentioned in the biographical dictionaries devoted to his particular *madhhab*. This does not mean, however, that such identities should in all cases be construed as professional identities, far from it. Even those notoriously schematic and reified artifacts of pre-modern ulama culture, the biographical dictionaries, preserve evidence of the existence of a much more fluid and porous entity than one might be led to believe. In fact, if one was to spend just a bit of time thumbing through standards such as Subkī's *Ṭabaqāt al-shāfiʿiyya* or Ibn Rajab's *Dhayl ʿalā ṭabaqāt al-ḥanābila*, one would come across plenty of individuals who could never claim the status of *ʿālim* per se, for in fact most *ḥadīth* transmitters or those who busied themselves in the study and perpetuation of religious learning were simply engaging in a pious avocation. As made clear in the previous chapter, however, there were those, like Suhrawardī, who vested such activities with both soteriological *and* professional meaning.

Such identity was maintained through adhering to the generally accepted conventions which determined those things which an *ʿālim* should (and should not) do and in turn how such things were to be done. In his capacity as a Shāfiʿī *ʿālim*, Suhrawardī did these things. Not only did he study jurisprudence and engage in the transmission of *ḥadīth*, but he even went a step further by professionalizing his efforts through producing a curriculum vitae (*mashyakha*) intended for general circulation. Such documents were an important feature of the science of *ḥadīth* transmission, serving as an instrument of legitimacy during the lifetime of their authors as well as upon their death, becoming an object transmitted as a discrete text, being treated in the same manner as other collections of *ḥadīth*. This vita has been preserved.

In the Arabic collection of the Chester Beatty Library in Dublin there exists an anthology of *ḥadīth*-related material which contains a short text of some ten folios entitled *Mashyakhat Shihāb al-Dīn al-Suhrawardī.*[61] Although mentioned in the Arabic bio-bibliographical literature as well as having been taught and transmitted by the author himself among his disciples, the Chester Betty text appears to be a unicum. Consisting of fifteen individual teachers, Suhrawardī's *Mashyakha* begins, naturally, with his paternal uncle Abū ʾl-Najīb—from whom he heard his first *ḥadīth*—extends through a number of famous, and some less than famous Baghdadi *muḥaddithūn*, and closes with one Bishāra bt. al-Raʾīs Abī ʾl-Saʿādāt Masʿūd b. Mawhūb (d. c. late 6th/12th cen.). Because it seems to have been compiled fairly early in Suhrawardī's career in Baghdad, the *Mashyakha* is not a complete record of all the individuals from whom he heard *ḥadīth*, but it does provide a good sense of the type of individuals with whom the young Suhrawardī associated during his student days under Abū ʾl-Najīb.

As with those to whom he would eventually transmit to himself, the individuals from whom Suhrawardī heard *ḥadīth* represent a group of individuals whose avocations, professional pursuits, and legal affiliations were common in late 6th/12th-century Baghdad. Namely, a group of largely Shāfiʿī ulama who in addition to transmitting *ḥadīth* engaged in other pursuits such as preaching, jurisprudence, Qurʾānic recitation, and of course, Sufism. Some, like his uncle Abū ʾl-Najīb—from whom he relates three *ḥadīth* in his *Mashyakha* and many more in the *ʿAwārif al-maʿārif*—were well known *ḥadīth* transmitters in their own right, cited frequently in the *rijāl* works as energetic participants in Baghdad's bustling *ḥadīth* culture, whereas others simply served as quiet parts of the backdrop. None too surprisingly, a number of them were formal disciples of Abū ʾl-Najīb. The predominance of individuals associated with the Shāfiʿī school in this resume further evinces the long-standing connection between Shāfiʿī jurists and this particular strand of the Sufi tradition.

Upon Abū ʾl-Najīb's death in Jumādā II, 563/1168, ʿUmar al-Suhrawardī was but a young man of twenty-four. It had only been eight years since his uncle initiated him into the religious sciences and the Sufi path, and he was far away from establishing himself as an *ʿālim* of any standing. His first datable treatises would not be composed until some thirty-five years later, and the accession of his eventual patron, the

[61] C.B., MS. Arab. 495_9, fol. 84a–95; for a description of which see A.J. Arberry, "The Teachers of Shihāb al-Dīn ʿUmar al-Suhrawardī," *BSOAS* 13 (1950): 339–356.

energetic Abbasid caliph al-Nāṣir li-Dīn Allāh, was still a dozen years down the road. Although a great personal loss for the budding Sufi shaykh, Abū ʾl-Najīb's death seems to have left him with an opportunity to cultivate the skills which would eventually bring him to the attention of the caliphal court as well as enough prestige to attract and retain disciples, but this would take some time.

As with the issue of Abū ʾl-Najīb and the directorship of Wajīh al-Dīn's Sufi *ribāṭ*, the Saʿādat al-Khādim, there is no direct evidence that Suhrawardī took over Abū ʾl-Najīb's position as director of the latter's Tigris *ribāṭ* and *madrasa* immediately following his death. Despite his young age, which may not have necessarily precluded him from taking over his uncle's position, the issue was complicated by the presence of Abū ʾl-Najīb's three sons, one of whom we just happen to know something about. Although he had been absent from Baghdad for many years, this son, Abū Muḥammad ʿAbd al-Laṭīf al-Suhrawardī[62] (534–610/1140–1213), returned to the city sometime around his father's death, perhaps expecting to take over his position. A young man with a propensity for reclusiveness, ʿAbd al-Laṭīf had gotten into some serious trouble as a youth and fled Baghdad for points east. Studying with numerous ulama in Khurāsān and Transoxiana, he developed a reputation for religious learning, a skill which he would ply quite successfully later in life. Returning to Baghdad for a time, according to Ibn al-Mustawfī (who personally interviewed ʿAbd al-Laṭīf in Irbil) he eventually came to blows with his older brother, ʿUmar al-Suhrawardī's cousin and later father-in-law ʿAbd al-Raḥīm b. Abī ʾl-Najīb al-Suhrawardī, and left the city once again, this time for Syria.[63] Once in Damascus, he put himself into the service of the celebrated Ayyubid general Saladin, who appointed him judge (*qāḍī*) and Friday preacher (*khaṭīb*) over Acre (and perhaps other jurisdictions) following his famous campaign against the Crusaders in 583/1187.[64] After this, according to al-Ṣafadī, ʿAbd al-Laṭīf "moved from province to province, finally returning once again to Baghdad where he taught (*darrasa*) in his father's

[62] Ibn Nuqṭa, *Taqyīd*, 2:155–156 (no. 492); *KW*, 19:103–104 (no. 95); *TIsl*, 49:374–375 (*anno* 610, no. 524); *ṬShK*, 8:312 (no. 1216); *ṬSh*, 2:66; and, Ibn Ḥajar al-ʿAsqalānī, *Lisān al-mīzan*, ed. Muḥammad ʿAbd al-Raḥmān al-Marʿashlī (Beirut: Dār al-Turāth al-ʿArabī, 1995–1996), 4:437–438 (no. 5304).

[63] *TIr*, 1:171.

[64] *MZ*, 8:395; *TIr*, 1:161; *TIsl*, 47:30 (*ḥawādith, anno* 583), and, 49:375; and, *KW*, 19:104; cf. al-Nuʿaymī, *Dāris*, 2:179.

madrasa",[65] after which he left for Irbil, where he made something of a name for himself among the city's Sufis, notables, and governor.[66] After a protracted illness, which even the royal doctors could not cure, he died there in Jumādā I, 610/September, 1213 and was buried in the graveyard of the Sufis.

Although we do not know for how long ʿAbd al-Laṭīf stayed in Baghdad before coming to blows with his brother ʿAbd al-Raḥīm, it seems that one or both of them took over Abū ʾl-Najīb's Tigris *ribāṭ* and *madrasa* for according to a first hand account of one of Suhrawardī's disciples in Baghdad, Ibn Bātīsh, after Abū ʾl-Najīb's death Suhrawardī became a student of Ibn Faḍlān (d. 595/1199), a Shāfiʿī *faqīh* known for his mastery of the sciences of juridical divergence (*al-khilāf*) and juridical disputation (*al-jadal*).[67] Although it is impossible to determine how long Suhrawardī stayed in Baghdad under the tutelage of Ibn Faḍlān, it appears that at some point he left and traveled down to Basra where he associated with a certain Mālikī Sufi master named Abū Muḥammad Ibn ʿAbd al-Baṣrī.[68]

We are informed that while under Abū ʾl-Najīb's tutelage in addition to pursuing a course of legal and religious studies, Suhrawardī also engaged in wayfaring on the Sufi path, but it seems that it was only quite some time after his uncle's death that he left his studies to pursue a life of renunciation. Much like his early life as a student under the tutelage

[65] *KW*, 19:104.

[66] Associating with the *faqīr* Abū Saʿīd Kawkabūrī, transmitting *ḥadīth*, as well as teaching his own treatise, the *K. maʿnā al-ḥaqīqa*, to none other than Ibn al-Mustawfī himself. (*TIr*, 1:181–182; Ibn Ḥajar al-ʿAsqalānī, *Lisān*, 4:437) His wife, a freed slave called Rājiyya al-Armaniyya who was a respected *muḥadditha* in her own right, outlived him by some ten years, dying in Irbil in 622/1225 (*TIsl*, 51:106 [*anno* 622, no. 87]).

[67] Born in Baghdad, Ibn Faḍlān—also known as Wāthiq—was a student of Saʿīd b. Muḥammad b. al-Razzāq, the *mudarris* of the Niẓāmiyya. He also traveled to Khurāsān where he studied jurisprudence with Muḥammad b. Yaḥyā Najā al-Nīsābūrī, the teacher of Abū Ḥāmid al-Ghazālī as well as studying with the grandson of the Sufi master al-Qushayrī, Abū ʾl-Asʿad al-Qushayrī (d. 532/1137–1138), with whom he seems to have forged close ties. Back in Baghdad, he taught first in the Mosque of the Lawziyya neighborhood, later obtaining a position at the Dār al-Dhahab Madrasa which was built for him by Fakhr al-Dawla Abū ʾl-Muẓaffar b. al-Muṭṭalib. He was also the father of the famous Shāfiʿī jurist, *qāḍī al-quḍāt*, and *mudarris* at the Mustanṣiriyya Madrasa, Muḥammad (d. 631/1233). On him, see: Ibn Nuqṭa, *Taqyīd*, 2:637 (s.v. Wāthiq), 305 (no. 659); *KT*, 10:168 (*anno* 595); Ibn al-Dubaythī, *Mukhtaṣar*, 128; *TW*, 2:172–174 (no. 491); *DhR*, 15; *JM*, 9:11 (*anno* 595); *SN*, 21:257; *MZ*, 3:479 (*anno* 595); and, *ṬShK*, 7:322–323.

[68] *WA*, 3:446; *SN*, 22:374; *TIsl*, 52:112; al-ʿUmarī, *Masālik*, 8:225; *TIbW*, 2:232 (where his name is given as Abū Muḥammad b. ʿAbdūn); *ṬShK*, 8:339; and, *ṬFSh*, 2:835 (where his name is given as Abū Muḥammad b. ʿUbayd al-Baṣrī).

of Abū ʾl-Najīb, the trajectory of his middle years closely mirrored that of both Wajīh al-Dīn and Abū ʾl-Najīb, for just like them he entered a period of withdrawal before emerging as a public preacher and Sufi master. On the issue, however, Suhrawardī's biographers present a narrative which is more conventional and tropological than reflective of a discrete, datable, biographical fact. Returning to the account of Ibn Bāṭīsh we find that Suhrawardī studied with Ibn Faḍlān until

> ...he achieved mastery in jurisprudence and then he embarked upon busying himself with God and wayfaring on the path of the Hereafter, spending all his time in devotions and private worship and cleaving unto God until God made him the foremost of his time.[69]

Similar reports are found elsewhere. In his lengthy biographical entry on Suhrawardī, the shaykh's student Ibn al-Najjār says that Suhrawardī left his studies to engage in the sustained practice of pious retreat, continuous fasting, *dhikr*, and worship until it occurred to him—when he reached a 'dignified age' (*ʿinda ʿuluww sinnihi*)—that he should appear in public and discourse to people, and so he did just that, holding preaching sessions (*majlis al-waʿẓ*) in his uncle's *madrasa* located on the Tigris[70] where he made a name for himself as a preacher, "discoursing with useful speech without embellishment or pretension, drawing large crowds and achieving great fame among both the elites and the commoners."[71] Whether or not Suhrawardī actually took over the directorship of the Tigris *ribāṭ* and *madrasa* from either one of his cousins, or simply engaged in preaching there alongside one or both of them, however, is impossible to tell.

Although sketchy, the evidence contained in the reports of the contemporaries of ʿAbd al-Laṭīf suggests it was first Abū ʾl-Najīb's eldest son, ʿAbd al-Raḥīm, who took over his role as director of the Tigris *madrasa* and that he was followed by ʿAbd al-Laṭīf, who only assumed the position sometime after his return from Palestine, perhaps as little as a year after 583/1187. Although we do not know when ʿAbd

---

[69] al-Subkī, *Ṭabaqāt al-shāfiʿiyya al-wusṭa*, op. cit; in the anonymous *Wafāt al-Suhrawardī*, the compiler states that "...he entered Baghdad in the year 555 [1160], entered the path (*ṭarīq*) of seclusion, religious devotions, and cleaving unto God in the year 566 [1170–1171], and died on the first Wednesday of Muḥarram in the year 632 [27 September, 1234], living for a total of 93 years". (fol. 322b; the date 566/1170–1171 is the same in Khwāfī, *Mujmal*, 1.2:558)

[70] *DhTB*, 5:180, and, *TIsl*, 53:114; cf. *WA*, 3:446; *KḤ*, 102; *SN*, 22:375; al-Dimyāṭī, *Mustafād*, 327; *ṬShK*, 8:340; and, *ṬFSh*, 2:835; all of whom quote Ibn al-Najjār.

[71] *TIsl*, 53:114; the same is said about Abū ʾl-Najīb's preaching style.

al-Laṭīf left Baghdad for Irbil, it was probably quite late as the first thing which his contemporary Ibn al-Mustawfī reports about him, after narrating the events of his death, is that he heard *ḥadīth* from him, in the company of Ibn Nuqṭa, during the latter's visit to the city in Ramaḍān, 609/January–February, 1213.[72] As the first datable instance of Suhrawardī serving in an official capacity of any sort, in this case director of the Ribāṭ al-Maʾmūniyya whose *mashyakha* he assumed in 579/1183, it makes sense to infer that ʿAbd al-Laṭīf did indeed come back to Baghdad for a time to take up the duties which Suhrawardī had inherited from ʿAbd al-Raḥīm and then left for his position as director of the Ribāṭ al-Maʾmūniyya. There is, of course, much room for speculation on the details. The biographers of ʿAbd al-Laṭīf only mention that he 'taught' (*darrasa*) at the Tigris *madrasa*, and although he was certainly classified as a Sufi later at Irbil, there is no mention of him taking on the role of *shaykh al-tarbiya* or investing anyone with the *khirqa* in either Baghdad or Syria.

Although it is difficult to determine exactly when Suhrawardī reappeared in public life, Ibn al-Najjār's report is at least partially confirmed in that Suhrawardī virtually disappears from the annals of Baghdad's *muḥaddithūn* during this period as the vast majority of individuals who heard *ḥadīth* from him certainly did not do so until much later in his life or at the very least not until the last few years of this period. The same, in fact, can be said regarding the record of his formal disciples, none of whom are recorded as having associated with him until the first few years of the 7th/13th century. It was probably around this time when Suhrawardī married Abū ʾl-Najīb's granddaughter, Sayyida bt. ʿAbd al-Raḥīm,[73] their union later giving birth to Suhrawardī's son, and eventual successor in Baghdad, ʿImād al-Dīn Muḥammad al-Suhrawardī in 578/1182. Beyond this, little else can be gleaned from the sources about this period of his life.

[72] *TIr*, 1:249.

[73] The daughter of Suhrawardī's cousin, ʿAbd al-Raḥīm b. Abī ʾl-Najīb al-Suhrawardī, Sayyida bt. ʿAbd al-Raḥīm b. Abī ʾl-Najīb ʿAbd al-Qāhir b. ʿAbdullāh al-Suhrawardī was born in 563/1167–1168 and is recorded by Dhahabī to have been a *muḥadditha* who transmitted *ḥadīth* to numerous individuals in Baghdad. She died on the 16th of Rajab, 640/9 January, 1243. (*TIsl*, 52:436 [*anno* 640, no. 656])

Enter al-Nāṣir li-Dīn Allāh

We are partially informed about Suhrawardī's reentry into public life, however, by way of an event which occurred three years after Suhrawardī's eventual patron, al-Nāṣir li-Dīn Allāh, assumed the caliphate, for in Shawwāl, 579/April or May, 1183, an important new *ribāṭ* was opened in Baghdad. Formerly the house of one of al-Nāṣir's *mamlūks*, Sunqur al-Ṣaghīr, after his arrest in 577/1181, al-Nāṣir ordered the building seized and the house transformed into a Sufi *ribāṭ*.[74] This institution, the Ribāṭ al-Maʾmūniyya, was financed by al-Nāṣir li-Dīn Allāh's mother, a Turkish slave called Zumurrud Khātūn (d. 599/1202–1203) who had already made something of a name for herself during the caliphate of al-Mustaḍīʾ through her extensive patronage of pious foundations.[75] According to al-Dhahabī, who does not quote his source and whose account appears nowhere else, the opening of the Ribāṭ al-Māʾmuniyya was attended by government officials, judges, *imāms*, and notables, Suhrawardī being installed as its director (*shaykh*) and made responsible for its special endowments.[76]

Now forty years of age and thus having attained what Ibn al-Najjār called a "dignified age", Suhrawardī was now at the height of his intellectual and spiritual maturity according to the conventions of his day. The trajectory of his life, which as we have seen closely mirrored that of his forebears, was about to enter its culminating stage. Having successfully made the transition from student to *ʿālim*, and from aspirant (*murīd*) to master (*shaykh*), Suhrawardī had emerged from his lengthy period of withdrawal, just as Wajīh al-Dīn and Abū ʾl-Najīb had done before him, to assume the role of *shaykh al-tarbiya*. He was now ready to take on the responsibilities of initiating and directing students, writing treatises and transmitting religious learning, managing the affairs of what would come to be a network of endowed institutions, and serving his patron al-Nāṣir in a capacity which the authority he now possessed allowed him to do.

---

[74] *MZ*, 8.1:365 (*anno* 577); and, *Nṣr.*, 127, 180, fn. 59.

[75] *KT*, 10:192; *MZ*, 8.2:513–514; *DhR*, 33; *JM*, 9:102; *TIsl*, 48:386; *KW*, 14:213; *BN*, 13:36; *Nṣr.*, 180–181; idem, "Al-Nāṣir," *EI*², 7:997; and, Renate Jacobi, "Zumurrud Khātūn," *EI*², 11:570.

[76] *TIsl*, 46:50 (*ḥawādith*, *anno* 579); cf. *KT*, 9:478 (*anno* 579) where only the opening of the *ribāṭ* is mentioned; and, *MZ*, 8.1:365 (*anno* 577!?).

In 588/1192, some nine years after having assumed the directorship of the Ribāṭ al-Maʾmūniyya, Suhrawardī was sent on the first of four diplomatic missions which he would performs for al-Nāṣir over the course of the next thirty years. This particular year was a critical one for al-Nāṣir, for following the death of the İldigüzid ruler Qızıl Arslān in 587/1191, the Seljuk sultan Ṭoghrıl III had finally been able to throw off the yoke of İldigüzid domination in Azerbaijan, Arrān and the Northern Jibāl, taking advantage of the weakness of Qızıl Arslān's successor, Qutlugh İnānç, to reconsolidate power in his own person.[77] This mission, which is scarcely mentioned in the sources, was to the then ruler of the Armenian town of Akhlāṭ (Khilāṭ—located on the north-western shore of Lake Van), a slave commander named Begtimur (r. 581–589/1185–1193).[78] Taken from the Seljuks in 493/1100 by the Turkish slave commander Sökmen al-Quṭbī (d. 506/1112), Akhlāṭ was the capital of the short-lived dynasty of the Shāh-i Armanids (493–604/1100–1207)[79] which, at the time, was under the control of the less than illustrious successor to Sökmen b. Ibrāhīm (d. 581/1185)—under whose long rule the Shāh-i Armanid dynasty had reached its apogee—ultimate control of which his slave commander Begtimur had allowed to fall into the hands of the powerful İldigüzids of Azerbaijan. Akhlāṭ was a strategic town for al-Nāṣir, for under the Shāh-i Armanids it had become an integral part of a group of powerful Turkish principalities of the Jazīra and eastern Anatolia, after the death of Sökmen b. Ibrāhīm in 581/1185 becoming a prize which both the Saladin and the İldigüzid ruler, Muḥammad b. İldigüz Pahlavān (r. 571–582/1175–1186), fought over, the İldigüzids eventually subjecting it to vassalage.[80] In his bid to win over the İldigüzids as allies against Ṭoghrıl III as well as to check the designs of the Ayyubids on the town following the death of Qızıl Arslān, he seems to have sent Suhrawardī to cultivate Begtimur as an

[77] *KT*, 10:112–115, 118 (*anno* 587), 128 (*anno* 590); al-Ḥusaynī, *Akhbār*, 72–176; *Nṣr.*, 74–75; and, M.T. Houtsma [C.E. Bosworth], "Ṭoghrïl III," *EI*², 10:554.

[78] *TIsl*, 47:77 (*ḥawādith*, *anno* 588); on Begtimur and the rather interesting events surrounding his death, see *MZ*, 8.1:423; and, *SN*, 21:277–278.

[79] On the Shāh-i Armanids, see: Vladimir Minorsky and Franz Taeschner, "Akhlāṭ," *EI*², 1:329; Osman Turan, *Doğu Anadolu Türk devletleri tarihi*, 2nd ed. (Istanbul: Turan Nakışlar Yayınevi, 1980), 83–106, 243, 279; Carole Hillenbrand, "Shāh-i Arman," *EI*², 9:193; and, C.E. Bosworth, *The New Islamic Dynasties* (New York: Columbia University Press, 1996), 197 (no. 97).

[80] Hillenbrand, op. cit., 193; Bosworth, op. cit., 197; cf. Gibb, *The Life of Saladin*, 41–42, fn. 4.

ally, perhaps sending him to invest the commander with a diploma of investiture over the territory.

For al-Nāṣir, choosing an individual such as Suhrawardī to lead such mission was nothing new, for upon assuming the caliphate some thirteen years before he had strategically employed another Sufi master and Shāfiʿī *ʿālim* to do much the same thing. This individual, whom one of his biographers describes as "unique in his era, a man who struck a perfect balance between *dīn* and *dunyā*",[81] was none other than the *shaykh al-shuyūkh* of Baghdad, Ṣadr al-Dīn ʿAbd al-Raḥīm (d. 580/1185). Upon his accession to the caliphate in 575/1180 al-Nāṣir sent him as part of a delegation to Isfahan, Khurāsān, Azerbaijan, Syria, and Egypt (where he met with Saladin) with orders to take the oath of loyalty (*bayʿa*) from their rulers,[82] Suhrawardī's teacher Raḍī al-Dīn al-Ṭālqānī[83] (the Shāfiʿī *mudarris* of the Niẓāmiyya) being sent to Mosul to do the same. The following year, in response to a letter which Saladin sent to Baghdad, the *shaykh al-shuyūkh* went to Damascus and presented him with a diploma of investiture and a caliphal robe of honor, confirming his rule over Diyār Muḍar as a bulwark against the Crusaders.[84] Two

---

[81] *TIbW*, 2:135.

[82] The meeting with Saladin is described by Ibn Wāṣil (*Mufarrij*, 2:92; see also: Ehrenkreutz, *Saladin*, 166; Gibb, *The Life of Saladin*, 14; and, Mason, *Two Statesmen*, 91). Although largely successful, Ṣadr al-Dīn did run into some trouble, however, having to return to the İldigüzid *atabeg*, Muḥammad b. İldigüz Pahlavān, a second time because he had initially refused his request. (*KT*, 9:443 [*anno* 575]; and, *Nṣr.*, 72, 295).

[83] Raḍī al-Dīn al-Ṭālqānī (d. 590/1194) studied Shāfiʿī *fiqh* and heard *ḥadīth* in Qazvīn and Nīshāpūr before coming to Baghdad, first on his way to the *ḥajj*, and then in 555/1160 during which time he established a preaching circle (*majlis al-tadhkīr*), and again sometime after 560/1165 where he taught Shāfiʿī *fiqh* at the Niẓāmiyya and the Jāmiʿ al-Qaṣr, being officially appointed as a teacher in the former in 569/1173–1174. As a Sufi, al-Ṭālqānī invested disciples with the *khirqa* on the authority of the aforementioned Abū ʾl-Asʿad al-Qushayrī, who had invested him in his grandfather's *ribāṭ* in Nīshāpūr, investing. In addition to this, al-Ṭālqānī is remembered as being something of a storyteller known for orally translating Persian tales into Arabic, as well as preaching, as would Suhrawardī later, at the Badr al-Sharīf Gate in Baghdad. According to a report preserved by Dhahabī, he is said to have been the first to preach at this gate, saying that the caliph al-Mustaḍīʾ (r. 566–575/1170–1180) would attend his sessions, listening from behind a screen, he preaching on some days and Ibn al-Jawzī on others (*SN*, 21:193). Known for his outspoken views, al-Ṭālqānī eventually ran into trouble in Baghdad on account of his refusal to curse Yazīd b. Muʿāwīya whereupon he was forced to return to Qazvīn, dying there in Muḥarram, 590/January, 1194 (*MZ*, 8.2, 443–444). On him, see: al-Samʿānī, *Ansāb*, 8:178–179 (s.v. al-Ṭālqānī); al-Rāfiʿī, *Tadwīn*, 2:144–148; Ibn Nuqṭa, *Taqyīd*, 1:138 (no. 147); *LTA*, 2:76–77; Ibn al-Dubaythī, *Mukhtaṣar*, 1:174–176 (no. 337); *TW*, 1:368–371 (no. 224); and, *KW*, 6:253–255 (no. 2736).

[84] Ibn Wāṣil, *Mufarrij*, 2:94–95 (text of letter preserved there); and, *Nṣr.*, 86–87, 295. On Diyār Muḍar (Diyār al-Jazīra)—an area in the Jazīra comprising the towns of

years later, in 579/1183–1184, and again in 580/1184–1185—in an attempt to negotiate in the conflict between Saladin and the new ruler of Mosul 'Izz al-Dīn—Ṣadr al-Dīn was sent to him as an emissary of the caliph, conducting his negotiations in Mosul from one of the city's Sufi *ribāṭs*.[85]

A New Ribāṭ: 599/1203

In Jumādā I, 599/January or February, 1203, al-Nāṣir's beloved mother Zumurrud Khātūn passed away. Stricken with grief, the caliph himself preceded her bier on foot, her body being transported via the Tigris to a mausoleum (*turba*) which she had already built, along with a *madrasa*, at the grave of the famous early Baghdadi Sufi Ma'rūf al-Karkhī (d. 200/815–816).[86] An active player in political life, during the caliphate of al-Mustaḍī' (r. 566–575/1170–1180) Zumurrud Khātūn proved herself an energetic champion of one of al-Mustaḍī''s favorites, Ibn al-Jawzī, and the Ḥanbalites of Baghdad in general, continuing to intercede for them during the reign of her son al-Nāṣir.[87] She was a founder of numerous charitable works, including *madrasas*, *ribāṭs*, and congregational mosques as well as public works such as repairing—at the cost of 300,000 dinars—the water supplies of Mecca and Medina.[88] In her memory, a month after her death, al-Nāṣir distributed a large amount of money to the *zāwiyas*, *ribāṭs*, and *madrasas* of the city, ordering his mother's personal possessions, including gold, jewels, and fine clothing to be distributed among her household and the precious drugs and medical preparations in her treasury to be given to Baghdad's al-'Aḍudī Hospital.[89]

---

al-Raqqa, Ḥarrān, Edessa, and Sarūj—see: Claude Cahen, "Diyār Muḍar," *EI²*, 3:247.

[85] *KT*, 9:461–465; Ibn Wāṣil, *Mufarrij*, 2:155–157; *TIbW*, 2:135; Mason, *Two Statesmen*, 92; *Nṣr.*, 88–89, 295; Gibb, *The Life of Saladin*, 34; and, Ehrenkreutz, *Saladin*, 178, 185.

[86] *KT*, 10:192; *MZ*, 8.2:513–514; *DhR*, 33; *JM*, 9:102; *TIsl*, 48:386; *KW*, 14:213; *BN*, 13:36; *Nṣr.*, 180; Jacobi, "Zumurrud Khātūn," *EI²*, 11:570. Located east of the famous Basra Gate in the Convent Gate Cemetery, Ma'rūf al-Karkhī's mausoleum was destroyed by fire in 459/1067, subsequently being rebuilt in brick and plaster. (Wiet, *Baghdad*, 116, 141, 170)

[87] *Nṣr.*, 180–181; and, Jacobi, op. cit., 11:570.

[88] *MZ*, 8.2:514; *DhR*, 33; *TIsl*, 47:91, 48:386; *Nṣr.*, 180; and, Jacobi, op. cit., 570.

[89] *MZ*, 8.2:514; *DhR*, 33. Located in the Karkh neighborhood in the Sūq al-Māristān, this justly famous hospital was built by the Buyid prince 'Aḍud al-Dawla (d. 338/944). According to Ibn Jubayr, the al-'Aḍudī hospital was an extremely large

Although it is not mentioned if it occurred before or after Zumurrud Khātūn's death, it was during this year that the construction of an important new *ribāṭ* was finally completed. Known at the time as Ribāṭ al-Mustajadd ('the new *ribāṭ*'), the building was located in the Marzubāniyya Neighborhood alongside the Nahr ʿĪsā, and once finished was handed over to Suhrawardī and his disciples, he and his group of students being provided with everything which they might require while living there.[90] This *ribāṭ*, which came to be known simply as the Ribāṭ al-Marzubāniyya, also included an attached private home, complete with a bath and gardens, for the shaykh and his family.[91]

Two years after having settled into the Ribāṭ al-Marzubāniyya, Suhrawardī received an important order from the caliph. According to Ibn al-Sāʿī, on Thursday the 21st of Jumādā I, 601/21 May, 1205, Suhrawardī was ordered to begin preaching at the Badr al-Sharīf Gate, a duty which he seems to have discharged on a weekly basis for at least the next four years.[92] Located near the Palace Congregational Mosque (Jāmiʿ al-Qaṣr), the position of preacher here was an official one, and for many years Ibn al-Jawzī himself held regular Saturday preaching sessions there on the caliph's orders.[93] His being assigned to this position by al-Nāṣir not only publicly confirmed his status as a legitimate religious authority, but also evinces the extent of the relationship between Suhrawardī and his patron because such appointments were not given out casually. By all accounts, Suhrawardī was a popular preacher, addressing his audience from a clay pulpit while wearing his everyday clothing, like his uncle Abū ʾl-Najīb before him discoursing in an unaffected and unpretentious manner.[94]

---

and well-funded medical center, approaching the dimensions of a palace in proportions, containing chambers and closets and all the appurtenances of a royal dwelling. (Wiet, *Baghdad*, 140)

[90] *JM*, 99 (*anno* 599); *MZ*, 8.2:513; and, *BN*, 13:34. In an *ijāza* for the *ʿAwārif al-maʿārif* written for his disciple Najm al-Dīn al-Tiflīsī, Suhrawardī specifically refers to al-Nāṣir as the one responsible for building this *ribāṭ* (MS. Süley., Turhan Vâlide Sultan 186_4, fol. 420b).

[91] *KH*, 102; and, Wiet, *Baghdad*, 151.

[92] *JM*, 145 (*anno* 601); and, *KH*, 102.

[93] *JM*, 231–232, fn. 1; e.g., *TIsl*, 46:5–6, 12–13, 17–18, 24, 27.

[94] *BN*, 12:138–139; cf. *TIsl*, 45:164. Sibṭ Ibn al-Jawzī admits seeing him during one of these sessions, saying: "In 590 [1194] saw him at the Ribāṭ Darb al-Maqbara preaching from a pulpit of clay (*minbar ṭīn*) with a simple wool wrap (*miʾzar ṣūf*) upon his head." (*MZ*, 8.2:679; and, *NZ*, 6:284 [*anno* 631])

Mission to the West: The Ayyubids, 604/1207–1208

In 604/1207–1208 Suhrawardī was sent on a diplomatic mission which took him to the courts of al-Malik al-Ẓāhir in Aleppo, al-Malik al-ʿĀdil in Damascus, and al-Malik al-Kāmil in Cairo. Upon concluding an armistice with the Crusaders at Ṭarāblus, al-Malik al-ʿĀdil had sent a mission to Baghdad requesting a diploma of investiture (al-tashrīf wa-l-taqlīd) from the caliph for suzerainty over Egypt, Syria, the Jazīra, and Akhlaṭ. The mission was lead by two high ranking officials, the majordomos (ustādār) Amīr Aldukuz al-ʿĀdilī and the Ḥanafī qāḍī of Syria Najm al-Dīn Khalīl al-Maṣmūdī, who received a good reception from the caliph and a reply in the form of a return mission led by Suhrawardī.[95]

Accompanied by Sunqar al-Silḥadār and his disciple Saʿd b. Muẓaffar al-Yazdī (d. 637/1239) and bearing the caliphal robe of honor (khilaʿ), neckband (ṭawq), and trousers of the futuwwa (sirwāl) Suhrawardī's first stop was in Aleppo, where he was greeted by al-Malik al-Ẓāhir Ghāzī and his army,[96] three days thereafter convening a preaching session at the Dār al-ʿĀdil[97] in which he addressed both the amir and the city's notables, hammering home his message until "hearts were filled with fear and eyes gushed".[98] During the course of his address he conveyed a message to the effect that in Baghdad and elsewhere, the caliph gave a break on taxes and natural produce which amounted to 300,000 dinars, al-Malik al-Ẓāhir then granting Suhrawardī some 3,000 dinars in the form of largesse (nithār) to be distributed in Damascus upon the investiture of al-Malik al-ʿĀdil and his sons with the caliphal robes of honor.[99]

---

[95] MẔ, 8.1:534; DhR, 60; Ibn Wāṣil, Mufarrij, 3:180; al-Maqrīzī, K. al-sulūk fī maʿrifat duwal al-mulūk, ed. Muḥammad Muṣṭafā Ziyāda (Cairo: Lajnat al-Taʾlīf wa-l-Tarjamat wa-l-Nashr, 1956–1973), 1.1, 167; and, NẔ, 6:165.

[96] BN, 13:47; and, DhR, 61. Both giving the word *سروان for the last item which the editors failed to correct to the more appropriate سروال.

[97] The 'Palace of Justice', an institution first established by Nūr al-Dīn in Aleppo and then later in Damascus. Essentially a maẓālim court, Nūr al-Dīn would sit there twice weekly (along with the qāḍī and jurists) in order to hear petitions. (P.M. Holt, The Age of the Crusades: The Near East from the Eleventh Century to 1517 [London: Logman, 1986], 73)

[98] Ibn Wāṣil, Mufarrij, 3:180; and, al-Maqrīzī, al-Sulūk, 1.1, 167.

[99] Ibn Wāṣil, op. cit., 3:180–181; Abū ʾl-Fidā, al-Mukhtaṣar fī akhbār al-bashar (Cairo: Maṭbaʿat al-Ḥusayniyyat al-Miṣriyya, 1325 [1907]), 135; al-Maqrīzī, op. cit., 1.1:167; NẔ, 6:165; and, Nṣr., 246–247. Or 30,000 dinars; there are variants in the manuscripts.

Upon the orders of al-Malik al-Ẓāhir, in Aleppo Suhrawardī was joined by the former confidant, chronicler, and *qāḍī al-ʿaskar* of Saladin, Bahāʾ al-Dīn b. Shaddād[100] (d. 631/1234), and the two traveled together from there to Damascus, encountering along the way more largesse sent from Ḥamā by al-Malik al-Manṣūr and al-Malik al-Mujāhid. Upon their arrival at the outskirts of the ancient city, the delegation was greeted with much fanfare, being received by the army and then personally by al-Malik al-ʿĀdil and his sons al-Ashraf Mūsā and al-Muʿaẓẓam ʿĪsā who then lead them into the Citadel. The whole event was something of a spectacle for the city's inhabitants who came out in large numbers to gawk at the proceedings, no doubt in part because the markets had been ordered closed on account of the visit.[101] The investiture ceremony itself took place the next day and was conducted by both Suhrawardī and Ibn Shaddād. It is described in some detail by Ibn Wāṣil:

> When he [al-Suhrawardī] entered, al-ʿĀdil sat in the inner court of the palace with the tokens of investiture spread out before him. They consisted of a black satin *jubba* trimmed all the way around with gold embroidery, a black turban with gold embroidery, and a heavily bejeweled gold neckband (*ṭawq*). Likewise, he [al-ʿĀdil] was invested with a sword with a pure gold scabbard. He mounted a gray stallion fitted with a golden saddle, and a black standard on a golden pole, upon which was written in white the agnomens of the caliph, was hoisted above his head. The *qāḍī* Ibn Shaddād came forward scattering gold and brought five robes of honor: first he distributed them to the kings' emissaries and then invested al-Ashraf and al-Muʿaẓẓam with their robes, black turbans, and thickly brocaded *thawbs*. The vizier Ṣafī al-Dīn b. Shukr was invested in a similar manner. After this, Malik al-ʿĀdil rode off with his sons and vizier, wearing the caliphal robes of honor. The city had been decorated and [after parading through it] they returned to the Citadel. The city continued in its decoration for eight days more and the diploma of investiture was read aloud from the pulpit by Ṣafī al-Dīn and the *khuṭba* in the name of al-ʿĀdil: 'King of Kings' and 'Intimate Friend of the Commander of the Faithful' (*shāhinshāh wa-malik al-mulūk wa-khalīl amīr al-muʾminīn*), and during the vizier's reading, he stood up upon the pulpit as did al-ʿĀdil and the rest of the people in attendance in reverence for the caliph.[102]

[100] The former secretary of Saladin's enemy, ʿIzz al-Dīn of Mosul, and later close confident to Saladin himself. On him, see: Gibb, *The Life of Saladin*, 2; and, Ehrenkreutz, *Saladin*, 177–178, 237.

[101] Ibn Wāṣil, *Mufarrij*, 3:181; and, al-Maqrīzī, *al-Sulūk*, 1.1, 168.

[102] Ibn Wāṣil, *Mufarrij*, 3:181–182; cf. Abū ʾl-Fidā, *Mukhtaṣar*, 3:109 where the same description of the tokens are given. Ibn Wāṣil's account is repeated almost verbatim by al-Maqrīzī in *al-Sulūk*, 1.1:168; Ibn Taghribīrdī paraphrases the account (*NZ*, 6:166); cf.

In addition to participating in the investiture ceremony, while in Damascus Suhrawardī also held a number of preaching assemblies, during one of which he addressed al-Ashraf Mūsā himself, telling him that he personally sought out each and every copy of Ibn Sīnā's *K. al-shifā'* in the libraries of Baghdad and washed the ink from every page. Apparently, the sultan was not pleased with the shaykh's attempts at purification for later during the course of his address, Suhrawardī mentioned that over the past year much of the populace of Baghdad had fallen violently ill, to which the sultan replied: "and why not, since you have eliminated the *Shifā'* from it!"[103] It was also during this visit to Damascus when Suhrawardī is said to have also met with the popular maverick ascetic ʿAlī al-Kurdī (d. 622/1225). After this Suhrawardī traveled on to Egypt, where he presided over a similar investiture ceremony for the son of al-Malik al-ʿĀdil, al-Malik al-Kāmil, the amir then riding out of his palace to triumphantly display his robe of honor to the populace of Cairo.[104]

An Indiscretion

According to Ibn al-Sāʿī, it was on the 4th of Ṣafar, 605/18 August, 1208 that Suhrawardī returned to Baghdad from his mission to the Ayyubids. Accompanied by two emissaries of al-Malik al-ʿĀdil (who had previously come to the court to petition for the diploma of investiture in the first place) the majordomos Shams al-Dīn Aldukuz and the *qāḍī al-ʿaskar* Najm al-Dīn Khalīl al-Maṣmūdī, the retinue arrived at the entrance to the royal court where they were met by a large group of officials, ulama, and Sufis. From here, the group was given a royal procession, led by the *naqīb al-ṭālibiyīn* al-Ṭāhir Fakhr al-Dīn Abū 'l-Ḥusayn b. al-Mukhtār (d. 649/1251–1252), which made its way through the city, crossed over the Tigris to the western side of the city, and finally ended up at the Jāmiʿ al-Sulṭān, Shams al-Dīn Aldukuz being received with honor at the Bāb al-Nūbī Gate.[105]

Although there was little to prevent Suhrawardī from receiving a welcome befitting an ambassador of the caliphal court from the Ayyubids, returning to a city in which he was known as a pious Sufi shaykh

Humphreys, *From Saladin to the Mongols: The Ayyubids of Damascus, 1193–1260* (Albany: State University of New York Press, 1977), 139–140.

[103] *SN*, 22:377; and, *TFSh*, 2:837. For this event, see Chapter Five.

[104] Ibn Wāṣil, *Mufarrij*, 3:182; Abū 'l-Fidā, *al-Mukhtaṣar*, 3:109; and, *NZ*, 6:166.

[105] *JM*, 259.

demanded a different tact. The gifts which he had accumulated from the grateful Ayyubid princes caused quite a stir when he reappeared with them in Baghdad:

> In this year [605/1208] shaykh Shihāb al-Dīn al-Suhrawardī returned from his mission to Syria, entering Baghdad with the majordomos of the Dār al-ʿĀdil, Shams al-Dīn Aldukuz. He was given a procession of honor and had with him gifts and presents, but Usāma and others disclaimed and resented the shaykh because he stretched out his hand to riches in Syria and honored the invitations of princes. Prior to his mission to Syria he had been a poor ascetic, and the *ribāṭ*s which had been under his possession—namely, Ribāṭ al-Zawzanī and Ribāṭ al-Marzubāniyya—were taken from him and he was prohibited from preaching. He said, 'I did not accept these riches except to distribute them to the Sufis (*fuqarā'*) of Baghdad.' Therewith, he began distributing the riches and fine clothing (*thiyāb*) in the *zāwiya*s and *ribāṭ*s.[106]

According to Ibn al-Mustawfī, the standing appointment to preach at the Badr al-Sharīf Gate on Tuesdays which Suhrawardī had previously enjoyed was revoked (ostensibly by the caliph) and Ibn al-Jazwī's son, Muḥyī 'l-Dīn Abū Muḥammad Yūsuf, was ordered to take his place,[107] his first order of business being to public criticize Suhrawardī for what he had done, saying:

> It is not seemly for a man to take property without a right to it and then distribute it to those who actually have a right to it. If he had left it alone in the first place, then he would have also been free of having to distribute it in the second! However, he wanted to improve his reputation by distributing it and then return to his previous state as if he had not distributed a thing! The servant should be cautious of the world for she is a temptress who enslaves even the luminaries among the ulama and God's servants.[108]

Likewise, the directorship (*mashyakha*) of the *ribāṭ*s which Suhrawardī possessed were subsequently passed on to others. According to Ibn Rajab, the directorship of the Ribāṭ al-Zawzanī (the date when Suhrawardī obtained its *mashyakha* is never mentioned) was handed over to Ibn al-Tānrāyā who also became responsible for managing the institution's pious foundations (*awqāf*).[109] The names of the new director(s) of the

---

106 *DhR*, 64–65; *BN*, 13:51; synopsis in *TIsl*, 49:21 (*ḥawādith, anno* 605); and, *GE*, 11.
107 *DhR*, op. cit.; and, *JM*, 231–232.
108 *BN*, 13:51–52.
109 Ibn Rajab, *al-Dhayl ʿalā ṭabaqāt al-ḥanābila*, ed. Muḥammad Ḥamīd al-Faqī (Cairo: Maṭbaʿat al-Sunna al-Muḥammadiyya, 1952–1953), 2:163.

Ribāṭ al-Marzubāniyya and the Ribāṭ al-Maʾmūniyya, however, are not mentioned. In any event, according to Ibn al-Mustawfī, Suhrawardī remained separated from his directorship of the Ribāṭ al-Marzubāniyya until 611/1214, when he returned and resumed his previous role as its director.[110] It is unclear if the other two *ribāṭs* still remained outside of his control, although he was most certainly in possession of them some ten years later after having effected a certain reconciliation with al-Nāṣir, being called upon to perform yet another mission, one quite different that his visit to the Ayyubids.

Mission to the East: The Khwārazm Shāh, 614/1217–1218

In 614/1217–1218, Suhrawardī was once again sent out of the city on behalf of the caliph, although in much less cordial circumstances than his previous mission. This year was a bad one for al-Nāṣir. At the beginning of the year, yet another serious riot broke out between the residents of the Maʾmūniyya and Bāb Azaj Neighborhoods, many losing their lives until a tense order was restored by one of the caliph's *mamlūks*. At the same time, the Tigris rose to unprecedented levels, causing a particularly terrible flood which caused widespread panic, numerous drownings, and severe damage to many buildings on both banks, including to the mausoleums of Abū Ḥanīfa and Aḥmad Ibn Ḥanbal.[111] In addition to all of this, al-Nāṣir's long-running dispute with the Khwārazm Shāhs was about to come to a head. Having given up on his demands that his name be mentioned in the *khuṭba* in Baghdad and that he be granted the title of sultan, early in the year the current Khwārazm Shāh, ʿAlāʾ al-Dīn Muḥammad (r. 596–617/1200–1220), had produced a fatwa which declared al-Nāṣir deposed, nominated an ʿAlid anti-caliph from Tirmidh, and was preparing to march on Baghdad itself.

Even though his father, the Khwārazm Shāh Tekish (r. 567–596/1172–1200), had rendered a great service to al-Nāṣir by eliminating Ṭoghrıl III and thereby extinguishing the Great Seljuk dynasty for ever (in 590/1192), his personal ambitions certainly outweighed any formal alliances which he had forged with the caliph early in his reign. After the death of Ṭoghrıl III, these ambitions collided with al-Nāṣir's policies of territorial expansion in the Jibāl and even though the Ghūrids in

[110] *TIr*, 1:192; cf. *MZ*, 8.2:679.
[111] *KT*, 10:311–312; and, Wiet, *Baghdad*, 156.

southern Khurāsān and Ghazna were able to check Tekish's advances on behalf of the caliph by keeping him busy in Khurāsān, he was eventually able to assert control over key parts of the Jibāl, which in addition to Northern Khurāsān, Rayy and Khwārazm, were already under his control, leaving al-Nāṣir with only a small part of Khūzistān under his direct suzerainty.[112] The situation appeared to have stabilized after the Ghūrids, close and loyal allies of al-Nāṣir, exacted a heavy toll on Tekish's main allies, the non-Muslim Qara Khiṭay, and in a calculated move of pacification al-Nāṣir formally invested Tekish and his son Quṭb al-Dīn Muḥammad with suzerainty over these regions on his behalf in 595/1199.[113] Tekish, however, died the next year and was succeeded by his ambitious son, ʿAlāʾ al-Dīn Muḥammad, an individual in whom al-Nāṣir was to find an even greater challenge to his authority.

Faced with a complicated power struggle between the Ghūrids, Qara Khiṭay, the Kıpçak of the northern steppe, and the Qarakhānid ruler in Samarqand, ʿUthmān Khān, before confronting al-Nāṣir himself ʿAlāʾ al-Dīn Muḥammad had to first deal with his opponents. With Qara Khiṭay support, in 598/1202 ʿAlāʾ al-Dīn Muḥammad was finally able to drive the Ghūrid ruler, Muʿizz al-Dīn Muḥammad Ghūrī, from Khurāsān, and after his death in 602/1206 was able to incorporate the former Ghūrid domains,[114] however briefly, into his own empire, six years thereafter killing ʿUthmān Khān and thus adding the remainder of the Qarakhānid territories in Transoxiana to his domains as well.[115] Now secure in his position as master of most of the eastern Islamic world, ʿAlāʾ al-Dīn Muḥammad—who in a powerful enunciation of authority had already proclaimed himself the 'Second Alexander', the 'Shadow of God on Earth, and 'Sultan Sanjar'[116]—set upon resurrecting his father's dream of reestablishing the old Seljuk ideal of a universal

---

[112] Siddiqi, "Caliphate and Kingship in Mediæval Persian," *Islamic Culture* 11.1 (1937): 51–52; Mason, *Two Statesmen*, 103–104; *Nṣr.*, 75–78; and, Bosworth, "Khʷārazm-Shāhs," *EI²*, 4:1067.

[113] That is, without conceding to Tekish's demand that his name be mentioned in the *khuṭba* in Baghdad, al-Nāṣir simply sending him and his son caliphal robes of honor (*khilaʿt*) and a diploma of investiture (*taqlīd*) over western Persia (ʿIraq al-ʿAjamī), Khurāsān, and Turkistan. (*KT*, 10:167; *TIsl*, 48:21 [*ḥawādith, anno* 595]).

[114] Juvaynī, *World-Conqueror*, 1:327–332, 341–354, esp. 332, where the Ghūrid amir Maḥmūd orders the Khwārazm Shah's name mentioned in the *khuṭba* and new coins struck with his title.

[115] Mason, *Two Statesmen*, 104; Bosworth, "Khʷārazm-Shāhs," *EI²*, 4:1067; and, idem, *The New Islamic Dynasties*, 299; cf. Juvaynī, op. cit., 1:341–349.

[116] Juvaynī, op. cit., 1:349; Siddiqi, "Caliphate and Kingship," 52–53; *Nṣr.*, 80.

sultanate in his own person. On the pretext that al-Nāṣir had earlier conspired with the Ghūrids against him, as well as committing other injustices, ʿAlāʾ al-Dīn ordered the removal of the caliph's name from the *khuṭba* in Khwārazm and the other territories under his control and convened a council of ulama whom he induced to issue a fatwa to the effect that:

> ...the Imāmate [caliphate] of any Imām [caliph] who committed such acts as have been mentioned is not a valid Imāmate; and that when such an Imām perpetrated an attack upon a sultan who had aided Islam and had passed an entire lifetime in jihad, that sultan had the right to depose that Imām and install another in his stead. Furthermore it is the *sayyid*s from the line of Ḥusayn who had the right to the caliphate for the Abbasids were usurpers.[117]

ʿAlāʾ al-Dīn's assertion that al-Nāṣir had acted in an unbefitting manner was based on his claim that after having conquered Herat in 612/1215, he entered Ghazna and discovered there a cache of 'secret correspondence' which, among other things, implicated al-Nāṣir in the murders of ʿAlāʾ al-Dīn's governor in Hamadhān, Ighlamış, and the brother of the Sharīf of Mecca as well as provided evidence which proved that the *fidāʾī*s of Alamūt were in his service and that he had conspired against the Khwārazm Shāhs with both the Ghūrids and the Qara Khiṭay.[118] After making the fatwa public, ʿAlāʾ al-Dīn named as anti-caliph a Shiite from Tirmidh called Sayyid ʿAlāʾ al-Mulk al-Tirmidhī and immediately set off for Baghdad in order to depose al-Nāṣir and install the *sayyid* in his stead.[119]

Unknowingly, al-Nāṣir himself had set the stage for the Khwārazm Shāh's march against the city, for some four years earlier the governor of the Jibāl, Menglī, had seized control of Hamadhān, Isfahan, Rayy and the areas surrounding them from one of al-Nāṣir's allies, an

[117] Juvaynī, op. cit., 2:292 (as above with a few adjustments to Boyle's translation based on *The Taʾríkh-i-Jahán-Gushá*, ed. M.M. Qazvini, G.M.S., no. 3 [Leiden and London: E.J. Brill and Luzac and Co., 1912–1937], 2:121–122). Earlier in the text Juvanyī adds: "Moreover, the Abbasid Caliphs had been backward in undertaking the jihad [i.e., against the Crusaders] in the way of Almighty God and, though possessing the means thereto, had failed to defend the frontiers, to extirpate the heterodox and the heretical and to call the infidel to the true faith, as is incumbent upon, nay, obligatory to all in command; and so had neglected this pillar, which is the main pillar of Islam." (*World-Conqueror*, 2:364–365)

[118] Juvaynī, op. cit., 1:353–354, 2:364–365, 390–392; Siddiqi, op. cit., 54; Mason, *Two Statesmen*, 109; and, Bosworth, "Khʷārazm-Shāhs," *EI*², 4:1067.

[119] Juvaynī, op. cit., 2:365; and, Mason, *Two Statesmen*, 108.

action which had forced the caliph to enter into a plot with the former Ismāʿīlī-turned-Sunnī Jalāl al-Dīn of Alamūt and the İldigüzid governor of the northern Jibāl, Muẓaffar al-Dīn Özbeg b. Jahān Pahlavān, against him.[120] Although Menglī was defeated, the largest share of the captured provinces, which by agreement were to be given to Özbeg b. Jahān Pahlavān, were succeeded to Ighlamış, a *mamlūk* of Özbeg b. Jahān Pahlavān's brother who, in turn, allied himself to ʿAlāʾ al-Dīn Muḥammad and thus became the latter's governor over Menglī's former possessions.[121] Shortly thereafter, Ighlamış was assassinated, ostensibly on al-Nāṣir's orders, by a *fidāʾī* from Alamūt and in the confusion which followed the Khwārazm Shāh seized his chance, taking Rayy, Sāva, Qazvīn, Zanjān, Abhar, and finally Hamadhān, in addition to asserting control over Isfahan, Qumm, and Kāshān after which he received assurances from a frightened Özbeg b. Jahān Pahlavān that his name would be mentioned in the *khuṭba* in the provinces under his control.[122]

Arriving in Hamadhān, the Khwārazm Shāh is reported to have mustered an army of some 400,000 or more troops (sic!), and announced that he intended to march on Baghdad itself. Preparing for a direct attack on the city, al-Nāṣir began to muster his own forces, sending Suhrawardī out ahead of them in order to intercede with the Khwārazm Shāh on his behalf. In contradistinction to his mission to the Ayyubids, here Suhrawardī capitalized upon a different type of authority which he held, that of an *ʿālim*, although it is not quite so clear why al-Nāṣir choose him as his representative over one of the many Shiites who were in his service. There are three versions of the audience which Suhrawardī had with the Khwārazm Shāh, the first, given by Sibṭ Ibn al-Jawzī runs as follows:

> In this year [614/1217] Muḥammad the Khwārazm Shāh, came to Hamadhān en route to Baghdad along with some 400,000 to 600,000 troops. The caliph [al-Nāṣir li-Dīn Allāh] prepared for him, distributing provisions and weapons, and he sent al-Shihāb al-Suhrawardī to him as an envoy in order to humble him. Once there, the Khwārazm Shāh called for him and when he came to his throne, he did not permit him to sit. Al-Shihāb has related an account of all of this, saying: "He called me and I was brought to a great tent with a vestibule, the likes of which

[120] *KT*, 10:290–291; Mason, op. cit., 106; and, *Nṣr.*, 80–81.
[121] Mason, op. cit., 106; and, *Nṣr.*, 80; cf. *KT*, 10:291.
[122] *KT*, 10:299–300; and, Juvaynī, *World-Conqueror*, 2:366 (where he says that Özbeg did indeed strike coins and have the *khuṭba* read in his name).

have never been pitched in this world. The tent's vestibule and flaps were made of satin and its ropes of silk; and in the vestibule the Kings of Persia were arranged according to their rank, among them the rulers of Hamadhān, Isfahan, Rayy, and others. I then entered into another tent of silk brocade and in the vestibule beheld the Kings of Khurāsān, Marv, Nīshābūr, Balkh, and others. Finally, I entered yet another tent just like the others and in its vestibule was the King of Transoxiana. We approached him and he was seated in a grand tent (*kharkāh*) of gold covered by a bejeweled veil. He was a young man with a full head of hair, sitting on a simple throne. He wore a Bukharan *qabā*ʾ worth about five dirhams and perched upon his head was a scrap of leather worth about two. I greeted him but he neither returned my greeting nor ordered me to sit. So, straight away I began to discourse most eloquently on the excellencies of the Abbasids and described the qualities of the caliph, his asceticism, pious scrupulosity, fear of God, and piety, all the while the interpreter helping him with my words. When I had finished, he said to the interpreter: "Tell him that the one whom he has described is not in Baghdad and I am coming to install a caliph who goes by this description." And so he dismissed me without a reply, and snow fell on them and killed their riding beasts, and the Khwārazm Shāh was out riding one day when his horse stumbled, and in that he saw a bad omen. Ruin befell his army, provisions ran short, and by God's grace 70,000 of the Khiṭā withdrew and by this a great misfortune was adverted.[123]

The second version of the encounter is preserved by al-Nasawī (d. 647/1249–1250) in his biography of ʿAlāʾ al-Dīn's successor, Jalāl al-Dīn Mangübirdī, related to him by the *qāḍī* Majīd al-Dīn ʿUmar al-Khwārizmī who reports being present at the meeting:

When Shihāb al-Dīn came to the sultan—possessed as he was of a sound creed by the loftiness of his station and the height of his rank and his precedence over all the shaykhs of his age, it was not necessary to distinguish him with an excess of honor and respect as he was already distinguished over all other ambassadors who had previously come to him from the caliphal court—he was left standing in the courtyard of the *dār*. Eventually, he was given permission to enter and when the council (*majlis*) took its place around the shaykh, he said, 'because it brings good fortune and blessings it is customary (*sunna*) for a messenger (*dāʿī*) to a victorious kingdom to begin with a *ḥadīth* of the Prophet before discharging his mission.' So the sultan gave him permission to do so and sat on his knees as is proper for hearing a *ḥadīth*. The shaykh recited a *ḥadīth* whose gist was a warning against giving trouble to the House of ʿAbbās

[123] *MZ*, 2:582–583; cf. Wiet, *Baghdad*, 150–151 (condensed translation); *KT*, 10:300, who only mentions the Khwārazm Shāh's withdrawal; *NZ*, 6:219–220, 224; *SN*, 22:231 (synopsis); and, *TIsl*, 50:15–17 (*ḥawādith, anno* 614).

> and when he finished his recitation, the sultan said, 'I am but a Turk with very little comprehension of the Arabic language but I understood the gist of what you mentioned, however I have given no trouble to any of the children of ʿAbbās nor do I mean them any harm. In fact, it has reached me that the number of people from among them whom the Commander of the Faithful has imprisoned has been multiplying endlessly. If the shaykh might repeat this *ḥadīth* in person to the Commander of the Faithful it would certainly be more appropriate and beneficial.' The shaykh replied, 'Since the beginning of his rule, the caliph has pledged to abide by the Book of God, the Sunna of His Messenger, and the pious exertion (*ijtihād*) of the [office of] the Commander of the Faithful, and if his pious exertion leads to a ruling that the imprisonment of a small faction (*shirdhima*) will improve the entire community (*umma*) then he cannot be blamed for doing so!' And he continued to explain the meaning of this and did not avoid the issue, but all to no avail, and so Shihāb al-Dīn returned empty handed.[124]

The third version of the encounter, preserved by Ibn Wāṣil in his general account of the entry of the Mongols into the lands of Islam in 616/1219, casts the meeting a bit differently:

> Since he [ʿAlāʾ al-Dīn Muḥammad b. Tekish] had turned his army towards Baghdad, the caliph al-Nāṣir li-Dīn Allāh sent the shaykh Shihāb al-Dīn al-Suhrawardī—may God be merciful with him—to repel his advance. Upon reaching the sultan ʿAlāʾ al-Dīn, he was honored and invited in as a guest. The shaykh Shihāb al-Dīn began his audience with a prophetic *ḥadīth* praising the Family of the Prophet and rebuking those who rose up against them for such an offense. As he recited it, the sultan fell down upon his knees in respect for the *ḥadīth* of the Prophet—may God bless and greet him—and when the shaykh Shihāb al-Dīn had finished, the sultan addressed him, saying, 'it would be more proper if the shaykh would recite this *ḥadīth* to the Commander of Faithful for it is he who has injured the Family of the Prophet by incarcerating them in prison, as for me, I have done nothing of the sort.' So, the sultan resolved to aim for Baghdad in order to appropriate the same position the Seljuks had enjoyed previously. But after a time, a large snow storm fell and frustrated his plans, and thus he returned to his country with the intent of returning to Iraq the next year, but in that year the Tatars entered [his land].[125]

---

[124] al-Nasawī, *Sīrat al-Sulṭān Jalāl al-Dīn Mankbunī*, ed. Ziia M. Buniiatov (Moscow: Izdatel'skaia firma "Vostochnaia lit-ra" RAN, 1996), 15–16; cf. *SN*, 22:195 for al-Nāṣir's reaction.

[125] Ibn Wāṣil, *Mufarrij*, 4:35–36; condensed translation in Siddiqi, "Caliphate and Kingship," 53.

Although Suhrawardī was unable to convince ʿAlāʾ al-Dīn to turn back, fortunately for al-Nāṣir other forces did. Unusually heavy snowfalls in the mountains of Kurdistan had wrought a toll on his force's mounts and when coupled with the incessant pilfering of Kurdish and Turkic tribesmen of his camps and the news of Kıpçak unrest on the Khwārazmian frontiers, he decided to return to Khwārazm and mount another expedition against the caliph the following year,[126] only to be consumed for the last three years of his life by serious troubles at home, not the least of which was the Mongol invasion which eventually forced him to flee to an island in the Caspian where he died in 617/1220.

Later Missions: 618–621/1221–1224

Following this encounter, Suhrawardī is recorded to have untaken one, if not two, other diplomatic missions on behalf of al-Nāṣir. In 618/1221, al-Nāṣir sent Suhrawardī to the court of the celebrated ʿAlāʾ al-Dīn Kayqubād (r. 616–632/1211–1220), the Seljuk sultan of Rūm in Konya who had just succeeded his brother Kay Kāwūs I (r. 608–616/1205–1211). This mission, during which Suhrawardī presented the sultan with the tokens of investiture, met the Sufi author Najm al-Dīn al-Rāzī Dayā, and developed contacts with the Akhīs of Anatolia, is dealt with in full in Chapter Five. The other, said to have taken place in 621/1224, probably never actually occurred. According to Angelika Hartmann—who does not quote any primary source but instead relies upon a similarly unsupported statement made by Hans Gottschalk some years earlier—in 621/1224 al-Nāṣir once again sent Suhrawardī to the Ayyubids, this time to the son of al-Malik al-ʿĀdil, al-Malik al-Ashraf.[127] According to her, this mission occurred in 621/1224, a year in which the fortunes of the Khwārazm Shāhs looked bright. First, early in the year the brother of the last Khwārazm Shāh Jalāl al-Dīn Mangübirdī, Ghiyāth al-Dīn, had seized control over Fārs.[128] Second, having successfully escaped from the vicious pursuit of Genghis Khān some four years earlier, Jalāl al-Dīn himself appeared in Kirmān.[129] Here, he married the daughter of the Salghūrid *atabeg* of

[126] *KT*, 10:300; Juvaynī, *World-Conqueror*, 2:366–367; Bosworth, op. cit., 4:1068.

[127] *Nṣr.*, 90, 295.

[128] *KT*, 10:384–385; Juvaynī, *World-Conqueror*, 2:469; Ibn Wāṣil, *Mufarrij*, 4:136; and, *BN*, 13:103–104.

[129] The details of which are described in fantastic detail by Juvaynī in *World-Conqueror*, 2:403–417.

Fārs and patron of the great Persian poet Saʿdī, Muẓaffar al-Dīn Saʿd b. Zangī (r. 594–623/1198–1126) and then traveled to western Persia where he deposed his brother and took control of the province.

Although it is not clear whether he did it before or after deposing Ghiyāth al-Dīn, at some point Jalāl al-Dīn sent an envoy to al-Nāṣir requesting (according to Juvaynī) the caliph's 'assistance' against the advancing Mongol armies, a favor which al-Nāṣir was not willing to grant him.[130] Ostensibly, it was at this point that al-Nāṣir sent Suhrawardī to win the support of al-Malik al-Ashraf against the 'threat' which Jalāl al-Dīn Mangübirdī posed to Baghdad, for having made good headway on the Khurāsān road sometime after Muḥarram the Khwārazm Shāh and his army were at the key town of Baʿqūbā, a mere seven *farsakh*s away from Baghdad itself.[131] Gottschalk, not quoting any sources, states:

> The caliph al-Nāṣir, who held an irreconcilable hatred for Jalāl al-Dīn, sent al-Suhrawardī along with the *muqaddam al-najībīn* Sayf al-Dīn b. Balāḥ to al-Ashraf with valuable gifts. Up until this time relations between the Ayyubids and the caliph had been cool since he had refused to side with al-Ashraf in providing assistance against the Mongols in 618/1221–1222, and before that against the Franks after their march on Damietta. The objective of the envoys could only have been one thing: to win al-Ashraf as an ally against the Khwārazm Shāh.[132]

Relying on this statement, Hartmann has asserted the same thing, namely that al-Nāṣir hoped to repair his relationship with al-Malik al-Ashraf in hopes of finding an ally against the Khwārazm Shāh, ostensibly sending an envoy with whom al-Ashraf was previously familiar, Suhrawardī. As for Sayf al-Dīn b. Balāḥ, neither Gottschalk, Hartmann, nor myself for that matter have been able to determine who he was nor to what the title *muqaddam al-najjābīn* ('administrator of the courier service'?) refers. More importantly, however, is that I have been unable to locate any mention of this mission in the historiography, not even in the chronicles of Abū Shāma al-Maqdisī or Ibn Wāṣil, both of whom furnish detailed accounts of al-Ashraf's activities during that year.

---

[130] Juvaynī, op. cit., 2:366–367, 417–421; J.A. Boyle, "Djalāl al-Dīn Kh^{w}ārazm-Shāh," *EI*^{2}, 2:393.

[131] *KT*, 10:389; and, Ibn Wāṣil, *Mufarrij*, 4:144.

[132] Hans Gottschalk, *Al-Malik al-Kāmil von Egypten und seine Zeit; eine Studie zur Geschichte Vorderasiens und Egyptens in der ersten Hälfte des 7./13. Jahrhunderts* (Wiesbaden: Otto Harrassowitz, 1958), 126.

Given the state of affairs which had obtained between the warring Ayyubid princes following the Fifth Crusade and the death of al-Malik al-ʿĀdil in 615/1218—in which Jalāl al-Dīn himself was involved in the form an alliance with al-Muʿaẓẓam ʿĪsā against al-Malik al-Ashraf—it is certainly possible that al-Nāṣir might have proposed an alliance with him,[133] but no such alliance was obtained and it fell to al-Nāṣir himself to move upon Jalāl al-Dīn. Certainly remembering the previous Khwārazm Shāh's challenge to his rule, al-Nāṣir responded to Jalāl al-Dīn's apparent request for assistance against the Mongols by sending a large force under the command of his *mamlūk* Jamāl al-Dīn Qush-Temür which was joined by another force from Irbil under the command of the Begtiginid governor Muẓaffar al-Dīn Gökböri b. ʿAlī Küçük (d. 630/1233) to route him.[134] Due to some deft maneuvering on Jalāl al-Dīn's part, however, the attack was ultimately unsuccessful and he set out for Azerbaijan, in Rabiʿ I, 622/March–April, 1225 sacking the town of Daqūqa and four months later easily taking Tabriz, after which he set about waging a very successful campaign against the Georgians.[135] For his part, the caliph al-Nāṣir li-Dīn Allāh died just two months later.

Quite prior to the time in which the last Khwārazm Shāh was threatening al-Nāṣir, his great alliances had already come to an end. During the last three years of his life the caliph lived in relative isolation, and although suffering from severely diminished eyesight and a number of serious health problems, tried hard to maintain direct control over his office. He dictated letters to a slave girl who had mastered his handwriting and kept himself out of the reach of physicians lest, in conspiring with his enemies, they contribute to his demise.[136] During his final days, only a few people remained close to him, one of the most important being the son of Ibn al-Jawzī, Muḥyīʾ l-Dīn, who had succeeded his father as preacher at the Jāmiʿ al-Qaṣr, served al-Nāṣir as an envoy a number of times, as well as upon the caliph's death on the last day of Ramaḍān, 622/6 October, 1225, being the one to prepare his body for burial.

[133] The events are described fully in Humphreys, *From Saladin to the Mongols*, 170–178; see also: Ibn Wāṣil, *Mufarrij*, 4:134–158.

[134] *KT*, 10:389; Ibn Wāṣil, op. cit., 4:145, 138–152; Juvaynī, op. cit., 2:421–423; and, Ibn Duqmāq, *Nuzhat*, 52–53.

[135] *KT*, 10:389–390, 393–395; Ibn Wāṣil, op. cit., 4:148–149; and, Humphreys, *From Saladin to the Mongols*, 177; cf. *BN*, 13:105–106.

[136] Mason, *Two Statesmen*, 113–114; and, *KḤ*, 126.

Shaykh al-shuyūkh?

Overall, the official status of Suhrawardī vis-à-vis the caliph al-Nāṣir and his administrative apparatus is difficult to judge. While he served the caliph as an emissary and certainly supported his program, it is unclear exactly what this meant beyond his being granted the *mashyakha* over a couple of the city's *ribāṭ*s and other such honors which al-Nāṣir bestowed upon him. According to Gramlich it was due "to his good personal relationship with the caliph al-Nāṣir, that Suhrawardī was first in line to receive the title and office of the Grand Shaykh (*shaykh al-shuyūkh*) of Baghdad and with it precedence among the city's Sufis".[137] Although Ibn Khallikān accords Suhrawardī the title *shaykh al-shuyūkh*, which is repeated by his later biographers, the title is not mentioned in connection with Suhrawardī in the earliest biographical materials which bear upon him and, more importantly, neither do we find it mentioned in connection with him in the historiography bearing on al-Nāṣir's Baghdad. One of his earliest biographers, Ibn al-Najjār simply states that he was "the master (*shaykh*) of his age in the science of divine realties and the Sufi path".[138] Outside of the Suhrawardiyya corpus—where the title is certainly honorific—the closest we come to it, in fact, is in a later source, where Ibn Kathīr states that Suhrawardī was the *shaykh al-ṣūfiyya bi-Baghdād*,[139] the same title accorded to Abū 'l-Najīb by his contemporary Ibn al-Mustawfī.[140] In the end, this title seems to have been largely rhetorical or, at best, honorific. Although the position of *shaykh al-shuyūkh* following the lifetime of Suhrawardī became more of a clearly delineated office, especially under the Mamluks in Egypt[141] what it entailed under al-Nāṣir is wholly unclear. Similarly, Yāqūt's statement that al-Nāṣir "made him a *muqaddam* over the shaykhs of Baghdad" provides little in the way of explanation as nothing approaching this title or office is mentioned in the historiography of the period and what such an office might have entailed is difficult if not impossible to account for.

According to Massignon, who tended to conflate disparate pieces of historical evidence, the *mashyakhat al-shuyūkh* of Baghdad was established

137 *GE*, 10.
138 *DhTB*, 5:180.
139 *BN*, 12:138.
140 *TIr*, 1:108.
141 See Leonor Fernandes, *The Evolution of a Sufi Institution in Mamluk Egypt: The* Khanqah (Berlin: Klaus Schwarz Verlag, 1988), 47–54.

by the vizier Ibn al-Muslima in 437/1045 in order to provide a liaison between the city's Sufi *ribāṭ*s and the administration as well as, ostensibly, to oversee the pious endowments (*awqāf*) which sustained them.[142] Clearly (although not approaching the status of the Sunni *niqābat al-hāshimiyīn* and the Shiite *niqābat al-ṭālibiyīn*) it appears to have been largely a hereditary office. However, in light of the very meager evidence which is preserved in the historiography of the period on the individuals who held the office, it does not seem that it functioned in the manner which Massignon alluded to and may not have existed at all. There is, in fact, no evidence of any overarching authority responsible for all of the *ribāṭ*s of Baghdad in the latter 6th/12th and 7th/13th centuries nor for any type of generalized authority for representing the city's Sufis as with the other *naqīb*s. On the contrary, even up through the Mongol invasion and the period of Naṣīr al-Dīn al-Ṭūsī's reconfiguring of the various *nuqabāʾ* of Baghdad, the city's most popular *ribāṭ*s were possessed of multiple directors who seem to have overseen their own affairs, including the family of ʿAbd al-Qādir al-Jīlānī, the descendants of Aʿazz al-Suhrawardī, and the actual '*shaykh al-shuyūkh*' family itself, the latter of whose history runs as follows.

According to Massignon, the first to hold the office, from its creation in 437/1045 until his death in 441/1049 was Abū ʾl-Barakāt Ismāʿīl b. Aḥmad b. Muḥammad Dūstzādā al-Nīsābūrī,[143] a Shāfiʿī jurist and Sufi who immigrated to Baghdad from Nīshāpūr and quickly established himself as a scholar of some standing. He is rarely mentioned in the historiography of the period and certainly not as having done anything in an official capacity. He was followed by his brother, Abū Saʿd Aḥmad b. Muḥammad b. Dūstzāda al-Nīsābūrī, a disciple of Abū Saʿīd b. Abī ʾl-Khayr, who is said to have held the office from 441/1049 until his death in 479/1086 and is mentioned as having constructed a *ribāṭ* on the Nahr Muʿallā.[144] From 479/1086 to 541/1146–1147 the office was held by the son of Abū Saʿd, Abū ʾl-Barakāt Ismāʿīl b. Saʿd[145] (d. 541/1146–1147), one of the *shaykh*s whom Aḥmad-i Ghazālī is said to have met with during his time in Baghdad and a target of

[142] Louis Massignon, "Caliphs et naqībs bagdadiens," *WZKM* 51 (1948): 114.

[143] *MZ*, 8.1:188 (*anno* 541, s.v. Ismāʿīl b. Aḥmad); Massignon, op. cit., 114.

[144] *MT*, 9:11; *MJ*, 3:132; Massignon, op. cit., 114; and, Meier, *Abū Saʿīd*, 375–379.

[145] On him, see *MT*, 10:121 (*anno* 541); *KT*, 10:148 (*anno* 541); *TIr*, 1:32 (s.v. Abū ʾl-Futūḥ Aḥmad al-Ghazālī), 2:16–17 (*ḥawāshī*, no. 21); *MZ*, 8.1:188 (*anno* 541); al-Dhahabī, *ʿIbar*, 3:294; *MJ*, 3:274; *GE*, 10, fn. 72; and, Richter-Bernburg, *Der syrische Blitz*, 48.

Ibn al-Jawzī who criticizes him for hosting a particularly ostentatious wedding feast.[146] Although a very active figure in the culture of Sunni religious learning, especially the transmission of *ḥadīth*, during the time, his activities seem to have been largely confined to his own circles, and although he did have a relationship with the court, it seems to have been being largely ceremonial.

Abū 'l-Barakāt was followed by his son, Ṣadr al-Dīn ʿAbd al-Raḥīm[147] who held the post from 541/1146 until his death in 580/1184. It was he who founded the *ribāṭ* in the Mashraʿa Neighborhood in the eastern part of Baghdad which came to be known as Ribāṭ Shaykh al-Shuyūkh.[148] Like many of the city's *ribāṭs*, this particular institution would become a family possession. A respected Shāfiʿī *ʿālim*, jurist, and *ḥadīth* transmitter, the *shaykh al-shuyūkh* Ṣadr al-Dīn was closely cultivated by al-Nāṣir, prefiguring much of what Suhrawardī would do later. As we have already seen, he was sent on a number of key missions on behalf of the caliph, first to various provinces to secure the oaths of loyalty (*bayʿa*) to al-Nāṣir as caliph, to Saladin in 576/1180–1181 and 579/1183–1184, and finally to Mosul in 580/1184–1185 to negotiate in a conflict between Saladin and ʿIzz al-Dīn over control of the city.[149] Beyond this, his recorded activities are mainly confined to teaching and the transmission of *ḥadīth*, there being little in the way of information on exactly what his role as *shaykh al-shuyūkh* (if any) entailed.

Ṣadr al-Dīn was followed by his brother ʿAbd al-Laṭīf (d. 596/1200), an individual who according to his biographers was quite dull-witted.[150] According him the title *shaykh al-shuyūkh*, Ibn al-Sāʿī relates only that after the death of his brother Ṣadr al-Dīn, ʿAbd al-Laṭīf took over the directorship (*mashyakha*) of his father's *ribāṭ* and oversaw its pious

---

[146] *MT*, 10:121; cf. *MZ*, 8.1:188.

[147] *DhR*, 17 (*anno* 596, s.v. ʿAbd al-Laṭīf); *NZ*, 6:97–98; *GE*, 10, fn. 72.

[148] *JM*, 9:37–38 fn. 2; cf. *KT*, 9:386, 10:203–204.

[149] *TIsl*, 46:53 (*ḥawādith*, *anno* 579); Mason, *Two Statesmen*, 92; *Nṣr.*, 72, 86, 88 fn. 131, 293; Gibb, *The Life of Saladin*, 34, 39; and, Ehrenkreutz, *Saladin*, 185.

[150] On ʿAbd al-Laṭīf (Ṣafī al-Dīn Abū 'l-Maḥāsin b. *shaykh al-shuyūkh* Ismāʿīl b. Aḥmad b. Muḥammad b. Dūstzādā al-Nīsābūrī al-Baghdādī) (523–596/1129–1200) see *MZ*, 8.2:473 (*anno* 596); *JM*, 9:36 (*anno* 596); *DhR*, 17; al-Dhahabī, *ʿIbar*, 4:293, *SN*, 21:334–335 (no. 177); *TIsl*, 48:253 (*anno* 596); *TIbW*, 2:135; al-ʿAynī, *ʿIqd al-jumān fī taʾrīkh ahl al-zamān*, ed. Muḥammad Amīn (Cairo: al-Hayʾat al-Miṣriyya al-ʿĀmma li-l-Kitāb, 1987–1992), 17:247; *NZ*, 6:159; and, *GE*, 10, fn. 72. Ibn al-Dubaythī said he was: "an idiot who did not understand a thing... only people who did not care to inquire about the veracity of the transmitters or who did not want to investigate the completeness of the *isnād* would hear *ḥadīth* from him." (*SN*, 21:335 fn. 2)

endowments (*awqāf*), providing no further details on what other duties, if any, his title entailed. There is no evidence that he took over the management of the *waqf*s of any other institutions nor served as a spokesperson on behalf of any particular group of Sufis. Sometime after this, ʿAbd al-Laṭīf left the city on pilgrimage, thereafter visiting Egypt, Jerusalem, and Damascus where he died and was buried in the graveyard of the Sufis. It is wholly unclear whether or not an interim *shaykh al-shuyūkh* was appointed in his absence or what, if anything, this title might have meant in an official sense.

If such an appointment did indeed occur, this would be the logical point at which al-Nāṣir might have appointed Suhrawardī *shaykh al-shuyūkh*, for after the death of ʿAbd al-Laṭīf the title is used only indiscriminately in the historiography to describe those who took over the hereditary Ribāṭ Shaykh al-Shuyūkh. The first of those to whom it is applied in this way was the son-in-law of ʿAbd al-Laṭīf, Ibn Sukayna[151] (d. 607/1210–1211), a personal associate of both Abū ʾl-Najīb and ʿUmar al-Suhrawardī[152] who served as the representative of the Shāfiʿīs to whom al-Nāṣir transmitted his *Rūḥ al-ʿārifīn.*[153] Having established contact with al-Nāṣir at the beginning of his reign, the caliph sent him on an official mission to the Ayyubids in 585/1189–1190.[154] Apparently also an associate of Ibn al-Jawzī—whose son Yūsuf he is said to have invested with the *khirqa* on the authority of his grandfather[155]—Ibn Sukayna was a typical Baghdadi Shāfiʿī Sufi *shaykh*, receiving and transmitting *ḥadīth* to numerous individuals as well as directing disciples and investing individuals with the *khirqa* in the *ribāṭ* which he had inherited from his forefathers. By all accounts, an important figure who deserves

[151] On him, see *DhTB*, 1:256–258 (no. 141); Ibn al-Dubaythī, *Mukhtaṣar*, 3:58 & 59 (no. 846); *KT*, 10:280 (*anno* 607); *TIr*, 1:283 (s.v. ʿUmar b. Khallikān), 417 (s.v., al-Mūqānī), and, 2:244–245 (*ḥawāshī*, no. 80); *DhR*, 70 (*anno* 607); al-Dhahabī, *Duwal al-islām* (Hyderabad: Dāʾirat al-Maʿārif, 1919), 2:113; *SN*, 21:502–505 (no. 262); *TIsl*, 49:252–256 (no. 355); *MJ*, 4:15; *ṬShK*, 8:324–325; *ṬSh*, 2:60 (no. 647); *BN*, 13:61 (*anno* 607); Ibn al-Mulaqqin, *ʿIqd*, 165; Ibn al-Jazarī, *Ghāyat al-nihāyat fī ṭabaqāt al-qurrāʾ*, ed. Gotthelf Bergstraesser and Otto Pretzl (Cairo: Maktabat al-Khānjī, 1932–1933), 1:480 (no. 1998); *ṬFSh*², 2:390–391 (no. 359); *NZ*, 6:201 (*anno* 607); *ShDh*, 7:48–49 (*anno* 607); Ghazzī, *Dīwān*, 3:135 (no. 1213); Massignon, "Cadis," 114; *Nṣr.*, 213; and, *GE*, 10, fn. 72.

[152] He transmitted *ḥadīth* on the authority of Abū ʾl-Najīb (*ṬShK*, 7:174) and Suhrawardī quotes him first-hand in the *ʿAwārif*, calling him "our shaykh" (*GE*, 4.1; 29.1, 9, 20; 30.18, 21, 41, 44, 47, 56, 67, 75; 31.6; 35.4; 41.3; 51.8, 17; and, 52.12).

[153] *MZ*, 8.2:543; and, *Nṣr.*, 213.

[154] *Nṣr.*, 146 fn. 90, 295.

[155] *DhR*, 70.

further study, like Suhrawardī his funeral prayers were conducted at the Jāmiʿ al-Qaṣr to a much bereaved crowd.

Upon the death of Ibn Sukayna, the office of *shaykh al-shuyūkh*, or perhaps simply the *mashyakha* of the family *ribāṭ*, passed to an individual who is occasionally accorded the title *shaykh al-shuyūkh* by his biographers, a son of Ibn Sukayna named Ṣadr al-Dīn ʿAbd al-Razzāq[156] (d. 635/1237–1238). As a boy, ʿAbd al-Razzāq lived for two years in Mecca with his mother as a *mujāwir*. After the death of his father Ibn Sukayna he became the controller of the al-ʿAḍudī Hospital in Baghdad for a time as well as taking over the directorship of the Ribāṭ Shaykh al-Shuyūkh. Like Suhrawardī, he heard *ḥadīth* from Ibn al-Baṭṭī[157] as well as transmitting *ḥadīth* in Damascus, including to famous individuals such as al-Birzālī and Ibn ʿAsākir. From here, the office passed to his son Quṭb al-Dīn Muḥammad b. ʿAbd al-Razzāq, who held it from 635/1237–1238 until 644/1246 and then to ʿAlī b. Nayyār who held it from 644/1246 until his execution, along with other public notables, by the Mongols in 656/1258.

Ibn ʿAsākir in Damascus

Although there is no explicit evidence that Suhrawardī obtained the title of *shaykh al-shuyūkh* in any official capacity, according to his student Ibn al-Najjār, after his mission to the Khwārazm Shāh he was 'appointed as a shaykh' (*ruttiba shaykhᵃⁿ bi-*) in, or over, three of Baghdad's *ribāṭ*s, namely: the Ribāṭ al-Nāṣirī, Ribāṭ al-Bisṭāmī, and the aforementioned Ribāṭ al-Maʾmūniyya which he seems to have lost possession of along with the Ribāṭ al-Marzubāniyya after the indiscretion of 605/1208. According to Ibn al-Najjār, he held this position until the end of his

Ibn al-Najjār was a student of al-Suhrawardī

---

[156] On him, see: *SN*, 23:19–20 (no. 12); Ibn Duqmāq, *Nuzhat*, 107 (*anno* 635); *NZ*, 6:301 (*anno* 635); and, *ShDh*, 7:300 (*anno* 635).

[157] Number three in Suhrawardī's *Mashyakha*—where he gives three *ḥadīth* he heard from him on 2 Rabīʿ II, 566/31 Mar., 1161 (*Mashyakha*, fol. 86b–87a)—during his youth Ibn al-Baṭṭī (d. 564/1169) served the chief general of the caliphal armies (*amīr al-juyūsh*) as a chamberlain (*ḥājib*), during which time he gained something of a reputation for his influence over his patron and thus became quite a popular intercessor on people's behalf. Known for his altruism and generosity to the poor, Ibn al-Baṭṭī remained in the amir's house until the latter's death, after which he became a popular Baghdadi *muḥaddith* and Qurʾān reciter. Ibn al-Jawzī admits to hearing many *ḥadīth* from him and al-Samʿānī attended his sessions for the same reasons. He is frequently quoted in the *ʿAwārif* as the authority for Suhrawardī's citations from al-Iṣfahānī's (d. 420/1038) *Ḥilyat al-awliyāʾ* (e.g., *GE*, 3.21, 4:12, 7.10, 14.8 & 9, 15.15, 51.22 & 26, 62.1). On him, see: al-Samʿānī, *Ansāb*, 2:262 (s.v. al-Baṭṭī); *MT*, 10:229 (*anno* 564, no. 325); Ibn Nuqta, *Taqyīd*, 1:84–85 (no. 77); *LTA*, 1:130 (s.v. al-Baṭṭī); *TMA*, 4.3:334–335 (no. 2365); Ibn al-Dubaythī, *Mukhtaṣar*, 1:77–78 (no. 145); *TIsl*, 45:205–208 (*anno* 564, no. 162); *SN*, 20:481–482 (no. 304); and, *KW*, 3:209 (no. 1196).

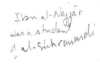

life, fulfilling his duties despite ill health and the ailments of old age,[158] something confirmed by the presence of multiple dated *ijāza*s which explicitly state the Suhrawardī was transmitting texts in at least one of these *ribāṭ*s (the Ribāṭ al-Maʾmūniyya) as early as 621/1224 and as late as 627/1230.[159] If we are to take Ibn al-Najjār's report as mirroring an actual chronology, then some time shortly after his return from his mission to the Khwārazm Shāh, Suhrawardī seems to have held the *mashyakha* of a total of five *ribāṭ*s:

1. Ribāṭ al-Nāṣirī.[160] Better known as the Ribāṭ al-Ḥarīm al-Ṭāhirī, it was founded by al-Nāṣir li-Dīn Allāh in Rabīʿ I, 589/March, 1193 in the Ḥarīm al-Ṭāhirī Neighborhood located in the western part of the city and was endowed with many valuable books. The caliph installed the Shāfiʿī *faqih* Bahāʾ al-Dīn al-Mīhanī as its first director. At some point, Suhrawardī's former disciple Saʿd b. Muẓaffar al-Yazdī was appointed director of this institution.
2. Ribāṭ al-Marzubāniyya. Built by al-Nāṣir specifically for Suhrawardī in 599/1203.
3. Ribāṭ al-Maʾmūniyya. Built by Zumurrud Khātūn in 579/1183, Suhrawardī being installed as its director thereupon.
4. Ribāṭ al-Bisṭāmī. Originally built for the Baghdadi ascetic and Sufi Abū ʾl-Ḥasan al-Bisṭāmī (d. 493/1100) on the Tigris in the western part of city by an caliphal official named Abū ʾl-Ghanāʾim b. al-Maḥlabān [Pahlavān?].[161]
5. Ribāṭ al-Zawzanī. Built by Abū ʾl-Ḥasan ʿAlī b. Ibrāhīm al-Baṣrī (d. 371/981–982), and took its name from the celebrated Sufi and student of ʿAbd al-Raḥmān al-Sulamī, Abū ʾl-Ḥasan ʿAlī b. Ibrāhīm al-Zawzanī (d. 451/1059). Located near the Jāmiʿ al-Manṣūr, a graveyard, the Maqbarat al-Ṣūfiyya eventually grew up around it.[162]

---

158 *DhTB*, 5:180–181; *TIsl*, 53:114; *ṬShK*, 8:340; and, *MS*, 2:355.

159 E.g., MS. Süley., Reisülküttap 465_1, fol. 1a; and, MS. Süley., Yeni Câmi 717, fol. 1a.

160 *KT*, 10:125; *Nṣr.*, 126; Jawād, "al-Rubuṭ," 242; and, Jacqueline Chabbi, "La fonction du ribat à Bagdad de Vᵉ siècle au début du VIIᵉ siècle," *REI* 42 (1974): 117–119.

161 Jawād, "al-Rubuṭ," 238–239; cf. *KḤ*, 19, fn. 3.

162 *KT*, 8:167 (*anno* 451); and, Jawād, "al-Rubuṭ,", 236–237.

Meetings with Remarkable Men

As with the historiographers and prosopographers who narrated the political and learned activities of Suhrawardī from the particular perspectives inherent in the very genres in which they were writing, so too did the hagiographers narrate a figuration of Suhrawardī which was constrained by equally powerful rules, conventions, and expectations. As we have seen, although each had access to a shared body of sources, what Suhrawardī was allowed to become for someone like Subkī was very different from what he meant for someone like his disciple Ibn al-Najjār, for a chronicler like Abū Shāma al-Maqdisī, or for Dārā Shukūh some four centuries later. Just as the chorographical writings and biographical dictionaries of ulama are guided by certain rules of inclusion and exclusion and configure their representations thusly, so too are the Sufi hagiographies guided by an internal logic which determines how a particular biographee can be represented. Oftentimes, the narratives which obtain in such sources do more to illuminate the particular concerns of their authors than to offer any 'positive' historical data, and when dealing with a figure such as Suhrawardī, the paragonic status of his eponymic role in the rise of *ṭarīqa*-based Sufism generally and the visible success of the Suhrawardiyya in North Indian Sufi landscapes in particular, inevitably cast him as a 'paragon' who could be used as a powerful symbol of legitimization vis-à-vis later hagiographic representations of his contemporaries. This is well evinced in a series of anecdotes which place Suhrawardī together with a number of 'remarkable men', most notably the aforementioned ʿAbd al-Qādir al-Jīlānī (d. 561/1166), the mysterious shaykh Ibn ʿAbd (d. c. 580/1184–1185) of Basra, the maverick Damascene ascetic ʿAlī al-Kurdī (d. 622/1225), and four celebrated early 7th/13th-century Sufi luminaries: Bahāʾ al-Dīn Valad (d. 628/1231), Ibn al-Fāriḍ (d. 632/1235), Muʿīn al-Dīn Chishtī (d. 633/1236), and Muḥyī ʾl-Dīn Ibn ʿArabī (d. 638/1240).[163]

[163] In addition to these individuals, during his diplomatic mission to the court of ʿAlāʾ al-Dīn Kayqubād in 618/1221, Suhrawardī met with the Sufi author and disciple of Najm al-Dīn Kubrā, Najm al-Dīn al-Rāzī Dāya (d. 654/1256); on which see Chapter Five. There is, as well, another meeting related by al-Qazwīnī in his account of the remarkable men of Qazvīn in the *Āthār al-bilād*. Not mentioned elsewhere, this meeting is said to have taken place in Irbil where Suhrawardī encountered the outspoken ascetic Pākbāz-i Qazvīnī (d. c. 620/1223) (*Āthār al-bilād* [Beirut: Dār Ṣādir, 1970], 439; and, *GE*, 12 [no. 50]). The tradition of a relationship between the great Persian moralist Saʿdī Shīrāzī (d. 691/1292) and Suhrawardī (like many events in the poet's

ʿAbd al-Qādir al-Jīlānī (d. 561/1166)

As to the first, the issue of the relationship between Suhrawardī and the aged ʿAbd al-Qādir al-Jīlānī is, like that of relationship with other 'paragons' of his day, a complicated one. Beyond a few vague references in the prosopographical literature,[164] there is only one source which presents a sustained narrative on any 'relationship' which obtained between Suhrawardī and the eponym of the Qādirī brotherhood between the five years after Suhrawardī's arrival in Baghdad and Jīlānī's death in 561/1166. Based on this narrative, in fact, there is little to say that Suhrawardī had anything to do with ʿAbd al-Qādir save for a chance meeting with the aged preacher when he was still under the tutelage of his uncle, and there is certainly no mention of him having associated with him as a disciple or studied under him as a student as the biographers might lead us to believe. The episode, which as we have seen would later be repeated in various hagiographies of ʿAbd al-Qādir such as those of al-Tādifī and Dārā Shukūh, appears first in Ibn Rajab's entry on Jīlānī, where he preserves two distinct reports concerning their 'relationship'. The first was transmitted to him, interestingly enough, by Ibn Taymiyya (d. 728/1328):

> Shaykh Taqī al-Dīn Abū ʾl-ʿAbbās b. Taymiyya said that shaykh ʿIzz al-Dīn Aḥmad b. Ibrāhīm al-Fārūthī[165] related to him that he heard shaykh

life) as well as the verses referring to him in the *Bustān* are later constructions (*Kuliyyāt-i Saʿdī*, ed. Muḥammad ʿAlī Furūghī [Tehran: Nashr-i Muḥammad, n.d.], 75–76, fn. 3; cf. E.G. Browne, *A Literary History of Persia* (Cambridge: Cambridge University Press, 1902–1924), 2:32, 527–528.

[164] *WA*, 3:446; *SN*, 22:374; *TIsl*, 52:112; *TIbW*, 2:232; *ṬFSh*, 2:835; Ibn Duqmāq, *Nuzhat*, 60; *ṬFSh*², 1:400; and, *ShDh*, 7:268. In his necrology on Suhrawardī, Ibn al-Wardī quotes a couplet first cited by Ibn Khallikān which Suhrawardī is reported to have recited from the pulpit, saying that ʿAbd al-Qādir al-Jīlānī used to recite the same couplet from the pulpit during his own preaching sessions (*Taʾrīkh*, 2:232). Although the couplet is cited by almost all of Suhrawardī's later biographers, Ibn al-Wardī is the only one to provide this detail.

[165] ʿIzz al-Dīn al-Fārūthī was a Shāfiʿī *muḥaddith*, Qurʾānic scholar, *muftī*, Sufi, and preacher who, in 629/1231–1232—at the age of thirteen—heard *ḥadīth* from Suhrawardī, and others, in Baghdad as well as reportedly taking the *khirqa* from him. According to Ibn al-Ṣuqāʿī, he was also possessed of the *nibsa* 'al-Rifāʿī', an attributive not being given by his other biographers (*Tālī kitāb wafayāt al-aʿyān*, ed. & trans. by Jacqueline Sublet [Damascus: al-Mahʿad al-Faransī bi-Dimashq li-l-Dirāsāt al-ʿArabiyya, 1974], 9 [no. 10]). This designation, however, seems quite appropriate given al-Fārūthī's apparent association with Aḥmad al-Rifāʿī as evinced in the following *khabar* preserved by al-Wāsiṭī d. 744/1343) in his *Ṭiryāq al-muḥibbīn*: "ʿIzz al-Dīn Aḥmad al-Fārūthī said: 'I associated with Shihāb al-Dīn ʿUmar al-Suhrawardī (*ṣuḥbat al-tabarruk*) and attended his courses. One day he suggested investing me with their *khirqa*, but when it was conveyed

> Shihāb al-Dīn ʿUmar b. Muḥammad al-Suhrawardī, author of the *ʿAwārif*, say: "I was determined to read something from the science of dialectical theology (*ʿilm al-kalām*) but I was hesitant to do so; for how could I read the *Irshād* of the Imām al-Ḥaramayn, or the *Nihāyat al-aqdām* of al-Shahrastanī, or another book which mentions it? So, I went with my maternal (sic!) uncle Abū ʾl-Najīb—who used to pray beside ʿAbd al-Qādir—and he said, 'so go on then, catch the attention of the shaykh ʿAbd al-Qādir!' And he said to me. 'O' ʿUmar, that is not among the provisions of the grave! That is not among the provisions of the grave!' So, I refrained from it." Shaykh Taqī al-Dīn said: 'I saw this story preserved in the handwriting of the shaykh Muwaffaq al-Dīn b. Qudāma al-Maqdisī'.[166]

Ibn Rajab cites his second report from the lost *Taʾrīkh li-madīnat al-salām* of the famous Iraqi historian and student of Suhrawardī, Ibn al-Najjār, which although ostensibly a first-hand account, still preserves a clear expression of the cardiognostic acumen (*firāsa*) for which ʿAbd al-Qādir was famous:

> I heard ʿUmar b. Muḥammad al-Suhrawardī, the shaykh of the Sufis, saying: "When I was a young man, I was studying *fiqh* in the Niẓāmiyya Madrasa and it occurred to me that I should read something from the science of dialectical theology. I resolved in myself to do this without talking to anyone about it. It so happened that one day I was praying the Friday prayer with my paternal uncle Abū ʾl-Najīb in the congregational mosque and shaykh ʿAbd al-Qādir happened to be present among the congregation. He [Abū ʾl-Najīb] asked him to say a supplication for me, mentioning to him that I was currently busying myself with *fiqh*. He [al-Suhrawardī] said: "I rose and kissed his hand, then he took my hand and said, 'Repent from what you are resolved to busy yourself with, and you will achieve success [in the Hereafter].' Then he fell quiet and let go of my hand." He [al-Suhrawardī] said: "but my resolve to busy myself with it did not change until it completely confounded all of my interior states and consumed all of time, and only then did I realize that this came about because of contradicting the shaykh." He [al-Suhrawardī] said: "So, I repented to God from doing it that very day and refrained from it; and my interior state became sound and my heart agreeable.[167]

---

to him that my *khirqa* was Aḥmadiyya, he said: "Please excuse me, but all of us are embraced within the *khirqa* of Aḥmad al-Rifāʿī!" (al-Wāsiṭī, *Ṭiryāq*, 60, as quoted by Trimingham, *Sufi Orders*, 183, fn. 2). He is reported to have invested individuals with the *khirqa*, although it is not clear if he did so on the authority of al-Rifāʿī or Suhrawardī or exactly what type of *khirqa* he was transmitting. On him, see: *TIsl*, 58:206–209 (*anno* 694, no. 206); *KW*, 6:219–220 (no. 2678); al-Kutubī, *Fawāt*, 1:55–56 (no. 21); Ibn Rāfiʿ, *Muntakhab*, 18–20 (no. 11); *MJ*, 4:223–224 (*anno* 694); al-Nuʿaymī, *al-Dāris*, 1:355–357 (s.v. al-Madrasa al-Ẓāhiriyya al-Jawwāniyya); and, *GE*, 8 (no. 36).

[166] Ibn Rajab, *Dhayl*, 1:296–97; and, *GE*, 3.

[167] Ibn Rajab, op. cit., 1:297.

The kernel of the story, whatever details may frame it, certainly may contain a ring of truth, but given both the rhetorical features of the report as well as its various incarnations in later hagio-historiography, the importance of this meeting seems to have been more tropological than factual. Even though Suhrawardī cites Jīlānī (four times) as an authority in the *ʿAwārif al-maʿārif*, he only does so in second hand reports ('I have heard that he...'), something which stands in striking contrast to many of his other contemporaries with whom he studied or associated who are quoted in the text. In addition, in the large body of contemporary and near-contemporary biographical material preserved on Abū ʾl-Najīb, he is never mentioned as having associated with Jīlānī. Furthermore, Ibn Rajab's narrative, in fact, is embedded within a much larger series of similar episodes concerning al-Jīlānī, each of which clearly evince Ibn Rajab's rhetorical strategy, namely to cast the Ḥanbalī shaykh as a paragonic figure duly noted as such by his contemporaries. As has been shown in the case of al-Tādifī and Dārā Shukūh, much can extrapolated from such a kernel.

Shaykh Ibn ʿAbd of Basra (d. c. 580/1184–1185)

As already noted, after the death of Abū ʾl-Najīb, Suhrawardī is reported to have associated with at least two other teachers, studying jurisprudence with the aforementioned Shāfiʿī *faqih* Ibn Faḍlān (d. 595/1199) as well as traveling down to Basra where he met with one Ibn ʿAbd.[168] A mysterious individual about whom little is known, the exact relationship between Ibn ʿAbd and Suhrawardī is difficult to determine, although his later biographers count him among Suhrawardī's earliest 'teachers', repeating the report of Ibn Khallikān who says that "after studying with Abū ʾl-Najīb and ʿAbd al-Qādir al-Jīlanī, Suhrawardī went down Basra where he studied with one Abū Muḥammad Ibn ʿAbd."[169] In the *ʿAwārif al-maʿārif*, Suhrawardī affirms the latter, saying that he was with

---

[168] His name being given as Abū Muḥammad al-Qāsim Ibn ʿAbd[in] al-Baṣrī. On him, see al-Tādifī, *Necklaces*, 422–427; and, al-Shaʿrānī, *Ṭabaqāt*, 2:330–332. He is mentioned in conjunction with Suhrawardī by Ibn Khallikān (*WA*, 3:446; cf. *SN*, 22:374; *TIsl*, 52:112; and, al-ʿUmarī, *Masālik*, 8:225; *TIbW*, 2:232 [where his name is given as Abū Muḥammad b. ʿAbdūn]; *ṬShK*, 8:339; *ṬFSh*, 2:835 [where his name is given as Abū Muḥammad b. ʿUbayd al-Baṣrī]; and, by Ibn Duqmāq, *Nuzhat*, 60 [where his name is given as Abū Muḥammad b. ʿAbdūn]); see also *GE*, 3 (no. 6); and, Düzenli, "Şihâbuddin," 12–13 (no. 12).

[169] *WA*, 3:446–447 (also, *TW*, 6:122, in a similar form, thus revealing an earlier source); cf., *MJ*, 4:80.

the shaykh Muḥammad Ibn ʿAbd in Basra and directly quoting him on a point having to do with the issue of 'passing thoughts' (*khawāṭir*).[170] Beyond the curt reference to him first noted by Ibn Khallikān and Suhrawardī's own short admission, however, al-Tādifī preserves the only report placing the two together in any meaningful way, in his entry on Ibn ʿAbd quoting Suhrawardī as saying:

> I once traveled down to Basra to visit the shaykh. On my way there, I passed by many cattle, crops and date palms, so I thought to myself, 'I must be experiencing the spiritual state of kings.' As I entered Basra, I was reciting the Chapter of the Cattle [Qurʾān 6], so I said to myself, 'I wonder which verse I shall have reached by the time I arrive at the shaykh's house? That will surely be a good omen (*faʾl*) for my visit with him.' At the moment when I set my foot on the threshold of his house, I was reciting: 'They are those whom God guides, so follow their guidance.'[171] His servant met me at the door, and instructed me to enter at the shaykh's command. Before I had even entered his presence, the first thing the shaykh said to me was, 'O' ʿUmar, as for everything that is upon the earth, it is upon the earth, and nothing of it is inside my heart.' Great indeed was my astonishment at his knowledge of something that no one apart from God could have known about me!'.[172]

According to al-Tādifī and al-Shaʿrānī, Ibn ʿAbd was one of the great Sufi shaykhs of Iraq who, in addition to lecturing on mystical topics and law, served as a Mālikī mufti in Basra. Both state that "his authority in the training of disciples (*murīdīn*) in Basra and the neighboring regions was paramount" and that a "large number received training from him, subsequently propagating his teachings", and in his usual style al-Tādifī preserves a number of miracle stories about him, especially in regard to his sheer otherworldly presence among his disciples. Was he perhaps associated with a later incarnation of the Sālimiyya? Certainly the *aqwāl* attributed to him by both authors contain a hint of the teachings of Sahl al-Tustarī, and Suhrawardī himself quotes extensively from Sahl al-Tustarī both in the *ʿAwārif al-maʿārif* and elsewhere, although not on Ibn ʿAbd's authority.

170 *ʿAM*, 2:259/*GE*, 57.9.
171 Qurʾān 6:90.
172 al-Tādifī, *Necklaces*, 424–425.

ʿAlī al-Kurdī (d. 622/1225)

As already mentioned, while in Damascus during his official mission to the Ayyubids in 604/1207–1208 Suhrawardī is reported to have met with the maverick ascetic ʿAlī al-Kurdī, an individual whom the historiographers characterize as a 'fool of God' (*muwallah*) famous for his disregard of the divine law and socially deviant behavior which included a filthy appearance and public nakedness.[173] His second claim to fame (which is mentioned only by the hagiographers)[174] is an encounter which he is reported to have had with Suhrawardī. The source of this anecdote is found in the *Risāla* of Suhrawardī's younger contemporary, the Egyptian Sufi Ṣafī al-Dīn b. Abī ʾl-Manṣūr al-Khazrajī (d. 682/1283):

> When the shaykh and imam al-Suhrawardī came to Damascus on a mission from the caliph to invest al-Malik al-ʿĀdil with the robe of honor, neckband, and so forth, he said to his companions, 'I want to visit ʿAlī al-Kurdī,' but the people said, 'O' master, do not do that for you are the imam of existence and that man does not perform the canonical prayers and walks around naked most of the time!', to which he replied, 'It is necessary for me to do so.' Now, shaykh ʿAlī al-Kurdī used to inhabit the Grand Mosque of Damascus, but when a *muwallah* called Yāqūt entered it, by sunset the very same day ʿAlī had already left Damascus and set up residence in the cemetery near Bāb al-Ṣaghīr. He remained there until his death and Yāqūt prevailed in the Grand Mosque. I saw this Yāqūt in the Grand Mosque after ʿAlī's departure. When the shaykh Shihāb al-Dīn al-Suhrawardī searched the Grand Mosque for ʿAlī, Yāqūt told him that he was now living in the cemetery and so he mounted his donkey and with a guide set off to find ʿAlī. Upon reaching the place, he dismounted and walked towards him. When ʿAlī al-Kurdī saw him drawing near, he defiantly displayed his nudity, but the shaykh Shihāb al-Dīn said, 'This is not a thing which will stop me, for you must see me as I am your guest!' And so he approached and sat with him. Later, some porters came bearing savory food, and they were asked, 'who do you want?', to which they replied, 'the shaykh ʿAlī al-Kurdī'. He said, 'put it before my guest!', and then turning to the shaykh Shihāb al-Dīn said, 'Did you not say that you

[173] *MZ*, 8.2:638; *DhR*, 146; and, *BN*, 13:108–109.

[174] Ṣafī al-Dīn b. Abī ʾl-Manṣūr, *Risālat Ṣafī al-Dīn*, ed. and trans. by Denis Gril as *La Risāla de Ṣafī al-Dīn Ibn Abī l-Manṣūr Ibn Ẓāfir: Biographies des maîtres spirituels connus par un cheikh égyptien du VIIe/XIIIe siècle* (Cairo: IFAOC, 1986), 36, 125; which is quoted both by al-Munāwī (*Kawākib* [*Ṭabaqāt al-kubrā*], 2:272 [no. 433] and [*Ṭabaqāt al-sughrā*] 4:463–464 [no. 441]; and by Nabhānī (*Jāmiʿ*, 2:331–332).

were my guest? In God's name, eat! This is your reception.' And so the shaykh ate and he held him [ʿAlī al-Kurdī] in great esteem.[175]

As Denis Gril points out in his introduction to the *Risāla*, Ṣafī al-Dīn was particularly interested in narrating the exploits of *muwallahs*, time and time again highlighting their importance in the 'economy of sanctity' and function in the invisible 'spiritual government' structuring the world in which he moved. The outcome of the meeting between Suhrawardī and ʿAlī al-Kurdī reflects this attitude, implicitly answering one of the main criticisms which Suhrawardī leveled against the Qalandariyya and other antinomian groups, namely their propensity to flout established social custom (*ʿādāt*).[176] At the same time, this narrative evinces how early Suhrawardī came to be endowed with the paragonic status which later hagio-historiographers—such as Aflākī in his account of the shaykh's meeting with Bahāʾ al-Dīn Valad—would employ in their own projects of sanctification.

Bahāʾ al-Dīn Valad (d. 628/1231)

In his account of the life of Bahāʾ al-Dīn Valad in the *Manāqib al-ʿārifīn*, the 8th/14th-century Mevlevi hagiographer Shams al-Dīn Aflākī places Suhrawardī together with the famous father of Jalāl al-Dīn Rūmī on two occasions. The first meeting, which is not mentioned in the other sources on Bahāʾ al-Dīn's life, is said to have occurred during the family's wanderings in the period between their departure from Khurāsān and their arrival in Konya around 618/1221. Naturally enough, Aflākī situates the meeting in Baghdad, which if it actually occurred would have taken place in Shaʿbān, 613/November–December 1216.[177] According to his account, the arrival of the retinue was announced to the caliph al-Nāṣir, who perplexed at the answer which Bahāʾ al-Dīn gave to his guards called upon Suhrawardī to discern who he was. Upon hearing the guard's story, the shaykh announced that it could be none other than Bahāʾ al-Dīn Valad, and al-Nāṣir sent him to deliver an invitation to visit the court.

---

[175] Ṣafī al-Dīn, *Risālat*, 36, 125.

[176] *ʿAM*, 1:231–233; cf. Ahmet Karamustafa, *God's Unruly Friends: Dervish Groups in the Islamic Later Middle Period, 1200–1550* (Salt Lake City: University of Utah Press, 1994), 34–36.

[177] See: Frank Lewis, *Rumi: Past and Present, East and West* (Oxford: Oneworld, 2000), 69.

Accompanied by a large group of well-wishers, Suhrawardī met Bahā᾽ al-Dīn on the outskirts of the city, dismounted from his mule, and greeted the shaykh with the utmost of politeness and respect. According to Aflākī, the family was put up at the Mustanṣiriyya Madrasa—an impossibility given that the institution was not opened until 632/1234—and Suhrawardī personally attended to his settling in there, treating him with every kindness. Bahā᾽ al-Dīn, however, refused the gifts sent to him by al-Nāṣir, and during a well-attended public sermon at the Palace Congregational Mosque criticized him severely for his impious behavior and warned him that the Mongols would descend upon him and exact revenge for his transgressions of the divine law.[178] This was neither the first nor the last time Bahā᾽ al-Dīn exhorted a ruler with the same threat.

The second meeting is said to have taken place in Konya during Suhrawardī's mission to ʿAlā᾽ al-Dīn Kayqubād, the same year in which the family is said to have settled down in the city (618/1221). During this time, Bahā᾽ al-Dīn is reported to have repaid the kindness which Suhrawardī had shown him some years prior in Baghdad, proclaiming that: "the people of Suhraward are an ancient people, as well as near relations of ours."[179] Later that night, the sultan had a perplexing dream which he immediately submitted to both Suhrawardī and Bahā᾽ al-Dīn for interpretation, the former deferring it to the latter who offered an interpretation which, as with his pronouncement on al-Nāṣir, predicted the utter ruin which the Mongols would bring upon the house of the Seljuks.

Later in his account, Aflākī recounts another meeting which Suhrawardī had with a member of Bahā᾽ al-Dīn's circle in Konya, this time with the teacher of Jalāl al-Dīn Rūmī, Sayyid Burhān al-Dīn Muḥaqqiq (d. 637/1239–1240). This meeting, in fact, mirrors al-Yāfiʿī's account of the meeting between Suhrawardī and Ibn ʿArabī (see below), employing the well-worn conceit of the 'speechless conversation':

> When the *shaykh al-islām* Shihab al-Dın-i Suhrawardı came from the abode of the caliphate to the sultan of Rūm he wished to visit the Sayyid [Burhān al-Dīn]...when the shaykh went in to see him, he found him sitting motionless on the ground. The shaykh lowered his head and sat down at a distance. No words were exchanged between them. Weeping,

---

[178] Aflākī, *The Feats of the Knowers of God*, trans. John O'Kane (Leiden: Brill, 2002), 14–17.

[179] Ibid., 34.

> the shaykh stood up and departed. The disciples asked: 'What is it that not a single question, answer, or any speech between you?' The shaykh replied: 'Before the people of spiritual states (*ḥāl*) what is required is the language of spiritual states (*zabān-i ḥāl*), not the language of words (*qāl*)... Later, Ṣāhib Shams al-Dīn and his companions asked the shaykh: 'how did you find the Sayyid?' To which he replied: 'He is a wave-tossed sea of pearls of meaning and ornaments of the realities of Muḥammad's secrets, clear to the utmost degree and hidden in the utmost degree. Nor do I think that anyone else in the entire world, with the exception of our master Jalāl al-Ḥaqq wa-l-Dīn will attain his spiritual achievement and overtake him'.[180]

Unlike Suhrawardī's supposed meeting with Ibn ʿArabī, however, given that its interest would have been limited to Mevlevī circles, Aflākī's account is not repeated by later narrators.

Ibn al-Fāriḍ (d. 632/1235)

A similar situation occurs in connection with the celebrated Egyptian Sufi poet Ibn al-Fāriḍ. In the proem (*dībāja*) to his famous *Dīwān*, his grandson ʿAlī Sibṭ Ibn al-Fāriḍ relates an anecdote told to him by his uncle concerning a meeting which is said to have taken place between Ibn al-Fāriḍ and Suhrawardī in the precincts of the Holy Mosque in Mecca in 628/1231:

> When Shihāb al-Dīn al-Suhrawardī went on pilgrimage in the year 628 [1231], many people from Iraq went with him and during the circumambulation of the Kaʿba and the standing at ʿArafāt he noticed a huge crowd of people gathered around him, imitating his every word and action. It reached al-Suhrawardī that the shaykh [Ibn al-Fāriḍ] was there in the sacred precincts. He longed to see him, and he wept while saying inwardly, "Do you believe that God regards me as these folk do? Do you believe that I am remembered in the Beloved's presence today?" Then the shaykh appeared to him and said, "O' Suhrawardī: Good news for you, so strip off what is on you,/for you have been remembered despite your crookedness!" Shihāb al-Dīn screamed and stripped himself bare [i.e., of his *iḥrām*] as did the Sufi masters (*mashāyikh*) and the novices (*fuqarāʾ*) present. He looked for the shaykh but could not find him, so he said, "This is news from one who was in the Divine Presence [*ḥaḍra*]!" Some time later, the two met there in the Noble Sanctuary, and they embraced and spoke together in private for a long while. He asked my father's permission to invest me and my brother ʿAbd al-Raḥmān with the Sufi habit (*khirqat al-ṣūfiyya*) according to his way (*ʿalā ṭarīqatihi*), but my father

---

[180] Ibid., 53–54.

> would not permit it, saying, "This is not our manner (*laysat hādhihi min ṭarīqinā*)." But he persisted until my father consented, and I was invested as was my brother, together with Shihāb al-Dīn Aḥmad Ibn al-Khiyāmī and his brother Shams al-Dīn, who also has my father's permission, for both of them were like sons to him. In addition, a large group of people were also invested by al-Suhrawardī in the presence of the shaykh and a group of Sufi masters such as Ibn al-ʿUjayl al-Yamanī and others.[181]

Although dismissing its details, Boullata affirms the historicity of the report, arguing that there is little reason to doubt that Suhrawardī performed the pilgrimage of 628/1231 as it was his habit to make it annually near the end of his life and to engage in the practice of pious retreat (*jāwara*) while there.[182] In addition, Suhrawardī is reported to have made the pilgrimage in the preceding two years, during which he invested numerous individuals with the *khirqa*, transmitted the *ʿAwārif al-maʿārif*, and held preaching sessions. Although only mentioned by ʿAlī Sibṭ Ibn al-Fāriḍ in this anecdote, Ibn al-Fāriḍ was no stranger to Mecca and it is quite probable that he could have been there at the time.

Although Homerin does not dispute the possibility of Ibn al-Fāriḍ meeting with Suhrawardī in Mecca on chronological grounds, he is quite justified in questioning its historicity for a number of other reasons. First, as he quite rightly points out, within the internal organization of the *Dībāja* this anecdote clearly serves as a climatic hagiographic device aimed at exemplifying the saintly qualities of his grandfather following a long string of strategically crafted anecdotes. Second, a similar incident is related by a younger contemporary of ʿAlī Sibṭ Ibn al-Fārid, al-Fayyūmī, in which Suhrawardī is replaced with one Abū Fatḥ al-Wāsiṭī who upon hearing the same couplet strips of himself of his *iḥrām* and then presents it to the poet as a gift of appreciation. Third, the implications of Ibn al-Fāriḍ's refusal to allow his sons to be invested with the *khirqa* by Suhrawardī cannot be glossed over, having something to do with the manner in which ʿAlī Sibṭ Ibn al-Fāriḍ envisioned his

---

[181] Homerin, trans., *From Arab Poet to Muslim Saint: Ibn al-Fāriḍ, His Verse, and His Shrine* (Columbia, S.C.: University of South Carolina Press, 1994), 47–48; and, idem, *ʿUmar Ibn al-Fāriḍ: Sufi Verse, Saintly Life* (Marwah, NJ: Paulist Press, 2000), 324–325. I have made a number of changes and amendments to this translation based on the original text ("Dībājat Ibn al-Fāriḍ", in *Dīwān Ibn al-Fāriḍ* [Cairo: ʿAyn, 1995], 182–183) in order to conform with the terminological conventions employed in this book. A condensed version of the anecdote is given by al-Yāfiʿī (*MJ*, 4:77–78; and, Jāmī, *Nafaḥāt*, 542; see also: *Nṣr.*, 237; and, *GE*, 5 [no. 18]).

[182] Issa Boullata, "Toward a Biography of Ibn al-Fāriḍ," *Arabica* 38.1 (1981): 51–52.

grandfather vis-à-vis the increasingly formalized *ṭarīqa*-based modes of Sufi organization proliferating in the Egypt of his day.[183]

On the last point, Homerin speculates that not only was al-Fayyūmī's telling less appealing to the narrator as a hagiographic device but that his narrative may reflect a move among the poet's descendents to organize a distinct *ṭarīqa* around Ibn al-Fāriḍ in which case his refusal, and subsequent consent that his sons be invested with the *khirqa*, provides a proof-text for an earlier articulation of a distinct order. However, and this is something which is taken up much more fully in Chapter Four of this study, this interpretation relies upon how we understand the term *ṭarīqa*, for I read Ibn al-Fāriḍ's response "*laysat hādhihi min ṭarīqinā*" as meaning: 'as an act, investiture with the *khirqa* is not our way of doing things', and not that Sibṭ Ibn al-Fāriḍ meant to say that his grandfather was rejecting Suhrawardī's way (*ṭarīqa*) in terms of it being construed as a distinct lineage or order (e.g., the Suhrawardiyya) in favor of another (e.g., a fictitious 'Fāriḍiyya'), but rather that he was simply attempting to enunciate the spiritual prestige of his subject through employing the figure of a paragonic Sufi master as a foil against which it could be measured.

Muʿīn al-Dīn Chishtī (d. 633/1236)

The same seems to occur in the alleged instance of Suhrawardī's meeting with the famed Sufi, and eponym of one of the earliest *ṭarīqa*-lineages and eventual competitor to the Suhrawardiyya in the Indian Subcontinent, Muʿīn al-Dīn Chishtī. According to Gramlich, during a period of wandering following his departure from his master ʿUthmān-i Hārwanī (d. 607/1211 or 617/1221) and before his arrival in Ajmer (after already having met with both ʿAbd al-Qādir al-Jīlānī and Najm al-Dīn Kubrā) Muʿīn al-Dīn Chishtī visited Baghdad and while there cultivated a friendly relationship with ʿUmar al-Suhrawardī.[184] Much like the famous legend of the 'three schoolfellows' (Niẓām al-Mulk—ʿUmar

---

183 Homerin, *From Arab Poet to Muslim Saint*, 48–49; on the latter quoting ʿAlī b. Muḥammad al-Fayyūmī, *Nathr al-jumān fī tarājim al-aʿyān*, MS. Topkapı Sarayı, Ahmet III 1746, 2:69a–69b. In his article "ʿUmar ibn al-Fāriḍ, A Saint of Mamluk and Ottoman Egypt," in *Manifestations of Sainthood in Islam*, ed. Grace Martin Smith and Carl W. Ernst [Istanbul: The Isis Press, 1987], 85–94) Homerin charts this project of Ibn al-Fāriḍ's sanctification.

184 *GE*, 4 (no. 11); and thus Hartmann, "al-Suhrawardī," *EI*^{2}, 9:779; Knysh, *Islamic Mysticism*, 196; cf. Fritz Meier, *Die Fawāʾiḥ al-Ǧalāl des Naǧm ad-Dīn al-Kubrā* (Wiesbaden: Franz Steiner Verlag, 1957), 38–39.

Khayyām—Ḥasan-i Sabbāḥ), however, the association between these eponyms of four of the earliest *ṭarīqa*-lineages is but a later construction. Although important linkages were forged, and then broken, early-on between the Chishtiyya and Suhrawardiyya in India, there is no reliable evidence that Suhrawardī either met or corresponded with Muʿīn al-Dīn Chishtī, quite to the contrary. As P.M. Currie has established, disentangling the Muʿīn al-Dīn of history from the Muʿīn al-Dīn of legend is a difficult task,[185] and as with the other narratives which link Suhrawardī with such 'remarkable men', this tradition must be read carefully.

Although the work of Currie and others on the construction of the figure of Muʿīn al-Dīn in later South Asian hagio-historiography excuses me from discussing the permutations of narratives placing him in the presence of Suhrawardī, it is important to make note of the first reference to the two which is found—over three centuries after the supposed fact—in the *Siyar al-ʿārifīn* of the 10th/16th-century Suhrawardī poet and traveler Ḥāmid b. Faḍlullāh Jamālī-yi Dihlawī (d. 942/1542):

> When Muʿīn al-Dīn arrived in Hārwan in Nīshāpūr he found the blessed shaykh of the shaykhs ʿUthmān-i Hārwānī...and remained in his service for two-and-a-half years...when he completed his task, ʿUthmān invested him with the *khirqat-i khilāfa* and he then asked for permission to go to Baghdad. He came to the town of Sijz where at the time Najm al-Dīn [Kubrā] lived and he remained in his company for some two-and-a-half months. From there, he went to Jīl and there found Muḥyī ʾl-Dīn ʿAbd al-Qādir [al-Jīlānī] and remained in his company for some fifty-seven days...after meeting Muḥyī ʾl-Dīn ʿAbd al-Qādir, he went to Baghdad where he encountered Ḍiyāʾ al-Dīn [al-Suhrawardī], the master (*pīr*) of Shihāb al-Dīn [al-Suhrawardī] and for a time enjoyed his company. At that time Awḥad al-Dīn Kirmānī was in Baghdad at the beginning of his novitiate and it is related by the *khalīfa* of the author of the *Mathnavī*, Mawlānā Jalāl al-Dīn [Rūmī], Ḥusām al-Dīn Chelebī, that Muʿīn al-Dīn invested Kirmānī with the *khirqat-i khilāfa* and that Shihāb al-Dīn ʿUmar reached the state of the perfect man (*insān-i kāmil*). It is also related by Ḥusām al-Dīn that Muʿīn al-Dīn came from Baghdad to Hamadhān where he met Yusūf Hamadhānī and from there set out for Tabrīz where he met Abū Saʿīd Tabrīzī, the master of Jalāl al-Dīn Tabrīzī...[186]

[185] *The Shrine and Cult of Muʿīn al-Dīn Chishtī of Ajmer* (Delhi: Oxford University Press, 1989), 20–96. In addition, see the comments of Ernst and Lawrence on Chishtī hagiographical sources and the construction of the Chishtī tradition in *Sufi Martyrs of Love*.

[186] As quoted, with modifications, by Currie, *The Shrine and Cult*, 32–33.

Although mentioning Suhrawardī—alongside a truly magnificent list of the brightest stars in the Sufi universe of the time—according to Jamālī's account it was Abū ʾl-Najīb and not ʿUmar with whom Muʿīn al-Dīn met, this ostensibly having occurred sometime before ʿAbd al-Qādir al-Jīlānī set out for Baghdad in 488/1095[187] (some forty-eight years before Muʿīn al-Dīn Chishtī's birth) and his emergence in the city as a public preacher in 521/1127 (there is no mention of him having returned to Jīlān), Abū ʾl-Najīb's death in 563/1168, Kirmānī's first visit to Baghdad c. 575/1180,[188] and Muʿīn al-Dīn's arrival in India around 588/1192! When faced with such egregious chronological inconsistencies, one must ask other questions of such narratives, and as discussed in-depth by Currie, Ernst, and Lawrence, such questions have everything to do with the complex inter-*ṭuruq* relationships of the Indian Subcontinent and almost nothing to do with the situation of late 6th/12th–early 7th/13th century Baghdad.[189] As is made apparent in the narratives of those figures associated with the development of both the Chishtiyya and Suhrawardiyya orders in India, the respective histories of these two lineages are intimately intertwined.

Muḥyī ʾl-Dīn Ibn ʿArabī (d. 638/1240)[190]

The final meeting is both the most remarkable and the most telling as all, that which is alleged to have taken place between Suhrawardī and the Andalusian *magister maximus* Muḥyī ʾl-Dīn Ibn ʿArabī (d. 638/1240), who

---

[187] al-Shaṭṭanawfī, *Bahjat*, 20; and, al-Tādifī, *Necklaces*, 11; see also: Demeerseman, *Nouveau regard*, 7; and, Gürer, *Abdülkâdir Geylânî: Hayatı, Eserleri, Görüşleri* (Istanbul: İnsan Yayınları, 1999), 64.

[188] On which see Mikâil Bayram, *Şeyh Evhadü'd-din Hâmid el-Kirmânî ve Evhadiyye Tarikatı* (Konya: Damla Matbaacılık ve Ticaret, 1993), 23–24, 27.

[189] Chishtī sources forge all manner of connections between Muʿīn al-Dīn and Suhrawardī (alongside Najm al-Dīn Kubrā, Ibn ʿArabī, Awḥad al-Dīn Kirmānī, Ṣadr al-Dīn Qūnawī, Bahāʾ al-Dīn Valad, etc.), some dated such an anecdote in the apocryphal *Dalīl al-ʿārifīn* (composed c. 756/1355–787/1385) which places Suhrawardī alongside him at the investiture of Quṭb al-Dīn Bakhtiyār in 613/1216 in Baghdad (Currie, *Shrine*, 48), another in a mid-11th/17th-century Indian hagiography, the *Siyar al-aqṭāb*, which has Suhrawardī, Awḥad al-Dīn al-Kirmānī, and many others coming to 'kiss his feet in order to obtain blessings' at the sessions of *samāʿ* which he would hold in Baghdad (ibid., 69, 95), a text which a bit later in the narrative also places Suhrawardī and Awḥad al-Dīn Kirmānī in India performing *dhikr* with Muʿīn al-Dīn! (ibid., 82)

[190] This section is a much condensed version of my article "Between Historiography, Hagiography and Polemic: The 'Relationship' between Abū Ḥafṣ ʿUmar al-Suhrawardī and Ibn ʿArabī," *JMIAS* 34 (Autumn, 2003): 59–82.

according to Osman Yahia met Suhrawardī in Baghdad in 608/1211,[191] although as Claude Addas has quite rightly pointed out, the passage from Ibn al-ʿImād's *Shadharāt al-dhahab* which he cites provides neither place nor date for such a meeting[192] and Gramlich points out that: "the meeting between this renowned and uncontested representative of speculative mysticism with his twenty-year elder Suhrawardī carries certain legendary elements, much like the meeting between Abū Saʿīd b. Abī ʾl-Khayr and Ibn Sīnā."[193] Gramlich is quite right, for not only are there no mutually verifiable points of biographical intersection between the two but the biographies of each tell us that they could only have met during a rather limited window of time: either in Baghdad during the latter part of the year 608/1212 or almost ten years later in Malatya in the year 618/1221 during the course of Suhrawardī's mission to ʿAlāʾ al-Dīn Kayqubād. Despite the reception which Ibn ʿArabī received in Baghdad in 608/1212—having been interviewed by the important Iraqi historiographers Ibn al-Dubaythī and Ibn al-Najjār, both of whom were students of Suhrawardī—and the well-documented receptions which Suhrawardī received during his journey to Anatolia in 618/1221, there is no corroborating evidence which places the two together during either of these times.

There is, in fact, only one narrative which places the two shaykhs together at all, and for reasons which will become clear shortly, it provides no real clues as to time or place. The earliest occurrence of this story—which would serve as the template for all to follow—is found in the *Mirʾāt al-jinān* of the 8th/14th-century Shāfiʿī jurist and Sufi Abū ʿAbdullāh b. Asʿad al-Yāfiʿī (d. 768/1367). His account runs as follows:

> It has been said that he [Ibn ʿArabī] met with Imām Shihāb al-Dīn al-Suhrawardī and that during this meeting everyone was looking at one another in expectation, but the two departed without saying a word. Later, Ibn ʿArabī was asked about shaykh Shihāb al-Dīn and he replied, 'he is filled with the *sunna* from head to toe'. Likewise, Shihāb al-Dīn was asked about him and he said, 'he is an ocean of divine verities' (*baḥr al-haqāʾiq*).' As I have mentioned in some of my books, everyone

[191] *Histoire et classification de l'oeuvre d'Ibn ʿArabī* (Damascus: Institut Français de Damas, 1964), 2:98.

[192] *Quest for the Red Sulpher: The Life of Ibn ʿArabī*, trans. Peter Kingsley (Cambridge, UK: The Islamic Texts Society, 1993), 240; cf. *ShDh*, 7:337.

[193] *GE*, 4. Hartmann says the same (*Nṣr.*, 236–237; idem, "al-Suhrawardī," *EI*², 9:779); but cf. Meier, *Abū Saʿīd*, 26–28 on the issue of their correspondence.

> disagrees over the question of declaring him [Ibn ʿArabī] a heretic, but my personal opinion in the matter is to withhold judgment and entrust his affair to God Most High.[194]

The same report, with various accretions and inclusions, can be found in later biographical works such as, for example, the *Shadharāt al-dhahab* of the 11th/17th-century Ḥanbalī biographer Ibn al-ʿImād which Yahia cited as proof of their meeting:

> It is reported that al-Yāfiʿī used to censure him by saying that he was a heretic. One day some of his companions said to him, 'I want you to point out the *quṭb* to me', and he said 'it is he'. It was said to him: 'but you normally censure him', to which he responded: "I maintain the exotericity of the reveled law", although in his *Irshād* he has described it in terms of mystical knowing (*maʿrifa*) and its verities. And he said: 'the two shaykhs, these two *imams*—both of them gnostics, verifiers of divine realities, and respected divines—al-Suhrawardī and Ibn ʿArabī met; and during this meeting each of them sat in silence for an hour after which they departed without saying a word. Later, it was said to Ibn ʿArabī, 'so, what do you say about al-Suhrawardī?', to which he replied, 'he is filled with the *sunna* from head to toe.' Likewise, it was said to al-Suhrawardī, 'so, what do you say about him?', and he replied, 'he is an ocean of divine verities'.[195]

Based on such retellings, it is clear from the outset that the issue here is not whether or not Ibn ʿArabī and Suhrawardī actually met, but rather that their meeting serves a polemical agenda, namely to position one or another biographer or historiographer in terms of his stance on the issue of *takfīr*. As Alexander Knysh has shown, the controversy over Ibn ʿArabī consumed a great deal of the collective energy of medieval Muslim thinkers from the 7th/13th century onwards, it being something of a standard obligation to define one's own position vis-à-vis the controversial Sufi master. As he has convincingly argued, in fact, the manner in which the figure of Ibn ʿArabī was reimagined and reproduced in later Muslim discursive arenas can in many ways be better understood when viewed as a literary discourse; as a series of narratives both masking and reflecting broader theological tensions and controversies of concern to a particular discursive community at a given time and place. What this amounts to, then, is the production of a body of literature which for all intents and purposes engages the legacy

---

[194] *MJ*, 4:101.
[195] *ShDh*, 7:337.

of the shaykh only inasmuch as pronouncements—or more often than not, equivocations—on that legacy serve, to quote Alexander Knysh: "...as a convenient rallying point for various religio-political factions vying for power and supremacy...this, in turn, leads to the historical Ibn ʿArabī becoming fictionalized into a polemical image, for once the rules of the debate had been established by a few authoritative scholars, they were, some exceptions and variations apart, meticulously observed by both parties to the debate, leading, as it were, to the routinization and stabilization of the polemical discourse."[196]

In the case of al-Yāfiʿī, the intention is clear, namely that in his well-known personal disagreement over negative assessments of the shaykh by vituperative critics such as Ibn Taymiyya or less-than-flattering biographical portrayals such as that of Dhahabī, the learned Shāfiʿī scholar and Sufi sympathizer self-consciously and programmatically set out to vindicate—although in rather ambivalent terms—Ibn ʿArabī from charges of infidelity, grave sin, and even heresy. By coupling Ibn ʿArabī with a well-known and by then paradigmatic representative of a creditable, thoroughly *jamāʿī-sunnī*, essentially unimpeachable, 'Islamically-correct' and 'ulama-sanctioned' tradition of organized, *ṭarīqa*-based Sufism, al-Yāfiʿī was able to mitigate questions over the shaykh's standing vis-à-vis the very tradition which he claims. What better way to rehabilitate the image of a potential *kāfir* then to place him squarely in the lap of an unquestionably unobjectionable and, especially during the 8th/14th century, authoritative icon of all that is right with the Sufi tradition such as Abū Ḥafṣ ʿUmar al-Suhrawardī? Interestingly enough, however, by no means did al-Yāfiʿī's figuration do much to soften potential polemics, and the use of such 'face-saving' narratives did not go unnoticed by Ibn ʿArabī's critics, one such critic in fact later remarking that "the al-Suhrawardi story was transmitted from one anonymous [narrator] to another" and that al-Yāfiʿī mentioned it because, as an advocate of Sufis, he was keen on "finding excuses for them no matter how far-fetched they may be."[197]

In later Sufi hagio-historiography, the meeting between the two which we first encounter in al-Yāfiʿī became something of a trope, a trope at

[196] *Ibn ʿArabi in the Later Islamic Tradition: The Making of a Polemical Image in Medieval Islam* (Albany, NY: State University of New York Press, 1999), 274, 275.

[197] Ibid., 119 (quoting the vituperative Yemeni critic, Ibn al-Ahdal, in his *Kashf al-ghiṭāʾ ʿan ḥaqāʾiq al-tawḥīd wa ʾl-radd ʿalā Ibn ʿArabī al-faylasūf al-ṣūfī* [Tunis: Aḥmad Bakīr, 1964], 274).

least inasmuch as it came to take on a certain ideological weight vis-à-vis whatever partisan leanings guide the narrative vision of this or that hagiographer. Within Sufi hagio-historiography the *locus classicus* of the supposed meeting between Ibn ʿArabī and Suhrawardī is found in Jāmī's *Nafaḥāt al-uns*. Although he quotes al-Yāfiʿī as a source, in Jāmī's retelling of the meeting the tables are turned. Here, a paradigmatic Ibn ʿArabī is put in service of Suhrawardī, lending, it would seem, a measure of credibility and importance to the eponym of one of the most active Sufi brotherhoods of Jāmī's time. Curiously enough, this connection does not appear in his entry on Ibn ʿArabī[198]—where he simply repeats the episode we find in al-Yāfiʿī—but rather is programmatically embedded within his account of Suhrawardī where he quotes from al-Simnānī's *Chihil majlis*:

> In the *Risāle-ye iqbāliye*[199] it is mentioned that shaykh Rukn al-Dīn ʿAlāʾ al-Dawla said that shaykh Saʿd al-Dīn Ḥammūya was asked, 'how do you find shaykh Muḥyī ʾl-Dīn?' to which he said [in Arabic], 'he is a surging ocean without a shore'. It is also said that he was asked. 'How do you find shaykh Shihāb al-Dīn Suhrawardī?' to which he replied [in Arabic]: "the perpetual light of the Prophet—may God bless and greet him—shines upon his forehead, and that is something else indeed![200]

Here, Jāmī makes two interesting connections. The first is between Ibn ʿArabī and two *silsila*s: the Kubrawiyya and the Suhrawardiyya, both of which underwent a rapid expansion in the eastern Islamic lands of Jāmī's time, each in fact vying for patronage and legitimacy vis-à-vis the other as well as finding themselves in competition with Jāmī's own Naqshbandī lineage. In choosing al-Simnānī's quote, and thus placing the disciple of the celebrated Najm al-Dīn Kubrā, Saʿd al-Dīn Ḥammūya (d. 650/1252), alongside Suhrawardī, Jāmī is able to effect, in one fell swoop, an immediate connection between two contemporary *ṭarīqa*-based Sufi traditions, both of which were not only very active in the Persianate milieu for which Jāmī was writing, but were also known for their mutual hostility to the school of Ibn ʿArabī. By having both of these iconic representatives of their respective brotherhoods praise Ibn ʿArabī, Jāmī is able to further solidify his vision of what he sees as constituting an 'authentic' mystico-theosophical Sufi tradition, a

[198] Jāmī, *Nafaḥāt al-uns*, 546.
[199] al-Simnānī, *Chihil majlis*, ed. ʿAbd al-Rafīʿ Ḥaqīqat (Tehran: Intishārāt Asāṭīr, 1378 sh.), 215.
[200] Jāmī, *Nafaḥāt*, 474.

vision which he programmatically lays out in the *Nafaḥāt*'s sizeable introduction. The second connection concerns the *nūr muḥammadiyya*, an image which is integral not only to Ibn ʿArabī's system, but one which came to figure prominently in certain Naqshbandī appropriations of the Akbarian tradition. For Jāmī, al-Yāfiʿī's 'ocean of divine verities' ultimately cannot serve his agenda well enough, for although the most obvious meaning of the figure of speech which the speaker is made to employ in this account is quite intelligible without reference to the *nūr muḥammadiyya*, for those attuned to such imagery—as indeed most of Jāmī's audience would have been—the allusion is unmistakable.

The final meeting between Ibn ʿArabī, *al-shaykh al-akbar*, and Abū Ḥafṣ ʿUmar Suhrawardī, *shaykh al-ṣūfiyya*, is in fact both the earliest and the latest of the three. It is a meeting which in the first place differs from all others, a meeting which takes place not in the texts of historiographers and hagiographers, not in the narratives of the Other, but rather in a world within which both subjects appear on equal footing, a world within which both were equally immersed, a world which is comprised of narratives of the self—or so it would seem. This is the universe of the authorial text, a field of experience and self-immortalization within which both Ibn ʿArabī and Suhrawardī were undisputedly prolific. It was in this world where the two shaykhs did in fact meet each other, at least one of them interrogating the other through the medium of pen and ink, inserting themselves into the broader discursive fields which each shared by default. It must be said, however, that as tantalizing as this sounds, this meeting was but a brief, fleeting, encounter; for both Ibn ʿArabī and Suhrawardī devote little to no space to his contemporary, and from what I have been able to determine neither had much interest in the other, certainly not to the extent to which the historiographical and hagiographical narratives would lead us to believe.

Let us start at the beginning. In his *al-Futūḥāt al-makkiyya*, Ibn ʿArabī refers to Suhrawardī twice. Both of these references occur within the context of the shaykh's thoughts on the ontological differentiation between divine witnessing, or God's self-unveiling (*al-mushāhada*), the divine word or speech (*al-kalām*) and the primordial polarity of the divine will, namely its bifurcation into two modes: the engendering command, *al-amr al-takwīnī*, and the prescriptive command, *al-amr al-taklīfī*.[201] In both cases, the shaykh employs the figure of Suhrawardī, or

[201] On this, see William Chittick, *The Self-Disclosure of God* (Albany: State University of New York Press, 1998), 250–251.

in the following case that of his uncle Abū ʾl-Najīb, as an example of an individual for whom the two are wholly undifferentiated; one whose spiritual state has not yet matured to a point which would allow him to distinguish between these two modalities. Thus, in chapter 550 on the subject of knowing the state of the *quṭb*, Ibn ʿArabī writes:

> It is inevitable that he who has directly tasted the two commands becomes aware of their distinction. It has reached me on the authority of the aged shaykh Shihāb al-Dīn al-Suhrawardī, that his cousin [sic!] Abū ʾl-Najīb maintained the unity between divine witnessing and the divine word. Although I know his station and his tasting in regards to this, I do not know if he advanced after this or not. I do know, however, that he was at the level of 'imaginalization' (*al-takhayyul*) and this is a common station widespread among the generality of Sufis; but as for the elect, they know it and through a certain affair have surpassed that which the generality of Sufis have tasted. This is what we, al-Sayyārī, and anyone who follows the same route of realization have alluded to.[202]

Likewise, in chapter 71 on the mysteries of fasting, in a section dealing with the question of whether or not the faster is allowed to kiss or be kissed by someone, Ibn ʿArabī once again mentions al-Suhrawardī, saying:

> With regard to this question of kissing: among the doctors of the law there are those who approve of it unconditionally, those who disapprove of it without exception, and those who disapprove of it for the novice but approve of it for the shaykh. The answer to this question is the opposite of the issue of Moses—peace be upon him—for he requested the vision (*al-ruʾya*) after experiencing the divine word. As for divine witnessing and the divine word, the two do not occur simultaneously save in the isthmithic theophany (*al-tajallī al-barzakhī*). This was the station of Shihāb al-Dīn ʿUmar al-Suhrawardī who died in Baghdad—may God be merciful to him—for it has been narrated to me about him by a transmitter from among his companions whom I trust, that he maintained the unity of the vision and the divine word, and for this reason I know for certain that his witnessing took place in the isthmithic theophany, and there is no doubt about it, for without that, it could not have been so.[203]

Interestingly enough, in the entry on Suhrawardī in his *al-Kawākib al-dhurriya*, the 11th/17th-century Egyptian scholar and Khalwatī Sufi al-Munāwī not only quotes the passage from this chapter in his account, but misconstrues its meaning, saying that: "it should be pointed out to

---

[202] Ibn ʿArabī, *al-Futūḥāt al-makkiyya*, photo-reproduction of the Cairo 1867 edition (Beirut: Dār Ṣādir, 1968), 4:192.
[203] Ibid., 1:609.

you that the gnostic Ibn ʿArabī praised him by saying this".[204] For Ibn ʿArabī, however, Suhrawardī, as with many other similar individuals whom he uses to support such points, serve only as examples of lesser attainments, and not as praiseworthy exemplars of the perfect man.

So what about Suhrawardī? As was mentioned earlier, it is 'common scholarly knowledge' that Suhrawardī harshly criticized the shaykh on the grounds that he had somehow adulterated or sullied the pure and simple mystical experience of the classical Sufi tradition by introducing the abstract and speculative language of Islamic philosophy into the once "venerable tradition of Prophetic *taṣawwuf*"—or did he? While later Muslim thinkers such as Ibn Khaldūn (d. 780/1382) made such a charge against the shaykh,[205] it is unclear if Suhrawardī should be counted among them. In her entry "al-Suhrawardī" in the second edition of the *Encyclopaedia of Islam*, Angelika Hartmann states:

> Though referring to the doctrine of the "pious forefathers", al-Suhrawardī in his mystical ideas went far beyond this, up to the point of even accepting, be it in a limited way, the *anā ʾl-ḥaḳḳ* of al-Ḥallad̲j̲. Yet the freedom which al-Suhrawardī permitted himself in his judgment of the executed mystic did not bring him into agreement with the doctrines of contemporary "freethinkers". In strong words, he turned against the pantheism of his contemporary Ibn al-ʿArabī. According to al-Suhrawardī, the latter had started to establish a despicable connection between *taṣawwuf* and elements of Greek philosophy.[206]

This statement, as with much of her entry, is in fact nothing but a direct translation of some passages in her otherwise excellent 1975 German monograph *an-Nāṣir li-Dīn Allāh*,[207] this statement itself being based upon some rather confusing evidence provided by Massignon in his monumental *La passion d'l-Ḥallâj*—which, incidentally, Hartmann does not cite in the above quoted entry. In fact, this is the only place in her rather sizable *oeuvre* on Suhrawardī where she mentions this fact. No place is it stated exactly where Suhrawardī criticizes Ibn ʿArabī, and no wonder because no such mention of Ibn ʿArabī is made in either of Suhrawardī's polemics against the *falāsifa*, the *Rashf al-naṣāʾiḥ* or the *Idālat al-ʿiyān ʿalā ʾl-burhān*, nor in fact throughout his entire corpus!

---

204 al-Munāwī, *Kawākib*, 2:517.
205 On this, see Knysh, *Ibn ʿArabī*, 190–197.
206 Hartmann, "al-Suhrawardī, S̲h̲ihāb al-Dīn Abū Ḥafṣ ʿUmar," *EI*², 9:778.
207 *Nṣr.*, 236–237.

More than any of Suhrawardī's meetings with 'remarkable men', this episode serves as an excellent example of the way in paradigmatic or 'iconic' figures constitute a special class of persons within pre-modern biographical literary traditions. Functioning as loci of broader networks of values, ideologies, and religio-philosophic discourses, the way in which the 'biographies' of such figures are written often tell us much more about those who wrote them then about the biographee himself. In the case of Muḥyī 'l-Dīn Ibn ʿArabī and Abū Ḥafṣ ʿUmar al-Suhrawardī it is apparent just how easily their iconic value could be capitalized, coming to serve as a sort of discursive unit of exchange in the economy of medieval Muslim polemic; although the concerns of Yāfiʿī and Jāmī differed considerably, both were able to make good use of a common legal tender.

The Farewell Pilgrimage

Alongside of these meetings with individual remarkable men, there are a number of reports that Suhrawardī made the pilgrimage to Mecca numerous times, often accompanied by a large retinue of disciples and others.[208] Stories of the activities of he and his disciples in the holy city are common in later hagio-historiography, especially in the South Asian materials where the 'Sufi shaykh in Mecca' is a common trope. Despite their rhetorical coloring, however, there is little reason to doubt that Suhrawardī preformed the pilgrimage numerous times for not only does Suhrawardī explicitly state that the *Aʿlām al-hudā* was composed in Mecca, but his handbook for pilgrims, the *Ḥilyat al-nāsik fī 'l-manāsik*, evinces his first-hand knowledge of the rites of the pilgrimage and a personal familiarity with the topography of the Hejaz.[209] Although

awk

[208] *WA*, 3:447; al-ʿUmarī, *Masālik*, 8:225; *TIbW*, 2:233; *BN*, 12:138; Ibn Duqmāq, *Nuzhat*, 61; *ṬShK*, 8:340; al-Dāwūdī, *Ṭabaqāt al-mufassirīn*, ed. ʿAlī Muḥammad ʿUmar (Cairo: Maktabat Wahba, 1972), 2:10; *MS*, 2:355–356; and, *ShDh*, 7:268.

[209] *AH*, 46; idem, *Ḥilyat al-nāsik*, MS. Süley., Ayasofya 1136_3, fol. 98b–121b. What we can say for sure is that during his time in Mecca, Suhrawardī would also hold preaching sessions (*majlis al-waʿz*), a typically accentuated example (from outside the Suhrawardiyya sources) of one such session being preserved by al-ʿUmarī: "al-Wadāʿī has related that Shaykh Quṭb al-Dīn b. al-Qurṭubī said: 'I was present in a gathering of Shaykh Shihāb al-Dīn al-Suhrawardī in Mecca, and he was preaching. Near the end of his sermon, he recited the following [verses]: 'He is inaccessible and his places of abode are his places alone/he alights, and in the dead of night sees with his own eyes what afflicts him; among his companions a brother falls into ecstasy by disputing with him/for in conversation, no outpouring can keep pace with him.' Thereupon, a Sufi (*faqīr*) came up to him and said: 'I will discourse with you, O' preacher!' and he

we do not know when he made his first pilgrimage, later in his life he seems to have made it on a regular basis well as often staying in the city as a 'pious resident' (*mujāwir*), stopping the practice only when he became too infirm to travel.[210] Some of these pilgrimages, in fact, are dated, such as the one of 626/1229 during which he granted Bahā' al-Dīn Zakariyyā Multānī written permission to train disciples and the one of the following year when he invested Ḍiyā' al-Dīn al-Sabtī with the *khirqa* as well as transmitting his *'Awārif al-ma'ārif* to a large group of students, including to Ibn al-Qasṭallānī (d. 686/1287).[211]

Beyond its religious and spiritual significance, the pilgrimage seems to also have also served an important function in the diffusion of Suhrawardī's Sufi system. As with business men and traders who forged commercial relationships with individuals whom they would have otherwise never met, for scholars and Sufis such as Suhrawardī the grand microcosm of the Abode of Islam which was the medieval hajj served as an ideal setting where personal connections could be made, relationships forged, *ḥadīth* gathered, works transmitted, and *khirqa*s given. This is not only well evinced in the datable instances of investiture and transmission but also reflected in hagiographical anecdotes, such as Suhrawardī's alleged meeting with Ibn al-Fāriḍ in 628/1231 or a tradition preserved by the 9th/15th-century Persian chronicler Khwāfī who states that in 616/1220 a meeting of prominent Sufis took place at the Holy Mosque in Mecca and that Suhrawardī was among the gathering.[212] Mecca as a center of Sufism throughout the 7th/13th–8th/14th centuries is well evinced in the numerous *ribāṭ*s which are known to have existed in the city, and Suhrawardī is certainly not the only great

---

sat down and placed his head between his knees, and the shaykh said: 'prepare your brother for burial for he has died!" And so they went to him and found him dead, prepared him and buried him." (*Masālik*, 8:226)

[210] *SN*, 22:376.

[211] al-Suhrawardī, *Ijz. li-Bahā' al-Dīn Zakariyyā Multānī*, MS. Tüb., Ma VI 90_4, fol. 71b; for al-Sabtī's investiture see *SN*, 22:377, and, *TIsl*, 53:115; and, for Ibn al-Qasṭallānī's *riwāya* of the *'Awārif* (who states he finished hearing the text from Suhrawardī during a *majlis*, in the shade of the Ka'ba, in Dhū 'l-Ḥijja, 627/Oct., 1230) MS. Köp., Fazıl Ahmed Paşa 750, fol. 130b, which he subsequently transmitted to one Khalīl b. Badrān al-Ḥalabī in 649/1251 in the famous Sa'īd al-Su'adā' Khānaqāh in Cairo.

[212] Here, Suhrawardī is placed along with such luminaries as Sa'd al-Dīn Ḥammūya and Awḥad al-Dīn Kirmānī. (Khwāfī, *Mujmal*, 1.2:290) For Khwāfī such connections are many. In his obituary for the early Kubrawī master, Sayf al-Dīn Bākharzī (d. 659/1261), for instance Khwāfī states that he heard *ḥadīth* from Suhrawardī, although given the details of his biography it is quite unclear when or where the two could have met. (ibid., 1.2:316).

shaykh to be associated with the city, whether in physical visits or the more common spiritual visits which are so well known to us from South Asian hagiographic traditions. At least one of Suhrawardī's successors—the above mentioned Ibn al-Qasṭallānī—followed his master's precedent of spending time in Mecca, investing disciples with the *khirqa* on Suhrawardī's authority and transmitting the *ʿAwārif al-maʿārif* to a large groups of individuals who came to the city from as far away as Morocco and Andalusia.

What is certain, is that after the death of al-Nāṣir the public activities of Suhrawardī began to slip quietly into the background. By this time, the era of ambassadorial missions and embassies had long since ended and it seems that in the final few years of his life, the shaykh spent his time quietly in the city of Baghdad, perhaps living in the Ribāṭ al-Maʾmūniyya which would later be passed on to his son ʿImād al-Dīn and from him to a long line of hereditary Sufi shaykhs who trained disciples within its precincts. Nothing substantial is reported about these final years save that although suffering from blindness and debilitation, the venerable old shaykh did not fail to keep up with the duties required of him, his biographers being careful to point out that he was fastidious in attending the Friday congregational prayer even though he had to be carried to the mosque on a litter.[213]

He died, at the age of ninety-three, on the evening of Tuesday, the 1st of Muḥarram, 632/26 September, 1234[214] and the following morning—after his funeral prayer at the Jāmiʿ al-Qaṣr—was interred in the Wardiyya, a cemetery located on the east bank of the city near the Ẓafariyya Neighborhood near the Bāb Abraz.[215] Perhaps in vindication

---

213 According to his contemporary and student Ibn al-Najjār (as quoted by *SN*, 22:375, and, *TIsl*, 53:114; see also: *TW*, 6:1223; *ṬShK*, 8:340; *ṬFSh*², 1:401; *MS*, 2:355; and, al-Daljī, *al-Falākat wa-l-maflūkūn* [Beirut: Dār al-Kutub al-ʿIlmiyya, 1993], 124). Ḥamd Allāh Mustawfī provides another interesting account of his devotional program, underscoring the trope of the 'spiritual athlete' so common in retellings of such Sufi shaykhs: "In the presence of the caliph, it is said that he completed the recitation of the Qurʾān in the span of only two units of prayer, and that everyday he would complete two full courses of litanies (*waẓīfa*). One time, the caliph put him to a test: to stand before him while reciting the (entire) Qurʾān, a task which he completed in less than three hours without neglecting a single rule of proper recitation. (*Tārīkh-i guzīda*, 669)

214 *Nasab al-Suhrawardī*, fol. 52b; *SN*, 22:377, and, Tashköpruzāde, 2:355. For his part, al-Mundhirī states the first night of Muḥarram (*TW*, 6:121), and Ibn al-Dimyāṭī on the night of Wednesday in the beginning of Muḥarram (*Mustafād*, 368).

215 *TIr*, 2:320 (*ḥawāshī*, no. 1); *TW*, 6:122; *WA*, 3:448; (pseudo-)Ibn al-Fuawaṭī, *KḤ*, 103; and, al-ʿUmaraī, *Masālik*, 8:227; cf. Sibṭ Ibn al-Jawzī who says that he was buried

over his indiscretion of 605/1208, his biographers are careful to mention that he died without a penny to his name.[216] At some point prior to his death a mausoleum had already been constructed for him, a building which was later restored by the Ottoman sultan Murād IV along with the sanctuaries of Abū Ḥanīfa and ʿAbd al-Qādir al-Jīlānī after he took the city from the Safavids in 1048/1638.[217] Since that time, the mausoleum has witnessed a number of repairs and despite the tragedies which Baghdad has suffered in recent memory, still stands today.

* * *

In the narratives of the historiographers, prosopographers, and Sufi hagiographers we are presented with a figuration of Suhrawardī which finds him, often at one and the same time, playing the role of a Shāfiʿī *ʿālim* and *muḥaddith*, a charismatic public preacher, a respected Sufi master whose membership in the ranks of the *ṣulahāʾ* is unimpeachable, a gnostic who has reached the heights of spiritual perfection, and a diplomat whose religious and spiritual authority was of enough value to al-Nāṣir and his opponents to be employed to effect political gain. Here, we find an ʿUmar al-Suhrawardī who played roles, alongside many others, which were of consequence in all three clusters of before and after which came to coalesce in late 6th/12th and early 7th/13th-century Baghdad, ensuring the permanence of his memory in multiple narratives and for multiple groups of individuals. While these authors and compilers tell us a great deal about the shape of Suhrawardī's world as they choose to represent it vis-à-vis the expectations and constraints of their respective genres and historiographical or biographical projects, at the same time such representations tell us next to nothing about how Suhrawardī actually envisioned himself and the world in which he moved. For this, we need to turn to a different set of texts and traces.

---

in his *ribāṭ*, apparently confusing him and Abū ʾl-Najīb (*MZ*, 8.2:689). According to Yāqūt, the Wardiyya Cemetery was located after the Bāb Abraz on the eastern side near the walls of the Ẓafariyya neighborhood (*Muʿjam al-buldān*, 4:61, 5:371; see further Wiet, *Baghdad*, 115–116).

216 *SN*, 22:375; *ṬShK*, 8:340; and, *ṬFSh*, 2:835.

217 *KḤ*, 103; al-Dimyāṭī, *Mustafād*, 327; Ernst Herzfeld, "Damascus: Studies in Architecture—I," *Ars Islamica* 9 (1942): 26–27; and, *Nṣr.*, 249.

CHAPTER THREE

WRITING AUTHORITY

At some point later in his life, al-Suhrawardī received a request from some of his companions and friends (*aṣḥāb wa-aṣdiqāʾ*) to explain to them the meaning of voluntary poverty (*faqr*). Such a request was nothing new, and he received many others like it from, as Ibn Khallikān stated, "masters of the path (*arbāb al-ṭarīq*) from among the shaykhs of his era who would write to him from their home countries asking for 'legal opinions' (*fatāwā*) on things having to do with their spiritual states."[1] Indeed, in addition to an assemblage of letters, testaments, and compendiums written at the behest of various petitioners, a collection of such legal opinions composed at the behest of an anonymous 'group of imams of Khurāsān' have been preserved in the manuscript record.[2] For some reason, however, in response to this particular request from his associates, Suhrawardī set about composing a short epistle which, with obvious delight and conviction, he chose to preface with an extended first-person narrative:

> I have traveled through parts of this world and have learned and accomplished many great things. I have kept company with great men, and have tasted both the sweet and bitter things of this world. I have studied many books, associated with the ulama, witnessed many wonders, and after all of this, would say that I have not seen a thing more fleeting then the life of this world or anything closer than death and the Hereafter. Indeed, I have not seen a thing better than the latter! I have never seen anything more precious in this world or the next than true contentment, nor a more debased person than the one who spends his life in vain and hopeless pursuits. I have come to see humility as the most precious ornament and stinginess as the worst. I have not seen anything comprised of more evil than envy, nor have I seen anything comprised of more good

[1] *WA*, 3:447; *TIbW*, 2:233; Dāwūdī, *Ṭabaqāt*, 2:11; and, *ShDh*, 7:270.

[2] *Ajwibat ʿan masāʾil baʿḍ aʾimmat Khurasān* which has been edited with a useful introduction and notes by Aḥmād Ṭāhirī ʿIrāqī as "Pāsukhhāʾi Shihāb al-Dīn ʿUmar-i Suhravardī," *Maqalāt u Barrasīhā* 49–50 (1369/1411/1991): 45–64. In addition, al-Mundhirī—who never visited Baghdad—states that: "we are in possession of *ijāza*s from him which he sent to us (*katabahā ilaynā*) more than once, including one dated 618 [1221]." (*TW*, 6:123)

> than beautiful manners. I have seen no greater insult than pandering and nothing which prolongs life more than abstinence. I have seen that success comes with diligence and assiduity, and I have never seen a more deprived person than the greedy nor a more grief stricken person than one who seeks this world. I have seen disgrace in obedience to created beings and nobility and honor in obedience to the Creator, and I have seen nothing harder nor more grim than the hearts of kings. I have not seen a more intelligent person than one who focuses on the Hereafter nor a more ignorant person than one who focuses on this world... indeed, I have seen the blessing of life and livelihood in obedience to God Most High and happiness in this world and the next in following His Messenger.[3]

Beyond a few curt passages scattered here and there, this moralizing homily constitutes the limit of Suhrawardī's autobiographical voice, a voice which much like al-Ghazālī in his celebrated *al-Munqidh min al-ḍalāl* is more formulaic than personal, and more rhetorical than autobiographical *sensu stricto*.

One should not expect too much from such works however. The absence of such a voice is not unusual, for first-person narratives represent but a small fraction of the collective literary output of 6th/12th–7th/13th-century Sufis and are scarcely evinced in the generic categories upon which Suhrawardī drew in composing his own works in any case.[4] Meaningful autobiographical statements—and this seems to be the manner in which he would have wanted to represent himself to both his colleagues and to future generations—are not to be found in biographical anecdotes (although he occasionally uses them to prove a point) nor in the direct quotations of those few prosopographers who interviewed him such as his disciple Ibn al-Najjār, but rather in his

[3] Suhrawardī, *R. fī 'l-faqr*, MS. Süley., Esad Ef. 1761_5, fol. 52a–52b/Amravhī (trans.), "Faqr o darveshī ke li'e bunyādī umūr: Vaṣiyyat bi-nām ba'ḍ fuqarā' aur darvīsh," in *Vaṣāyā Shaykh Shihāb al-Dīn Suhravardī* (Lahore: al-Ma'ārif, 1983), 39–40.

[4] There are, of course, exceptions to this rule, especially in the case of 'visionary diaries' such as the fascinating autobiographical portion of the *Kashf al-asrār* of Ruzbihan-i Baqlı (translated by Carl Ernst as *The Unveiling of Secrets: Diary of a Sufi Master* (Chapel Hill, NC: Parvardigar Press, 1997) or the numerous biographical anecdotes scattered throughout the massive *œuvre* of Ibn 'Arabī (see: Addas, *The Quest for the Red Sulphur*, passim; and, Stephen Hirtenstein, *The Unlimited Mercifier: The Spiritual Life and Thought of Ibn 'Arabī* [Oxford: Anqa Publishing, 1999]). Earlier examples include the 'conversion narrative' of al-Muḥāsibī (d. 243/857) in his *K. al-naṣā'iḥ* (*al-Waṣāyā*) and al-Ḥakīm al-Tirmidhī's (d. between 292 and 297/905 and 910) autobiography (*Bad' sha'n Abī 'Abdullāh... al-Tirmidhī*) which has been translated by Bernd Radtke and John O'Kane in *The Concept of Sainthood in Early Islamic Mysticism* (Richmond, Surrey: Curzon Press: 1996, pp. 15–36).

family genealogy, his *Mashyakha*, his *nisbat al-khirqa*, the *ijāza*s which he granted, the testaments and letters which he wrote, and the treatises which he dictated, precisely those things which served as instruments of authority and legitimacy in the both the *madrasa* and the Sufi *ribāṭ*.

While the biography of Suhrawardī has a great deal to tell us about how power, authority, and status were configured, deployed, and maintained among a particular subsection of the religious classes of the urban centers of the central and eastern lands of Islamdom at the end of the Earlier Middle Period, it has its limits. As we have seen, the almost Weberian ideal types which the prosopographers, chroniclers, and Sufi hagiographers employ in narrating the biography of a figure such as Suhrawardī and the different ways in which their narratives are emplotted in particular rhetorical modes of narration by genre, project, and convention, inevitably obscures what such an individual may have actually thought about himself and, in turn, how he might have envisioned his own role in the activities which he is represented as having engaged in.

Although it is impossible to completely mitigate such a schematized picture, it is possible to add a bit of depth and nuance to such narratives by reading their retellings alongside Suhrawardī's own representation of himself and the particular *Personengruppe* (*ṭā'ifa*) for which he claimed to speak. This representation is offered nowhere save in the collective body of his written works, an *œuvre* in which traces of his presence were kept alive by those of his disciples and their successors who copied, transmitted, and anthologized these works in an effort to preserve a living testament to their eponymous spiritual master. Many of these works, of course, were not originally intended to be collated and anthologized, but as with the collection of *fatāwā* and letters among the *fuqahā'* or the posthumous compilation of *dīwān*s among the *udabā'*, the act of anthologizing served as an important instrument for preserving memory and identity. Thus, the textual artifacts which constitute this trace of Suhrawardī serve a dual function. First, they offer us a synchronic distillation of a particular discursive moment, showing us, through the medium of texts, how an early 7th/13th-century urban Shāfi'ī *'ālim* and Sufi master navigated the multiple social, religious, and discursive spaces in which he, his teachers, students, and disciples moved. Here, we find an author who just like his biographers emplotted his retelling in established rhetorical modes, engaging in the composition and programmatic dissemination of texts as part of a broader program of reform and centralization which aimed to circumscribe various self-constituted commonalities and sectarian affiliations within the orbit of what Suhrawardī perceived as a comprehensive and increasingly accommodationist *ribāṭ*-based Sufi system. Second, in their life as aftertexts among Suhrawardī's disciples and their successors, they offer us a diachronic distillation of the movement, transplantation, and (re)articulation of this particularly influential system of organization, theory, and praxis into social, political, and discursive arenas far removed from Suhrawardī's Baghdad. It is in the intersections and divergences between and among these representations where the figure of Abū Ḥafṣ ʿUmar, the son of Muḥammad from Suhraward is to be sought.

Genealogies of Mystical Knowing

It is clear that for Suhrawardī Sufism was as much about contested identities and claims to authority and legitimacy as it was about the search for veridical knowledge and spiritual perfection. In this, his modus operandi differed little from that of the Sufi systematizers of the 4th/10th–5th/11th century, for like them he strived to assert the identity of a particular *ṭāʾifa* vis-à-vis other *Personengruppen* by constructing a comprehensive vision of identity through an instrument shared with the entirety of the learned classes of Islamdom at the end of the Earlier Middle Period, the discourse and authority of the text. In doing this, Suhrawardī vigorously engaged multiple contested spaces, often in a single text, asserting exegetical authority over the Qurʾān, Ḥadīth, and the exempla of the *salaf al-ṣāliḥ* in an effort to co-opt the authority of those religious professionals whom he called, pejoratively, the worldly-ulama (*ʿulamāʾ al-dunyā*) and place it back in the hands of its rightful owners, the otherworldly-ulama (*ʿulamāʾ al-ākhira*), while at the same time striving to position the Junaydī Sufi tradition (*ṭarīqat al-qawm/al-ṣūfiyya*) to which he considered himself an heir in a position of preeminence over all other self-identified mystical and ascetic movements through strategically employing the recorded sayings and doings of past Sufi paragons as argumentative proofs. As attested in the manuscript record, Suhrawardī not only disseminated such texts to large groups of disciples in the physical space of his Baghdadi *ribāṭ*s through the instrument of personal transmission, but also authorized numerous individuals to transmit them on his authority through written permission, often coupling an *ijāzat ʿāmma* to transmit his works with the bestowal of the *khirqa*.[5]

Throughout these works, Suhrawardī presents himself as a spokesmen for a particular *ṭāʾifa* who marked themselves out from other self-identified groups populating the Muslim body politic in certain ways, constantly reinforcing the point that what differentiates the *ṣūfiyya* from other *Personengruppen* (*ṭawāʾif*) is that they are in possession of something comprehensive and veridical, namely a body of sciences or knowledge (*ʿulūm*) which conserve and perpetuate the original dispensation in time and space in the most perfect and sound manner. In delineating and explicating this body of knowledge, Suhrawardī engages is a totalizing discourse, a discursive strategy which he strategically employed in other arenas as well where the sciences of the Sufis are scarcely even mentioned,[6] a strategy which in the case of the *ṣūfiyya* was simultaneously rooted in a genealogy, a metaphysics, a special technical language, and a praxis. For Suhrawardī, the *ṣūfiyya* were in possession of something comprehensive and totalizing, something perfect and veridical, something which no other *ṭāʾifa* could rightfully lay claim to and it was his job to consolidate, systematize, and enunciate this to the world.

In his *ʿAwārif al-maʿārif* in particular Suhrawardī expends a great deal of energy in trying to establish an identity and write a genealogy for the Sufis, systematically positioning their sciences within a larger complex of genealogies of knowledge, self-identified group commonalities, and contested claims to religious authority. His aim was to write a norm, to circumscribe the sciences of the Sufis (*ʿulūm al-ṣūfiyya/al-qawm*) both vertically through time and space and horizontally in the context of his own day and age. In systematically delineating this genealogy, Suhrawardī emplots his narrative as nothing less than a salvation history, arguing—from within the structure of religious and spiritual authority subsumed under the term 'bearers of knowledge' (*ʿulamāʾ*) as enunciated in the *ḥadīth* of heirship[7] which was understood to refer to the corporate body of 'religious professionals' (*ʿulamāʾ*) populating

[5] E.g., al-Suhrawardī, *Ijz. li-ʿAlī b. Aḥmad al-Rāzī*, MS. Süley., Musalla Medresesi 20_{13}, fol. 295b; and, idem, *Ijz. li-Bahāʾ al-Dīn Zakariyyā Multānī*, fol. 72a.

[6] In particular in his theological and philosophical polemics. On this, see Chapter Five.

[7] Based on the oft-quoted, and even more often contested, *ḥadīth*: "the 'bearers of knowledge' are the heirs of the prophets" (*inna ʾl-ʿulamāʾ warathatu ʾl-anbiyāʾ*). (A.J.

the Abode of Islam—that ultimately, spiritual, and thus soteriological, authority rested solely in the hands of a single *ṭāʾifa* and that this group, in fact, served as key actors in the process of perpetuating the original dispensation in time and space.

A number of themes emerge from his reading of this complex and the position of the Sufis within it. First, it is the *ṣūfiyya* who are the true 'heirs of the prophets' and not those whom Suhrawardī calls the worldly-ulama, for although the latter play an essential role in the maintenance and perpetuation of the original dispensation in what Suhrawardī envisioned to be a universal *jamāʿī-sunnī* Muslim community, they fall far short in their claims to heirship. Second, that the *ṣūfiyya* are possessed of specific characteristics which legitimize their claims of heirship, namely their perfect coupling of veridical knowledge with faultless praxis. Third, that the sciences of the *ṣūfiyya* themselves are but a particular articulation of a universal Adamic knowledge and praxis which the Prophet Muḥammad vouchsafed to his immediate companions, a knowledge which was subsequently passed down from generation to generation up to Suhrawardī's own day and age. Fourth, that this very knowledge is encoded in the Sunna of the Prophet and the exempla of the *salaf al-ṣāliḥ*, and that the *ṣūfiyya* are the ones who possess both the key and the authority to revivify it in time and space. Fifth, that the *ṣūfiyya* themselves are differentiated intra-communally in terms of individual grades of spiritual attainment and the hierarchy of authority which that entails. Sixth, that the *ṣūfiyya* are differentiated from other group commonalities and types of individuals who either claim to belong to them or are considered as such by society at large.

The Ursprung *of Knowledge*

In the first chapter of the *ʿAwārif al-maʿārif*, entitled "On the Origin of the Sciences of the Sufis", Suhrawardī cites a *ḥadīth* in which the Prophet likens the knowledge (*ʿilm*) and guidance (*hudā*) which God has charged him to dispatch to an abundant rain shower, a portion of which falls upon fertile ground which then yields verdant herbage, a portion of which is caught in cisterns and is then parceled out by men for various life-sustaining purposes, while the remaining portion simply falls upon

Wensinck, *Concordance et indicies de la tradition musulmane* [Leiden: E.J. Brill, 1936–1971]: 4:321; al-Ghazālī, *Iḥyāʾ*, 1:15–16; and, *AdM*, 22/Milson, *Sufi Rule*, 39).

dead earth and yields nothing.[8] In an extended commentary on this *ḥadīth* and the Qurʾānic verse, "He sends down water from the heavens and the channels flow each according to their measure",[9] Suhrawardī builds up an argument which reads the two as a metaphor for the disposition of the original dispensation in time and space, likening those 'learned in religion' (*al-faqīh fī ʾl-dīn*) to the fields upon which the rain shower of knowledge and guidance falls and their hearts to the water channels through which it flows.

Like Ghazālī, Suhrawardī singles out two groups in particular as recipients of this rain shower of guidance and knowledge, the first being a group whom he calls the conventional and worldly-ulama, in particular the jurists (*fuqahāʾ*), scholars of the Ḥadīth (*aʾimma al-ḥadīth*), and Qurʾānic exegetes (*ʿulamāʾ al-tafsīr*), while the second are those whom he calls the 'Sufis from among the world-renouncing scholars and the Sufi masters' (*al-ʿulamāʾ al-zāhidīn fī ʾl-dunyā min al-ṣūfiyya wa-l-shuyūkh*), or simply the 'otherworldly-ulama'.[10] Although each group receives the rainfall of the dispensation, they do so only according to the relative capacities of their particular vessels, which in reference to the Qurʾānic verse are qualified by their respective ability to receive and retain the water. The worldly-ulama are like the fertile lands which absorb the rain shower and yield a verdant herbage, benefiting the community through the various religious sciences which they cultivate, conserving and perpetuating the externals of the original dispensation in time and space, without however comprehending its internal dimensions. The latter group on the other hand serve as the cisterns which collect and preserve the live-giving water of knowledge, internalize its verities, and then distribute it to humankind as guidance.[11]

---

[8] *ʿAM*, 1:143–144/*GE*, 1.2; the *ḥadīth* is cited in Ibn al-Ṣiddīq, *ʿAwāṭif al-laṭāʾif min aḥādīth ʿawārif al-maʿārif*, ed. Idrīs al-Kamdānī and Muḥammad Maḥmūd al-Muṣṭafā (Mecca: al-Maktabat al-Makkiyya, 2001), 1:6; idem, *Ghaniyyat al-ʿāwārif*, ed. idem (Mecca: al-Maktabat al-Makkiyya, 2001), 1:13–14; see also al-Ghazālī, *Iḥyāʾ*, 1:21.

[9] Qurʾān 13:17.

[10] *ʿAM*, 1:144–147/*GE*, 1.3–8; cf. al-Ghazālī, *Iḥyāʾ*, 1:73–88 (in which he enumerates eight primary characteristics of the otherworldly-ulama); Suhrawardī calls the elect among this group, the 'fully-actualized scholars' (*al-ʿulamāʾ al-muḥaqqiqūn*). (*JQb*, fol. 2a, 6a); but, cf. Abū ʾl-Najīb Suhrawardī who singles out three *ṣinf*, the *ḥadīth* transmitters (*aṣḥāb al-ḥadīth*), jurists (*fuqahāʾ*), and Sufi scholars (*ʿulamāʾ al-ṣūfiyya*) (*AdM*, 14/Milson, *Rule*, 34).

[11] *ʿAM*, 1:147–149/*GE*, 1.12–13. This entails a number of things, most notably translating what one has come to know into direct action which in the case of the world-renouncing *ʿālim* means perpetuating the prophetic function of 'moral guidance' (*hudā*) through admonishment (*indhār*), the 'most perfect and highest station' of

In contradistinction to the worldly-ulama, the cisternal hearts of the world-renouncing Sufi scholars are able to receive and retain the rain shower of knowledge and distribute the water of guidance because they are sound, having been made spotless and pure through renunciation of the world and the perfection of the ethical quality of god-fearing piety (*taqwā*).[12] This group of world-renouncing scholars are like the conventional ulama in terms of having taken a share of discursive knowledge (*ʿilm al-dirāsa*) but are unlike them in that they couple discursive knowledge with inherited knowledge (*ʿilm al-wirātha*), the Adamic inheritance bequeathed to the Prophet which allows them to see things as they truly are.[13] In turn, this state is predicated upon the Sufis' disposition for diligent attunement (*ḥuṣn al-istimāʿ*) to the significances of the revelation as contained within the Qurʾān and Ḥadīth,[14] finding in every verse of the former "an ocean possessed of both exoteric and esoteric significances" and in the latter an inspired speech which concretizes its verities in a model of exemplary behavior and praxis.[15]

These significances, however, can only be grasped once the fires of the 'soul commanding to evil' (*al-nafs al-ammārat bi-sūʾ*) have been extinguished by the water of knowledge and guidance and its position as the instrument through which the specificities of the revelation are cognized is replaced with that of the heart (*qalb*), an epistemic shift obtained through systematically rejecting the world and its vanities and perfecting the quality of *taqwā*.[16] Barring divine intervention (which according to Suhrawardī represents a valid way of reaching this state) such a position is achieved only through a particular set of sciences

---

those learned in religion (*al-faqīh fī ʾl-dīn*). In the *Jadhdhāb al-qulūb* Suhrawardī explains how this guidance is effected through the art of public preaching (fol. 12b–13a; *ʿAM*, 2:332/*GE*, 63.25; idem, *W. li-Naṣīr al-Dīn al-Baghdādī*, MS. Süley., Şehid Ali Paşa 1393_6, fol. 64b).

12 *ʿAM*, 1:145–146/*GE*, 1.5; cf. *JQb*, fol. 7b–8a.

13 *ʿAM*, 1:151–153/*GE*, 1.18–22; idem, *W. li-Naṣīr al-Dīn al-Baghdādī*, fol. 65a. The classic expression of this idea and what it entails is found in al-Junayd's letter to ʿAmr b. ʿUthmān al-Makkī and, to a lesser degree, in his letter to Abū Yaʿqūb al-Rāzī (*The Life, Personality and Writings of al-Junayd*, ed. & trans. A.H. Abdel-Kader [London: Luzac & Co., 1962], 127–147, 7–26 [Arabic text] & 147–151, 27–30 [Arabic text]) the vision, although perhaps not the nuance, of which is wholly replicated by Suhrawardī in his discourse on the subject.

14 The general subject of the second chapter of the *ʿAwārif* (1:155–169/*GE*, 2.1–26).

15 *ʿAM*, 1:149, 155, 161–165/*GE*, 1.13, 2.2 & 12–18.

16 Ibid., 1:155–156/*GE*, 2.3; *HT*, fol. 93a–94b; and, idem, *W. li-Naṣīr al-Dīn al-Baghdādī*, fol. 64a.

(*ʿulūm*), a body of knowledge which in his day and age was the sole possession of the *ṣūfiyya*.

The Sciences of the Sufis

As a member of the ulama, Suhrawardī situated himself and these sciences within a broader discourse of learning and the pursuit of knowledge (*ṭalab al-ʿilm*), considering it to be a religious duty (*farīḍa/farḍ*) and citing various authorities on exactly what types of knowledge one is duty bound to seek. For his part, Suhrawardī explicitly states that his inclination is to agree with Abū Ṭālib al-Makkī, namely that what is obligatory for every Muslim (as per the *ḥadīths* "seek knowledge be it as far as China" and "the pursuit of knowledge is an obligation for every Muslim")[17] is limited to knowledge of the five pillars and knowledge of 'commanding the right and forbidding the wrong'.[18] For the world-renouncing ulama and the Sufi masters (*mashāyikh al-ṣūfiyya*), however, who pour all they have into pursuing the knowledge of obligatory actions through their virtue of steadfastness (*istiqāma*), the pursuit of the 'sciences of the folk' (*ʿulūm al-qawm*) are considered to be an obligatory religious duty (*farḍ*), even though they are not obligatory upon others.[19]

What differentiates these sciences, and there are many, from the discursive sciences of the worldly-ulama is that they are experiential sciences (*ʿulūm dhawqiyya*) which like the sweetness of sugar cannot be described discursively, but must be tasted; they cannot be learned anywhere save in the '*madrasa* of *taqwā*' and cannot be accessed save through the practice of renunciation.[20] It is only through the perfection of renunciation and *taqwā* that internal spiritual purity is effected, transforming the individual into the Qurʾānic paragon of the 'one firmly-rooted in knowledge' (*rāsikh fī ʾl-ʿilm*), an epistemic state which simultaneously comprehends the apparent meanings and significations of discursively apprehensible knowledge while at the same time allowing for the direct apprehension of the ontological significances underlying

[17] *ʿAM*, 1:171, 282–283/*GE*, 1.3, 16.2; the two of which Suhrawardī conjoins as "seek knowledge be it as far as China for (*fa-inna*) the pursuit of knowledge is obligatory upon every Muslim". Extensive references to the sources for both by Ibn al-Ṣiddīq in *ʿAwāṭif*, 1:53–58; and, idem, *Ghaniyyat*, 1:48–53.

[18] *ʿAM*, 1:170–175/*GE*, 3.1–11; *JQb*, fol. 3b; and, Abū Ṭālib al-Makkī, *Qūt al-qulūb*, 1:265/Gramlich (trans.), *Die Nahrung*, 31.8; cf. al-Ghazālī, *Iḥyāʾ*, 1:25.

[19] *ʿAM*, 1:174–177, 1:187/*GE*, 3.11–15, 3.32; *JQb*, fol. 7b.

[20] *ʿAM*, 1:179, 182/*GE*, 3.18, 3.22.

them.[21] In a letter to the famous theologian and exegete Fakhr al-Dīn al-Rāzī (d. 606/1209), Suhrawardī places himself and his addressee in this category, saying:

> God's favor has been made great for he who has been appointed to disseminate knowledge in this era, and it is necessary for the clever sages among the masters of religion to persist in righteous supplication so that God Most High will make his religion and knowledge pure through the verities of *taqwā*...and this is the level of those 'firmly rooted in knowledge' and they are the heirs of the prophets (*wurrāth al-anbiyā*ʾ); those who have refined their knowledge (*ʿulūm*) with praxis (*aʿmāl*) and their praxis with knowledge until their praxis has become purified and made subtle, their nightly conversations mystical, and their daily conversations spiritual; those whose praxis assumes the form of knowledge and knowledge the form of praxis.[22]

These sciences or bodies of knowledge (*ʿulūm*) are, of course, the inherited knowledge (*ʿilm al-wirātha*) spoken of earlier, which Suhrawardī likens to butter extracted from pure milk, the milk being the discursive sciences (*ʿulūm al-dirāsa*) and its quintessence, the butter, inherited knowledge; or put in another way the relationship between the two is like that between simple submission to the divine law (*islām*) and true faith in its reality (*īmān*), the former in its focus on externals being the domain of the discursive sciences (*ʿulūm al-lisān*) and the domain of the worldly-ulama, and the latter in its focus on internal belief being the sciences of the heart (*ʿulūm al-qulūb*) and the domain of the otherworldly-ulama.[23]

The way in which the *ṣūfiyya* actually came into possession of these sciences is a matter which Suhrawardī discusses at some length. Directly quoting the standard Junaydī sources, he points out that even the paragons of the past debated the derivation of the words *taṣawwuf* and *ṣūfī*, some attributing it the precedent of past prophets wearing wool (*ṣūf*) as a sign of their rejection of the vanities of the world, some deriving it from the *ahl al-ṣaffa* meaning those who occupy the first row (in the mosque), and some attributing it to the 'Folk/Companions of the Veranda' (*ahl/aṣḥāb al-ṣuffa*) of the time of the Prophet Muḥammad.[24]

---

[21] Ibid., 1:172–175, 2:315/*GE*, 3.22–28, 62.2; and, *JQb*, fol. 13b. The reference is to Qurʾān 3:7, 4:162.

[22] al-Suhrawardī, *R. ilā Fakhr al-Dīn al-Rāzī*, MS. Süley., H. Hüsnü Paşa $585_{\text{mü/6}}$, fol. 220a; cf., idem, *W. li-Naṣīr al-Dīn al-Baghdādī*, fol. 64a.

[23] *ʿAM*, 1:175–176/*GE*, 3.30–31.

[24] Ibid., 1:209–214/*GE*, 6.1–8; idem, *Irshād al-murīdīn wa-injād al-ṭālibīn*, MS. Süley., Şehid Ali Paşa 1397_1, fol. 29b–30a; *Suh.*, 89–95; cf. al-Kalābādhī, *K. al-taʿarruf li-madh-*

Neither words are found in the Qur᾽ān or the Ḥadīth, and following Qushayrī, Suhrawardī situates its appearance as an appellative coined before the close of the 2nd/8th century, defining it as the model behavior and spiritual insight which the Prophet transmitted to his immediate companions (*ṣaḥāba*) and they to their successors (*tābiʿūn*).

According to this narrative, after this there ensued a period of fragmentation and struggle among various groups, each with its own claims and opinions. Out of this, one *ṭāʾifa* in particular distinguished themselves through their pious actions, illuminated spiritual states, and renunciation of the world and its vanities, gathering together in the corners of mosques (*zawāyā*) in the manner of the 'Folk of the Veranda', developing a specific science (*ʿilm*) and technical language (*iṣṭilāḥāt*) to delineate and describe that which had been passed down to them, something which they in turn passed on to the generations following the *salaf al-ṣāliḥ* up to Suhrawardī's own day and age.[25]

In his works, Suhrawardī tends to organize these 'Sciences of the Folk' (*ʿulūm al-qawm*) in an hierarchical scheme, clustering them in such a way so that they correspond with his vision of the gradated nature of individuals vis-à-vis the reception and disposition of the original dispensation in time and space while at the same time drawing them into a specific relationship with the particular practices of his own *ribāṭ*-based Sufi system. Although certainly enumerated elsewhere, it is in the 8th chapter of the *ʿAwārif al-maʿārif*, entitled "On Explaining the Excellencies of the Sciences of the Sufis", where Suhrawardī enumerates his most comprehensive list of these obligatory sciences (*ʿulūm farḍ*), the first cluster of which, naturally enough, is concerned with the very thing which differentiates the otherworldly and world-renouncing ulama from the worldly-ulama, the purity of their souls and the soundness of their hearts.

Delineated along the same threefold scheme as his conception of the Sufi path, this synopsis begins with what he sees to be the most precious of the Sciences of the Folk, the 'science of the carnal soul and the knowledge of it and its behaviors' (*ʿilm al-nafs wa-maʿrifatihā wa-maʿrifat akhlāqihā*). Comprising, among other things, knowledge of the subtle desires and hidden passions of the soul, its voracity, evil intentions, and

hab ahl al-taṣawwuf, ed. A.J. Arberry (Cairo: Khānjī, 1938), 21–23/English translation by Arberry as *The Doctrine of the Ṣūfīs* (Cambridge: Cambridge University Press, 1935), 5–9; *SL*, 14.4–5; *KM*, 34–41/Nicholson, *The Kashf*, 31–35; *SQ*, 41.1–2.

[25] *ʿAM*, 1:215–216/*GE*, 6.11–12; *PGB*, 256–257.

destructive inclinations, this science provides a means by which one can subjugate it by identifying and then limiting its influence. This is not only the most characteristic science of the *ṣūfiyya* but also represents the beginning of their path (*ṭarīq*). Following this is the 'science of passing thoughts' (*ʿilm al-khawāṭir*), a body of knowledge comprised of things such as how to identify and deal with the sinful inner motivations and passing fancies which distract from one's advancement on that path. Here, the sciences of 'scrupulous examination and observation' (*ʿilm al-muḥāsaba wa-l-riʿāya*) and 'vigilant awareness' (*ʿilm al-murāqaba*) are paramount, providing the means through which the aspirant can cultivate both the outer and inner stability necessary to perfect his knowledge of 'the verities of trust in God' (*ʿilm ḥaqāʾiq al-tawakkul*). This cluster of sciences belongs to the beginning of the medial stage of the Sufi path. After this comes sciences such as 'the science of contentment' (*ʿilm al-riḍā*), 'renunciation; (*ʿilm al-zuhd*), 'renunciation of renunciation' (*maʿrifat al-zuhd fī ʾl-zuhd*), the science of 'turning [to God] and seeking refuge [with Him]' (*ʿilm al-ināba wa-l-iltijāʾ*), and the 'science of divine love' (*ʿilm al-maḥabba*) among others. This cluster of sciences are subsumed under the latter medial stage of the Sufi path. The final cluster is comprised of the 'sciences of direct witnessing' (*ʿulūm al-mushāhadāt*) and is the domain of the 'Masters of Divine Verities' (*arbāb al-ḥaqāʾiq*), comprising the final and most advanced of the sciences of the Sufis.[26]

Mapping Boundaries

This does not mean of course that the experiences which these sciences capture do not antedate this time, they most certainly do, for according to Suhrawardī as an appellative of particular individuals, the term *ṣūfī* is a cognate to those individuals whom the Qurʾān describes as 'the patient'

[26] *ʿAM*, 1:177–179/*GE*, 3.15–18; and, idem, *W. li-Naṣīr al-Dīn al-Baghdādī*, fol. 63b–64a. According to Suhrawardī, the last cluster is comprised of sciences such as those of awe (*ʿilm al-hayba*), intimacy (*uns*), contraction and expansion (*al-qabḍ wa-l-basṭ*) and the differences between contraction and 'worry' (*hamm*), expansion and 'cheerfulness' (*nashāṭ*), annihilation and subsistence (*al-fanāʾ wa-l-baqāʾ*) and the differences in the states of annihilation; 'veiling' (*istitār*) and theophany (*tajallī*), union and separation (*al-jamʿ wa-l-farq*), 'flashes' (*lawāmiʿ*), 'risings' (*ṭawāliʿ*), and 'pangs' (*bawādī*), sobriety (*ṣaḥw*) and intoxication (*sukr*), and so forth and so on. Although lengthy, this enumeration is compressed as Suhrawardī himself states: "if time had permitted we would explain all of what we have mentioned in some volumes (*majalladāt*), but life is short and time precious, so this then is the author's compendium (*mukhtaṣar*) of the 'Sciences of the Folk'." (*ʿAM*, 2:179/*GE*, 3.18); cf. Abū ʾl-Najīb al-Suhrawardī who also sticks closely to this hierarchical enumeration (*AdM*, 14–15/Milson, *Rule*, 35).

(*ṣābirūn*), 'the sincere' (*ṣādiqūn*), 'those who recollect' (*dhākirūn*), and most notably those who are 'drawn nigh [to God]', the *muqarrabūn*:

> Know that every noble state which we attribute to the Sufis in this book is the state of the one 'drawn nigh' (*muqarrab*). The '*ṣūfī*' is the '*muqarrab*', and the term '*ṣūfī*' is not found in the Qur'ān, but rather has been coined to refer to the '*muqarrab*' as we will explain in the appropriate chapter. Furthermore, in the far corners of the lands of Islam, east and west, the Folk Drawn Nigh are normally not known by this name, although 'those who copy them' (*mutarassimūn*) often are. How numerous have been the *muqarrabūn* in the western lands and the regions of Turkistan, Transoxiana, and Farghāna who were not known by this term because they did not dress in the dress of the Sufis; and there is no quarrel over words. Know then that what we mean by the term *ṣūfiyya* are the *muqarrabūn* and that all of the eponymous authorities (*mashāyikh*) of the Sufis who are named in the *Ṭabaqāt* [of al-Sulamī] and in other such books pursued the path of those drawn nigh and that their sciences are the sciences of the states of the *muqarrabīn*.[27]

Whereas the *muqarrabūn* are the paragons and ideal models of the fully actualized Sufi, it is in another Qur'ānic verse "...God chooses for Himself those whom He pleases and guides to Himself those who turn [to Him]"[28] where Suhrawardī finds an allusion to the entire corporate body of the *ṣūfiyya* as they existed in his own day, maintaining that there are only two *ṭā'ifa*s who can rightly claim membership within its ranks, a membership which is ontologically determined and which, theoretically, is only diagnosable by an accomplished Sufi master. These are

[27] Ibid., 1:154/*GE*, 1.23. The term is drawn from the Qur'ān (3:45, 4:172, 7:114, 26:42, 56:11, 56:88, 83:21 & 28). Throughout his writings, Suhrawardī makes a distinction between the *muqarrabūn* and the godly (*abrār*), positioning the former above the latter in terms of their higher spiritual attainments and relative rarity. In his *Futūḥ* I, for instance, he employs the figure of each to explain the distinction between merely dealing with the machinations of the soul and actually conquering it, saying: "...among men there are two paths of escape from the turbidity of the characteristics of the soul and its behaviors: that of the *abrār* and that of the *muqarrabūn*. As for the *abrār*, when the soul is roused into action by its characteristics and bad behaviors such as malice, jealously, and spite...their inner state whispers to them the knowledge of how to handle it, and they embark on the path of contentment (*riḍā*) by compliance (*qaḍā'*) and submission (*taslīm*), just as the Master has commanded...as for the *muqarrabūn*, however, they directly perceive the attachments of the soul in its agitation and the manifestations of its behaviors and characteristics...and because they have been divested of the shirt of existence and clothed in the garment of the light of proximity, the attachments of the soul do not bother them. Indeed, they are thinly spread throughout the earth and are rarer than red sulfur." (MS. Tüb., Ma VI 90_{12}, fol. 80a; and, idem, *W. li-Naṣīr al-Dīn al-Baghdādī*, fol. 63b–64a).

[28] Qur'ān 42:13.

the two basic classes from which all others derive, namely those who are 'desired by God' (*murād*) and those who 'desire Him' (*murīd*).

The first group, God's 'desired beloveds' (*al-maḥbūb al-murād*), are those who have been favored through 'sheer selection' (*al-ijtibā' al-ṣirf/maḥḍ*) without any choice or effort on their own part, experiencing unveiling immediately, mysteriously, and without having striven to obtain it. Contrary to the generality of Sufis, the desired beloveds traverse the path in an inverted manner, beginning with unveiling and mystical knowing (*ma'rifa*) and ending with the acts of pious self-exertion (*mujāhadāt*) characteristic of the lower stages of the path.[29] The second group are those who desire God, turning to Him in eager anticipation of their moment of unveiling, those who when they reach the goal are characterized not as beloveds but rather as 'lovers' (*muḥibb*).[30] As Suhrawardī describes it: "the end of the affair of the lovers is the beginning of the affair of the beloveds",[31] for in contradistinction to them their unveiling is effected through action, specifically through adhering to the obligations and conditions which God has established as the path of approach to Him, beginning with the exercise of pious self-exertion and then proceeding through the various stages of the Sufi path.

In addition to these two groups, Suhrawardī identifies two types of individuals whose paths are not counted among the 'ways of realization by Sufism' (*ṭuruq al-taḥqīq bi-l-taṣawwuf*). The first of these are a variation of the *murādūn*, those who are simply 'pulled to God' (*majdhūb*), but unlike then do not return to pious striving after their unveiling. The second is the 'striving worshipper' (*mujtahid muta'abbid*), individuals who are simply not granted an unveiling despite their pious strivings. In a similar manner, although Suhrawardī considers voluntary poverty (*faqr*) to be Sufism's foundation and point of departure, he is careful to differentiate Sufism from both voluntary poverty and asceticism (*zuhd*) as ends in and of themselves. Rather, he maintains that the qualities of each are subsumed under the term Sufism (*taṣawwuf*) which, as a collective noun, comprises and comprehends the qualities of both while at the same time adding to them, coupling, for instance, the abandonment

[29] *'AM*, 1:196–197/*GE*, 4.8–9; idem, *Futūḥ* VI, MS. Süley., Şehid Ali Paşa 1393_{10}, fol. 69b; and, idem, *W. li-Naṣīr al-Dīn al-Baghdādī*, fol. 65b–66b.

[30] *'AM*, 1:196, 2:334/*GE*, 4:8, 63.32.

[31] Idem, *Futūḥ* VI, fol. 70a.

of material possessions and worldly achievement with the abandonment of one's desire for such things.[32]

As with the hierarchical nature of the responses and reactions of those who are confronted with the original dispensation among the generality of Muslims (*ʿāmm*), the worldly-, and the otherworldly-ulama, there are also various grades of Sufis, each representing both a stage and a stopping point on the Sufi path.[33] The lowest grade is that of the 'pretender' (*mutashabbih*), an individual who out of love for the Sufis desires to be close to them but whose inability to persevere in their way precludes him from advancing on the path. This individual, however, is neither to be blamed nor disparaged, for his desire is a noble one, a result of the awakening of his spirit by an encounter with the enlightened spirits of the Folk of Proximity, his own proximity to whom is, in and of itself, of benefit to him. He is the possessor of *īmān*, the first foundation of the Sufi path, and is at the station of watching over his soul through pious self-exertion (*mujāhada*) and scrupulous examination (*muḥāsaba*), although his spiritual state is not subjected to change (*talwīn*).[34]

The second grade is the 'one who aspires to become a Sufi' (*mutaṣawwif*), an individual who is waiting to obtain the state of Sufihood. The defining characteristic of this group is that they have made a conscious and deliberate choice to become a formal disciple (*murīd*) of a Sufi master (*shaykh*) and pursue his path. Consequently, this group is composed of various grades beginning with the novice (*mubtadiʾ*).[35] The medial stage (*mutawwasiṭ*), is the *mutaṣawwif* who is a possessor of knowledge (*ʿilm*), comprehending both the state of the *mutashabbih* and *mubtadiʾ* in terms of possessing *īmān* and formal adherence to the path while at the same time standing below the Sufi in terms of not yet having obtained the level of direct tasting (*dhawq*). Generally, Suhrawardī refers to this group as the possessors of spiritual states (*arbāb al-aḥwāl*), placing them at the station of vigilant awareness (*murāqaba*) and characterizing them

---

[32] *ʿAM*, 1:203–205/*GE*, 5.6–7; idem, *W. li-Naṣīr al-Dīn al-Baghdādī*, fol. 66b; and, *Suh.*, 98–104, 294–295. On the idea of the *madhjūb* see: Gramlich, *Derwischorden*, 2:189–194; and, idem, "Madjdhūb," *EI*², 5:1029.

[33] *ʿAM*, 1:217–221 & 242–243/*GE*, 7.3–6 & 10.16–20.

[34] Ibid., 1:220/*GE*, 7.6; and, *Suh.*, 104–106.

[35] *ʿAM*, 2:323–329/*GE*, 63.2–19; same in Abū ʾl-Najīb al-Suhrawardī who refers to the *mubtadiʾ* simply as the *murīd*. (*AdM*, 16/Milson, *Rule*, 35).

by the changeability of their spiritual states, first in the realm of the soul and, once they have advanced, in the realm of the heart.[36]

The final grade is the *ṣūfī* properly speaking, those who are among the possessors of verities (*arbāb al-ḥaqāʾiq*), tasting, and direct apprehension (*mushāhada*). These are those who have reached the goal (*muntahī*) and in contrast to the *mutaṣawwif*, their spiritual state is characterized by its fixity (*tamkīn*) and resistance to changeability.[37] Both the outer (*ẓāhir*) and inner (*bāṭin*) beings of this group, who Suhrawardī describes as the 'possessors of endings' (*arbāb al-nihāyāt*), are permanently settled in God and their spirits are completely free of the *nafs*, being those who serve to guide others on the path through the completeness of their knowledge and the perfection of their spiritual insight.[38] It is this final group which not only represent the otherworldly-ulama but also those individuals who serve as the masters of the lower tiers of seekers, having reached this particular state constituting the *sine qua non* of shaykhood (*mashyakha*). Although gradated, according to Suhrawardī each of these groups belong to the 'circle of the chosen' (*dāʾirat al-iṣṭifāʾ*) and each are counted among those who will achieve success and salvation in the Hereafter, being distinguished only through what they have been granted and what they have taken.[39]

At the same time, there were other *ṭawāʾif* associated with Sufism which Suhrawardī took pains to distinguish from the *ṣūfiyya* themselves. In his description of these groups, which is clearly articulated in the generic form of the heresiography, he singles out three main *Personengruppen* who either deliberately associated themselves with the *ṣūfiyya* or were understood as such in the mind of the public, arguing that they

[36] *ʿAM*, 1:220, 2:322, 334/*GE*, 7.6, 62.22, 30; *Suh.*, 106–107; and, *AdM*, 16/Milson, *Rule*, 35.

[37] *ʿAM*, 1:220, 2:322/*GE*, 7.6, 62.22; and, *AdM*, 16/Milson, *Rule*, 35.

[38] *ʿAM*, 2:329–330/*GE*, 63.20–21.

[39] Such three-fold gradations are common in the literature, viz. Hujwīrī: *ṣūfī-mutaṣawwif-mustaṣwif*, the latter being used pejoratively (*KM*, 39–40/Nicholson, *The Kashf*, 34–35); Abū ʾl-Najīb al-Suhrawardī: *murīd-mutawassiṭ-ʿārif/muntahī* (*AdM*, 16ff./Milson, *Rule*, 35ff.; and, Najm al-Dīn Kubrā: *mubtadiʾ-mutawassiṭ-muntahī* (*Fawāʾiḥ*, ed. Meier, 87; same with al-Simnānī [Jamal Elias, *The Throne Carrier of God: The Life and Thought of ʿAlāʾ ad-Dawla as-Simnānī* (Albany, NY: State University of New York Press, 1995), 116]), but are not standard. While differentiating between various levels of attainment, for instance, the great 7th/13th-century Sufi and theosophist ʿAzīz-i Nasafī drew a clear distinction between the Sufis and the Folk of Unity (*ahl-i waḥdat*), both of whom stand above the ulama and the philosophers (Lloyd Ridgeon, *Persian Metaphysics and Mysticism: Selected Treatises of ʿAziz Nasafī* [Richmond: Curzon Press, 2002], 14ff.).

neither belonged to nor could be counted among them. The first group are the Malāmatiyya, a loosely structured Khurāsānī ascetic movement first appearing in the 3rd/9th century in Nīshāpūr whom Suhrawardī seems to have known primarily through al-Sulamī's *R. al-malāmatiyya* (which he quotes directly in the *ʿAwārif al-maʿārif*) as well as claiming that in his day a group (*ṭāʾifa*) of them were active in Khurāsān and that in Iraq he personally had contact with devotees of their school, although they did not go by this specific name in the region.[40] As described by Suhrawardī (through al-Sulamī), the Malāmatiyya are those who 'incur blame' by concealing their spiritual states and pious acts while at the same time publicly revealing blameworthy behaviors, considering overt secrecy to be a mark of true inner sincerity (*ikhlāṣ*), a quality which he lauds as praiseworthy but one which he argues is already comprehended by the Sufis who transcend the outward dimensions of sincerity by internalizing its verities. This, however, does not mean that the Malāmatiyya are to be disparaged all together, and he distinguishes between the true *malāmatī*, whom he situates ahead of the *mutaṣawwif* but behind the Sufi, and an altogether unspecified group of 'seducers' (*maftūnūn*) who call themselves 'Malāmatiyya' and dress in the style of the Sufis, claiming an affiliation but actually having nothing in common with them.[41]

In contrast to the Malāmatiyya, who in Suhrawardī's view possess a noble spiritual state and distinguished spiritual station because they adhere to the Sunna of the Prophet and the exempla of the *salaf al-ṣāliḥ*, stand a second group, the antinomian Qalandariyya, whom we have already met in the figure of the Damascene *muwallah* ʿAlī al-Kurdī. According to Suhrawardī, like ʿAlī al-Kurdī in his nakedness the Qalandariyya are those who systematically flout established social customs (*ʿādāt*) and have only minimal respect for the divine law, focusing their efforts solely on maintaining the 'tranquility of their hearts' (*ṭībat qulūbihim*) through complete disinterest in the gaze of society. For Suhrawardī, this mode of piety is sharply contrasted with that of the Sufis, who in contradistinction to both the Malāmatiyya and the

---

[40] *ʿAM*, 1:228–229/*GE*, 8.8–11; and, *Suh.*, 209–210. Specifically, Suhrawardī quotes Sulamī's account of the Malāmatī attitude towards *samāʿ* and their idea of a fourfold *dhikr* (*R. al-malāmatiyya*, in *al-Malāmatiyya wa-l-ṣūfiyya wa-ahl al-futuwwa*, ed. Abū ʾl-ʿAlāʾ ʿAfīfī [Cairo: Dār Iḥyāʾ al-Kutub al-ʿArabiyya, 1945], 103–104].

[41] *ʿAM*, 1:225–230, 232/*GE*, 8.1–8.12, 9.4.

Qalandariyya put everything in its proper place, concealing and showing only what is appropriate, every action being guided by their perfectly cultivated virtues and strict adherence to the dictates of the *sharīʿa* and the Sunna of the Prophet.[42]

In addition to these groups, Suhrawardī singles out those who subscribe to the doctrine of incarnation (*ḥulūl*), arguing those who maintain such a doctrine have lapsed into heresy (*zandaqa*).[43] At the same time, however, he defends the 'ecstatic elocutions' (*shaṭaḥāt*) of both al-Ḥallāj and al-Bisṭāmī, saying:

> God forbid that we believe that Abū Yazīd said that [i.e., *ṣubḥānī*—'glory be to me'] except in the sense that he related these words from God Almighty (*ʿalā maʿnā al-ḥikāyat ʿan Allāh taʿālā*). Likewise, it is appropriate to understand the words of al-Ḥallāj [i.e., *anā ʾl-ḥaqq*—'I am the Truth'] in the same way. If we would know that such words concealed some kind of incarnationism, then we would reject them just as we reject the incarnationsts.[44]

Although he does not apply a name to them, at the end of this chapter the same is said for another *ṭāʾifa* who, like the Qalandariyya, systematically flout the dictates of the *sharīʿa*, justifying their actions by maintaining that they are involuntarily compelled by God to behave in such a manner. For Suhrawardī, they are nothing but heretics who in transgressing the limits and rulings of the *sharīʿa* voluntarily depart from the Muslim community.

The Interior Dimension

It is also clear that for Suhrawardī the production, conservation, and dissemination of texts was neither an exercise in documenting abstract ideas or personal spiritual experiences nor merely an academic exercise in commentary and exegesis, but rather part of a larger program of

---

[42] Ibid., 1:231–233/*GE*, 9.1–5; *Suh.*, 209–210; and, Karamustafa, *God's Unruly Friends*, 34–36.

[43] *ʿAM*, 1:233–235/*GE*, 9.7–9. Incarnationism, or the indwelling of two spirits in one body, was often associated with Christian doctrine and here Suhrawardī provides an objection to *ḥulūl* on the grounds that it derives from 'the Christian doctrine of the *lāhūt* and *nāsūt*'. (Ibid., 1:234/*GE*, 9.7; and, *Suh.*, 210)

[44] *ʿAM*, 1:234/*GE*, 9.7; and, *Suh.*, 119–120. For his part, al-Yāfiʿī includes Suhrawardī among those who accepted al-Ḥallāj on the basis of the allegorical interpretation (*taʾwīl*) of his *shaṭaḥāt*. (*MJ*, 2:253)

consolidation and centralization expressed in the form of a broader discourse which was unified and totalizing in its vision and systematic in its articulation. Posterity has remembered Suhrawardī as a number of things, first and foremost as a paragonic *shaykh al-tarbiya* and systematizer of a *ribāṭ*-based Sufi system which exerted a decisive influence on subsequent articulations of Sufi religiosity throughout Islamdom in the period following the rise of the Sufi brotherhoods. Although the praxis, organization, and complex of social behaviors of the Sufi *ribāṭ* certainly constitute a major theme of his writings, by no stretch of the imagination is it the only one, nor can his contribution to this particular genre of Sufi literature be understood without reference to his other works. There are, in fact, a number of central themes which Suhrawardī treats again and again throughout his *oeuvre*, themes which on the surface seem to have little to do with the particular concerns of the denizens of the Sufi *ribāṭ* but, when read as a whole, present a consistent and coherent argument which in the end has everything to do with that particular 'institution of place' and the 'institutions of process' which define it.

Although Suhrawardī was undoubtedly a premier systematizer of organization and praxis, his written works evince that he was also a deeply mystical thinker. In contradistinction to individuals such as Ḥakīm al-Tirmidhī or Ibn ʿArabī, however, this dimension of his thought is not so easily divorced from the broader vision structuring his program. For Suhrawardī, the sciences of the Sufis were not only authorized and legitimated through a genealogy and a replicable model of exemplary praxis but also through a comprehensive ontology and metaphysics. Maintaining that existential location serves—over and against the usual socio-religious and ideological demarcations—as a factor in the classification of certain *ṭāʾifa*s, opens up a powerful discursive space, and Suhrawardī took full advantage of the possibilities which such a space offered. In writing this ontology and metaphysics, Suhrawardī employed the same rhetorical strategies and modes of emplotment which informed his other works, asserting exegetical authority over contested proof-texts and articulating his vision in pre-established generic categories. While it is quite evident that Suhrawardī distinguished between what we might call the 'practical' and what we might call the 'theoretical' in many of his writings, when read as a whole it is not difficult to see how deeply the former is woven into the latter and that, in fact, neither can be fully understood without reference to the other. As shown in the following chapter, in many ways it is ultimately the 'theoretical' which frames and directs the 'practical' and the 'practical' which embodies and gives form and definition to the 'theoretical'.

It is, of course, the well-worn narrative of 'origin and return' which serves as the primary thematic frame for Suhrawardī's exposition of the sciences of the Sufis in their ontological and metaphysical dimension, an ancient narrative well known to all theosophical, gnostic, and mystical traditions of the Mediterranean Basin, a narrative which Suhrawardī chose to emplot as an Islamic salvation history. For Suhrawardī, the manner in which this narrative unfolds in time and space was, as for most Sufi authors both before and after, construed as a path or journey comprised of levels of personal experience and spiritual refinement arranged hierarchically, each stage of the journey presupposing the actualization of certain attitudes, experiences, and beliefs, and ultimately the realization of particular significances and verities.

In describing this path, Suhrawardī generally employs metaphors which divide up the journey into broad, comprehensive stages, such as in the first chapter of his *Irshād al-murīdīn*, where he describes the individual paths (*ṭuruq*) through which the seeker must pass as tripartite, joining the well-worn metaphor of the search for the pearl of great price with the equally well-worn expression of *sharīʿa-ṭarīqa-ḥaqīqa*:

> The paths are three, consisting of the *sharīʿa*, the *ṭarīqa*, and the *ḥaqīqa*. It is said that the *sharīʿa* is like the ship, that the *ṭarīqa* is like the sea, and that the *ḥaqīqa* is like the pearls. He who wishes to obtain the pearls sails on the ship and then plunges into the sea, thereupon obtaining the pearls. But as for the one who violates this sequence, he obtains nothing.[45]

Such a systematic division is echoed in some of Suhrawardī's other texts, such as in his *R. fī ʾl-sayr wa-l-ṭayr*, a short but dense treatise which delineates the geography of the spiritual path through an extended commentary on the *ḥadīth*:

> God's Messenger—may God bless and greet him—said, 'journey onward, the *mufarridūn* have already gone ahead.' It was said to him, 'And who are the *mufarridūn* O' Messenger of God?' To which he replied, 'Those who

---

[45] *IrM*, fol. 1b–2a; the reference being to an oft-quoted *ḥadīth* in which the Prophet is reported to have said: "The *sharīʿa* are my words (*aqwālī*), the *ṭarīqa* are my actions (*aʿmālī*), and the *ḥaqīqa* my interior states (*aḥwālī*)." (ʿAzīz-i Nasafī, *Maqṣad-i aqṣa*, in Lloyd Ridgeon (trans), *Persian Metaphysics and Mysticism*, 45; and, Schimmel, *Mystical Dimensions*, 99) In his *R. fī ʾl-sulūk*, Najm al-Dīn al-Kubrā uses the exact same expression. (*Fawāʾiḥ*, ed. Meier, 49)

> are zealous in remembering God, bearing the burden of remembrance so that they show up at the Day of Resurrection lightly'.[46]

In his commentary on this *ḥadīth*, Suhrawardī reads it as an allusion to the stages comprising the journey of the elite (*khawāṣṣ*) among the Muslims, dividing it into broad stages which correspond to the ternary *sharīʿa-ṭarīqa-ḥaqīqa*, namely a preparatory stage characterized by pious exertion (*ijtihād*) on the path of the *sharīʿa*, followed by a two-fold movement of wayfaring (*sulūk*) and voyaging (*sayr*) which corresponds to the Sufi *ṭarīqa*, and a final movement characterized as flying (*ṭayr*) which corresponds to the *ḥaqīqa*. In his discussion of the geography of this journey, Suhrawardī relates each of these stages to a specific domain of the human being's psycho-spiritual constitution, the first movement being associated with the soul (*nafs*), the second with the heart (*qalb*), and the third with the spirit (*rūḥ*). It is in the manner in which he defined each of these constituent parts of the human psycho-spiritual constitution which furnishes the key to understanding the essential connection between the ontological and metaphysical dimensions of his vision and its articulation in the actual practices and patterns of institutionalized praxis and organization characterizing his *ribāṭ*-based Sufi system.

The Psycho-Spiritual Body

For Suhrawardī, the psycho-spiritual constitution of the human being is a battleground which plays host to a violent struggle (*fitna*) between the carnal or lower soul (*nafs*) and the spirit (*rūḥ*), the heart (*qalb*) being caught somewhere in the middle:

> The spirit is the source of good and the soul the source of evil. The intellect is the army of the spirit and passion the army of the soul. Success from God are the auxiliaries of the spirit and disappointment the auxiliaries of the soul. And the heart joins whichever army happens to be more powerful.[47]

As the shaykh points out, there is little which has engendered as much debate among men of understanding than the question of exactly what constitutes the *rūḥ*, and in his *ʿAwārif al-maʿārif* he quotes various

---

[46] al-Suhrawardī, *R. fī ʾl-sayr wa-l-ṭayr*, MS. Süley., Bağdatlı Vehbi Ef. 2023_8, fol. 67b; also, al-Bidlīsī, *Bahjat al-ṭāʾifa*, ed. Edward Badeen in *Zwei mystische Schriften des ʿAmmār al-Bidlīsī* (Beirut and Stuttgart: In Kommission bei Franz Steiner Verlag, 1999), 49. This *ḥadīth* is evinced, with minor variants, in the major collections.

[47] *IrM*, fol. 11b; same in *AdM*, 33/Milson, *Rule*, 44.

opinions on the subject representing a wide variety of perspectives.[48] Although he states that his first inclination is to remain quiet on the subject, Suhrawardī does offer an answer to the question in the form of an elaborate anthropogenic theory which he develops much further in his later works,[49] a theory whose Neoplatonic and Gnostic underpinnings are clear. His earliest articulation of this theory—as stated in those of his works explicitly dealing with Sufism—states that the spirit is of two types: 1) the 'human translunar spirit' (*al-rūḥ al-insānī al-ʿulwī*) which proceeds from the world of divine command (*ʿālam al-amr*); and, 2) the 'human animal spirit' (*al-rūḥ al-ḥayawānī al-basharī*) which proceeds from the world of creation (*ʿālam al-khalq*).[50]

For its part, the human animal spirit is a subtle bodily substance (*jismānī laṭīf*) which bears the faculties of sensation and movement emitted from the physical heart. In this, the human being does not differ from any other living being, for all created beings are possessed of an animal spirit (*rūḥ ḥayawānī*), a physical heart, and natural drives such as hunger and thirst. At the same time, the animal spirit of the human being is differentiated from other animal spirits in that it is possessed of 'human' (*basharī*) qualities, qualities which are attractive to the human translunar spirit and which prompt it to settle down upon it and not upon other animal spirits. As the place of descent (*maḥall/mawrid*) of the human translunar spirit, the human animal spirit thus serves as the seat of the human translunar spirit in the world of creation, the former becoming tied to the latter due to a strong mutual affinity obtained between them at the moment of their meeting, an affinity which Suhrawardī likens to the strong affinity which obtained between Adam and Eve at the moment of their coupling.[51]

As a potentiality, the soul (*nafs*) is created by God from the translunar spirit in the *ʿālam al-amr* prior to its manifestation in the *ʿālam al-khalq*,

---

[48] *ʿAM*, 2:242–247/*GE*, 56.2–15.

[49] Specifically in his polemic against the *falāsifa* the *Kashf al-faḍāʾiḥ al-yūnāniyya wa-rashf al-naṣāʾiḥ al-īmāniyya* (ed. ʿĀʾisha Yūsuf al-Manāʿī [Cairo: Dār al-Salām, 1999]). The antecedents of this theory are present in Abū ʾl-Najīb's *K. ādāb al-murīdīn* (e.g., 33/Milson, *Rule*, 44).

[50] This theory is presented in the latter half of the 56th chapter of the *ʿAM* (2:247–255/*GE*, 56.15–34), in an abridged form in his *al-Lawāmiʿ al-ghaybiyya fī ʾl-rūḥ* (MS. Süley., Bağdatlı Vehbi Ef. 2023_{38}, fol. 186a–187a) and elsewhere (noted below). In the section on the *nafs* and *rūḥ* in his *Irshād al-murīdīn*, however, Suhrawardī simply repeats Qushayrī (*IrM*, fol. 11a–11b; *SQ*, 2.26).

[51] *ʿAM*, 2:247/*GE*, 56.15; and, idem, *al-Lawāmiʿ al-ghaybiyya fī ʾl-rūḥ*, fol. 186a/idem, *Tarjama-yi al-lawāmiʿ al-ghaybiyya fī ʾl-rūḥ*, MS. Tüb. Ma VI 90_{10}, fol. 75a.

this potentiality being actualized in its physical engenderment through the coupling of the two spirits in the matrix of the human frame (*qālab*), the human animal soul becoming transfigured into the *nafs* proper in the process. Following this coupling there is another, this time between the *nafs* and the translunar spirit, the product of which is the heart (*qalb*), a subtle organ (*laṭīfa*) whose seat is the physical heart. As with the creation of the soul, the potentiality of the heart is created in the *ʿālam al-amr* and is engendered in the *ʿālam al-khalq*. It is the simultaneous presence of each of these three constituent parts (*rūḥ-qalb-nafs*) which comprise the psycho-spiritual constitution of the human being, and in analyzing the relationship between each of the three parts Suhrawardī again draws upon the figures of Adam and Eve, identifying the *rūḥ* as the father Adam, the *nafs* as the mother Eve, and the heart as the progeny produced from their coupling.[52]

Just as in the Gnostic and Manichean struggle to free the entrapped particles of divine light from the dark human body or the yearning of the soul to rise from its material existence in the generative world back to its source in the *Nous* in the system of Plotinus, this anthropogony is deeply connected to man's spiritual destiny. According to Suhrawardī, just as some children incline towards their father and others towards their mother, so too are there certain hearts which incline towards the translunar spirit (*ab* = Adam = *al-rūḥ al-ʿulwī*) and others which incline towards their mother (*umm* = Eve = *al-nafs al-ammārat bi-sūʾ*), a situation which puts the spirit in a precarious position, for:

> ...from its yearning and affection for its Master, the translunar spirit desires to move upwards and to be raised above created things, yet the heart and the soul are created things, and when the spirit ascends, the heart yearns for it just like the yearning of an obedient child for his father; in the same way, the soul yearns for the heart—which is their child—just like a yearning mother longs for her little one.[53]

On the familiar Neoplatonic model, it only in breaking away from the longings which continuously pull it back to its earthly entrapments, that the spirit can ascend back to its origin. The consequences of this are both epistemological and ethical, for the various bodies comprising the

[52] *ʿAM*, 2:248/*GE*, 56.16; idem, *Lawāmiʿ*, fol. 186a–186b/idem, *Tarjama-yi al-lawāmiʿ*, fol. 75a; and, *Suh.*, 131–132. The same process is described by Najm al-Dīn Rāzī Dāya (*PGB*, 192, 268, 334–335).

[53] *ʿAM*, 2:248–249/*GE*, 56.18; and, idem, *Lawāmiʿ*, fol. 186b–187a/idem, *Tarjama-yi al-lawāmiʿ*, fol. 75a–75b.

psycho-spiritual constitution of the human being play a direct role in his capacity to effect such an ascension, which in Suhrawardī's emplotment centers upon the Muslim's ability to receive and negotiate the original dispensation in time and space through the instrument of the intellect (*ʿaql*), and in the second place the ability to deploy the knowledge (*ʿilm*) and wisdom (*ḥikma*) effected through the intellect to engage in a praxis which tames the soul, thus reaching a state wherein his spirit is able to begin its ascension.

For Suhrawardī, the position of the intellect is an important one, for it is the instrument through which knowledge (*ʿilm*) is apprehended, and within the geography of the *ṭarīqa*, knowledge—coming as it does after the level of *īmān* but before the level of direct tasting (*dhawq*)—is essential, for it is a means to praxis (*ʿamal*), and praxis is the key to those things which the seeker must perfect if his spirit is to set out on its journey of ascent to its Master.[54] At its base, Suhrawardī defines knowledge as a light which differentiates between inspiration (*ilhām*) and devilish whisperings (*waswasa*), something which is mediated through the intellect, in which case it is called wisdom (*ḥikma*).[55] The intellect, located in the brain and whose light filters down into the heart where actual cognition occurs, is thus connected to the spirit, serving as its 'tongue and conductor' in managing the heart and the soul just as a father manages (*tadbīr*) his son (the *qalb*) and his wife (the *nafs*).[56] The primary task of the intellect is to deal with the manifold psychological events which transpire in the heart.

The analysis of various forms of thought constitute a perennial theme in Sufi psychology, and in his continual focus on the problems and opportunities created by the manifold fancies, notions, ideas, images, and inspirations which continually pass through the human conscience (*ḍamīr*), Suhrawardī differed little from what went before him. Collectively, these psychic phenomena (*khawāṭir*; sing., *khāṭir*) consist

[54] *JQb*, fol. 2b; see also: *Suh.*, 269–275; *AdM*, 16, 22, 25/Milson, *Rule*, 35, 39, 40–41. According to Suhrawardī, epistemically, knowledge (*ʿilm*) is of two types, discursive knowledge which is mediated through the instrument of the intellect (*ʿaql*) and disclosed knowledge (*al-ʿilm al-kashfī*) which is mediated through direct witnessing (*mushāhada*). (*JQb*, fol. 3b).

[55] *JQb*, fol. 2a. Another version of the text begins by defining knowledge (*ʿilm*) as "the mediated, discursive and sensual apprehension of the verities (*ḥaqāʾiq*) of existing things (*ashyāʾ*) through the instrument of the intellect." (MS., Süley., Lâleli 3685, fol. 1a); cf. *Suh.*, 268–271.

[56] *ʿAM*, 2:248, 253–254/*GE*, 56.18, 32–33; idem, *Lawāmiʿ*, fol. 186b/idem, *Tarjama-yi al-lawāmiʿ*, fol. 75b; and, *JQb*, fol. 2b.

of articulable messages (*khiṭāb*) which come upon the conscience from one of a number of sources of which Suhrawardī (following al-Junayd) identifies four: 1) satanic (*shayṭāniyya*) which consist of devilish whisperings (*wasāwis*); 2) carnal (*nafsāniyya*) which consist of notions (*hawājis*); 3) angelic (*malakiyya*) which consist of inspirations (*ilhāmāt*); and, 4) divine (*ilāhiyya*) which consist of pure inspired knowledge (*al-ʿulūm al-ṣāfiyya al-ilhāmiyya*).[57] Each of these forms of thought exert pressure or, more properly, 'inscribe' the locus of their cognition (the heart), either inhibiting or facilitating the progress of the seeker on the Sufi path. In turn, these types of thoughts are to be distinguished from the 'oncoming' (*wārid*; pl. *wāridāt*) which are a more general category of praiseworthy thoughts which come upon the heart independent of any action on the part of their recipient and are non-verbal in nature.[58]

The major combatant in this soteriological battle is that subtle body which serves as the first obstacle in the spirit's ascent, the soul (*nafs*). As with the heart, Suhrawardī considers the soul to be an embodied thing, a dark existent (*al-wujūd al-ẓulmānī*) located between the two flanks of the body which is the source of all blameworthy characteristics (*awṣāf madhūma*) just as the spirit is the source of all praiseworthy characteristics (*awṣāf maḥmūda*). These blameworthy characteristics, and there are many, manifest themselves in outward behaviors (*akhlāq*) deriving from two primary foundations: 1) heedlessness (*ṭaysh*), which is the result of the soul's innate ignorance; and, 2) voracity (*sharah*), which is the result of the soul's innate cupidity (*ḥirṣ*). If an individual hopes to fully actualize his humanity (*insāniyyat*) and move beyond his state of entanglement

[57] al-Suhrawardī, *Futūḥ* IX, MS. Süley., Musalla Medresesi 20_6, fol. 292a; idem, *Futūḥ* VII, MS. Süley., Şehid Ali Paşa 1393_{11}, fol. 70a; *IrM*, fol. 137a–138b; *ʿAM*, 2:259–261/*GE*, 57.10–14; *Suh.*, 282; cf., *SQ*, 2.21. Here, Suhrawardī draws upon the description of al-Junayd (*Adab al-muftaqir ilā ʾllāh*, in *The Life, Personality and Writings*, 178–183, 58–63 [Arabic text]); same in Kalābādhī, *Taʿarruf*, 90–91/Arberry (trans.), *Doctrine*, 80; *SL*, 120.43–44; Najm al-Dīn al-Kubrā, *Fawāʾiḥ*, ed. Meier, 11–14 (save *ilāhī* is replaced with *raḥmānī*; see 127–134 [Einleitung]; but cf. idem., *R. al-sāʾir al-ḥāʾir* [ed. Marjian Molé in "Traités mineurs", *Annales Islamologiques* 4 (1963), 52] where five are mentioned, viz. divine, angelic, satanic, and the *khawāṭir* of the heart); ʿAzīz-i Nasafī, *Kashf al-ḥaqāʾiq*, trans. Ridgeon in *Persian Metaphysics and Mysticism*, 208; cf. Abū Ṭālib al-Makkī, *Qūt al-qulūb*, 1:234–235/*Die Nahrung*, 30.6–8 (who defines six: *khawāṭir* of the soul, Satan, the spirit, angels, the intellect, and certainty (*yaqīn*) which are repeated by Jīlānī [*GhT*, 2:204–205]). See also: Badeen, *Zwei mystische Schriften*, 45–46; and, Peter Awn, *Satan's Tragedy and Redemption: Iblīs in Sufi Psychology* (Leiden: E.J. Brill, 1983), 66–69. These thoughts, in turn, produce an influence (*lamma*) which move both soul and the spirit, the former being effected by satanic thoughts and the latter by angelic thoughts. (*ʿAM*, 2:262–263/*GE*, 57.20–21)

[58] *IrM*, fol. 137b; *ʿAM*, 2:261/*GE*, 57.17 (quoting *SQ*, 2.23).

in the animal qualities of the soul, these blameworthy behaviors must be broken and replaced with praiseworthy ones.[59] This can only occur when the soul has been purified.

This purification takes place in predictable ways, for according to Suhrawardī the soul is but one thing possessed of three changeable states, a scheme developed quite early on in Sufi psychology which took its inspiration from the Qurʾānic descriptions of the *nafs* as 'commanding to evil' (*al-nafs al-ammārat bi-l-sūʾ*), blaming (*al-nafs al-lawwāma*), and tranquil (*al-nafs al-muṭmaʾinna*).[60] Generally, the first state is the natural state of the soul, full of appetites and destructive influences which have yet to be fully disciplined thus inducing its possessor into sinful actions. The second state is that of reproach, when the soul rebukes its possessor for his sinful behavior and induces him to repentance and turning to God (*tawba/ināba*). The state of tranquility is the highest state of the soul, a state which it reaches only when the heart has been raised to the station of the spirit and the servant has completely acquiesced to all of God's commands.[61] According to Suhrawardī, the sciences of the Sufis provide the surest means to effect this tranquility. The soul, however, is not the only subtle body which figures in the discipline of the Sufi path, for the heart too plays an essential role in the process of the spirit's ascension back to its Master.

For its part, the heart is an organ comprised of both a bodily and a spiritual dimension. Physically, the heart consists of two chambers (*tajāwīf*), an inner chamber (*bāṭin*) where hearing and vision reside, and an outer (*ẓāhir*) chamber where the light of the intellect (*ʿaql*) resides. Spiritually, the heart is an 'illuminated existent' (*al-wujūd al-nūrānī*) which, as the seat of the light of the intellect, is the center of discursive understanding (*fahm*), the instrument through which the external (exoteric) dimensions of belief and praxis are cognized and

[59] *ʿAM*, 2:250–251/*GE*, 56.20–22; cf., idem, *Futūḥ* II, MS. Tüb. Ma VI 90_{16}, fol. 85a–85b; idem, *R. fī ʾl-faqr*, fol. 53a; *AdM*, 33/Milson, *Rule*, 44–45; and, al-Suhrawardī, *Ḥilyat al-faqīr al-ṣādiq fī ʾl-taṣawwuf*, MS. Süley., Yazma Bağışlar 1971_3, fol. 115b (on location of the soul between the two flanks).

[60] *ʿAM*, 2:251/*GE*, 56.22; idem, *Tarjama-yi al-lawāmiʿ*, fol. 75b–76a; *IrM*, fol. 16b; idem, *Sayr*, fol. 62b–63a; and, *Suh.*, 132–134. The references are to Qurʾān 12:53, 75:2, and 89:27 respectively.

[61] *IrM*, fol. 16b. Because of its inherent lower earthly nature, the soul can never rise as does the spirit, but rather remains domiciled in the body where it takes over the spirit's regulatory function which, in its tranquility, it manages in a sound manner (idem, *Futūḥ* IV, MS. Süley., Şehid Ali Paşa 1393_{14}, fol. 72a; idem, *Futūḥ* XIX, MS. Tüb. Ma VI 90_{37}, fol. 97a–97b).

understood, it being the medium through which the particularities of the proper modes of behavior and belief are delineated, organized, and regulated.[62] Such a mode of cognition is essential, for it allows for both the understanding and perpetuation of the *sharīʿa*, the divine law which serves simultaneously as the overarching framework within which God's creatures relate to Him and His creation *qua* their creatureliness, as well as the initial mode of access to the realization and unmediated apprehension of its verities.

The heart is also the primary spiritual instrument of the Sufi path, whose work (*ʿamal al-qalb*) consists of pursuing the disciplines of *muḥāsaba* and *murāqaba*, the twin practices which allow for the breaking of the *nafs* and the effectuation of its tranquility, the *sine qua non* of the beginning and medial stages of the path by which the aspirant prepares himself to advance to its higher stages.[63] At the same time the heart is also an independent organ of discernment possessed of an instrument of apprehension separate from that of the intellect. This is the 'vision of the heart' (*baṣar al-qalb*), which according to Suhrawardī is that instrument which allows for direct apprehension (*mushāhada*), a non-discursive and immediate mode of cognition which is characteristic of the final stage of the Sufi path, the *ḥaqīqa*.[64]

In addition to serving as a cognitive instrument, the heart also serves as the locus of the seeker's encounter with the divine attributes and essence. For Suhrawardī, the theophany (*tajallī*) is spoken of in terms familiar to the Junaydī tradition to which he considered himself an heir, namely through the motif of the light and the veil.[65] A typical definition of this complex comes in the *Irshād al-murīdīn*:

> The theophany is a light and divine disclosure (*mukāshafa*) from God Most High which appears in the heart of the gnostic (*ʿārif*), overwhelming and scorching him, and the veil (*sitr*) is the withholding of this theophany from him so that it he is not completely burned and melted away in its light. The veil is a mercy from God Most High to the gnostic just as the theophany is a favor.[66]

Generally, Suhrawardī speaks of this theophany as an outpouring of the 'lights of divine favor' (*anwār faḍl al-ḥaqq*), an outpouring which

[62] *JQb*, fol. 10b; and, *ʿAM*, 1:239/*GE*, 10.9–10.
[63] Idem, *Futūḥ* XI, MS. Tüb., Ma VI 90_{27}, fol. 92a.
[64] *ʿAM*, 1:157–160/*GE*, 2.8–11; and, idem, *Futūḥ* XI, fol. 92a.
[65] E.g., *SQ*, 2.13.
[66] *IrM*, fol. 136a; cf. *ʿAM*, 2:318–319/*GE*, 62.9.

reaches the heart where it effects an existential shift, or reorientation, in the very being of the recipient, progressively burning away the traces of individual existence.[67] It is divided into the theophany of the divine attributes (*ṣifāt*), which occurs in the penultimate stage of the Sufi path, and the theophany of the essence (*al-dhāt*), which occurs at the cusp of the final stage of the journey, the former being associated with divine disclosure (*mukāshafa*) and the latter with direct witnessing (*mushāhada*).[68]

In addition to the spirit, the heart, and the soul, there is a fourth component which is usually counted as part of the human being's psycho-spiritual constitution, the 'secret' (*sirr*), a term which Suhrawardī is careful to point out is neither possessed of a Qur'ānic precedent nor understood in a consistent manner among the Sufis. Although reticent to do so, in the *ʿAwārif al-maʿārif* Suhrawardī offers his own definition, a reading which contradicts that of other Sufi metaphysicians:

> What is called a secret (*sirr*) does not refer to a thing independent in and of itself, something possessed of an ontological existence and essence (*dhāt*) like the spirit and the soul. Rather, when the soul is purified and made clean, the spirit departs from its dark strictures and when it commences its ascent to the fatherlands (*awṭān*) of proximity, the heart emigrates from its firmly-established residence, rising to the spirit, and at that moment it acquires an extra quality (*waṣf zāʾid*) on top of its regular quality, and this quality is unintelligible to the ecstatics (*wājidīn*) so they differentiate it from the heart and call it a 'secret'.[69]

It is these three constituent parts then which comprise the entirety of man's psycho-spiritual constitution, and as such it is the job of the sciences of the Sufis to deal with each in a manner which effects the return of the spirit to its Master. In analyzing how this is to occur, Suhrawardī contends that as a created existing being (*khalq wujūd*) man is composed of two halves, or polarities, the first spiritual and heavenly and the second corporeal and earthly.[70] Although the first is higher than

---

[67] Idem, *Futūḥ* VII, fol. 70a; and, idem, *Futūḥ* VIII, MS. Köp., Fazıl Ahmed Paşa 1605_{12}, fol. 38b.

[68] *ʿAM*, 1:326–327, 2:309, 322/*GE*, 20.2–3; 61.34, 62.22; cf. *HT*, fol. 90a–90b where Suhrawardī describes the hierarchical nature of the two primary theophanies and the epistemological distinction between *mukāshafa* and *mushāhada*.

[69] *ʿAM*, 2:251–252/*GE*, 56.25; *Suh.*, 131. In the *Irshād al-murīdīn*, however, Suhrawardī contradicts himself by quoting Qushayrī's definition of the *sirr* which identifies it as a subtle bodily container (*laṭīfat mawdiʿat fī ʾl-qalāb*) which is the seat of direct witnessing. (fol. 11b; cf. *SQ*, 2.27)

[70] al-Suhrawardī, *Futūḥ* III, MS. Köp., Fazıl Ahmed Paşa 1605_{14}, fol. 39a.

the second, both are intimately connected in a relationship of mutual influence and co-dependency, the state of one directly influencing that of the other.[71] As a phenomenal existent, the psycho-spiritual constitution is necessarily possessed of the attribute of existence (*wujūd*), but at the same time it is an aggregative existent whose ontological status is indeterminate. Accordingly, Suhrawardī differentiates between two beings, or modalities of existence (*wujūdān*) based on the basic existential polarity which together constitute the aggregate of the phenomenal human person: the mental or intellectual being (*wujūd al-dhihnī*) which he uses interchangeably with 'inner being' (*bāṭin*) and which is generally connected with the first half; and, the physical or corporeal being (*wujūd al-ʿaynī*) which he uses interchangeably with 'outer being' (*ẓāhir*) and is generally connected with the second.[72] As two distinct, yet mutually co-substantial existents, both are subject to the same laws and processes of purity and corruption, movement and quiescence, annihilation and subsistence, and so forth. As will be discussed shortly, the existential status of these two polarities of existence, in fact, relate directly to Suhrawardī's idiosyncratic conception of the 'stations and states' of the mystical path as well with the actual practices of the Sufi *ribāṭ* itself.

The Geography of the Mystical Path

As with Sufi theorists before and after him, the various organs, subtle bodies, and cognitive instruments of the human are deeply embedded in descriptions of the geography of the spiritual path itself. As both the *raison d'être* of the existence of the spiritual path in the first place and

[71] To take a typical example, in *Futūḥ* V Suhrawardī states: "The servant's reality (*ḥaqīqa*) is drawn from the *kiswa* of existence just as a sword is drawn from its scabbard, and it is brandished by the hand of the spiritual state in the plain of proximity, but whenever the soul is stirred by its characteristics the servant's reality is drawn back into its existence, and whenever its is quiet it is divested (*tajarrud*), and both the body and the physical senses follow in its divestment and the light of the inner being (*bāṭin*) overcomes the outer being (*ẓāhir*)." (MS. Süley., Şehid Ali Paşa 1393_9, fol. 69b)

[72] As evinced in his letters to Kamāl al-Dīn al-Iṣfahānī (MS. Tüb., Ma VI 90_{28}, fol. 92b) and ʿIzz al-Dīn Muḥammad b. Yaʿqūb (MS. Tüb. Ma VI 90_{57}, fol. 123b) where he explains the synonymy of the two terms in reference to the implications of the practices of vigilant awareness (*murāqaba*) which is concerned with the former and scrupulous examination (*muḥāsaba*) which is concerned with the latter. In some places, Suhrawardī also uses the pair 'inner secret' (*sirr*) and 'visible form' (*ʿalāniyya*) to refer to the *bāṭin/wujūd al-dhihnī* and *ẓāhir/wujūd al-ʿaynī* (e.g., *JQb*, fol. 3bff.; *HT*, fol. 90b) or simply *wujūd basharī* to refer to the latter (e.g., *Futūḥ* VII, fol. 70a).

the primary loci of the experiences which effect its traversal, one can scarcely be analyzed without reference to the other. In this, Suhrawardī deviated little, for the model of ascent he describes is articulated as a process of progressive purification of these bodies, in particular the soul and the heart, delineated along both 'practical' and 'theoretical' lines, the first concerned with the actual praxis associated with the journey of ascent and the latter with the analysis of the experiences generated through such praxis. Although understood as a comprehensive whole, for the purposes of discussion and interpretation Suhrawardī tends to divide the 'practical' and the 'theoretical' into more or less independent units, in the former presenting a detailed method of disciple and spiritual praxis revolving around the actual practices in which the aspirant engages in the course of his journey and in the latter presenting an equally detailed exposition of the spiritual content generated through or, more appropriately, guiding such praxis. Following his predecessors, Suhrawardī describes this content in terms of 'spiritual stations' (*maqāmāt*, sing. *maqām*; or, *manāzil*, sing. *manzil*) and 'spiritual states' (*ḥāl*, pl. *aḥwāl*).[73]

Basing his discussion on an observation that there is a great deal of confusion over the meaning of the mystical stations and states, in the 58th-61st chapters of the *'Awārif al-ma'ārif*, Suhrawardī offers a reading which attempts to mitigate such confusion by questioning what he identified as a tendency towards generalization and reification among the Sufis of his day. For him, a heuristic which differentiates between states and stations solely on the basis of the mystical state being defined by its free bestowal and changeability and the mystical station being defined solely by its permanence and volitive acquisition, is not entirely accurate.[74] According to Suhrawardī, such definitions are facile and have

---

[73] Dhū 'l-Nūn al-Miṣrī (d. 245/859) is usually credited as the first to describe the Sufi path in terms of stations and states, and theorists both before and after Suhrawardī provide different enumerations of each. Abū Naṣr al-Sarrāj, for instance, enumerates seven stations and ten states (*SL*, 21.1–37.6), Abū Ṭālib al-Makkī nine stations and numerous states (e.g., *Qūt al-qulūb*, 364/*Die Nahrung*, 32.1), 'Abdullāh-i Anṣārī literally hundreds of both, and Abū 'l-Najīb fourteen stations and twelve states (*AdM*, 20–21/ Milson, *Rule*, 49–50). See also: Anawati and Gardet, *Mystique musulmane*, 4th ed., 77ff.; L. Gardet, "Ḥāl," *EI*², 3:83; Gramlich, *Derwischorden*, 2:273–280; Schimmel, *Mystical Dimensions*, 109–148; and, Knysh, *Islamic Mysticism*, 303–309.

[74] Generally, the *maqāmāt* are understood to be acquired things (*makāsib*) and the *aḥwāl* freely given gifts (*mawāhib*), e.g., *SL*, 83; al-Sulamī, *Manāhij*, 38; *KM*, 224–228/Nicholson, *The Kashf*, 180–183; *SQ*, 2.3; al-Ghazālī, *Iḥyā'*, 4:139; *AdM*, 20–21. In the *IrM*, however, Suhrawardī differentiates between the 'state' (*ḥāl*) and the 'inhering state' (*ḥāll*) (from

little to do with the actual experiences which the aspirant undergoes as his spirit makes its ascent. For Suhrawardī, in fact, those attainments which most Sufi theorists have interpreted as comprising discrete mystical stations cannot be limited in such a way, because each station is in fact possessed of both a *ḥāl* and a *maqām*. In the opening of the 58th chapter of the *ʿAwārif al-maʿārif*, he offers an example:

> In its essence, something is a state before it becomes a station, for example: A man receives a call from his inner being to engage in the scrupulous examination [of his soul] (*muḥāsaba*) and conquer its bad characteristics, but they reappear, and then vanish again, and thus he persists in the state of *muḥāsaba*...(until) finally with God's help he conquerors the bad characteristics of the soul, defeats it, disciplines it, and restrains it. At this point, the state of *muḥāsaba* becomes his fatherland (*waṭan*), dwelling place (*mustaqarr*), and station (*maqām*). He obtains the station of *muḥāsaba* only after having obtained the state of *muḥāsaba*. After this, the state of vigilant awareness (*murāqaba*) descends upon him, for when *muḥāsaba* becomes his station then *murāqaba* becomes his state, and similarly...the state of *murāqaba* is transformed into a station only after it had become a state for him. Just as the station of *muḥāsaba* is not made permanent except through the descent of the state of *murāqaba* the station of *murāqaba* is not made permanent except through the descent of the state of direct witnessing (*mushāhada*), for when the state of *mushāhada* is bestowed upon a man, his *murāqaba* is made permanent and becomes his station after it had been his state.[75]

Having taken care of the issue of changeability and permanence, Suhrawardī then tackles the issue of bestowal and attainment, challenging what he cites as being the views held by both the authorities (*mashāyikh*) of Iraq, who considered that the *ḥāl* is something freely given (*manna*) by God, and the authorities of Khurāsān, who considered

ḥ-l-l, meaning 'to dismount', 'alight', 'settle down upon') saying: "The *maqām* is where a man is situated among the stopping places (*manāzil*) and they differ. The first of them is straightening out affairs, renouncing illicit things, and knowledge of the soul's blemishes, and the last of them is cleansing the soul of its blameworthy blemishes...the *ḥāll*, with a doubling of the letter 'l', is that which descends upon (*nazala ʿalā*) the heart such as rapture (*ṭarab*), contraction (*qabḍ*), expansion (*basṭ*), longing (*shawq*), and direct tasting (*dhawq*). It is said that the *ḥāll* is like a lightening flash, meaning that it does not subsist but rather persists for a short time; if it remains then it is but a notion (*ḥadīth al-nafs*) and not a *ḥāll*." (fol. 4a–4b)

[75] *ʿAM*, 2:264/*GE*, 58.2; *Suh.*, 165–167. A similar reading is given for the station/states of *zuhd*, *tawakkul*, and *riḍā* later in the same chapter (2:267–268/*GE*, 58.9). A great admirer of Suhrawardī, ʿAzīz-i Nafasī quotes this interpretation as the correct one (Ridgeon [trans.], *Kashf al-ḥaqāʾiq*, in *Persian Metaphysics and Mysticism*, 215).

the *ḥāl* to be the inheritances (*mawārīth*) of worshipful actions (*aʿmāl*),[76] neither in Suhrawardī's view being entirely correct:

> In general, the Sufi authorities (*shuyūkh*) have said that the stations are acquired things (*makāsib*) and that the states are gifts (*mawāhib*), but in terms of the way in which we have arranged them, they are all gifts. This is because acquired things comprise gifts (*al-makāsib maḥfūfat bi-l-mawāhib*) and gifts comprise acquired things. In fact, the states are ecstatic experiences (*mawājīd*) and the stations the paths (*ṭuruq*) to them. Acquisition is apparent in the stations, but gifts are hidden, and in the states acquisition is hidden, but gifts are apparent. In fact, the states are translunar, heavenly gifts (*mawāhib ʿulwiyyat samāwiyya*) and the stations the paths to them.[77]

The next issue is concerned with the seeker's role in making the transition from one station to the next, and in turn how such an ascent is ordered. According to Suhrawardī, the authorities provide two possibilities, either the seeker can advance to the next station only when he has mastered the station which stands below it, or he advances first and then perfects the lower station after the fact, being in an advantageous position to survey the imperfections of his previous station from a new height and thus correct it. There is, however, another option which is more nuanced and sophisticated in its implications, an option which begins with the bifurcation of the traditional station into a state/station coupled with the absence of free acquisition:

> An individual in a particular station acquires a state from the station above that which he is currently in and to which he is about to advance, and it is by this that he straightens out the affair of the station which he is currently in. God has free disposal over this, and the worshiper has no say in the matter of whether he advances or not.[78]

What this amounts to is a difference between entering a particular station and actually making it sound or permanent, a key distinction in Suhrawardī's system and a potential cause for confusion. For Suhrawardī, the stations and states are not discrete units of experience in and of themselves, but rather a comprehensive whole into which the aspirant dips again and again in his journey towards subsistence in the divine. The moral and ethical underpinnings of each of the stations and states as discussed by the early Sufi authors serve as repositories of

---

[76] *ʿAM*, 2:266/*GE*, 58.5.
[77] Ibid., 2:265/*GE*, 58.4; cf. Gramlich, *Derwischorden*, 2:273–280.
[78] *ʿAM*, 2:266/*GE*, 58.7.

certain qualities, but not as actual demarcations of the progress of the seeker along the path strictly speaking. In the *Hudā al-ṭālibīn*, Suhrawardī makes it clear what he means by this distinction:

> The stations overlap, one with the other, and for each one of them, entering into what comes after it requires the perfection of the former's result and the completion of its benefits, but at the same time to make it sound (*ṣiḥḥa*, i.e., permanent) each one of them requires entering into something from the entirety of the stations themselves, for some are conditional upon others and some necessitate others.[79]

In Suhrawardī's view, the manner in which the seeker proceeds through the various stations and states is through a process of progressive layering. In his journey the seeker does not progress through a strict hierarchy of stations and states, completing or receiving one after the other, but rather makes multiple passes across the entire field of the stations and states, appropriating certain qualities associated with certain stations in an initial pass and then progressively obtaining more and more qualities in subsequent passes. For him, the journey of the seeker is envisioned as an upward spiral which sees the wayfarer reaching certain 'ground stations' (of which there are four, one preparatory and three actual) and then continually perfecting his actualization of the qualities of every other station, state, or station/state by 'revisiting' and 'drawing upon' them as he moves through subsequent ground stations.

The idea is one of cumulative acquirement, the seeker does not actually leave behind any one station after having acquired the next but rather progressively adds to what he has already acquired from the totality of the stations as a whole, perfecting the qualities of each relative to the particular ground station in which he finds himself at any one particular point along his journey. Only when he has dipped into a particular station/state enough times, or has fulfilled certain requirements necessary to actualize its verities is it made permanent. This is why Suhrawardī characterizes each station as a path (*ṭarīq*) in and of itself,[80] for like the *ṭarīqa* as a whole, proceeding through each means to accomplish certain things which in and of themselves are gradated and whose perfection is relative to multiple contingencies.

---

[79] *HT*, fol. 88b. As Suhrawardī points out, there are numerous states which, although necessary to effect the permanence of particular stations, do not themselves become stations. (*ʿAM*, 2:268, 320/*GE*, 58.11, 62.19)

[80] *IrM*, fol. 2b; and, *ʿAM*, 2:265/*GE*, 58.4.

Prior to even entering the realm of stations and states, however, the potential seeker must first arrive at a suitable point of departure. In his *R. fī 'l-sayr wa-l-ṭayr*, Suhrawardī identifies this point of departure in reference to the ternary laid out in the *Irshād al-murīdīn*, positing that entry into the *ṭarīqa* is contingent upon actualizing the verities of submission (*al-taḥaqquq bi-ḥaqā'iq al-islām*), "preparing oneself to strike out on the path of wayfaring (*sulūk*) by perfecting the foundations of submission (*mabānī al-islām*) through 'pious exertion' (*ijtihād*)".[81] This is a contingency which cannot be avoided, for only once the striver has actualized the verities of submission through perfecting pious striving can he then be raised to the verities of faith (*ḥaqā'iq al-īmān*) and actually become one of the Folk of Wayfaring (*ahl al-sulūk*). It is the perfection of faith which is the key to entering the initial station of the spirit's ascent, the station of repentance (*tawba*), both the first stage of the *ṭarīqa* proper and the "foundation of every other station and key to every spiritual state."[82] This station is followed by two other ground stations which, as explained in the *'Awārif al-ma'ārif*, comprise the station of renunciation (*zuhd*) and the station of worshipfulness (*'ubūdiyya*):

> To the extent of my knowledge and the limits of my ability and personal exertion, I have weighed the stations and the states and their results and have found them to consist of but three things—that is three things after the soundness of faith and its binding stipulations and requirements by which they total four... He who actualizes the verities of these four enters into the dominion (*malakūt*) of the heavens, sees the divine decree and the signs (*āyāt*) unveiled, comes to possess both direct tasting and discursive understanding of God's revealed words, and obtains all of the states and stations, for their entirety are produced from these four, and by them are prepared and confirmed. After faith, the first of the three is sincere repentance (*al-tawba al-naṣūḥ*), the second renunciation of the world (*al-zuhd fī 'l-dunyā*), and the third the actualization of the station of worshipfulness (*taḥqīq maqām al-'ubūdiyya*) which is none other than the perpetual worship of God (*dawām al-'amal li-Llāh*) both in the inner and outer beings, in the worship of the heart and in the body, without slackening a bit or cutting short... and the world-renouncing ulama and the eponymous authorities

---

[81] Idem, *Sayr*, fol. 67b–68a; idem, *R. dar kār-i murīd*, MS. Tüb., MA VI 90_{8}, fol. 73b, where *taqwā* is singled out as the beginning of the work of the *murīd* and making repentance (*tawba*) sound as the first station of *taqwā*; cf. idem, *W.* IV, MS. Tüb., Ma VI 90_{13}, fol. 80b.

[82] *'AM*, 2:269–270/*GE*, 59.2; idem, *IrM*, fol. 12a; idem, *Mukhtaṣar min kalām al-Suhrawardī*, MS. Süley., Ayasofya 4792_{46}, fol. 799a (on the margins); idem, *R. dar kār-i murīd*, fol. 73b; and, idem, *W.* IV, fol. 81a.

(*mashāyikh*) are all agreed that by these four, the stations are made permanent dwelling places and the states are straightened out.[83]

To move through these stations is to make a three-fold journey. First, from the *sharīʿa* to the *ṭarīqa*, during which the aspirant is characterized as a striver (*mujtahid*) whose *nafs* is inevitably 'commanding to evil'. Second, from the *ṭarīqa* to the *ḥaqīqa*, during which the aspirant engages in a two-fold movement of wayfaring (*sulūk*) and voyaging (*sayr*), the former concerned with rectifying the soul (*tahdhīb al-nufūs*) and the latter with fortifying the heart (*taqwīyat al-qulūb*), over the course of which he defeats the 'soul commanding to evil' at which point it becomes blaming (*lawwāma*). In the final part of this movement, the aspirant pushes beyond the *ṭarīqa* to the *ḥaqīqa*, a movement during which his soul becomes tranquil (*muṭmaʾinna*) and his spirit released from the strictures of the created bodily entrapments which have so far restrained its ascent, from whence he flies upwards, meets his Lord, is annihilated from himself, and then subsequently returned to existence and ensconced in a station of perpetual worship from which nothing can detract.[84]

The First Station: Repentence (tawba)

As the first ground station of the path, repentance (*tawba*) is not only the most fundamental, but is also the most permanent of all of the stations. In this, Suhrawardī differed little from those who came before

[83] *ʿAM*, 2:270/*GE*, 59.4; idem, *W. li-Rashīd al-Dīn Abī Bakr al-Ḥabash*, MS. Tüb., Ma VI 90_{53}, fol. 117a–117b; and, *Suh.*, 168. The 60th chapter of the *ʿAwārif* (entitled "On the Allusions of the Eponymous Authorities (*mashāyikh*) to the Stations According to their Arrangement") enumerates them in a manner reflecting earlier schemes: *tawba, waraʿ, zuhd, ṣabr, faqr, shukr, khawf wa-rajāʾ, tawakkul, riḍā*; cf. al-Sarrāj: *tawba, waraʿ, zuhd, faqr, ṣabr, tawakkul, riḍā*; and, Abū Ṭālib al-Makkī: *tawba, ṣabr, shukr, rajāʾ, khawf, zuhd, tawakkul, riḍā, maḥabba*; Abū ʾl-Najīb: *intibāh, tawba, ināba, waraʿ, muḥāsabat al-nafs, irāda, zuhd, faqr, ṣidq, taṣabbur, ṣabr, riḍā, ikhlāṣ, tawakkul.* As with most, his enumeration of the states in the following chapter (i.e., *maḥabba, shawq, uns, qurb, ḥayāʾ, ittiṣāl, qabḍ wa-basṭ, baqāʾ wa-fanāʾ*) differ from others (e.g., al-Sarrāj: *murāqaba, qurb, maḥabba, khawf, rajāʾ, shawq, uns, iṭmaʾnīna, mushāhada, yaqīn*; Abū ʾl-Najīb the same but adding *ḥayāʾ* between *rajāʾ* and *shawq*). (*ʿAM*, 2:280–314/*GE*, 60.1–61.47; *SL*, 21.1–37.6; al-Makkī, *Qūt al-qulūb*, 1:364/*Die Nahrung*, 32.1; *AdM*, 21; *Suh.*, 168–198) In the *Hudā al-ṭālibīn*, however, Suhrawardī analyzes ten 'essential' stations: *tawba, zuhd, muḥāsaba, mujāhada, ṣidq, ināba, murāqaba, mukāshafa, mushāhada*, and *ṣabr*, explaining how each are connected with the others in a mutual relationship of interdependence. (fol. 88b–90b)

[84] al-Suhrawardī, *Sayr*, 67b–69a; and, idem, *Futūḥ* IX, fol. 292a–292b.

him.[85] Repentance, in fact, comprehends everything else, constituting the frame within which each station and every state is obtained and the matrix within which the qualities of each are made sound. Just as the station of *tawba* cannot be approached without first having actualized the verities of submission and faith, neither can any other station be made sound and permanent without first actualizing the verities of repentance.[86] In the *ʿAwārif al-maʿārif* and elsewhere, Suhrawardī fleshes out the details of this process, outlining a scheme in which effecting the permanence of repentance is made contingent upon the wayfarer coming into possession of certain qualities associated with particular states and stations.

The first of these is 'reproach' (*zājir*), a state in which the potential repenter (*tāʾib*) feels a sense of disgust with himself and his current aims and resolves to amend them. From here, the individual obtains the state of 'attentiveness' (*intibāh*), a state characterized by turning away from the path of sin and error and placing oneself on the path towards God to the exclusion of all other considerations. The final state is that of 'wakefulness' (*yaqẓa*), in which the potential repenter awakens to the mournful sighs of his spirit whose grief over its alienation from created beings and loneliness in its earthly entrapment induces in him a realization that he will never be happy until his spirit is reunited with its Master. It is at this point when the seeker actually makes the transition from the state of repentance to the station of repentance and begins to acquire certain qualities from other states and stations which help him to perfect it and make it permanent. This stage of the journey is

[85] The station of repentance is almost unanimously considered the first station of the Sufi path, e.g., *SL*, 21.1–21.3; al-Makkī, *Qūt al-qulūb*, 1:364–394/Gramlich (trans.), *Die Nahrung*, 31.2–79; ʿAbdullāh-i Anṣārī, *Sad maydān*, ed. Qāsim Anṣārī (Tehran: Kitābkhāna-yi Ṭūrī, 1376 sh. [1997]), 15–18; and, de Beaurecueil, "Le retour à Dieu (*tawba*): élément essential de la conversion, selon ʿAbdullāh Anṣārī," *MIDEO* 6 (1961): 55–122; *KM*, 378–386/Nicholson, *The Kashf*, 294–299; *SQ*, 3.1–27; al-Ghazālī, *Iḥyāʾ*, 4:3–62; see also: Anawati and Gardet, *Mystique musulmane*, 4th ed., 147–149; Gramlich, *Derwischorden*, 2:280–286; Schimmel, *Mystical Dimensions*, 109–110.

[86] Idem, *Sayr*, fol. 68a. In an oft used expression, Suhrawardī states that the soundness of the station of *tawba* is obtained when the "recording angel perched on the right shoulder has nothing left to write in his register of one's misdeeds" (ibid., fol. 68a; idem, *R. dar kār-i murīd*, fol. 73b; idem, *W.* IV, fol. 81a; idem, *R. ilā ʿIzz al-Dīn Muḥammad b. Yaʿqūb*, fol. 123b; *ʿAM*, 1:288/*GE*, 16.14, quoting a saying attributed by Qushayrī to Abū Bakr al-Zaqqāq).

concerned wholly with taming the *nafs* and accordingly is associated with the stage of wayfaring (*sulūk*).[87]

After having set out on the path of repentance (*ṭarīq al-tawba*) through acquiring the three states of reproach, attentiveness, and wakefulness, the wayfarer begins to perfect its permanence through cultivating the two states/stations of 'scrupulous examination and observation' (*al-muḥāsabat wa-l-riʿāya*) and 'vigilant awareness' (*murāqaba*), both of which begin as states but are eventually concretized as stations when the wayfarer has fully actualized their verities.[88] Here, the wayfarer works from the outside in, his first task being to gain mastery over his outer members through the disciple of scrupulous examination and observation, an attitudinal commitment focused on the persistent examination of the destructive influence of the *nafs* on outward actions and behaviors and a concerted effort to restrain them.[89]

This stage of the journey is comprised of a number of distinct stages which witness the wayfarer perfecting the stations of pious self-exertion (*mujāhada*) and sincerity (*ṣidq*), both of which are contingent upon his taking something from the stations of patience (*ṣabr*), contentment (*riḍā*), fear and hope (*khawf wa-rajāʾ*), and thankfulness (*shukr*).[90] In effecting the permanency of the station of pious self-exertion, the primary activity of the wayfarer is to do battle against the drives of his soul, constantly opposing its passions and desires, and systematically depriving it of its pleasures (*ḥuẓūẓ*) until he reaches the state/station of sincerity, the domain of vigilant awareness and struggle with the stray thoughts and inclinations which hinder his advancement on the path.[91] Once he has reached the station of vigilant awareness through drawing upon the qualities of the station of sincerity the makes the critical transition from outward acts of spiritual effort and disciple to the inward dimensions of the *ṭarīqa*.

---

[87] *ʿAM*, 2:270–271/*GE*, 59.4–5; and, idem, *Futūḥ* XIX, fol. 97a. According to Abū ʾl-Najīb it is at this point when the aspirant is enjoined to seek a shaykh (*AdM*, 26/Milson, *Rule*, 41).

[88] *ʿAM*, 2:271–273/*GE*, 59.6–10; and, idem, *Mukhtaṣar min kalām al-Suhrawardī*, fol. 799a (on the margins). In the *Hudā al-ṭālibīn*, Suhrawardī identifies both *muḥāsabat wa-l-riʿāya* and *murāqaba* as stations (*maqāmāt*) whereas in the *ʿAwārif* they are first identified states and then later as stations; cf. idem, *R. dar kār-i murīd*, fol. 73b; *W.* IV, fol. 81a.

[89] *ʿAM*, 2:272/*GE*, 59.8; *HT*, fol. 89a; idem, *R. ilā ʿIzz al-Dīn Muḥammad b. Yaʿqūb*, fol. 123b; and, *AdM*, 32–33/Milson, *Rule*, 44.

[90] *ʿAM*, 2:270–278/*GE*, 59.2–17; and, *HT*, fol. 90b (for *ṣabr*).

[91] Idem, *Futūḥ* II, fol. 85a–85b; idem, *Futūḥ* XIV, Süley., Şehid Ali Paşa 1393_{15}, fol. 72a–72b; and, *HT*, fol. 89a–89b.

For its part, vigilant awareness picks up where scrupulous examination and observation leave off, being concerned with inner restraint and self-control rather then outer restraint,[92] an attitude which springs from "the worshipper knowing that he is being scrutinized by God and through that knowledge...preserving his every action, word, and what comes in the way of passing thoughts (*khawāṭir*) from what might be displeasing to God."[93] This station is associated with the station of sincerity, the quality of which Suhrawardī often characterizes as the wayfarer's careful examination of the aims, desires, and intentions of his soul and the inspirations which he receives in an effort to ascertain whether his actions are really directed to God or are actually directed to something other than Him.[94] In his continual perfection of the stations of vigilant awareness and sincerity, the wayfarer proceeds to a second level of repentance, which begins as the state of 'return' (*ināba*), a state in which the 'repenter' (*tāʾib*) becomes a 'returner' (*munīb*), an individual who "has no place of return except Him, returning to Him from his return and then returning from the return of his return" and is perfected in the actualization of the verities of the station of repentance itself.[95]

Dealing with the most characteristic states and stations of the first level of wayfaring, this part of the journey is an imminently purificatory one, and in his analysis of the cluster of experiences which the wayfarer undergoes in traversing it, Suhrawardī consistently employs a language of purity and corruption. In a letter to one of his disciples, the famous Persian poet Kamāl al-Dīn al-Iṣfahānī (d. c. 635/1237–8), he describes it in just such a way, saying:

---

[92] Idem, *Mukhtaṣar min kalām al-Suhrawardī*, fol. 799a (on the margins); *R. dar kār-i murīd*, fol. 73b; idem, *R. ilā Kamāl al-Dīn al-Iṣfahānī*, fol. 92b–93a; and, idem, *R. ilā ʿIzz al-Dīn Muḥammad b. Yaʿqūb*, fol. 123b.

[93] *IrM*, fol. 20b; *HT*, fol. 89b; idem, *Futūḥ* XIX, fol. 98a; and, idem, *W. li-Najm al-Dīn al-Tiflīsī*, MS. Tüb., Ma VI 90_{14}, fol. 83b. Gramlich translates Suhrawardī's use of *murāqaba* in the *ʿAwārif* as 'Gott-vor-Augen-haben' ('having God before the eyes'/'keeping God in mind') which accords with the definitions which Suhrawardī provides; cf. Qushayrī where he identifies *murāqaba* as the third act in the ternary *islām-īmān-iḥsān* referred to in the famous 'Ḥadīth of Gabriel' (*SQ*, 23.2; the *ḥadīth* is attested in all the major collections [Wensinck, *Concordance*, 1:467]).

[94] *HT*, fol. 89a–89b; *JQb*, fol. 8a–8b; idem, *Futūḥ* XV, MS. Süley., Şehid Ali Paşa 1393_{16}, fol. 72b; idem, *Futūḥ* XVI, MS. Tüb. Ma VI 90_{34}, fol. 95b. A key concept in early Islamic mysticism (see A. Knysh, "Ṣidḳ," *EI*², 9:548–549).

[95] *ʿAM*, 2:273/*GE*, 59.11; and, *HT*, fol. 89b.

> God's contentment is obtained by purifying the soul, and that by avoiding vices (*radhā'il*), and that by restraining the limbs through the prohibitions of the divine law, and that by sincere repentance (*al-tawba al-naṣūḥ*). The perfection of repentance necessitates continuous scrupulous examination and observation. These vices include blameworthy character traits such as malice, envy, cupidity, hypocrisy, duplicity, and the desire to show off in front of people. When one has been cleansed of these aforementioned vices, he then turns his attention to the vices of his inner being and seeks God's help in overcoming them, and by this becomes one of the possessors of vigilant awareness (*arbāb al-murāqaba*), his outer being safeguarded by *muḥāsaba* and his inner being by *murāqaba* and thus his mental (*dhihnī*) and physical (*'aynī*) beings are purified. When these two beings are purified, his worship and prayer are perfected and he reaches the station called 'do not worship the Lord as if you do not see Him' and his acts of worship become like those of the angels.[96]

As the first stage of the Sufi *ṭarīqa* proper, repentance has a beginning and an end, "its beginning being that the worshipper leaves behind in word, deed, and desire that which does not concern him after having repented from what has passed and what is to come, and its end turning away from everything which is 'other than God' in both his outer and inner beings."[97] The wayfarer proceeds in this way until the station of repentance has become permanent, it being at that point when the second ground station, renunciation (*zuhd*), is brought forth.[98]

The Second Station: Renunciation (zuhd)

Having entered the state of repentance after perfecting his submission and faith, cultivated its virtues, actualized its verities, and made it his permanent abode and dwelling place, the wayfarer then proceeds on to the second major movement in his journey back to his Maker. As the second ground station of the Sufi path, renunciation of the world (*al-zuhd fī 'l-dunyā*) is, like repentance, a station possessed of a beginning, a middle, and an end.[99] Like repentance, this station demands that the

---

[96] Idem, *R. ilā Kamāl al-Dīn al-Iṣfahānī*, fol. 92a–92b; and, idem, *W. li-Rashīd al-Dīn Abī Bakr al-Ḥabash*, fol. 117a; cf. *'AM*, 2:273/*GE*, 59.10.

[97] *HT*, fol. 88b; and, *IrM*, fol. 138b.

[98] *'AM*, 2:302/*GE*, 61.16; idem, *R. dar tawba*, MS. Tüb. Ma VI 90_9, fol. 74b.

[99] In the *'Awārif*, Suhrawardī defines three levels of *zuhd*: 1) rejecting the pleasures of the *nafs* in all worldly affairs which is effected for the sake of God (*li-'llāh*); 2) 'renunciation in renunciation' (*al-zuhd fī 'l-zuhd*) which entails the resignation of free choice in renunciation in a desire that it be effected by God and not by oneself; and, 3) a third type of renunciation which is wholly effected by God. (*'AM*, 2:283–284/*GE*, 60.8–9)

wayfarer dip into the qualities of numerous other stations and states in order to perfect it and actualize its verities. According to Suhrawardī, the beginning of renunciation entails rejecting rank and wealth, preoccupation with secondary causes, material things, and people, abandoning what one possesses except for what is absolutely necessary to sustain life, and not laying up store for the morrow, whereas its end is comprised of renouncing all activities, thoughts, and states of being which are concerned with 'other than God'.[100]

Like the station of repentance, the station of renunciation is also possessed of a wide middle, and as with its predecessor its perfection is contingent upon the aspirant dipping into the qualities of other stations and states, many of which the seeker has already visited such as trust in God (*tawakkul*), contentment (*riḍā*), and patience (*ṣabr*). In this pass, however, the wayfarer comes to appropriate qualities which were not necessary for the actualization of the station of repentance, such as the qualities of satisfaction (*qanāʿa*) with worldly poverty which is drawn from the station of contentment and 'humility and humbleness' (*tawāḍuʿ wa-dhull*) which are drawn from the station of patience.[101] In his quest to perfect the station of renunciation, the wayfarer begins by dipping into the qualities of each of these stations, appropriating them first as states and then, through the progressive actualization of the station of renunciation, eventually effecting their permanency as stations.

It is in this process of progressive acquisition, effected solely through the will of God and not acquired through personal volition in the normal sense, that the wayfarer begins to effect the perfection of the station of renunciation, a process which not only witnesses his dipping into the qualities of other stations but one which also sets into motion a process of progressive actualization of certain groups of interrelated stations. According to Suhrawardī, for example, in their higher levels, the four stations of renunciation, trust, contentment, and patience are tied together in an intimate relationship of mutual co-dependence, the actualization of the station of renunciation effecting the actualization of the station of trust, its actualization effecting the actualization of the

[100] *HT*, fol. 88b–89a; and, idem, *Sayr*, fol. 68a–68b. According to Abū ʾl-Najīb, it is at this point when the aspirant should begin wearing the patched frock (*muraqqaʿa*) as a symbol of his having entered the state of renunciation (*AdM*, 28/Milson, *Rule*, 42).

[101] al-Suhrawardī, *R. dar tawba*, fol. 74b. According to Suhrawardī, *ṣabr* is a part of each and every station, the aspirant progressively traversing its levels (*darājāt*) as he passes through the various stations (*HT*, fol. 89a).

station of contentment, and its actualization effecting the actualization of the station of patience.[102]

To reach this point, however, the wayfarer must make a transition from the domain of repentance and the *nafs* to the domain of renunciation and the heart. It is in the space between the wayfarer's actualization of the station of repentance and the actualization of the station of renunciation where his psycho-spiritual constitution undergoes this transition, a critical existential transformation which marks the point of his actual transition from wayfaring (*sulūk*) to voyaging (*sayr*).[103] In other places, Suhrawardī positions the moment of this transformation at the point when the state of direct witnessing (*ḥāl al-mushāhada*) becomes the station of direct witnessing (*maqām al-mushāhada*), a point at which the 'knowledge of certainty' (*ʿilm al-yaqīn*) becomes the 'essence of certainty' (*ʿayn al-yaqīn*) and the aspirants acts like the worship of the angels.[104] At whichever moment it occurs, this critical transition from wayfaring to voyaging, from *mubtadiʾ* to *mutawwasiṭ*, happens in a moment of annihilation.

Throughout his writings, Suhrawardī distinguishes between two primary types of annihilation, the annihilation of the outer being (*fanāʾ al-ẓāhir*) and the annihilation of the inner being (*fanāʾ al-bāṭin*). The first of them, the annihilation of the outer being, occurs when the wayfarer has been liberated from the dark strictures of the 'soul commanding to evil' through his perfection of the stations of scrupulous examination and observation and vigilant awareness, or in other words

---

[102] *ʿAM*, 2:278/*GE*, 59.20.

[103] Idem, *Sayr*, fol. 68b.

[104] Idem, *R. dar kār-i murīd*, fol. 74a; *HT*, fol. 90a–90b; and, idem, *Futūḥ* XXI, MS. Süley., Musalla Medresesi 20_3, fol. 291b. The essence of certainty in turn is followed by the 'truth of certainty' (*ḥaqq al-yaqīn*) (idem, *W.* IV, fol. 82a). In his works, Suhrawardī provides a number of different explanations of these terms, saying in the *Jadhdhāb*, for instance, that: "the knowledge of certainty is knowledge of the inevitability of death and being prepared for its coming, the essence of certainty the supervision of the angels over death, and the truth of certainty tasting the sip of death; and the outcome of certainty is being prepared for the Hereafter and its mark, disassociation from the world before being removed from it." (fol. 8b, 10b) In the *Irshād*, however, he simply repeats the definition of Qushayrī: "According to the terminology of the Sufis the knowledge of certainty is based on decisive proof (*bi-sharṭ al-burhān*), the essence of certainty on demonstrative proof (*bi-ḥukm al-bayān*), and the truth of certainty on self-evidence (*bi-naʿt al-ʿiyān*)." (fol. 10a–10b; *SQ*, 2.22; similar in the *ʿAwārif* [2:320/*GE*, 62.16]) These three also have a certain connection with the epistemological and existential modes of presence, disclosure, and direct witnessing (*muḥāḍara, mukāshafa, mushāhada*) in terms of their implications (*IrM*, 136a–136b; *ʿAM*, 2:321/*GE*, 62.20; and, al-Qushayrī, op. cit., 2.14).

the actualization of the station of repentance. The effects of this outer annihilation directly impact the manner in which the wayfarer proceeds along his journey, for it ushers in a new set of challenges which must be navigated with a new type of spiritual discipline. This outer annihilation is the annihilation of blameworthy characteristics and the subsistence of praiseworthy ones in the first place and the dissolution of his free choice in the second.[105] It is at this moment when the aspirant actually makes the transformation from wayfaring to voyaging, from *sālik* to *sāʾir*, from earthliness to heavenliness, from darkness to illumination, experiencing a 'second birth' (*al-waldat al-thāniya*) through the delivery of his heart from the darkness of the *nafs*, now a fragile infant who must be tenderly cared for.[106] Here, through the persistence of his inner aspiration (*taṭalluʿ*) for the presence of his beloved, the newly minted voyager and his fragile infant heart are blessed with a theophany which induces a direct, immediate, and non-discursive realization that God is the only true agent (*fāʿil ḥaqīqat*[an]) and that his actions cannot be attributed to any other agent but Him.[107]

Although having experienced the annihilation of his outer being, at this point in his journey the wayfarer turned voyager is still far from reaching his goal. His transition from wayfaring to voyaging, which corresponds to the second movement of his journey on the *ṭarīqa*, has but ushered in another stage which presents its own set of obstacles, the primary one being the heart, which although essential to his advance-

---

[105] *ʿAM*, 2:313–314/*GE*, 61.43–44. In the *Hudā al-ṭālibīn*, Suhrawardī distinguishes between four levels (*darājāt*) of annihilation: 1) the annihilation of the will in the will of God (*fanāʾ al-irāda fī irādat allāh*) which is characterized by relinquishing free choice, adhering completely to the stipulations of the *ṭarīqa*, and submitting the *nafs* to God; 2) the annihilation of individual existence and the *nafs* (*fanāʾ al-kawn wa-l-nafs*) which is characterized by the unveiling of the *ḥaqīqa* and annihilation in the essence of divine unicity (*ʿayn al-tawḥīd*); 3) the annihilation of the wayfarer's knowledge of the attributes (*fanāʾ al-ṣifat fī ʿayn maʿrifat al-sālik*) which is characterized by an oncoming of the states of *hayba* and *uns*; and, 4) the annihilation of annihilation (*fanāʾ al-fanāʾ*) which alludes to the unveiling of the divine essence and attributes and is characterized by the oncoming of the state of sobriety (*ṣaḥw*) after the state of intoxication (*sukr*). (fol. 91b–92a) In one of his letters, al-Junayd identifies three types, or stages, of annihilation: 1) the annihilation of consciousness of attributes, characteristics, and natural qualities; 2) the annihilation of individual desire in the divine will; and, 3) the annihilation of the awareness of one's manifest vision of the Ipseity (*ruʾyat al-ḥaqīqa*) and the complete obliteration of individual consciousness in the majesty of the Godhead. (*Life, Personality and Writings*, 175–176 & 54–55 [Arabic text])

[106] Idem, *Futūḥ* IX, fol. 292a–292b; idem, *Sayr*, fol. 68a; and, idem, *Futūḥ* XVIII, MS. Tüb. Ma VI 90_{36}, fol. 96b.

[107] Idem, *Sayr*, fol. 68b; idem, *R. dar kār-i murīd*, fol. 74a; *ʿAM*, 2:309/*GE*, 61.34.

ment up to this point places demands on his spirit which fetter its ability to ascend. Like the *nafs*, the heart is a created existent, and as such is something which withholds the spirit from entering the divine presence (*al-ḥaḍrat al-ilāhiyya*), constantly exerting pressure on it and thus inhibiting its ability to ascend, being a veil of light just as the *nafs* was a veil of darkness.[108] In his attempt to free his spirit from attachment to the heart, the first station which the voyager must perfect is the station of trust, a station which is characterized by contentment with God's plan and absolute reliance on him in every affair, both physical and spiritual, a station which is intimately connected with the virtues of freely chosen poverty (*faqr*).[109] From here, the voyager passes into the station of contentment and from there into the other stations which are subsumed under the station of renunciation, each one of which witnesses the progressive dissolution of his individual existence (*wujūd/kawn*) until, in the language of the *R. fī al-sayr wa-l-ṭayr*, he begins to approach the station of the *mufarridūn*.[110]

The Third Station: Worshipfulness (ʿubūdiyya)

It is the actualization of the stations of repentance and renunciation which lead the voyager to the fourth ground station, a station which Suhrawardī identifies as the station of worshipfulness (*ʿubūdiyya*), a state of ceaseless remembrance and perpetual worship (*dawām al-ʿamal*) with which nothing interferes except the requirements of the divine law or those duties which are absolutely necessary to the maintenance of life. At the same time, however, even when such an individual is compelled to occupy himself with a necessary duty, his interior does not cease in its worship.[111] Prior to fully actualizing this station, however, the voyager must undergo yet another existential transformation, namely make the transition from voyaging, which is the domain of the heart and the *ṭarīqa*, to flying (*ṭayr*) which is the domain of spirit and the *ḥaqīqa*.[112]

---

[108] *ʿAM*, 2:311/*GE*, 61.37–38.
[109] Idem, *Sayr*, fol. 68b; and, *JQb*, fol. 15a–15b. On *faqr*, see Chapter Four.
[110] Idem, *Sayr*, fol. 68b.
[111] *ʿAM*, 2:278/*GE*, 59.22; cf. *IrM*, fol. 21b–22a.
[112] In one short Persian synopsis of the events leading up to this state, Suhrawardī outlines a scheme in which: "contentment (*qanāʿat*) is the key to renunciation (*zuhd*), renunciation the key to steadfastness (*istiqāma*), steadfastness the key to the *ḥaqīqa*, and the reality of worshipfulness (*ḥaqīqat-i ʿubūdiyya*) the path (*rāh*) to the 'special love of the Truth' (*maḥabbat-i khāṣṣ-i ḥaqq*). The offspring of love (*natīja-yi maḥabbat*) is direct witnessing (*mushāhada*) and unveiling (*mukhāshafa*). Direct witnessing becomes the ornament of

As Suhrawardī explains in his *R. fī ʾl-sayr wa-l-ṭayr*, this stage is called flying because the very otherness of such an act in regard to ordinary human experience aptly captures its significance as an act of the Real effected upon the spirit.[113] Here, through the continual outpouring of divine assistance (*imdād ilāhiyya*) the light of the spirit is strengthened to such an extent that it begins to emanate in the direction of the *nafs*, effecting its acquisition of the quality of equanimity (*ṭumaʾnīna*) and thus it becomes tranquil (*muṭmaʾinna*), at which point the heart rises to the seat of the spirit and the *nafs al-muṭmaʾinna* takes over its managerial functions.[114] Now free, the spirit of the voyager turned flier (*ṭāʾir*) is unveiled through the sheer purity of the divine disclosure (*mukāshafat al-rūḥ bi-ṣarīḥ al-futūḥ*) experiencing various higher spiritual states beginning with special love (*al-maḥabbat al-khāṣṣa*), and then states such as awe (*hayba*), which is an intensification of the state of contraction (*qabḍ*), and intimacy (*uns*), which is an intensification of the state of expansion (*basṭ*).[115] This is followed by all manner of psychic oncomings (*wāridāt*) such as descents (*nawāzil*), flashes (*lawāmiʿ*), glimmerings (*lawāʾiḥ*), and risings (*ṭawāliʿ*), each with a special significance.[116] The fliers who have reached this stage have joined the ranks of the Folk of Divine Dis-

---

the heart through the light of certainty (*nūr al-yaqīn*) and the light of certainty is a ship (*sakīna*) and the ship of the aspirant is faith. As long as he restrains the existence of the passions, he will set his foot in the field of the 'truth of certainty' (*maydān-i ḥaqq al-yaqīn*), and the truth of certainty is the most precious gifts of the Truth which are bestowed upon the elite (*khawāṣṣ*)." (*R. dar tawba*, fol. 74b)

[113] Idem, *Sayr*, fol. 68b.

[114] al-Suhrawardī, *Futūḥ* XIX, fol. 97b; cf. *ʿAM*, 2:322/*GE*, 62.22; and also ibid, 2:275/*GE*, 59.15, in which Suhrawardī posits that the transformation of the blaming soul into the tranquil soul occurs with the actualization of the station of patience. In *Futūḥ* XXVI, Suhrawardī likens the light of the spirit to the light of the sun and the light of the heart to the light of the moon, both fall upon the earth (the *nafs*) but the latter is not strong enough to produce any effect. (MS. Süley., Şehid Ali Paşa 1382_9, fol. 8a)

[115] Idem, *Futūḥ* XIX, fol. 97b; *IrM*, fol. 133a–133b (on *hayba* and *uns*); *ʿAM*, 2:309–312/*GE*, 61.35–40. According to Suhrawardī, this love, which is the love of the elite (*maḥabbat al-khawāṣṣ*), is utterly unlike 'ordinary love' (*maḥabbat ʿāmma*), and in the *ʿAwārif* he spends a great deal of time analyzing the differences as well as the category of love itself, developing a very nuanced analysis which is reminiscent of the theories of Ghazālī. As it relates to the path of ascent outlined here, essentially the love of the elite is love of the divine essence and all other types of love, love of the divine attributes and acts; see: *ʿAM*, 2:292–307/*GE*, 61.3–26; *JQb*, fol. 13b–14b; *IrM*, fol. 33b–34b; and, *Suh.*, 185–189.

[116] al-Suhrawardī, *Sayr*, fol. 68b–69a; and, *IrM*, fol. 136a–136b; cf. *ʿAM*, 2:321/*GE*, 62.21.

closure (*ahl al-mukāshafa*) and are at the cusp of making the transition from *mutaṣawwif* to *ṣūfī*.

It is this status which allows the flyer to be conveyed to the station of 'relinquishing self-disposal and freewill' (*maqām tark al-tadbīr wa-l-ikhtiyār*), a station in which his freewill is replaced with the will of God in a moment of absolute annihilation (*fanāʾ muṭlaq*), the annihilation of his inner self (*fanāʾ al-bāṭin*) which is the result of his spirit having become free from the illuminated existent (*al-wujūd al-nūrānī*) of the heart just as he had formally been liberated from the dark existent (*al-wujūd al-ẓulmānī*) of the *nafs*.[117] It is here where the flier is annihilated from himself (*fanāʾuhu min nafsihi*) and completely effaced in the divine qualities, after which, by God's leave, the existential demand (*al-muṭālabat al-wujūdiyya*) pulls him back into existence and to a reconstituted state of being. This is the station of subsistence (*maqām al-baqāʾ*), a station which Suhrawardī describes as nothing less than the station of perpetual worship:

> It is the complete withdrawal (*insilākh*) of the worshipper from existing by himself and the effectuation of existence through the Real. In this station not even an atom of deviation remains upon him and his outer and inner beings are permanently ensconced in a state of worshipfulness. Knowledge and action fill both and he is firmly settled down in the presence of proximity (*qurb*) between the hands of God through his utter submission and need.[118]

This stage is the station of the *mufarridūn* fully actualized, whose remembrance (*dhikr*) is not merely the recollection of the divine attributes and names by either the tongue or the heart but rather the constant recollection of the divine essence (*al-dhāt*) in the inner being unrestricted by either name or attribute.[119] Although the flight of the flier ultimately results in his annihilation, the culmination of this flight and what makes him a *muntahī* consists of his settling into the station of subsistence (*maqām al-baqāʾ*), the station which Suhrawardī considered to be "the

---

[117] *ʿAM*, 1:327/*GE*, 20.4; and, idem, *Futūḥ* IX, 292a–292b; which Suhrawardī describes as: "whereas the possessor of the *nafs* is earthly (*ʿarḍī*) and the possessor of the heart heavenly (*samāwī*), he who has been freed from both of them is divine (*ilāhī*)." (ibid., 292b)

[118] *ʿAM*, 2:279/*GE*, 59.25; idem, *Futūḥ* I, fol. 69b; and, idem, *W. li-Naṣīr al-Dīn al-Baghdādī*, fol. 65b; cf. al-Junayd, *K. al-fanāʾ*, in *The Life, Personality and Writings of al-Junayd*, 153–156, 32–36 (Arabic text).

[119] *Futūḥ* I, fol. 69a; and, idem, *Futūḥ* IX, fol. 292a.

loftiest level and furthest station (*al-martabat al-aʿlā wa-l-maqām al-asnā*)".[120] It is at this point that the flier obtains the highest of all the spiritual states, the truth of certainty (*ḥaqq al-yaqīn*) which is granted to him as a result of his having obtained the station of subsistence.[121] This constitutes the end of his journey and the beginning of his Sufihood.

The aftereffects of this final movement in the journey of the spirit are comprised of a number of things, and Suhrawardī singles out three in particular which are worthy of extended analysis. First, he states that the individual who is ensconced in the station of subsistence returns to all of the outward acts of worship and obedience which are enjoined upon him by the divine law but not to the spiritual austerities (*ʿaẓāʾim*) and supererogatory devotions (*nawāfil*) which he formally practiced, because he no longer stands in need of them as he has already been ensconced in a state of perpetual worship.[122] Second, the multiplicity of thoughts (*tanawwuʿ al-khawāṭir*) which were effaced in the moment of his annihilation return, but only in the form of either carnal (*nafsiyya*) or angelic (*malakiyya*) thoughts, satanic thoughts having no mode of approach to such an individual and divine thoughts being unnecessary because of his perpetual proximity (*qurb*) to the divine.[123]

Both of these assertions are deeply tied to the concepts of spiritual and religious authority which Suhrawardī lays out in his genealogy of the sciences of the Sufis and the status of the otherworldly-ulama vis-à-vis that of the worldly-ulama, which in turn are tied to his broader program of consolidating a *ribāṭ*-based Sufi system in a language which resonated with the *jamāʿī-sunnī* revivalist climate of early 7th/13th-century Baghdad. Here, religious authority was both praxic and genealogical, undergirded by an outward adherence to the dictates of the revealed law in a manner which was neither ostentatious nor questionable—as were many of the practices associated with the *ṣūfiyya* and other *Personengruppen* associated with them—which was reinforced and strengthened, in a familiar metaphysical and philosophical language, by the inscription of authority in existential terms. The enunciation of identity in such bold and categorical terms evinces, as we will see over

[120] *HT*, fol. 90b.
[121] *ʿAM*, 2:265/*GE*, 58.3.
[122] *ʿAM*, 2:330–332/*GE*, 63.21–24; cf., *AdM*, 8–9/Milson, *Rule*, 31.
[123] Idem, *Futūḥ* IX, fol. 292b.

the next two chapters, both the self-assuredness of urban Sufi elites such as Suhrawardī and, more importantly, the power and prestige which they held in both the eyes of the state powers who patronized them and the various types of individual who flocked to the *ribāṭ*s, teaching circles, and *madrasa*s in which they moved, hearing *ḥadīth*, listening to sermons, receiving their blessing through investiture with the *khirqat al-tabarruk*, and for some striving for annihilation and subsistence in God through staying on and pursuing their way.

Closely tied to this is Suhrawardī's third observation on the state of the *muntahī*, an observation which asserts that in his return the fully-actualized Sufi comes to resemble the Prophet, people being attracted (*jadhb*) to him just as the first Muslims were to the Prophet Muḥammad.[124] This attraction, which is most visibly manifest in the figure of the Sufi shaykh, is effected by a certain spiritual charisma which the fully-actualized Sufi comes into possession of as a result of his having successfully achieved the goal, a charisma which directly mirrors the state of the Prophet himself:

> The state of the *muntahī* becomes similar to the state of God's Messenger in calling people to the Real...and in this is a great secret, and this is that the Messenger would call people to the Real through an affinitive connection of the soul (*bi-rābiṭat al-jinsiyya al-nafs*), there being a deep mutual connection (*rābiṭat al-ta'līf*) between his spotless soul and the souls of those who followed him just as there was a deep mutual connection between his spirit and theirs.[125]

As Fritz Meier has shown in a lengthy study of Naqshbandī conceptions of the *pīrī-murīdī* relationship, this concept of natural or affinitive connection (*rābiṭat al-jinsiyya*) between master and disciple came to serve as one of the defining features of *ṭarīqa*-based Sufism following the rise of the Sufi brotherhoods in the era of Suhrawardī's successors,[126] and as with many of the formal and conceptual characteristics of this broader tradition, Suhrawardī seems to be the first to have discussed and analyzed the concept in the manner in which it came to be under-

---

[124] *ʿAM*, 2:332–333/*GE*, 63.26–27; *HT*, fol. 93a; and, idem, *W. li-Naṣīr al-Dīn al-Baghdādī*, fol. 64b–65a.

[125] *ʿAM*, 2:232–233/*GE*, 63.27; echoed in *HT*, fol. 93a–93b.

[126] Fritz Meier, "Die Herzensbindung an den Meister," in idem, *Zwei Abhandlungen über die Naqšbandiyya* (Istanbul and Stuttgart: Franz Steiner Verlag, 1994).

stood (with various nuances and expansions certainly) by later Sufi masters who consciously situated themselves in the particular tradition of Junaydī-inspired *ṭarīqa*-based Sufism which he championed.

* * *

It is the question of how this journey was to be effected in time and space, the various actors in its production, their costumes and props, and the places and spaces in which they staged this soteriological drama which forms a third point of entry into the details of this process of institution building and our understanding of a figure who by all accounts played an important role in its unfolding. While Suhrawardī's enunciation of authority and identity on behalf of the particular *ṭā'ifa* for whom he spoke, grounded as it was in the discourse and authority of the text, does indeed add a layer to the retellings of his biographers, it leaves a number of important questions unanswered, most notably how did Suhrawardī go about projecting this comprehensive vision onto the actual physical and social spaces in which he moved and, in turn, how successful was he in doing so? How was an individual who so clearly challenged the status of the majority of the ulama as the heirs to the prophets and the final arbiters of the religious law able to not only attract a large group of well-documented and thoroughly unimpeachable students, disciples, and petitioners from among its ranks but also enjoy the support of a caliph who himself was deeply concerned with maintaining good relations with such groups themselves? Where can Suhrawardī be situated within the particular Junaydī tradition of Sufism to which he considered himself an heir and on whose behalf he appointed himself a spokesmen, and in turn, how and where did he situate himself among the other Sufis of his day? Finally, to what extent did the organized and institutionalized system of *ribāṭ*-centered Sufism which he champions in his written works reflect an actual reality on the ground?

Although each set of texts which we have interrogated thus far furnish material which helps to clarify some of these issues, complete answers to these questions cannot be found wholly in the works of Suhrawardī's biographers, nor in the historiography bearing upon the people and places with who he was associated, nor in what we might initially interpret as a largely self-contained description of mystical theory and metaphysics. To answer such questions, we need to move from the interior to exterior, employing the historical subtext and biographical narratives to map this veridical geography of ascent onto the horizontal realm of practices, relationships, social spaces, and the actual physical institutions which housed them.

CHAPTER FOUR

MAʿRIFA DISCIPLINED AND INSTITUTIONALIZED

There were, of course, no Sufi brotherhoods as we know them today in the early-7th/13th century, no self-identified groups of individuals looking back to an eponymous founder under whose name a particular teaching lineage might differentiate itself from others based on an inherited body of practices, texts, foundational narratives, and accoutrements. This would come later, and in the case of the earliest teaching lineages—the Suhrawardiyya being among the first—was invariably the work of a particular eponym's disciples and their successors and never that of the eponym himself.[1] As with ʿAbd al-Qādir al-Jīlānī (d. 561/1166), Aḥmad al-Rifāʿī (578/1182), Muʿīn al-Dīn Chishtī (d. 633/1236), Abū ʾl-Ḥasan al-Shādhilī (d. 656/1258), and Jalāl al-Dīn Rūmī (d. 672/1273) neither Abū ʾl-Najīb nor ʿUmar al-Suhrawardī 'founded' an order or brotherhood as such. In many cases, the particular teaching lineages which bore the names of such eponyms did not come to be construed as distinct orders (*ṭuruq*) as such until subjected to the centralizing pressures and institutionalizing policies of the Mamluk, Ottoman, and Mughal imperial projects. What these eponyms did do, however, is bring a certain measure of closure to a long and complex period of transition characterized by the progressive routinization of Sufism as a distinct mode of religiosity, identity, and social affiliation by championing, or at least setting into motion, an institutionalizing vision of organization, accoutrement, and praxis which was self-regulating, self-propagating, and most importantly, reproducible. It was during this age of transition—underway by middle of the 5th/11th century and finding a certain measure of consummation in the latter 6th/12th through the

[1] The literature on the development and diffusion of the early *ṭarīqa* lineages is widely scattered, and much research remains to be done before any broad synthetic conclusions can be offered. Overviews and further references in Trimingham, *The Sufis Orders*, 31–104 (dated); Gramlich, *Derwischorden*, 1:4–18; Popovic and Veinstein, eds., *Les voies d'Allah*, 44–67, 104–120, 205–212, 451–517 and esp. the bibliography 636–672; Eric Geoffroy, *Le soufisme en Égypte et Syrie sous les derniers Mamlouks et les premiers Ottomans* (Damascus: Institut Français de Damas, 1995), 205–282; idem, et al., "Ṭarīḳa," *EI*^{2}, 10:243–257; and, Knysh, *Islamic Mysticism*, 169–244.

late 7th/13th centuries—when certain particularly well-positioned Sufi masters such as Abū ʾl-Najīb and ʿUmar al-Suhrawardī began to codify the collective theoretical, practical, and institutional weight of the past which they had inherited into discrete, self-regulating, and replicable forms of organization and praxis which would eventually come to characterize transregional forms of institutional organization and praxis associated with *ṭarīqa*-based Sufism from North Africa to Iraq, and from Anatolia to India during the centuries which followed.

It is only at the end of this transitional period, occurring somewhere between the late-7th/13th and mid-8th/14th centuries where the shift from the precedence of particular self-referential methods (*ṭarīq/madhhab*)[2] of individual Sufi shaykhs as primary loci of spiritual authority and group identity to the beginnings of the precedence of a formally definable institutional entity, the organized Sufi brotherhood (*ṭarīqa*, pl. *ṭuruq*), took place. Generally this shift is understood to have been one of the outcomes of a much earlier transition from the generic pattern of the 'teaching-shaykh' or 'master of instruction' (*shaykh al-taʿlīm*) to the 'directing-shaykh' or 'master of training' (*shaykh al-tarbiya*) and the concomitant proliferation of the physical institutions which sustained them, namely the Sufi *ribāṭ*s and *khānaqāhs*. In no small number of cases (as with Abū ʾl-Najīb al-Suhrawardī's Tigris *ribāṭ* for example), such institutions were underwritten by powerful political patrons, supported through the instrument of pious endowment (*waqf*), constructed with living quarters and, in some cases, supplied with adjoining *madrasas*.[3]

Living as he did in the heart of this transitional period, we find in Suhrawardī an individual who exemplifies the role which such directing-shaykhs played in this process, individuals who in their endowed *ribāṭ*s and *khānaqāh*s trained students along the lines of a specific *ṭarīq* which, if they happened to become eponyms such as Suhrawardī, would later be replicated, in progressively more self-identified and institutionalized ways, under their name by future generations who envisioned

[2] On the connotations of the term *ṭarīq* (way, road, path; pl. *ṭuruq*; fem. *ṭarīqa* [way, method, course]; pl. *ṭarāʾiq* [rare in this sense]) as it came to be used in Sufism, see: Eric Geoffroy, "Ṭarīḳa," *EI²*, 10:243–246.

[3] On this, see Fritz Meier, "Khurāsān and the End of Classical Sufism," in *Essays on Islamic Piety and Mysticism*, trans. John O'Kane (Leiden: Brill, 1999), 189–219; Malamud, "Sufi Organization," 427–442; Kiyānī, *Taʾrīkh-i khānaqāh dar Īrān*, 311–322 (on *khānagāh-madrasa* complexes); and, Arthur Buehler, *Sufi Heirs of the Prophet: The Indian Naqshbandiyya and the Rise of the Mediating Sufi Shaykh* (Columbia, SC: University of South Carolina Press, 1998), 29–54.

themselves as direct heirs to their particular method. Just as it came to refer to a formally constituted Sufi brotherhood, as the second term in the ternary *sharī'a—ṭarīqa—ḥaqīqa*, the term *ṭarīq(a)* also refers to the individualized and idiosyncratic ways of particular Sufi masters, connotations whose implications were sublimated but not subsumed with the rise of the fraternal *ṭuruq* long after the age of Suhrawardī.[4] As with many technical terms, it is in the first chapter of his *Irshād al-murīdīn* where Suhrawardī offers his most telling definition of what he intends by the term *ṭarīq(a)*, informing the group of friends and companions who had requested that he write this particular "compendium on the method of the Masters of Wayfaring" (*mukhtaṣar fī bayān madhhab arbāb al-sulūk*) that:

> The term 'path' (*ṭarīqa*) refers to the acquisition of god-fearing piety (*taqwā*) and what draws you near to the Master by way of traversing stopping places (*manāzil*) and stations (*maqāmāt*). Every station is a path in and of itself, and the respective paths (*ṭuruq*) of the Sufi masters (*mashāyikh*) differ because their station and states (*aḥwāl*) differ. Every master devises a path which accords with his state and station. Some of them follow the path of assembling with people and training them while others select only a certain individual or group [to train]. Still others follow a path consisting of the recitation of many litanies, extensive fasting, prayer, and the like. Others pursue a path of serving people by carrying firewood and hemp upon their backs and selling it in the market, being honest in its price. In this way, each one of them chooses from among the various paths.[5]

Used in such a manner, the term *ṭarīqa* does not refer to the kind of corporate entities or self-regulating group solidarities which would come to characterize *ṭarīqa*-based Sufism with the rise of the formally constituted Sufi brotherhoods, but rather individual 'ways' or 'methods' of negotiating the bridge connecting the domain of submission and faith, the *sharī'a*, with the domain of the ground of existence and the really real, the *ḥaqīqa*, and as with the authorities upon which he drew, Suhrawardī's figuration of the term *ṭarīq(a)* is grounded in the recognition that there is, in fact, a multiplicity of methods, various paths of

[4] Gilles Veinstein, "Un islam sillonné de voies," in Popovic and Veinstein, eds., *Les voies d'Allah*, 12–13; Geoffroy, "Ṭarīḳa," *EI*[2], 10:244; Ernst, *Sufism*, 121–123; and, Ernst and Lawrence, *Sufi Martyrs of Love*, 11–26.

[5] al-Suhrawardī, *Irshād al-murīdīn*, MS. Süley., Ayasofya 2117_5, fol. 131b; cf., *'AM*, 1:282–295 / *GE*, 16.1–25. Abū 'l-Najīb presents a similar explanation of the term *ṭarīq*, providing more examples of the various routes (*masālik*) which may be followed (*AdM*, 22 / Milson, *Rule*, 38–39).

negotiating this bridge which are characteristic of any one socially-recognized or existentially designated *ṭāʾifa* or any one Sufi master. Thus, to take a typical example, he speaks of two separate methods (*ṭarīqān*) of escape from slavery to the soul: the method of those drawn nigh (*ṭarīq al-muqarrabīn*) and the method of the godly (*ṭarīq al-abrār*).[6]

As discussed in the previous chapter, for Suhrawardī some of these methods were deemed better and more perfect than others and, never one to leave things ambiguous, he invariably refers to his own path, or method, as either the *ṭarīq al-ḥaqq* ('path of the Real'), the *ṭarīq al-muttaqīn* ('path of the God-fearing'), or simply as the *ṭarīq al-qawm* ('path of the Folk', i.e., the path of al-Junayd),[7] constantly enjoining his audience to adhere to its terms and regulations (*sharṭ*, pl. *sharāʾiṭ*) and the rights or obligations (*ḥaqq*, pl. *ḥuqūq*) of its methods and those who populate its byways. It was in this spirit that Suhrawardī systematically laid out his own *ṭarīq*, a method or modality comprised of specific forms of organization, praxis, manners, customs, and accoutrements. For an individual like Suhrawardī, this path could not be construed except in institutional terms, and it is in his particular structuration of its essential features which gave institutional shape and form, and ultimately replicability, to the comprehensive soteriological vision encoded in his analysis of the origins, aims, and outcome(s) of the sciences of the *ṣūfiyya* for which he appointed himself a spokesman. In turn, it was in writing the norms which define the scope, content, and boundaries of this particular *ṭarīq* which provided the template which his disciples and their successors would use to construct a distinct *ṭarīqat al-suhrawardiyya* in the two or so generations following his death.

The Exterior Dimension

Contrary to the way in which Suhrawardī set up polarities among the contenders to prophetic heirship, the manner in which he mapped

---

[6] al-Suhrawardī, *Futūḥ* I, fol. 69a–69b; *ʿAM*, 2:218 / *GE*, 52.3; idem, *W.* IV, fol. 80b; and, idem, *W. li-Naṣīr al-Dīn al-Baghdādī*, fol. 63b–64a.

[7] For example, *R. ilā Fakhr al-Dīn al-Rāzī*, fol. 220a; *ʿAM*, 1:247, 2:218 / *GE*, 11.1, 52.3; and, idem, *W. li-Naṣīr al-Dīn al-Baghdādī*, fol. 63b ff.; the former, *ṭarīq al-ḥaqq*, being by far the most common. The connection between Suhrawardī's *ṭarīq* (i.e., the Suhrawardiyya) and, a real or imagined, *ṭarīqat al-Junayd*, was not lost on later authors, e.g. al-Sanūsī (d. 1276/1859), *al-Salsabīl al-maʿīn fī al-ṭarāʾiq al-arbaʿīn*, in *al-Majmūʿat al-mukhtārat min muʾallafāt Muḥammad b. ʿAlī al-Sanūsī* (Beirut: Dār al-Kitāb al-Lubnānī, 1968), 47–49; and, idem, *al-Manhal al-rawī fī asānīd al-ʿulūm wa-uṣūl al-ṭarāʾiq*, in op. cit., 98–103; on this see: Geoffroy, *Le soufisme*, 211–213.

and inscribed the comprehensive mystical vision of ascent into the actual physical and social spaces in which he moved was not through a process of exclusion but rather through one of systematic inclusion, a program articulated in a rhetoric of circumscription and regulation. Just as al-Nāṣir projected his centralizing vision of a unified Abode of Islam under the aegis of a universal caliphate through formal policies of circumscription, the particular *ribāṭ*-based system (*ṭarīq*) of organization and praxis which Suhrawardī carefully describes in his works ultimately derived its vitality from the manner in which it went about demarcating a hierarchy of participation and affiliation, assigning specific roles, expectations, and conditions to each of its constituents through a body of prescriptions (i.e., policies), authorized and legitimated through a comprehensive and totalizing enunciation of authority. In its specifically Islamic emplotment, this *ṭarīq* was supported on religious grounds through proof texts mined from the Qurʾān, the Ḥadīth, and the exempla of the *salaf al-ṣāliḥ* and on intracommunal grounds through the strategic appropriation of the exempla of the paragonic Sufi authorities of the Junaydī past as heirs, exemplars, and mediators of this body of knowledge and praxis into a very real present. At the same time this *ṭarīq* was both universal and specific, universal in that it was legitimated through a comprehensive ontology and metaphysics, and specific in the manner in which it came to situate itself in the very socio-religious and discursive milieux in which its constituents moved by attending to a wider body of social acts, cultural codes, and symbols which extended far beyond the Sufi *ribāṭ* itself.

As in the *madrasa* and the culture of religious learning among urban ulama generally, in the Sufi *ribāṭ* authority was mediated through a complex of behaviors and codes authorized and legitimated, in part at least, by enunciating connections to authoritative bygone paragons through inserting oneself into an either real or imagined process of perpetual renewal (*tajdīd, iḥyāʾ*) concretized in the conservation, dissemination, and replication of the exemplary and soteriologicaly-focused behavior of past authorities. This idea of renewal through replication is one of, if not the most, defining characteristics of the particular Junaydī strand of Sufism to which Suhrawardī considered himself an heir, a tradition which rooted much of its identity in a perceived continuity articulated and concretized, in the first place, in very specific modes of behavior and praxis. As we have seen, such assertions of identity were enunciated early, most visibly in that supremely influential group of Sufi systematizers of the 4th/10th–5th/11th-centuries to whose collective output Suhrawardī was deeply indebted. Such enunciations are rife throughout this corpus, well evinced in multiple discursive and rhetorical configurations such as, for instance, by the eminent late 4th/10th-century Sufi scholar ʿAbd al-Raḥmān al-Sulamī in one of his own compendia of the sciences of the Sufis:

> Among the regulations (*sharāʾiṭ*) of Sufism to which the classical authorities (*mashāyikh mutaqaddimūn*) held fast are: the renunciation of the world in favor of recollection (*dhikr*) and acts of worship; self-sufficiency and complete contentment with a modicum of food, drink, and clothing; attending to the poor and breaking with vain desires; pursing the path of spiritual exertion and pious scrupulosity; sleeping and talking little, restraining ambition, and vigilant awareness; separation from created beings in favor of meeting with the shaykhs; eating only out of bare necessity, speaking only when compelled to do so, and sleeping only when it overtakes; sitting in mosques and wearing the patched frock (*muraqqaʿa*)...indeed, in our age it is necessary for the one possessed of intellect to follow all of this and to know something of the fundamentals (*uṣūl*) of Sufism and the path of the Folk of Sincerity among them so that he may disassociate himself from those pretenders (*mutashabbih*) who imitate them, those who don their dress, and those who wrongly take their name, and thus not become one of them. Verily, the *ṣūfiyya* are God's trust on His earth, the confidents of His secrets and knowledge, and those whom He has chosen from among all His creatures.[8]

As for al-Sulamī, for Suhrawardī it is in the continuity and replicability of such fundamental behaviors which both differentiate the *ṣūfiyya* from other *Personengruppen* while at the same time authorizing and legitimating their claims to heirship. In the *ribāṭ*, the exempla of the past serve as both a device of legitimization and a model of praxis, and not only does Suhrawardī claim the status of prophetic heirship for the *ṣūfiyya*, finding in them the "only *ṭāʾifa* among all the *ṭawāʾif* of Islam who revivify the Sunna in time and space",[9] but also assigns each and every one of the practices characteristic of this group a precedent in the exempla of the Prophet and the *salaf al-ṣāliḥ*, an authoritative articulation in the exempla of the Sufi paragons of the past, a grounding in the ontology and metaphysics of the mythic journey of ascent, and a connection to wider social-cultural and religious symbols and practices.

---

[8] al-Sulamī, *al-Muqaddima fī ʾl-taṣawwuf*, ed. Yūsuf Zaydān (Beirut: Dār al-Jīl, 1999), 72; idem, *Jawāmiʿ ādāb al-ṣūfiyya*, in *MA*, 1:352, 383, 387)—on eating, sleeping, and talking little.

[9] *ʿAM*, 2:56, 2:222 / *GE*, 29.1, 52.13.

At the same time, the works of Suhrawardī are infused with the spirit of *jamāʿī-sunnī* communalism which one would expect to find in the *œuvre* of an early 7th/13th-century Shāfiʿī *ʿālim, muḥaddith*, preacher, and Sufi master living and working in al-Nāṣir's Baghdad, a type of socially-conscious activism well evinced in the heyday of the so-called Seljuk Sunni Revival by individuals such as Abū Ḥāmid al-Ghazālī, and in Suhrawardī's own time by the Ḥanbalī *ʿālim*-cum-Sufi revivalist ʿAbd al-Qādir al-Jīlānī, an orientation which by all accounts guided the program of his uncle Abū ʾl-Najīb and one which Suhrawardī himself was careful to replicate. While Suhrawardī was a Sufi shaykh, he was also a member of the ulama, publicly enunciating his membership in their ranks through participating in their culture and, what is more, counting among his many teachers, students, associates, and disciples individuals who clearly identified themselves as full-fledged members of that body, transmitting *ḥadīth*, teaching in the *madrasa*s, serving as muftis and *qāḍī*s, preaching, and leading prayers in Friday congregational mosques. Judging from both Suhrawardī's lengthy argument for the Sufis, in their capacity as the otherworldly-ulama, as the legitimate possessors of prophetic heirship and their very public presence in multiple arenas of power and influence, the sheer self-assuredness of Suhrawardī and his associates is as astounding as it is telling. For Suhrawardī, it was not a matter of effecting some type of reconciliation between the ulama and the Sufis through answering criticisms voiced by individuals such as Ibn al-Jawzī, but rather consolidating a position of a group who were already well-established, deeply entrenched in a culture of religious professionals toward whom the state looked for support and legitimacy and the people for religious guidance and intercession.

While it is clear that Suhrawardī posits both a qualitative and quantitative distinction between the generality of Muslims (*ʿawwām*) and the elite (*khawāṣṣ*) on metaphysical grounds, as evinced in the structure of his *ribāṭ*-based system considered in its totality, the world of the *ṣūfiyya* as he envisioned it was neither esoteric nor exclusionary. Certainly, Suhrawardī's *ribāṭ* privileges the centrality of the master-disciple dyad as the core discipline of an intentional community of like-minded individuals, but at the same time this discipline did not define the institution as a whole. While certainly retaining the insularity and parochialism of the *ribāṭ*s, *khānaqāh*s, and private residences of the Sufi masters of previous generations at its center, at its periphery Suhrawardī's *ribāṭ* mirrored the porousness of the *madrasa*s and the culture of religious learning generally. The *ribāṭ*-based system which Suhrawardī championed was simultaneously an open and a closed space, programmatically making room for varying levels of participation and affiliation by inviting those who had neither the desire, capacity, or wherewithal to become full-time disciples the opportunity to participate in its life, and thus in Suhrawardī's view, benefit from the blessing which such a space contains. Although neither the first nor the only representative of this trend, Suhrawardī is certainly the best documented, and perhaps most representative, figure in this important transitional moment in the history of Sufism and its institutions.

As with the genealogy which Suhrawardī programmatically laid out for the sciences of the Sufis in terms of their representing a particular inherited knowledge passed down from the Prophet Muḥammad to his companions, known at the time neither by a particular name nor a discrete body of accoutrements, he also casts the actual physical institution of the *ribāṭ* and the practices which transpire within it as praiseworthy innovations first evinced in the exempla of the paragonic authorities of the past. As to be expected, it is in the *ʿAwārif al-maʿārif* where he lays out a genealogy for this institution, seeing it as both a recreation of the state of the Folk of the Veranda[10] and a response to the famous *ḥadīth* in which the Prophet is reported to have said "we have returned from the lesser jihad to the greater jihad" about which he was asked, "and what is the greater jihad", to which he replied "the struggle against oneself (*mujāhadat al-nafs*)".[11] Providing an etymology for the word which plays upon its military connotations, Suhrawardī casts this space as an outpost for spiritual warriors who, as 'frontline fighters' (*murābiṭ mujāhid*) in the struggle against the *nafs*, are obligated to follow a certain 'military order of formal regulations' (*sharāʾiṭ*), saying:

> These are the regulations of the resident (*sākin*) of the *ribāṭ*: 1) that he cut off relations (*muʿāmala*) with created beings in favor of establishing relations with the Real; 2) that he renounce acquisition and be content with the guaranty of the causer or causes; 3) that he restrain his soul from undue social intercourse and avoid its consequences; and, 4) that he embrace worshipful devotions day and night as a counterweight to every bad habit. And these are his occupations (*shughl*): 1) that he busy himself

---

[10] *ʿAM*, 1:213, 267–269, 272 / *GE*, 6.7, 14.1–4, 9.

[11] Ibid., 1:263 / *GE*, 108.4; idem, *Tarjama-yi al-lawāmiʿ*, fol. 76a–76b; *ḥadīth* in Ibn al-Ṣiddīq, *ʿAwāṭif*, 1:188–189 (no. 79); and, idem, *Ghaniyyat*, 1:183–185 (no. 79); see also: *KM*, 252 / Nicholson, *The Kashf*, 200.

> in preserving his moments (*hifẓ al-awqāt*); 2) that he persist in his litanies (*awrād*); 3) that he wait eagerly for the time of canonical prayer; and, 4) that he assiduously avoid heedless mistakes. By this, he will become a 'frontline fighter' (*murābiṭ mujāhid*).[12]

It is in waging this greater jihad through acts of supererogatory piety and self-exertion (*mujāhadāt*) where Suhrawardī finds one of the most powerful arguments for the necessity of such a space vis-à-vis the Sufi path, for according to the long-standing interpretation of this particular *ḥadīth*, the Prophet's definition of the greater jihad against oneself (*nafs*) refers to the struggle against 'the enemy within', namely those things within man which divert him from responding to the dictates of revelation, in Sufi terminology none other than the *nafs al-ammārat bi-sūʾ*.

In the first chapter of this study we noted the connection between the *ribāṭ* as an institution associated with the frontiers (*thughūr*) of the *dār al-islām* and its connection to the jihad, asceticism, and the early paragons of the collective Sufi past. In the urban centers of the central lands of Islamdom during the late 6th/12th through the 7th/13th centuries such associations did not seem to go unnoticed. This was the age of the Crusades, a period during which Sufi shaykhs such as the celebrated patron saint of Damascus Arslān Dimashqī (who played an active role in the jihad) were cultivated by individuals such as the famed anti-Crusader Nūr al-Dīn b. Zangī as sources of authority in legitimizing their bids to garner support for the jihad, funding the construction of *madrasas* and *ribāṭ*s on a hitherto unprecedented scale.[13] Saladin himself did the same, financing among many other institutions the construction of the important Saʿīd al-Suʿadāʾ Khānaqāh in Cairo, a space which played host to at least one of the individuals responsible for the diffusion of Suhrawardī's *ʿAwārif al-maʿārif* in Egypt, Ibn al-Qasṭallānī. As has already been discussed in great detail, the caliph al-Nāṣir did the same, drawing upon the authority of individuals such as Suhrawardī by tying them into patronage relationships which, as discussed in the next chapter, brought with it certain obligations. Despite widespread debate over the permissibility of accepting such patronage among Sufis in general, like both Wajīh al-Dīn and Abū ʾl-Najīb, ʿUmar

---

[12] *ʿAM*, 1:265–266 / *GE*, 13.7.

[13] Nūr al-Dīn b. Zangī, in fact, founded a *ribāṭ* in Damascus for Shaykh Arslān; on this, see Eric Geoffroy, *Djihad et contemplation: vie et enseignement d'un soufi au temps des croisades* (Paris: Éditions Dervy, 1997), 13–36; and, idem, "L'apparition des voies: les *khirqa* primitives," in Popovic and Veinstein, eds., *Les voies d'Allah*, 52–53.

al-Suhrawardī had little aversion to enjoying such support, a policy which he makes clear in a response to a question put to him by his anonymous interlocutors from Khurāsān:

> We ask: is it permissible for aspirants to reside in *ribāṭs*, *khānaqāhs*, or *zāwiyas* built with the money of sultans or political powers and to eat from its endowments? We answer: it is permissible to reside in them but not to eat from their endowments unless one is engaged in a full-time program of spiritual devotions.[14]

This is an important point, and cannot be glossed over lightly, because as Suhrawardī makes clear through his writings it is the actual physical space of the *ribāṭ* and the organizational structures and practices which fill it which define and particularize, more than anything else, both his *ṭarīq* and the particular *ṭāʾifa* associated with it vis-à-vis others. The *ribāṭ* as the primary locus of identity is further evinced in the way in which Suhrawardī speaks about the group solidarity of its inhabitants. As evinced in the detailed rules and regulations which Suhrawardī outlines for traveling from *ribāṭ* to *ribāṭ*, there is no doubt that this solidarity was diffuse and transregional, something which Suhrawardī hints at in the very language he uses to describe this space, saying that *ribāṭ* is the encampment (*bayt*) of a particular tribe (*qawm*), the permanent homestead (*dār*) of a family group (*jamāʿa*), and a stopping place (*manzil*) for a wider community of affiliates who are brethren (*ikhwān*) tied together in a bond of brotherhood (*ukhuwwa*) rooted in a single aim and shared existential situation (*qasḍ wāḥid wa-ʿazm wāḥid wa-aḥwāl mutanāsaba*).[15] This brotherly solidarity and sense of community (*ijtimāʿ*) shared among the constituents of the *ribāṭ* is highlighted time and time again throughout Suhrawardī's works, an enunciation of identity which envisions a community tied together by a comprehensive body of shared manners and customs, allegiances to both each other and to the masters who oversee their activities, and by the presence of discrete psycho-spiritual affinities engendered by their collective spiritual endeavors.[16] When tied to a comprehensive political program such as

---

[14] *AdM*, 61 (no. 12).

[15] *ʿAM*, 1:267, 311 / *GE*, 14.1, 18.11.

[16] E.g., Ibid., 1:268, 273–276, 2:223–237 / *GE*, 14.1, 15.1–6, 53.1–55.16. It is important to recall that Arabic has two plurals for the word brother (*akh*), *ikhwa* which is normally used to refer to biological brothers and *ikhwān* whose meaning is well captured by the English word 'brethren'. The use of the term in this way is evinced in both the logia of the Sufi paragons, and in Sulamī's *Jawāmiʿ ādāb al-ṣūfiyya* and *K. ādāb al-ṣuḥba*

that of al-Nāṣir, the possibilities which such spaces offered to a patron extended far beyond the spiritual charisma of the individual Sufi masters who stood at their apex.

In addition to serving as the space of a larger family of spiritual warriors, the *ribāṭ* was also a space within which the charismatic community of 1st/7th-century Medina was replicated, the shaykh taking on the role of the Prophet and the constituents of the *ribāṭ* that of his Companions (*ṣaḥāba*). Here, we move into the realm of symbol, and accordingly throughout his works Suhrawardī makes it explicitly clear that the manners and customs (*ādāb*), accoutrements, and practices associated with the *ribāṭ* are not only fully in accordance with the dictates of the divine law but are derived directly from the Sunna and the exempla of the *salaf al-ṣāliḥ*. It is in the systematic explication of each of these connections and continuities where Suhrawardī maps his comprehensive vision of mystical ascent unto the actual physical and social spaces and institutions in which it transpired.

This being said, Suhrawardī offers precious little information on how such spaces were organized structurally. In contrast to later descriptions of *ribāṭ*s and *khānaqāh*s, neither his writings nor contemporary sources provide much in the way of information on the day-to-day operations of such institutions, although Suhrawardī does make note of some of its most important features including the 'common room' (*bayt al-jamā'a*) and the cell (*zāwiya*, pl. *zawāyā*). When he speaks about the former, it is either in connection with communal activities such as the shaykh's public lectures and teaching sessions (*majlis* / *ḥalqa*) or the ritual of the spiritual concert (*samā'*) as well as its use as a prayer hall (*muṣallā*). On the latter, he consistently uses the term *zāwiya* to refer to the individual cells in which the discipline of solitary spiritual retreat (*khalwa* / *arba'īniyya*) is carried out. Beyond this, nothing else substantial is offered.

Although certainly a desideratum, such structural details are ultimately less important than details regarding the people who inhabited them and the practices they engaged in, and in *'Awārif al-ma'ārif*, and to a lesser extent in some of his other writings, Suhrawardī presents

---

wa-ḥusn al-'ishra (ed. M.J. Kister [1954], rpt. in *MA*, 2:62–132) where, clearly reflective of the ethos of the early *futuwwa* / *javānmardī* tradition, he consistently uses the term *ikhwān* to describe the proper manners and behaviors (*adab*) structuring the social relationships between and among fellow seekers on the Sufi path. Similarly, just like Abū 'l-Najīb and 'Umar al-Suhrawardī, Jīlānī uses the same term in his own prescriptions on *adab* for the constituents of the *ribāṭ* specifically (e.g., *GhṬ*, 2:287, 296).

us with a systematic description of the organization of this charismatic community of frontline fighters. Although hinted at in earlier works and most certainly proliferating with the widespread establishment of *ribāṭ*-based Sufi communities in the two centuries following his death, to my knowledge his description of the hierarchy of this institution, the rights, obligations, duties, and roles of its various members, the activities which they engage in, and the manners and customs by which they interact with one another is the earliest we have. It was the replication of this system, preserved, transmitted, translated, and expanded in the form of his *ʿAwārif al-maʿārif* and those Sufi manuals which drew upon it which was to color the diffusion of his particular *ṭarīq* under the aegis of a number of his most erstwhile disciples following his death.[17]

Master and Disciple

One of the primary features of the processes informing the increasing institutionalization of Sufism during the era preceding Suhrawardī was

[17] In addition to the translations, reworkings, and commentaries on the *ʿAwārif al-maʿārif* of Qāsim Dāwūd Khaṭīb Darācha (c. 639/1241–1242), Ismāʿīl b. ʿAbd al-Muʾmin Māshāda (in 665/1266), Ṣadr al-Dīn Junayd al-Shīrāzī (d. 716/1316) and others (on which, see William Chittick, "ʿAwāref al-Maʿāref," *EIr*, 1:114–115), portions of both this work and Abū ʾl-Najīb *K. ādāb al-murīdīn* made their way, via Persian, into early Kubrawī circles, beginning with Najm al-Dīn al-Kubrā himself in his own *Ādāb al-murīdīn*, a text wrongly attributed to ʿAbdullāh-i Anṣārī by Serge de Laugier de Beaurecueil based on an attribution of authorship in one, and only one, of the many mss. of the text (MS. Süley., Şehid Ali Paşa 1393, fol. 39a–49a; ed. and trans., idem, in "Un opuscule de Khwāja ʿAbdullah Anṣārī concernant les bienséances des soufis," *Bulletin de l'Institut Français d'Archéologie Orientale du Caire* 59 [1960]: 203–240; translated by Gerhard Böwering in "The *Adab* Literature of Classical Sufism: Anṣārī's Code of Conduct," in Barbara Metcalf, ed., *Moral Conduct and Authority: The Place of* Adab *in South Asian Islam* [Berkeley: University of California Press, 1984], 61–87], a text which both Fritz Meier, who translated it into German based on MS. Süley., Ayasofya 4792, fol. 738a–741b, and Masʿūd Qāsimī, who edited it based on five more mss., have quite rightly argued actually belongs to Najm al-Dīn Kubrā and his circle (Meier, "A Book of Etiquette for Sufis," in *Essays on Islamic Piety and Mysticism*, 49–92; and Qāsimī's introduction to *Ādāb al-ṣūfiyya* [Tehran: Kitābfurūshī-yi Zavvār, 1363 sh. (1984)], esp. 4–7; cf. Böwering, op. cit., 69–70 who argues for the attribution to Anṣārī). The continued diffusion of these works, and the actual organizational and institutional apparatus which they prescribe, is well evinced in the masterful Sufi handbook of Yaḥyā Bākharzī, the *Fuṣūṣ al-ādāb* (ed. Īrāj Afshār in *Awrād al-aḥbāb wa-fuṣūṣ al-ādāb*, vol. 2. [Tehran: Dānishgāh-yi Tihrān, 1966] which, like Kāshānī in the *Miṣbāḥ al-hidāya*, draws heavily upon the works of both Abū ʾl-Najīb and ʿUmar al-Suhrawardī. ʿAlāʾ al-Dawla Simnānī recommended that his disciples consult Abū ʾl-Najīb's *K. ādāb al-murīdīn* (Elias, *Throne Carrier*, 123).

a shift in the status of the figure of the master (*shaykh*)[18] who, standing as he did at the apex of the pyramidal hierarchy of the *ribāṭ*, combined in his very personhood the collective identity of the *ṣūfiyya* as a distinct and self-regulating *Personengruppe* and the mediatory, and ultimately soteriological, status entailed by his claim to prophetic heirship. At its most fundamental, the formal recognition of an individual's shaykhood (*mashyakha*) by a disciple demanded accepting the consequences of two oft-quoted statements, namely the old Sufi dictum that "he who has no master takes Satan as his leader",[19] and a *ḥadīth* in which the Prophet is reported to have said: 'among his group the shaykh is like the prophet among his people.'[20] The first encapsulates the recognition that formal attachment to a shaykh is essential for traversing the Sufi path, and the second that the disciple owes absolute obedience to his shaykh, carrying out his commands without question and acting only with his permission.[21]

For Suhrawardī, it is this master-disciple dyad which lies at both the heart of Sufism as an individual enterprise and at the very center of the institutional forms and structures which sustain it. As with a student receiving a *ḥadīth* from the lips of an authoritative transmitter, at the moment of his initiation, the *murīd* enters into a process where he is linked not only to a transcendent and trans-historical knowledge vouchsafed to the Prophet, but at the same moment reaffirms his identity as part of, and a participant in, a community attempting to work out that legacy in their own time and space. For Suhrawardī and his disciples, this mode was deeply informed by the authoritating practices

[18] Etymologically, "someone whose age appears advanced and whose hair has gone white" (Ibn Manẓūr, *Lisān al-'arab* [Beirut: Dār Ṣādir, 1988], 7:254 as cited in Éric Geoffroy, "Shaykh," *EI*², 9:396), the elder of a tribe and, by extension, the leader of any social group who enjoys authority and prestige, ideally earned. For Suhrawardī, *shaykh* (with the plural *shuyūkh*) refers—as in the biographical dictionaries of ulama—to one who has achieved distinction in a particular field of learning and is qualified to transmit such learning to others, viz. knowledge of the Sufi path. He enjoys the prerogatives of 'shaykhood' (*mashyakha*) which in the person of the directing-shaykh (*shaykh al-tarbiya*) include complete obedience from his formal disciples (*murīd*, pl.-*ūn*). In addition, the term *shaykh* (with the plural *mashāyikh*) also refers to the 'eponymous authorities' of a particular field of learning (i.e., Sufism) whose opinions are considered authoritative.

[19] Usually attributed to Bāyazīd Bisṭāmī, e.g., *SQ*, 54.5; *'AM*, 1:252 / *GE*, 12.3; and, *IrM*, fol. 38a.

[20] *KM*, 62 / Nicholson, *The Kashf*, 55; *AdM*, 37 / Milson, *Rule*, 46; al-Bidlīsī, *Bahjat al-ṭā'ifa*, 93; and, *PGB*, 235; see also: Meier, "Khurāsān," in *Essays*, 203.

[21] Expressed throughout Suhrawardī's works; see also *PGB*, 235–242, 255–256, 283–283; 'Azīz-i Nasafī, *Maqṣad-i asnā*, trans. Ridgeon in *Persian Metaphysics and Mysticism*, 47; idem, *Zubdat al-ḥāqā'iq*, in ibid., 186; and, Elias, *Throne Carrier*, 123–124.

surrounding the transmission of religious learning generally, and notions of authority bound up in the 'institution of process' of the master-disciple relationship (*ṣuḥba*), the relationship between mentor (*maṣḥūb / ustādh*) and protégé (*ṣāḥib / tilmīdh*), and the concomitant complex of formal manners (*adab*) surrounding its effectuation. Given both the *jamāʿī-sunnī* revivalist climate of Suhrawardī's Baghdad as well as the clear foregrounding of claims of prophetic heirship in Suhrawardī's vision of the sciences of the *ṣūfiyya*, it is not surprising that his enunciation of what this authority entailed is clear and unequivocal:

> In a report about God's Messenger—may God bless and greet him—it is mentioned that [he said]: "By He in whose hand is the soul of Muḥammad, I swear to you that the most beloved servants of God are those who inspire the love of God in His servant, make His servant lovable to God, and who spread good admonitions (*naṣīḥa*) over the earth." That which God's Messenger mentioned here is the rank of shaykhood (*mashyakha*) and summoning (*daʿwa*) [people] to God, because the *shaykh* inspires His servant to love God in a true sense and makes God's servant lovable to Him. The rank of shaykhood is the highest rank of the Sufi path (*ṭarīqat al-ṣūfiyya*) and the representative (*niyāba*) of prophethood (*nubuwwa*) in summoning to God.[22]

As a member of the otherworldly-ulama and heir to the Adamic *ʿilm al-wirātha*, the shaykh exercises his *niyāba* through educating and refining his disciples (*taʾdīb / tarbiya*), doing so as the Prophet with his companions and as a father with his son.[23] The latter is in fact just as important as the former, and Suhrawardī is much more apt to describe the aspirant as the shaykh's 'spiritual child' (*walad maʿnawī*) who at the moment of his initiation undergoes a second, spiritual, rebirth (*wilādat maʿnawiyya*) and thus comes into possession of a spiritual father (*ab maʿnawī*) who takes responsibility for educating, refining, and training him just as his natural

---

[22] *ʿAM*, 1:236 / *GE*, 10.1; see also: idem, *W.* III, MS. Süley., İbrahim Ef. 870_9, fol. 81b–82a; idem, *W.* IV, fol. 80b; idem, *W. li-Naṣīr al-Dīn al-Baghdādī*, fol. 65a–65b, 67a; and, *Suh.*, 148–149; *ḥadīth* in Ibn al-Ṣiddīq, *ʿAwātif*, 1:158–159; and, idem, *Ghaniyyat*, 1:134–135.

[23] *ʿAM*, 1:236–237 / *GE*, 10.1–5; idem, *W.* III, fol. 82b; cf. al-Sulamī, *Jawāmiʿ*, *MA*, 1:377–378, 389, 408–409). In describing the mentor-protégé relationship ʿAbd al-Qādir al-Jīlānī makes a very similar statement, laying out an unbroken genealogy of *mashyakha* extending from Adam, who was the *tilmīdh* of the archangel Gabriel, through Seth, Noah and his descendents, Abraham and his, Moses (from his father ʿImrān), Aaron, Joshua and the Israelites, Jesus and the Apostles (*ḥawāriyyūn*), Muḥammad (who like Adam was instructed by Gabriel), the first four caliphs, the *salaf al-ṣāliḥ*, Ḥasan al-Baṣrī and his students, Sarī al-Saqaṭī, and from him to al-Junayd. (*GhṬ*, 2:280–281)

father (*ab ṭabīʿī*) was responsible for doing when he was a child.[24] This is why in various testaments (*waṣāyā*), Suhrawardī inevitably addresses individual disciples as his 'righteous son' (*al-walad al-ṣāliḥ*).[25]

Not everyone, however, is qualified to become a shaykh, and in identifying the type of individual who can rightfully claim the rank of shaykhood, Suhrawardī proposes a four-fold typology of individuals, here again writing a norm based on existential designations.[26] First, there is the simple wayfarer (*sālik mujarrad*), an individual who is not qualified to claim the rank of shaykhood because he is still immersed in the 'station of devotions and self-control' (*maqām al-muʿāmalat wa-l-riyāḍa*), having achieved neither the equanimity nor spiritual experience necessary to guide others on the path. Second, there is the one who is simply 'attracted' (*majdhūb mujarrad*), an individual who although having reached the goal is immediately disqualified because he has never traversed the path himself. Third, there is the one who has reached a state of striving through attraction (*sālik mutadārak bi-l-jadhba*), an individual qualified to assume the rank of shaykhood, but only in a less than perfect way because of the reverse order of his arrival and the consequent imperfections in his spiritual state. Finally, there is the one who has obtained the state of one attracted through wayfaring (*majdhūb mutadārak bi-l-sulūk*), an individual more qualified than the others to assume the rank of shaykhood because the unveiling of his heart was effected through traversing the path, giving him the experiential knowledge necessary to direct aspirants along the same arduous journey.

The highest rank of shaykhood is that of the 'absolute shaykh' (*al-shaykh al-muṭlaq*), an individual who has become free from the veil of both the *nafs* and the heart, having reached the station of 'those drawn nigh', the *muqarrabūn*, God's desired beloved (*al-maḥbūb al-murād*) whose

---

[24] *ʿAM*, 1:238–241 / *GE*, 10.8–15; idem, *W. li-Naṣīr al-Dīn al-Baghdādī*, fol. 66b–67a; and, *Suh.*, 151–152. Najm al-Dīn Rāzī Dāya, who quotes a saying of Jesus as a proof text ("he who is not born twice shall not penetrate the kingdom of the heavens and the earth"; cf. John 3:3), also characterizes the aspirant's attachment to a shaykh as a 'second birth', explaining it through the metaphor of the hen and the egg (*PGB*, 247–250; this egg imagery is prefigured in Suhrawardī's *Aʿlām al-hudā* (88).

[25] E.g., *W. li-ʿAlī al-Mawqānī*, MS. Tüb., Ma VI 90_{52}, fol. 116a; idem, *W. li-Jamāl al-Dīn al-Isfahānī*, ed. Hartmann in "Bemerkungen zu Handschriften," 140–142. In the *ʿAM*, Suhrawardī reports that his paternal uncle Abū ʾl-Najīb would often say: "he one who travels my path and follows my guidance is my son (*waladī man salaka ṭarīqī wa-ihtadā bi-hudā*)." (*ʿAM*, 1:231 / *GE*, 10.15)

[26] *ʿAM*, 1:242–246 / *GE*, 10.16–26; and, idem, *W. li-Naṣīr al-Dīn al-Baghdādī*, fol. 65b–67a.

spirit is free and *nafs* tranquil, the *muntahī* who is permanently ensconced in a state of perpetual subsistence (*baqāʾ*). According to Suhrawardī, it is this type of individual who is most qualified to assume the position of shaykh, the only one having the existential authority to receive, initiate, direct, and guide disciples on their individual journeys on the path of ascent. As we have seen, it is through his perfection that such an individual comes into possession of a certain charisma, an attractive quality which draws students to him in a bond of affinitive connection (*rābiṭat al-jinsiyya al-nafs*) which is not only concretized in an existentially validated relationship grounded in the reality of the human psycho-spiritual constitution but also replicates the almost tangible *charismata* by which the prophets themselves attracted and retained followers.[27] Although perhaps not originating with Suhrawardī himself, such ideas came to be systematized in Naqshbandī figurations of the master-disciple relationship in the key concepts of *tawajjuh* and *rābiṭa*.[28]

The authority of such a shaykh is comprehensive. He is both a 'superintendent of souls' (*ishrāf ʿalā ʾl-bawāṭin*) who has the right of free disposal over every aspect of the program of his disciples, determining what they should wear and when they should fast, when they should work and when they should beg, as well as ensuring that they persist in their litanies, pray the proper supererogatory prayers, and hold fast in their recitation of the Qurʾān.[29] At the same time, the shaykh does not enjoy unrestricted disposal over life in the *ribāṭ*, and Suhrawardī is careful to prescribe the proper behaviors (*ādāb*), duties (*waẓāʾif*), and mutual rights and obligations (*ḥuqūq*) which the shaykh is required to observe in dealing with its constituents, saying that it is obligatory for the him to:

1. shun those whose motivations for seeking his company are impure or misdirected;
2. look upon his disciples as his children, and accordingly, give them good counsel in both spiritual and material matters;
3. carefully diagnose and scrutinize his disciples so that they can be directed in a manner consistent with their different spiritual states and aspirations;

---

[27] *ʿAM*, 1:238–239, 2:232–233 / *GE*, 10.8–10, 63.27.

[28] In addition to the study of Meier cited previously ("Die Herzensbindung an den Meister"), on this, see Buehler, *Sufi Heirs of the Prophet*, 99, 131–134.

[29] *ʿAM*, 1:258 / *GE*, 12.13.

4. avoid fraternizing, socializing, chumming, or chatting with his disciples, and to carefully calculate when it is necessary to be present among them;
5. treat his disciples with the utmost courtesy, respect, and humility;
6. treat his companions (*aṣḥāb*) with affection and tenderness and respect the rights (*ḥuqūq*) which they have over him;
7. not accept property, services, and voluntary charity (*ṣadaqa*) from disciples as gratuity;
8. not speak directly to a disciple about a reprehensible action which he has committed, but rather to allude to it while discoursing to the community so that all may benefit from his mistake;
9. pick up the slack, forgive, and gently spur on a disciple who has become lax in his assigned duties;
10. and, maintain strict confidentiality regarding the spiritual experiences and inner state (*sirr*) of individual disciples.[30]

In the day-to-day life of the *ribāṭ*, the shaykh also plays the role of community director and manager of its affairs, admitting and rejecting newcomers, arbitrating disputes, managing the affairs of its permanent staff, while at the same time overseeing its endowment (*waqf*) and determining who may receive support from its coffers.[31] While many of these tasks were delegated to his superintendent (*khādim*)—to whom we will return shortly—this comprehensive authority, legitimated through genealogical, praxic, spiritual, and metaphysical claims to prophetic heirship was mediated through a number of channels, most notably through a formally definable complex of manners and proper behaviors which served to reinforce such a position, *adab*.

Proper Manners (adab)

Like the relationship between students and teachers in the *madrasa*, between viziers, courtiers and officials in the caliphal palace and bureaus, between littérateurs and men of culture in their salons, and between a master and apprentices in the trade and craft markets, so too was the

[30] Ibid., 2:217–222 / *GE*, 51.1–13; and, *Suh.*, 161–163. ʿAbd al-Qādir al-Jīlānī prescribes a very similar set of rules for the *adab* required of the shaykh to his disciples, see: *GhṬ*, 2:284–286; cf. al-Bidlīsī, *Bahjat al-ṭāʾifa*, 94–96 who spiritualizes the requirements and Najm al-Dīn Rāzī Dāya who stipulates twenty conditions of shaykhood rooted mainly in moral and ethical affect (*PGB*, 250–253).

[31] *ʿAM*, 1:269, 279 / *GE*, 14.5, 15.11.

Sufi *ribāṭ* possessed of a commonly accepted code of proper behaviors and manners which all were expected to observe, commonly expressed by the term *adab*.[32] As we have already discussed in the first chapter of this study, such codes of social interaction served as an integral component of a much larger process of constructing and maintaining identity, social relationships, legitimacy, authority, and group definition within the literate, urbanized, and cosmopolitan ulama culture of which Suhrawardī was a part. In short, the culture of *adab* as a formalized externalization of deeper religious, social, and cultural mores was in the air, something which Suhrawardī was careful to point out to his young son ʿImād al-Dīn, counseling him:

> For you, there is a proper mode of behavior (*adab*) in every situation (*aḥwāl*) and with everyone, godly man and profligate alike. Treat everyone with honor, both those younger and older than you, and never regard them except with a merciful eye.[33]

Such sentiments are neither unusual nor noteworthy, neither for Sufis or other self-reflective *Personengruppen* of the late-6th/12th-early-7th/13th century possessed of a prescriptive literature of one type or another, and one often meets with the famous saying attributed to the 3rd/9th-century Sufi paragon and alleged founder of the Malāmatiyya, Abū Ḥafṣ al-Ḥaddād of Nīshāpūr: "Sufism consists entirely of proper manners (*ādāb*), for every moment (*waqt*) there is a manner, for every station (*maqām*) a manner, and for state (*ḥāl*) a manner".[34] One could

---

[32] As is well known to all students of classical and medieval Islam, the term *adab* (sing. *adab* in the sense of etiquette, culture, learning, refinement; pl. *ādāb* in the sense of particular manners and proper behaviors) is possessed of a wide range of meanings and associations (see: F. Gabrieli, "Adab," *EI²*, 1:175–176; and, George Makdisi, *The Rise of Humanism*, 97 ff. and index s.v. *adab*).

[33] al-Suhrawardī, *W. li-ibnihi*, 34; cf. *GhṬ*, 2:288. Something of a final, comprehensive compendium of his great-uncle's *K. ādāb al-murīdīn* and his father's *ʿAwārif al-maʿārif*, later in his life ʿImād al-Dīn penned a treatise entitled *Zād al-musāfir wa-ādāb al-ḥāḍir* (extant in MS. Köprülü 1603_2, fol. 11a–52b; and, MS. Topkapı Sarayı, Ahmet III, 1416_5, fol. 197a–241b, of which the former will be cited here) in which he systematically enumerates 120 points of *adab* organized in twelve sections (*faṣl*): 1) on the manners of travel (*safar*) for the *muntahī*; 2) on the manners of travel for the *mutaṣawwif* and *faqīr*; 3) on the manners of the *mutaṣawwif* and *faqīr* upon entering the a city and the *ribāṭ*; 4) on manners pertaining to residing in the *ribāṭ* (*ḥuḍūr wa-muqām*); 5) on the manners of retreat in the *ribāṭ* (*mujāwara*); 6) on the manners of eating during travel and while in residence; 7) on the manners of drinking; 8) on the manners of sleeping and rising; 9) on the manners of dress; 10) on the manners of attending the mystical concert (*samāʿ*); 11) on the rending of the *khirqa* during *samāʿ*; and, 12) on the ways and means (*majārī*) of the constituents of *ribāṭ* in relating to one another.

[34] al-Sulamī, *Ṭabaqāt*, 106; *KM*, 47 / Nicholson, *The Kashf*, 41–42; and, *ʿAM*, 1:203,

cite many such aphorisms from the logia of the early Sufi paragons, but what is important for us here is to recall that the particular strand of the largely-urban, *sharīʿa*-minded, Khurāsānī-Junaydī Sufi tradition which Suhrawardī so vigorously attempted to codify in texts such as the *ʿAwārif al-maʿārif* placed a great deal of emphasis on the cultivation of ethics and their articulation in formally definable acts of etiquette and proper behavior.

The valuation of moral character framing Suhrawardī's formal prescriptions on *adab*, in fact, evinces a clear continuity with those of his predecessors, especially the strand of the *futuwwa* / *javānmardī* tradition which, as evinced in the works of al-Sulamī, was squarely centered on cultivating a host of formal attitudes and modes of behavior which look to structure and regulate social relationships through the shared application of chivalric, altruistic, and self-effacing life-orientational values.[35] Like Sulamī, when taken as a larger complex of behaviors set within the framework of Suhrawardī's totalizing vision, the particulars of *adab* are intimately tied to the cultivation of the moral and spiritual person through ethics (*akhlāq*, sing. *khulq* / *khuluq*), a subject to which Suhrawardī devotes one of the longest chapters of the *ʿAwārif al-maʿārif* to explaining, describing in great detail both the inner (*bāṭin*) and outer (*ẓāhir*) dimensions of virtues such as humility (*tawāḍuʿ*), obsequiousness (*mudāra*), altruism (*īthār*),[36] abstention (*tajāwuz*), forgiveness (*ʿafw*), cheerfulness (*al-bishr wa-l-ṭalāqat al-wajh*), simplicity and pliancy (*suhūla wa-l-līn al-jānib*), informality (*tark al-takalluf*), indifference to storing up for the morrow (*al-infāq min ghayr iqtār wa-tark al-idkhār*), mutual affection with one's brethren (*tawaddud wa-l-tāʾluf maʿa al-ikhwān*), thankfulness for God's

---

2:208 / *GE*, 5.4, 51.6; on Abū Ḥafṣ al-Ḥaddād see: Richard Gramlich, *Alte Vorbilder des Sufitums* (Wiesbaden: Otto Harrassowitz, 1995–1996), 2:113–154.

[35] Namely, in the *Jawāmiʿ ādāb al-ṣūfiyya* which begins by discussing the importance of *adab* by locating it squarely in the pedagogy of the Prophet Muḥammad who educated and refined (*taʾdīb*) his companions in the proper manners (*ādāb*) after which he prescribes some 160 individual points of proper manners based mainly on the exempla of the Sufi paragons; idem, *K. ādāb al-ṣuḥba, MA*, 2:22–28, on the connection between ethics and *adab*, and 28 ff. containing prescriptions which are focused mainly on interpersonal relations (*muʿāmalāt*) as circumscribed by the social relationship of *ṣuḥba* ('intimate companionship'), which here is used as a synonym of *ʿishra* ('kin-like closeness') and not in the sense of *ṣuḥba* as used to refer to the master-disciple relationship (*shaykh-murīd, ustādh-tilmīdh, maṣḥūb-ṣāḥib*), the virtues cultivated in such relationships spilling over into all others; idem, *Darajāt al-muʿāmalāt, MA*, 1:485; also *AdM*, 34–40, 43–44 / Milson, *Rule*, 45–48, 50; and, of course, *ʿAM*, 2:231–240 / *GE*, 54.1–55.16.

[36] On which, see my entry "Altruism," *Encyclopaedia of Islam Three* (Leiden: Brill, forthcoming).

bounty (*shukr ʿalā ʾl-iḥsān wa-duʿāʾ lahu*), and sacrificing worldly rank not only for one's brethren but for the entire Muslim community (*badhl al-jāh li-l-ikhwān wa-l-muslīmīn kāffat*[an]).[37] Grounded solidly in Qurʾānic models of piety and the ethical and moral practice of the Prophet, and supported by the exempla of the *salaf al-ṣāliḥ* and Sufi paragons, this long list of ethics are none other than those praiseworthy characteristics (*awṣāf / akhlāq maḥmūda*), those sound dispositions (*sajāyā ṣāliḥa*) of the spirit which are literally 'effectuated through *adab*', effacing and replacing the blameworthy characteristics and vices (*radhāʾil*) of the *nafs*.[38] As we have seen, for Suhrawardī this is accomplished only through engaging in the dual disciples of *muḥāsaba* and *murāqaba*, both of which require the direction of a shaykh, a shaykh a *ribāṭ*, a *ribāṭ* a community of affiliates, and a community of affiliates a shared body of definable, replicable, and normative patterns of behavior through which they structure the relationships amongst themselves as a community (*jamāʿa*) of brethren (*ikhwān*) as well as individually as disciples and students organized in a radial network around a single shaykh, in short *adab*.

The Superintendent (khādim)

Standing below the shaykh in the hierarchy of the *ribāṭ* is the superintendent (*khādim*, pl. *khuddām*), an individual whom Suhrawardī considered important enough to distinguish from the shaykh, devoting an entire chapter of the *ʿAwārif al-maʿārif* to doing so.[39] The reasons for this are ultimately unclear, although according to his comments in his day and

---

[37] *ʿAM*, 1:56–97 (also: 2:236–240) / *GE*, 29.1–30.87 (55.1–16); and, *Suh.*, 225–233, which is not an atypical enumeration. On the connection between ethics and *adab*, and similar values: al-Sulamī, *Jawāmiʿ*, *MA*, 1:353, 381–382 (on altruism); *KM*, 432–478 / Nicholson, *The Kashf*, 334–366; *AdM*, 19–20 / Milson, *Rule*, 38–39; and, *GhṬ*, 2:287–291; see also: R. Walzer and H.A.R. Gibb, "Akhlāq," *EI*², 1:325–329.

[38] *ʿAM*, 2:98–99 / *GE*, 31.1–3, that is, "*fa-l-adab istikhrāj mā fī al-qūwat ilā ʾl-fiʿl*", which as per his Ashʿarism Suhrawardī considers acquired acts (*fiʿl al-ḥaqq*) and which, as such, are situated within his broader vision of the path of ascent; see: *Suh.*, 214–224; cf. al-Bidlīsī, *Bahjat al-ṭāʾifa*, 96–98 where the idea, much further developed by Ibn ʿArabī, of 'taking on the attributes of God' (*al-takhalluq bi-akhlāq allāh*) is fronted, something which is present in the thought of Suhrawardī, but only in a limited manner (e.g., *ʿAM*, 2:233 / *GE*, 54.7).

[39] That is, chapter 11 (*ʿAM*, 1:247–250 / *GE*, 11.1–8). At the same time, the true *khādim* must be distinguished from the *mutakhādim*, the former being distinguished by the sincerity of his intention (*niyya*) whereas the latter engages in service out of desire for praise and adulation from the people whom he serves, both of whom must be distinguished from the *mustakhdim*, the servant who when approached by the mendicants for a handout, treats them with open contempt and cuts them off from the *waqf*, and thus actually assists them in their poverty by disciplining them.

age there was a problem of certain superintendents claiming a rank to which they were not entitled, presenting themselves as shaykhs while in reality they were not qualified to do so. In typical fashion, Suhrawardī differentiates this particular group from the others on existential grounds, arguing that although outwardly the superintendent may seem to play a role similar to that of the shaykh, he is differentiated from him in that his actions are effected by his desire for divine reward, which although pious and sound, arises from intentional volition. Whereas the shaykh is a member of the *muqarrabūn* and thus 'accomplishes things through God' (*yafʿalu al-shayʾ bi-Llāh*) the superintendent is a member of the godly (*abrār*) and 'accomplishes things for God' (*yafʿalu al-shayʾ li-Llāh*), and whereas the shaykh acts through God's will, the *khādim* acts through an intentional desire to be self-sacrificing and altruistic in his acts of service (*khidma*).[40]

Potential confusion between the shaykh and the *khādim* however seem to have been of external concern, for nowhere in his *oeuvre* does Suhrawardī cast the *khādim* as being in the position of actually directing aspirants in the discipline of the *ribāṭ*. His role, which is not clearly described in any case, seems to have been simply to act as a personal assistant to the shaykh, taking care of tasks such as soliciting donations for the *ribāṭ*, receiving and dealing with complaints from its residents, serving food to incoming mendicants (*fuqarāʾ*), and rendering general service to the *ribāṭ*'s population (*qawm*).[41] According to Suhrawardī, the upshot of his service is that it serves as a spiritual disciple, a device by which the *khādim* can subdue his *nafs* and advance on the spiritual path through the practice of altruism (*īthār*), self-sacrifice (*badhl*), and service, three virtues which Suhrawardī argues are more advantageous for him than supererogatory devotions.

In the *Ādāb al-murīdīn*, Abū ʾl-Najīb states that "service is a rank second only to that of shaykhood"[42] and given that Suhrawardī almost invariably couples the two terms *shaykh-khādim* and *shaykh-muqaddam* when discussing the conditions which certain individuals lower in the hierarchy (such as the mendicants or companions of service) are to observe in negotiating the formal structures of the *ribāṭ*, it seems that the position of *khādim* was generally given to a senior disciple (*murīd*) of a

---

[40] Ibid., 1:247 / *GE*, 11.1; also: *AdM*, 18, 29 / Milson, *Rule*, 43, 45–46; cf. *SQ*, 54.23–34.

[41] *ʿAM*, 1:248, 276, 313 / *GE*, 11.3, 15.6, 18.15–16.

[42] *AdM*, 45 / Milson, *Rule*, 50.

particular shaykh. This accords with the figure of the *khādim* associated with *ribāṭ*-based Sufi communities in the period following Suhrawardī in Syria and Egypt and the description of the position given by Bākharzī in the early 8th/14th century.[43]

The Aspirant (murīd)

The aspirant (*murīd*, pl. *-ūn*), who is also called the *mutaṣawwif*—or collectively the 'Folk of Desire' (*ahl al-irāda*) or the practitioners of pious retreat (*arbāb al-khalwa*)—on the other hand is one who has either moved up the hierarchy of the *ribāṭ* to assume the position of a true disciple of the shaykh, or has been accepted as such straight away.[44] Unlike those below him, because he is engaged in a full-time program of spiritual discipline the aspirant is entitled to full support from the *ribāṭ*'s endowment (*waqf*) and is not required to actively seek sustenance outside of its precincts unless so directed by the shaykh.[45] At the same time, the aspirant is expected to adhere to a much stricter discipline than those who stand below him, being obligated to engage in a sustained program of spiritual practice under the direction of the shaykh, being enjoined to neither become slack in his duties lest he slip into the realm of the practitioners of dispensations (*arbāb al-rukhṣa*) nor leave his shaykh lest he be cut off from his guidance at a critical moment in his spiritual development.

Metaphysically, the key distinction between such individuals and others populating the *ribāṭ* is that the *murīd* ('the one desiring') possesses *irāda* (desire), a technical term whose origin (*aṣl*) Suhrawardī finds in the Qurʾānic verse: "send not away those who call upon their Lord morning and evening, seeking His Face".[46] According to Suhrawardī, this verse was revealed as a command to the Prophet Muḥammad to respect the rights of the 'Folk of Desire' from the poor among his companions (*ḥaqq ahl al-irāda min fuqarāʾ aṣḥābihi*), a command which by extension came to be a stipulation binding upon the Sufi shaykhs who, as his representatives, are required to nurture the desire of the aspirants entrusted to them.[47]

---

[43] Geoffroy, *Djihad et contemplation*, 26; idem, *Le soufisme*, 280; Bākharzī, *Fuṣūṣ al-ādāb*, 128–132.

[44] *ʿAM*, 1:273 / *GE*, 15.1; see also: *GhṬ*, 2:272–273.

[45] *ʿAM*, 1:279 / *GE*, 15.11; and, *AMKh*, 61 (no. 12).

[46] Qurʾān 6:42.

[47] al-Suhrawardī, *W. li-Naṣīr al-Dīn al-Baghdādī*, fol. 63a–63b; there is no such inter-

This desire is not, however, willed by the individual himself, rather it is a desire which God casts into the inner being of the potential aspirant when he awakens to the loneliness and isolation of his spirit and becomes sensitized to its yearning for its Maker. According to Suhrawardī, it is this desire which pulls the aspirant into a state where his individual will is completely submerged in the will of his shaykh, all previous attachments, individual desires, and wants and needs of his soul and heart being redirected into the very personhood of the shaykh so that he becomes "like a corpse in the hands of the washer". As we have already seen in Suhrawardī's delineation of the journey of ascent, the aspirant must necessarily proceed in such a manner until his desire is effaced in the will of God, at which point he emerges from the liminal state of dependence upon the mediating agency of the shaykh to obtain a state of subsistence in the agency of the ground of existence and the really real.[48]

The Sufi Habit (khirqa)

As with the spiritual disciplines in which he engages, the aspirant is also distinguished from other constituencies of the *ribāṭ* by a special raiment, the *khirqa*, a symbol of his status as a formal disciple of a particular shaykh and his commitment to the master-disciple relationship. One of Suhrawardī's anonymous interlocutors from Khurāsān wrote to him asking if there was a prophetic precedent for the practice of investiture with the *khirqa*[49] and if so, how exactly did the Prophet do it?[50] In response to this question, the shaykh responds in the affirmative, saying that the practice has its origin (*aṣl*) in the Sunna and quite predictably

pretation, however, of this verse in his *Nughbat al-bayān* where Suhrawardī simply accounts for the *sabb al-nuzūl* (same in Ṭabarī, Ibn Kathīr, etc.) and the standard glosses (Düzenli, "Şihâbuddin Sühreverdî," 122 [Arabic text]).

[48] Idem, *W. li-Naṣīr al-Dīn al-Baghdādī*, fol. 67b; cf. PGB, 255.

[49] From the root *kh-r-q*, with the connotation of 'ripping', 'rending', 'tearing', as a physical object the *khirqa* (pl. *khiraq*)—to be distinguished from the *muraqqa'a* (see below)—refers to the worn and tattered outer cloak or frock worn by the Sufis as a sign of poverty and rejection of the world in place of the *qabā'* or 'workaday cloak' (see: Dozy, *Dictionnaire détaillé*, 153–155, 352–362). On the nature, role, and iconic value of the *khirqa* in pre-modern Sufism generally, see Trimingham, *Sufi Orders*, 181–185; Gramlich, *Derwischorden*, 2:172–174; J.-L. Michon, "Khirḳa," *EI*^{2}, 5:17–18; Geoffroy, *Le soufisme*, 195–196, *passim*; and, Jamal Elias, "The Sufi Robe (Khirqa) as a Vehicle of Spiritual Authority," in Gordon Stewart, ed., *Robes of Honor: The Medieval World of Investiture*. (New York: Palgrave, 2001), 275–289; and my entry "Kerqa," *EIr* (forthcoming).

[50] *AMKh*, 56–57 (no. 6).

quotes the *ḥadīth* of Umm Khālid[51] to support his statement, an episode which Ibn al-Jawzī considered a ridiculous precedent upon which to base such a practice.[52] In the *ʿAwārif al-maʿārif*, where he is always careful to qualify such etiologies, Suhrawardī implicitly recognizes such objections, saying that while the practice draws its inspiration from the Prophet's 'investiture' of Umm Khālid, the *salaf al-ṣāliḥ* did not actually invest anyone with the *khirqa* and that it is a praiseworthy innovation, the permissibility of which all of the eponymous Sufi authorities affirm.[53] As evinced in Suhrawardī's account of his own *nisbat al-khirqa*, the idea was that initiatic authority was transmitted first through the medium of *ṣuḥba* and only later, beginning with al-Junayd, explicitly through investiture with the *khirqa* (see Chart 4).

On the practice itself, according to Suhrawardī there were two main methods of investiture prevalent among the Sufis of his day and age, namely an investiture which occurred at the end of the aspirant's period of training in which case it served as a symbol of his having successfully traversed the path or an investiture which occurred at his point of entry in which case it served as a symbol of his commitment to training under a particular master.[54] In his own *ṭarīq* Suhrawardī followed the second, and in the twelfth chapter of the *ʿAwārif al-maʿārif* sums up the essential features of investiture with the *khirqa*, defining it as the threshold (*ʿataba*) of entering into the discipline of *ṣuḥba*, an outward symbol of the establishment of a commitment between the shaykh and the aspirant and the aspirant's appointment of the shaykh to a position of jurisdiction over his affairs.[55] As an instrument, the *khirqa* is an

---

[51] Umm Khālid (Ama bt. Khālid b. Saʿīd b. al-ʿĀṣ), the mother of the famous Khālid b. al-Zubayr al-ʿAwwām, was born in Abyssinia among the first group of emigrants who later returned to the Hejaz, she being a young girl at the time of the investiture. The *ḥadīth* runs as follows: "Umm Khālid b. Khālid related: Some garments (*thiyāb*) were brought to the Prophet and among them was a small black *khamīṣa* and he said: 'whom shall I clothe with this?' The people were silent, and the Prophet said: 'bring me Umm Khālid!' And I was brought to him and he clothed me with it by his own hand saying: 'wear it and make it shabby! (*ablī wa-akhliqī*)'." (*ʿAM*, 1:253 / *GE*, 12.5; Ibn al-Ṣiddīq, *ʿAwāṭif*, 1:174–172 [no. 60]; and, idem, *Ghaniyyat*, 1:158–159 [no. 60])

[52] Ibn al-Jawzī, *Talbīs Iblīs* (Beirut: Dār al-Kitāb al-ʿArabī, 1995), 236–237.

[53] *ʿAM*, 1:260 / *GE*, 12.20; and, *Suh.*, 153–154.

[54] *IrM*, fol. 40b–41b; in the *ʿAM* he also mentions that he has observed shaykhs in his own day and age who do not practice investiture with the *khirqa* but train disciples nonetheless (*ʿAM*, 1:260 / *GE*, 12.20; and, *Suh.*, 154).

[55] *ʿAM*, 1:251 / *GE*, 12.1; *AMKh*, 57 (no. 6); and, idem, *W. li-Rashīd al-Dīn Abī Bakr al-Ḥabash*, fol. 117b where he states that *ṣuḥba* with the shaykh is not permissible without the aspirant first having been invested with the *khirqa* and instructed in all of its obligations (*ḥuqūq*); see also: Trimingham, *The Sufi Orders*, 181–182.

Chart 4.

Al-Suhrawardī's *nisbat al-khirqa**

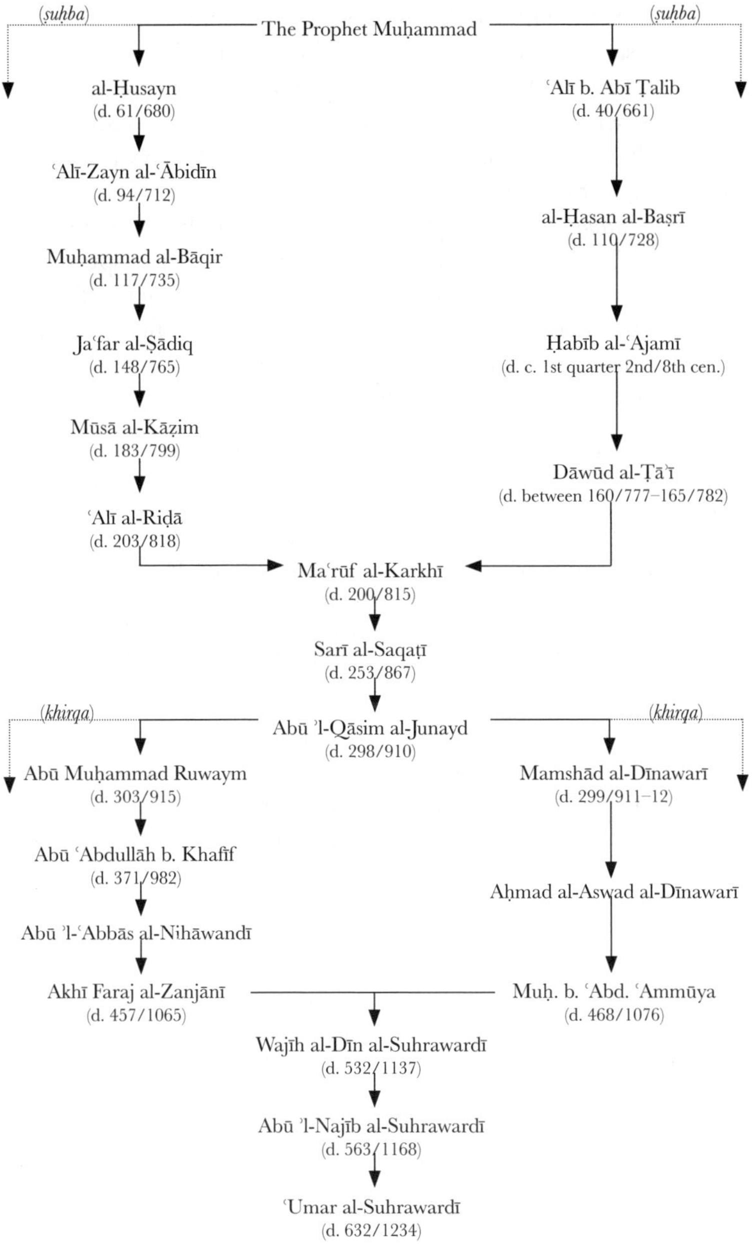

* al-Suhrawardī, *Ijz. li-ʿAlī b. Aḥmad al-Rāzī*, fol. 295b; *Nisbat al-khirqat al-Suhrawardī* I, fol. 132a; *Nisbat al-khirqat al-Suhrawardī* II, fol. 1a; Ibn al-Qasṭallānī, *Irtifāʿ*, 85–86; *MJ*, 3:40–41 (s.v. Najm al-Dīn Kubrā); Jāmī, *Nafaḥāt*, 558–559 (no. 546); and, Maʿṣūmʿalīshāh, *Ṭarāʾiq*, 2:309–310, 322, 442.

outward mark of the aspirant's inner commitment to place himself in a state of submission to the complete jurisdiction of the shaykh over all of his affairs, which as a symbol of the oath of fidelity (*mubāyaʿa* / *ʿahd al-wafāʾ*) is the entry point for a form of discipleship (*ṣuḥba*) which self-consciously replicates the master-disciple relationship which obtained between Muḥammad and his immediate companions, the hand of the shaykh representing the hand of the Prophet and the oath of fidelity that which his companions took with him at Ḥudaybiyya.[56]

According to Suhrawardī, the *khirqa* is of two types: 1) the 'habit of aspiration' (*khirqat al-irāda*); and, 2) the 'habit of benediction' (*khirqat al-tabarruk*). The former is intended only for the true aspirant (*murīd ḥaqīqī*), and is an outer symbol of his inner commitment. The *khirqat al-tabarruk*, on the other hand, is an imitation of the first, and as such is acquired only by the *mutashabbih*.[57] The difference between the two is summed up by Suhrawardī as follows:

> As for the *khirqat al-tabarruk*, it is requested by one whose aim is to acquire blessing (*tabarruk*) from the 'ornament of the Folk' (*bi-zayy al-qawm*); and in the same way the conditions of discipleship (*sharāʾiṭ al-suḥbat*) are not required of him, but rather he is only counseled to adhere to the limits of the divine law. By associating with this group (*ṭāʾifa*) he accumulates their blessing and is educated in their manners, and through this he might be raised to a level of suitability for the *khirqat al-irāda*. The *khirqat al-tabarruk* is offered to every seeker whereas the *khirqat al-irāda* is prohibited except for the one who is sincere in his intention.[58]

The availability of the *khirqa* to every seeker is an extremely important detail which cannot be passed over lightly. Some ninety years after the death of Suhrawardī, the famous traveler Ibn Baṭṭūṭa reports being invested with the *khirqat al-tabarruk* from, among others, a director of a *ribāṭ* in Isfahan on the authority of Suhrawardī, being careful in his

---

[56] *AMKh*, 57 (no. 6), *ʿAM*, 1:251–255, 2:33 / *GE*, 12.1–10, 25.9; idem, *W.* III, fol. 81b; and, *Suh.*, 154–156; referred to in the Qurʾān (48:10), the oath, usually referred to as the 'pledge of good fortune' (*bayʿat al-riḍwān*) occurred in 628 CE when the Prophet and a large group of followers from Medina, who had set out on an expedition to perform the lesser pilgrimage, were stopped outside of Mecca by the Quraysh. According to the usual account, during the ensuing stalemate, the Prophet asked those present to swear an oath to follow him whatever the circumstances might be. On this episode, see: Watt, "al-Ḥudaybiyya," *EI²*, 3:539.

[57] *AMKh*, 57–58; *ʿAM*, 1:256 / *GE*, 12.12 (also trans. in Trimingham, *The Sufi Orders*, 185); and, *Suh.*, 156.

[58] *ʿAM*, 1:259 / *GE*, 12.17.

account to give the *nisbat al-khirqa* of the habit which he had received.[59] In addition, as we have already seen al-Suhrawardī himself invested numerous individuals with the *khirqat al-tabarruk* in Baghdad, including men of note such as the aforementioned Ibn al-Dubaythī, Ibn al-Najjār, and Ibn al-Sāʿī. As evinced in Suhrawardī's discussion of the *mutashabbih* (see below) such investitures were common practice, providing an alternate means of affiliation to a particular shaykh and his *ribāṭ* for those who had neither the desire, wherewithal, or capacity to become formal disciples.

As with all of the distinctive practices and accoutrements of the *ribāṭ*, Suhrawardī is careful to provide both an etiology for the habits of dress of his particular *Personengruppe* in terms of their precedents in the Sunna, as well analyzing their symbolic dimensions. The color of the *khirqa*, for instance, was an important enough issue for Suhrawardī to discuss it, mentioning that dark blue (*azraq*) is the preferred color for the vestment, one of the reasons being that it is useful for one practicing voluntary poverty in that it easily hides the dirt which inevitably comes with such a state.[60] Furthermore, associated as they were with worldliness and decadence neither red nor yellow were appropriate colors, and whereas the preferred color for the *khirqat al-irāda* of the aspirant is dark blue, for the Sufi shaykhs, following prophetic precedent, black is deemed more appropriate.[61] Furthermore, Suhrawardī states that it is only permissible for the shaykh to wear the traditional outfit of the scholars (*farajiyya*), each of its parts symbolizing their perfection of a particular quality while simultaneously underscoring their membership in both the ranks of the ulama and that of the Sufi authorities (*mashāyikh*).[62]

---

[59] Ibn Baṭṭūṭa, *The Travels of Ibn Baṭṭūṭa*, trans. H.A.R. Gibb (Cambridge: The Hakluyt Society, 1962), 2:297–298.

[60] *ʿAM*, 1:259–260 / *GE*, 12.18–20; *JQb*, fol. 16a; *Suh.*, 156–157; same in Hujwīrī (Per. *kabūdī* / *kabūd* = *azraq*), *Kashf*, 59 / Nicholson, *The Kashf*, 53; see also: Meier, "A Book of Etiquette," in *Essays*, 69–70 fn. 65 & 68–69; cf. Abū ʾl-Najīb al-Suhrawardī who opts for green (the color of the Prophet) and white (*AdM*, 9–10 / Milson, *Rule*, 32; white wool in Daylamī, *Sīrat al-shaykh al-kabīr Abū ʿAbd Allāh ibn al-Khafīf al-Shīrāzī*, ed. Annemarie Schimmel [Ankara: Türk Tarih Kurumu Basımevi, 1955], e.g. 58).

[61] *IrM*, fol. 42a–42b.

[62] Ibid., fol. 42a–43a; same in *AdM*, 54 / Milson, *Rule*, 56. Generally the *farajiyya* (pl. *farājī*; Suhrawardī saying *libs al-farajī*), was a costume worn by the ulama, (see Dozy, *Dictionnaire détaillé*, 327–334). In his chapter on the *adab* of dress and clothing in the *ʿAwārif*, however, Suhrawardī makes it a point to say that his paternal uncle Abū ʾl-Najīb did not care one way or the other about the appearance of his clothing, wearing what came his way, that ʿAbd al-Qādir al-Jīlānī wore a distinctive costume including the

The Master-Disciple Relationship (ṣuḥba)

For Suhrawardī, the relationship between the aspirant and the shaykh represents the heart of the discipline of the *ribāṭ*. At the point of his initiation, symbolized by investiture with the *khirqa*, the aspirant enters into a state where he completely relinquishes his will and right of free disposal to his shaykh until such time that he reaches the stage on the path where his will is then relinquished to God.[63] In annihilating himself in the shaykh through relinquishing free choice (*fanā fī 'l-shaykh bi-tark ikhtiyār nafsihi*) the aspirant becomes his spiritual child, a liminal state which Suhrawardī calls the aspirant's period of suckling (*awān al-irtiḍā*ʿ), a period during which he submits (*taslīm*) to the shaykh's complete jurisdiction (*ḥukm*) over all of his affairs. To enter into such a state is to enter into a relationship which is first and foremost an explicit reenactment of the relationship of complete emulative dependency (*iqtidā*ʾ) between the Prophet and his Companions. In his description of this institution, Suhrawardī is unequivocal that as the representative (*nāʾib*) of the Prophet, the aspirant's submission to the jurisdiction of the shaykh is equivalent to entering under the Prophet's jurisdiction and, by extension, under the jurisdiction of God Himself. Like the relationship between Moses and the mysterious Khiḍr, the aspirant is to neither question nor contradict the shaykh, but rather place complete trust in the veracity of his instructions and to fulfill the 'rights and conditions of the *khirqa*' (*sharāʾiṭ / ḥuqūq al-khirqa*) by adhering to the oath of fidelity (*ʿahd al-wafā*ʾ) which the shaykh took from him at the time of his investiture. At the same time, the jurisdiction of the shaykh does not extend to innovation or infidelity, something which Suhrawardī was careful to counsel his young son ʿImād al-Dīn on in his oft-copied testament to the boy, saying:

> Be a servant (*khādim*) for the *shaykh*s through wealth, body, and rank and be heedful of their hearts, moments, and way of acting, and do not contradict them a thing except what contradicts the community (*jamāʿa*) for if you contradict them, you will never achieve success.[64]

ṭaylasān (cowl, head shawl) over his turban, a sign of rank (see Dozy, op. cit., 254–262 [s.v. *ṭarḥa*], 278–280), and that another shaykh, ʿAlī b. al-Hītī (or perhaps al-Haythī) simply wore the peasant clothing of the Sawād (*ʿAM*, 2:163 / *GE*, 44.7; *Suh.*, 238).

[63] In the following, I am relying on *ʿAM*, 1:251–256 / *GE*, 12.1–11; and, *Suh.*, 151–153; see also: Badeen, *Zwei mystische Schriften*, 7–8 (with further references to the term in al-Bidlīsī's *Bahjat al-ṭāʾifa*, 61; also, ʿAzīz-i Nasafī, *Maqṣad-i asnā*, trans. Ridgeon in *Persian Metaphysics and Mysticism*, 54–56.

[64] al-Suhrawardī, *W. li-ibnihi*, 34; similar in *AdM*, 38 / Milson, *Rule*, 46–47; same in

It is in the person of the shaykh where the prophetic function of guidance (*hidāya*) is vested, for as with the aspirant's natural father it is his duty as a spiritual father (*ab maʿnawī*) to transmit knowledge (*ʿulūm*) to his spiritual child and educate him in the proper manners (*ādāb*). According to Suhrawardī, this occurs through the institution of discipleship (*ṣuḥba*), an instrument which provides the means through which the shaykh transmits his own spiritual state directly to the aspirant's inner being, his words flowing into and literally infusing or impregnating (*yulaqqin/yulaqqiḥ*) it.[65] Much like the *ṣuḥba* of the *madrasa*, this transmission can only take place when the aspirant, observing all of the proper manners, listens attentively to the discourse (*maqāl*) of his shaykh, not recording the knowledge being transmitted to him on a quire of paper but rather on the tablet (*lawḥ*) of his heart.

It is in his description of the complex of formal behaviors and attitudes to which the aspirant is held which yield one of the clearest pictures of life within the *ribāṭ*, a complex of behaviors which in the case of the aspirant are subsumed under what Suhrawardī calls the 'proper behaviors of aspirantship' (*ādāb al-irāda*), a set of conditions and expectations which can be summarized as follows:

1. he should only devote himself to one shaykh at a time and should cleave to him until he has reached the goal;
2. he is not to enter into discipleship (*ṣuḥba*) with the shaykh until he has been instructed in its proper manners;
3. while in the presence of his shaykh, he is to observe a quiet propriety, neither speaking unless spoken to nor raising his voice over that of the shaykh;
4. he is not to conceal any of the spiritual events which he has experienced from his shaykh;

GhṬ, 2:279; but cf. Najm al-Dīn Rāzī Dāya who adds no such caveat (*PGB*, 283). At the same time, the question of the veracity of particular shaykhs was an issue, Suhrawardī's anonymous interlocutors from Khurāsān asking him: "even if a shaykh invests people with the *khirqa*, calls aspirants to the path of wayfaring, and prompts people to repent from their heedlessness, how can we know if he is a true shaykh (*shaykh ḥaqīqī*) and if he actually has the authority (*idhn*, 'permission') to call people to God?", to which Suhrawardī replied: "a true and veridical shaykh is not evinced simply on account that he calls people to God and attracts seekers, rather the hearts of the Folk of Sincerity find the breath of the All-Merciful (*nafas al-raḥmān*) to be with them and consequently repair to him and seek him out." (*AMKh*, 63 [no. 17]; see also ibid., no. 18)

[65] al-Suhrawardī, *W. li-Naṣīr al-Dīn al-Baghdādī*, fol. 65b–66a, 67b.

5. he is not to unfurl his prayer mat in front of his shaykh save during the times of canonical prayer;
6. he is to adhere to the *adab* of *samāʿ* (see below);
7. he should defer to the shaykh in all matters, strive to emulate his example, and not undertake any endeavor without his guidance;
8. when he wishes to speak with his shaykh about any matter, whether spiritual or worldly, he should neither pester nor barrage him with questions, but rather be curt and attentive;
9. he should maintain the highest opinion of his shaykh, constantly strive to serve and honor him, and follow his orders without question, although it is prohibited to consider him infallible (*ʿiṣma*); and,
10. he should not seek a rank above that of his shaykh.[66]

Two main points are worth nothing here. First, the foregrounding of rules of *adab* which not only reinforce the status of the shaykh in the hierarchy of the *ribāṭ*, but also evince a striking continuity with the same complex of *adab* prescribed by individuals such as al-Zarnūjī for the relationship between student and teacher in the *madrasa*. Second, is the issue of multiple affiliation, which although becoming something of a standard practice in Syria and Egypt under the Mamluks and Ottomans, is clearly prohibited by Suhrawardī. Much like the concentration of authority in juridical affiliations, where individuals were expected to identify themselves with only one school of jurisprudence, the aspirant is to pledge his allegiance to one and only one shaykh, an individual whom Suhrawardī—following the ruling of Qushayrī—is careful to point out should not be considered infallible.

[66] *ʿAM*, 2:206–212 / *GE*, 5.2–13; *Suh.*, 157–161; *IrM*, fol. 37b–40b (portions of which are drawn from al-Qushayrī's *W. li-murīdīn* [in *SQ*, 54.1–30]), including the stipulation that the aspirant is not to consider his shaykh infallible); see also: *AdM*, 37 / Milson, *Rule*, 46–47 (on the necessity of complete obedience); and, al-Sulamī, *K. ādāb al-ṣuḥba*, *MA*, 2:69, 115 on the respect [*ḥurma*] due to the shaykh; idem, *Jawāmiʿ*, in *MA*, 1:367–368, 374, 389, 396–297 where he adds, among other things, that one should accept what the shaykh has alluded to even if one does not understand it); also, *PGB*, 283–284 (on the prescription to have only one shaykh at a time). For his part, ʿAbd al-Qādir al-Jīlānī prescribes almost exactly the same set rules concerning the *adab* required of the aspirant in dealing with his shaykh (*GhṬ*, 2:279–284; cf. al-Bidlīsī, *Bahjat al-ṭāʾifa*, 94–96; and, *PGB*, 260–267).

The Aspirant's Program

It is telling that when discussing the praxic dimensions of the Sufi path, Suhrawardī constantly speaks in terms of the regulations (*sharṭ*, pl. *sharāʾiṭ / shuruṭ*) and proper manners which define and structure every individual practice. As we have seen, in Suhrawardī's system each stage of the journey of ascent is possessed of distinct conditions which the aspirant must fulfill prior to advancing to the next stage, the first being to preserve one's outer being from engaging in prohibited actions through strict adherence to the divine law, the second to preserve one's inner being through perfecting the quality of faith (*īmān*), and the third to prepare the spirit for its journey of ascent by cultivating an attitude of repentance.[67] All of this is aimed at establishing the moral, ethical, and praxic foundation necessary to commence wayfaring on the Sufi path, all funneling into that transitional moment when the seeker is formally accepted in the master-disciple relationship and thus obligated to adhere to each of the regulations structuring that particular stage of the Sufi path.[68]

It is such regulations which position the aspirant within the hierarchy of the *ribāṭ*, differentiating him from others both existentially in terms of the spiritual identity which his discipline entails and practically in that he is supported from its coffers, something which as per the fatwa which Suhrawardī provided to his anonymous interlocutors from Khurāsān is permissible, even if he is eating from endowments set up by sultans

[67] al-Suhrawardī, *Futūḥ* XVI, fol. 95b; idem, *W* III, fol. 81b; idem, *W.* IV, fol. 83a; idem, *W. li-ʿAlī b. Aḥmad al-Rāzī*, MS. Süley., Musalla Medresesi 20_{15}, fol. 295b; idem, *W. li-baʿd al-murīdīn*, MS. Süley., İbrahim Ef. 870_{10}, fol. 82b–83a; and, idem, *W. li-Rashīd al-Dīn Abī Bakr al-Ḥabash*, fol. 117a; see also: *PGB*, 151, 179–189, 201–234 whose description follows the same conceptual scheme.

[68] *ʿAM*, 2:323–329 / *GE*, 63.1–21. Enumerated endlessly in the Sufi texts following the time of Suhrawardī, such as ʿAzīz-i Nasafī's regulations of wayfaring: 1) constant reaffirmation of faith; 2) constant renewal of repentance; 3) continual application of *taqwā* and *waraʿ* to all daily circumstances; 4) adherence to a shaykh; 5) inner and outer detachment; 6) inner and outer obedience to the shaykh; and, 7) inner and outer constancy in the spiritual disciples of the path (*Kashf al-ḥaqāʾiq*, trans. Ridgeon in *Persian Metaphysics and Mysticism*, 206–207), or the famous eight-plus-three Naqshbandī 'sacred precepts' (*kalimāt-i qudsiyya*) said to have been formulated by ʿAbd al-Khāliq Ghijduvānī (d. 617/1220) and later supplement by Bahāʾ al-Dīn Naqshband (d. 791/1389) himself: 1) awareness of breath (*hūsh dar dam*); 2) watching over one's steps (*naẓar bar qadam*); 3) self-introspection (*safar dar vaṭan*); 4) solitude in company (*khalvat dar anjuman*); 5) remembrance (*yād kard*); 6) restraint (*bāz gard*); 7) watchfulness (*nigāh dāsht*); 8) recollection (*yād dāsht*); and, 9–11) numerical pause (*wuqūf-i ʿadadī*), temporal pause (*wuqūf-i zamānī*), and the pause of the heart (*wuqūf-i qalbī*), these last three being concerned specifically with the practice of *dhikr* (Trimingham, *The Sufi Orders*, 203–204).

and princes. Like everything else associated with the *ribāṭ*, Suhrawardī provides a clear and defined statement of what comprises the particular discipline which allows for such status. In one of his *Futūḥ*, for instance, Suhrawardī enjoins the wayfarer on the path of God (*sālik ṭarīq al-ḥaqq*) to preserve in the three spiritual disciplines of prayer, recitation of the Qur'ān, and *dhikr*, as these three constitute the straightest path and surest means for him to reach to goal.[69] Indeed, throughout his works there are finite number of spiritual practices which Suhrawardī recommends for aspirants at the initial stages of the Sufi path, formal acts of worship (*ʿibādāt*), recollection *dhikr* (pl. *adhkār*), recitation of the Qur'ān (*tilāwa / qirā'a*), reflection (*fikr*), and the night vigil (*qiyām al-layl*) being discussed most often.[70] Some of these practices, such as recollection, are associated specifically with the forty-day retreat (*arbaʿīniyya*), although according to Suhrawardī each can be practiced independent of the formal discipline of that particular practice, the most important thing being that none of them can interfere with the aspirant's fastidious execution of both the obligatory (*farā'iḍ*) and recommended (*sunan*) acts of devotion enjoined by the *sharīʿa*.[71]

On the first, and following in the footsteps of the Junaydī tradition to which he considered himself an heir, Suhrawardī's analysis of those formal acts of worship prescribed and regulated by the divine law (*ʿibādāt*) interiorize their outward regulations into a complex of inward significances (*asrār*). Thus, like Abū Ṭālib al-Makkī, Ghazālī, and ʿAbd al-Qādir al-Jīlānī, in a series of lengthy chapters in the *ʿAwārif al-maʿārif* Suhrawardī deals with both the legal requirements attached to ablution, prayer, and fasting as well as well as discussing how each relate to the spiritual disciple of the Sufi path and the effects of each on the

[69] al-Suhrawardī, *Futūḥ* XI, fol. 92a.

[70] *ʿAM*, (see below); *JQb*, fol. 10a; idem, *Mukhtaṣar min kalām al-Suhrawardī*, fol. 799a (on the margins); idem, *W.* IV, fol. 80b–81a; idem, *W.* V, MS. Tüb., Ma VI 90_{15}, fol. 85a; idem, *W. li-ʿAlī b. Aḥmad al-Rāzī*, fol. 295b; idem, *W. li-baʿḍ aṣḥābihi*, 31–32; idem, *W. li-Najm al-Dīn al-Tiflīsī*, fol. 83b–84a; and, idem, *W. li-Rashīd al-Dīn al-Farghānī*, MS. Tüb., Ma VI 90_{30}, fol. 93b. Reflection (*fikr / tafakkur*) consists of a number of things, most notably meditation on key Qur'ānic verses and concepts such as God's 'promise and threat' (*al-waʿd wa-l-waʿīd*), constant recollection of the reality of death, and meditation upon the predicament of this world. (*JQb*, fol. 10b–11a; idem, *W. li-baʿḍ aṣḥābihi*, 32) The classic treatment is by Ghazālī who devotes an entire book (*K. al-fikr*) to the subject in the *Iḥyā'* treating in great detail the various types of reflection and contemplation, their relative merits, epistemological dimensions, modalities, and effects on the spiritual state of the practitioner (4:449–474).

[71] *IrM*, fol. 39a.

inner beings of their practitioners.[72] In this, he was deeply indebted to what had gone before, his explanation of the outer dimensions clearly following the Shāfiʿī school in the typical matters of divergence on particular points of ritual practice, and his discussion of their inner dimensions being taken (in many cases through direct quotation) from the *Qūt al-qulūb* of Abū Ṭālib al-Makkī. In addition, Suhrawardī gives detailed instructions on how to correctly perform certain devotions and rites, such as the ritual of *istikhāra*,[73] supplications for any number of occasions, detailed instructions on how to perform the night vigil, as well as a set of daily and nightly devotional programs (*waẓīfa*, pl. *waẓāʾif*) complete with a lengthy set of litanies culled, as Suhrawardī himself admits, from the *Qūt al-qulūb*.[74]

At the same time, in his prescriptions on the day-to-day discipline of the aspirant, Suhrawardī draws a clear distinction between the beginning and medial stages of wayfaring on the Sufi path, mapping the particulars of the journey of ascent in a defined program of actual, replicable, practices. Thus, supererogatory devotions (*nawāfil*)—while integral for lower stages of the path—are generally discouraged for the aspirant because they detract from his practice of *dhikr*.[75] As such, the

[72] *ʿAM*, 2:107–150 / *GE*, 33.1–41.11; idem, *Futūḥ*, XIX, fol. 98a–98b; idem, *R. ilā Kamāl al-Dīn al-Iṣfahānī*, fol. 92b–93a; idem, *W* IV, fol. 81a–82b; idem, *W* V, fol. 84b–85a; and, idem, *W. li-Najm al-Dīn al-Tiflīsī*, fol. 84a. In the *ʿAwārif*, much of his discussion (by his own admission) drawing heavily on Abū Ṭālib al-Makkī's *Qūt al-qulūb*.

[73] That is, the incubatory prayer which is preformed when one is trying to choose between options, the answer usually being given during sleep (see T. Fahd, "Istikhāra," *EI*², 4:259). A widespread practice, Suhrawardī gives detailed instructions on how it is to be preformed based on a *ḥadīth* transmitted to him by Abū ʾl-Najīb (*ʿAM*, 1:294–295/ *GE*, 16.25).

[74] *ʿAM*, 1:294–295 (instructions for *istikhāra*), 300–302, 307 (supplications for traveling), 319 (supplication for requesting sustenance) / *GE*, 16.25, 17.9–13, 18.1, 19.6, 49.1–50.23; and, esp. 2:180–205 / *GE*, 45.1–50.23 where Suhrawardī lays out a twenty-four hour program of devotions for the beginning aspirant (*al-murīd al-sālik*), prescribing in a very specific and detailed manner how and when to pray and perform the required ablutions, what litanies, supplications, portions of the Qurʾān, and formulas of recollection (*tasbīḥ, adhkār*) to recite, when to sleep or how to avoid it, and so forth and so on. Space precludes a thorough discussion of the details, but the daily routine which he prescribes—ultimately drawn from Abū Ṭālib al-Makkī—in many ways evinces a continuity with the general prescriptions of Abū Saʿīd Ibn Abī ʾl-Khayr's famous 'ten-point rule', the *rusūm-i Bū Saʿīdī* (see: Nicholson, *Studies*, 76; and, Meier, *Abū Saʿīd*, 310–311) and was replicated by later Kubrawī shaykhs (see, e.g., Elias, *Throne Carrier*, 114–116). On the scope of various prayers, supplications, daily offices, etc. associated with these acts of Muslim piety generally, in addition to the relevant *EI*² entries (s.v., *dhikr, duʿāʾ, istikhāra, ṣalāt, subḥa, wird*, etc.), see also Trimingham, *The Sufi Orders*, 198–202, 204–207.

[75] *IrM*, fol. 39a; according to Suhrawardī this includes undertaking the pilgrimage

heart of the aspirant's spiritual disciple consists of engaging in the twin disciplines of scrupulous examination (*muḥāsaba*) and vigilant awareness (*murāqaba*), the first concerned with purifying the outer being through regulating the influence of the *nafs*, and the second with purifying the heart and cleansing it from heedlessness towards God.[76] As the 'devotional program' (*waẓīfa*) of the body and the heart respectively, these two disciples are not properly cultivated in the company of others and thus require, in the first place, actual physical withdrawal from society (*khalwa*) and in the second, a certain inward solitude in which the aspirant maintains a continual focus on God in those instances where he finds himself in the midst of social gatherings (*ʿuzla*).[77]

Solitary Retreat (arbaʿīniyya / khalwa)

Intimately associated with the discipline of vigilant awareness and the purification of the heart, in Suhrawardī's system the practice of the forty-day retreat (*arbaʿīniyya*) takes pride of place, the shaykh devoting three chapters of the *ʿAwārif al-maʿārif* to its explication as well as dealing with both its practical and spiritual aspects in various places throughout his *œuvre*.[78] Forming a synergy with social withdrawal and

---

(hajj) on a voluntary basis, in which case it is prohibited for the aspirant to do so unless so directed by his shaykh because "he must first have knowledge of the Lord of the House before visiting His House." (ibid.)

[76] Idem, *Futūḥ* XIII, MS. Süley., Şehid Ali Paşa 1393_7, fol. 68a; idem, *Mukhtaṣar min kalām al-Suhrawardī*, fol. 799a (on the margins); idem, *R. dar kār-i murīd*, fol. 73b–74a; idem, *R. ilā Kamāl al-Dīn al-Iṣfahānī*, fol. 92b; idem, *W.* IV, fol. 81a; idem, *W. li-Rashīd al-Dīn Abī Bakr al-Ḥabash*, fol. 117a; and, idem, *W. li-Rashīd al-Dīn al-Farghānī*, fol. 93b–94a.

[77] *ʿAM*, 1:269, 2:224–225 / *GE*, 14.4, 53.6; idem, *Futūḥ* XI, fol. 91b-92a; idem, *Futūḥ* XIII, fol. 68a; idem, *Futūḥ* XVI, fol. 95b; idem, *Futūḥ* XIX, fol. 97a; idem, *Mukhtaṣar min kalām al-Suhrawardī*, fol. 799a (on the margins); idem, *R. ilā ʿIzz al-Dīn Muḥammad b. Yaʿqūb*, fol. 123b; idem, *W. li-baʿḍ aṣḥābihi*, 31–32; idem, *W. li-baʿḍ al-murīdīn*, fol. 82b–83a; idem, *W. li-Najm al-Dīn al-Tiflīsī*, fol. 83b; and, *JQb*, fol. 9a–9b (on the necessity of silence [*samṭ*] for spiritual advancement).

[78] In particular *ʿAM*, 2:37–55 / *GE*, 56.1–58.11, where the bulk of the discussion is devoted to establishing a precedent for the practice in the exemplary practice of the past prophets—evinced most visibly in the forty-night vigil of Moses (Qurʾān 2:51, 7:142) and Muḥammad's custom of periodic retreat to a cave in Mt. Ḥirāʾ where he is reported to have received his first revelation—and the exempla of the Sufi paragons as well as to differentiating it from what Suhrawardī identifies as Christian and Hindu (*barāhima*; e.g., 'Brahmanic') monastic practices (2:37–44 / *GE*, 26.1–16). Already a well-established discipline, the practice of *khalwa*—also referred to as *arbaʿīniyya* ('forty-[day retreat]; Per. *chilla*, fr. *chihil* 'forty')—became one of the most distinctive features of *ṭarīqa*-based Sufism in the period following the rise of the Sufi brotherhoods; see: Trimingham, *The Sufi Orders*, index; Herman Landolt, "Khalwa," *EI*², 4:990; and, Knysh, *Islamic Mysticism*, 314–317.

inner solitude (*khalwat wa-ʿuzla*), the periodic practice of solitary retreat is an integral and necessary practice for the aspirant, but at the same time it is a powerful and dangerous undertaking, one which must be approached with all seriousness, proper intentions, and sincerity, and never without the guidance of a shaykh.

Neither mentioned as a distinct practice in the earliest Sufi manuals nor discussed beyond its ethical, moral, and spiritual dimensions in the works of Abū Ṭālib al-Makkī and Ghazālī, the analysis of the formal practice of solitary retreat given by Suhrawardī appears to be one of the earliest accounts we have, a practice which as with the Kubrawiyya after him was clearly modeled on the 'eight rules' (*al-sharāʾiṭ al-thamān*) traditionally associated with the 'Path of al-Junayd' (*ṭarīqat al-Junayd*):

> 1) the constant observance of ritual purity; 2) constant fasting; 3) constant silence; 4) constant seclusion (*khalwa*); 5) constant recollection (*dhikr*) using the *tahlīl*; 5) constancy in keeping the heart fixed on the shaykh (*rabṭ al-qalb bi-l-shaykh*); 6) referring all spiritual experiences to the shaykh; 7) constancy in negating 'passing thoughts' (*nafī al-khawāṭir*); and, 8) to continually desist from opposing everything, good or bad, which God brings one's way and to refrain from asking Him for Paradise or seeking refuge with Him from the Fire.[79]

As with the other practices and accoutrements associated with the Sufi *ribāṭ*, in his analysis the rules of solitary retreat are clearly defined.[80] The place of retreat (*zāwiya*—'cell') must be an enclosed space situated away from people and impervious to light, and the aspirant should approach as if it were his grave. As such, before entering his grave the aspirant must first ensure that his clothing and the actual place of retreat are ritually pure. Once this has been established, he is to perform the major ablution (*ghusul*), pray two units of prayer, and turn to God in sincere repentance. From here, the aspirant enters into the actual place of his retreat, neither leaving it or having contact with anyone save during

---

[79] As cited by Najm al-Dīn al-Kubrā, *Fawāʾiḥ*, ed. Meier, 2–3; also *PGB*, 280–283; and, Elias, *Throne Carrier*, 119–120. For his part, Najm al-Dīn al-Kubrā added two more regulations: 1) to consume only a modicum of food and drink; and, 2) to observe moderation in breaking the fast. These rules were subsequently circulated under the title *al-ʿUṣūl al-ʿashara*, or "The Ten Principles".

[80] The following description is based on Suhrawardī's discussions of the practice of the *arbaʿīniyya* in *AMKh*, 55–56 (nos. 4–5); *ʿAM*, 2:43–45, 50–51 / *GE*, 27.1–6, 28.1–3; idem, *Ḥilyat*, fol. 115a–115b; *IrM*, fol. 12b–13a; idem, *Mukhtaṣar min kalām al-Suhrawardī*, fol. 799a–799b (on the margins); idem, *R. dar kār-i murīd*, fol. 74a–74b; idem, *R. dar ṣifat-i khalvat va ādāb-i ān*, MS. Millet, Ali Emiri Ef. Farsca 1017_3, fol. 21b–23a; idem, *Futūḥ* XVI, fol. 95b; *AMKh*, 55; and, *Suh.*, 141–148.

the times in which he must quit his cell to pray in congregation. Even when he has left his retreat, however, the aspirant must neither speak with nor acknowledge anyone but rather remain silent and keep his eyes cast towards the ground lest his concentration be broken.

During the period of his retreat, the aspirant is to devote himself to only one activity at a time as so directed by the shaykh, activities which may include the continual performance of a single *dhikr*, recitation of the Qurʾān, prayer, or engaging in the disciple of vigilant awareness, all of which should be performed facing the direction of prayer (*qibla*). Whichever activity the aspirant has been assigned to do, he is allowed to stop only when sleep overtakes him or when he is forced to attend to mandatory or necessary duties such as performing the five obligatory and recommended (*sunan*) prayers, answering the call of nature, making the ablutions necessary to maintain a state of ritual purity, or eating the modicum of food necessary for the maintenance of life.[81] The final regulation which Suhrawardī prescribes is that throughout the period of his retreat the aspirant should continually employ incense (*ṭīb / bukhūr*) to keep his cell fresh and keep account of the spiritual experiences or visions (*wāqiʿa*, pl. *waqāʾiʿ*)[82] which he undergoes so that they can later be submitted to the shaykh for interpretation.

Recollection (dhikr)

As for other disciplines, there is *dhikr* (recollection, remembrance, anamnesis), a polyvalent term possessing a range of moral, ethical, and devotional associations. As a specific discipline of the Sufi *ribāṭ*, *dhikr* refers to the methodical and ritualized repetition of particular formulae,

---

[81] Hunger and fasting are important components of the disciple of the pious retreat and Suhrawardī provides precise and detailed prescriptions on the dietary regime to which the aspirant is to adhere (*ʿAM*, 2:51–55 / *GE*, 28.1–16; and, idem, *R. dar ṣifat-i khalvat va ādāb-i ān*, fol. 21b–22b).

[82] In the Qurʾān, the term refers to the Final Hour (56:1), and in the sources upon which Suhrawardī was drawing to a class of psychic events connected with both 'passing thoughts' (*khawāṭir*) and 'oncomings' (*wāridāt*)—inasmuch as each are external forces which impress themselves upon the heart (see Chapter Three, s.v. "The Interior Dimension")—which come upon the aspirant as a result of his spiritual exertion; see: *KM*, 502 / Nicholson, *The Kashf*, 387; Badeen, *Zwei mystische Schriften*, 47–52 (with further references to the term in al-Bidlīsī's *Bahjat al-ṭāʾifa*); *PGB*, 286–293; ʿAzīz-i Nasafī, *Kashf al-ḥaqāʾiq*, trans. Ridgeon in *Persian Metaphysics and Mysticism*, 211–212; and, Kāshānī, *Miṣbāḥ*, 171–179; also: Meier, *Fawāʾiḥ*, 109–113; and, Gramlich, *Derwischorden*, 2:215.

a practice familiar to many contemplative disciplines.[83] For Suhrawardī, the practice of recollection represented the surest and most immediate means to effect one's advancement on the Sufi path, a practice without which the wayfarer would most certainly not reach his goal.[84] According to him, at its most fundamental there are two modalities of recollection, recollection by the tongue (*dhikr bi-l-lisān*) and recollection by the heart (*dhikr bi-l-qalb*), the first specific, fleeting, and discursive, and the second unrestricted, perpetual, and immediate:

> The recollection of the tongue is remembering him through His most beautiful names and lofty attributes and speaking of His blessing, whereas the remembrance of the heart is completely preserving Him [in the heart] (*yaḥfaẓuhu*) and not forgetting Him (*lā-yansāhu*).[85]

The first leads to the second, the recollector (*dhākir*) reciting the formula which he has been assigned by his shaykh loudly at first and then progressively softer and quieter until it disappears from his lips

[83] The practice of *dhikr* has often been compared to the Jesus prayer of the Russian Eastern Orthodox Church, the Hesychasm of the monks of Mt. Athos, various Buddhist and Hindu meditative practices surrounding the use of mantras, and certain meditative practices of Jewish mysticism (see, e.g., Anawati and Gardet, *Mystique musulmane*, 4th ed., 189–194). Arguably the most defining feature of Sufi spiritual praxis in any of its historical manifestations, the ritualized practice of recollection, its rules, regulations, effects, and significance have been discussed, debated, and explained in detail by every major Sufi writer from the time of the great systematizers of the 4th/10th–5th/11th century up to the present, see: *SL*, 89.7; Kalābādhī, *Ta'arruf*, 103–106 / Arberry (trans.), *The Doctrine*, 93–98; Abū Ṭālib al-Makkī, *Qūt al-qulūb* (index in Gramlich [trans.], *Die Nahrung*, 4:123–124 [s.v., Gedenken, Gottgedenken]; al-Sulamī, *Mas'alat ṣifāt al-dhākirīn wa-l-mutafakkirīn*, in *MA*, 2:445–456; *SQ*, 32.1–11; al-Ghazālī, *Iḥyā'*, 1:349–360; (pseudo?)-Ibn 'Aṭā' Allāh al-Iskandarī, *Miftāḥ al-falāḥ wa-miṣbāḥ al-arwāḥ* (Cairo: Īsā al-Bābī al-Ḥalabī, 1961 (relevant passages translated and discussed by Ernst Bannerth in "Dhikr et khalwa d'après Ibn 'Aṭā' Allāh," *MIDEO* 12 [1974]: 75–88); *PGB*, 269–278; and, Elias, *Throne Carrier*, 124–134 (on al-Simnānī's rules for *dhikr*). See also: Meier, *Kubrā*, 200–214; Anawati and Gardet, *Mystique musulmane*, 4th ed., 187–234; Gramlich, *Derwischorden*, 2:370–430; Trimingham, *The Sufi Orders*, 200–207 & index (s.v. *dhikr*); Schimmel, *Mystical Dimensions*, 167–178; Gardet, "Dhikr," *EI*², 2:223; Geoffroy, *Le soufisme*, 408–411; Popovic and Veinstein, eds., *Les voies d'Allah*, index (s.v., *dhikr*); M.I. Waley, "Contemplative Disciples in Early Persian Sufism," in Lewisohn, ed. *The Heritage of Sufism*, 1:502–511; and, Knysh, *Islamic Mysticism*, 317–322.

[84] al-Suhrawardī, *R. fī 'l-dhikr*, MS. Dār al-Kutub al-Miṣriyya (Cairo) 776_4, Ṭasawwūf Taymūr, fol. 19a (quoted in *Suh.*, 134–135); and, *JQb*, fol. 5a-5b; also, *SQ*, 32.2; al-Bidlīsī, *Bahjat al-ṭā'ifa*, 44–53. These two modalities and their qualities are, of course, not the only possible types of recollection analyzed by Sufis both before and after Suhrawardī, e.g., recollection of the tongue, heart, secret (*sirr*), and spirit (al-Sulamī, *Mas'alat ṣifāt al-dhākirīn*, 446 ff.).

[85] *IrM*, fol. 24b; cf. *SQ*, 32.1–11; and, *PGB*, 215–216.

and sinks into his heart at which point it is interiorized, serving as a barrier against the chatter of the soul (*ḥadīth al-nafs*).[86]

In his prescriptions to aspirants, Suhrawardī prescribes numerous formulas of recollection which the aspirant is enjoined to recite.[87] The first, and most effective, is the first-half of the Muslim proclamation of faith (*shahāda*), the *tahlīl*: "there is no God but God" (*lā ilāha ilā 'llāh*), whose practice follows a *ḥadīth* in which the Prophet is reported to have said "the best *dhikr* is to say 'there is no god but God' and the best supplication 'all praise is due to God' (*al-ḥamdu li-llāh*)".[88] The second, beginning with the same formula, is: 'there is no god but God, unique without partner' (*lā ilāha ilā 'llāh waḥdahu lā sharīk lahu*). The third, which alludes to the famous 'throne verse' (*āyat al-kursī*) of the Qur'ān (2:255), is: 'there is no god but God, the Living, the Self-Subsisting' (*lā ilāha ilā 'llāh al-ḥayy^{u} al-qayyūm*).

In Suhrawardī's system, the inculcation of the formula of recollection (*talqīn al-dhikr*) was concomitant to investiture with the *khirqat al-irāda*, like it being supported by a chain of authorities (*nasab / isnād*) and subject to certain rules and regulations. In his account of his own reception of the formula of recollection from his uncle Abū 'l-Najīb—which unlike the *khirqa* transmitted through Wajīh al-Dīn, was transmitted through Aḥmad-i Ghazālī—Suhrawardī explains that both the *dhikr* itself and the ritual of its inculcation (*ṭarīqat talqīn al-dhikr*) has its origins in an encounter between the Prophet Muḥammad and ʿAlī b. Abī Ṭālib:

> He [the Prophet] said, 'O' ʿAlī what prophecy has bestowed [upon me] is incumbent upon you', and he said, 'and what is that O' Messenger of God', to which he replied, 'preserving in the recollection of God in moments of isolation (*khalwāt*).' ʿAlī considered this for a while and eventually said, 'and how should I recollect O' Messenger of God?', to which he replied, 'close you eyes and listen to what I say three times, and then repeat it to yourself thrice.'[89]

---

[86] *ʿAM*, 2:45–46, 51 / *GE*, 27.7–8, 28.3; idem, *W* IV, fol. 81a–81b; idem, *W. li-Najm al-Dīn al-Tiflīsī*, fol. 83b; and, *Suh.*, 140.

[87] Not always mentioned together; here I am combining his discussions in: *ʿAM*, 2:45–47 / *GE*, 27.7–14; idem, *Futūḥ* XXIX, trans. Amravhī in *Vaṣāyā*, 46 (*iqtibāsāt*, no. 4); idem, *Ḥilyat*, fol. 117a; *JQb*, fol. 4b–6a; idem, *Mukhtaṣar min kalām al-Suhrawardī*, fol. 799b (on the margins); idem, *Tarjama-yi al-lawāmiʿ*, fol. 76b; and, idem, *W.* IV, fol. 81a–82b; also, *Suh.*, 134–141.

[88] *JQb*, fol. 4b; and, *Suh.*, 136.

[89] al-Suhrawardī, *R. fī 'l-dhikr*, fol. 19b–20a (as quoted in *Suh.*, 136–137).

He goes on to state that ʿAlī subsequently transmitted the *dhikr* to al-Ḥasan al-Baṣrī through the same procedure from whence it eventually passed to al-Junayd and so on and so forth up to Abū ʾl-Najīb al-Suhrawardī who formally inculcated him with the formula in the same way, replicating the ritual of inculcation in which "the aspirant shuts his eyes and listens to his shaykh pronounce the *dhikr* three times, after which the his shaykh listens as he recites it back to him thrice."[90] This ritual of transmission, as Suhrawardī explains in response to a question on the subject, is not merely the transmission of a verbal formula but is rather the impregnation (*talqīḥ*) of the inner secret of the formula and its meaning into the inner being of the aspirant through the breath (*nafas*) of the shaykh, stating further that to engage in *dhikr* without having first undergone this ritual of inculcation will yield little benefit.[91]

The Patched Frock (muraqqaʿa)

In addition to investiture with the *khirqa* and the inculcation of the formula of recollection, Suhrawardī also speaks about a third initiatic event, saying that when the aspirant has reached a certain point in his education and spiritual development he is allowed to be invested with the patched frock (*muraqqaʿa*)[92] a garment which, like the *khirqat al-irāda*, serves as an outward symbol (*ʿalāma*) of his inner state (*aḥwāl al-bāṭin*).[93] A traditional Sufi symbol of renunciation whose use is well attested in the logia of the paragons, the early manuals, and descriptions of Sufis by contemporaries of Suhrawardī such as Ibn al-Jawzī (who of course finds the practice laughable)[94] Suhrawardī associates the *muraqqaʿa* with the second ground station of the Sufi path, renunciation of the world (*al-zuhd fī ʾl-dunyā*).[95] According to him, the *muraqqaʿa* has its precedent

[90] Ibid. 137. The same ritual is described in greater detail by Najm al-Dīn Rāzī Dāya (*PGB*, 275–276). For Suhrawardī's *nisbat talqīn al-dhikr*, see Chapter One, Chart 2.

[91] *AMKh*, 62–63 (no. 16); same in *PGB*, 242, 273–274, 277.

[92] Attested in both the masc., *muraqqaʿ*, and fem. *muraqqaʿa*; see: *KM*, 55–57 / Nicholson, 48–51; Najm al-Dīn Kubrā, *Ādāb*, 29, 30 (with a symbolic etymology from '*marra wa-waqaʿa*', or 'he went and fell down', which he explains means: "he who flees from the patched frock [*muraqqaʿ*] falls in such a way that he will never get up again").

[93] *IrM*, fol. 41b–42a; cf. Najm al-Dīn Kubrā's detailed discussion of the correspondences between clothing (color, type, etc.) and the interior state of the aspirant (*Ādāb*, 29–31; detailed notes on terms and significance in Meier, "A Book of Etiquette," in *Essays*, 68–75; and, Böwering, "The *Adab* Literature," 75–78).

[94] *Talbīs Iblīs*, 234–237.

[95] See also, *AdM*, 28 / Milson, *Rule*, 42.

in the figure of Jesus, the first to wear the patched frock, a symbolic object which like the *khirqat al-irāda* carries with it certain conditions to which its wearer must adhere.[96]

Mendicants, Servants, and Lay Affiliates

Below the aspirant stands another type of individual who is differentiated from others based on existential designations, the mendicant (*faqīr* / pl. *fuqarāʾ*). Within the hierarchy of the *ribāṭ*, the mendicant, or more properly the 'sincere mendicant' (*al-faqīr al-ṣādiq*) to use Suhrawardī's terminology, is accorded a lower position than that of the *murīd*. Generally speaking, the distinction between the aspirant and the mendicant is one of degree, the latter being a probationary disciple who is not actively engaged in a comprehensive program of spiritual training under the direction of the shaykh and consequently is not held to the regulations binding upon *ahl al-irāda*. As such, in contradiction to the aspirant the mendicant is not entitled to receive support from the *ribāṭ*'s coffers, but rather is counseled to obtain his sustenance outside of its precincts through his own devices.[97]

Writing in the early 5th/11th century, Hujwīrī remarks that when a seeker comes to a Sufi shaykh with the intention of renouncing the world it is their established custom (*sunnat*) to subject him to a three-year period of probation, the first year devoted to serving people, the second to serving God, and the third to watching over the heart (*murāʿāt-i dil-i khud*); if he fails to fulfill the requirements of each then he is not accepted into their path (*ṭarīqat*).[98] Although neither Suhrawardī nor his near contemporaries lay out such a formal temporal structure, from the perspective of the *R. fī ʾl-sayr wa-l-ṭayr* the mendicant is an individual

---

[96] *JQb*, fol. 16a. Similarly, Suhrawardī assigns a particular prophet as a precedent for each type of dress; Moses, for instance, being the first to wear a hair shirt and Solomon the first to wear the scholar's overcoat (*abāʾ*) (ibid., fol. 16a–16b). In the *ʿAwārif*, Suhrawardī associates the *khirqa* with the shirt (*qamīṣ*) of Joseph, a heavenly silken vestment which the archangel Gabriel gave to Abraham when he emerged naked from Nimrod's fire which was then inherited by Isaac and then by Jacob who stuffed it into an amulet (*taʿwīdh*) which he hung around his son Joseph's neck, which after he fell into the well Gabriel came to rescue him, removed the shirt from the amulet, and then invested Joseph with it, completing the cycle of investiture which began with his ancestor, Abraham (*ʿAM*, 1:258 / *GE*, 12.16).

[97] *ʿAM*, 1:279 / *GE*, 15.11.

[98] *KM*, 61 / Nicholson, *The Kashf*, 54.

who has clearly yet to enter the domain of wayfaring, an individual who has yet to fully actualize the verities of faith (*īmān*) and god-fearing piety (*taqwā*), and thus has yet to enter into the domain of the master-disciple relationship and wayfaring on the path. As such, the mendicant is rarely spoken of in connection with the spiritual disciplines associated with the aspirant, rather being connected with the two lower, or perhaps preparatory, disciplines of voluntary poverty and traveling.

Voluntary Poverty (faqr)

Among the eighteen questions put to him by his anonymous interlocutors from Khurāsān, five deal with the interrelated issues of work, begging, and marriage, by all accounts an important set of questions which Suhrawardī dutifully answered in a series of short responsa (*fatāwā*) as well as treating them, at some length, in the *ʿAwārif al-maʿārif*.[99] From the perspective of the Sufi path, each of these questions have to do with the interrelated practices of poverty (*faqr*) and asceticism (*zuhd*), two issues which Ibn al-Jawzī singled out for extended discussion in his account of the errors and excesses of the Sufis of Baghdad.[100] In his own discussion of these contentious issues, Suhrawardī attempts to counter such criticisms in his usual way, namely trying to control and delimit the potential for excess by laying out precise prescriptions and regulations, and then authorizing and legitimatizing their practice through evincing their conformity with Qurʾānic models of piety, precedents in the Sunna, the exempla of the *salaf al-ṣāliḥ* and the paragonic Sufi authorities, and their rootedness in a comprehensive metaphysical and psycho-spiritual reality.

In contradistinction to other technical terms, Suhrawardī tends to analyze poverty (*faqr*) as a spiritual virtue or life-orientational attitude comprehending a wide range of religious, spiritual, ethical, and moral concerns. It is this figuration of the term, for example, that we encounter in his beautifully written *Ḥilyat al-faqīr al-ṣādiq fī ʾl-taṣawwuf*, where the shaykh associates the virtue of poverty with a long list of behaviors, beliefs, commitments, and practices which in most treatises are connected with the terms submission (*islām*), faith (*īmān*), and god-fearing

[99] *AMKh*, nos. 2, 8, 9, 13, 14; *ʿAM*, 1:317–350 / *GE*, 19.1–21.24; and, *Suh.*, 178–179.
[100] Ibn al-Jawzī, *Talbīs Iblīs*, 340–361.

piety (*taqwā*).[101] At the same time, however, Suhrawardī also uses the term *faqr* and the adjective *faqīr* (pl. *fuqarā'*) to refer to the actual practice of voluntary poverty and its practitioner, in which case it is both comprehended by and distinct from renunciation (*al-zuhd fī 'l-dunyā*), comprehended in that its own perfection is an outcome (*thamar*) of the actualization of the station of renunciation and distinct in that, as a virtue, its articulation in attitudinal and practical commitments is also a means to effect the actualization of renunciation itself. The idea is a very common trope in Sufi literature, namely that as an antonym to *ghānī* ('one who is not in need', 'self-sufficient') the *faqīr* ('one in need') asserts his ontological status as a created being entirely dependent upon the truly self-sufficient (*al-ghānī* being one of the names of God) an assertion which can be exteriorized in the existential condition of worldly poverty.[102] It is here where the practice of poverty associated with the *faqīr* as a specific type of individual carries over into the higher stages of the Sufi path associated with the *mutaṣawwif.*

The practical outcome of engaging in the practice of *faqr* is that the *faqīr* must still somehow obtain his daily sustenance while at the same time preserving his inner state from being disturbed, meaning that he must adhere to both an attitude and particular set of manners, something which Suhrawardī makes clear in his counsel to his son ʿImād al-Dīn:

> O' my son, renounce this world for pursuing it will destroy your religion. Your duty is fasting, prayer and maintaining a state of poverty (*faqr*) which is clean, light, proper, scrupulous, informed, and clear from the ignorant Sufis and their generality... do not ask anyone for anything nor take a loan from them and do not store away anything for the morrow for each day God gives a fresh sustenance (*rizq*)... Trust in God's promises in the matter

[101] al-Suhrawardī, *Ḥilyat*, fol. 116a–117b; and, idem, *R. fī 'l-faqr*, fol. 52b–53b.

[102] *JQb*, fol. 15a–15b; idem, *R. fī 'l-faqr wa-l-ghinā*, MS. Süley., Reisülküttap 465_2, fol. 109b–110b; idem, *W.* IV, fol. 83a; and, *Suh.*, 178–179; cf. *SL*, 89.8–9; Sulamī, who affirms the basis of but provides a different (i.e., Malāmatī) perspective on the outward manifestations of spiritual poverty, e.g.: *K. bayān zalal al-fuqarā' wa-l-ādābihim*, ed. Süleyman Ateş in *Tisʿa kutub fī uṣūl al-taṣawwuf wa-l-zuhd.* (Beirut: al-Nāshir li-Ṭibāʿa wa-l-Nashr al-Tawzīʿ wa-l-Iʿlān, 1993), 429–465 / trans. Kenneth Honerkamp as "The Stumblings of Those Aspiring and the Conduct Required of Them," in idem, *Three Early Sufi Texts* (Louisville, KY: Fons Vitae, 2003), 129–153; idem, *Bayān aḥwāl al-ṣūfiyya*, ed. Süleyman Ateş in op. cit., 366–368; idem, *K. sulūk al-ʿārifīn*, ed. Süleyman Ateş in op. cit., 400–407; but cf. idem, *Jawāmiʿ*, in *MA*, 1:376–377, 396, 397–398, 403–405; *KM*, 21–34 / Nicholson, *The Kashf*, 19–29; Kāshānī, *Misbāḥ*, 375–379; *SQ*, 40.1–19; and, al-Bidlīsī, *Bahjat al-ṭā'ifa*, 35–41. See also Gramlich, *Derwischorden*, 431–451; and, K.A. Nizami, "Faḳr," EI^2, 2:757.

> of sustenance for God has guaranteed a sustenance for every creature as He said: "there is nothing which crawls on the earth save that God has given it a sustenance." Do not become disappointed by depending upon people for sustenance and do not be too much inclined to them, always speak the truth, but do not depend upon any one.[103]

In the *'Awārif al-ma'ārif*, Suhrawardī explains that there is only one proper way for the *faqīr* to obtain his daily bread, and that is through alms or charity (*futūḥ*—lit. 'opening') given to him by others. Here, Suhrawardī delineates two modes of obtaining this sustenance, either through active begging and solicitation or through a quiet perseverance and trust that God will send something one's way without having asked for it.[104] As to be expected, he prohibits the *faqīr* from engaging in the former, an injunction which he extends to asking God to provide something save only in the most dire of circumstances for which he then prescribes a ritual supplication which one should use to effect an 'opening' and if that fails, a dispensation to actively seek alms.[105] At the same time, the permissibility of accepting an opening must be guided by the inner insight of the *faqīr*, and he should try to endeavor to determine whether or not a particular opening has come to him by some inner aspiration or is an act of God (*fi'l al-ḥaqq*).[106]

Closely tied with this issue is that of marriage and family, something which Suhrawardī devotes an unusually lengthy chapter to discussing in the *'Awārif al-ma'ārif*.[107] As with the ruling which he gave to his anonymous interlocutors from Khurāsān, despite a lengthy argument which weighs the respective advantages and disadvantages of marriage and family life vis-à-vis the Sufi path, for Suhrawardī it boils down to one thing: for both the *faqīr* and aspirant bachelorhood and isolation (*tajarrud*) is always preferable to marriage and family. He gives three main reasons for this, first that because sexual desire is of the *nafs* it should

[103] al-Suhrawardī, *W. li-ibnihi*, MS. Süley., Nâfiz Paşa 428_4, fol. 190a–190b.

[104] *'AM*, 1:317–324 / *GE*, 19.1–13; but cf. *GhṬ*, 2:291–294, who provides a bit more latitude in the *adab* of worldly poverty.

[105] *'AM*, 1:319, 321, 335 / *GE*, 19.6, 9, 20.21; cf. *AdM*, 70–72 / Milson, *Rule*, 68–69). None of this, of course, applies to the fully actualized Sufi who because he has passed through the state of relinquishing his free will (*tark al-ikhtiyār*) in the will of God possesses both 'a license to beg' and 'a license to work' because he considers asking or patiently waiting for an opening, working or not working, to be one and the same thing. (*'AM*, 1:330–335 / *GE*, 20.10–20; cf. al-Sulamī, *Jawāmi'*, in *MA*, 1:358–363)

[106] *'AM*, 1:327–330 / *GE*, 20.5–10.

[107] Ibid., 1:337–350 (also 2:225) / *GE*, 21.1–24 (53.7); cf. *AdM*, 68–80 / Milson, *Rule*, 67–68; cf. *KM*, 470–479 / Nicholson, *The Kashf*, 360–366.

be rejected, second that the legal obligations which come with having a family inevitably place great constraints on the time the aspirant can devote to pursing the path, and third—with a misogyny typical of his day and age—that women entice men into all manner of trials and tribulations. If, however, an individual has such a strong desire to marry that it continually disturbs and interferes with his devotions, then he should carefully consider the matter, seek the guidance of a shaykh and his brethren, perform the *istikhāra*, and only after he has received a veridical answer on the issue from God, make his choice.[108]

Travel (safar)

At the same time, almost invariably Suhrawardī describes the mendicant in association with the spiritual discipline of travel, a well worn trope in both the logia of the Sufi paragons and something which served as a key component of the *ribāṭ*-based system which Suhrawardī describes in his works. In this, his discussion was neither novel nor unusual, for the discipline of travel and its manners and customs is something which both Abū ʾl-Najīb and ʿUmar al-Suhrawardī's own son ʿImād al-Dīn wrote about themselves in their own manuals of Sufi *adab*.[109] Playing with the etymological associations of the root of the word, in the *ʿAwārif al-maʿārif* Suhrawardī envisions travel (*safar*) as a type of spiritual disciple which unveils (*yusfiru ʿan*) the bad character traits of the *nafs* by subjecting it to hardship and unfamiliar situations,[110] and following Qushayrī, he analyzes four permutations practiced by the Sufis, namely those who travel early on in their career on the Sufi path and then settle down at its end, those who settle down first and then travel at its end, those who never travel, and those who continually travel and never settle down.[111] The first does so in pursuit of knowledge, in order to meet authoritative shaykhs and fellow travelers on the Sufi path and benefit from their company, to discipline the soul and break it of

[108] *ʿAM*, 1:342–344 / *GE*, 21.9–13; cf. *AMKh*, 59 (no. 8).

[109] *AdM*, 48–52 / Milson, *Rule*, 52–55; and, ʿImād al-Dīn al-Suhrawardī, *Zād al-musāfir wa-adab al-ḥāḍir*, fol. 14b–32a; cf. *SQ*, 54.9–10; who advises the aspirant that travel is for the spiritually weak.

[110] *ʿAM*, 1:285 / *GE*, 16.7; first attested in al-Sarrāj (*SL*, 68.9, 75.5, 142.2), same in Qushayrī (*SQ*, 43.9). As a spiritual discipline, it is important to remember that, like others, Suhrawardī draws a distinction between journeys with a specific destination or purpose (*safar*, pl. *asfār*) and itinerant wanderings (*siyāḥa*, pl. *-āt*; also, *ightirāb*).

[111] *ʿAM*, 1:282–292 / *GE*, 16.1–19; and, *Suh.*, 239–240. Clearly drawing on Qushayrī (*SQ*, 43.1–2); cf. al-Sulamī, *Jawāmiʿ*, in *MA*, 1:356.

habits bred by familiarity by subjecting it to unfamiliar situations, to take a lesson from seeing the sheer diversity of God's signs and effects in the world, and to cultivate a sense of alienation from it by not relying on acceptance by others. The second does not pursue travel at the beginning of his career on the path because God favors him with the formal acceptance of a shaykh without his having needed to travel to find him, only setting out on a journey when he has benefited fully from his companionship with that shaykh. The third is the state of the *majdhūb* who in being pulled directly to God has nothing to gain by traveling. The final state is that of the true itinerant, the perpetually wandering seeker exemplified in the figure of Ibrāhīm al-Khawwāṣ (d. 291/904), a disciple of al-Junayd who is said to have never stayed in one place for more than forty days.[112]

In the *Kashf al-maḥjūb*, Hujwīrī mentions that aspirants are divided into two categories: intentional travelers (*musāfirān*) and residents (*muqīmān*), the latter superior to the former in both rank and spiritual station.[113] In his discussion of the praxis of the *ribāṭ*, Suhrawardī follows this division and in a number of places, most notably in his two handbooks the *'Awārif al-ma'ārif* and *Irshād al-murīdīn*, devotes a considerable amount of space to the practice, outlining a detailed set of regulations concerning the individual, ritual, and social manners which the mendicant is required to observe in the course of his travels. These rules, constituting an entire *adab al-safar*, are anchored by two axial events, namely departing from and entering into the *ribāṭ*. Both of these moments represent a highly ritualized break with the sacralized space of the *ribāṭ* and entering into the profane space of the outer world, a transition whose gravity is highlighted in the manner in which Suhrawardī lays out the regulations governing the ritual of departure:

> The customs of the Sufis on exiting from the *ribāṭ* are comprised of the following: first the one departing should pray two units of prayer at daybreak on the day which he is to travel. He should take out his traveling-shoes (*khuff*)[114] and shake them off, and then tuck up his right

---

[112] On him, see: al-Sulamī, *Ṭabaqāt*, 220–222 (no. 47); idem, *Jawāmi'*, in *MA*, 1:363; *KM*, 193–194 / Nicholson, *The Kashf*, 153–154; al-Iṣfahānī, *Ḥilyat*, 10:347–352; *SQ*, 1.43; Ibn al-Jawzī, *Ṣifat al-ṣafwā*, 2:305–308 (no. 675); *'AM*, 1:291–292, 303 / *GE*, 16.19, 17.14; and, Jāmī, *Nafaḥāt*, 138–140 (no. 154).

[113] *KM*, 442–443 / Nicholson, *The Kashf*, 340.

[114] Generally, as per the root *k-f-f* (connoting lightness), *khuff* (usually a collective noun, but also attested with the dual *khuffayn* ['a pair of *khuffs*'] and the plurals *khifāf* and *akhfāf*, with the latter also referring to the footpad of a camel, ostrich foot, and sole), refers to

> sleeve and gird his waist with a girdle (*miyāband*) after which he should take out a satchel for his slippers (*madās*),[115] shake it off, and then take it to the place where he intends the put on his traveling-shoes. There, he should unfurl his prayer mat, rub the soles of his slippers together, and then taking them in the right hand and the satchel in the left, slide them down into the satchel, tie-up its top, and then with his left hand, stow them away on his back. After this, he should sit on his prayer mat and with his right hand place his traveling-shoes out in front, shake them off, and beginning with the right put them on, being careful to not allow either his breeches (*rānīn*) or girdle (*minṭaqa*) to touch the ground.[116] After this, he should wash his hands and proceed to the place of his departure, taking leave of those who are present; and if some of the brethren take his shoulder bag (*rāwiya*) to the exit of the *ribāṭ* [for him] he should not stop them, and likewise his walking stick (*ʿaṣā*) and ewer (*ʾibrīk*). He should bid farewell to those who see him off, and then gird himself with his shoulder bag by lifting up his right hand and sliding the bag up under his right armpit and then back around over to his left side—so that his right shoulder is free—and then secure it on his left side.[117]

The use of the Persian words *miyāband* (girdle) and *rānīn* are of significance in this account, in that they help us to locate the particular

---

a short, ankle length leather slipper, sock, or half-boot whose use, according to Dozy, was "already attested in the era of Muḥammad, the Prophet carrying them himself but prohibiting the faithful to wear them on the pilgrimage unless they were unable to procure sandals (*niʿāl*)" (*Dictionnaire détaillé des noms des vêtements chez les Arabes*, 155). Gramlich translates Suhrawardī's use of the term as 'traveling- shoe' (*Reiseschuh*) which based on other references given by Dozy (*Dictionnaire détaillé*, 155–159) seems correct, although one cannot rule out the possibility of the *khuff* being possessed of symbolic value as a symbol of worldly poverty based on the *ḥadīth* cited by Dozy.

[115] That is, *kharīṭat al-madās*. A type of footwear, the *madās* or *midās* which Gramlich translates as 'slipper' (*Hausschuh*), was a type of high shoe affixed to the foot with straps.

[116] The edited text reads "*wa-lā yadaʿu shayʾan min al-rān aw al-minṭaqa yaqaʿu ʿalā ʾl-ʿarḍ*" with the editor glossing *al-rān* as *al-khuff*. A better reading, attested in most manuscripts, is *al-rānayn* which Gramlich has rightly corrected to the Persian *ranīn* (fr. *rān*, 'thigh') with the meaning of breeches (Gr. *Hose*) (*GE*, 134 fn. 52). We can assume that *minṭaqa* here is an equivalent for the Persian *miyāband*.

[117] *ʿAM*, 1:304–305 / *GE*, 17.18–19; and *IrM*, fol. 45b–46b with a clearer ending: "After having put on his traveling-shoes he should wash his hands and then carry his shoulder bag upon his left shoulder and his walking stick and pot in his left hand; and if someone carries his shoulder bag [for him], he should not prohibit him from doing so. When he exits the *ribāṭ* he should secure the shoulder bag upon his back, bid farewell to those who followed him out in order to see him off, and then turn his attention to the residents (*qawm*) who might happen to be standing there waiting for him and acknowledge them by nodding his head three times in a spirit of service and humility." (fol. 46a) Najm al-Dīn Kubrā affirms girding the waist and rolling up the sleeves (*Ādāb*, 37).

strand of the Junaydī tradition in which Suhrawardī positioned himself. As Suhrawardī himself states in his lengthy enumeration of the regulations of travel, they are given according to the custom (*sunna*) of the mendicants of Khurāsān and the Jibāl, a body of regulations which the shaykh argues the mendicants of Iraq, Syria, and the Maghrib do not adhere to and which they debate, the former saying that they are evinced in the exempla of the ancient authorities (*mutaqqadimūn*) and the latter that they are mere vanities. He resolves this dispute curtly, saying that these are sound customs (*adab ḥasan*) which are not disapproved (*munkar*) by the *sharīʿa* and that furthermore each of them are evinced by a precedent in the Sunna and the practice of the *salaf al-ṣāliḥ*.[118]

Furthermore, like the *khirqat al-irāda*, the *muraqqaʿa*, and the *farajiyya* of the ulama, according to Suhrawardī each of the accoutrements and acts associated with this ritual are possessed of symbolic significance, something which extends, in fact, to each and every aspect of the mendicant's travels. In the case of the ritual of departure specifically, for example, the girding of the *madās* in a special satchel symbolizes the traveler's preservation of the solitude and focus associated with the *ribāṭ* in the midst of the hustle and bustle of the outer world, girding the waist and rolling up the sleeves symbolizes his readiness to engage in spiritual combat with the drives of his *nafs* while on the road, and securing the shoulder bag on the left side symbolizes his distain for the space he is about the enter.[119] The traveler then proceeds, accoutrements in hand, to step outside the walls of the fortified encampment of the frontline fighters into the battlefield of the outside world, struggling with his *nafs* until such a time that he reaches the safety of another *ribāṭ*, finding comfort and solace among his comrades in arms.

Having made the transition from the inner sanctity of the *ribāṭ* to the profane space of the outer world, the mendicant begins his journey, and just as with the ritual of departure, and later the ritual of arrival, Suhrawardī carefully outlines a body of regulations and conditions structuring the mendicant's travels, prescribing a complex of manners, customs, and accoutrements which can be summarized as follows:[120]

---

118 *ʿAM*, 1:305–306, 312 / *GE*, 17.21, 18.12.

119 *IrM*, fol. 47b–48a.

120 *ʿAM*, 1:292–312 / *GE*, 16.21–18.22; *IrM*, fol. 43b–48a; and, *Suh.*, 240–241; cf. *GhṬ*, 2:300–302.

1. the traveler (*sāfir*) must investigate his spiritual state, be sound in his intention, and should perform the *istikhāra* before making any resolution to travel;
2. he must know the conditions attached to the legal dispensations granted to travelers;[121]
3. he must never travel alone, but rather with a traveling companion (*rafīq*) or in the company of others, in which case a leader (*pīshraw*) should be chosen;[122]
4. when calling his fellow travelers to set off, the leader should rouse them with supplications (*dūʿāʾ*);
5. in dealing with his traveling companions, the traveler should speak little, be generous in sharing what he has received by ways of alms (*futūḥ*), and perform acts of service for them;[123]
6. he should perform two units of prayer at every way station;
7. he should carry with him a walking stick, prayer mat, and a small ewer (*ibrīq* / *rakwa*) which is to serve as a vessel for ritual ablutions;[124]

[121] Here, Suhrawardī gives detailed instructions on the dispensations (*rukhaṣ*, sing. *rukhṣa*) granted to travelers for both ritual ablution and canonical prayer, namely the conditions attached to performing the ablution with sand or soil (*tayammum*), the conditions attached to the act of 'passing the hands over the socks' (*al-masḥ ʿalā ʾl-khuffayn*) in lieu of directing washing the feet, and the conditions attached to combining and shortening the canonical prayers. Needless to say, he follows the Shāfiʿī school in his enumeration of the conditions of each of these dispensations (ibid., 1:296–299 / *GE*, 17.1–7).

[122] The regulation is based on a *ḥadīth* in which the Prophet is reported to have prohibited traveling alone (quoted by Ibn al-Ṣiddīq, *ʿAwāṭif*, 245–246 [no. 103]; idem, *Ghaniyyat*, 1:222 [no. 103]; cf. Najm al-Dīn Kubrā, *Ādāb*, 37 not mentioning the *ḥadīth* but affirming the necessity of like-minded traveling companions). For his part, Suhrawardī prohibits it save for the "Sufi who has full knowledge of the machinations of his *nafs*" (*ʿAM*, 1:299 / *GE*, 17.8). His use of the Persian *pīshraw* (leader; lit. 'one who goes before') here accords with his reliance on the custom of the Sufis of Khurāsān and the Jibāl, explaining that: "the Sufis call such a leader *pīshraw*, and he is a group-leader (*amīr*) who should be chosen from among the most ascetic of the group and the most abounding in god-fearing piety." (ibid.) In his testament to his son ʿImād al-Dīn, Suhrawardī counsels him to look for five qualities in such a companion (*rafīq*): "do not take a companion until you have distinguished five qualities in him: 1) that he voluntarily chooses poverty over wealth; 2) the Hereafter over this world; 3) humility over pride; 4) has insight into the actions of both the inner and outer beings; and, 5) that he is prepared for death." (*W. li-ibnihi*, fol. 190b)

[123] Echoed in al-Sulamī, *Jawāmiʿ*, in *MA*, 1:348–349, 401–402; and, *KM*, 456 / Nicholson, *The Kashf*, 350; also Kubrā, *Ādāb*, 32.

[124] The *rakwa* refers to a leather canteen or bowl, a term which Suhrawardī uses interchangeably with *ibrīq*. The walking stick (*ʿaṣā*) is of particular importance in that its use is attested in the Sunna. In the *ʿAwārif*, Suhrawardī provides another list of small provisions, citing the example of the paragonic Sufi traveler Ibrāhīm al-Khawwāṣ—who was never without a pot, needle, thread, and scissors—as a model, as well as quoting

8. he should observe the proper manners of dress while traveling;[125]
9. if he encounters a group of brethren (*ikhwān*) or a shaykh of the *ṭā'ifa*, he is to greet them with the formula 'peace be upon you';
10. the visitation (*ziyāra*) of graves is a laudable practice;
11. when entering a city the first thing he must do is find a mosque—a congregational mosque being preferable—perform two units of prayer, and then proceed directly to the city's *ribāṭ*;[126] and,
12. he is not to enter a *ribāṭ* after the time of the mid-afternoon prayer (*'aṣr*).[127]

As with everything else, according to Suhrawardī each of these accouterments and manners of travel are possessed of a spiritual meaning (*sirr*), some of which he explicates and others of which intentionally leaves unexplained out of 'fear of divulging the secrets of the folk to the uninitiated'. Certain accoutrements serve as icons, and in the *Irshād al-murīdīn*, for instance, Suhrawardī states that if the traveler's *ibrīq* happens to break while on the road, he should not dispose of it but rather retain a shard so that when he enters a *ribāṭ* the residents there will

---

a *ḥadīth* which states that the Prophet always carried five or six things on his person while traveling: a mirror, a case of collyrium, a hair pin (*midrā*), a tooth stick, a comb, and nail scissors. (*'AM*, 1:303 / *GE*, 17.14; *ḥadīth* in Ibn al-Ṣiddīq, *'Awāṭif*, 1:255–256 [no. 112]; and, idem, *Ghaniyyat*, 1:228–229 [no. 112]; cf. *AdM*, 51–52 / Milson, *Rule*, 54–55). Hujwīrī prescribes a patched frock (*muraqqa'a*), prayer mat, walking stick, *rakwa*, rope, and shoes or pair of sandals (*kafsh* / *na'layn*) as essential and adds the comb, nail scissors, needle, and case of collyrium as praiseworthy additions (*Kashf*, 450 / Nicholson, *The Kashf*, 345). In addition to the walking stick and *ibrīq*, Najm al-Dīn Kubrā prescribes a toothstick, comb, nail scissors, and case of collyrium as necessary. (*AdM*, 37; further references in Meier, "A Book of Etiquette," in *Essays*, 89, fn. 184).

[125] According to Suhrawardī these include: 1) girding the waist and rolling up the sleeves, practices considered obligatory as they have a precedent in the Sunna; 2) considering the cotton overcoat (*milḥafa*) to be a shroud (*kafan*) as a reminder that one should always be prepared for death; 3) placing one's slippers (*madās*) in a satchel which should then be secured behind the back and, if worn, underneath the *khirqa*; and, 4) purifying the comb, tooth stick, and other small provisions at the same time one makes their ritual ablution. (*IrM*, fol. 44a–45b; *'AM*, 1:309–310 / *GE*, 18.5–6)

[126] This injunction follows that of performing two units of prayer at every way station, the two units prayed in the mosque representing both the 'prayer of greeting' (*ṣalāt al-taḥiya*)—according to most schools a recommended practice to be executed upon entering a mosque as per its precedent in the Sunna—and a prayer of thanksgiving for having arrived safely at this particular way station, prayer in a mosque always being preferable; cf. Abū 'l-Najīb who only prescribes that the traveler should seek out the town's Sufis (*AdM*, 50 / Milson, *Rule*, 109).

[127] That is, because it is after the mid-afternoon prayer when the brethren begin the first round of their nightly cycle of spiritual devotions and to enter at that time would cause a disturbance (*'AM*, 1:313–315 / *GE*, 18.16–17).

know that he is one of them.[128] Similarly, the custom of loading up the shoulder bag with the left hand and carrying it on the left shoulder symbolizes the mendicant's disdain for the world because, according to the Sunna, everything despicable is done with the left hand, and likewise dressing to the right and undressing to the left is in emulation of the practice of the Prophet.[129]

Having reached his destination the mendicant performs the ritual of departure in reverse, preparing himself to move from the profane space of the outer world back into the sacralized space of the *ribāṭ*:

> When he draws near to the gate of the *ribāṭ* he should take off what is on his back such as his prayer mat, overcoat, and such like and drape them over his left shoulder. He should then take his *ibrīq* and walking stick into his left hand, thus leaving his right hand empty. When entering the precincts of the *ribāṭ* in such a manner, he is not to greet its denizens with the formula 'peace be upon you'[130] and if one of them comes and takes his shoulder bag from him he should not stop him from doing so. He should then ungird his waist and take out his slipper satchel (*kharīṭat al-madās*), untie it with his right hand, and remove the slippers with his left in such a way that he does not stir up the dust on the satchel, after which he should carefully close it so that no dust is scattered about. Then, he should wrap his girdle around the middle of the satchel, lay it on his shoulder bag, and then commence unwrapping the boot straps (*lifāfa*) on his left foot and remove its traveling-shoe. If anyone wants to do this for him, he should not stop them, attending to the other foot himself while they are doing so. He should see to it that the straps do not touch the ground and should coil them up and place them in his traveling-shoes or in the slippers which he had worn while on the road.

---

[128] *IrM*, fol. 44a; Abū ʾl-Najīb says the same about the *rakwa* serving as a symbol of affiliation (*AdM*, 51–52 / Milson, *Rule*, 54–55); same in al-Sulamī, *K. al-arbaʿīn fī ʾl-taṣawwuf* [Hyderabad: Dāʾirat al-Maʿārif al-ʿUthmāniyya, 1950], 12; and, idem, *Jawāmiʿ*, in *MA*, 1:363).

[129] *IrM*, fol. 47a–47b; and, *ʿAM*, 1:312 / *GE*, 18.12; *ḥadīth* in Ibn al-Ṣiddīq, *ʿAwāṭif*, 2:283–285 [nos. 129–130]; and, idem, *Ghaniyyat*, 1:243–244 [nos. 129–130]; often attested in Sufi *adab*, e.g. *KM*, 451 / Nicholson, *The Kashf*, 346.

[130] Based ultimately upon a *ḥadīth*, as Suhrawardī explains there are three main reasons for this. First, the word peace (*salām*) is one of the names of God and it is not proper to utter it without having first performed a proper ritual ablution after the termination of travel. Second, as the *ribāṭ* is a place where individual aspirants are constantly engaged in the contemplative disciple of vigilant awareness, it is unseemly to disturb them by uttering a loud greeting. Third, as the *ribāṭ* is the shared dwelling place (*bayt*) of a larger spiritual family of brethren (*ikhwān*), it is presumptuous for the mendicant to address them by uttering such a formal greeting. (*ʿAM*, 1:310–311 / *GE*, 18.7–10; *IrM*, fol. 47b; cf. *AdM*, 46–47 / Milson, *Rule*, 51–52 where excessive formality [*takalluf*] is discouraged [same in Kubrā, *Ādāb*, 33; further references in Meier, "A Book of Etiquette", 79, fn. 123]).

> If there is any dirt on his feet he should take his [undefiled] slippers in his left hand, search out some water, and renew his ablution. After this, he should look for a place [inside the *ribāṭ*] to unfurl his prayer mat and then take it there and perform two units of prayer. If he is accompanied by traveling companions, however, he should wait for them so that they can perform the ablution together. When he has finished his prayer he should look for the superintendent (*muqaddam*) of the folk of the *ribāṭ*, go to him, and greet him with the formula 'peace be upon you' and treat him with humility after which he should return to his prayer mat and not speak unless asked a question in which case he should only answer [and not chat further]. He should sit quietly and observe the goings on of the folk of the *ribāṭ*, the shaykh, and their conversations, promising himself to conceal what emanates from them, and if he sees anything reprehensible he should not speak about it since he is among a people (*qawm*) much greater than himself.[131]

When entering such a space, the mendicant becomes a guest (*musāfir*) and as such is bound to the observe, and enjoy, the customs binding between guest and host, namely the three-day rule of hospitality. During this time, his task is to observe and learn from the denizens of the *ribāṭ*, endeavoring to discover the secrets of their goings on and to learn their ways, inquiring about them with the utmost of graciousness and polite behavior and promising to hold what he learns in strict confidence. Prior to leaving, he must seek out the permission of the shaykh who, in certain cases, may require him to stay in which case his status as *musāfir* is dissolved and he becomes bound to the same rules and regulations binding upon the other residents of the *ribāṭ*.[132]

Youths (shubbān) *and Servants* (aṣḥāb al-khidma)

The next to last constituency in the hierarchy of the *ribāṭ* is comprised of two overlapping, but mutually distinguishable, groups, namely the youths (*shubbān*, sing. *shābb*) and the servants (*aṣḥāb al-khidma*), the first of whose presence within the *ribāṭ* Suhrawardī feels obliged to defend. In his *Talbīs Iblīs*, one of the main objections which Ibn al-Jawzī levels against the Sufis of Baghdad concerned their practice of associating with young men (*ṣuḥbat al-aḥdāth*), an issue which was just as contentious

[131] *IrM*, fol. 44b–45a; similar in *'AM*, 1:309 / *GE*, 18.5; cf. Abū 'l-Najīb who prescribes a similar but much less detailed procedure (*AdM*, 50–51 / Milson, *Rule*, 53–54) and Kubrā who repeats the same (*Ādāb*, 32–33, 37; correspondences noted by Meier, "A Book of Etiquette," in *Essays*, 77–78, fn. 120).

[132] *IrM*, fol. 45b; and, *'AM*, 1:316 / *GE*, 18.21.

for *sharī'a*-minded Sufis like Suhrawardī as it was an ideal vehicle of mystical praxis for certain Sufis such as his contemporary Awḥad al-Dīn al-Kirmānī (d. 635/1238) or the celebrated Persian mystical poet—and long-time disciple of one of Suhrawardī's own disciples Bahā' al-Dīn Zakarriyā Multānī—Fakhr al-Dīn 'Irāqī (d. 688/1289).[133] In his description of the place of the youth in the hierarchy of the *ribāṭ* in the *'Awārif al-ma'ārif*, Suhrawardī hints at such objections:

> As for the youth, his freedom of movement is restricted to sitting in the common room (*bayt al-jamā'a*), for when he is exposed to the gaze of others most eyes will inevitably fall upon him. Because of that, he is restricted and is limited to being educated in the proper manners. This, however, only happens when the congregation of the *ribāṭ* are gathered together in the common room, engaged in controlling their moments, regulating their breath, and guarding their senses, just like the companions of God's Messenger: 'on that day each one of them will have enough concern to make him indifferent to others.'[134] They had so much ambition for the Hereafter that they had nothing to do with one another. Likewise, it is seemly for the Folk of Sincerity and the Sufis to be together in congregation without spoiling their moments.[135]

Whether or not the youth served as an intentional object of gaze for the congregation is difficult to judge from such comments, although the tensions associated with the practice of *naẓar ilā al-murd / shāhidbāzī* are clearly present in his prescriptions and indeed the possibility of his presence at the communal spiritual concert (*samā'*) is noted elsewhere.[136] At the same time, as a resident of the *ribāṭ* Suhrawardī states that the

---

[133] Ibn al-Jawzī, *Talbīs Iblīs*, 324–331. Within the context of the *ribāṭ* such objections were most often raised in connection with the ritualized 'Platonic stare' of gazing upon beardless youths (*naẓar ilā 'l-murd/aḥdāth*; Per. *shāhidbāzī*), a practice most often associated with the spiritual concert (*samā'*) which quickly became a conceit in Persian poetry. On the practice, see: *KM*, 542 / Nicholson, *The Kashf*, 416; *SQ*, 54.16—who considers *ṣuḥbat al-aḥdāth* one of the 'worst disasters of the path'; see also: Massignon, *Essay on the Origins of the Technical Language of Islamic Mysticism*, trans. B. Clark (South Bend, IN: University of Notre Dame Press, 1997), 75, 81; Schimmel, *Mystical Dimensions*, 290–291; and, Knysh, *Islamic Mysticism*, 325.

[134] Qur'ān 80:37.

[135] *'AM*, 1:269–270 / *GE*, 14.5.

[136] Ibid., 2:32 / *GE*, 25.7; loosely quoting Abū 'l-Najīb al-Suhrawardī (*AdM*, 63 / Milson, *Rule*, 62) on the permissibility of the presence of youths at the concert and, if present, a rule prohibiting them from standing up or moving; see also ibid., 39 / Milson, *Rule*, 47–48 on companionship with young men (*ṣuḥbat al-aḥdāth*) being reprehensible, something intimately associated with the spiritual concert in that the singer or reciter (*qawwāl*) is normally spoken of as being a youth (e.g., *KM*, 542 / Nicholson, *The Kashf*, 416); something which Najm al-Dīn Kubrā sternly forbids (*Ādāb*, 36).

youth is under the direct control of the shaykh, being a seeker (*ṭālib*) whose primary duty is to perform acts of service (*khidma*) to those denizens of the *ribāṭ* who are actively engaged in wayfaring on the Sufi path, who because of his age has not yet attained the position of being able to embark on the same path but shares in the fruits of their labors nonetheless through his acts of service.[137]

It is in such acts of service where the youths overlap with the next to last constituency populating the *ribāṭ*, the 'companions of service' (*aṣḥāb al-khidma*), individuals who are differentiated from the *khādim* in that their sole duty is to serve and assist those denizens of the *ribāṭ* who are actively engaged in wayfaring. Unlike the youths, whom we can assume were slaves (*ghulām*, pl. *ghilmān*) of the director of the *ribāṭ*, and the *khādim*, who was an advanced disciple of the shaykh, according to Suhrawardī the *aṣḥāb al-khidma* enter the *ribāṭ* as novices (*mubtadi'*) with the intention of setting out on the formal path of discipleship, but who have yet to commence wayfaring, their acts of devotion being service to the brethren (*ikhwān*) under the direction of the shaykh.[138]

Mystical Audition (samāʿ)

Closely associated with these lower tiers of the *ribāṭ*, and with the practice of *naẓar ilā al-murd / shāhidbāzī*, was the communal ritual of the spiritual concert (*samāʿ*), during which the congregation would 'hear' or 'listen to' (*samāʿ / istimāʿ*) the recitation of poetry, often accompanied by music, as a devotional practice aimed at engendering spiritual experiences.[139] In his often copied testament (*waṣiyya*) to his son ʿImād al-Dīn, Suhrawardī counsels him on the subject, simultaneously disparaging and affirming its practice:

---

137 *'AM*, 1:271, 279 / *GE*, 14.7, 15.12; cf. al-Sulamī, *K. ādāb al-ṣuḥba*, 52–53 (92–93). According to ʿAzīz-i Nasafī, the proper time for wayfaring on the Sufi path is between the ages of twenty to forty (*Kashf al-ḥaqā'iq*, trans. Ridgeon in *Persian Metaphysics and Mysticism*, 204).

138 *'AM*, 1:270–272 / *GE*, 14.7–9; *AMKh*, 55.

139 As with the practice of *dhikr*, the literature on *samāʿ* is extensive, the standard studies and overviews include Fritz Meier, "The Dervish Dance: An Attempt at an Overview," in *Essays*, 23–48; Marjian Molé, "La danse extatique en Islam," in *Les danses sacrées* (Paris: Éditions du Seuil, 1963), 145–280; Jean During, *Musique et extase: l'audition spirituelle dans la tradition soufie* (Paris: Albin Michel, 1988); idem, "Samāʿ," *EI*², 8:1018–1019 (with further references); idem, "Musique et rites: le *samâʿ*," in Popovic and Veinstein, eds., *Les voies d'Allah*, 157–172; see also Schimmel, *Mystical Dimensions*, 178–186; Ernst, *Sufism*, 179–198; and, Knysh, *Islamic Mysticism*, 322–325.

> Do not engage frequently in sitting in *samāʿ* for it plants the seeds of hypocrisy (*nifāq*) and then the heart dies, but do not disavow it for it has its masters. The spiritual concert is not appropriate except for one whose heart is alive and whose *nafs* is dead, but as for the one who has not yet attained this state he is better advised to engage in fasting, prayer, and the recitation of litanies (*awrād*).[140]

As reflected in Suhrawardī's counsel, the practice of *samāʿ* was a contentious and much discussed issue. Certain Sufis such as Aḥmad-i Ghazālī defended its practice with little reservation whereas authorities such as Abū Ṭālib al-Makkī, Sulamī, Hujwīrī, Qushayrī, and Ghazālī were much more cautious, accepting it only with certain stipulations.[141] At the same time, critics of Sufism and its practices such as Ibn al-Jawzī and Ibn Taymiyya rejected it out of hand.[142] The early Chishtiyya, who early-on oriented themselves largely on the *ʿAwārif al-maʿārif*, were noted for their love of music and their avoidance of royal patronage—the exact opposite of Suhrawardī's program—and as is well known, their commitment to *samāʿ* provided fertile ground for the development of the *qawwālī* tradition in Indo-Muslim culture.[143]

As evinced in the four lengthy chapters which he devotes to it in the *ʿAwārif al-maʿārif*, in the late-6th/12th and early-7th/13th century, the practice of *samāʿ* was clearly a prominent feature of *ribāṭ*-based Sufi culture as well as being of particular concern to the shaykh himself.[144] In these chapters, the bulk of his discussion is devoted to answering questions concerning the permissibility of the *samāʿ* and the various practices associated with it such as dancing, weeping, and the ritual of 'rending the clothes' (*kharq al-libās*). Basing his argument on certain *ḥadīth*,

---

[140] al-Suhrawardī, *W. li-ibnihi*, 35; also, *AdM*, 62 / Milson, *Rule*, 61.

[141] *KM*, 508–546 / Nicholson, *The Kashf*, 393–420; *SQ*, 51.1–27; Abū Ṭālib al-Makkī, *Die Nahrung*, 32.744–762; al-Sulamī, *Darajāt al-muʿāmalāt*, in *MA*, 1:286; idem, *K. nasīm al-samāʿ*, in ibid., 2:162–170; idem, *K. al-samāʿ*, in ibid., 2:25; idem, *Uṣūl al-malāmatiyya wa-ghalaṭāt al-ṣūfiyya*, ed. ʿAbd al-Fattāḥ Aḥmad al-Fāwī Maḥmūd (Cairo: Maṭbaʿat al-Irshād, 1975), 174; and, pseudo-Aḥmad-i Ghazālī, *Bawāriq al-ilmāʿ*, ed. and trans. by James Robson in *Tracts on Listening to Music* (London: Royal Asiatic Society, 1938), 63–184 (the treatise was actually penned between the late 7th/13th and early 8th/14th-century by one Aḥmad b. Muḥammad al-Ṭūsī).

[142] Ibn Taymiyya, *K. al-samāʿ wa-l-raqṣ*, in *Majmūʿāt al-rasāʾil al-kubrā* (Cairo: al-Maṭbaʿat al-Amīriyya al-Sharqiyya, 1905), 284–291; Ibn al-Jawzī, *Talbīs Iblīs*, 274–307.

[143] See, e.g., Carl Ernst, *Eternal Garden: Mysticism, History, and Politics at a South Asian Sufi Center*. 2nd ed. (New Delhi: Oxford University Press, 2004), 147–154; and, Regula Burckhardt Qureshi, "Samaʿ in the Royal Court of Saints: The Chishtiyya of South Asia," in *Manifestations of Sainthood in Islam*, 111–127.

[144] *ʿAM*, 2:5–36 / *GE*, 22.1–25.17; also *IrM*, fol. 35a–36b, 43a–43b; Abū ʾl-Najīb also devotes a sizable amount of space to the issue (*AdM*, 61–68 / Milson, *Rule*, 61–66).

the exempla of the *salaf al-ṣāliḥ*, the logia of the Sufi authorities of the past, the rulings of the Shāfiʿī and Mālikī schools, the opinions of Abū Ṭālib al-Makkī, and his own observations of the practice of the Sufis of his day and age, Suhrawardī lays out a position which ultimately condones the practice but only with certain stipulations. Following what he cites to be the ruling of Abū Ṭālib al-Makkī, Suhrawardī states that when applied to specific circumstances and a specific class of people and practiced with certain conditions (*shurūṭ*), *samāʿ* is possessed of an 'indifferent' (*mubāḥ*) legal status.[145]

In terms of the specific circumstances and people, he states that as the goal of *samāʿ* is to obtain a state of ecstasy (*wajd*) it is appropriate only for those *mutaṣawwif* and Sufis who have reached a stage in their spiritual development where ecstatic experiences are filtered through the heart and not through the *nafs*. In this, he accords with the positions advanced by most others situated in the Junaydī-tradition, essentially deriving rulings based on existential condition and identity, the same process informing his prescriptions of the different disciplines associated with the mendicant and aspirant. In terms of its conditions, as with each of the disciplines and practices of the Sufi *ribāṭ*, the ritual spiritual concert is also subject to a complex of proper behaviors and manners (*ādāb al-samāʿ*), the particulars of which can be summarized as follows:[146]

---

[145] That is, belonging to the legal category of acts which are neither obligatory (*wājib*) nor recommended (*mandūb*), neither illicit (*ḥarām*) nor licit (*ḥalāl*); *ʿAM*, 2:7 / *GE*, 22.6. Similarly, Rūzbihān-i Baqlī declared the practice of *samāʿ* licit for the '*fidèles d'amour*' (*ʿāshiqīn*) while prohibiting, or at least qualifying, its practice for those at a lower spiritual station (*Le traité de l'Esprit saint* [*R. al-quds*], trans. Stéphane Ruspoli. [Paris: Les Éditions du Cerf, 2001], 221); cf. Najm al-Dīn Kubrā (*Ādāb*, 35–37), who describes the ritual and deals with the issue of the permissibility of musical instruments (which he advises against) but does not explicitly limit participation to specific individuals, simply stating that one must only attend it with 'like-minded' brethren following the oft-quoted rules of al-Junayd: "the *samāʿ* requires three things: time (*zamān*), place (*makān*), and brethren (*ikhwān*)." (*SL*, 72.1; *SQ*, 51.11; al-Ghazālī, *Iḥyāʾ*, 2:328; pseudo-Aḥmad-i Ghazālī, *Bawāriq*, 72–74 [123–126])

[146] Here I am relying upon Suhrawardī's discussion in *ʿAM*, 2:19–36 / *GE*, 23.1–25.17; and, *IrM*, fol. 35a–36b, 43a–43b (much repetition from *AdM*, 61–68 / Milson, *Rule*, 61–66, and, much of the same in *KM*, 542–546 / Nicholson, *The Kashf*, 417–420). In his prescriptions for the proper *adab* of the aspirant to his shaykh, Jīlānī prescribes rules 3 and 4 (*GhṬ*, 2:283–284); see also: al-Sulamī, *K. al-samāʿ*, 66; and, idem, *Jawāmiʿ*, in *MA*, 1:390.

1. The participant must approach the *samā*ʿ with proper intention (*bi-niyyat ḥasana*);
2. one may only participate in the *samā*ʿ with individuals who are possessed of a sound creed and proper motivations;
3. one is never to move in the presence of the shaykh unless involuntarily overcome by a state of ecstasy;
4. one must not make a feign ecstasy (*tawājud*) nor impugn one's brothers for doing so;
5. one must neither rend one's clothing nor cast one's *khirqa* to the singer or director (*ḥādī*) of the *samā*ʿ without the proper intention, and never as a result of the prompting of the *nafs*; and,
6. those present must adhere to the rules for the rending and division of a *khirqa* which has been cast off; namely: a) the shaykh is to decide if a cast off *khirqa* is to be rent and distributed or returned to its owner; and, b) if so directed by the shaykh, it may be rent and its pieces distributed equally among those in attendance by the singer/director so that all can benefit from its blessing.[147]

Despite such prescriptions, and in contrast to the expansion of the conditions and proper behaviors to which *samā*ʿ was subjected to in the Sufi manuals of Kāshānī and Bākharzī (each of which drew heavily upon the *ʿAwārif al-maʿārif*) in comparison to the other practices which Suhrawardī prescribes for his disciples, the spiritual concert does not seem to have been of great importance to his system.[148] Not only does his discussion of the topic in the *ʿAwārif al-maʿārif* and *Irshād al-murīdīn* evince a certain ambivalence to the practice, but in the collective body of his testaments to individual disciples and others works which deal specifically with the praxis of the *ribāṭ*, the spiritual concert is rarely if ever mentioned.

[147] The rules regarding the casting off of the *khirqa* and its division upon the conclusion of the spiritual concert are given much more fully by Abū ʾl-Najīb (*AdM*, 68–69 / Milson, *Rule*, 64–66; which are very similar to those Qushayrī prescribes in his *W. li-murīdīn* [*SQ*, 54.19]. As with many of his other prescriptions, ʿAbd al-Qādir al-Jīlānī prescribes much of the same *adab* for the spiritual concert as Suhrawardī, see: *GhṬ*, 2:302–305; cf. al-Sulamī, *K. al-samā*ʿ, 24 (*Majmūʿāt-i āthār*, 2:66). Najm al-Dīn Kubrā prescribes the rule of trying to keep still when overcome by ecstasy, mentions the issue of feigning, as well as the casting of the cloak (*Ādāb*, 36); also, cf. *PGB*, 265.

[148] Kāshānī, *Miṣbāḥ*, 179–202; and, Bākharzī, *Fuṣūṣ al-ādāb*, 180–253.

'Lay Affiliates' (mutashabbih / mustarshid)

At the lowest tier of the *ribāṭ* were the 'lay affiliates' (*mutashabbih / mustarshid*), and we have already seen that Suhrawardī accords a place to the *mutashabbih* within the fold of those belonging to the 'circle of the chosen', delineating a strict hierarchy of spiritual development, and citing the *ḥadīth* in which the Prophet is reported to have said: "he who emulates a people (*qawm*) is one of them" as a proof text for the spiritual favor which the *mutashabbih* enjoys by associating himself with the *ribāṭ* and its shaykh. We have also seen that Suhrawardī prescribes that such individuals are candidates for investiture with the *khirqat al-tabarruk*, entering into a relationship with the shaykh as token disciples (*murīd rasmī*) as opposed to true disciples (*murīd ḥaqīqī*) who are invested with the *khirqat al-irāda*.[149] Alongside the *mutashabbih* is another type of individual who inhabits the margins of the *ribāṭ*, the *mustarshid*, literally 'the one asking for guidance'.[150] Such individuals were important enough that in his *waṣiyya* to Rashīd al-Dīn Abū Bakr al-Ḥabash, Suhrawardī tells him that it is obligatory for him to provide seekers with good guidance (*yurashshidu al-ṭālibīn*) and the *mustarshid* with moral guidance (*yahdī al-mustarshidīn*).[151] Beyond formal modalities of affiliation such as the *khirqat al-tabarruk*, the manner in which such individuals actually related to or participated in the religiosity of the *ribāṭ* however is not entirely clear. Generally, traces of such modes of participation appear in discussions of the actual praxis and spiritual discipline of the *ribāṭ*, most notably in discussions concerning various levels of commitment to particular modes of behavior.

One of the most interesting features of Abū 'l-Najīb's Sufi handbook, the *Ādāb al-murīdīn*, is that it includes a section devoted to 'dispensations' (*rukhṣa*, pl. *rukhaṣ*), various exemptions from the code of ethics and manners which the constituents of the *ribāṭ* are obligated to uphold.[152] In Islamic legal terminology the term *rukhṣa* refers to the conditional relaxation or suspension of one or another of the legislations (*ḥukm*, pl. *aḥkām*) of the divine law (*sharī'a*) granted under specific circumstances such as distress or hardship, whereas its opposite *'azīma* ('strictness', pl. *'azā'im*) refers to general legislations (*aḥkām 'āmma*) not concerned with

---

149 *AMKh*, 57 (no. 6).
150 *'AM*, 2:217–218 / *GE*, 52.2–3.
151 Idem, *W. li-Rashīd al-Dīn Abī Bakr al-Ḥabash*, fol. 117a.
152 *AdM*, 80–99 / Milson, *Rule*, 72–83.

one or another specific circumstance.[153] As trained jurists and members of the ulama themselves, Sufis such as ʿAbd al-Qādir al-Jīlānī, Abū ʾl-Najīb, and ʿUmar al-Suhrawardī extended both the legal definitions of *rukhṣa* and *ʿazīma* and the conceptual apparatus surrounding them to the particular circumstances met with on the Sufi path, applying the terms, and indeed the very process of adducing legal decisions based on them, to the various conditions (*sharāʾiṭ*) of the *ṭarīqa* in the same way that jurists applied them to the various legislations (*ḥukm*) of the *sharīʿa*. Thus, at the end of the *Ādāb al-murīdīn*, Abū ʾl-Najīb summarizes the content of his manual in a language which is so clear in its employment of the terminology and standard expressions used by the *fuqahāʾ* that anyone with a familiarity with works of *fiqh* cannot but help to notice the associations:

> Now, this school (*madhhab*) is possessed of three dimensions, namely spiritual stations and states (*maqāmāt wa-aḥwāl*), ethics and proper manners (*akhlāq wa-ādāb*), and dispensations (*rukhaṣ*), and dispensations are the lowest of the three. He who adheres (*tamassaka bi-*) to the whole is one of the verifiers (*mutaḥaqqiqīn*), he who adheres to the external aspects of ethics and proper manners is one of the symbolic disciples (*mutarassimīn*), and he who adheres to the dispensations—being educated and refined in the proper manners about which we have already spoken—is one of the sincere imitators (*al-mutashabbihīn al-ṣādiqīn*) about whom the Prophet said: 'he who imitates a people (*qawm*) is one of them'. This, however, is conditional upon adhering to three fundamental principles (*uṣūl*), namely to discharge the obligatory dictates of the divine law (*farāʾiḍ*) whether they be difficult or easy, to avoid all illicit things great and small, and to renounce the world and its denizens save what the Prophet mentioned as necessary for the believer: 'there are four things which are in this world but not of it, namely a scrap of bread to satisfy your hunger, a piece of cloth (*khirqa*) to cover your nakedness, a tent (*bayt*) to shelter you from the elements, and a virtuous wife in whom you can confide'. One has no right to possess anything more than these four. All of the eponymous authorities (*mashāyikh*) are unanimous in their consent (*ajmaʿa ʿalā*) that to violate (*akhalla*) even one of these principles is to depart from (*kharaja ʿan*) the legislations of this school (*aḥkām al-madhhab*) and to disassociate from it (*taʿarrā ʿanhu*).[154]

[153] al-Tahānawī, *Khashshāf al-iṣṭilāḥāt al-funūn*, ed. Muḥammad Wajīh and ʿAbd al-Ḥaqq and Ghulām Qādir (1862; reprint: Istanbul: n.p., 1984), 1:560; see further Goldziher, "ʿAzīma," *EI²*, 1:822; R. Peters and J.G.J. ter Haar, "Rukhṣa," *EI²*, 8:595; and, *Suh.*, 211–212.

[154] *AdM*, 98 / Milson, *Rule*, 81–82, who in his translation not only skirts the key passage where Abū ʾl-Najīb defines his conception of the institution but also completely

Thus, Abū ʾl-Najīb lays out forty individual dispensations through which the *mutashabbih* is able to affiliate with this particular *madhhab* without completely removing himself from society or jeopardizing his livelihood, a group of allowances ranging from permission to engage in business ventures to permission to indulge in joke and jesting, and from permission to associate with the wealthy and powerful to a dispensation which allows one to revile insolent persons by disparaging their ancestors.

None of these dispensations, of course, have anything to do with the discipline of the *ribāṭ* itself as the *mutashabbih* has absolutely nothing to do with the types of exercises, devotions, and austerities which its other constitutions, such as the mendicants and the aspirants, are required to adhere. Like the *khirqat al-tabarruk* what they provide rather is both a formalized and replicable modality of affiliation which allows one to participate in the culture of the *ribāṭ* through cultivating some of its manners and customs. In this, the dispensations granted to the *mutashabbih* were much like the system of ethics and *adab* which, as discussed in the following chapter, Suhrawardī prescribed for the lower tier of the *futuwwat-khāna*.

For the Sufi *ribāṭ* specifically, like his paternal uncle Abū ʾl-Najīb, ʿUmar al-Suhrawardī admits the permissibility of certain dispensations but only at the most elementary stages of the path and only for those who have yet to reach the state of discipleship,[155] but unlike his uncle no where in his *œuvre* does the shaykh prescribe a comprehensive enumeration of such dispensations. What he does do is to juxtapose the terms *rukhṣa* and *ʿazīma*, defining modalities of individual commitment, affiliation, and relative capacities of spiritual stamina or lack thereof (*nashāṭ* vs. *fatra*) by comparing those whom he calls possessors of dispensations (*arbāb al-rukhṣa*) with the possessors of strictness (*arbāb al-ʿazīma*), speaking of them only in those instances where the latter literally 'slides down' into the status of the former, moving from *ʿazāʾim* such as little talk, little food, little sleep, seclusion from society (*iʿtizāl*), marriage, and practices such as *muḥāsaba* and *murāqaba* to their opposites, which are dispensations for them.[156] As in their legal sense, such *ʿazāʾim* and

misses the legal rhetoric which frames this passage. On the latter, I have supplied the references in transliteration above. Such language is so common that to cite parallels in juridical works would be superfluous.

[155] *ʿAM*, 2:220 / *GE*, 52.9; *IrM*, fol. 38a; idem, *W.* III, fol. 81b–82b; idem, *W.* VI, MS. Süley., Musalla Medresesi 20_{17}, fol. 296a; and, *Suh.*, 212–213; cf. *GhṬ*, 2:284–285.

[156] *ʿAM*, 1:339, 2:163, 165 / *GE*, 21.5, 44.7, 12; idem, *W.* III, fol. 81a–82a; idem, *W.* VI, fol. 296a; idem, *W. li-Rashīd al-Dīn Abī Bakr al-Ḥabash*, fol. 117a; and, *Suh.*, 212.

rukhaṣ are applied only to specific individuals in specific circumstances, such as was noted in the preceding chapter in the case of the *muntahī*, an individual who is no longer subject to *ʿazāʾim* because of the change in his existential state.

* * *

The manner in which Suhrawardī went about mapping both the genealogy of the sciences of the *ṣūfiyya* and the journey of ascent which they aim to effect upon the actual discursive, social, and physical landscapes in which he, his teachers, students, and disciples moved well evinces his sensitivity to the multiple locations of legitimacy and authority of his time and space as well as his attunement to particularly potent socio-cultural and religious symbols deeply embedded in the collective conscience of those to whom he addressed his message. While Suhrawardī emplotted the deeper psycho-spiritual structures embedded in the mythic journey of ascent in the form of an Islamic salvation history, and was thus able to escape the inevitable stigma attached to other articulations of the same generic narrative—whether expressed in Neoplatonic, Peripatetic, Illuminationst, Gnostic, or Hermetic idioms—cultivated by those who often, but not always, inhabited spaces far removed from those circles of power and influence associated with the ulama and the amirs, sultans, and caliphs who so carefully cultivated their support, at the same time the culture of the *ribāṭ* was at its heart an elite and exclusionary space. By definition, a life of withdrawal and spiritual athleticism cannot be anything if not inaccessible, indeed unimaginable, to most, something which Suhrawardī himself affirms in his clear delineation of a hierarchy of affiliation and participation defined in existential terms.

At the same time, although its center was closed, the periphery of the *ribāṭ* was open and accommodating. As we have seen, according to Suhrawardī as the only true and legitimate heirs to the prophets the *ṣūfiyya* play an integral role in the revivification and perpetuation of the original dispensation in time and space, and as such possess a certain responsibility. It was the way in which he went about bridging the tensions between this responsibility, the inner life of the *ribāṭ* and its constituents, and the larger world which lay outside of its walls which, in the end, provided a substantial portion of that which made the comprehensive system or theory, praxis, and organization which he inherited and systematized sustainable, effective, and successful, that which made it attractive to an individual such as al-Nāṣir as well as replicable to a long line of successors who cultivated it from Egypt to India in the centuries which followed. It was in forging connections where many of these tensions were bridged, the very polysemy of certain symbols, modes of behavior, expressions of religiosity, and notions of authority and legitimacy already embedded in the broader socio-cultural milieu framing the activities of an early 7th/13th-century Shāfiʿī *ʿālim* and Sufi master serving as a particularly fecund repository of spiritual, religious, social, and cultural capital which in a sense financed a broader program of institutionalization.

In Suhrawardī's system, the forms of social practice and ritualization of religious knowledge already embedded in the culture of learning among the ulama and their well established self-image as custodians of religious knowledge (*mashyakha, adab, ṣuḥba*, the text, *fatāwā*), the ethical praxis of the *futuwwa* and those groups of urban craftsmen associated with them (*adab*, ethics, brotherhood, service), Shiite notions of the transmission of spiritual authority and the importance of unbroken genealogies (*nisbat al-khirqa*, initiatic investiture, oaths of fidelity, radial community), and the complex relationship between *faqīh*s, imams, and other members of the ulama with the masses (*ʿawāmm*) who looked to them for religious guidance, instruction, and blessing (*mustarshid*, moral guidance, *mutashabbih, baraka*), all coalesced in the basic symbols and modalities mediating authority and legitimacy embedded in Suhrawardī's enunciation of the comprehensive system of theory, praxis, and organization to which he considered himself an heir and which he set out to systematize and disseminate.

It is in transposition of this system into the final cluster of 'before' and 'after' which converged in Suhrawardī's historical moment, the dominance of political program, which closes the circle opened up in the first chapter of this study. Why was an individual such as the caliph al-Nāṣir so vigorous in his support of an individual such as Suhrawardī and the *ribāṭ*-based system of organization and praxis which he championed? And in turn, what did Suhrawardī actually offer to his patron which was valuable enough to engender such a patronage relationship in the first place? To answer such questions we must turn to yet another set of texts and traces, a cluster of works which on the surface appear quite different than those which have been interrogated thus far, but which when read alongside the collective body of material constituting Suhrawardī's *œuvre* and the linkages which they forge with a larger body of texts and the discursive arenas to which they ultimately belong, evince the same continuity of vision and program framing the discourse which has been mapped up to this point.

CHAPTER FIVE

IMPERIAL AND OTHER PROJECTS

According to a license of audition (*ijāzat al-samāʿ*) written on the verso of the first leaf of the earliest known copy of the *ʿAwārif al-maʿārif* the text was transmitted along with al-Suhrawardī's manual for pilgrims to Mecca, the *Ḥilyat al-nāsik fī ʾl-manāsik*, and his ten-chapter creed, the *Aʿlām al-hudā wa-ʿaqīdat arbāb al-tuqā*, to the copyist and owner of the manuscript, Sharaf al-Dīn al-Mālīnī, sometime before 605/1208–1209 when it was dictated to a group of students in the Ribāṭ al-Marzubāniyya by Suhrawardī's disciple and personal secretary Najm al-Dīn al-Tiflīsī (d. 631/1234).[1] Although not specifically mentioned in this particular *ijāza*, other licenses of audition evince that the *ʿAwārif al-maʿārif* was not the only text transmitted in Suhrawardī's *ribāṭ*s, and it is reasonable to assume that the *Aʿlām al-hudā* was transmitted in the shaykh's *majlis* alongside other texts such as his polemic against Peripatetic philosophy,

[1] MS. Süley., Lâlâ İsmail Ef. 180, fol. 1a. This occurred in the same year when Suhrawardī returned from his mission to the Ayyubids, his ostentatious entry into the city resulting in his being stripped of the *mashyakha* of the *ribāṭ*s which al-Nāṣir had formerly granted him as well as his removal from the position of Tuesday preacher at the Badr al-Sharīf Gate (see Chapter Two, s.v. "An Indiscretion"). A Sufi, poet, and *muḥaddith* who distinguished himself through his knowledge of jurisprudence and its fundamentals (*al-uṣūl*), Arabic, traditions (*akhbār*), poetry, and Sufism (*sulūk*), Tiflīsī would assist his master by correcting the mistakes which he found in his writings. It is not clear how long al-Tiflīsī stayed with Suhrawardī, but according to al-Mundhirī—who expresses regret over not having met him but did hear some of his poetry from Najm al-Dīn's companions—he is said to have gone to Egypt as an emissary of the caliphal court (*al-dīwān al-ʿazīz*), perhaps accompanying his master on his diplomatic mission to the Ayyubids in 604/1207–1208. At some point al-Tiflīsī left Baghdad for good, journeying to Syria. Ibn al-Mustawfī met him in Irbil in 612/1215, saying that he settled down at the Junayniyya Khānaqāh for a time and composed poetry there. His final stop, however, was Damascus, where he served as the *shaykh* of the Asadiyya Khānaqāh, becoming known as an expert in Sufism and poetry, occupying himself, as his biographers say, with the 'pursuit of knowledge in the sciences of the *sharīʿa* and *ṭarīqa*'. Known for his good hand, al-Tiflīsī's collection of books were bequeathed to the Shumayṣātiyya Khānaqāh upon his death, in Damascus, on the 17th of Jumāda I, 631/18 February, 1234. He was buried in the graveyard of the Sufis. He is one of the disciples for whom Suhrawardī wrote a *waṣiyya*. On him, see *TIr*, 1:258–260 (no. 157); *TW*, 6:102 (no. 2529); *DhR*, 162 (*anno* 631); al-Dhahabī, *Ishārat*, 333 (*anno* 631), and, *TIsl*, 52:57–59 (*anno* 631, no. 16); and, *NZ*, 6:286.

the *Kashf al-faḍāʾiḥ al-yūnāniyya wa-rashf al-naṣāʾiḥ al-īmāniyya*, and his Qurʾānic commentary, the *Nughbat al-bayān fī tafsīr al-qurʾān*.[2]

As discussed in the first chapter of this book, to participate in the transmission of texts in such a manner was an important enunciation of affiliation and identity, the transmission event itself, whether occurring in a *madrasa* or Sufi *ribāṭ*, being framed by a well-established complex of behaviors, practices, ideas, and symbols which defined and regulated the transmission of religious learning and the very social relationships through which it was effected. Authority was literally written in the act of transmission itself. For those who might have happened to be present in a *majlis* during which the shaykh was transmitting his *Aʿlām al-hudā*, after what must have been many hours of dictation, one of the final statements which they would have transcribed in their own copies is the creed's penultimate article of faith, an affirmation which while neither novel nor unusual, is possessed of a certain potency when read against both the creed as a whole and Suhrawardī's quite public relationship with the individual who financed the very *ribāṭ*s in which such transmissions took place:

> We believe (*naʿtaqidu*) that the caliphate resides with the Quraysh until the Day of Resurrection and that it will not be bestowed upon anyone else other than them. We believe in the necessity of obedience to the Imam of the time, who is from the Abbasids, and who grants the right to rule to those who govern on their behalf, and we deem fighting one who revolts against the caliph (*imām*) as necessary.[3]

Followed as it is with an affirmation of his adherence to the collective consensus (*ijmāʿ*) of the broader Sunni community (*ahl al-sunna wa-l-jamāʿa*), Suhrawardī's affirmation of this article of faith is telling. Referencing the juridical configuration of authority particular to the *siyāsa sharʿiyya* works, Suhrawardī clearly enunciates that the particular *Personengruppe* on whose behalf he speaks fully supports the so-called

---

[2] al-Suhrawardī, *Rashf al-naṣāʾiḥ*, MS. Süley., Reisülküttap 465$_1$, fol. 1a (transmitted over a series of sessions in the Ribāṭ al-Maʾmūniyya which ended on Thursday, the 16th of Shawwāl, 621 / 31 Oct., 1224); idem, *Nughbat al-bayān*, MS. Aleppo, al-Madrasa al-ʿUthmāniyya 25 (currently Asadiyya 14769), fol. 2a & 282a (autographed *talqīn al-dhikr*, *ijāza* for the text, and an *ijāzat ʿāmma* granted to his disciple Jalāl al-Dīn al-Tabrīzī (d. 641/1243); and, ibid., MS. Süley., Hacı Beşir Ağa Eyüb 24, fol. 1a (autographed *ijāza* in which al-Suhrawardī records the transmission of both this copy of the *Nughbat al-bayān* as well as Iṣfahānī's *Ḥilyat al-awliyāʾ* to al-Tiflīsī in 610/1214).

[3] *AH*, 91; cf. idem, *Idālat al-ʿiyān ʿalā ʾl-burhān*, MS. Bursa, Ulu Cami 1597$_4$, fol. 85a–85b (not the best copy, but the most complete manuscript).

'classical theory of the caliphate', a formally constituted doctrine collectively worked out by individuals such as the Mālikī jurist and Ashʿarite theologian al-Bāqillānī (d. 403/1013), the Shāfiʿī jurist al-Māwardī (d. 450/1058), and the famous Ashʿarite-Shāfiʿī scholar al-Juwaynī (d. 419/1028) and his student Abū Ḥāmid al-Ghazālī during the period in which the Abbasid caliphate witnessed its lowest ebb at the hands of various dynastic and military contenders, most notably the Seljuks.[4]

Briefly put, the *siyāsa sharʿiyya* theorists attempted to bridge the reality of the *de facto* authority of military powers such as the Seljuks with the now *de jure* moral and religious authority of the caliphate through re-imagining the constitution of power and authority in terms of a compromise formulated in legal terms. Thus, we find al-Bāqillānī laying out a defense of the caliphate and the formal conditions which effect its legitimacy,[5] al-Māwardī coupling such prescriptions with a vision of how the caliph functions as the supreme executor of the *sharīʿa* whose *de jure* moral and religious authority is implemented by the *de facto* coercive power of the sultans,[6] and then al-Juwaynī and al-Ghazālī who refine the implications of a legally validated compromise between *de jure* and *de facto* authority in what has been called a fiction by which the Sunni jurists 'reunited' religious and temporal rule in order to assure the continuity of *sharʿī* government.[7]

[4] The classic treatment is to be found in two oft-quoted articles of H.A.R. Gibb "Some Considerations of the Sunni Theory of the Caliphate," (1939), and, 401–410; and, "Al-Mâwardî's Theory of the Khilâfah," (1937), both reprinted in idem, *Studies on the Civilization of Islam* (Boston: Beacon Press, 1962), 141–150, 151–165; see also: A.K.S. Lambton, *State and Government in Medieval Islam: An Introduction to the Study of Islamic Political Theory* (Oxford: Oxford University Press, 1981), 69–129; and, Anthony Black, *The History of Islamic Political Thought* (New York: Routledge, 2001), 81–90.

[5] Yusuf Ibish, *The Political Doctrine of al-Baqillani* (Beirut: American University of Beirut Press, 1966), 71–105.

[6] Affirming, on Qurʾānic dictate, that it is God who delegates authority to the imam (caliph) and that the legitimacy of his office is derived from the *sharīʿa*, al-Māwardī argues that the institution is essential for the continued existence of the Islamic community, and as with al-Bāqillānī prescribes a number of qualities and conditions which the imam must possess as well as discussing the implications of the usurpation of caliphal power by the amirate and the vizierate, see: al-Māwardī, *al-Aḥkām al-sulṭāniyya*, trans. Wafaa H. Wahba as *The Ordinances of Government: Al-Aḥkām al-Sulṭāniyya w'al-Wilāyāt al-Dīniyya* (Reading, UK: Center for Muslim Contribution to Civilization & Garnet Publishing Ltd., 1996), 3–22; see also: Laoust, "La pensée et l'action politiques d'al-Māwardī (364–450/974–1058)," *REI* 36.1 (1968): 16–36.

[7] Following al-Māwardī, both Juwaynī and Ghazālī defended the caliphate by affirming its necessity on the basis of revelation and consensus (*ijmāʿ*) as well as prescribing certain qualities and conditions the caliph must possess (W. Montgomery Watt, "Authority in the Thought of al-Ghazālī," in Makdisi, et al., eds., *La notion d'autorité*

At the same time, the *siyāsa sharʿiyya* discourse represents neither the only, nor in many respects the most powerful, figuration of power and authority characteristic of the Earlier Middle Period, for there were wholly alternative figurations of power and authority which just like the *siyāsa sharʿiyya* discourse were enunciated in texts, most notably the type of political thought embedded in what Lambton has called the literary and philosophical tradition of political theory. Generally speaking, in contradistinction to the *siyāsa sharʿiyya* discourse such materials—constituted in a collective body of *Fürstenspiegelen* ('Mirrors for Princes'), administrative handbooks, and works of philosophical ethics—emphasizes the divine right of kings, the primacy of justice, practice over theory, and the assimilation of Islamic notions of authority and power to older Sasanian ideas of kingship and Turkic patterns of rule and governance, configuring the ruler as a type of philosopher-king whose primary role is to assure that universal law becomes the basis and foundation of an ideal and orderly state whose object is the achievement of happiness (*saʿāda*).[8]

In a sense, the caliph al-Nāṣir both rejected and affirmed the configuration of *khilāfa/imāma* of the *siyāsa sharʿiyya* discourse. He rejected it in that over the course of his rule he denied, time and time again, its compromise in both theoretical and practical terms, widening the scope of the *de jure* moral and religious authority associated with the caliphate through a systematic program of propaganda, circumscription, and daring public enunciations of power and authority, while at the same time trying to chip away at the *de facto* power of the sultans through strategically implemented military and ideological policies. Politically, this denial found a certain culmination in the death of the last Seljuk sultan Ṭoghrıl III in 590/1194, an event which constituted something of a moral victory in a bitter struggle which al-Nāṣir's immediate predecessors had negotiated with varying levels of success since the mid-5th/11th century. At the same time, al-Nāṣir affirmed the *siyāsa sharʿiyya* discourse in that he strategically deployed the political apparatus which had grown up around it in his dealings with regional

au Moyen Age Islam, Byzance, Occident, 66–67; Lambton, *State and Government*, 107–117; and, Carole Hillenbrand, "Islamic Orthodoxy or Realpolitik? Al-Ghazālī's Views on Government," *Iran* 26 (1988): 81–94).

[8] On which, see A.K.S. Lambton, "Justice in the Medieval Persian Theory of Kingship," *StI* 17 (1962): 91–119; and, idem, "*Quis Custodiet Custodes*: Some Reflections on the Persian Theory of Government," *StI* 5 (1956): 125–148; 6 (1956): 125–146.

powers, collecting the *bayʿa*, granting formal diplomas of investiture, and exchanging embassies just as his predecessors had done with various sultans and amirs before him, although with a new ideology underlying such acts.

It was trying to mitigate the compromise of the *siyāsa sharʿiyya* discourse long since associated with the Abbasid caliphate and those alternative figurations of power and authority associated with those who for so long had actually wielded power in the Abbasid domains which in many ways prefigured the field of discourse which al-Nāṣir was to confront in his relationships with various sultans and amirs. Clashes were inevitable, something well evinced in his confrontation with the Khwārazm Shāh ʿAlāʾ al-Dīn Muḥammad, an individual who was clearly set on reestablishing the old Seljuk ideal of a universal sultanate in his own person, publicly proclaiming himself the 'Second Alexander', the 'Shadow of God on Earth, and 'Sultan Sanjar'.[9] Thus, while al-Nāṣir retained the theoretical underpinnings and forms of effectuation of the *siyāsa sharʿiyya* ideal through formal recognition of coercive power wielded on his behalf when it was politically expedient, such as with the Ayyubids, he was equally vigorous in asserting his identity as the axis of the entirety of the Abode of Islam when it was challenged.

While retaining the ideal of the caliph as executor of the *sharīʿa* al-Nāṣir further negotiated such tensions through no small number of formal apparatus aimed at strengthening and consolidating that authority, programmatically promulgating a sophisticated body of policies which looked to push the *jamāʿī-sunnī* vision of a comprehensive *sharʿī* government to its logical conclusion. Here, we are presented with an ideal which envisioned a unified Abode of Islam organized like the members of a Sufi *ribāṭ*, the students of the *ḥalqa* of a *mudarris* in a *madrasa*, or the apprentices of a master craftsmen in the trade markets, namely radially around a central figure, being linked to one another through their shared allegiance to a common master. In the case of al-Nāṣir, the center of this network was none other than the very 'shadow of God upon earth', at one and the same time the Qurayshī-ʿAbbāsī representative of the Prophet, the champion of the *ahl al-bayt*, the recognized master of the *futuwwa*, a master jurisconsult recognized by

---

[9] Juvaynī, *World-Conqueror*, 1:349; Siddiqi, "Caliphate and Kingship," 52–53; and, *Nṣr.*, 80.

all four Sunni *madhhab*s, and perhaps even a fully actualized Sufi,[10] an individual whose very personhood was envisioned as a focal point of the collective soteriological ambitions of all those who could reasonably be circumscribed under its very comprehensiveness.

Numerous ulama and Sufis such as Suhrawardī were drawn in as participants in this program, entering into patronage relationships in which their posts in Baghdad's *ribāṭ*s and *madrasa*s seems to have been directly tied to their willingness to serve as ambassadors, transmit certain texts, and hold public preaching sessions at pulpits associated with the caliphate. As we have already seen, Suhrawardī was part of this group, but Angelika Hartmann's characterization of him as al-Nāṣir's advisor (*Ratgeber*) and court theologian (*Hoftheologe*) is something of an overstatement, and her reading of the role which he played in the caliph's comprehensive program of reform and centralization is a bit too optimistic.[11] While it is certain that Suhrawardī served al-Nāṣir as an ambassador and public preacher and did indeed support the caliphate, such a grand role is not easily extracted from the sources.

When read in the aggregate, what the sources evince rather is that the figure of Suhrawardī represents but a particularly well-documented example of a type and an instance, an individual whom we know so much about not because he was the court theologian of one of the last Abbasid caliphs but rather because he was something else first, something important enough to certain individuals that they took it as their task to preserve his memory and the texts which he composed. There are many others whose presence in the historiography and prosopography bearing directly upon al-Nāṣir's Baghdad are just as, and often much more, visible than Suhrawardī, but because they neither became eponyms of a particular *ṭarīqa* lineage nor possessed a

---

[10] Dhahabī mentions that at one point during the middle of his reign, al-Nāṣir threatened to renounce the caliphate and become a Sufi, donning a *khirqa* made expressly for him in one of Baghdad's *ribaṭ*s (*SN*, 22:202). On this, see Hartmann, "Wollte der Kalif Ṣūfī werden? Amtstheorie und Abdankungspläne des Kalifen an-Nāṣir li-Dīn Allāh (reg. 1180–1225)," in U. Vermeulen and D. de Smet, eds., *Egypt and Syria in the Fatimid, Ayyubid and Mamluk Eras* (Leuven: Uitgeverij Peeters, 1995), 175–205.

[11] *Nṣr.*, 245–254; and, idem, "al-Nāṣir," *EI*², 7:999–1000. Many years earlier Ritter similarly characterized al-Suhrawardī: "er wurde von dem Khalifen Nāṣir (575–622 h) zum šaiḫaš-šuyūḫ von Bagdad ernannt und scheint die Rolle eines Hoftheologen gespielt zu haben" ("Philologika IX", 37), something which I have come across in the works of Taeschner and other German scholars before Hartmann, all using the same term (*Hoftheologe*). I suspect a bit of textual archeology would uncover an earlier (late 19th-century?) *Urtext* for this problematic characterization.

body of disciples and heirs who took it as their task to preserve their memory and the texts which they composed, they are easily pushed into the background.

In fact, it is only many years after al-Nāṣir's grand program of consolidation and centralization had come to an end when we find Suhrawardī explicitly enunciating a vision which moves beyond his earlier affirmation of allegiance to a Qurayshī-ʿAbbāsī Imām in the terms laid out by the *siyāsa sharʿiyya* theorists, and whether or not one can advance the idea, as Hartmann has done, that such an enunciation constitutes the thought of a powerful *Hoftheologe und Ratgeber* and that it represents a coherent ideology which fueled Suhrawardī's earlier ambassadorial activities on behalf of al-Nāṣir between 588/1192 and 618/1221, is a matter of how far one wants to push the sources. The fact is that it is only in those two very late polemics against Peripatetic philosophy—the first composed a year before al-Nāṣir's death in 621/1224 and the second during the reign of al-Mustanṣir (r. 623–640/1226–1242)—where Suhrawardī explicitly devotes space to the subject of the caliphate and its relationship with the *ṭāʾifa* for whom he spoke, the most telling enunciation, brief as it is, being found in two short sections of the latter work. Here, the shaykh locates the *ṣūfiyya* as mediators between the caliphate and those below them, but in turn binds the caliphate to the very existential specificities which give the *ṣūfiyya* their authority in the first place:

> God has made the caliphate a mediator (*wāṣita*) between Him and His creatures, and the Sufi, when he has reached the end of his journey and has attained the rank of shaykhood (*mashyakha*), the mediator between him and the sincere aspirant (*murīd ṣādiq*). The caliph (*imām*) is the absolute mediator and the Sufi the one who serves to mediate the *sunna* to both the aspirant (*murīd*) and the seeker (*ṭālib*). This connection (*munāsaba*) is rooted in the fact that the caliph's order (*amr*) is God's order and his ruling (*ḥukm*) God's ruling, just as my paternal uncle Abū ʾl-Najīb al-Suhrawardī has informed us... God's Messenger said: 'He who has obeyed me has obeyed God and he who has disobeyed me has disobeyed God, and he who obeys the commander (*al-amīr*) obeys me and he who disobeys the commander disobeys me.' Furthermore, as God said: 'if We had made it an angel, We should have sent him as a man, and We certainly have caused them confusion in a matter which they have already confused'; that is, 'in the form of a man' because his power is disposed in the phenomenal world (*ʿālam al-shahāda*) through measuring out wisdom (*ḥikma*) and as such the phenomenal world is kept in order by the caliph, and through his beneficial agency its maintenance is ensured. God does not choose one for the caliphate save that he has demonstrably perfected the actualization of the divine attributes (*akhlāq allāh*) in his own ethical

> constitution, his final attainment being none other than the state of the Sufi, who is perfect and has reached the furthest limit, and only the state of prophethood is more powerful than this.[12]

Preceded by a section which makes reference to the new rule of al-Nāṣir's grandson (*al-dawla al-mustanṣiriyya*), following this enunciation Suhrawardī goes on to once again articulate his vision of the existential and epistemic changes effected upon the psycho-spiritual constitution by pursing the Sufi path, legitimizing the authority of the caliphate on grounds already familiar to us from his earlier discourse on the state of the otherworldly-ulama and *ṣūfiyya*. In a certain sense, he adds a layer to the established *siyāsa sharʿiyya* discourse by fusing its vision and prescriptions on the constitution of caliphal authority and legitimacy with those possessed by his own *ṭāʾifa*, a group whom in turn he situates within a soteriologicaly consequential figuration of mediatory power and providential responsibility for maintaining the integrity of the original dispensation in time and space. However, when read bearing in mind Suhrawardī's vision of the soteriological authority of his *ṭāʾifa*, effected as it is by pursing the Sufi path and either circumscribing or excluding all those who do not, then the caliph is a mediator only if he possesses the existential state of the Sufi who, by default then, actually stands above him. While certainly adding to the other locations of authority in which al-Nāṣir strategically inserted himself, this statement tells us more about the broader symbolic implications of claiming such status rather than a new *Chalifatstheorie* which, as Hartmann has characterized it, rejected the principle of consensus (*ijmāʿ*) in electing, maintaining allegiance to, and defending a legitimate imam as understood in the juridical formulation of *khilāfa/imāma*.

Indeed, Suhrawardī did defend the caliphate, but only in ways familiar to the *siyāsa sharʿiyya* discourse, enunciating his allegiance not only in his *Aʿlām al-hudā*, but on numerous public occasions, not the least of which was his mission to the Khwārazm Shāh ʿAlāʾ al-Dīn during which he unsuccessfully argued for the legitimacy and authority of a Qurayshī-ʿAbbāsī imam in Baghdad on the basis of al-Nāṣir's lineage,

[12] al-Suhrawardī, *Idālat al-ʿiyān*, fol. 88a–89b; the Qurʾānic reference is to 6:9. In what seems to be the oldest of the three copies of the text (MS. Bursa, Ulu Cami 1597_4), this section on the caliphate is comprised of two *faṣl*s (fol. 84a–90b), of which the mid 7th/14th-century copy MS. Süley., Hamidiye 1447_{27} preserves only the second (fol. 135a–135b), and the early 8th/15th-century copy MS. Köp. 1589, fol. 74a–97b (on the margins) neither.

not on the basis of his possessing the qualities of a Sufi shaykh. Defending the caliphate was not Suhrawardī's first order of business in any case, rather it was quite secondary to something which was ultimately of much greater consequence. When those texts which Hartmann has read as documents reflecting Suhrawardī's role as al-Nāṣir's *Hoftheologe* such as the *Aʿlām al-hudā, Kashf al-faḍāʾiḥ, Idālat al-ʿiyān*, and even his two Persian *Futuwwat-nāma*s are read alongside those works concerned with his primary forte, the sciences of the *ṣūfiyya*, it quickly becomes apparent that Suhrawardī pursued what amounted to a 'dual policy', one whose first aim was to establish and enunciate the authority of his own *ṭāʾifa* and to either circumscribe or exclude all competing group solidarities under its master *isnād*. While each of these texts can certainly be situated within al-Nāṣir's program in spirit, it is clear that their primary aim was not to support the caliphate and defended its policies, and when the fact of the very late dates of composition of two of them are brought into consideration it becomes all the more necessary to re-examine them.

The question then is what did someone like al-Nāṣir find in an individual such as Suhrawardī—or for that matter Ibn Sukayna, Raḍī al-Dīn Ṭālqānī, or Abū Ṣāliḥ Naṣr b. ʿAbd al-Razzāq—which was valuable enough to enter into a patronage relationship with them in the first place and then to deploy it for political gain in the second? Similarly, how should the statements of an individual who served neither as a 'court theologian' nor whose primary concern lay in defending the caliphate be understood vis-à-vis the policies of the patron who supported the very *ribāṭ*s in which he lived and worked? To answer these questions each of the three textual instances of what might be construed as Suhrawardī's participation in al-Nāṣir's program must be interrogated, beginning with a creed composed sometime before 605/1208–1209, then his two *Futuwwat-nāma*s composed sometime around 618/1221, and finally the two polemics against Peripatetic philosophy which he composed in 621/1224 and sometime after 622/1226 respectively.

A Sufi Creed

Unlike the manuals of Qushayrī and Abū ʾl-Najīb al-Suhrawardī, or later those of Kāshānī and Bākharzī, the *ʿAwārif al-maʿārif* does not begin with a creed, something which might seem a bit unusual until one recalls that Suhrawardī was already transmitting a creed, the *Aʿlām al-hudā*, among his disciples, a text whose ten chapters Kāshānī later reproduced almost verbatim at the beginning of his *Miṣbāḥ al-hidāya* before launching into a rewriting of the first chapter of the *ʿAwārif al-maʿārif* proper.[13] As we have seen, Suhrawardī considered adherence to a sound creed a *sine qua non* for entering the Sufi path, and in addition to the *Aʿlām al-hudā* in fact, he treats such issues in his two shorter handbooks, the *Jadhdhāb al-qulūb* and *Irshād al-murīdīn*, as well as in his *Ḥilyat al-faqīr al-ṣādiq fī ʾl-taṣawwuf*.

In all of these texts, Suhrawardī leaves little room for doubt as to his particular juridico-theological affiliation, presenting his readers with a creed which is clearly Shāfiʿī-Ashʿarite in perspective but which is at the same time quite reconciliatory and moderate. In this, the text can be situated in the ethos of al-Nāṣir's ideological program, the *daʿwa hādiya*, a program of propaganda which called for a certain rapprochement between various sectarian communities and dogmatic trends and the (re)centralization of identity and allegiance in a broader *jamāʿī-sunnī* community under the all-embracing shadow of the caliph himself. This program was propagated early on by, among many others, Shāfiʿī ulama and Sufi masters such as the *shaykh al-shuyūkh* Ṣadr al-Dīn al-Nīsābūrī, and seems to have continued in one form or another throughout al-Nāṣir's reign.

What is included and left out such a creed is telling, serving as a diagnostic for locating a particular author within a broader field of discourse populated by certain theological trends, clusters of texts, and group affiliations. Here we find Suhrawardī firmly situating himself within the urban Shāfiʿī-Sufi tradition long associated with Baghdad, a tradition which although rooted in a diffuse Shāfiʿī-Ashʿarite identity was framed by a broader *jamāʿī-sunnī* communalism and *sharʿī*-mindedness which, as evinced in the synonymity between his and al-Jīlānī's prescriptions dealing with *ribāṭ*-based Sufism, transcended juridical identities.[14] As with most Sunni creeds, however, in the *Aʿlām al-hudā*

[13] *SQ*, 0.8–36 (his doctrine on God's attributes and acts being discussed further in his creed, the *Lumaʿ fī ʾl-iʿtiqād*, at the beginning of a work on the conditions of discipleship, the *Bulghat al-maqāṣid*, and in another creed, the *al-Fuṣūl fī ʾl-uṣūl* [each in *Thalāth rasāʾil li-qushayrī*, ed. al-Ṭablāwī Saʿd (Cairo: Maṭbaʿat al-Amāna, 1988)]; *AdM*, 1–5 / Milson, *Rule*, 28–30; Kāshānī, *Miṣbāḥ*, 14–55; and, Bākharzī, *Fuṣūṣ al-ādāb*, 3–7. Chapters 5–28 of al-Kalābādhī's *Taʿarruf* can also be considered a creed inasmuch as they deal with the questions usually treated in such works and are arranged in the typical fashion (33–57/Arberry [trans.], *The Doctrine*, 14–72). The same holds for the lengthy Ḥanbalī creed furnished by ʿAbd al-Qādir al-Jīlānī in the *Ghunya* (1:121–167).

[14] Much the same is evinced in the juridical and professional identities of those with

Suhrawardī does not speak explicitly on behalf of a particular juridical or theological school in any case, but rather on behalf of the Sunni community as a whole, the *ahl al-sunna wa-l-jamāʿa*. Such should not be taken as solely as an enunciation of adherence to the Nāṣirian *daʿwa hādiya*, but rather as reflective of an established discourse among the ulama on primary matters of faith (*uṣūl al-dīn*), a discourse which is inevitably possessed of a certain intra-theological syncretism in any event. Thus while clearly adhering to the Shāfiʿī-Ashʿarite definition of faith (*īmān*), on other questions such as the nature of the beatific vision (*ruʾyat allāh*) and saintly miracles (*karāmāt*) he follows a Ḥanafī-Māturīdī line of thinking and presentation as well as displaying a certain anti-rationalism characteristic of the Ḥanbalites.[15] Such divergences should not be taken *prima facie* as a programmatic attempt at ecumenicalism as such, but rather *inter alia* as both a reflection of the fluidity and amorphous nature of theological discourse among early 7th/13th-century urban ulama generally and the idiosyncrasies of Suhrawardī's conception of the particular *Personengruppe* for whom he appointed himself a spokesmen.

---

whom Suhrawardī studied as well as those students, disciples, and seekers who heard *ḥadīth* and took the *khirqat al-tabarruk* from him, a group while comprised largely of self-identified Shāfiʿīs also counted in its ranks no small number of Ḥanbalites such as the aforementioned Ibn Nuqṭa, or Kamāl al-Dīn al-Shahrāyānī (d. 672/1273), ʿAbd al-Ṣamad al-Baghdādī (d. 676/1277), Ibn al-Mukharrimī (d. 688/1289), Rashīd al-Dīn al-Sallāmī (d. 707/1307), and others.

[15] In his definition of faith, Suhrawardī does not stray far from the typical Sunni elaboration of the Qurʾānic formula as generally understand by Shāfiʿī-Ashʿarites, namely stressing both verbal profession (*iqrār bi-l-lisān*) and internal conviction (*taṣdīq al-jinān*) on belief in God's unicity, His angels, books, messengers, the Last Day, and the predestination of both good and evil, and that faith is subject to increase and decrease, works (*ʿamal*) generally seen as perfecting, but not necessary, to faith (*JQb*, fol. 3a–3b, 10a; idem, *Ḥilyat*, 115b); see, e.g., al-Ashʿarī, *K. al-lumaʿ*, ed. and trans. R.J. McCarthy as *The Theology of al-Ashʿarī* (Beirut: Imprimerie Catholique, 1953), 75/104; but cf. idem, *ʿAqīda*, art. 24 (a creed embedded in idem, *al-Ibāna ʿan uṣūl al-diyāna*, trans. W.C. Klein as *The Elucidation of Islām's Foundation* [New Haven: AOS, 1940], 49–55. Generally, the Shāfiʿī-Ashʿarite definition differed from the Ḥanafī-Māturīdī which held that faith cannot increase or decrease and which stressed verbal profession, e.g., *Fiqh akbar* II, art. 18; al-Ṭahāwī, *Bayān al-sunna*, art. 23; and, al-Nasafī, *ʿAqāʾid*, art. 20 (all trans. Watt, op. cit., 48–56, 62–67; 80–85), although this was often joined with both inner conviction and/or 'knowing by the heart' (*maʿrifat bi-l-qalb*), such as in the *W. Abī Ḥanīfa* (trans. Watt, op. cit., 57–60). The Ḥanbalī position, on the other hand, tended to privilege verbal profession (*qawl*) and works (*ʿamal*) as necessary for faith, often adding intention (*niyya*) as well (e.g. *ʿAqīda* I, art. 1 [trans. Watt, op. cit., 33–39; and, Ibn Baṭṭa, *K. al-sharḥ wa-l-ibāna ʿalā uṣūl al-sunnat wa-l-diyāna*, ed. and trans. Henri Laoust in *La profession de foi d'Ibn Baṭṭa* (Damascus: Institut Français de Damas), 47–50/77–83.

As with his forays into the *futuwwa* and his engagement in polemics against the *falāsifa*, Suhrawardī's creed evinces his dual strategy, arguing for the heirship of the otherworldly-ulama/*ṣūfiyya* and the necessity of their *niyāba* in ensuring the perpetuation of the original dispensation in time and space, implicitly locating that authority under the umbrella of a universally recognized, Qurayshī-ʿAbbāsī *imām* who in patronizing such a *ṭāʾifa* ensures both the integrity and continuity of that *niyāba* and the maintenance of the comprehensive *jamāʿī-sunnī* unity which it effects. In pursuit of this dual strategy Suhrawardī's creed further softens the type of *via media* associated with certain watersheds in the history of the Islamic religious sciences such as al-Shāfiʿī (d. 204/820) and al-Ashʿarī (d. 324/935), like both looking to secure legitimacy for a particular epistemological element (in this case the mystical and not the rational) alongside the traditional sources (Qurʾān, Ḥadīth, *ijmāʿ*) championed by the Ḥadīth Folk/Ḥanbalites as the sole generative materials of belief and praxis.

In this, Suhrawardī was in no way unique, for all such ulama of any consequence, 'rationalist' and 'traditionalist' alike, constructed their respective projects as comprehensive enunciations of interpretive authority which, whether explicitly or implicitly, through exclusion or circumscription, situated themselves within and among whichever competing discourses might happen to share, contest, or even simply impinge upon the same discursive space. For the early 4th/10th-century theologian al-Ashʿarī it was the Muʿtazilites and traditionists/Ḥanbalites, for a late 4th/10th-century Sunni revivalist such as Ghazālī, the dialectical theologians, Ismāʿīlis, and philosophers, for a late-5th/11th-century jurist and *ʿālim* such as Ibn ʿAqīl (d. 513/1119) the Shāfiʿī/Ḥanafī-Ashʿarites and certain circles of his own Ḥanbalī *madhhab*, and for a mid-to-late 6th/12th-century jurist, *muḥaddith*, polemicist, and all-around Ḥanbalī *ʿālim* like Ibn al-Jawzī all of those dialectical theologians, Sufis, philosophers, and hidden heretics sowing dissension among the populace of Baghdad. For an early 7th/13th-century Shāfiʿī *ʿālim* and Sufi shaykh such as Suhrawardī, it was those worldly-ulama, Peripatetic philosophers, traditionists (Ḥanbalites), and rationalists (Ashʿarites) whose varying claims to exegetical authority and mutual antagonism posed a challenge to his own ideal of a cohesive community of spiritual brethren organized under an authoritative shaykh, and, perhaps by extension, a challenge to his patron's ideal of a unified Abode of Islam organized under his own person.

Although reflective of the ethos of al-Nāṣir's *daʿwa hādiya* in its attempt to effect a certain détente between the Ḥanbalites and Ashʿarites by counseling both to soften their position on contentious issues and to take seriously the destructive consequences of impugning and antagonizing one another, the *Aʿlām al-hudā* does not mention al-Nāṣir. At the same time, however, like al-Nāṣir's *daʿwa hādiya* the work was clearly directed at a broader public, being composed in Mecca at the request of an individual whom Suhrawardī simply calls a 'brother Muslim', a request which as a member of the otherworldly-ulama he felt duty bound to oblige:

> While I was in pious residence (*mujāwir*) in Mecca I was asked by a brother Muslim whilst he and I were circumambulating the Holy Kaʿba to compose for him a creed to which he could adhere... but I delayed for a while because I considered time in Mecca to be very precious, too precious to be occupied by things other than prayer, circumambulation, and reciting the Qurʾān, in addition to such diversions such as eating, sleeping, and the matters of necessity. However, this bother's question was demanding that its right (*ḥaqq*) be fulfilled, and at that point I knew that if I were to slacken the bridle of desire—by that which the soul embraces the study of books, quoting authoritative works, restricting it to what is mentioned in supported *ḥadīths*, and studying divergent teachings—then there would be too many distractions from my main task for which my limited time could not allow. So, I sought what was best and supplicated at the *multazam* hoping for a good omen, adhered to the pillars and the covering of the Kaʿba, beseeching God to keep up my determination in hopes that my prayer be answered, that my work be made sincere in its objective, and that I be safeguarded from error and mistake. After seeking what was best and supplicating, I drew out the sweet uses of this compendium from my inner being. While composing it, I imposed upon myself that my heart would look to God and seek recourse with Him, and whenever my mind began to hesitate in anything concerning it, I would circumambulate the Kaʿba until I was capable of expressing it; and thus I entitled it: *The Signs of Guidance and the Creed of the God-fearing*, arranging it into ten sections.[16]

The autodidactic procedure of composition which Suhrawardī describes here is important, for although only mentioning the Sufis by name once throughout the entire treatise, when read alongside the enunciation of the genealogically and existentially predicated authority of the *ṣūfiyya*

[16] *AH*, 46.

which frames his thinking, this creed clearly evinces the comprehensive reach of his vision, furnishing a particularly telling example of how he envisioned that authority being translated into actual discursive spaces in a systematic form. In essence, this creed is none other than that of the world-renouncing *ʿālim*, the *muntahī* whose soul has reached a state of equanimity and whose heart is perpetually enveloped in the light of the divine effusion:

> Praise be to God who lifts the veils of the heart from the spiritual insight (*baṣāʾir*) of the Folk of Love (*ahl al-widād*), and guides them by the light of him whom He has chosen to the straightest ways of guidance. He purifies their souls from worldly desire so that they travel the most balanced path of renunciation and protects their hearts through sound belief against deviation caused by the carnal passions. He conveys them to the spring of pure certainty so that their minds are cut off from the stuff of doubt and obstinacy, and the cups of their understanding are filled to the brim from the Kawthar of marvelous knowledge. By means of the constant outpourings of His assistance, the splendor of the felicity of mystical knowing (*maʿrifa*) and the glad tidings of having achieved the goal are recognized on their faces...Know—may God assist you!—the creed which is protected against passions is a creed produced in a living heart through the recollection of God, a heart bedecked by piety and supported by guidance, a heart in which shines the light of faith, a light whose effects are apparent on the outer being...it is a heart which God has returned to the splendor of its original nature (*fiṭra*) and a heart which He has cleansed from the effects of every hearsay which accrue to the *nafs*, effects which imprint it with various idle suppositions and chimeras. It is a heart so fully preoccupied that suppositions and imaginative fancies are denied access, and indeed there is nothing like this heart except for the heart of the world-renouncer (*al-zāhid fī ʾl-dunyā*), because he has a heart surrounded by light, and verily the heart surrounded by light is none other than the heart of the renunciant.[17]

As he would do later with the *futuwwa*, in this work Suhrawardī circumscribes the authority of the worldly-ulama by attending to the language and structure of a familiar discourse, writing in a genre intimately associated with group identities (the *ʿaqīda*) yet at the same time placing himself above it and those with whom it is associated by not seeking recourse with established authorities, analogical reasoning, or rational argument. His account of the composition of this *ʿaqīda* is not an apology, but rather a co-optative device which in its very rhetoric

[17] Ibid., 49.

repositions exegetical, and thus mediatory and ultimately soteriological authority, into the hands of the only legitimate heirs to the prophets, those otherworldly-ulama and *ṣūfiyya* like himself who in clinging to the Kaʿba and supplicating God for right guidance could not be guided but to the straightest of paths.

Whether or not the 'worldly-ulama' would have accepted such a configuration of authority (course most would not) is a moot point, for in this creed Suhrawardī was not speaking to them, but rather to those who have already vested this type of authority with meaning, an enunciation of authority which, as we have seen in each and every step of Suhrawardī's career, not only outwardly adhered to the collective body of rules, norms, behaviors, genres, institutions, and forms of individual and collective practice shared and accepted as natural and proper in the broader culture of religious learning of the ulama but envisioned itself as participating from within that very structure in the same process of working out a comprehensive soteriology in real terms:

> Most Muslims adhere to a creed whose apodictic proofs (*adilla*) are firmly established among them, and whose decisive proofs (*barāhīn*) are obvious through consideration. When the world-renouncing scholar considers them, however, he finds them remaining forever in imitation (*taqlīd*), yet they persist in believing they are possessed of a complete and perfect theology, but when you consider their states you will find them to be but mere imitators of those whom they consider to be the best among them. Their opinions are none other than those of their eponymous authorities (*mashāyikh*) and religious leaders (*aʾimma*), and they believe that these men possess the capacity of knowledge and mastery of what is sound, and thus receive their creed and its demonstrative proofs from them, dictating their imaginative fancies from what they hear and thinking that they possess mastery, 'each party rejoicing in that which is with itself'.[18]

Here, Suhrawardī situates himself within the general Shāfiʿī-Ashʿarite distain for imitation (*taqlīd*) on the part of commoners on basic matters of faith (*uṣūl al-dīn*), but in his discussion quickly moves towards a characteristically Ḥanbalī conception which tended to understand the term, non-pejoratively, in reference to the imitation of the traditions of the Prophet and his Companions.[19] Finding only unanimity and no dissention on a single point of belief among that community due to

[18] Ibid., 50. The final reference is to Qurʾān 30:32.

[19] See, e.g., *Fiqh Akbar* III, art. 1; Laoust, *La profession de foi*, 7 fn. 2, 9–10, fn. 1; Makdisi, *Ibn ʿAqil*, 66–68; and, for the Shāfiʿī-Ashʿarite position, Norman Calder, "Taḳlīd," *EI*[2], 10:137.

the presence of the Prophet, Suhrawardī implicitly connects this type of *taqlīd* with the genealogically and existentially derived representative authority (*niyāba*) of the world-renouncing *ʿālim* who, if he happens to be a director of a *ribāṭ*, possess an obligation to provide the ordinary believer (e.g., *mustarshid*) with guidance:

> As for one who does not keep much company with scholars, he may still adhere to a creed, but hears it from the company he keeps and from those of his neighborhood and locality with whom he fraternizes. Thus, he adheres to that to which they adhere and charges with unbelief those who does not believe as they do. Sometimes, many of those who think such things join up with some commoner who claims that he has obtained a demonstrative proof, and like him they become imitators. Their souls are such that they absorb, are imprinted, and inscribed by various things of which their possessors take no notice, for they are naturally disposed to and have an innate propensity for such, and for this there is a profoundly deep and unusual interpretation. When this trial (*fitna*) becomes a widespread affliction, there is no path to salvation save for sincerity of want and the goodness of seeking refuge with a master (*mawlā*) who removes obscurity and guides whosoever from the Muslim community (*umma*) who happens to be knocking upon the door of request to the Absolute Truth (*al-ḥaqq al-ṣarf*). Such a one is he whose heart has been denuded of passion and who has obtained the position of giving good guidance (*ihtidā'*). He looks upon those who are veiled with a merciful eye and not even for an instant is hard-hearted towards any and all of the religious scholars (*arbāb ikhtilāf al-ārā' kāffat*[an]) or any and all of the Muslim masses (*ahl al-qibla min al-muslīmīn kāffat*[an]); and we seek God's assistance in understanding the needs of those seekers asking for guidance (*al-ṭālibīn al-mustarshidīn*).[20]

Like many Sunni creeds, the *Aʿlām al-hudā* is apologetic in nature and hortatory in tone, utilizing the explicative and defensive method familiar to medieval Muslim polemic in general and dialectical theology in particular (e.g., 'if they say *x*, I say *y*') yet the opponent whom it engages and the nature of its arguments are idiosyncratic to its author, colored by Suhrawardī's vision of various *Personengruppen* being demarcated in existential terms and an epistemological position which privileges direct and unmediated experience over and against discursive reasoning and logic, something which inevitably limits him to traditional arguments, namely those arguments from scriptural authority, for those in need of

[20] *AH*, 50–51; cf. al-Ghazālī, *Fayṣal al-tafriqa bayna 'l-islām wa-l-zandaqa*, trans. Sherman Jackson as *On the Boundaries of Theological Tolerance in Islam* (Oxford and New York: Oxford University Press, 2002), 88–89.

such a creed (i.e., non-Sufis) by definition could not validate its articles on epistemological grounds. Such was the type of authority which al-Nāṣir purchased, something which if it had not possessed a ready market would have most certainly been more trouble than it was worth.

Arranged into ten chapters, the *Aʿlām al-hudā* more or less follows the standard outline of such creeds, organized into discrete sections devoted first to the typical theological questions (*ilāhiyyāt*) and then to the typical traditional questions (*samʿiyyāt*), affirming those things which would be acceptable to most within the *jamāʿī-sunnī* fold, and glossing over or repositioning those things which might be causes for controversy and division. Thus, on the nature of God Suhrawardī affirms the typical Ashʿarite and Māturīdī position of 'declaring incomparability' (*tanzīh*), affirming that God is one, utterly unique and other, existing sempiternally (*azaliyya*) and eternally *a parte post* (*abadiyya*), unrestricted by spatial, temporal, or modal signifiers, named 'only by what He named Himself', and known by attributes but only amodally. As with the divine will, the attributes of the essence and the attributes of the acts are inscrutable and are to be accepted without inquiring into their modality, they are known only through revelation and fall far beyond the capacity of the intellect (*ʿaql*) and its rational judgments to even begin to conceive their nature and significance.[21]

Likewise, on the complicated issue of freewill and predestination, Suhrawardī generally follows the Ashʿarite-Māturīdī doctrine of trying to reconcile the divine decree (*qadar*) with human moral responsibility, stating that human acts and their outcomes are created by God and appropriated by creatures through the modality of acquisition (*kasb/iktisāb*), God simultaneously creating both the act and the power to

---

[21] *AH*, 52–60, 69–73; cf. idem, *Ḥilyat*, fol. 115a; and, *IrM*, fol. 32a–32b; *KF*, 110–111, 169, 232. Following the typical differentiation between the attributes of the divine essence (*ṣifāt dhātiyya*) and the attributes of acts (*ṣifāt fiʿliyya*), Suhrawardī states that the seven attributes of the essence are necessarily connected with the divine essence (*al-dhāt*) but are known only through their corresponding qualificatives, e.g. life to living (*ḥayyāt* to *ḥayy*), power to powerful (*qudra* to *qādir*), knowledge to knowing (*ʿilm* to *ʿālim*), and so forth. The quintessential expression—the primary points of which Suhrawardī's statement is in full accordance—is found in al-Ghazālī's "Exposition of the Sunni Creed Embodied in the Two Phrases of the Profession of Faith" (*Tarjamat ʿaqīdat ahl al-sunna fī kalamtay al-shahāda*) in the first section (*faṣl*) of the second book of the *Iḥyāʾ* (2:108–110 [the points of which are expounded upon in the 3rd section of the same book in a résumé of his *R. qudsiyya fī qawāʿid al-ʿaqāʾid*, a creed written for the people of Jerusalem during the period of his famous crisis]; trans. W.M. Watt in *Islamic Creeds*, 73–79), hereafter cited as *Tarjamat ʿaqīda*.

act but the latter possessing no casual efficacy. While referencing the doctrine of acquisition however, Suhrawardī's analysis is elusive and he ultimately shifts the focus away from speculation to unqualified adhere to the divine law as made know through revelation without 'asking how'.[22] Similarly, on the decisive issue of God's speech, Suhrawardī attempts to strike a balance between opposing views on the relationship between the Qur'ān as *verbum dei* and its actual sounds and letters as reproduced on the tongues of men and sheets of paper, saying:

> Some say: there is no letter or sound for one who is too great to be present in them; while others say: there is a letter and a sound for one who is too exalted to be absent from them... O' brothers from among these two factions, the ideal path and the most balanced way is that you should abandon controversy... for it is obvious to every intelligent person that when a servant says that the Qur'ān is the word of God, he does so while believing that he is required to follow His commands and prohibitions, cling to His commandments and what He has made licit and illicit, give ear to His promise and threat, and carry out His rights and punishments... otherwise, when you deal with the eternal, your opponent deals with the created; you call him an unbeliever while he calls you the same. What then is your opinion about doing so without really acting in accordance with it?... Rather, engage in the recitation of God's Book day and night and treat your prayers and other religious duties with circumspection, for although the Book was sent down to you it can just as easily become an argument against you. The controversy in this matter is like their receiving a letter from a sultan which commands and prohibits, yet they quarrel over its handwriting, its manner of expression, and what it contains in terms of eloquent speech and felicitous expression; and thus their attention becomes distracted from that with which they were charged to do in the first place![23]

On the equally contentious issue of the anthropomorphic statements of the Qur'ān and Ḥadīth he pursues the same détente, enjoining his reader to neither betake to anthropomorphism (*tashbīh*) nor to 'divesting God of His attributes' (*ta'ṭīl*), saying:

[22] *AH*, 62–63. Conceptualizations of the doctrine of acquisition and its moral implications differed among various Ash'arite and Māturīdī thinkers, although was invariably mentioned as an article of faith, e.g., *W. Abī Ḥanīfa*, art. 15; al-Ash'arī, *'Aqīda*, arts. 15–16 (reflective of, idem, *Ibāna*, 103–104, 107–111; *K. al-luma'*, 54–69/76–96); *Fiqh Akbar* II, art. 6; al-Kalābādhī, *Ta'arruf*, 46–47/Arberry (trans.), *The Doctrine*, 30–31; *Fiqh Akbar* III, art. 19; *SQ*, 0.35; idem, *Luma' fī 'l-i'tiqād*, 28–29; al-Ghazālī, *Iḥyā'*, 1:131–135; and, *GhT*, 1:138–139 (whose use of the idea deserves further study). On the issue in general, see Louis Gardet, "Kasb," *EI*[2], 4:693–694; and, idem, *Les Grandes problèmes de la théologie musulmane: Dieu et la destinée de l'homme* (Paris: J. Vrin, 1967), 60–64, 116–120, 128–132.

[23] *AH*, 65–67 (much condensed translation).

> O' brother Ḥanbalite, know that your brother Ashʿarite does not betake to figurative interpretation except for whatever he imagines in regard to people being deceived by anthropomorphism and similarity. If sheer sitting is conceded to him he does not figuratively interpret it, so what need does he have for interpreting it figuratively if not for his fear of anthropomorphism? O' brother Ashʿarite, your brother Ḥanbalite is driven to debate and insistence due to his fear that denying and divesting is to recognize a hidden deception [in the revelation]. So, one should make peace with the other, the Ḥanbalite driving away from his mind the fear of hidden deception so that nothing of the sitting will elude him, and the Ashʿarite driving away his fear of anthropomorphism and not persisting in figurative interpretation, so that the recognition of sheer sitting will not harm him. So let them both confirm without anthropomorphism and deny without divesting![24]

Asserting that the best position is to affirm, along with Mālik b. Anas, that "His sitting is known, but its modality (*kayfiyya*) is unknown, belief in it is obligatory and questioning it an innovation (*bidʿa*)" Suhrawardī states that as one of the most complete acts of worship is the amelioration of enmity, it is imperative to understand that differences in interpretation are evinced only as per the relative intellectual and spiritual capacity of the interpreter, and that even the Prophet used to speak with people in accordance with their capacity to comprehend what he was saying.[25]

On the equally contentious issue of the beatific vision (*ruʾyat allāh*) Suhrawardī affirms its reality based on the Qurʾān and Ḥadīth, but qualifies it in typical Māturīdī fashion through an argument which differentiates between mere visual perception (*bi-l-abṣār*) and actual apprehension or comprehension (*idrāk*), positing that the vision (*ruʾya*) is apprehended not through the modality of physical sight but rather through a certain 'spiritual eye' which serves, like the heart, as an alternative instrument of perception.[26] He goes on to state, however,

---

[24] Ibid., 70–71; al-Ṭahāwī, *Bayān*, art. 8; and, al-Ghazālī, *Fayṣal*, 93, 107–108.

[25] *AH*, 61–63.

[26] Ibid., 75–78; *Fiqh Akbar* II, art. 17; al-Ṭahāwī, *Bayān*, art. 6; al-Nasafī, *ʿAqāʾid*, art. 10; but cf. al-Kalābādhī, *Taʿarruf*, 42–43 / Arberry (trans.), *The Doctrine*, 24–26, which only presents al-Ashʿarī's argument without mentioning the Māturīdī notion of vision by the heart, viz., al-Ashʿarī, *ʿAqīda*, art. 22; idem, *Ibāna*, 56–65; *K. al-lumaʿ*, 32–36/45–52; idem, *Maqālāt*, 157, 213–217, 292; and, *Fiqh Akbar* III, art. 17; also al-Ghazālī, *Iḥyāʾ*, 4:577–578; but cf. the Ḥanbalī position which affirms visual perception (*bi-l-abṣār*) and generally denies spiritual perception or perception by the heart, e.g., *ʿAqīda* V, art. 6; *GhṬ*, 1:123; and, Ibn Qudāma, *ʿAqīdat*, 109. On the debate and its origins, which was connected with much wider issues which Suhrawardī does not cover, see Gimaret, "Ruʾyat Allāh," *EI²*, 8:648–649.

that the vision, which may or may not be the same as the *visio beatifica*, is not limited to the Hereafter, the common believers experiencing it in the Hereafter just as the saints (*awliyāʾ*) experience it in this world, and the elect of the saints experiencing it in the Hereafter just as the Prophet Muḥammad did during his nocturnal journey.[27] In positing this idea, something which would have been vigorously objected to by most Ḥanbalīs, Suhrawardī certainly contradicts his stated aim of theological reconciliation, and one is left to wonder how this might have supported al-Nāṣir's *daʿwa hādiya*.

On those subjects generally construed as comprising the traditional questions (*samʿiyyāt*), that is those things known only *ex auditu* (through the Qurʾān and Ḥadīth), Suhrawardī affirms the basic articles of faith found in the vast majority of Sunni creeds. At the same time, however, his discussion of certain articles clearly evinces its grounding in the overarching vision framing his discourse on the sciences of the *ṣūfiyya* and the role which they play in the disposition of the original dispensation in time and space. Thus, in his discussion of prophethood and in particular the veracity of the prophethood of Muḥammad being evinced through evidentiary miracles (*muʿjizāt*), Suhrawardī posits a close connection typical of Ḥanafī-Māturīdī thinking—not generally shared by Ashʿarites and Ḥanbalites as an article of faith—between such miracles and the reality of saintly miracles and supernatural feats (*karāmāt/ijābāt*), arguing that the latter are an affirmation of the former.[28] At the same time, he adheres closely to the line of thinking found in both the earlier Sufi handbooks and typical among Ashʿarite thinkers, stipulating that saintly miracles and supernatural deeds are real but are qualitatively different from evidentiary miracles, and if they are displayed by an individual who does not perfectly adhere to the divine law are to be considered mere trickery and should be rejected.[29]

---

[27] *AH*, 78; *JQb*, fol. 14b.

[28] *AH*, 79–82, which also affirms the importance of dream-visions and thus for his continual insistence on the necessity of *istikhāra* (same in the Ḥanbalī *ʿAqīda* I, art. 11); cf. *JQb*, fol. 17a; and, *IrM*, fol. 36b–37a. The connection between evidentiary miracles and saintly miracles is made clear in a number of Ḥanafī-Māturīdī creeds, e.g. *Fiqh Akbar* II, art. 16; al-Nasafī, *ʿAqāʾid*, art. 26, but is clearly absent in Shāfiʿī-Ashʿarite creeds, including those written by Sufis such as Qushayrī, e.g., *Lumaʿ fī ʾl-iʿtiqād*, 29–31; and, idem, *Bulghat al-maqāṣid*, 70–72; the various positions have been covered exhaustively by Richard Gramlich in *Die Wunder der Freunde Gottes* (Wiesbaden: Franz Steiner Verlag, 1987), 19–73.

[29] *AH*, 80; and, *IrM*, fol. 2a, 36b–37b; see *SL*, 113.1–118.6; Kalābādhī, *Taʿarruf*, 71–79 / Arberry (trans.), *The Doctrine*, 57–66; *SQ*, 0.35, 38.4, 52.1–61; and, *KM*, 276–303/ Nicholson, *The Kashf*, 218–239. See further my entry "Karāma," *EIr* (forthcoming).

Having taken care of this issue, Suhrawardī then moves on to the perennially vexing issue of the Family and Companions of the Prophet. Here, he is transparently apologetic in his pronouncement, prefacing his discussion with a broad statement of inclusion which circumscribes the respective positions of the Sunnis and Shiites in a nebulous comprehensiveness which links his vision of spiritual maturation as embedded in his delineation of the Sufi path with the politics of partisanship:

> Know that the inheritance (*mīrāth*) of prophethood is knowledge (*ʿilm*), and that both the Prophet's Companions (*aṣḥāb*) and the members of his House (*ahl baytihi*) have inherited it. It is incumbent upon you to love all of them without inclining towards one or the other, for that is not but mere passion. This desire will not be taken away from you until something of the special love of God (*maḥabbat khāṣṣa*) settles down in your inner being. At that moment you will be freed from passion and will occupy yourself solely with what you have been given. Possessing a new clarity of vision, their good qualities will be revealed to you and whatever you may object to about one of them will be covered up, for being preoccupied with partisanship and examining their affairs is the occupation of the idle.[30]

Perhaps articulated in support of al-Nāṣir's program of cultivating the Imāmīs, Suhrawardī states that it is incumbent upon all believers to unconditionally love each and every companion and member of the *ahl al-bayt* without inclining to one or the other, saying that it is obligatory to love not only Abū Bakr, ʿUmar, ʿUthmān, and ʿAlī but also Fāṭima, al-Ḥasan, and al-Ḥusayn, it being but the machinations of the *nafs* which engenders debate about their affairs and relative virtues.[31] Implicitly, then, those in possession of the higher state of special love (*maḥabbat khāṣṣa*)—which as we have already seen Suhrawardī connects with that critical point at which the *nafs* makes its transition from blaming (*lawwāma*) to tranquil (*muṭmaʾinna*) and the voyager his transition from voyaging to flying—are existentially non-partisan in their leanings, embodying the *jamāʿī-sunnī* ideal of comprehensive moral and communal unity which al-Nāṣir tried so hard to localize the caliphate and Suhrawardī in the Sufi *ribāṭs*.[32]

[30] *AH*, 83; cf. idem, *Ḥilyat*, fol. 115b; similar in al-Ṭahāwī, *Bayān*, arts. 38–41; also *ʿAqīda* I, art. 12; and, al-Ashʿarī, *ʿAqīda*, art. 34; cf. Ibn Baṭṭa, *Ibāna*, 64–65/123–125.

[31] The pro-Imāmī policies of al-Nāṣir were open and well known, something often earning him the disparagement of later historiographers who often speak about his Shiite leanings (*mutashayyiʿ*). On this and for references, see: *Nṣr.*, 136–172; and, idem, "Al-Nāṣir," *EI*², 7:1001.

[32] *AH*, 83–86; the typical article in Sunni creeds being to posit only the excellence,

On the final traditional questions normally dealt with in such creeds, eschatological matters, Suhrawardī affirms the cardinal points shared between the Shāfiʿī-Ashʿarites, Ḥanafī-Māturīdīs, and Ḥanbalites as opposed to the Muʿtazilites and Philosophers, namely the cognizance of the deceased, the interrogation, pressure, and punishment of the grave, the physical resurrection of the body, the eschatological portents, the sensate nature of punishment and bliss, and, although debated, the eventual removal of the believing sinner (*fāsiq*) from the Fire. Likewise, the possibility of intercession is affirmed as is the reality of the pool (*ḥawḍ*), the scales (*mīzān*), and the bridge (*ṣirāṭ*), all of which Suhrawardī asserts—in a veiled criticism of those *falāsifa* and materialists who 'do not know how to weigh things save by essences and accidents yet believe themselves to be the salt of the earth'—cannot be subject to rationalization and figurative interpretation but must be accepted as realities without inquiring about their nature or modality.[33] He closes the creed with the affirmation of the veracity of the caliphate and his adherence to the *ijmāʿ* of the Sunni community quoted earlier.

While the *Aʿlām al-hudā* unequivocally enunciates its author's adherence to the Qurayshī-ʿAbbāsī caliphate and the disposition of its authority as envisioned by the *siyāsa sharʿiyya* theorists, and while its call for reconciliation is reflective of al-Nāṣir's program, it is clear that Suhrawardī wrote this work neither to defend the caliphate nor to localize sectarian identity under his person. What he did, rather, is

---

in descending order, of the Prophet, Abū Bakr, ʿUthmān, ʿAlī, and—either explicitly or by implication—their right to the caliphate, e.g., *W. Abī Ḥanīfa*, art. 10; *ʿAqīda* I, art. 13; *ʿAqīda* II, art. 13; al-Ashʿarī, *ʿAqīda*, art. 35; idem, *Ibāna*, 133–136; *Fiqh Akbar* II, art. 10; Ibn Baṭṭa, *Ibāna*, 61/113–115; al-Ṭahāwī, *Bayān*, art. 39; al-Qushayrī, *Lumaʿ fī ʾl-iʿtiqād*, 32; idem, *Bulghat al-maqāṣid*, 77; al-Ghazālī, *Tarjamat ʿaqīda*, art. 25; idem, *Iḥyāʾ*, 1:137; idem, *al-Iqtiṣād fī ʾl-iʿtiqād*, ed. İbrahim Agâh Çubukçu and Hüseyin Atay (Ankara: Nur Matbaası, 1962), 242–246; al-Nasafī, *ʿAqāʾid*, arts. 27–28; *GhṬ*, 1:157–162; and, Ibn Qudāma, *ʿAqīdat*, 111.

[33] *AH*, 87–91; cf. *W. Abī Ḥanīfa*, arts. 19–21, 25; *ʿAqīda* I, arts. 6–8; *ʿAqīda* V, arts. 9–12; al-Ashʿarī, *ʿAqīda*, arts. 4–5, 26–27, 30–31, 44–45, 48; idem, *Ibāna*, 130–132; al-Kalābādhī, *Taʿarruf*, 54–57/Arberry (trans.), *The Doctrine*, 39–42; *Fiqh Akbar* II, arts. 20–21, 23, 29; al-Ṭahāwī, *Bayān*, arts. 10–11, 25, 32–33, 43; Ibn Baṭṭa, *Ibāna*, 53–55/93–100, 58/106–107; al-Nasafī, *ʿAqāʾid*, arts. 17, 19; *Fiqh Akbar* III, arts. 25–27; al-Ghazālī, *Tarjamat ʿaqīda*, arts. 17–24; idem, *Iḥyāʾ*, 1:135–137, 4:525–535, 543–563; idem, *Iqtiṣād*, 213–220; *GhṬ*, 1:140, 142–158; and, Ibn Qudāma, *ʿAqīdat*, 110–111. It should be noted that on each and every one of these points, the vast majority of Sunni creeds are in concordance with one another, the issue being to defend against metaphorical interpretation or denials of the corporality of those things associated with the eschatological narratives found in the Qurʾān and Ḥadīth by the Muʿtazilites and other rationalist thinkers.

to argue for the authority of the particular *Personengruppe* for which he appointed himself a spokesmen, using the generic vehicle of the *ʿaqīda* to engage, and then circumscribe, the exegetical authority of those non-Sufi, worldly-ulama, populating the same discursive and physical spaces in which he himself moved, grounding his exposition in the same existential and epistemological arguments framing his exposition of the sciences of the *ṣūfiyya*, something which many years later he would again deploy in his polemic against Peripatetic philosophy. Before reaching this point, however, Suhrawardī had to negotiate yet another aspect of his patron's program, one concerned not with fundamental beliefs and theological arguments but rather with another source of potential disunity within the Abode of Islam, the *fityān*.

A Sethian Genealogy

It is important to remember that a major part of al-Nāṣir's broader program of centralization centered upon a sweeping project aimed at reorganizing the young-men's clubs (*futuwwa*), a largely urban form of intentional social organization often identified with both the Iraqi-Iranian ʿAyyārūn and Syrian Aḥdāth who since the 4th/9th century had caused major headaches for rulers in times of crisis, transition, and political weakness.[34] Forging contacts with the *fityān* of Baghdad shortly after his accession, al-Nāṣir was initiated into one of their branches in 578/1182–1183 and thereafter slowly began to promulgate a series of moral and legal injunctions which eventually concentrated absolute authority for its rites and regulations in his own person.[35] The caliph's

[34] Research on the *futuwwa* during the Islamic Middle Periods is fairly substantial, the works of Franz Taeschner and Claude Cahen being fundamental. Overviews with further references in Süleyman Uludağ and Ahmet Yaşar Ocak, "Fütüvvet," *TDVİA*, 13:259–265; Claude Cahen, "ʿAyyār," *EIr*, 3:159–160; and, idem and Franz Taeschner, "Futuwwa," *EI²*, 2:961–962.

[35] The branch, which the Baghdadi *fityān* called a *bayt* (pl. *buyūt*), being the Rahhāṣiyya and the initiation taking place at the hands of its current master, Shaykh ʿAbd al-Jabbār b. Ṣāliḥ al-Ḥanbalī (Ibn al-Miʿmār, *K. al-futuwwa*, ed. Muṣṭafā Jawād and Muḥammad Taqī al-Dīn al-Hilālī [Baghdad: Maktabat al-Muthannā, 1958], 146–147; al-Malik al-Manṣūr, *Miḍmār al-ḥaqāʾiq wa-sirr al-khalāʾiq*, ed. Ḥasan Ḥabashī [Cairo: Aʿlām al-Kutub, 1968], 86; *TIsl*, 46:47 [*ḥawādith, anno* 578]; idem, *ʿIbar*, 4:232; and, *MJ*, 3:409; also: Claude Cahen, "Notes sur les débuts de la futuwwa d'al-Nāṣir," *Oriens* 6 (1953): 18–19; Deodaat Breebaart, "The Development and Structure of the Turkish Futūwah Guilds" [Ph.D. diss., Princeton University, 1961], 52–53; and, *Nsr.*, 94–96). Reforms included things such as a prohibition on shooting with pellets (*ramy bi-l-bunduq*) save

relationship with the *futuwwa* was a life-long one, and some twenty-five years after having become an initiate, in 604/1207 he finally issued a decree in which he proclaimed himself its *qibla* and the apex of its hierarchy, outlining a series of principles and norms with which non-compliance was a capital offense.[36]

An important part of this reform was genealogical, for in addition to concentrating absolute authority for the *futuwwa* in his own person on the basis of prophetic *ḥadīth*, al-Nāṣir promulgated a new initiatic chain which brought it from ʿAlī b. Abī Ṭālib down to his own person, and on its basis sent out specially designated agents to initiate sultans and princes, instituted what developed into a *niqāba* intended to represent the entire corporate body of Baghdadi *fityān*, and sponsored the composition and dissemination of manuals outlining its principles and practices.[37] It is in conjunction with one of his official missions on behalf of al-Nāṣir where we find Suhrawardī engaging in at least one of these reforms, composing two handbooks on the *futuwwa* which seem to have been intended for dissemination in Seljuk Anatolia.

Perhaps more so than the others, however, these treatises call into question the nature of Suhrawardī's support for his patron's program, clearly evincing his dual strategy of privileging his own program of

---

with his permission as well as a prohibition on flying carrier pigeons (*al-ṭuyūr al-manāsīb*) save with birds obtained from his own aviary, the latter obviously aimed at regulating communications networks (*KT*, 10:400; al-Malik al-Manṣūr, *Miḍmār*, 180; *MZ*, 8.1:437; Breebaart, op. cit., 52–53, 58; *Nṣr.*, 97–98; and, idem, "Al-Nāṣir," *EI*², 999).

[36] *JM*, 221–222 (text of decree cited on 223–225; also idem, *al-Manāqib al-ʿabbāsiyya wa-l-mafākhir al-mustanṣiriyya*, MS. Bibliothèque Nationale de France 6144, fol. 138b–139b, in Ibn al-Miʿmār, *K. al-futuwwa*, 297–301); al-Khartabirtī, *Tuḥfat al-waṣāyā*, fol. 117a-117b (citation, next note); Cahen, "Notes," 20–21; *Nṣr.*, 101–102; and, idem, "Al-Nāṣir," *EI*², 7:999.

[37] Franz Taeschner, "Futuwwa, eine gemeinschaftbildende Idee im mittelalterlicher Orient und ihre verschiedene Erscheinungsforme," *Schweizerisches Archiv für Volkskunde* 52.2–3 (1956): 136–143; Cahen, "Notes," 18–23; *Nṣr.*, 92–107; and, idem, "Al-Nāṣir," *EI*², 7:998–999. Despite the quick demise of the Nāṣirian *futuwwa* following the Mongol destruction of the Abbasid caliphate in 656/1258—although it did survive in Mamluk Egypt for a time—at least two such manuals have been preserved, namely the aforementioned *K. al-futuwwa* composed by a high-ranking Ḥanbalī *futuwwa* master known as Ibn al-Miʿmār (d. 646/1248) and a short treatise entitled *Tuḥfat al-waṣāyā* composed by one Aḥmad b. Ilyās al-Naqqāsh al-Khartabirtī. The first was edited by Muṣṭafā Jawād and Muḥammad Taqī al-Dīn al-Hilālī on the basis of a single unique manuscript (MS. Tüb. MA VI 197) as *K. al-futuwwa* (ref. above), whereas the second, found in the same collection as Suhrawardī's two *Futuwwat-nāmas* (MS. Süley., Aya Sofya 2049, fol. 108a–117b) was published in facsimile with a Turkish translation by Abdülbaki Gölpinarlı in his collection of *futuwwat-nāmas*: "İslam ve Türk illerinde fütüvvet teşkilatı ve kaynakları," *İstanbul Üniversitesi İktisat Fakültesi Mecmuası* 11.1–4 (1949–1951): 205–231.

consolidation and dissemination at the expense of that of the patron who installed him in the very *ribāṭ*s from which he pursued it in the first place. Although Baghdad's mutually antagonistic Ḥanbalites and Ashʿarites could most certainly be targeted as groups for circumscription by the *ṣūfiyya*, in the case of the city's *fityān* this would have been quite unwise, for to try to circumscribe or co-opt their institutions would be to challenge al-Nāṣir himself, and thus the shaykh had to look elsewhere. For this, he found a space just as heavily populated by Sufis, sympathetic ulama, and a particular grouping of *fityān* who by all accounts were closely associated with the Sufis, Seljuk Konya.

Sometime after the death of his brother Kay Kāwūs I in 617/1220 and his subsequent accession to the throne, the celebrated Seljuk sultan of Rūm ʿAlāʾ al-Dīn Kayqubād (r. 616–634/1219–1237) seems to have sent word to Baghdad requesting a diploma of investiture over the domains he had inherited and perhaps with it the trousers of the Nāṣirian *futuwwa*, his brother having received them from an envoy of al-Nāṣir (Majd al-Dīn Isḥāq) after the conquest of Sinop in 611/1214. As with a similar request sent many years earlier by the Ayyubid sultan al-Malik al-ʿĀdil, al-Nāṣir responded by sending Suhrawardī, an individual who despite his age of almost eighty lunar years was by all accounts still an active and vigorous presence in the *ribāṭ*s over which al-Nāṣir had confirmed his *mashyakha* following his mission to the Khwārazm Shāh some four years earlier. By all accounts too, this was an important journey for Suhrawardī, one during which the shaykh not only received an honorable welcome from the sultan and met the aspiring Kubrawī master Najm al-Dīn al-Rāzī Dāya, but also seems to have developed important contacts with certain groups of *fityān* and *ribāṭ*-based Sufis populating the flourishing city of Konya.

Certainly an event of little interest to the Iraqi and Syrian historiographers, the details of the shaykh's journey and his meeting with ʿAlāʾ al-Dīn Kayqubād are preserved solely in the chronicle a chancellery official of the Rūm Seljuk administration, Ibn-i Bībī (d. c. 683/1284), an account which in a florid Persian typical of the time evinces the well-known policy of the Rūm Seljuks of supporting and patronizing religious scholars and Sufis. He begins:

> When the news of the waxing political power and good fortune of sultan ʿAlāʾ al-Dīn Kayqubād became known to the Caliphal Presence and the Court of the Imamate, al-Nāṣir li-Dīn Allāh, a decree of dominion and vicegerency over the jurisdiction of the lands of Rūm was promulgated, and the caliph recognized his rulership by sending the divine—the Abū

> Yazīd of the age and the second Junayd, who sits in the center of the dome of the saints and the god-fearing, heir to the knowledge of the prophets, quintessence of virtue and pure of the pure, knower of divine realities and scaler of heights and divine mysteries, the Flame of the Community and the Faith, Shaykh of Islam and of the Muslims, guide to kings and sultans, he who calls people to cleave to the Master of the Day of Judgment—Abū ʿAbdullāh ʿUmar b. Muḥammad al-Suhrawardī—may God be pleased with him—to present him with the tokens of kingship: the sword and the signet ring.[38]

The honorifics which Ibn-i Bībī heaps upon Suhrawardī—while certainly not stylistically unusual—clearly resonate with the representations of the shaykh we have already encountered in the hagiographies, namely the unification of *sharʿī* and mystical knowledge, heirship to the knowledge of the prophets (*vārith-i ʿulūm-i anbiyā*), and most importantly his role as guide to sultans and kings. In fact, Suhrawardī addressed a letter of recommendation to ʿAlāʾ al-Dīn Kayqubād on behalf of the aspiring Najm al-Dīn Rāzī Dāya, the author later dedicating his comprehensive Sufi manual, the *Mirṣād al-ʿibād*, to this particular patron, a manual which includes sections devoted specifically to the wayfaring (*sulūk*) of kings and ministers.[39]

Like al-Nāṣir, as well as Saladin and a number of the later Ayyubid princes, ʿAlāʾ al-Dīn Kayqubād was a patron of religious scholars and Sufis, something well evinced in his having installed Bahāʾ al-Dīn Valad in Konya's Altın Apa Madrasa upon his arrival in the city some years later (c. 626/1229), perhaps replicating the practice of Niẓām al-Mulk whose *Siyāsat-nāma* he is said to have read.[40] The setup complete, the stage was now set for the meeting of these two luminaries, one a patron of ulama and Sufis, and the other no stranger to such men. Ibn-i Bībī continues:

> When the sultan was informed of the arrival of the luminous shaykh at Ak Sarāy he sent numerous amirs with supplies to receive him, and when

[38] This and the translations which follow are based on the combined reports preserved in Ibn-i Bībī, *al-Awāmir al-alāʾiyya*, ed. Necati Lugal and Adnan Sadık Erzi (Ankara: Türk Tarih Kurumu Basımevi, 1957), 1:229–231; idem (anonymous Persian epitome), *Mukhtaṣar-i saljūqnāma*, in *Recueil de textes relatifs à l'histoire des seldjoucides*, ed. M. Th. Houtsma (Leiden: E.J. Brill, 1902) 4:94–97; and the Turkish epitome of Yazıcıoğlu ʿAlī, *Tawārikh-i āl-i saljūq*, in ibid., 3:220–227/H.W. Duda (trans.), *Die Seltschukengeschichte des Ibn Bībī* (Copenhagen: Munksgaard, 1959), 101–104.

[39] *PGB*, 11–12, 45–46, 48–49, 56–57, 395–444.

[40] Claude Cahen, *The Formation of Turkey*, trans. P.M. Holt (London: Logman, 2001), 53, 162–163, 168; and, Lewis, *Rumi*, 74–81.

he arrived at the way station of Zinjīrlū as many groups as possible went out to greet him: judges, imams, shaykhs, Sufis (*mutaṣavvifa*), notables, and 'Akhīs' (*ikhwān/fityān*).[41] With a fully decorated army, the sultan himself set out to meet him, and when his eyes fell on the blessed countenance of the shaykh he said, 'this face resembles that visage which during the night a day ago freed me from the imprisonment of sleep, mounted me on a steed, and said that the special favor (*himmat*) of ʿUmar Muḥammad-i Suhravardī will be with me continuously.' When he finally drew near, they embraced and shook hands, and the shaykh said. 'since the night of imprisonment the thoughts (*khāṭir*) of ʿUmar Muḥammad-i Suhravardī have been continuously directed towards the sultan of Islam and we owe thanks to God that before descending into the orbit of ease, it is necessary for one to acquire that which cannot be replaced, so 'praise be to God who has removed from us all sorrow'.' After exchanging greetings, and with an extraordinary sense of happiness and elation, the sultan hurried to kiss the shaykh's blessed hand. By this, the 'articles of his creed' were doubled and his reverence for the shaykh reached the utmost limit, and thereupon he wished, like Ibrāhīm b. Adham, to take the way (*ṭarīq*) of Jesus, son of Mary.[42] However, the shaykh—by way of his illuminated vision (*naẓar-i nūrānī*)—was able to apprehend the inspirations and thoughts of the sultan and he gave a reply to each and every one of them, allaying the confusion born of a desire which had been placed in his being on the Day of the Primordial Covenant (*rūz-i alast*).[43] He offered an interpretation, reciting: 'not one of us but has a place appointed', and 'every duty has its man', enjoining him to dispense justice and nourish religion. And so by the time the sultan arrived in the city he had disposed of all his royal trappings, pride, haughtiness, and forgetfulness; and like the soul of an angel, he could do no wrong.

[41] The lists and designations differ somewhat. The *Awāmir* itself reads: "judges, imams, shaykhs, Sufis, notables, brethren (*akhīs*?), and the *fityān* of Konya" (*quḍāt o aʾimma o mashāyikh o mutaṣavvifa o aʿyān o ikhwān o fityān-i qūnya*) (1:230); the *Mukhtaṣar* leaves out 'the *fityān* of Konya' (94–95); whereas Yazıcıoğlu ʿAlī has only "judges, *imāms*, shaykhs of the Sufis, and notables" (*qāḍīları ve aʾimma ve mashāyikh-i mutaṣavvıfa ve aʿyānı*" (*Tawārikh*, 220).

[42] Ibrāhīm b. Adham (d. c. 161/778), one of the earliest paragons of the Sufi tradition, is remembered as a prince from Balkh who underwent a sudden conversion experience which led him (like the figure of Gautama Buddha) to renounce his position and pursue the path of spiritual asceticism; see al-Sulamī, *Ṭabaqāt*, 35–42 (+ fn. 3 for refs. to other sources); and, al-Iṣfahānī, *Ḥilyat*, 7:426–452.

[43] That is, the primordial 'Day of the Covenant' (*yawm al-mīthāq*) referred to in Qurʾān 7:172 when God called out the pre-created human souls from the loins of the not-yet-created progeny of Adam and asked them: "am I not your Lord?" (*a-lastu bi-rabbikum*), to which they replied: "Yes, we witness it" (*balā shahidnā*), a reference which came to be endlessly expounded upon—as existential event, idea, and poetic image—in the works of numerous Sufis and others; see: Louis Massignon, "Le "jour du covenant" (*yawm al-mīthāq*)," *Oriens* 15 (1962): 86–92.

Beyond the typical hagiographical figuration of Suhrawardī as a Sufi master possessed of great cardiognostic skills (*firāsa*) and the standard trope of the king renouncing his kingdom to pursue the spiritual life, Ibn-i Bībī's enumeration of those particular groups who came out to meet Suhrawardī is important, in particular the last group which he mentions, the brethren (*ikhwān*) and *fityān* of Konya.

As in Baghdad, Seljuk Konya was possessed of a well-entrenched form of 'chivalric' organization, a grouping of *fityān* which seems to have existed alongside the courtly *futuwwa* as envisioned by al-Nāṣir and the organized solidarities of the Sufi *ribāṭ*s and *khānaqāh*s as envisioned by Suhrawardī. These were the Turkic Akhī brotherhoods, a specific form of the *futuwwa* (*akhī-fityān*) known to us through a number of contemporary accounts, documents, treatises and inscriptions.[44] As a form of social organization, *akhilik* was an urban phenomenon, an intentional community of like-minded, usually unmarried, young men linked to certain collectivities of urban artisans and neighborhood militias who adhered to the ideals of the *futuwwa* and pursued a communal way of life centered around a lodge (*zāwiya/āstāna*). It is to this group in particular, to whom we shall return presently, where Suhrawardī seems to have directed the bulk of his attention after discharging his official duties on behalf of the caliph:

> The following day, the shaykh was called to the royal pavilion so that the sultan could don the caliphal robe of honor and place upon his head the turban which had already been wrapped in Baghdad. And in front of an assemblage of people forty blows were struck on the sultan's back with a baton (*ʿaṣā*) which is customarily kept in an honored place in the *dār al-khilāfa*, and then a steed from the same place, shod in gold, was brought in, and in the presence of the assemblage the sultan kissed the hoof of the Imam's horse. Thereupon, the great shaykh mounted him upon the steed and the entire assemblage quietly observed the sultan in his new position. When things returned to normal and the tables were returned and set, professional singers (*qawwālān-i khāṣṣ*) began to perform the *samāʿ*. Some advanced aspirants—who were disciples of shaykhs Gūr and Najd—had been crossing through and they immediately fell into ecstasy (*wajd*). And from the tasting (*dhawq*) of that *samāʿ* desire manifested

[44] On which, see Neş'et Çağatay, "Fütüvvet-Ahi Müessesesinin Menşi Meselesi," *Ankara Üniversitesi İlâhiyat Fakültesi Dergisi* 1 (1952): 59–84, 1.2–3 (1952): 61–84; Taeschner, "Futuwwa, eine gemeinschaftbildende Idee," 144–151; Breebaart, "Development and Structure," 109–145; Taeschner, "Akhī," *EI²*, 1:321–323; Claude Cahen, "Sur les traces des premiers Akhis," in *Mélanges Fuad Köprülü* (Istanbul: Osman Yalçın Matbaası, 1953), 81–91; and, idem, *The Formation of Turkey*, 116–121.

itself in each and every person present. Thereupon, the sultan and the other *amirs*, especially Jalāl al-Dīn Qaraṭaj, carried out the ritual shaving (*miqrā-kārī*), and when the shaykh alighted upon the blessed station he favored the sultan with his absolute and undivided attention.

Both the presence of Sufis and the performance of the *samāʿ* in the court is of obvious importance, but beyond that is the investiture ceremony itself. Marked as it is with some familiar tokens, namely the caliphal robe of honor (*khilʿat-i khilāfat*), sword (*ḥusām*), and signet ring (*nigīn*), it is clear that the ceremony was indented to convey the delivery of a diploma of investiture (*tashrīf-i shahryārī*), similar to that conducted by Suhrawardī for the Ayyubids in Damascus many years earlier. As with this mission as well—al-Malik al-ʿĀdil and his sons already having received the trousers of the *futuwwa* some five years earlier (599/1203)[45]—it is not entirely clear if Suhrawardī actually initiated ʿAlāʾ al-Dīn Kayqubād into the Nāṣirian *futuwwa*, for Ibn-i Bībī does not mention the most important token of initiation: the trousers (*sirwāl*; pl. *sarāwīl*).

At the same time however, the presence of the turban, the ritualized striking, the performance of the ritual of shaving (*miqrā-kārī*), all seem to point to some type of initiation ceremony distinct from the delivery of a diploma of investiture, although in the absence of corroborating sources, it is difficult to define what it might have been. Perhaps it is reflective of a local form of initiation associated with the *akhī-fityān*, for the practice of the *samāʿ* among the Akhīs is mentioned by Ibn Baṭṭūṭa as well as in the versified late 7th/13th-century Persian *akhī-fityān* manual of Nāṣirī and in the late 8th/14th-century Turkish *akhī-fityān* manual of Yaḥyā b. Khalīl (Çoban) al-Burgāzī, as is the ritual of shaving.[46] Be that as it may, our court chronicler then ends his account with a statement reflective the type of authority which such individuals possessed in the eyes of such rulers, underscoring the sanctity associated with Sufi masters such as Suhrawardī:

All the while during the shaykh's residence in Konya, the sultan found himself again and again benefiting from his blessing (*baraka*). During the

---

[45] *MZ*, 8.2:513; *DhR*, 33; *SN*, 22:194, and, *TIsl*, 48:50 (*ḥawādith, anno* 599); *BN*, 13:34; Breebaart, "Development and Structure," 53–54; *Nsr.*, 107; and, idem, "Al-Nāṣir," *EI*², 7:998.

[46] Nāṣirī, *Futuwwat-nāma*, ed. Franz Taeschner (Leipzig: Deutsche Morgenländischen Gesellschaft, Kommission Verlag F.A. Brockhaus, 1944), lines 798–852; and, Yaḥyā b. Khalīl al-Burgāzī, *Fütüvvetnāme*, ed. Abdülbaki Gölpinarlı in "Burghazī ve Fütüvvetnāmesi," *İstanbul Üniversitesi İktisat Fakültesi Mecmuası* 15.1–4 [1953–1954], 137, 147.

> time when the shaykh was coming and going from his immediate presence, the *kharāj* of the Christians and Armenians amounted to 100,000 dirhams, and 5000 gold sultan's dinars, either 500 or 150 *mithqāl* in weight, were struck with the ʿAlāʾī mint stamp. Also, other types of good fortune came to him through associating (*dar suḥbat*) with Qaraṭaj and Najm al-Dīn Ṭūsī such as administrative expenditures remaining the same. He then bid farewell to Zinjīlī—which is one *farsakh* from Konya—and he would ask for help from the spiritual favor which accrued to the place from his being there.

By all accounts, Suhrawardī seems to have made quite an impression in Anatolia. In addition to the narrative of Ibn-i Bībī and Najm al-Dīn Rāzī Dāya's account of his meeting with the shaykh in Malatya, Suhrawardī's visit to Anatolia was also preserved in the collective memory of the Sufis of Konya for a least a century. In his *Manāqib al-ʿārifīn*, the great Mevlevi hagiographer Shams al-Dīn-i Aflākī vividly recounts the shaykh's—chronologically implausible—meetings with both Bahāʾ al-Dīn Valad and Sayyid Burhān al-Dīn during his visit to the Seljuk imperial capital, emplotting Suhrawardī's presence in his grand hagiographical drama as an legitimating device.[47] As already discussed, such meetings were re-imagined for other purposes, but what is important for us is the persistence of the memory. Alongside this, throughout his narrative Aflākī evinces connections between Anatolian *akhilik* and the Mevlevi masters, citing numerous episodes which find Sufis and Akhīs associating with one another and, in no small number of cases, frequenting the same masters. The persistence of such a memory evinces the early importance of social and institutional connections between the *futuwwat* and nascent *ṭarīqa*-based Sufism in Turko-Iranian Sufi landscapes which would become ubiquitous two centuries later,[48] a connection which although not easily discernable from Ibn-i Bībī's account of his visit, is clearly evinced in Suhrawardī's two *Futuwwat-nāma*s.

Unlike Ibn al-Miʿmār and al-Khartabirtī, Suhrawardī does not mention his patron's name in either of his two *Futuwwat-nāmas*, something which seems quite unusual for a *Ratgeber und Hoftheologe* who had

---

[47] Aflākī, *The Feats of the Knowers of God*, 14–17, 34–35, 53–54; see also Cahen, "Sur les traces," 83–91.

[48] This is well evinced in the *Futuvvat-nāma-yi sulṭānī* of Ḥusayn Vāʿiẓ-i Kāshifī (d. 910/1504), on which see Jean-Claude Vadet "La 'Futuwwa', morale professionnelle ou morale mystique?," *REI* 46:1 (1978) 57–90; and, Kathryn Babayan, *Mystics, Monarchs, and Messiahs: Cultural Landscapes of Early Modern Iran* (Cambridge, MA: Harvard University Press, 2002), 165–204.

developed a comprehensive new *Chalifatstheorie* predicated on a union between Sufism, the *futuwwa*, and the caliphate.[49] Given the content and language of the works, this would have made little sense anyway since they were clearly not written with the Nāṣirian *futuwwa* in mind, but rather for those Anatolian *akhī-fityān* whom Ibn-i Bībī reports came out in great numbers to greet the shaykh during his visit.

In a much more immediate way than what an Abbasid genealogy for the *futuwwa* might have done for him, Suhrawardī was already—or perhaps at this time enunciated—a personal connection to the *futuwwa*, in specific a connection to those particular *akhī-fityān* populating the cities of Anatolia. This connection in fact comes within Suhrawardī's own *nisbat al-khirqa*, an *isnād* he himself transmitted to one of his disciples, one which up until today is repeated as such and accepted without comment among the Suhrawardiyya. In the *nasab* of the very *khirqa* which was bestowed upon him by Abū ʾl-Najīb and which Suhrawardī then passed on his disciples and they to theirs, we find the figure of none other than Akhī Faraj Zanjānī (d. 457/1065), the patron saint of Anatolian *akhilik*.[50] In his account of his *nisbat al-khirqa*, Suhrawardī states that Akhī Faraj had invested his great-uncle Wajīh al-Dīn al-Suhrawardī

---

[49] Hartmann, "Conception governementale," 56–57, 60; *Nṣr.*, 111–118; idem, "Al-Nāṣir," *EI²*, 7:1000; idem, "al-Suhrawardī, S͟hihāb al-Dīn Abū Ḥafṣ ʿUmar," *EI²*, 9:779; often repeated (e.g., Black, *History of Islamic Political Thought*, 133–134). I am not the first to raise such objections (e.g., Vadet, "La futuwwa," 71–72, fn. 1). It is, of course, quite possible that at some point Suhrawardī did claim an Abbasid genealogy for the *futuwwa*. Such a connection, in fact, is found in the *Futuwwat-nāma* of Najm al-Dīn Zarkūb (d. 712/1313), the son of one of Suhrawardī's disciples from Shiraz, ʿIzz al-Dīn Zarkūb (d. 663/1264–65) in a section arguing for the legitimacy of the ritual of drinking salted water: "I heard that our master, king of the ulama and *fityān*, pillar of the community and the faith, is reported to have said: 'our genealogy (*shajara-yi mā*) is the genealogy of the shaykh of the shaykhs, paragon of the poles, master of seekers, the late Shaykh Shihāb al-Dīn-i Suhravardī. His method of training (*ṭarīqa-yi tarbiyyat*) in the *ṭarīqat, sharīʿat, ḥaqīqat*, and *futuwwat* was perfect, and he possessed an initiatic genealogy for the *futuvvat* from the caliph Nāṣir (*ū-rā nisbat-i futuvvat bā khalīfa-yi jahān nāṣir-i khalīfa būda ast*); it is written in his own hand that: the Commander of the Faithful ʿAlī b. Abī Ṭālib used to give salted water (*namak o āb mī-dād*)." (Najm al-Dīn Zarkūb, *Futuwwat-nāma*, ed. Sarraf in *Traites*, 191); cf. the detailed genealogies of the Nāṣirian *futuwwa* given by Ibn al-Miʿmār (*K. al-futuwwa*, 143–149) and Khartabirtī (*Tuḥfat al-waṣāyā*, 205–206).

[50] A contemporary of Hujwīrī, alleged *pīr* of the great Persian poet Niẓāmī (a chronological impossibility), and a disciple of Abū ʾl-ʿAbbās Nihāwandī (whence the link in Suhrawardī's *nisbat al-khirqa*), Hujwīrī mentions Akhī Faraj Zanjānī among the modern Sufis of Quhistān, Azerbaijan, Ṭabaristān, and Kumish, calling him "a man of good manners (*mardī nīgū-siyar*) and admirable doctrine (*sitūda ṭarīqat*)" (*Kashf*, 215/ Nicholson, *The Kashf*, 173; see also: Jāmī, *Nafaḥāt*, 150–151; Taeschner, "Futuwwa, eine gemeinschaftbildende Idee," 145; idem, "Ak͟hī," *EI²*, 1:322; idem and Cahen, "Futuwwa," *EI²*, 2:966; and, Cahen, "Sur les traces," 81–82).

with the *khirqa* in a simultaneous investiture ceremony connected alongside his father, Muḥammad b. ʿAbdullāh, both *khirqa*s reaching back to al-Junayd, and from him to the Prophet through a generic Junaydī *nasab al-ṣuḥba* evinced in many later *ṭarīqa*-lineages as well as through a second line through the Shiite Imāms up to ʿAlī al-Riḍā, also not usual in the initiatic genealogies of later *ṭarīqa*-lineages.[51] Although not mentioned in his two *Futuwwat-nāma*s, nor in any of his other texts save in a number of *ijāza*s, there is little reason to doubt that Suhrawardī would not have made this genealogy known to those whom he addresses as '*akhī*s'.

What then might have been Suhrawardī's connection, if any, to the Nāṣirian *futuwwa* and how have he might have envisioned himself and the *ṭāʾifa* for whom he spoke within it? Quite in contradistinction to the handbooks of Ibn al-Miʿmār and al-Khartabirtī, his two *Futuwwat-nāma*s offer no answer. In fact, throughout the nearly one-thousand pages of printed text and manuscript folios constituting his entire *œuvre*, he devotes no more than a dozen lines to the issue, certainly not developing any type of grand *Chalifatstheorie* revolving around some effective union between the caliphate, Sufism, and the *futuwwa* as Hartmann has asserted. Given what we have seen so far, and this should not be considered unusual, the sole reference which Suhrawardī makes to the 'Nāṣirian *futuwwa*' comes late, in fact very late, namely following his enunciation of the connection (*munāsaba*) between the caliphate and Sufism in the *Idālat al-ʿiyān* quoted earlier. As Suhrawardī makes quite clear, at this point the *futuwwa* itself was no longer Nāṣirian in any case, but rather Mustanṣirian:

> The honorable caliphate is a register (*daftar*) of which Sufism is a part (*juzʾ*) and Sufism a register of which the *futuwwa* is a part. The *futuwwa* is distinguished by pure morals (*akhlāq zakiyya*), Sufism by the unification of pious praxis with noble spiritual litanies (*bi-jamʿ bayna al-aʿmāl al-ṣāliḥa wa-l-awrād al-ʿazīza*), and the honorable caliphate by the unification of noble spiritual states (*aḥwāl sharīfa*), pious praxis, and pure morals. In a

[51] This *nasab* is given by Suhrawardī in an *ijāza* he wrote for ʿAlī b. Aḥmad al-Rāzī (MS. Süley., Musalla Medresesi 20_{14}, fol. 295b; also: *Nisbat al-khirqat al-Suhrawardī* I, MS. Tüb., Ma VI 90_{68}, fol. 132a; *Nisbat al-khirqat al-Suhrawardī* II, MS. Süley., Fatih 2741, fol. 1a; *MJ*, 3:40–41 [s.v. Najm al-Dīn Kubrā]; Jāmī, *Nafaḥāt*, 558–559 [no. 546]; and, Maʿṣūmʿalīshāh, *Ṭarāʾiq al-ḥaqāʾiq*, ed. Muḥammad Jaʿfar Maḥjūb [Tehran: Kitābkhāna-yi Bārānī, 1950], 2:309–310, 322, 442). Although completely lost on the later Suhrawardiyya sources, given the connections between the early Safavids and the Anatolian *akhī*s and the fact that this *nisbat al-khirqa* (from Abū ʾl-Najīb) figures in the early Ṣafawiyya *silsila* (see Chapter Two, Chart 3), this node probably retained some of its initial resonance even after the 7th/13th century.

> moment, we will recount some tales (*ḥikāyāt*) of the *fityān* and explain the *futuwwa* of the most munificent of successors, the fortunes of whose star has risen and whose rain clouds have burst forth to renew a most honorable dress (*libās*), a link between (*irtibāṭ bayna*) the two Imams, the Commander of the Faithful ʿAlī and the Commander of the Faithful al-Mustanṣir bi-Llāh, a link which strings the pearls: Hāshimī, then Qurayshī, then Muḍarī...all of the *fityān* being strung in an honorable, centuries-old order.[52]

Whether a comprehensive alternative to the *siyāsa sharʿiyya* discourse—which Suhrawardī upholds in a text which was actually composed during al-Nāṣir's heyday (the *Aʿlām al-hudā*) in any event—can be constructed in a few dozen lines seems highly unlikely. This point must be kept in mind when reading the shaykh's two *Futuwwat-nāma*s, for they really only make sense when disconnected from al-Nāṣir's vision of the *futuwwa* and situated where they rightly belong, in Suhrawardī's own program of disseminating his *ribāṭ*-based Sufi system, in this case in a very specific place and among a very specific group of *fityān*.

Like the *ʿAwārif al-maʿārif*, or the *K. al-futuwwa* of Ibn al-Miʿmār and the *Tuḥfat al-waṣāyā* of al-Khartabirtī, Suhrawardī's two *Futuwwat-nāma*s were written as guidebooks, and like them, and much like the *akhī-fityān* manuals of Nāṣirī and Yaḥyā b. Khalīl Çoban, the history of their preservation is deeply telling. Although the rest of Suhrawardī's *œuvre*, comprised of over fifty treatises in both Arabic and Persian was carefully preserved by Suhrawardiyya communities and others in Iran and India, and whose manuscript record is scattered from Cairo to Istanbul and from Tehran to Lahore, not one of the many anthologies (*majmūʿāt*) in which Suhrawardī's works are found preserve even a single quote from either of these two texts. In fact, only a few copies of Suhrawardī's two *Futuwwat-nāma*s are extant at all, the longer of the two only in an anthology of treatises on the *futuwwa* which was most certainly copied in Anatolia and is now held in Süleymaniye Library in Istanbul,[53] and

[52] al-Suhrawardī, *Idālat*, fol. 89a–89b; cf. Hartmann, "La conception gouvernementale," 58; idem, *Nṣr.*, 116; idem, "al-Nāṣir," *EI*^{2}, 7:1000; and, idem, "al-Suhrawardī," *EI*^{2}, 9:779, who save in all but one instance fails mention the reference to al-Mustanṣir. The relationship between the Nāṣirian *futuwwa* and the Sufism of Baghdad's *ribāṭ*s is unclear in any case. Although careful to differentiate the Nāṣirian *futuwwa* from it Ibn al-Miʿmār, for instance, states that there is no harm in the *fatā* frequenting *ribāṭ*s (*K. al-futuwwa*, 151, 233), but this tells us little. A thorough study is much needed, which would first require a careful sifting of the historiography and prosopography in search of individuals who populated both spaces.

[53] That is, the *K. fī ʾl-futuwwa* which is preserved solely in MS. Süley., Ayasofya

the shorter in three manuscripts copied in Turko-Persian milieux, the most important of which is contained in an anthology copied in the Crimea in the 8th/14th century now held in the Bibliothèque Nationale in Paris.[54]

As with the particularities of their contents, this textual memory certainly accords with the picture of a certain type of widespread, urban *futuwwa/javānmardī* tradition associated with trade guilds, *ṭarīqa*-based Sufism, and various urban collectivities as a phenomenon localized almost wholly in Turko-Persian landscapes after the Mongol invasions. In short, like the handbooks of Ibn al-Miʿmār and al-Khartabirtī which were no longer applicable following the destruction of the Abbasid caliphate at the hands of the Mongols in 656/1258, and consequently were not copied, Suhrawardī's two manuals were simply not of interest to those of his disciples who propagated his teachings outside of Anatolia—places like Syria, Egypt, Iran, and North India having little need for manuals on *akhilik*. At the same time, they did remain relevant to the *akhī-fityān* of Anatolia prior to the gradual submergence of their traditions in other social collectivities in the profound transformations wrought by the Ottoman imperial project, and thus like the *Futuwwat-nāmas* of Nāṣirī and Yaḥyā b. Khalīl Çoban, were copied for a time at least. Not in Baghdad, Cairo, Isfahan, or Ucch, but rather in places like southern Anatolia and the Crimea.

When read alongside Suhrawardī's other works, these two texts present a number of things worthy of note. First, as in his works on Sufism where we find him laying claim to and then refashioning the textual past of the particular strand of the Junaydī Sufi tradition to which he considered himself an heir, in these two works the past undergoes a decisive transformation, a shift in content, focus, and language which takes the moral and ethical elaborations characteristic of earlier Sufi

2049_{16}, fol. 158b–181b, part of an extremely important anthology comprised of 25 texts on the *futuwwa*. The text was edited by Morteza Sarraf in his important collection of Persian treatises on the *futuwwa* (*Traites des compagnons-chevaliers*, 104–166) which includes a short analysis of the work by Henry Corbin ("Introduction analytique", 49–59). Franz Taeschner has provided a summary of the work (*Zünfte und Bruderschaften im Islam*, 254–256; also, idem, "Eine Schrift des Šihābaddīn Suhrawardī über die Futūwa," *Oriens* 15 [1962]: 278–280).

[54] That is, MS. Bibliothèque Nationale de France, Supplément Persan 113, fol. 50b–60b, the *R. fī 'l-futuwwa* (*Shajarat al-futuwwa ḥilyat li-ahl al-muruwwa*). Much shorter than the *K. fī 'l-futuwwa*, this text was also edited by Sarraf (*Traites des compagnons-chevaliers*, 90–102), and is also extant in MS. Süley., Ayasofya 2049_{15}, fol. 154a–158b, and, MS. Süley., Ayasofya 3135_{4}, fol. 185a–190b.

discourse such as Sulamī's *K. fī 'l-futuwwa* or Qushayrī's chapter on the *futuwwa* in the *Risāla* and subjects them to the same institutionalizing vision.[55] Much like the transformation in Suhrawardī's conceptualization of the Sufi tradition, in fact, the transformation which the *futuwwa* undergoes in his works decidedly attends to the specificities of his historical moment, reconfiguring the past by blending the ethical and moral qualities constituting the discourse of Sulamī and Qushayrī with a systematized and thoroughly rule-governed vision of behavior and praxis situated squarely within the type of *jamāʿī-sunnī* communalism undergirding his vision of a complete and universal *ribāṭ*-based Sufi system.

As already noted, in the main this shift was from the personal to the institutional and from the theoretical to the practical, articulated in a rhetoric which self-consciously asserts control over multiple locations of authority and then systematical positions and deploys that authority from a new center. As in his works on *ribāṭ*-based Sufism, in Suhrawardī's two *Futuwwat-nāma*s three broad thematic clusters emerge as the primary pivots of a broader institutionalizing vision: 1) the enunciation of a mytho-historical genealogy which is programmatically projected into the present; 2) the systematization of hierarchies of affiliation; and, 3) the prescription of socially regulated and rule-governed modes of behavior through which such hierarchies are maintained. Let us take each in turn.

As with the praxic and institutional linkages which Suhrawardī draws between the *futuwwa* and the *ribāṭ*-based system of Sufism which he championed, the genealogical connections which he forges in his *Futuwwat-nāma*s were neither accidental nor chosen haphazardly. As in his other works, Suhrawardī programmatically unearths linkages both between and among self-constituted solidarities, in this case connecting Anatolian *akhilik*—and perhaps the urban artisan guilds from which at least some of their constituency was drawn—to the hierarchical yet socially open form of *ribāṭ*-based Sufism which he had quite successfully cultivated in Baghdad. As with the genealogy of the sciences of the Sufis which Suhrawardī lays out in the *ʿAwārif al-maʿārif*, in his *Futuwwat-nāma*s the shaykh characterizes the *futuwwa* as an Adamic inheritance,

---

[55] al-Sulamī, *K. al-futuwwa*, in *MA*, 2:220–333. In that ever important anthology of *futuwwa* texts (MS. Süley., Ayasofya 2049) there is also a is also a short work ascribed to ʿAbdullāh-i Anṣārī which covers much of the same ground (fol. 149a–154b; see: Ahmet Yaşar Ocak, "Fütüvvetnâme," *TDVİA*, 13:264).

a discrete body of knowledge and praxis grouped alongside the entirety of the crafts and trades (*ṣanʿat o ḥirfat*) which Adam bequeathed to his progeny. Genealogically, the *futuwwa* is associated with Adam's son Seth, an individual who according to Suhrawardī was not only the recipient of the complex of attitudes and praxis of the primordial *futuwwa* from his father Adam but also the first to practice the craft of weaving, being the first to weave a woolen garment and consequently the first human being who could properly be called a Sufi.[56] Here, we run into the issue of specification, for as Suhrawardī reminds us, just as the sciences of the Sufis were not formally constituted as a discrete body of transmittable knowledge and endeavor until the age of the *salaf al-ṣāliḥ* so too was the Sethian inheritance originally an undifferentiated science which comprised the totality of what would later become the *futuwwat* and the *ṭarīqat* proper.

According to Suhrawardī, the formal differentiation between the *futuwwat* and the *ṭarīqat* took place under Abraham in response to the difficulties inherent in the latter, some of his companions having complained that they were simply to weak to wear the *khirqa* of the *ṭarīqat* and thus he divided the complex into two into parts, he and his companions setting sail on the ocean of the *ṭarīqat* until they finally reached the island of the *futuwwat* at which point some disembarked.[57] In turn, Abraham passed on both the *futuwwat* and the *ṭarīqa* to his son Ishmael, and he to the generations which followed up to the Prophet

[56] al-Suhrawardī, *R. fī 'l-futuwwa*, 91–92. The idea of a Sethian genealogy for the *futuwwa* neither originated nor stopped with Suhrawardī, being evinced in the lost *futuwwa* manual of the 5th/11th-century littérateur and leader of a group of Baghdadi *fityān* (who was accused and tried as a propagandist for the Fāṭimids) Ibn Rasūlī (Abū Naṣr Muḥammad b. ʿAbd al-Bāqī Khabbāz) whom according to Ibn al-Jawzī posited the same genealogy from Adam to Seth to Muḥammad given by Suhrawardī (*MT*, 8:326–327). Likewise, the Sethian genealogy of the *futuwwa* given by Suhrawardī was repeated later, such as by Kāshifī (*Futuwwat-nāma-yi sulṭānī*, ed. Muḥammad Jaʿfar Maḥjūb [Tehran: Bunyād-i Farhang-i Īrān, 1350 (1972)], 6–7); cf. Sulamī who a century earlier than Ibn Rasūlī also mentions Seth, saying: "the first to follow the call of *futuwwa* was Adam... Abel (Hābīl) took it up when Cain (Qābīl) rejected it and Seth adhered to its right and protected it from everything improper." (*K. al-futuwwa*, in *MA*, 2:225–226).

[57] al-Suhrawardī, *R. fī 'l-futuwwa*, 92–94; Taeschner, "Eine Schrift," 278; and, Breebaart, "Development and Structure," 118; same in Kāshifī, *Futuwwat-nāma-yi sulṭānī*, 7; but cf. Ibn al-Miʿmār who clearly places the origin of the *futuwwa* and its initiatic lineage (*mabdaʾ al-futuwwa wa-manshaʾuhā*) in the figure of Abraham, the 'father of all chevaliers' (*abū 'l-fityān*). (*K. al-futuwwa*, 140–141); similar statement and somewhat different genealogy by Nāṣirī (*Futuwwat-nāma*, lines 47–84 [partial], 164–220, 462–486, 539–548 [Gabriel invests Abraham with the trousers (*shalvār*) + eventual transmission to the Banū Hāshim, Muḥammad to ʿAlī and on to Salmān-i Fārisī]).

Muḥammad who subsequently passed it on to his cousin and son-in-law ʿAlī. As Suhrawardī takes great pains to explain, from Seth to Abraham and from Ishmael to Muḥammad both the *futuwwa* and *ṭarīqat* were passed on concomitantly with prophethood (*nubuwwat*), but with ʿAlī only the former two became his inheritance (*mīrāth*).[58] From here, both the *futuwwat* the *ṭarīqat* became the patrimony of the house of ʿAlī, passed on to al-Ḥasan and al-Ḥusayn (and a portion to Fāṭima) at which point, where we would expect him to bring it down to the House of ʿAbbās, he ends the narrative. Certainly, for the authors of manuals on the Nāṣirian *futuwwa* such as Ibn al-Miʿmār and al-Khartabirtī leaving this out would have been unthinkable. For Suhrawardī and the *akhī-fityān* of Konya, however, it made little difference.

The second thematic cluster is institutional and organizational. While the moral and ethical dimensions of the *futuwwa* presented in the works of Sulamī and Qushayrī play an important role in Suhrawardī's two treatises on the subject, they are subordinated to the organizational and institutional particulars of the tradition as configured in the forms of social organization embedded in urban landscapes of medieval Islamdom. As in his works on *ribāṭ*-based Sufism, Suhrawardī's *Futuwwat-nāma*s display a marked concern with structure and form, configuring identity and process as a determinant of content and prioritizing the actual organizational and institutional structures of the *futuwwa* over and against the moral and ethical attitudes underlying them. This convergence is expressed in real terms, specifically in the overt linkages which Suhrawardī makes between the Sufism of the *ribāṭ*s and the *futuwwat* of the *akhī-fityān*, using the same terminology of hierarchy and affiliation found in the manuals of Nāṣirī and Yaḥyā b. Khalīl Çoban.

Here, a number of linkages stand out as primary. The first has to do with descriptive connections between the actual constituents of the *ribāṭ* and what Suhrawardī calls over and over again the '*futuwwat-khāna*', namely the hierarchy of affiliation and levels of participation which were allowed to obtain in each. Like the Sufis of Baghdad, he presents the

[58] al-Suhrawardī, *R. fī ʾl-futuwwa*, 100–101; and, idem, *K. fī ʾl-futuwwa*, 112; also Taeschner, "Eine Schrift," 278–279. His comments evincing what one would naturally expect from Suhrawardī as well as hinting at the particular context in which he wrote the work. He mitigates this, however, by quoting the typical *ḥadīth*s one often meets with in such *futuwwat-nāma*s, such as "there is no valiant youth (*fatā*) save ʿAlī, nor a sword save Dhū ʾl-Fiqar", "I am the city of knowledge and ʿAlī its gate", "O' ʿAlī, you are to me as Aaron was to Moses", and so forth (*K. fī ʾl-futuwwa*, 108–109; cf. Ibn al-Miʿmār, *K. al-futuwwa*, 136; and, Nāṣirī, *Futuwwat-nāma*, lines 15–27).

Akhīs of Anatolia as an intentional community, a group of brethren (*barādarān*) tied together by both a certain *esprit de corps* and commonality of purpose revolving around a shared allegiance to a particular master (*ustād*). In both spaces, the position of master is presented as central and absolute, and as long as his dictates do not contradict the *sharīʿa* or the rules of the *futuwwat*, he is not to be challenged or questioned for any reason. At the same time, the institutional organization of the *futuwwat-khāna* as represented by Suhrawardī mirrored the general trend towards a more open mode of affiliation and participation characteristic of his Baghdad *ribāṭ*s. In both spaces, individuals were invited to participate in the life and praxis of the community at a level of their own choosing, each bringing with it certain rights and responsibilities.

Like the Sufi *ribāṭ*, Suhrawardī describes the population of the *futuwwat-khāna* as being set into two main tiers, and in his *Futuwwat-nāma*s both of these tiers are explicitly identified as being equivalent to the two main tiers of the Sufi *ribāṭ*. Drawing an explicit connection between the two, the first differentiation he makes is between the 'verbal member' (*qawlī-fatā*) whom he equates with the *mutashabbih* who is characterized by his taking the *khirqa-yi tabarruk* and the 'sword-bearing member' (*sayfī-fatā*) whom he equates with the *murīd* who is characterized by his taking the *khirqa-yi bi-ḥaqq* (i.e., the *khirqat al-irāda*).[59] As with the *mutashabbih* in the Sufi *ribāṭ*, the *qawlī-fatā* of the *futuwwat-khāna* associates himself with the master and community as a 'lay member', making a verbal pronouncement to uphold the virtues of the *futuwwat* but not being obligated to fulfill all of its requirements. On the other hand, like the *murīd* of the *ribāṭ* the *sayfī-fatā* of the *futuwwat-khāna* is spoken of as a 'full member', one who makes a formal commitment (*ʿahd*), in this case to fully uphold all the rules and regulations of the *futuwwat* and place himself under the direction of a master.[60]

As with the *murīd* in the Sufi *ribāṭ*, Suhrawardī speaks of the *sayfī-fatā* in the *futuwwat-khāna* as being a student of a master, specifically an 'apprentice' (*tarbiyeh*) who just like his equivalent relates to his master (*ustād* / *ṣāḥib-i futuwwat*) as a child (*farzand*/*pesar*) to his father (*pedar*). This relationship is described in familiar terms, the *tarbiyeh* owing absolute and unfailing good will towards his *ustād* just like the *murīd* to his *shaykh*. In

[59] al-Suhrawardī, *R. fī 'l-futuwwa*, 101–102; and, Taeschner, "Eine Schrift," 279–280; cf. Yaḥyā b. Khalīl Çoban who uses the same (*kavlı, seyfi*) (*Fütüvvetnāme*, 123–125).

[60] al-Suhrawardī, *R. fī 'l-futuwwa*, 119–120; and, idem, *K. fī 'l-futuwwa*, 125–147; the same general distinctions are made by Nāṣirī and Yaḥyā b. Khalīl Çoban in their own descriptions of the difference between the *qawlī-* and *sayfī-fityān* (see following note).

the second place, just as there are various grades of *murīds* in the *ribāṭ* there are also various grades of apprentices in the *futuwwat-khāna*, from the actual *akhī* who, like the *mutaṣawwif* in the Sufi *ribāṭ*, has already been accepted and initiated into the *futuwwat* and has reached an intermediate stage, to the actual possessor of chivalry (*javānmard* / *futuwwat-dār*) who like the *muntahī* (or *ṣūfī* properly speaking) has reached the goal, but who may or may not serve as an actual master (*ṣāḥib-i futuwwat* / *ustād*). These correspondences can be represented as follows:

Table 1. Correspondences between the Hierarchy of the Sufi *ribāṭ* and the Hierarchy of the *futuwwat-khāna*

SUFI RIBĀṬ	***FUTUWWAT-KHĀNA***
mutashabbih: a 'pretender' affiliated through the *khirqa-yi tabarruk* who is not held to the discipline of the *ṭarīqat*.	***qawlī-fatā***: a 'vocal chevalier' who commits verbally but is not held to all the requirements of the *futuwwat*.
murīd: an 'aspirant' affiliated through the *khirqa-yi bi-ḥaqq* who is held to the discipline of the *ṭarīqat* through the master-disciple relationship.	***sayfī-fatā / tarbiyeh***: a 'sword-bearing chevalier' or 'apprentice' who is held to all the requirements of the *futuwwat*.
mutaṣawwif: an intermediate *murīd*.	***akhī***: an intermediate *tarbiyeh*.
ṣūfī (muntahī): the one who has obtained the goal of the *ṭarīqat* and is no longer a *murīd*.	***futuwwat-dār/javānmard***: 'possessor of chivalry', a fully accomplished chevalier.
shaykh: a Sufi who actually serves as a master, training *murīds* and counseling the *mutashabbih*.	***ṣāḥib-i futuwwat / ustād***: 'master of chivalry', a *futuwwat-dār* who actually trains apprentices.

Much like his delineation of the hierarchy of the Sufi *ribāṭ*, Suhrawardī's delineation of the hierarchy of the *futuwwat-khāna* does not seems to have been wholly a theoretical ideal, for both in the terms he applies to its constituents and their respective roles within the institution itself resonate in no small way with those found in the manuals of Nāṣirī and Yaḥyā b. Khalīl Çoban.[61] Furthermore, just as in the Sufi

[61] For his part, Nāṣirī distinguishes first between the *tarbiya* and *akhī* proper (derived from a Turkish root and not the Arabic 'my brother' as Ibn Baṭṭūṭa supposed [see Taeschner, "Akhī," *EI*², 1:321]) and then between the *qawlī-* and *sayfī-fityān* and *ṣāḥib-i*

ribāṭ Suhrawardī states that the affiliates of the *futuwwat-khāna* at all levels relate to each other as brothers (*barādarān*) and are held responsible for performing acts of generosity (*sakhāvat*) and service (*khidmat*) to their brethren, performing them solely for the good of the community and without expectation of recompense. Just as in the Sufi *ribāṭ* too, the relationship between each of these affiliates is governed by a complex set of formal manners (*adab*) and formally definable mutual expectations and rights (*ḥuqūq*), and as in the *ʿAwārif al-maʿārif*, in his *K. fī ʾl-futuwwa* Suhrawardī carefully lays out a set of conditions (*sharṭ*), rights, and proper manners (*tartīb o adab*) which the *tarbiyehgān* are expected to observe with the *ṣāḥib-i futuwwat* and vice versa. The bulk of the *K. fī ʾl-futuwwa*, in fact, is concerned with prescribing these manners and customs, divided into five sections which stipulate seven rights possessed by the master with regard to his apprentice and forty-one rules which the apprentice must observe in regard to his master, especially during the communal feast.[62]

---

futuwwat (*Futuwwat-nāma*, lines 135–163, 300–318; see also: Breebaart, "Development and Structure", 125–127). For his, Yaḥyā b. Khalīl Çoban distinguishes between three primary levels: 1) *yiūitlik* ('bravery' or 'courage'; *yiūit* = *fatā*); 2) *akhilik*; and, 3) *shaykhlik* first, and then the *qawlī-* and *sayfī-fityān* second (*Fütüvvetnāme*, 113–120; see further Breebaart, "Development and Structure,", 131–132). Later, as evinced in the 10th/16th-century Turkish 'Great *Fütüvvetnāme*' (*Futuwwat-nāma-yi kabīr*) of Sayyid ʿAlāʾ al-Dīn al-Ḥusaynī al-Raḍawī, the three principle grades of *akhilik* were absorbed into the three grades of tradesmen: apprentice (*terbiye/çırak*), journeyman (*kalfa*: Ott. *qalfa*), and master (*usta*).

[62] al-Suhrawardī, *K. fī ʾl-futuwwa*, 121–149; cf. *ʿAM*, 2:155–159, 206–212, 217–222/*GE*, 43.1–14, 51.1–13, 52.2–13; many being similar to the rules lain out by Nāṣirī (e.g., *Futuwwat-nāma*, lines 149–163, 445–459, 590–673). In terms of the early 7th/13th-century milieu, the institutionalizing vision which Suhrawardī applied to both the Sufi *ribāṭ* and the *futuwwat-khāna* of the *akhī-fityān* finds a parallel in the Nāṣirian *futuwwa* which (at least as described by Ibn al-Miʿmār) was highly organized and tightly controlled. In brief, the fundamental unit was the relationship between the *kabīr* or *ab* (senior/father, also *jadd* ['grandfather'] which is used to refer to the master or masters [*kabīr al-kubarāʾ*] of a particular house) and the *ṣaghīr* or *ibn* (junior/son). The former are responsible for training the latter in the art of the *futuwwa*, and demand much the same respect as a *murīd* to his *shaykh*. In turn, each individual *fatā* (*kabīr*, *ṣaghīr*, *jadd*) belongs to a particular house (*bayt*, pl. *buyūt*) such as the one into which al-Nāṣir was initiated (*bayt al-rahhāṣiyya*), individual *bayt*s being further sub-divided into parties (*ḥizb*, pl. *aḥzāb*) led by a single *kabīr*. Individual *fityān* associate with members of their own *ḥizb* as companions (*rafīq*, pl. *rufaqāʾ*) and are not allowed to move from *ḥizb* to another, although movement between individual *bayts* is allowed, admission being controlled by the *kabīr*. Admission was effected through a ceremonial girding of the waist (*shadd*) representing the oath of fidelity (*ʿahd*) taken by the *ṣaghīr* to uphold the precepts of the *futuwwa* as mediated through his *kabīr*. When his training was complete (*takmīl*), he was then invested with the *libās al-futuwwa* which consisted of the trousers (*sarāwīl*), a ceremony which according to al-Khartabirtī was conducted by a representative (*naqīb*) and not

After the genealogical and organizational linkages, the final thematic complex in which Suhrawardī forges linkages between the *futuwwat* and *ribāṭ*-based Sufism revolve around institutions and praxis. It is here where he makes the most overt connections, not only linking it to the Sufi *ṭarīqat* on an organizational level, but systematically attempting to co-opt its socio-religious authority—which is also reflective of his later comments on the Mustanṣirian *futuwwa*—by repositioning it as a derivative of Sufism. Once again employing the ternary *sharīʿāt-ṭarīqat-ḥaqīqat* to describe the totality of the spirit's journey back to its source, Suhrawardī makes room for the *futuwwa* in a larger soteriological scheme by identifying it, in no uncertain terms, as a part (*juz*) of the *ṭarīqat*.[63] This, as we have seen, was supported both genealogically and organizationally, but at the same time was also supported materially, for according to Suhrawardī the actual clothing of the *futuwwa*, the under-shirt (*zīr-jāme*) is in reality but a part (*juz*) of the Sufi *khirqa*, originally woven by Seth as the undergarment which completes the costume (*libās*) of the true worshipper (*ʿābid*).[64] In this way, both the universal *futuwwat* and its specific Anatolian articulation are cast as derivatives of the universal *ṭarīqat* and its specific Baghdadi articulation, the former being validated only inasmuch as it is linked with the former.

As such, to participate in the *futuwwat* meant to subscribe to rules and regulations which structure the *ṭarīqat*, although certainly at a lesser level and with certain dispensations (*rukhaṣ*) from its more difficult requirements. In his *futuwwat-nāma*s, such links are many. For example, as with the prerequisite for setting out on the *ṭarīqat* Suhrawardī prescribes that strict adherence to the *sharīʿat* is a fundamental condition for participation in the *futuwwat*. The requirements which are lain upon the *tarbiyeh* in this regard are the same as those expected of the *mubtadiʾ*. As in his works on Sufism, in fact, Suhrawardī expends a great deal of energy on trying to foreground the necessity of strict adherence to the *sharīʿat*

---

by the *kabīr* himself. (Ibn al-Miʿmār, *K. al-futuwwa*, 190–255; Ibn al-Khartabirtī, *Tuḥfat al-waṣāyā*, 221–224; and, Breebaart, "Development and Structure," 75–101).

[63] al-Suhrawardī, *R. fī ʾl-futuwwa*, 93–94; and, idem, *K. fī ʾl-futuwwa*, 105–106 (later adding *maʿrifat* as a fourth through the parable of the crossroads [ibid., 109–112; a discussion which deserves further study; see: Corbin, *Traites*, 51–55]); cf. Nāṣirī, *Futuwwat-nāma*, lines 443–444; and, Kāshifī, *Futuwwat-nāma-yi sulṭānī*, 5.

[64] al-Suhrawardī, *R. fī ʾl-futuwwa*, 94; but cf. Ibn al-Miʿmār, *K. al-futuwwa*, 150–151; just as with Ibn al-Miʿmār, both Nāṣirī and Yaḥyā b. Khalīl Çoban describe initiation through the ritual of girding the waist (*shadd*) and completion through investiture with the trousers (*Futuwwat-nāma*, lines 386–403, 443–576).

with the praxis of the *futuwwat*, going so far as to propose an alternative derivation for the term *futuwwat* itself, deriving it not from *fatā* but rather from *fatwā*. Although philologically implausible, the importance of this novel etymology lies in its signification for like the petitioner soliciting a legal opinion from a qualified mufti, the potential *futuwwat-dār* presents himself to a qualified master of the *futuwwat* (*ṣāḥib-i futuwwa*) in hopes of soliciting an informed and authoritative opinion on the 'legal validity' of his actions vis-à-vis its rules.[65]

Other convergences can be noted as well. In its capacity as part of the *ṭarīqat*, for example, Suhrawardī describes the *futuwwat* as being possessed of twelve pillars, six outward stations (*maqām-i ẓāhir*) and six inward stations (*maqām-i bāṭin*). The first six, to which the *akhī* must adhere after his initiation, are: 1) sexual purity (*band-i shalvār*); 2) restraining his stomach from illicit foods; 3) restraining his tongue from idle talk; 4) retraining his eyes and ears from distracting things; 5) restraining himself from meddling in the affairs of others; and, 6) restraining his desire for fame and fortune in this world in anticipation of the next.[66] The six inward stations, while enjoined upon the *akhī*, are obligatory for the *futuwwat-dār*: 1) generosity (*sakhāvat*); 2) nobility (*karam*); 3) humility (*tavāżuʿ*); 4) forgiveness and mercy (*ʿafv o raḥma*); 5) self-effacement (*nīstī az manīyat*); and, 6) prudence (*hushyārī*), a very similar complex of ethics (*akhlāq*) which we have already noted Suhrawardī outlines in the *ʿAwārif al-maʿārif*.[67] There is, of course, no discussion of the higher spiritual stations or mystical states which are integral to the Sufi *ṭarīqat*, for as a derivative and lower form of the *ṭarīqat*, such stations represent the same virtues, attitudes, and behaviors which Suhrawardī defines elsewhere as the preparatory stages of the Sufi path itself.

Thus, as a social space possessed of communal and spiritual authority, for Suhrawardī the *futuwwat-khāna* of the Anatolian *akhī-fityān* finds its equivalent in the Sufi *ribāṭ*. While such organizational forms seem to reflect the real state of the early 7th/13th-century *futuwwa* organizations

---

[65] al-Suhrawardī, *K. fī 'l-futuwwa*, 104–105, 117–119 (where he employs *ḥisāb* to equate the two, finding twenty five qualities [*khaṣlat*] each of which begin with one of the letters *f-t-w*); and like the Sufi *shaykh* the *ṣāḥib-i futuwwa* is qualified to train (*tarbiyat*) an *akhī* because of his fixed inner state. As to be expected, in the Nāṣirian *futuwwa* too, strict adherence to the *sharīʿa* was a cardinal principle (e.g., Ibn al-Miʿmār, *K. al-futuwwa*, 139, 163, 180).

[66] al-Suhrawardī, *R. fī 'l-futuwwa*, 94–96; and, idem, *K. fī 'l-futuwwa*, 116; cf. al-Khartabirtī, *Tuḥfat al-waṣāyā*, 209–210; and, Nāṣirī, *Futuwwat-nāma*, lines 749–797.

[67] al-Suhrawardī, *R. fī 'l-futuwwa*, 96–98; and, idem, *K. fī 'l-futuwwa*, 109.

at some level, for they are described as such shortly after Suhrawardī, it is the particular way in which he went about authorizing and legitimating them which betray the centralist aims of his program. As with the vision of *ribāṭ*-based Sufism which he enunciated in Baghdad, the vision of the *futuwwa* which he presented to his Anatolia audience inscribed authority in absolute and universal terms. In making the *futuwwat* a derivative of the *ṭarīqat* in the most comprehensive of terms (genealogy, organization, and praxis), Suhrawardī once again circumscribes through inclusion, inviting the *fityān* and their *futuwwat-khānas* to identify and affiliate with the *ṣūfiyya* and their *ribāṭs*, and thus just like the *mutashabbih*, and perhaps even the *mustarshid*, join the ranks of the circle of the chosen. In a sense, in Suhrawardī the prolonged flirtation between Sufism and the *futuwwa* finds a certain consummation, a textual one to be sure, but one which brings a certain closure to the sustained back and forth which had existed between the two since at least the time of Sulamī. In this, the shaykh seems to have made little room for the concerns of his patron, for that particular chaperone had been left back in Baghdad.

Polemic in Service of Statecraft?

We are informed by al-Dhahabī that while in Damascus during his mission to the Ayyubids of 604/1207–1208 in addition to participating in the investiture ceremony for al-Malik al-ʿĀdil and his sons, Suhrawardī also held a number of well attended preaching assemblies. During one of them, the shaykh addressed al-Ashraf Mūsā himself, telling him that he personally sought out each and every copy of Ibn Sīnā's *K. al-shifāʾ* in the libraries of Baghdad and washed the ink from every page. Later during the course of his address Suhrawardī mentioned that over the past year much of the populace of Baghdad had fallen violently ill, and apparently not pleased with the shaykh's attempts at purification, the sultan remarked: "and why not, since you have eliminated the *Shifāʾ* from it!"[68] Be this as it may, Suhrawardī seems to have been quite proud of his action, for many years later in his two polemics against

[68] *SN*, 22:377; and, *Ṭabaqāt*, 2:837; obviously in some confusion with Ibn Sīnā's *Qanūn fī ʾl-ṭibb*, but the iconicity is important. Some years later, the *shaykh al-shuyūkh* of Damascus, Ṣadr al-Dīn Ḥammūya (d. 617/1220) got in serious trouble for reciting a verse of Ibn Sīnā at the Umayyad Mosque during one of his preaching sessions (*TIsl*, 50:36 [*ḥawādith, anno* 617]).

the tradition of Peripatetic philosophy (*falsafa*) associated with Ibn Sīnā, he states that he did just that.[69]

In al-Nāṣir's Baghdad such a public act was nothing unusual, and in his vituperative attack on those whom he called the 'folk of innovation and misguided passions' (*ahl al-bidaʿ wa-l-ahwāʾ*), Suhrawardī's polemic against the Peripatetics, materialists (*dahriyya*), and all of those whom he saw as following their teachings was but part of a much larger program comprised of all manner of public denunciations, the deliberate destruction of philosophical literature, and the harassment of numerous prominent ulama who were unlucky enough to be caught dealing with the 'ancient sciences' (*ʿulūm al-awāʾil*).[70] At the same time however, as with the *Aʿlām al-hudā* and his two *Futuwwat-nāma*s the nature of the relationship between these texts and al-Nāṣir's policies are difficult to judge. The *Kashf al-faḍāʾiḥ* was composed very late in al-Nāṣir's reign, the shaykh completing it just a year before his patron's death in 622/1225 and although explicitly dedicating the work to al-Nāṣir and transmitting it publicly in Baghdad, like the *Idālat al-ʿiyān* it was a project which seem to have come far too late to be of any consequence to al-Nāṣir himself.[71]

Like the *Aʿlām al-hudā* and his two *Futuwwat-nāma*s, the content of these polemics can be located in al-Nāṣir's program, but in spirit only. Perhaps in regard to the *Idālat al-ʿiyān* at least there is something to be said for Suhrawardī maintaining an allegiance to the caliphal program in general. At the same time, however, although composed during the

---

[69] *KF*, 86; same in idem, *Idālat*, fol. 85b. The former was also translated into Persian by Muʿīn al-Dīn ʿAlī b. Jalāl al-Dīn Muḥammad al-Yazdī (d. 789/1387) which has been edited with a very useful introduction by Najīb Māyel Heravī (Tehran: Chap va Nashr-i Būnyād, 1365 sh. [1986]), and has been studied by Angelika Hartmann in "Eine orthodoxe Polemik gegen Philosophen und Freidenker," *Der Islam* 56.2 (1979): 274–293. Like al-Ghazālī's *Tahāfut al-falāsifa*, it also became the subject of a rejoinder, namely the *Kashf al-asrār al-īmāniyya wa-katk al-astār al-ḥuṭāmiyya* composed by Ḍiyāʾ al-Dīn b. Masʿūd b. Maḥmūd (d. 655/1257–1258), a disciple of Fakhr al-Dīn al-Rāzī.

[70] Individual cases covered by *Nṣr.*, 255–262; cf. idem, "al-Nāṣir," *EI²*, 8:1000; which included the public denunciation of the Ḥanbalī *faqīh* and uncle of ʿAbd al-Qādir al-Jīlānī, Rukn al-Dīn ʿAbd al-Salām al-Jīlānī (d. 611/1214) on account of being in possession of philosophical literature such as the *Rasāʾil* of the Ikhwān al-Ṣafāʾ and Ibn Sīnā's *K. al-shifāʾ* written in his own hand (Ibn al-Sāʿī, *Mukhtaṣar akhbār al-khulafāʾ*, quoted in idem, *JM*, 81–82, fn. 1; Ibn Rajab, *DhR*, 2:71; *TIsl*, 49:13 [*ḥawādith, anno* 603]; and, *Nṣr.*, 256–260). In his polemics against Peripatetic philosophy Suhrawardī also indicts dialectical theology (*ʿilm al-kalām*), seeing it as a derivative of the former (*KF*, 190) and in the *Idālat* refers specifically to al-Nāṣir's offensive against the *falāsifa* (fol. 85b).

[71] *KF*, 66–67 (dedication to al-Nāṣir); *SN*, 22:375; and, Dāwūdī, *Ṭabaqāt*, 2:10 (on the transmission of the text in Baghdad).

reign of al-Mustanṣir and providing an explicit enunciation of fidelity to the caliphate, given the fact that al-Mustanṣir denied Suhrawardī's son ʿImād al-Dīn the *mashyakha* of the Ribāṭ al-Marzubāniyya in favor of Awḥad al-Dīn Kirmānī upon the death of his father in 632/1234, one is left to wonder how cordial the relationship between the aged shaykh and the new caliph really was.[72] Should these two polemics be considered something of an anachronism or was Suhrawardī, in his continued transmission of the *Kashf al-faḍāʾiḥ* in Baghdad and his composition of the *Idālat al-ʿiyān* after al-Nāṣir's death, worried about al-Mustanṣir's support for the *mashyakha* of the *ribāṭ*s which he had been granted by his grandfather? Or, as with the *Aʿlām al-hudā* and his two *Futuwwat-nāma*s, were these two texts primarily concerned with self-referentially enunciating the legitimacy and authority of his own *ṭāʾifa* and only secondarily with the patron(s) who supported it and its institutions?

A partial answer to this question is found in the language, rhetoric, and content of the works themselves. In contradiction to the *Aʿlām al-hudā* and his two *Futuwwat-nāma*s where Suhrawardī pursues a clear policy of inclusion through circumscription, in his two polemics against Peripatetic philosophy he pursues a strict policy of exclusion, and although displaying a certain familiarity with the philosophic lexicon and the main currents of the Peripatetic tradition, identifies them as a single, unified *ṭāʾifa*, singling out by name al-Fārābī and Ibn Sīnā as their chief representatives and lumping them together with all manner of materialists, dualists (*thanawiyya*), Magians (*majūs*), Sabaeans and others.[73] In these polemics Suhrawardī casts these 'folk of passion and

[72] *KḤ*, 101, this however must be tempered with the fact that at some point, ʿImād al-Dīn served as one of the leaders of the hajj under al-Mustanṣir (ibid., 202–203) and well as later taking over the *mashyakha* of the Ribāṭ al-Maʾmūniyya. Like his grandfather, al-Mustanṣir continued to patronize Sufis and ulama from the same families, for instance endowing a new *ribāṭ* in the Dār al-Rūm neighborhood for the grandson of ʿAbd al-Qādir al-Jīlānī, Abū Ṣāliḥ and his disciples in 626/1229 as well as patronizing the *shaykh al-shuyūkh* family, in one instance sending an embassy led by one of the sons of Ibn Sukayna, Abū ʾl-Barakāt ʿAbd al-Raḥmān (to whom al-Mustanṣir had granted the *niqāba* of the Abbasid *futuwwa*) to Akhlāṭ to invest, of all people, the Khwārazm Shāh Jalāl al-Dīn Mangübirdī with its accoutrements. (ibid., 16, 21, 31, 116; on the latter, cf. *TIsl*, 50:38 [*ḥawādith*, *anno* 627]).

[73] Naming al-Fārābī and Ibn Sīnā as the twin icons of the *falāsifa* is also found in al-Ghazālī (*al-Munqidh*, McCarthy trans., 30–31; idem, *Tahāfut*, trans. Marmura as *The Incoherence of the Philosophers* [Provo: Brigham Young UP, 2000), 4; which also makes reference to *dahriyya*, the first order [*ṣinf*] and 'sect' [*ṭāʾifa*] of the Ancients whose views he explicitly connects with al-Fārābī and Ibn Sīnā [see Goldziher, "Dahriyya," *EI*[2],

innovation' as a group who present a particularly insidious threat to the Muslim community, sowing iniquity and dissention from within its very ranks by teaching their sciences under the guise of legitimate religious knowledge (*ʿilm al-sharʿiyya*). Stating in no uncertain terms that they fall far beyond the pale even of the People of the Book, he finds little trouble in branding them manifest apostates (*riddat ʿan islām*) and unbelievers (*kuffār*), individuals who are to be excluded from the Muslim community in the strongest of terms.[74] In no small measure, what this amounts to is a fatwa of *takfīr* promulgated by a trained Shāfiʿī jurist, one which portrays the *falāsifa* in categories of deviance easily separated from the Sunni moral center from which Suhrawardī was writing and whose population both al-Nāṣir and al-Mustanṣir clearly supported.

At the same time, Suhrawardī's polemics are intimately tied with his own program. Unlike Ghazālī in his infamous *Tahāfut al-falāsifa*, there is little in the way of turning the philosophers' rational methodology against them in order to refute their theses, and none too surprisingly in both the *Kashf al-faḍāʾiḥ* and *Idālat al-ʿiyān* Suhrawardī argues from the same two vantage points employed in the *Aʿlām al-hudā*, namely supporting his arguments on the basis of the existential authority derived from pursing the Sufi path supported, of course, through proof texts drawn from the Qurʾān and Ḥadīth. Here again, the shaykh's dual strategy is apparent, for in the process of excluding the philosophers from the corporate body of the Muslim community he programmatically reasserts each of the primary points framing his discourse on the sciences of the *ṣūfiyya* found in the *ʿAwārif al-maʿārif* and his other works

---

2:95–96]). In addition to these two moderns (*mutaʾakhkhirīn*) Suhrawardī also indicts those ancients (*mutaqaddimīn*) in the following order: 1) the celebrated 3rd/9th century 'philosopher of the Arabs' al-Kindī; 2–3) the Nestorian translators Ḥunayn b. Isḥāq (d. 260/873) and Yaḥyā al-ʿAdī (d. 363/974); 4) one Abū ʾl-Faraj al-Mufassir (probably the Nestorian philosopher Ibn al-Ṭayyib [d. 980/1043]); 5) the celebrated mid-4th/10th-century humanist Abū Sulaymān al-Sijistānī; 6) Abū Sulaymān Muḥammad al-Muqaddasī (al-Bustī), one of the authors of the *Rasāʾil Ikhwān al-Safāʾ*; 7) the famous Sabaean translator Thābit b. Qurra (d. 288/901); and, 8) Abū Tammām Yūsuf b. Muḥammad al-Nīsābūrī. (*KF*, 178)

[74] *KF*, 85–86, 89–92, 94–97, 119–120, 133–140, 159–160, 197–199; and, idem, *Idālat*, fol. 84b, 92a, 95a, 101b, 104b–105a; see also: Hartmann, "Cosmogonie et doctrine," 164, 173–174; idem, "Kosmogonie und Seelenlehre," 136–137; and, Muḥammad Karīmī Zanjānī, "Rashf al-naṣāʾiḥ," in *Dāʾirat al-maʿārif-i buzurg-i islāmī* (Tehran: Markaz-i Dāʾirat al-Maʿārif-i Buzurg-i Islāmī, 1367– sh. [1988–]), 8:251–252. This, of course, is much unlike Ghazālī who limited charging with unbelief (*takfīr*) to very specific points, seeing the bulk of the sciences and knowledge associated with the *falāsifa* as meriting only the charge of innovation (*tabdīʿ*) or that of neutral status (al-Ghazālī, *al-Munqidh*, 31–42; idem, *Fayṣal*, 109–112; and, idem, *Tahāfut*, 226–227 [where out of twenty specific errors, he identifies only three meriting *takfīr*]).

on Sufism, namely his conception of the journey of ascent, its anthropogony, epistemological bases, and their connection to the disposition of the original dispensation in time and space. As with the *Aʿlām al-hudā* as well, both the format and language of these polemics (although more so in the *Kashf al-faḍāʾiḥ* than in the *Idālat al-ʿiyān*) is telling, being written in a deliberately dense, stylized, and affected prose which was obviously carefully crafted for rhetorical effect.

In the *Kashf al-faḍāʾiḥ* at least, all of this is pervaded by an appeal to the authority of al-Nāṣir in his role as a member of the ulama. In the beginning of this text Suhrawardī states that his primary aim is to provide an anecdote for those otherwise well-intentioned seekers who have been beguiled by the philosophic sciences through refuting their arguments on the basis of the Qurʾān and Ḥadīth, something which he does specifically through recourse to a body of carefully chosen *ḥadīth* which he makes clear he had been granted an *ijāza* to transmit directly upon al-Nāṣir's authority.[75] Certainly drawn from al-Nāṣir's *Rūḥ al-ʿārifīn*, a work which Suhrawardī is reported to have disseminated in Aleppo,[76] the *isnād*s of the reports which he quotes in the *Kashf al-faḍāʾiḥ* are also telling in a wider sense, passing through individuals with whom both he, Abū ʾl-Najīb, the descendants of Aʿazz al-Suhrawardī, and a host of their teachers, associates, disciples, and students had direct dealings. These *isnād*s can be grouped as follows:

1. al-Nāṣir li-Dīn Allāh—ʿAlī b. ʿAsākir al-Baṭāʾiḥī—Abū ʾl-Waqt al-Sijzī—ʿAbdullāh-i Anṣārī; 1_a: ʿAlī b. ʿAsākir—Abū ʿAlī al-Ḥasan b. Muhra al-Ḥaddād—Abū Nuʿaym al-Iṣfahānī; 1_b: ʿAlī b. ʿAsākir—Abū Ṭālib ʿAbd al-Qādir b. Muḥammad b. Yusūf; 1_c: ʿAlī b. ʿAsākir—Abū

[75] *KF*, 67–70. In addition to the *ḥadīth* transmitted to him by al-Nāṣir, a number of *ḥadīth* which Suhrawardī collected during his student days under Abū ʾl-Najīb make an appearance in the *Kashf al-faḍāʾiḥ*, namely those transmitted to him by: 1) Abū ʾl-Najīb al-Suhrawardī (ibid., 111, 114); 2) Abū ʾl-Manṣūr Muḥammad b. ʿAbd al-Malik b. Khayrūn (ibid., 137); and, 3) Abū ʾl-Muʿammar Khudhayfa al-Wazzān (ibid., 170, 172, 173, 174, 175, 178).

[76] *SN*, 22:197. The *Rūḥ al-ʿārifīn* was a compilation of seventy *ḥadīth* collected by al-Nāṣir from prominent transmitters. He promulgated it in 607/1210–1211, from whence it was transmitted from Baghdad to Mecca, and from Damascus to Marv (*DhR*, 69; *MZ*, 8.2:543–544; *SN*, 22:197–198; and, *TIsl*, 49:29 [*ḥawādith*, *anno* 607]). A partial version entitled *Futūḥ al-waqt* was compiled by ʿAbd al-Laṭīf al-Baghdādī (d. 629/1231) and is extant (Br. Mus. Or. 5780 and 6332; see: Ellis and Edwards, *A Descriptive List of the Arabic Manuscripts Acquired by the Trustees of the British Museum Since 1894* [London: The British Museum, 1912], 16–18; list of transmitters in Georges Vajda, "Une liste d'autorités du Calife al-Nāṣir li-dīn Allāh," *Arabica* 6 [1959]: 173–177; contents in *Nṣr.*, 221–232]).

Zurʿa al-Maqdisī; and, 1_d: ʿAlī b. ʿAsākir—Abū ʾl-Waqt al-Sijzī—ʿAbd al-Raḥmān Muḥammad al-Dāwūdī.[77]

2. al-Nāṣir li-Dīn Allāh—ʿAbd al-Razzāq b. ʿAbd al-Qādir al-Jīlānī—Abū Zurʿa al-Maqdisī; 2_a: ʿAbd al-Razzāq—Sulaymān b. Masʿūd al-Shaḥḥāmī; and, 2_b: ʿAbd al-Razzāq—Abū ʾl-Waqt al-Sijzī—ʿAbd al-Raḥmān b. Muḥammad al-Dāwūdī.[78]
3. al-Nāṣir li-Dīn Allāh—ʿUbaydullāh b. ʿAlī al-Farrāʾ—Abū ʾl-Faḍl Muḥammad b. Nāṣir.[79]
4. al-Nāṣir li-Dīn Allāh—Ibn Kulayb—Ṣāʿid b. Sayyār al-Harawī.[80]
5. al-Nāṣir li-Dīn Allāh—ʿAbd al-Mughīth b. Zuhayr—Abū ʾl-Waqt al-Sijzī—ʿAbd al-Raḥmān b. Muḥammad al-Dāwūdī; and, 5_a: ʿAbd al-Mughīth b. Zuhayr—Hibatullāh b. Muḥammad b. al-Ḥuṣayn.[81]
6. al-Nāṣir li-Dīn Allāh—Shuhda bt. Aḥmad b. al-Faraj b. ʿUmar al-Ibarī—Ibn Bundār.[82]

---

[77] 12 *ḥadīth* (*KF*, 74, 77, 79, 81, 85, 92, 93, 94–95, 97); ʿAlī b. ʿAsākir (d. 572/1177) was a Ḥanbalī *muḥaddith* and Qurʾānic scholar (*MT*, 10:267 [no. 359]; *SN*, 20:548–550, and, *TIsl*, 46:100–101 [*anno* 572, no. 45]; Ibn Rajab, *Dhayl*, 1:335–337; and, Vajda, "Une liste," 175 [no. 12]); for the Ḥanbalī Sufi Abū ʾl-Waqt al-Sijzī, see Chapter Two, s.v. "Aʿazz b. ʿUmar al-Suhrawardī (d. 557/1162) and Sons"; ʿAbdullāh-i Anṣārī scarcely needs an introduction. 1_a = 5 *ḥadīth* (*KF*, 84, 150, 164, 177, 178); Abū ʿAlī al-Ḥaddād was a disciple of Abū Nuʿaym al-Iṣfahānī. 1_b = *KF*, 102, 159; Abū Ṭālib Yusūf was a Ḥanbalī *muḥaddith* (cf. *Tāʾrīkh*, 46:101). 1_c = 4 *ḥadīth* from Abū Zurʿa al-Maqdisī's (d. 566/1170) *riwāya* of the *Sunan Ibn Māja* which he also transmitted to al-Suhrawardī (*KF*, 153, 154–155 204). 1_d = 2 *ḥadīth* (*KF*, 212–213, 240); al-Dāwūdī was a prominent Ḥanbalī *muḥaddith*.

[78] 9 *ḥadīth* (*KF*, 79, 80, 82, 95 [2 *ḥadīth*], 110, 140, 168, 202); ʿAbd al-Razzāq (d. 605/1209) was the son of ʿAbd al-Qādir al-Jīlānī and a well-known Ḥanbalī *muḥaddith* and Sufi (on whom see, in addition to my entry "ʿAbd al-Razzāq b. ʿAbd al-Qādir al-Jīlānī," *Encyclopaedia of Islam Three* [Leiden: Brill (forthcoming)], *TW*, 2:116–117 [no. 980]; *JM*, 214–215; *TIr*, 1:296; *SN*, 21:426–428 [no. 222], *TIsl*, 49:119–121 [*anno* 605, no. 134]; Vajda, "Une liste," 174 [no. 9]); al-Maqdisī as above. 2_a = 2 *ḥadīth* (*KF*, 128, 227); al-Shaḥḥāmī could not be found. 2_b = 1 *ḥadīth* (*KF*, 143); al-Sijzī and al-Dāwūdī as above.

[79] 1 *ḥadīth* (*KF*, 117); ʿUbaydullāh was a prominent Ḥanbalī *muḥaddith* of Baghdad.

[80] 1 *ḥadīth* (*KF*, 121); Ibn Kulayb was another prominent Ḥanbalī transmitter.

[81] 1 *ḥadīth* (*KF*, 131–132); ʿAbd al-Mughīth b. Zuhayr b. ʿAlawī al-Harbī al-Hanbalī (d. 583/1187) was a Baghdadi *muḥaddith* who, among other things, composed a *Faḍāʾil Yazīd* for which he drew the ire of Ibn al-Jawzī, something which al-Nāṣir interrogated him on later (Ibn Nuqṭa, *Taqyīd*, 388–389 [no. 504]; *TW*, 1:63 [no. 11]; Ibn Rajab, *Dhayl*, 1:354–358 [no. 174]; *SN*, 21:159–161 [no. 79], and, *TIsl*, 47:155–157 [*anno* 583, no. 91]; and, Vajda, "Une liste," 174 [no. 6]); al-Sijzī and al-Dāwūdī as above. 5_a = 1 *ḥadīth* (*KF*, 211), al-Ḥuṣayn (not al-Ḥuṣīn) is often mentioned in the *isnād*s of the time.

[82] 1 *ḥadīth* (*KF*, 193); Shuhda al-Ibarī (d. 574/1178), known as Fakhr al-Nisāʾ was the daughter of Abū Naṣr Aḥmad al-Dīnawarī (d. 506/1112), a Shāfiʿī *muḥaddith* and Sufi who gave her hand to Abū ʾl-Ḥasan al-Duraynī (d. 549/1154), an official in the administration of the caliph al-Muktafī (r. 530–555 / 1136–1160) who endowed a Shāfiʿī *madrasa* and adjoining *ribāṭ* in the Azj neighborhood. A talented scribe (*kātiba*)

This list presents a couple of things worthy of note. First, the presence of Sufis, and Ḥanbalī Sufis in particular, in its lines of transmission is important. As we have already seen, al-Nāṣir's mother, Zumurrud Khātūn, was well known for patronizing Sufis and for her support for the Ḥanbalites in particular, and as al-Nāṣir must have received many of these *ḥadīth* early in his life—in the case of ʿAlī b. ʿAsākir and Shuhada bt. Aḥmad certainly before assuming the caliphate—and given the close relationship between him and his mother presented in the sources, there is little doubt that as a youth, he had contact with many such individuals. Although certainly reversing his father's policy of more-or-less blind support for Ḥanbalites upon assuming the caliphate, he certainly carried forward the policy of his mother regarding the Sufis, patronizing not only Suhrawardī (whose first *ribāṭ*, the Ribāṭ al-Maʾmūniyya, was financed by Zumurrud Khātūn herself) but also individuals such as the Shāfiʿī *ʿālims* and Sufi masters of the *shaykh al-shuyūkh* family, Ṣadr al-Dīn ʿAbd al-Raḥīm and Ibn Sukayna, as well as the grandson of ʿAbd al-Qādir al-Jīlānī, the latter two in fact also serving as the respective Shāfiʿī and Ḥanbalī representatives to whom he granted the first *ijāzas* for the *Rūḥ al-ʿārifīn*.[83]

Second, it is further telling that al-Nāṣir received the same recension of the *Sunan* of Ibn Māja which Suhrawardī received from Abū Zurʿa al-Maqdisī,[84] and as such the shaykh could have just as well quoted from

and very active *muḥadditha*, she transmitted to and from all of the 'big names' in Baghdad (al-Samʿānī, *Ansāb*, 1:118; *MT*, 10:288 [no. 374]; Ibn Nuqṭa, *Taqyīd*, 501 [no. 689]; *TIr*, 1:98 ff. (see index); Ibn al-Dubaythī, *Mukhtaṣar*, 2:263–265 [no. 1409]; *WA*, 2:477–478; *MZ*, 8.1:352; *KW*, 16:190–192 [no. 224]; *SN*, 20:542–543 [no. 344], and, *TIsl*, 46:145–147 [*anno* 574, no. 113]; and, Vajda, "Une liste," 176 [no. 27]; on Ibn Bundār (d. 566/1170), the seventh authority in Suhrawardī's *Mashyakha* (fol. 90a), see Arberry, "The Teachers," 348–349 (no. 7).

[83] The Ḥanafī representative being Ḍiyāʾ al-Dīn Aḥmad b. Masʿūd al-Turkistānī (d. 610/1213) and the Mālikī representative Taqī al-Dīn ʿAlī b. Jābir al-Maghribī. In addition, al-Nāṣir also granted *ijāzas* to numerous ulama for the *Musnad* of Aḥmad b. Ḥanbal (*DR*, 78; *MZ*, 8.2:556; and, *TIsl*, 49:35 [*ḥawādith*, *anno* 608]).

[84] The Shāfiʿī *muḥaddith* and native of Rayy, Abū Zurʿa al-Maqdisī, who is number four in Suhrawardī's *Mashyakha* (fol. 87a–88a), figures quite prominently in the *ʿAwārif*, where he is cited as the authority for over fifty prophetic *ḥadīth* and Sufi *akhbār*. Calling him a Sufi, in his *Mashyakha* Suhrawardī records five *ḥadīth* which he heard from him, the first on 13 Rabīʿ I, 588/29 March, 1192, as well as mentioning that Abū Zurʿa transmitted the entire *Sunan* of Ibn Māja to him, the *riwāya* of which Suhrawardī would later transmit to his disciple Ẓahīr al-Dīn al-Zanjānī (d. 674/1276). The less than illustrious son of the famous *muḥaddith*, author, and Sufi Abī ʾl-Faḍl Ibn al-Kaysarānī (d. 507/1113), Abū Zurʿa al-Maqdisī was a trader (*tājir*) and *muḥaddith* who after the death of his father set himself up at Hamadhān from where, every year, he would join the pilgrimage caravan and travel to Baghdad in order to engage in business and

his own *riwāya* for which he had an *ijāza* directly from al-Maqdīsī, but instead choose to quote it from al-Nāṣir's *riwāya*. In the *Idālat al-ʿiyān*, however, the situation is reversed, for although quoting many of the same *ḥadīth* Suhrawardī does not make use of al-Nāṣir's recension of Ibn Māja's *Sunan*, but rather his own. It is what Suhrawardī did with these *ḥadīth* however which, once again, evinces the dual nature of his program, for just as in the *Aʿlām al-hudā* and his two *Futuwwat-nāma*s, these two polemics evince much more of a concern with arguing for the legitimacy and authority of his own *ṭāʾifa* than with supporting the program of al-Nāṣir or later that of al-Mustanṣir.

The overarching argument which runs through the fifteen dense chapters of the *Kashf al-faḍāʾiḥ* and which is repeated, although not in its entirely, in the *Idālat al-ʿiyān* aims to prove the superiority of prophetic knowledge over the derived knowledge of the philosophers, the upshot of its critique being to show how the epistemological bases of apodictic knowledge necessarily preclude the philosopher from apprehending the truths and verities of the spiritual realms (*ʿawālim al-ghuyūb*) from which the prophets, and by extension those who are their heirs, derive veridical knowledge of the realities enunciated in revelation.

The root of Suhrawardī's argument lies in connecting the anthropogony which he laid out earlier in the *ʿAwārif al-maʿārif* and elsewhere with the philosophers' own system of thought, namely connecting it to a comprehensive ontology, cosmology, and epistemology articulated in the language of Neoplatonized Aristotelianism characteristic of the *falsafa* of the central and eastern lands of Islamdom since the time of al-Fārābī. Although explicitly rejecting the foundational Neoplatonic postulate that 'from the One only the one can emerge',[85] Suhrawardī pursues his critique squarely from within the framework of this system, positing what amounts to a series of successive 'higher emanations' proceeding from God through whose divine command (*amr*)—which he also identifies with the Qurʾānic *rūḥ qudsī* blown into Adam—proceeds what he calls either the 'greatest spirit' (*al-rūḥ al-aʿẓam*) or the 'universal spirit' (*al-rūḥ al-kullī*). According to Suhrawardī, the philosophers have

---

to transmit *ḥadīth*. On him, see: Ibn al-Dubaythī, *Mukhtaṣar*, 2:119–120 (no. 740); *WA*, s.v. Abū ʾl-Faḍl b. al-Kaysarānī; *SN*, 20:503–504 (no. 320), and, *TIsl*, 45:246–247 (*anno* 566, no. 223); and, *KW*, 16:406–407 (no. 441).

[85] *KF*, 103–104, 114, 124–126; idem, *Idālat*, fol. 109a–109b; the expression he uses being '*lā yūjid min al-wāḥid illā wāḥid*', which is usually expressed by the Muslim Neoplatonists as '*al-wāḥid lā yuṣduru ʿanhu illā al-wāḥid*' ('*ex uno non fit nisi unum*'); cf. Hartmann, "Kosmogonie und Seelenlehre," 141.

mistaken this necessitator (*mūjib*) as the 'being necessary in itself' (*wājib bi-ījāb wājib al-wujūd*) and the *prima causa* (*ʿillat al-ʿilal*) when in reality it is a contingent existent (*mumkin al-wujūd*). Assisted by God's command, from this spirit emerges the primordial intellect (*al-ʿaql al-fiṭrī*), in form and function akin to the first hypostasis of Plotinus (the masculine *Nous*) and the first intellect (*al-ʿaql al-awwal*) of the philosophers.[86]

Generally, Islamic Neoplatonism posited that the first intellect engages in two acts, an initial act of self-contemplation through which it effects the second intellect and then an act of contemplating its author through which it effects the third intellect, akin to the third Plotinian hypostasis, the feminine *Psyche*. In the emanationist scheme of both the Ikhwān al-Ṣafāʾ and Ibn Sīnā, this third effect (*al-maʿlūl al-thālith*) is called either the passive intellect (*al-ʿaql al-munfaʿil*) or the universal soul (*al-nafs al-kullī*), and although explicitly denying a dual act on the part of the primordial intellect and stating that the philosophers are wrong in identifying it as the third effect, Suhrawardī uses the very term *al-nafs al-kullī* to describe the 'hypostasis' engendered by the primordial intellect (*ʿaql fiṭrī*).

The type of Islamic Neoplatonism with which Suhrawardī seems to have been familiar generally posits that from the initial three acts of emanation proceed a series of creative cosmic emanations, each one engendering a constituent part of the cosmos (the higher celestial spheres, the sphere of fixed stars, the spheres of the planets, etc.), and although explicitly denying the creative agency of emanation, Suhrawardī implicitly validates its cosmological implications, positing that the effects (*taʾthīr*) of the universal spirit, primordial intellect, and universal soul constantly filter down from the world of divine command (*ʿālam al-amr* = *ʿālam al-ghayb*/*al-malakūt*) through the cosmic isthmus (*ʿālam al-jabarūt*; i.e., the celestial spheres) to the sublunar world. It is the continual descent of the effects of the three hypostases belonging to the world of divine command into the world of creation (*ʿālam al-khalq*/*al-shahāda*/*al-mulk*/*al-maḥsūs*) which according to Suhrawardī effects the vivification of individual sentient beings, beings which in their own bodies mirror the respective relationships obtained between the universal spirit, the primordial intellect, and the universal soul in the manner of

[86] *KF*, 65–66, 101–104, 112–113, 146–147, 165–166 (key passage), 197, 231–236 (key passage), 242, 245–246; and, idem, *Idālat*, fol. 94b–95a, 96a–96b, 97b–98a, 99b–100a, 108b–109a (key passage), 114a, and 128a; Hartmann, "Cosmogonie et doctrine," 168–169; idem, "Kosmogonie und Seelenlehre," 140–142; see further Majid Fakhry, *A History of Islamic Philosophy*, 2nd ed. (New York: Columbia University Press, 1983), 118–120, 152–157.

micro- to macrocosm.[87] After vivification, created beings continue to be influenced by way of sympathies with the corresponding universals.

Thus, according to Suhrawardī the human psycho-spiritual constitution as manifest in the *ʿālam al-khalq* is but a particularization of the corresponding universals of the *ʿālam al-amr*, the human translunar spirit (*al-rūḥ al-insānī al-ʿulwī*) being a particularized spirit (*rūḥ juzʾī*) proceeding from the universal spirit (*rūḥ kullī*) and the soul a particularized soul (*nafs juzʾī*) proceeding from the universal soul (*nafs kullī*). As with the *ʿaql fiṭrī* in the world of divine command which serves as the isthmus (*barzakh*) between the *rūḥ aʿẓam* and the *nafs kullī*, the heart (*qalb*) born from the meeting of the *rūḥ juzʾī* and *nafs juzʾī* in the world of creation serves as the isthmus between them. As a mediating agent, the heart then takes on one of two possible aspects, either being infused with the descending light of the primordial intellect (*ʿaql fiṭrī*) through the sympathies engendered by prophethood (*nubuwwa*), or by extension the sympathies engendered by the *ʿubūdiyya* of the accomplished Sufi, or remains mired in the darkness of the creatural intellect (*ʿaql khilqī*; sometimes *ʿaql ṭabʿ*) through its sympathetic connection with the universal soul in the case of all those who are not possessed of *nubuwwa* or *ʿubūdiyya*.[88]

Here, the essential argument which Suhrawardī advances is that due to its connection to the universal soul, the creatural intellect of the philosophers and all those who are spiritually immature can only apprehend the *ʿālam al-shahāda* whereas by virtue of the light of the *ʿaql fiṭrī*, the prophets and those who follow their path are able to penetrate into both it and the spiritual realms (*ʿawālim al-ghuyūb*).[89] This scheme can be represented as follows:

---

[87] In her two articles on the subject Hartmann has read this as a reiteration of a typical Late Antique Gnostic Mythos articulated in a Neoplatonic framework, the masculine *rūḥ kullī* playing the role of the *Logos* (= universal father/Adam) and the feminine *nafs kullī* that of *Sophia* (= universal mother/Eve) which, as we have already seen in the case of Suhrawardī's description of the psycho-spiritual constitution in the *ʿAwārif*, is replicated in the individual human person, a microcosm (*ʿālam ṣaghīr*) of the universal macroanthropos (*al-insān al-kabīr*); see: Hartmann, "Cosmogonie et la doctrine," 166 ff.; and, idem, "Kosmogonie und Seelenlehre," 138 ff.).

[88] *KF*, 116–117, 124–125, 130–131 (key passage), 159–167, 171–172, 227, 231, 233–235 (key passage), 242–243; and, idem, *Idālat*, fol. 99a–99b, 100a–102a; see also Hartmann, "Cosmogonie et doctrine," 165–168; cf. the parallel in al-Ghazālī, *Iḥyāʾ*, 3:17–19, which speaks of 'two doors of the heart', one opening to the *malakūt* and the other to the *ʿālam al-mulk*.

[89] *KF*, 113–119, 123–130, 141–142, 159–164, 180, 183–184, 206–207, 226–227, 229–231, 239–240, 246–247; idem, *Idālat*, fol. 93a, 95a–95b, 97a–97b, 100a, 104b; see also Hartmann, "Kosmogonie und Seelenlehre," 143; cf. al-Ghazālī, *Fayṣal al-tafriqa*, 87–88; and, idem, *al-Munqidh*, 60–62.

Table 2. Prophetic and Philosophic Consciousness

	Point of Origin	Active Agent	Mediating Agent (Isthmus)	Passive Agent	Locus of Apprehension
	ʿālam al-amr (masculine)	*rūḥ kullī* ↓	*ʿaql fiṭrī* ↓	*nafs kullī* ↓	*ʿālam al-ghayb* (*bāṭin*)
			← Prophetic Consciousness →		
Philosophic → Consciousness:	*ʿālam al-khalq* (feminine)	*rūḥ juzʾī*	← *ʿaql khilqī*/*qalb* →	*nafs juzʾī*	*ʿālam al-shahāda* (*ẓāhir*)

It is in this enunciation where Suhrawardī brings his earlier vision of the human psycho-spiritual constitution to its logical Neoplatonic conclusion, positing a microcosm-macrocosm relationship through mapping correspondences and then, in a fashion typical of most gnostic and Neoplatonic mysticisms, vesting it with epistemological and, ultimately, soteriological meaning. It is in the meeting of these two schemes where Suhrawardī's dual strategy is patently evinced. Throughout both polemics, the fundamental ideas of the *ʿAwārif al-maʿārif* all make a reappearance: the difference between the worldly- and otherworldly-ulama and the latter's claim to prophetic heirship, the idea of spiritual rebirth, the epistemological state of the illuminated prophetic or saintly heart and its resultant charisma, and the four-fold movement of the *ṭarīqa* are all woven into his discussion, serving as argumentative proofs against those "folk of innovation and misguided passions" posing such an insidious threat to the unity of the wider Muslim community and, by extension, to the prophetic heirs whose job it was to ensure its preservation in time and space.[90]

Arguing squarely from within the framework of this vision, like Ghazālī Suhrawardī identifies a number of specific points to refute as heretical, namely those three issues which the former saw as meriting the charge of *takfīr*, viz. the denial of the corporality and sentient nature of the Qurʾānic eschatological narrative, the denial of God's knowledge of particulars, and maintaining the eternity of the world

[90] *KF*, second spiritual birth (*wilādat maʿnawiyya*): 65–66, 188; prophetic charisma (*jadhba* and *rābiṭa*): 74–82, 161–162, 206–207, 211–214, 219–221 (idem, *Idālat*, fol. 90b–91b, 101a); heirship/combination of *ʿilm* and *ʿamal*: *KF*, 106–107, 132, 225, 229–230; the four-fold movement (i.e., *īmān—tawba naṣūḥ—zuhd fī ʾl-dunyā—ʿubūdiyya*) and its corresponding levels of attainment: idem, *Kashf*, 153–158, 187–188, 193–194, 201–202, 218; idem, *Idālat*, fol. 103b–104a.

sempiternally and eternally *a parte post*, a list to which Suhrawardī adds a number of others, the most important being what he sees as the philosophers' doctrine of the immortality of the soul (*nafs*) and their denial of miracles (*khawāriq al-ʿādāt*).[91] For Suhrawardī, however, there is no Ghazālian compromise, and in rooting each and every denial and challenge which the philosophers and materialists pose to revelation in the inability of their creatural intellects to penetrate the *ʿālam al-ghayb* and thus apprehend the ontological truths and spiritual verities which are apparent to the prophets and their followers, he programmatically connects *takfīr* with the superiority of gnostic and ecstatic cognition (*ʿirfāniyya wa-l-wajdāniyya*) over and against discursive cognition (*burhāniyya*),[92] and thus connects the otherworldly-ulama/*ṣūfiyya* to the Prophet and, although not explicitly but perhaps by extension, to the disposition of that spiritual authority through the authority of a caliph who serves to ensure its continuity by supporting and patronizing those who are its rightful heirs.

As with the publication of his creed and forays into the world of the *futuwwa*, ultimately Suhrawardī's stance on Peripatetic philosophy had already been prefigured by the constraints of his own program and that of his patron. While al-Nāṣir could easily accommodate the Sunni ulama, Imāmī Shia, *fityān*, and *ribāṭ*-based Sufis in his program, and Suhrawardī the competing strands of the Sufi tradition, Ḥanbalites, Ashʿarites, and Akhīs in his, unlike the *ṣūfiyya*, mutually antagonistic Sunni juridico-theological movements, or the *futuwwat*, the *falāsifa* were not as easily accommodated. Vesting authority and soteriological ambition in locations well outside the narrative of Abrahamic dispensation framing the very identity of *jamāʿī-sunnī*, *sharīʿa*-minded ulama such as Suhrawardī, the *falāsifa* were possessed of a vision of identity which could not readily be circumscribed under a master *isnād*, and since it

---

[91] *KF*, 97, 104–106, 112–114, 143–151, 194–198, 208, 217, 221–228, 240–243; and, idem, *Idalat*, fol. 95a–96a, 97a, 106b–107b, 109b–110a; see also: Zanjānī, "Rashf al-naṣāʾiḥ," 8:252; cf. al-Ghazālī, *Tahāfut*, 12–54, 134–143, 208–225; idem, *al-Munqidh*, 36; and, idem, *Fayṣal al-tafriqa*, 109–110.

[92] This is not to posit a strict, positive bifurcation between the respective epistemologies associated with dianoetic and mystical cognition in the minds of all Peripatetics and theosophically-inclined Sufis of the Middle Periods, but is rather simply indicative of a particular line of thinking associated with figures such as Suhrawardī. On this generally, see Oliver Leaman, *An Introduction to Classical Islamic Philosophy*, 2nd ed. (Cambridge: Cambridge University Press, 2002), 191–199; which, however, needs to be read within the still unresolved debate over the exact nature of Ibn Sīnā's 'mysticism' (on which, see D. Gutas, "Avicenna [V. Mysticism]," *EIr*, 1:79–83).

could not be co-opted, it had to be excluded. Whether this exclusion was enunciated in support of al-Nāṣir's program first—long after it had already come to an end in any case—and of his own program second is a matter of whether or not an ʿUmar al-Suhrawardī *als Ratgeber und Hoftheologe des Chalifen* first and *shaykh al-tarbiya* and champion of his own *ṭāʾifa* second can be extracted from the sources, something which in both the representation of himself in his own texts and the representation of him preserved in the texts of others, ultimately seems to favor the latter.

CONCLUSION

Although replicated in some measure by al-Nāṣir's grandson al-Mustanṣir and continuing on a much smaller scale with al-Mustaʿṣim (d. 656/1258), the destruction of the Abbasid caliphate at the hands of the Mongols just a mere twenty-four years after al-Suhrawardī's death brought a decisive end to what was already a very much yet-to-be-completed program. At the same time, however, this moment of destruction was possessed of great creative potential, and as with the moments of before and after which came to converge in the swan song of the once glorious and self-assured Abbasid caliphs of Baghdad, the vision of one of the many members of its choir came to serve as a moment of before and after for those who followed. Unlike the Nāṣirian *futuwwa* (although surviving for a brief time in Mamluk Egypt) the system of organization and praxis which Suhrawardī systematized in Baghdad became the inheritance of a number of just as important and influential beneficiaries, individuals who forged continuities with their benefactor by replicating many of his policies, and it is in their activities where the origins of the Sufi order bearing his name are to be sought.

In the case of the eponym himself, in charting the contours of the political history of the central and eastern lands of Islamdom between the 4th/10th and 7th/13th centuries as they came to converge in the figure of al-Nāṣir li-Dīn Allāh, we have seen why someone like this particular caliph may have found it useful to capitalize upon the authority wielded by someone like Suhrawardī. Here, the idea of a coherent and systematic political program simultaneously drawing upon multiple locations of authority and legitimacy already woven into the very social fabric of medieval Islamic urban landscapes is of primary importance. No small part of this program included capitalizing upon the authority of a group of literate, elite, urban *sharīʿa*-minded Sufi ulama populating the endowed *ribāṭ*s and *madrasa*s of Baghdad, and indeed, other major urban centers of the central and eastern lands of Islamdom during the 6th/12th–7th/13th centuries. In this, al-Nāṣir did nothing new, for his Seljuk and Abbasid predecessors did much the same, as did his contemporaries, most notably the Ayyubids in Syria and Egypt and the Rūm Seljuks in Anatolia. Although not the most important or consequential member of this group nor a powerful *Ratgeber und*

Hoftheologe, as a member of this body, Suhrawardī did participate and play a role in al-Nāṣir's program at some level, entering into a patronage relationship which brought with certain rights, obligations, and expectations for both parties.

This model, with differences certainly, would be replicated by individuals such as Bahā᾿ al-Dīn Zakariyyā Multānī (d. 661/1262), the most consequential propagator of Suhrawardī's vision in the Indian Subcontinent[1], and by Najīb al-Dīn ʿAlī b. Buzghush (d. 678/1279), the chief exponent of Suhrawardī's teachings in the important southern Iranian city of Shiraz.[2] Like their master, each of these men (and no small number of others who also participated in the dissemination of Suhrawardī's vision) belonged to the same broad group: both were trained Shāfiʿī ulama hailing from respectable scholarly families, both were active in the transmission of *ḥadīth* and other texts, both directed endowed *ribāṭ*s within which they invested individuals with the *khirqa* and trained disciples, and both passed on the *khirqa* which they received from Suhrawardī to many, many disciples, supported by the same ini-

[1] After ʿAlī b. Buzghush, certainly the most important figure in the spread of the Suhrawardiyya in the eastern lands of Islamdom. Allegedly of Qurayshī descent, his grandfather left Mecca, ended up in Khwārazm, and from there emigrated to Multan. Bahā᾿ al-Dīn left Multan for Khurāsān and spent a number of years studying in Bukhara, made the hajj, spent five years in Medina, went to Jerusalem, and finally arrived in Baghdad where he attached himself to Suhrawardī. According to his biographers, he spent a mere seventeen days under the tutelage of Suhrawardī before he was invested with the '*khirqat al-khilāfa*'. He was ordered by the shaykh to return to Multan, where he established a hereditary *silsila* which crystallized into the line which would give birth to the Indian Suhrawardiyya. His most important disciples included his son Ṣadr al-Dīn al-ʿĀrif (d. 684/1286), Sayyid Jalāl-i Bukhārī (d. 690/1291), Fakhr al-Dīn ʿIrāqī (d. 688/1289), and Ḥusayn-i Ḥusayn-i Sādāt (d. c. 718/1318). On him, see Dārā Shukūh, *Safīnat*, 114–115; ʿAbd al-Ḥayy al-Ḥusaynī, *al-Iʿlām bi-man fī ta᾿rīkh al-hind min al-aʿlām* (Beirut: Dār Ibn Ḥazm, 1999), 1:99–100 (no. 99); *GE*, 6 (no. 21); and, Athar Abbas Rizvi, *A History of Sufism in India* (New Delhi: Munshiram Manoharlal Publishers Pvt. Ltd., 1978–1983), 190–194, 202–206.

[2] Along with Bahā᾿ al-Dīn Zakariyyā Multānī, ʿAlī b. Buzghush was one of the major players in the diffusion of Suhrawardī's teachings in the eastern Islamic world after his death. Hailing from an immigrant family, his father (a wealthy merchant) came to Shiraz from Syria where he married the daughter of Sharaf al-Dīn Muḥammad al-Ḥusaynī. A man with a propensity for reclusiveness, we know little about his early life nor when he first met Suhrawardī, although he was definitely in Baghdad in the middle of Muḥarram, 624/January, 1227 where he was present at a reading of the *ʿAwārif* in the Ribāṭ al-Ma᾿mūniyya (MS. Süley., Lâlâ İsmail Ef. 180_4, fol. 234a). He died in Shiraz in Shaʿbān, 678/December, 1279, and came to serve as a node in the lines of a number of later Sufi teaching lineages. On him, see Zarkūb-i Shīrāzī, *Shīrāznāma*, ed. Bahman-i Karīmī (Tehran: Intishārāt-i Būnyād-i Farhang-i Īrān, 1350 sh. [1972]), 131–132; Junayd-i Shīrāzī, *Shadd*, 334–338; Khwāfī, *Mujmal*, 2:347; Dārā Shukūh, *Safīnat*, 114; Maʿṣūmʿalīshāh, *Ṭarā᾿iq*, 2:310–312; and, *GE*, 6 (no. 20).

tiatic genealogy that Suhrawardī claimed for himself when investing them. Like him too (although the details are much clearer in the case of Bahā᾿ al-Dīn) both of these individuals enjoyed the support and patronage of political powers, serving the interests of their respective patrons through the spiritual, social, and religious authority with which their status endowed them.

In the figure of Suhrawardī himself, we find al-Nāṣir patronizing an individual who was thoroughly convinced of the validity of the claim of his particular *Personengruppe* to prophetic heirship, an individual who in no uncertain terms presented himself as an authoritative spokesman for a group whom he saw as self-consciously marking itself out from all other *Personengruppen* who might impinge upon that claim. Given his life-long association with members of this group, it is naïve to assume that al-Nāṣir was not well aware of the categorical comprehensiveness with which Suhrawardī viewed his particular *ṭā᾿ifa*. Likewise, it is equally naïve to assume that such was lost upon those non-affiliates, both among the ulama and masses alike, who inhabited the neighborhoods which played host to the very *ribāṭ*s, *madrasa*s, and public pulpits which they populated.

At the same time, this particular Sufi shaykh and Shāfiʿī *ʿālim* was not the only one to do such, for although neither leaving behind texts nor becoming eponyms of later *ṭarīqa*-lineages much the same can be said for others such as the aforementioned members of the *shaykh al-shuyūkh* family Ṣadr al-Dīn ʿAbd al-Raḥīm and Ibn Sukayna, Suhrawardī's disciple and close associate Saʿd b. Muẓaffar al-Yazdī[3] (d. 637/1239), and the grandson of ʿAbd al-Qādir al-Jīlānī, Abū Ṣāliḥ Naṣr b. ʿAbd al-Razzāq

---

[3] Hailing from Yazd, Abū Ṭālib al-Yazdī set himself up at the Baghdad Niẓāmiyya teaching Shāfiʿī *fiqh*. After a time, he became a disciple of Suhrawardī and settled down in the Ribāṭ al-Zawzanī, abandoning jurisprudence in favor of the path of asceticism, solitary retreat, and spiritual austerities. He accompanied Suhrawardī to Syria during his mission to the Ayyubids of 604/1207–1208, and according to (pseudo-)Ibn al-Fuwaṭī also preached at the *madrasa* of Abū ᾿l-Najīb. At some point, he fell into the good graces of al-Nāṣir's vizier al-ʿAlawī and subsequently entered into his service, being granted the position of executor (*wakīl*). When al-ʿAlawī was removed from the vizierate, al-Yazdī "returned to the dress of the Sufis" until he was called upon by al-Nāṣir to perform a number of diplomatic missions which, according to Ibn al-Najjār, included one to the Khwārazm Shāh ʿAlā᾿ al-Dīn in Iraq—possibly in connection with Suhrawardī's mission to him in 614/1217–1218—and then to Syria, Egypt, Rūm, and Fārs. Near the end of his life, al-Mustanṣir granted him the *mashyakha* of the Ribāṭ al-Saljūqiyya, which he held until his death on the 26th of Muḥarram, 637/28 August, 1239 after which he was interred in the Shūnīziyya Cemetery. On him, see: Ibn al-ʿAdīm, *Bughyat al-ṭalab fī ta᾿rīkh Ḥalab*, ed. Suhayl Zakkār [Damascus: n.p., 1988], 9:4275–4276; and, *KḤ*, 153, 162–163.

(d. 633/1236), all of whom directed their own *ribāṭs*, invested individuals with the *khirqa*, and performed key tasks in support of al-Nāṣir's program, most of them to a much greater extent than Suhrawardī ever did. Important as they were however, because such individuals neither became eponyms of a particular *ṭarīqa*-lineage nor possessed a body of disciples and heirs who took it as their task to preserve their memory and the texts which they may have composed, any role which they might have played in the development and systematization of the particular form of institutionalizing *ribāṭ*-based Sufism which they most certainly championed is nearly unrecoverable. At the same time, there is little reason to doubt that such individuals—individuals located in the same social, discursive, political, and even physical spaces—would not have, at least in part, shared Suhrawardī's vision of the comprehensive spiritual and religious authority possessed by the 'otherworldly-ulama' and their responsibility to discharge that authority through the instruments—the institutions of process and institutions of place—which generated that authority in the first place.

Shielded as they were by the safety of a broader *jamāʿī-sunnī* commitment to the ideals embodied in the *siyāsa sharʿiyya* discourse rooted in the moral (and in al-Nāṣir's case increasingly politically validated) authority of the caliphate as the *de jure* guarantor of a broader *sharʿī* order supported and effectuated through a diffuse body of Sunni ulama, such individuals not only posed little challenge to al-Nāṣir's program as such, but in fact were in possession of a type of authority which could be deployed to effect it. Always carefully conscious of the wider implications of his public enunciations, it is doubtful if al-Nāṣir would have systematically capitalized upon the authority of Baghdad's Sufi *ribāṭs* and those who populated them if they did not already serve as repositories of types of authority already circulating in a broader socio-religious economy. As evinced in the particular figuration of authority in the circles in which Suhrawardī moved, those who populated the upper tiers of Baghdad's *ribāṭs* could be of consequence to such a patron precisely because they were linked with types of authority well embedded in the social world characterizing the major urban landscapes of medieval Islamdom, authority which, layered and multiply located to be sure, was neither insular nor unique.

It is here where the convergence between those twin institutions of the *madrasa* and the *ribāṭ* becomes especially important, for as we have seen not only did Suhrawardī and his teachers, students, disciples, and associates move seamlessly between both spaces but more importantly the very social practices, cultural codes, and figurations of authority and identity—its enunciation, conservation, and perpetuation through texts and social practices—structuring the transmission of both religious learning and mystical knowledge converged and overlapped in a shared language, practice, and symbol. In attending to these convergences, it becomes clear that it is both naïve and irresponsible to schematize Sufism generally, and the particular *ribāṭ*-based Junaydī tradition represented by Suhrawardī in particular, as a closed system set in binary opposition to some monolithic orthodoxy championed by certain bodies of well-situated ulama, certainly a foregone conclusion for those with any grounding in the literature of the period, but an idea which is still tenaciously clung to by many. If indeed the overlapping and converging nature of the *madrasa* and *ribāṭ* in Suhrawardī's Baghdad can be admitted (and I believe the sources evince that it can) then what we see is that at its core the *ribāṭ* was indeed highly regulated, almost curricular, in nature, designated solely for a particular self-identified group commonality and possessed of clear functional categories of individual participation at its center, but at the same time it was a place whose margins were porous, its fluidity providing for varying levels of affiliation and participation. Added to this is the clear presence of a certain transregional solidarity and group identity focused on the institution itself, something embedded in the very terms which Suhrawardī uses to describe the constituency of his *ribāṭ*s and something which is exemplified in his detailed prescriptions of travel for the *faqīr*. The convergence between this figuration of community and the practices which forge its identity and the transregionality of the culture of religious learning as evinced in that eminently important 'institution of process' of *ṭalab al-ʿilm* is so clear as to scarcely deserve further comment. Similarly, the configuration of social relationships obtaining in both spaces as being regulated by a complex of normative practices and behaviors rooted in a shared culture of formal manners (*adab*) and the clear semiological overlap between the transmission of religious learning in the *madrasa* and the transmission of mystical knowledge in the *ribāṭ* points to a broader institutional confluence which, in turn, is reflected in both Suhrawardī's own representation of himself and the *ṭāʾifa* for whom he spoke in rhetorical terms as well as in the seventy or so individual cases of members of his circle preserved in the historiography and prosopography in representational terms.

As it relates to both the systematic enunciation of the authority of his own *Personengruppe* and the Nāṣirian project in general, not only do we find in Suhrawardī an imminently public figure preaching at places such as Baghdad's Badr al-Sharīf Gate or inside the Ḥarām al-Sharīf in Mecca, but also an individual who in a very real sense looked to exteriorize the interiorizing, *baraka*-saturated, inner sanctum of the *ribāṭ* and its charismatic community of spiritual frontline fighters by attending to the porosity of its margins, investing any and all with the *khirqat al-tabarruk*, counseling those whom he granted permission to train their own disciples to respect the rights of those *mustarshidīn* who might come to them seeking guidance and religious or spiritual consul, and engaging in a public enunciation of spiritual and religious authority the depth of whose self-assuredness and moral confidence was as real to its affiliates as it was to its detractors, something well evinced in Suhrawardī's indiscretion of 605/1208. It is this institutional and social confluence which provides a link between the dominance of political program and the third cluster of before and after which converged in Suhrawardī's moment, the discourse and authority of the text.

As with the institutional confluence, in reading those traces which Suhrawardī left behind in his own texts, we have seen that the discursive enunciations of such an individual should be located within a broader economy of religious discourse among the ulama. In publicly writing his own identity through that of the particular *ṭāʾifa* for whom he spoke Suhrawardī pursued a strategy of inclusion through circumscription, programmatically attempting to draw various self-constituted commonalities and sectarian affiliations within the orbit of an increasingly socially-open and accommodationist *ribāṭ*-based Sufi system. In the case of those real or imagined *Personengruppen* who could not be accommodated under the master *isnād* of a broader *sharīʿa*-minded *jamāʿī-sunnī* identity in which Suhrawardī and the circles of elite, largely Shāfiʿī urban Sufi ulama of which he was a part located themselves, the same type of norm-writing was used as a device of exclusion. In the case of Suhrawardī and the particular strand of the Sufi tradition which he had inherited and for which he appointed himself a spokesman, this discourse proceeded from an established center, one populated, certainly, by otherworldly-ulama, but ulama nevertheless.

In this, the thrust of his project differed little from that of the Sufi systematizers of the 4th/10th–5th/11th centuries from whose works he quotes repeatedly (Sarrāj, Abū Ṭālib al-Makkī, Kalābādhī, Sulamī, Abū Nuʿaym al-Iṣfahānī, and Qushayrī), re-inscribing genealogies inherited from the past in a newly constituted, institutionalizing, present; a present where *niyāba* was existentialized solely through the sciences of the *ṣūfiyya* and the mediation of that *niyāba* to the aspirant, mendicant, pretender, and all those *mustarshidīn* seeking religious and moral guidance, solely through the very personhood of the shaykh, an individual who was at one and the same time a *muntahī* and *muqarrab*, an *ab maʿnawī* and *nāʾib nabawī*, a *wālī* and *ʿālim ṣāliḥ*, an individual who derived his authority from multiple locations but then centered it in the institutional forms of social organization and rule-governed praxis framing his presence in actual brick and mortar institutions. It is this underlying conception of authority and its articulation in the activities of the *ṭāʾifa* who possessed it which framed and guided Suhrawardī's policy of maintaining a 'dual-strategy' vis-à-vis his own program and that of his patron.

Furthermore, in examining the issue of the discourse and authority of the text as it came to express itself in Suhrawardī's historical moment, we have seen that in many ways the particular *ṭarīqa*-based trend of Sufism which Suhrawardī championed can be viewed as a textualizing tradition, a tradition which utilized textual strategies shared with a much larger culture of religious learning. As with jurists, *ḥadīth* transmitters, theologians, and others such individuals, Suhrawardī constructed the text as an instrument of affiliation, identity, and authority, vesting it with both social and soteriological meaning. Here, texts served as both repositories of memory and instruments of authority. As to the first, texts served as repositories of authoritative and, ultimately, salvific patterns of behavior which could be replicated in the present, whereas to the second, they served as instruments by which one could participate in a broader collective endeavor which conferred status and authority upon its practitioners. In this, his system was possessed of a built-in replicability. The interplay between the two clearly constituted a particularly powerful discursive technology, a contested instrument which as with Ibn Sīnā's *K. al-shifāʾ* could literally be washed away, an instrument of norm writing and institutionalization (*ʿAwārif al-maʿārif, Irshād al-murīdīn, Jadhdhāb al-qulūb*, the *R.* and *K. fī ʾl-futuwwa*), an enunciation of exegetical authority and religious or spiritual legitimacy (*Aʿlām al-hudā, Kashf al-faḍāʾiḥ, Idālat al-ʿiyān*), or even an instrument for preserving the near physicality of a relationship rooted in perceived psycho-spiritual affinities between master and disciple (*waṣāyā* and *ijāzāt ʿāmma*), between mentor and protégé, between spiritual father and spiritual son, between the very representative of the Prophet and those frontline fighters in the struggle against the *nafs* who saw themselves as his companions (*ṣaḥāba*). It is here where the position of Suhrawardī's own program seems to represent—when set alongside those of the other eponyms (and their immediate disciples) of the early *ṭarīqa*-lineages—a certain culmination, or final systematization, of a process of institution building which had been slowly gaining momentum since at least the late-4th/10th century.

There was a reason why Suhrawardī expended energy in writing an extended universalizing doxography in the *ʿAwārif al-maʿārif* and a reason why he was so careful in crafting a rhetoric of inclusion in his *Futuwwat-nāma*s for the *akhī-fityān* and a rhetoric of exclusion in his polemics against Peripatetic philosophy. Here, we witness the cumulative pressure of a particular *sharīʿa*-minded Junaydī past coalescing in Suhrawardī's moment, a past sensitized to discursive and social location and deeply concerned with securing identity in a discursive field where claims to religious and spiritual authority—and the very genealogies upon which they were predicated—were contested. It is vitally important to recall that in the particular Sufi *ribāṭ*s which al-Nāṣir patronized we meet with what was certainly a powerful and creative articulation of the Sufi tradition on the ascendancy, but nonetheless a strand of the Sufi tradition located within a broader complex of differing and often competing strands which in certain cases were equally as powerful players within the tradition itself. It was in keeping such competing strands in view (in what might be seen as a re-enactment of the earlier victory of the *ṣūfiyya* over the Malāmatiyya and Karrāmiyya) which in a sense frames Suhrawardī's contribution to the development of this particular figuration of the Sufi tradition, a figuration which would come to dominate, but in no way obliterate, others. While critiques such as those of Ibn al-Jawzī in the late 6th/12th century and Ibn Taymiyya in the early 8th/14th are certainly a bit exaggerated, they are nonetheless deeply telling in that they evince the presence of a very real polyphony within Sufism in the central lands of Islamdom before and after Suhrawardī. Much the same being be found in the comments of individuals such as Dhahabī and Ibn Kathīr, both of whom were keen observers of the various religious, political, and intellectual trends of their day and age, and who like Yāqūt in his entry on Suhraward quoted at the beginning of Chapter Two, knew what it meant to be a member of the *ṣulaḥāʾ* and what it meant to be a member of whichever antithesis—*qalandarī*, *malāmatī*, *ḥulūlī*, *ittiḥādī*, *falsafī*, etc.—might serve as its opposite in any one time, place, or—more often than not—discursive location.

While battling with these competing trends, located as he was near the moral center of a broader *jamāʿī-sunnī* communalist ethos, for

Suhrawardī enunciating the legitimacy of the *ṣūfiyya* was certainly not a matter of trying to effect some type of reconciliation between the ulama and the Sufis from the outside, but rather consolidating the position of a group who were already well-established; a group deeply entrenched in a culture of religious professionals toward whom the state looked for support and legitimacy and the people for religious guidance and intercession. Here, we find an author who just like his biographers emplotted his retelling in established rhetorical modes, engaging in the composition and programmatic dissemination of texts as part of a broader program of reform and centralization which aimed to circumscribe various self-constituted commonalities and sectarian affiliations within the orbit of what was perceived as a comprehensive and increasingly accommodationist *ribāṭ*-based Sufi system. Because of its privileging of the authoritating apparatus of genealogy, the delineation of strict hierarchies of affiliation, the foregrounding of detailed prescriptions for a program of praxis effected in actual brick and mortar institutions, and the way in which this vision would later come to constitute itself in discrete teaching lineages (*ṭuruq*), I have called this particular Junaydī mode of Sufism '*ṭarīqa*-based Sufism', although it is eagerly hoped that further research on the individuals, texts, and trends associated with the rise of the early teaching lineages will bring this term into question.

What is apparent, in fact, is that applying the attributive 'Suhrawardiyya' to those circles of Sufis comprised of Suhrawardī's immediate disciples is at best an anachronism. As with each of the early *ṭarīqa*-lineages, it not clear when those who saw themselves as heirs to Suhrawardī, or others for that matter, began to use the attributive 'Suhrawardiyya' to refer to a self-identified teaching lineage nor when an awareness of being initiated into a particular self-constituted and eponymicly-denominated *ṭarīqa* emerged. Part of the reason for this, although much more work needs to be done on the sources before a real answer can be furnished, seems to be rooted in the fluidity and indeterminate nature of what it meant during the 7th/13th–8th/14th century to enunciate affiliation with a particular *nisbat al-khirqa* or *nisbat talqīn al-dhikr*, something well evinced in the convergences of (mostly back-projected) lines of initiatic affiliation reaching back to Abū ʾl-Najīb al-Suhrawardī (see Chapter Two, Chart 3).

Contemporaries of Suhrawardī, such as the *shaykh al-shuyūkh* Ibn Sukayna, engaged in the same type of activities which Suhrawardī is remembered for, transmitting *ḥadīth*—including to Suhrawardī's son ʿImād al-Dīn (d. 655/1257)[4]—directing *ribāṭ*s, investing disciples with the *khirqa*, and enjoying the patronage of officials, yet did not become an eponym of a later *ṭarīqa*. Similarly, we know, for example, that the *khirqa* of al-Qushayrī was transmitted in Baghdad during the time of Suhrawardī (and indeed well into the 8th/14th-century), and that his *ribāṭ* in Nīshāpūr, which had become a hereditary possession, was an active center until at least the mid-7th/13th century, yet no *ṭarīqat al-qushayriyya* emerged from this lineage nor did he or his descendents become objects of hagiographic narration, two things which seem to be intimately connected. The same can be said for any number of others.

While his *waṣāyā* make it abundantly clear that Suhrawardī envisioned a transregional dissemination of the particular way (*ṭarīqa*) of a particular *ṭāʾifa* (the *ṣūfiyya*) throughout the lands of Islamdom, how systematic both the vision and consequence of such a dissemination might have been is not at all clear. Even though the South Asian hagiographies would have us think differently, neither the term *khalīfa* nor *muqaddam* is ever used by Suhrawardī himself, neither in the many *waṣāyā* in which he granted permission to disciples to return to their home countries and transmit on his authority, nor even in the extremely important *ijāza* which he granted to Bahāʾ al-Dīn Zakariyyā Multānī in Mecca on the 26th of Dhū ʾl-Ḥijja, 626/15 November, 1229 where he explicitly grants him permission to train disciples.[5] Ultimately, to understand how these documents might fit into the complex history

[4] Born in 578/1182, ʿImād al-Dīn was the product of Suhrawardī's marriage to Abū ʾl-Najīb's granddaughter, Sayyida bt. ʿAbd al-Raḥīm. Not much is preserved about him save that he went by the name 'Abū ʾl-Jaʿfar, the son of the shaykh Shihāb al-Dīn' and, along with many others, heard *ḥadīth* from both Ibn al-Jawzī and Ibn Sukayna. He is also reported to have traveled to Damascus where he heard *ḥadīth* from Bahāʾ al-Dīn al-Qāsim b. al-Ḥāfiẓ. Both his son, Jamāl al-Dīn ʿAbd al-Raḥmān, and his grandson, Abū ʾl-Qāsim ʿAbd al-Maḥmūd, are reported to have transmitted on his authority. According to al-Ṣafadī, ʿImād al-Dīn was well known as a Sufi and teaching shakyh. He invested individuals with the *khirqa*, and his *K. zād al-musāfir wa-adab al-ḥāḍir* evinces the continuity of his vision with that of his father. Although denied the *mashyakha* of the Ribāṭ al-Marzubāniyya by the caliph al-Mustanṣir, he inherited the *mashyakha* of the Ribāṭ al-Maʾmūniyya, being buried there on the 10th of Jumāda II, 655/Jun. 25th, 1257, its *mashyakha* then passing to his son Jamāl al-Dīn. On him, see *KḤ*, 353 (*anno* 655); *SN*, 22:377 (s.v. al-Suhrawardī), and, *TIsl*, 47:291 (births, *anno* 578), 49:255 (s.v. ʿAbd al-Wahhāb [Ibn Sukayna]), and 54:216 (*anno* 655, no. 221); *KW*, 4:262 (no. 1795); Ritter, "Philologika IX," 46 (no. 60); *GE*, 7 (no. 26); and, Düzenli, "Sühreverdî," 20–21 (no. 1).

[5] al-Suhrawardī, *Ijz. li-Bahāʾ al-Dīn Ẓakariyyā Multānī*, fol. 71b–72a.

of the diffusion of Suhrawardī's *khirqa*—as well as the diffusion of the *ʿAwārif al-maʿārif* through translations / re-writings and its incorporation in other manuals—requires us to make sense of what Suhrawardī might have envisioned when he prescribed in his rules of travel for the *faqīr* (prior to his investment with the *khirqa*) that one should visit multiple *ribāṭ*s in order to learn about the ways of its denizens, *ribāṭ*s which he characterizes as the outpost of a broader spiritual family of frontline fighters in the struggle against the *nafs*. Despite a careful enunciation of his own *nisbat al-khirqa*, whether or not Suhrawardī envisioned—as was to become increasingly common in the two centuries which followed—this broader commonality of brethren as organized primarily around a particular initiatic lineage is not readily apparent. What is clear, however, is the foregrounding of the ethos of the institution of *ṭalab al-ʿilm*, the *faqīr* traveling in search of knowledge of a particular science dispensed by particular masters located in particular places, a prominent part of the wider culture of religious learning throughout medieval Islamdom.

As it relates to the rise of the Sufi brotherhoods, what we can speak at this particular moment in time is the dissemination of a system of organization and praxis, a particular way or method of spiritual discipline supported by an initiatic lineage reaching back to Prophet Muḥammad through an eponym, orienting itself on his teachings, and affiliated with the physical space of endowed *ribāṭ*s and *khānaqāh*s. Although this can certainly be mitigated with further research, due to the fractured state of the sources, the general fluidity of the early *ṭarīqa*-lineages themselves, and the indeterminate nature of the activities of Suhrawardī's disciples and the generation following them, it is difficult to reconstruct anything beyond a rudimentary history of the diffusion of this particular '*ṭarīqa*' with any precision. As reflected in the sources interrogated in this study, there are, in fact, only three distinct lines of this lineage during the 7th/13th into the early-8th/14th century whose connection with the *khirqa* Suhrawardī inherited from Abū ʾl-Najīb can be ascertained with any certainty, the first in Shiraz which seems to have evolved into a hereditary *ṭāʾifa* stemming from ʿAlī b. Buzghush, an initial line in North India stemming from Bahāʾ al-Dīn Zakariyyā Multānī, and a hereditary line in Baghdad stemming from Suhrawardī's son ʿImād al-Dīn (see Charts 5–7).

Alongside these three lines, the diffusion of both Suhrawardī's *khirqa* and the *ʿAwārif al-maʿārif* in Syria, Egypt, and the Hejaz by individuals

Chart 5.

Suhrawardiyya Lineages Associated with ʿAlī b. Buzghush*

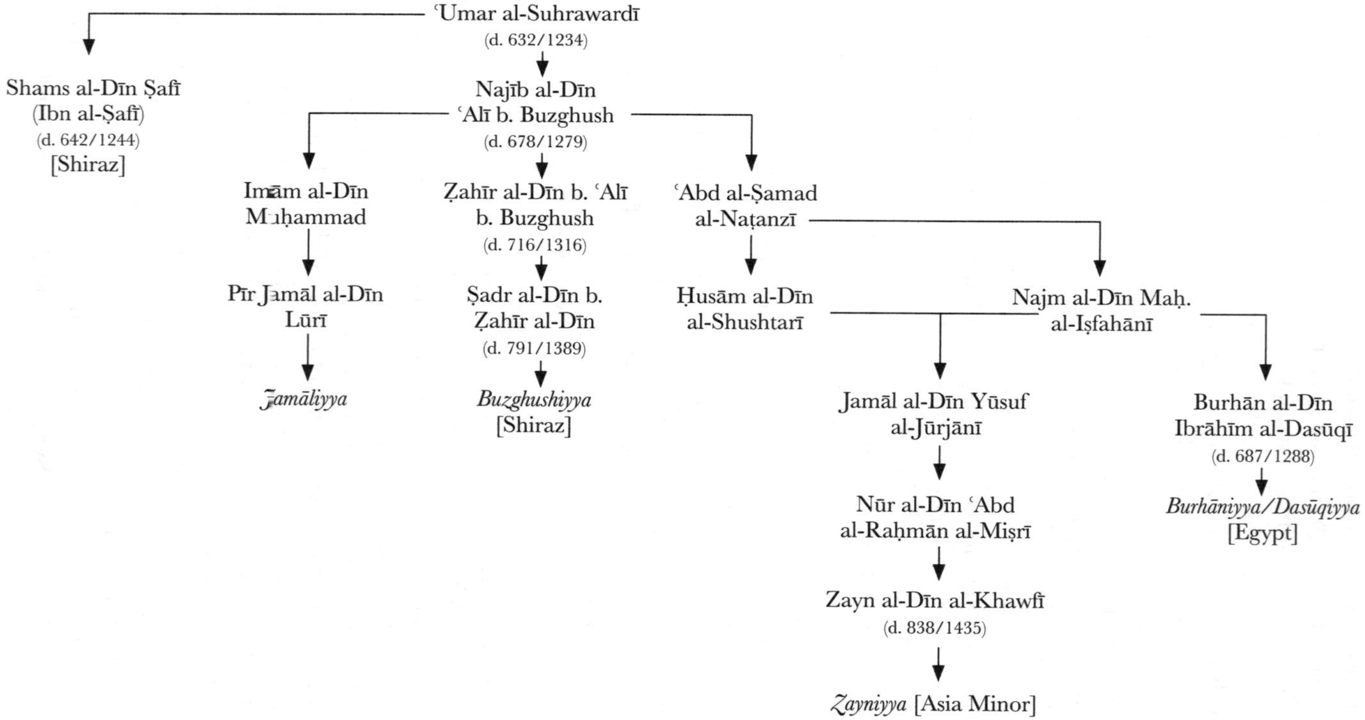

* al-Wāsiṭī, *Tiryāq*, 61; Jāmī, *Nafaḥāt*, 492–495 (nos. 510–511), 558 (no. 546); Chishtī, *Mirʾāt al-asrār*, 2:159–162; Dārā Shukūh, *Safīnat*, 114–115; Maʿṣūmʿalīshāh, *Ṭarāʾiq*, 2:311–312; al-Ḥusaynī, *al-Iʿlām*, 3:234 (no. 22), and 252 (no. 92); Kissling, "Aus der Geschichte des Chalvetijje Ordens," table 1; Trimingham, *Sufi Orders*, Appendix C; Norris, "The *Mirʾāt al-Ṭālibīn*"; Gramlich, *Derwischorden*, 1:10; 57–58; Shams, "ʿĀrifān-i suhravardiyya," 104–116; and, Mojaddedi, *Biographical Tradition*, Appendix 4.

Chart 6.

Early Suhrawardiyya Lineages in India (Simplified)*

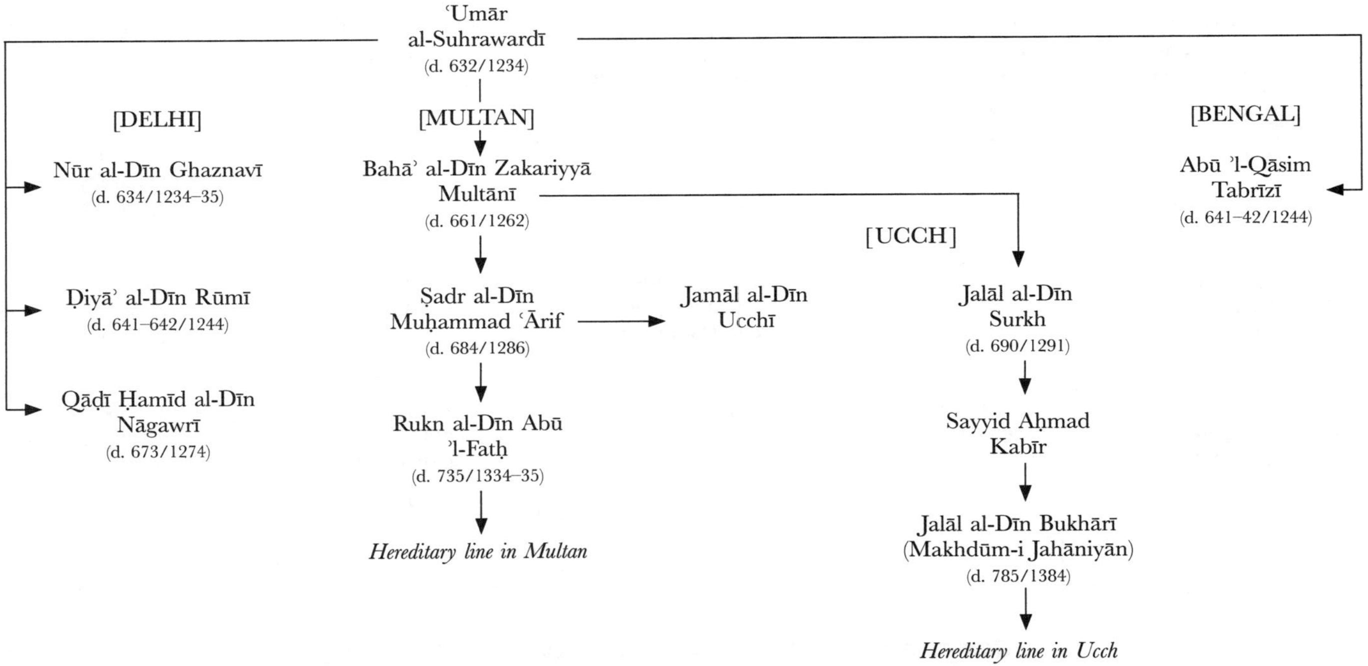

* Dihlavī, *Akhbār al-akhyār*, 28–29, 37–46, 61–66, 72–73; Chishtī, *Mirʾāt al-asrār*, 2:116–118, 136–141, 162–173, 255–263; Dārā Shukūh, *Safīnat*, 113, 115–116; Maʿṣūmʿalīshāh, *Ṭarāʾiq*, 2:312–313; al-Ḥusaynī, *al-Iʿlām*, 1:101 (no. 52), 1:99–100 (no. 99), 1:116 (no. 99), 1:122 (no. 110), 2:149 (no. 38); Trimingham, *Sufi Orders*, Appendix C; Rizvi, *A History*, 1:190–215; and, Steinfels, "Travels and Teachings," 45–58, 80.

Chart 7.

Early Suhrawardiyya Lineages in Iraq, Syria, and Egypt*

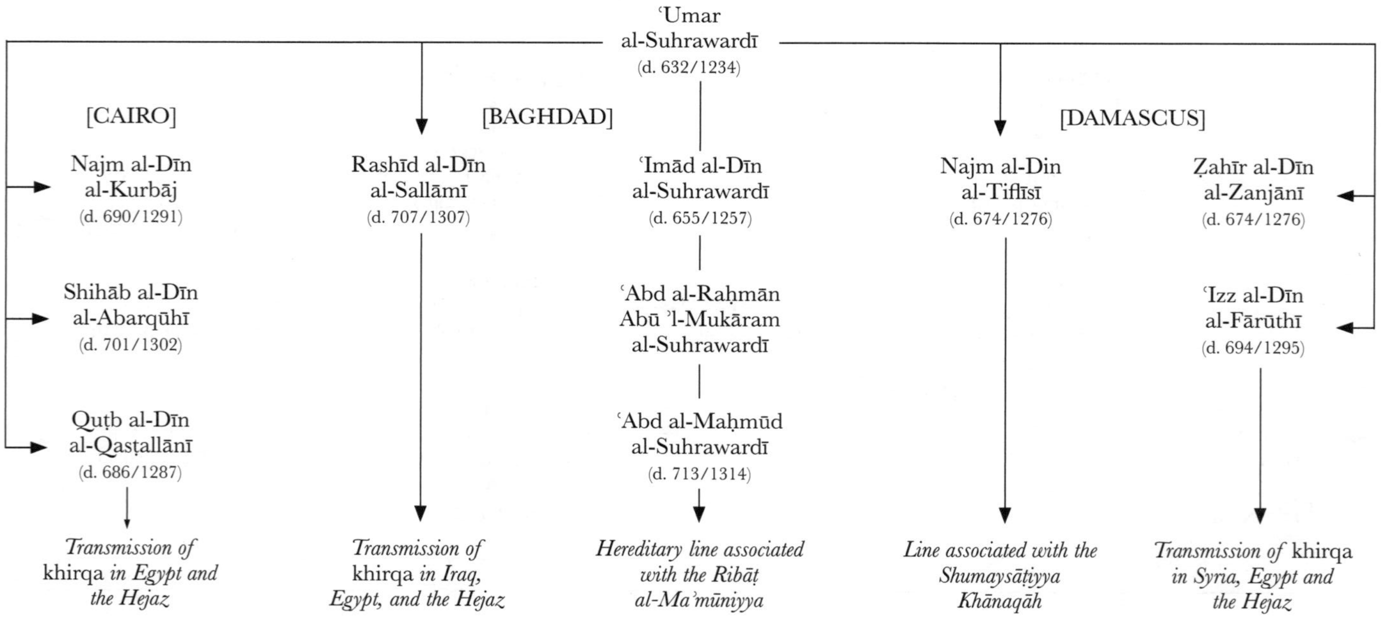

* Ibn al-Qasṭallānī, *Irtifāʿ*, Ɛ3; but, cf. Geoffroy, *Le soufisme*, 514.

such as Najm al-Dīn al-Tiflīsī and Ibn al-Qasṭallānī[6] (d. 686/1287) as well as the presence of disciples of the shaykh who directed *khānaqāh*s in Isfahan may have constituted others lines of transmission. Alongside this is the question of how and why both Abū ʾl-Najīb's *Ādāb al-murīdīn* and Suhrawardī's *ʿAwārif al-maʿārif* came to serve as such important texts in early Kubrawī circles and in turn what this may have meant for the development of other *ṭarīqa*-lineages associated with Transoxiana and Central Asia. As has already been noted in Chapters Three and Four, just as Suhrawardī preserved the works of Kalābādhī, Abū Ṭālib al-Makkī, Sulamī, and Qushayrī in his own manuals, so to do the manuals of Najm al-Dīn Kubrā, Najm al-Dīn Rāzī Dāya, and Yaḥyā al-Bākharzī preserve his, and given both the extent of the migration of 'Suhrawardī Sufis' from Transoxiana into the Indian Subcontinent beginning in the 8th/14th century and the connections between the nascent Suhrawardiyya and Yasawī and other lineages one occasionally comes across in the sources for the region, there is little reason to doubt that much could be gained from exploring the nature and extent of such associations. In addition to the massive amount of literature preserved on the early Suhrawardiyya in South Asia, the same, I think, should be done for the early Shādhiliyya in Egypt and North Africa,

---

[6] An individual whom Trimingham quite wrongly characterized as a man who "could barely be called a Sufi" (*The Sufi Orders*, 36), Ibn al-Qasṭallānī was a Shāfiʿī *muḥaddith* and Sufi known for his extraordinary asceticism and piety. Born in Egypt (27 Dhū ʾl-Ḥijja, 614/27 March, 1218) into a family of prominent Shāfiʿī ulama, as a young boy he was brought to Mecca and journeyed widely in search of *ḥadīth*, visiting Damascus and Baghdad, and from there Ḥimṣ, Aleppo, and Jerusalem. After the death of his brother, he took over his position as director of the Dār al-Ḥadīth al-Kāmiliyya in Cairo where—with frequent trips back to Mecca—he distinguished himself as a *muḥaddith*, mufti, *faqīh*, and author of treatises on *ḥadīth*, asceticism, and Sufism. In Dhū ʾl-Ḥijjā, 627/September, 1230, he heard the *ʿAwārif* from Suhrawardī in Mecca as well as taking the *khirqa* from him (*ʿAwārif al-maʿārif*, MS. Köprülü 750, fol. 130b; another copy of the same *riwāya* is preserved in ibid., MS. Süley., İzmir Yazmaları 293, fol. 302b). According to al-Shaʿrānī, he would invest individuals with the *khirqa* on the authority of the Suhrawardī (*Ṭabaqāt*, 2:349) and as attested in the manuscript record, was vigirous in transmitting the *ʿAwārif*, his *riwāya* being transmitted in Cairo for generations after his death. Ibn al-Qasṭallānī had something of a rivalry with Ibn Sabʿīn (d. 669/1269), and is reported to have polemicized against him quite often in Mecca as well as composing refutations against those whom he saw as following such teachings, beginning with al-Ḥallāj (d. 309/922) and ending with ʿAfīf al-Dīn al-Tilimsānī (d. 690/1291). He died while teaching in the Dār al-Ḥadīth al-Kāmiliyya (Cairo) on the 28th of Muḥarram 686/15 March, 1287. On him, see: *TIsl*, 57:277–279 (*anno* 686, no. 408); *KW*, 2:132–134 (no. 480); al-Kutubī, *Fawāt*, 3:310 (no. 433); *MJ*, 4:202–203 (*anno* 686); *ṬShK*, 8:43 (no. 1065); Ibn Rāfiʿ, *Muntakhab*, 173–175 (no. 148); *BN*, 13:310; *NZ*, 7:373; and, *ShDh*, 7:694–695 (*anno* 686).

the numerous instances of the transmission of the *ʿAwārif al-maʿārif* from the *riwāya* of Ibn al-Qasṭallānī in Cairo and Mecca up through at least the 8th/14th century to a diverse body of western Sufis (including scholars from as far away as Andalusia) needs to be examined, as does the presence of Suhrawardī's works in later Shādhilī literature and in the *nisbat al-khirqa*s of North African, Egyptian, and Syrian Sufis of the late 7th/13th through the late 9th/15th century found in the hagiographical compendia of al-Shaʿrānī and al-Munāwī.

In conclusion, to write the history of the institutionalization of Sufism (or perhaps a history of its particularly vocal institutionalizing trends) in a larger sense and the rise to prominence, and in no small way the rise to dominance, of this particular strand of Junaydī *ṭarīqa*-based Sufism within it, means to write the way in which such beneficiaries came to translate Suhrawardī's vision into the particular linguistic, geographic, political, discursive and social spaces in which they moved, attending to the same types continuities and disjunctions of before and after which I have attempted to attend to here. It is my sincere hope that the excavation and display of those traces which this particular actor left behind offered here will serve to frame that writing, for it is there where the history of Abū Ḥafṣ ʿUmar, the son of Muḥammad from Suhraward ends and the history of the *ṭarīqat al-suhrawardiyya* begins.

BIBLIOGRAPHY

Primary Sources

Abū 'l-Fidā. *al-Mukhtaṣar fī akhbār al-bashar*. 4 vols. in 2. Cairo: Maṭbaʿat al-Ḥusayniyyat al-Miṣriyya, 1325 [1907].

Abū Shāma al-Maqdisī. *Dhayl ʿalā 'l-rawḍatayn* (*Tarājim rijāl al-qarnayn al-sādis wa-l-sābiʿ*). Edited by Muḥammad Zāhid al-Kawtharī. Cairo: Dār al-Kutub al-Mālikiyya, 1947.

Aflākī, Shams al-Dīn Aḥmad. *Manāqib al-ʿārifīn*. 2 vols. Edited by Tahsin Yazıcı. Ankara: Türk Tarih Kurumu Yayınları, 1959–1961. English translation by John O'Kane as *The Feats of the Knowers of God*. Leiden: Brill, 2002.

Anṣārī, ʿAbdullāh-i. *Ṣad maydān*. Edited by Qāsim Anṣārī. Tehran: Kitābkhāna-yi Ṭūrī, 1376 sh. [1997].

ʿAqīda I, II, V. [s.v. Watt].

al-Ashʿarī, Abū 'l-Ḥasan ʿAlī b. Ismāʿīl. *al-Ibāna ʿan uṣūl al-diyāna*. Translated with an introduction and notes by Walter Conrad Klein as *The Elucidation of Islām's Foundation*. New Haven, CT: American Oriental Society, 1940.

——. *K. al-lumaʿ*. Edited and translated by R.J. McCarthy as *The Theology of al-Ashʿarī*. Beirut: Imprimerie Catholique, 1953.

——. *Maqālāt al-islāmiyyīn*. Edited by Helmut Ritter. Istanbul: li-Jamāʿiyyat al-Mustashriqīn al-Almāniyya, 1929–1933.

al-ʿAynī, Badr al-Dīn. *ʿIqd al-jumān fī taʾrīkh ahl al-zamān*. 4 vols. Edited by Muḥammad Amīn. Cairo: al-Hayʾat al-Miṣriyya al-ʿĀmma li-l-Kitāb, 1987–1992.

Bākharzī, Abū 'l-Mafākhir Yaḥyā. *Awrād al-aḥbāb wa-fuṣūṣ al-ādāb*. Edited by Īraj Afshār. Tehran: Dānishgāh-yi Tihrān, 1966.

Baqlī, Rūzbihān-i. *Le traité de l'Esprit saint* (*R. al-quds*). Translated by Stéphane Ruspoli. Paris: Les Éditions du Cerf, 2001.

Bayhaqī, Ẓahīr al-Dīn (Ibn Funduq). *Taʾrīkh al-ḥukamāʾ al-islām* (*Tatimmat ṣiwān al-ḥikma*). Edited by Muḥammad Ḥasan Muḥammad. Cairo: Maktabat al-Thaqāfat al-Dīniyya, 1996.

al-Bidlīsī, ʿAmmār. *Bahjat al-ṭāʾifa* and *Ṣawm al-qalb*. Edited with an introduction and synopses of texts by Edward Badeen in *Zwei mystische Schriften des ʿAmmār al-Bidlīsī*. Beiruter Texte und Studien, bd. 68. Beirut and Stuttgart: In Kommission bei Franz Steiner Verlag, 1999.

al-Burgāzī, Yaḥyā b. Khalīl (Çoban). *Fütüvvetnāme*. Edited by Abdülbaki Gölpinarlı as "Burghazī ve Fütüvvet-nāmesi." *İstanbul Üniversitesi İktisat Fakültesi Mecmuası* 15.1–4 [1953–1954]: 111–150.

Chishtī, ʿAbd al-Raḥmān. *Mirʾāt al-asrār*. 2 vols. Urdu translation from the Persian by Captain Wahid Bakhsh Siyal. Lahore: The Sufi Foundation, 1983.

al-Daljī, Aḥmad b. ʿAlī. *al-Falākat wa-l-maflūkūn*. Beirut: Dār al-Kutub al-ʿIlmiyya, 1993.

Dārā Shukūh. *Safīnat al-awliyāʾ*. Lithograph. Cawnpore: Munshī Nūlkishvār, 1301 [1884].

——. *Sakīnat al-awliyāʾ*. Edited by Tārā Chand and Sayyid Muḥammad Riḍā Jalālī Nāʾinī. Tehran: Muʾassasa-yi Maṭbūʿātī-yi ʿIlmī, 1965.

al-Dāwūdī, Shams al-Dīn. *Ṭabaqāt al-mufassirīn*. 2 vols. Edited by ʿAlī Muḥammad ʿUmar. Cairo: Maktabat Wahba, 1972.

Daylamī, Abū 'l-Ḥasan ʿAlī. *Sīrat al-shaykh al-kabīr Abū ʿAbd Allāh ibn al-Khafīf al-Shīrāzī* (*Sīrat-i Ibn-i Khafīf-i Shīrāzī*). Ankara Üniversitesi İlâhiyat Fakültesi Yayınlarından, XII. Edited by Annemarie Schimmel. Ankara: Türk Tarih Kurumu Basımevi, 1955.

al-Dhahabī, Shams al-Dīn. *Duwal al-islām*. 2 vols. Hyderabad: Dā'irat al-Ma'ārif, 1919.
——. *al-'Ibar fī khabar man ghabar*. 4 vols. Edited by Ṣalāḥ al-Dīn al-Munajjid and Fu'ād Sayyid. Kuwait: Dā'irat al-Maṭbū'at wa-l-Nashr, 1960–1963.
——. *al-I'lām bi-wafayāt al-a'lām*. Edited by Riyāḍ 'Abd al-Ḥamīd Murād and 'Abd al-Jabbār Zakkār. Beirut: Dār al-Fikr al-Mu'āṣir, 1991.
——. *al-Mu'īn fī ṭabaqāt al-muḥaddithīn*. Edited by Muḥammad al-Sa'īd b. Basyūnī Zaghlūl. Beirut: Dār al-Kutub al-'Ilmiyya, 1998.
——. *Siyar a'lām al-nubalā'*. 25 vols. Edited by Shu'ayb al-Arnāūṭ and Ḥusayn al-Asad. Beirut: Mu'assasat al-Risāla, 1981–1988.
——. *Ta'rīkh al-islām wa-wafayāt al-mashāhīr wa-l-a'lām*. 58 vols. Edited by 'Umar 'Abd al-Salām Tadmurī. Beirut: Dār al-Kitāb al-'Arabī, 1990–.
Dihlavī, 'Abd al-Ḥaqq b. Sayf al-Dīn al-Turk. *Akhbār al-akhyār fī asrār al-abrār*. Khayrpur, Pakistan: Fārūq Academy, 1977.
Fiqh akbar III. [s.v. Watt].
al-Ghazālī, Abū Ḥāmid. *Fayṣal al-tafriqa bayna 'l-islām wa-l-zandaqa*. Translated by Sherman Jackson as *On the Boundaries of Theological Tolerance in Islam*. Studies in Islamic Philosophy, no. 1. Oxford and New York: Oxford University Press, 2002.
——. *Iḥyā' 'ulūm al-dīn*. 5 vols. Beirut: Dār al-Kutub al-'Ilmiyya, 1996.
——. *al-Iqtiṣād fī 'l-i'tiqād*. Ankara Üniversitesi İlâhiyat Fakültesi Yayınları, no. 34. Edited by İbrahim Âgâh Çubukçu and Hüseyin Atay. Ankara: Nur Matbaası, 1962.
——. *al-Munqidh min al-ḍalāl*. Translated by R.J. McCarthy as *al-Ghazālī's Path to Sufism and his Deliverance from Error*. Louisville, KY: Fons Vitae, 1999.
——. *Tahāfut al-falāsifa*. Translated by Michael E. Marmura as *The Incoherence of the Philosophers*. 2nd edition. Islamic Translation Series. Provo, UT: Brigham Young University Press, 2000.
Ghazālī, (pseudo-)Aḥmad. *Bawāriq al-ilmā'*. In *Tracts on Listening to Music*, edited by James Robson. London: Royal Asiatic Society, 1938.
Ghazzī, Muḥammad b. 'Abd al-Raḥmān. *Dīwān al-islām*. 4 vols. Edited by Sayyid Kasrāwī Ḥasan. Beirut: Dār al-Kutub al-'Ilmiyya, 1990.
Ḥājjī Khalīfa (Katip Çelebi). *Kashf al-ẓunūn*. 2 vols. Edited by S. Yaltakaya and K.R. Bilge. Istanbul: Maarıf Matbaası, 1941–1943.
Ḥudūd al-'ālam min al-mashriq ilā maghrib. Translated by V. Minorsky and edited by C.E. Bosworth as *Ḥudūd al-'Ālam: "The Regions of the World"*. 2nd edition. E.J.W. Gibb Memorial Series, New Series, no. 11. London: Luzac & Co., 1970.
Hujwīrī, 'Alī b. 'Uthmān. *Kashf al-maḥjūb*. Edited by V.A. Zhukovsky. Leningrad: Dār al-'Ulūm Ittiḥād Jamāhīr Shūrawī Sūsiyālīstī, 1926. Reprint, Tehran: n.p. 1336 sh. [1959]. Abridged translation by R.A. Nicholson as *The Kashf al-Maḥjúb: The Oldest Persian Treatise on Sufism*. Gibb Memorial Series, no. 17. London: Luzac & Co., 1911.
al-Ḥusaynī, 'Abd al-Ḥayy Fakhr al-Dīn. *al-I'lām bi-man fī ta'rīkh al-hind min al-a'lām (Nuzhat al-khawāṭir wa-bahjat al-masāmi' wa-l-nawāẓir)*. 8 vols. in 3. Beirut: Dār Ibn Ḥazm, 1999.
al-Ḥusaynī, Ṣadr al-Dīn 'Alī b. Nāṣir. *Akhbār al-dawlat al-saljūqiyya*. Edited by Muḥammad Iqbal. Lahore: University of Punjab Press, 1933.
Ibn al 'Adīm. *Bughyat al ṭalab fī ta'rīkh Ḥalab*. 11 vols. Edited by Suhayl Zakkār. Damascus: n.p., 1988.
Ibn 'Arabī. *al-Futūḥāt al-makkiyya*. Photo-reproduction of the Cairo 1867 edition. Beirut: Dār Ṣādir, 1968.
Ibn al-Athīr. *al-Kāmil fī 'l-ta'rīkh*. 11 vols. Edited by 'Umar 'Abd al-Salām Tadmūrī. Beirut: Dār al-Kitāb al-'Arabī, 1997.
——. *al-Lubāb fī tahdhīb al-ansāb*. 3 vols. Cairo: Maktabat al-Quds, 1357 [1938].
——. *al-Ta'rīkh al-bāhir fī-l-dawlat al-atābikiyya*. Edited by 'Abd al-Qādir Aḥmad Ṭulaymāt. Cairo: Dār al-Kutub al-Ḥadītha, 1963.
Ibn Baṭṭa. *K. al-sharḥ wa-l-ibāna 'alā 'l-uṣūl al-sunna wa-l-diyāna* (*al-Ibāna al-ṣaghīra*). Edited

and translated by Henri Laoust as *La profession de foi d'Ibn Baṭṭa*. Damascus: Institut Français de Damas, 1958.

Ibn Baṭṭūṭa. *Travels of Ibn Battuta*. 5 vols. Translated by H.A.R. Gibb (vols. 1–3) and C.F. Beckingham (vols. 4–5). The Hakluyt Extra Series, nos. 110, 117, 141, 178, 190. Cambridge: Cambridge University Press for the Hakluyt Society, 1958–2000.

Ibn-i Bībī. *al-Awāmir al-ʿalāʾiyya fī ʾl-umūr al-ʿalāʾiyya*. Vol. 1, facsimile of MS. Aya Sofya 2985 as *Evāmirü ʾl-ʿAlāʾiyye fi ʾl-umūri ʾl-ʿAlāʾiyye*. Türk Tarih Kurumu Yayınlarından I, Seri, no. 4a. Ankara: Türk Tarih Kurumu Basımevi, 1956. Vol. 2 as *Evāmirü ʾl-ʿAlāʾiyye fi ʾl-umūri ʾl-ʿAlāʾiyye* (*Kılıç Arslan'ın vefatıdan I. ʿAlāʾuddīn Keykubād'ın cülûsuna kadar*). Ankara Üniversitesi İlâhiyat Fakültesi Yayınlarından, no. 19. Edited by Necati Lugal and Adnan Sadık Erzi. Ankara: Türk Tarih Kurumu Basımevi, 1957.

——. *Mukhtaṣar-i saljūqnāma*. Anonymous Persian epitome of *al-Awāmir al-alāʾiyya*. In *Recueil de textes relatifs à l'histoire des seldjoucides*. Edited by M.Th. Houtsma. Vol. 4, *Histoire des seldjoucides d'asie mineure d'après l'abrégé du Seldjouknāmeh d'ibn-Bībī*. Leiden: E.J. Brill, 1902.

——. *Tawārikh-i āl-i saljūq*. Turkish paraphrase of *al-Awāmir al-ʿalāʾiyya* by Yazıcıoğlu ʿAlī. In *Recueil de textes relatifs à l'histoire des seldjoucides*. Edited by M.Th. Houtsma. Vol. 3, *Histoire des seldjoucides d'asie mineure (texte turc)*. Leiden: E.J. Brill, 1902. German translation by H.W. Duda as *Die Seltschukengeschichte des Ibn Bībī*. Copenhagen: Munksgaard, 1959.

Ibn al-Dimyāṭī. *al-Mustafād min dhayl taʾrīkh baghdād*. Edited by Bashshār ʿAwwād Maʿrūf. Beirut: Muʾassasat al-Risāla, 1986.

Ibn al-Dubaythī. *al-Mukhtaṣar al-muḥtāj ilayhi*. 2 vols. Edited by Muṣṭafā Jawād. Baghdad: Maṭābiʿ Dār al-Zamān, 1963.

Ibn Duqmāq. *Nuzhat al-anām fī taʾrīkh al-islām*. Edited by Samīr Ṭabbārah. Beirut: al-Maktabat al-ʿAṣriyya, 1999.

Ibn al-Fuwaṭī. *Talkhīṣ majmaʿ al-ādāb fī muʿjam al-alqāb*. 3 vols. Edited by Muṣṭafā Jawād. Damascus: Mudīrīyat Iḥyāʾ al-Turāth al-Qadīm, 1962–1965.

(pseudo-)Ibn al-Fuwaṭī. *K. al-ḥawādith* (*al-Ḥawādith al-jāmiʿa wa-l-tajārib al-nāfiʿa fī ʾl-miʾa al-sābiʿa*). Edited by Bashshār ʿAwwād Maʿrūf and ʿImād ʿAbd al-Salām Raʾūf. Beirut: Dār al-Gharb al-Islāmī, 1997.

Ibn Ḥajar al-ʿAsqalānī. *Lisān al-mīzan*. 10 vols. Edited by Muḥammad ʿAbd al-Raḥmān al-Marʿashlī. Beirut: Dār al-Turāth al-ʿArabī, 1995–1996.

——. *Tabṣīr al-muntabih bi-taḥrīr al-mushtabih* (*al-Mushtabih fī asmāʾ al-rijāl*). 4 vols. Delhi: al-Dār al-ʿIlmiyya, 1986.

Ibn al-ʿImād. *Shadharāt al-dhahab fī akhbār man dhahab*. 10 vols. Edited by ʿAbd al-Qādir al-Arnāʾūṭ and Maḥmūd al-Arnāʾūṭ. Damascus and Beirut: Dār Ibn Kathīr, 1986–1993.

Ibn al-Jawzī. *al-Muntaẓam fī taʾrīkh al-mulūk wa-l-umam*. 10 vols. Hyderabad: Dāʾirat al-Maʿārif al-ʿUthmāniyya, 1939.

——. *Ṣifat al-ṣafwa*. 2 vols. Cairo: Dār al-Ṣafā, 1411 [1990–1991].

——. *Talbīs Iblīs*. Beirut: Dār al-Kitāb al-ʿArabī, 1995.

Ibn al-Jazarī. *Ghāyat al-nihāyat fī ṭabaqāt al-qurrāʾ* (*Die biographische Lexikon der Koranlehrer von Samsaddin Muhammad Ibn al-Gazari*). 2 vols. Edited by Gotthelf Bergstraesser and Otto Pretzl. Cairo: Maktabat al-Khānjī, 1932–1933.

Ibn Kathīr. *al-Bidāya wa-l-nihāya fī ʾl-taʾrīkh*. 14 vols. Cairo: Maṭbaʿat al-Saʿāda, 1932.

——. *Ṭabaqāt al-fuqahāʾ al-shāfiʿīyīn*. 3 vols. with vol. 3 as *Dhayl ṭabaqāt al-fuqahāʾ al-shāfiʿīyīn* by al-ʿIbādī. Edited by Aḥmad ʿUmar Hāshim and Muḥammad Zaynahum Muḥammad ʿAzab. Cairo: Maktabat al-Thaqāfat al-Dīniyya, 1993.

Ibn Khallikān. *Wafayāt al-aʿyān wa-abnāʾ al-zamān*. 8 vols. Edited by Iḥsān ʿAbbās. Beirut: Dār al-Ṣādir, 1977. Translated by William Mac Guckin de Slane as *Ibn Khallikan's Biographical Dictionary*. 4 vols. Paris: Printed for the Oriental Translation Fund of Great Britain and Ireland, 1843–1871. Reprint, Beirut: Librairie du Liban, 1970.

Ibn al-Miʿmār. *K. al-futuwwa*. Edited by Muṣṭafā Jawād and Muḥammad Taqī al-Dīn al-Hilālī. Baghdad: Maktabat al-Muthannā, 1958.

Ibn al-Mulaqqin. *al-ʿIqd al-mudhhab fī ṭabaqāt ḥamalat al-madhhab*. Edited by Ayman Naṣr al-Azharī. Beirut: Dār al-Kutub al-ʿIlmiyya, 1997.

Ibn al-Munawwar, Muḥammad. *The Secrets of God's Mystical Oneness*. Translated with notes and introduction by John O'Kane. Costa Mesa, CA and New York: Mazda Publishers in association with Bibliotheca Persica, 1992.

Ibn al-Mustawfī. *Taʾrīkh Irbil (Nabāhat al-balad al-khāmil bi-man waradahu min al-amāthil)*. 2 vols. Edited by Sāmī b. al-Sayyid Khamās al-Ṣaqqār. Baghdad: Dār al-Rashīd li-l-Nashr, 1980.

Ibn al-Najjār. *Dhayl Taʾrīkh Baghdād*. 5 vols. Edited by Caesar Farah. Hyderabad: Osmania Oriental Publications Bureau, 1978–1986.

Ibn Nuqṭa. *K. al-taqyīd li-maʿrifat al-ruwāt wa-l-sunan wa-l-masānīd*. 2 vols. Hyderabad: Maṭbaʿat Dāʾirat al-Maʿārif, 1983.

Ibn Qāḍī Shuhba. *Ṭabaqāt al-fuqahāʾ al-shāfiʿiyya*. 2 vols. Edited by ʿAlī Muḥammad ʿUmar. Cairo: Maktabat al-Thaqāfat al-Dīniyya, 1998.

Ibn al-Qasṭallānī. *Irtifāʿ al-rutbat bi-l-libās wa-l-ṣuḥbat*. Edited by Iḥsān Dhunūn al-Thāmarī and Muḥammad ʿAbdullāh al-Qadḥāt in *Rasāʾil min al-turāth al-ṣūfī fī lubs al-khirqa*. Amman: Dār al-Rāzī, 2002.

Ibn Qudāma. *ʿAqīdat al-Imām al-Maqdisī*. Edited by Hans Daiber in "The Creed (*ʿAqīda*) of the Ḥanbalite Ibn Qudāma al-Maqdisī: A Newly Discovered Text." In *Studia Arabica et Islamica: Feststschrift for Ihsan ʿAbbas on his Sixtieth Birthday*. Edited by Wadad Qadi. Beirut: American University of Beirut Press, 1981.

Ibn Rāfiʿ. *Muntakhab al-mukhtār (Taʾrīkh ʿulamāʾ Baghdād)*. Abridgement by Taqī al-Dīn al-Fāsī. Edited by ʿAbbās al-ʿAzzāwī. Baghdad: Maṭbaʿat al-Ahālī, 1938.

Ibn Rajab. *al-Dhayl ʿalā ṭabaqāt al-ḥanābila*. 2 vols. Edited by Muḥammad Ḥamīd al-Faqī. Cairo: Maṭbaʿat al-Sunna al-Muḥammadiyya, 1952–1953.

Ibn al-Sāʿī. *al-Jāmiʿ al-mukhtaṣar fī ʿunwān al-tawārīkh wa-ʿuyūn al-siyar*. Vol. 9. Edited by Muṣṭafā Jawād. Baghdad: al-Maṭbaʿat al-Siyāhiyya al-Kāthlūkiyya, 1934.

Ibn al-Ṣiddīq. *ʿAwāṭif al-laṭāʾif min aḥādīth ʿawārif al-maʿārif*. 2 vols. Edited by Idrīs al-Kamdānī and Muḥammad Maḥmūd al-Muṣṭafā. Mecca: al-Maktabat al-Makkiyya, 2001.

——. *Ghaniyyat al-ʿawārif*. 2 vols. Edited by Idrīs al-Kamdānī and Muḥammad Maḥmūd al-Muṣṭafā. Mecca: al-Maktabat al-Makkiyya, 2001.

Ibn al-Suqāʿī. *Tālī kitāb wafayāt al-aʿyān*. Edited and translated by Jacqueline Sublet. Damascus: al-Mahʿad al-Faransī bi-Dimashq li-l-Dirāsāt al-ʿArabiyya, 1974.

Ibn Taghrībirdī. *al-Nujūm al-ẓāhira fī mulūk miṣr wa-l-qāhira*. 16 vols. Cairo: al-Muʾassasat al-Miṣriyya al-ʿĀmma, 1963–1972.

Ibn al-Ṭiqṭaqā. *al-Fakhrī (Taʾrīkh al-duwal al-islāmiyya)*. Beirut: Dār Ṣādir, 1380 [1970].

Ibn al-Wardī. *Taʾrīkh Ibn al-Wardī (Tatimmat al-mukhtaṣar fī akhbār al-bashar)*. 2 vols. Najaf: al-Maṭbaʿat al-Ḥaydariyya, 1389 [1969].

Ibn Wāṣil. *Mufarrij al-kurūb fī akhbār Banī Ayyūb*. Vols. 1–3 edited by Jamāl al-Dīn al-Shayyāl. Cairo: al-Idārat al-ʿAmmāt li-Thiqāfa, 1954–1961. Vols. 4–5 edited by Ḥusayn Muḥammad Rabīʿ and Saʿīd ʿAbd al-Fattāḥ ʿĀshūr. Cairo: Maṭbaʿat Dār al-Kutub, 1972–1977.

al-Iṣfahānī, Abū Nuʿaym Aḥmad b. ʿAbd Allāh. *Ḥilyat al-awliyāʾ wa-ṭabaqāt al-aṣfiyāʾ*. 10 vols. in 5. Beirut: Dār al-Kitāb al-ʿArabī, 1967–1968.

Iṣfahānī, Ismāʿīl Māshāda. *Tarjama-yi ʿawārif al-maʿārif*. Edited by Qāsim Anṣārī. Tehran: Intishārāt-i ʿIlmī va Farhangī, 1985.

İsmail Paşa. *Hadiyyat al-ʿārifīn asmāʾ al-muʾallifīn wa-āthār al-muṣannifīn*. 2 vols. Edited by R. Bilge. Istanbul: Milli Eğitim Basımevi, 1951–1955.

al-Isnawī, Jamāl al-Dīn. *Ṭabaqāt al-shāfiʿiyya*. 2 vols. Edited by ʿAbdullāh al-Jubūrī al-Baghdādī. Baghdād: al-Irshād, 1390 [1970].

Jāmī, ʿAbd al-Raḥmān. *Nafaḥāt al-uns min ḥaḍarāt al-quds*. Edited by Maḥmūd ʿĀbidī. Tehran: Intishārāt-i Iṭilāʿāt, 1380 sh. [1991].

al-Jīlānī, ʿAbd al-Qādir. *al-Ghunya li-ṭālibī ṭarīq al-ḥaqq*. 2 vols. Beirut: Dār al-Kutub al-ʿIlmiyya, 1997.
al-Junayd. *Rasāʾil*. In *The Life, Personality and Writings of al-Junayd*, E.J.W. Gibb Memorial Series, New Series, no. 22. Edited and translated by A.H. Abdel-Kader. London: Luzac & Co., 1962.
Junayd-i Shīrāzī. *Shadd al-izār fī ḥaṭṭ al-awzār ʿan zuwwār al-mazār*. Edited by Muḥammad Qazvīnī and ʿAbbas Iqbāl. Tehran: Chāpkhāna-yi Majlis, 1328 sh. [1987].
Juvaynī, ʿAlāʾ al-Dīn ʿAṭāʾ-Malik b. Muḥammad. *The Taʾríkh-i-Jahán-Gushá*. 3 vols. Edited by M.M. Qazvini. Gibb Memorial Series, no. 3. Leiden and London: E.J. Brill and Luzac and Co., 1912–1937. English translation by J.A. Boyle as *The History of the World-Conqueror*. 2 vols. Manchester: Manchester University Press, 1958.
al-Kalābādhī, Abu Bakr. *K. al-taʿarruf li-madhhab ahl al-taṣawwuf*. Edited by A.J. Arberry. Cairo: Khānjī, 1938. English translation by Arberry as *The Doctrine of the Ṣūfīs*. Cambridge: Cambridge University Press, 1935.
Kāshānī, ʿIzz al-Dīn. *Miṣbāḥ al-hidāya wa-miftāḥ al-kifāya*. Edited by Jalāl al-Dīn Humāʾī. Tehran: Chāpkhānah-yi Majlis, 1367 sh. [1988].
Kāshifī, Ḥusayn Vāʾiẓ-i. *Futuwwat-nāma-yi sulṭānī*. Edited by Muḥammad Jaʿfar Maḥjūb. Tehran: Bunyād-i Farhang-i Īrān, 1350 [1972].
al-Khartabirtī, Aḥmad b. Ilyās al-Naqqāsh. *Tuḥfat al-waṣāyā*. MS. Süley., Aya Sofya 2049, fol. 108a–117b. Facsimile reproduction and Turkish translation by Abdülbaki Gölpinarlı in "İslam ve Türk illerinde fütüvvet teşkilatı ve kaynakları." *İstanbul Üniversitesi İktisat Fakültesi Mecmuası* 11.1–4 (1949–1951): 205–231.
al-Khazrajī, Ṣafī al-Dīn. *R. Ṣafī al-Dīn*. Edited and translated by Denis Gril as *La Risāla de Ṣafī al-Dīn Ibn Abī l-Manṣūr Ibn Ẓāfir: Biographies des maîtres spirituels connus par un cheikh égyptien du VIIᵉ/XIIIᵉ siècle*. Cairo: IFAOC, 1986.
Kubrā, Najm al-Dīn. *Ādāb al-ṣūfiyya* (*Ādāb al-murīdīn*). Edited by Masʿūd Qāsimī. Tehran: Kitābfurūshī-yi Zavvār, 1363 sh. [1984]. German translation based on MS. Süley., Ayasofya 4792, fol. 738a–741b by Fritz Meier in "Ein Knigge für Sufi's." *RSO* 32 (1957): 485–524. Translated as "A Book of Etiquette for Sufis." In *Essays on Islamic Piety and Mysticism*, ed. and trans. John O'Kane and Bernd Radtke. Leiden: Brill. 1999.
——. *Die Fawāʾiḥ al-Ǧalāl des Naǧm ad-Dīn al-Kubrā*. Edited by Fritz Meier. Wiesbaden: Franz Steiner Verlag, 1957.
Khwāfī, Faṣīḥ al-Dīn. *Mujmal-i faṣīḥī*. 3 vols. Edited by Maḥmūd-i Farrūkh. Mashhad: Kitābkhāna-yi Bāstān, 1960.
al-Kutubī, Muḥammad. *Fawāt al-wafayāt wa-l-dhayl ʿalayhi*. 4 vols. Edited by Iḥsān ʿAbbās. Beirut: Dār al-Ṣādir, 1973–1974.
al-Malik al-Manṣūr. *Miḍmār al-ḥaqāʾiq wa-sirr al-khalāʾiq*. Edited by Ḥasan Ḥabashī. Cairo: Aʿlām al-Kutub, 1968.
al-Makkī, Abū Ṭālib. *Qūt al-qulūb*. 2 vols. Cairo: Muṣṭafā al-Bābī al-Ḥalabī, 1381 (1961). German translation by Richard Gramlich as *Die Nahrung der Herzen: Abū Ṭālib al-Makkīs Qūt al-qulūb*. 4 vols. Freiburger Islamstudien, no. 16, pts.1–4. Wiesbaden: Franz Steiner Verlag, 1995.
al-Maqrīzī. *K. al-sulūk fī maʿrifat duwal al-mulūk*. 2 vols. in 6 fascs. Edited by Muḥammad Muṣṭafā Ziyāda. Cairo: Lajnat al-Taʾlīf wa-l-Tarjamat wa-l-Nashr, 1956–1973.
Maʿṣūmʿalīshāh. *Ṭarāʾiq al-ḥaqāʾiq*. 3 vols. Edited by Muḥammad Jaʿfar Maḥjūb. Tehran: Kitābkhāna-yi Bārānī, 1950.
al-Māwardī. *The Ordinances of Government: Al-Aḥkām al-Sulṭāniyya w'al-Wilāyāt al-Dīniyya*. Translated by Wafaa H. Wahba. Reading, UK: Garnet Publishing Ltd., 1996.
al-Munāwī, Muḥammad ʿAbd al-Raʾūf. *al-Kawākib al-durriyat fī tarājim al-sāda al-ṣūfiyya* (*Ṭabaqāt al-Munāwī al-kubrā wa-l-ṣughrā*). 4 vols. Edited by Muḥyī al-Dīn Dīb Mistū. Damascus: Dār Ibn Kathīr, 1993.
al-Mundhirī, ʿAbd al-ʿAẓīm. *al-Takmila li-wafayāt al-naqala*. 6 vols. Edited by Bashshār ʿAwwād Maʿrūf. Najaf: Maṭbaʿāt al-Ādāb al-Najaf al-Ashraf, 1968–1969.
al-Muqaddasī, Shams al-Dīn. *The Best Divisions for Knowledge of the Regions*. Translated by

Basil Anthony Collins. Reading, UK: Centre for Muslim Contribution to Civilisation, Garnet Publishing, 1994.

Mustawfī, Ḥamd Allāh. *Tārīkh-i guzīda*. Edited by ʿAbd al-Ḥusayn Navāʾī. Tehran: Intishārāt-i Amīr-i Kabīr, 1364 sh. [1985].

al-Nabhānī, Yūsuf b. Ismāʿīl. *Jāmiʿ karāmāt al-awliyāʾ*. 2 vols. Edited by Ibrāhīm ʿAṭwah ʿAwaẓ. Cairo: Muṣṭafā al-Bābī al-Ḥalabī, 1962.

Nasab al-Suhrawardī. MS. Tübingen, MA VI 90_2, fol. 52b.

al-Nasafī, ʿAzīz-i. [s.v. Ridgeon].

al-Nasafī, Najm al-Dīn Abū Ḥafṣ. [s.v. Watt].

al-Nasawī, Shihāb al-Dīn Muḥammad b. Aḥmad. *Sīrat al-Sulṭān Jalāl al-Dīn Mankbunī* (*Zhizneopisanie Sultana Dzhalal ad-Dina Mankburny*). Pamiatniki pis'mennosti Vostoka, vol. 107. Edited with Russian translation by Ziia M. Buniiatov. Moscow: Izdatel'skaia firma "Vostochnaia lit-ra" RAN, 1996.

Nāṣirī. *Futuwwat-nāma*. Edited by Franz Taeschner in *Der anatolische Dichter Nāṣirī und sein Futuvvet-name*. Abhandlungen für die Kunde des Morgenlandes, 29.1. Leipzig: Deutsche Morgenländischen Gesellschaft, Kommission Verlag F.A. Brockhaus, 1944.

Nisbat al-khirqat al-Suhrawardī I. MS. Tüb., Ma VI 90_{68}, fol. 132a.

Nisbat al-khirqat al-Suhrawardī II. MS. Süley., Fatih 2741, fol. 1a.

al-Nuʿaymī, ʿAbd al-Qādir b. Muḥammad. *al-Dāris fī taʾrīkh al-madāris*. 2 vols. Edited by Jaʿfar al-Ḥusaynī. Damascus: ʿUḍw al-Majmaʿ al-ʿIlmī al-ʿArabī, 1948–1951.

al-Qazwīnī, Zakariyyā b. Muḥammad. *Āthār al-balād wa-l-akhbār al-ʿibād*. Beirut: Dār Ṣādir, 1970.

al-Qushayrī, Abū ʾl-Qāsim. *al-Risālat al-qushayriyya fī ʾl-taṣawwuf*. 2 vols. Edited by ʿAbd al-Ḥalīm Maḥmūd and Maḥmūd b. al-Sharīf. Cairo: Dār al-Kutub al-Ḥadītha, 1385 [1966]. German translation by Richard Gramlich as *Das Sendschreiben al-Qušayris über das Sufitum*. Freiburger Islamstudien, no. 6. Wiesbaden: Franz Steiner Verlag, 1989.

——. *Thalāth rasāʾil li-qushayrī* (*Lumaʿ fī ʾl-iʿtiqād, Bulghat al-maqāṣid, al-Fuṣūl fī ʾl-uṣūl*). Edited by al-Ṭablāwī Saʿd. Cairo: Maṭbaʿat al-Amāna, 1988.

al-Rāfiʿī, ʿAbd al-Karīm. *al-Tadwīn fī akhbār qazwīn*. 4 vols. Edited by ʿAzīzullāh al-ʿAṭṭāridī. Beirut: Dār al-Kutub al-ʿIlmiyya, 1987.

Rāzī, Najm al-Dīn Dāya. *The Path of God's Bondsmen: From Origin to Return*. Translated by Hamid Algar. Persian Heritage Series, no. 25. Delmar, NY: Caravan Books, 1982.

Saʿdī Shīrāzī. *Kulliyāt-i Saʿdī*. Edited by Muḥammad ʿAlī Furūghī. Tehran: Nashr-i Muḥammad, n.d.

al-Ṣafadī, Khalīl b. Aybak. *K. al-wāfī bi-l-wafayāt* (*Das Biographische Lexikon des Ṣalāḥaddīn Ḫalīl ibn Aibak aṣ-Ṣafadī*). 30 vols. to date. Imprint varies, 1931–2004.

al-Sanūsī. *al-Majmūʿat al-mukhtārat min muʾallafāt Muḥammad b. ʿAlī al-Sanūsī*. Beirut: Dār al-Kitāb al-Lubnānī, 1968.

al-Sarrāj, Abū Naṣr ʿAbdullāh b. ʿAlī. *K. al-lumaʿ fī ʾl-taṣawwuf*. Edited by R.A. Nicholson. Gibb Memorial Series, no. 22. Leiden and London: E.J. Brill and Luzac & Co., 1914. Addenda in A.J. Arberry, *Pages from the Kitāb al-Lumaʿ of Abū Naṣr al-Sarrāj: Being the Lacuna in the Edition of R.A. Nicholson; Edited from the Bankipore MS., with Memoir, Preface, and Notes*. London: Luzac & Co., 1947. German translation by Richard Gramlich as *Schlaglichter über das Sufitum*. Freiburger Islamstudien, no. 13. Stuttgart: Franz Steiner Verlag, 1990.

al-Samʿānī, ʿAbd al-Karīm. *K. al-ansāb*. 5 vols. Edited by ʿAbdullāh ʿUmar al-Bārūdī. Beirut: Dār al-Jinān, 1988.

al-Shaʿrānī, ʿAbd al-Wahhāb. *al-Ṭabaqāt al-kubrā* (*Lawāqiḥ al-anwār fī ṭabaqāt al-akhyār*). 2 vols. Edited by ʿAbd al-Raḥmān Ḥasan Maḥmūd. Cairo: Maktabat al-Ādāb, 1993–2001.

al-Shaṭṭanawfī, Nūr al-Dīn. *Bahjat al-asrār*. Cairo: Muṣṭafā al-Bābī al-Ḥalabī, 1330 [1912].

Sibṭ Ibn al-Fāriḍ. "Dībājat Ibn al-Fāriḍ." In *Dīwān Ibn al-Fāriḍ*. Edited by ʿAbd al-Khāliq Maḥmūd. Cairo: ʿAyn li-l-Dirāsāt al-Buḥūth al-Insāniyyat wa-l-Ijtimāʿiyya, 1995. English translation by Th. Emil Homerin as "Adorned Proem to the Dīwān." In *ʿUmar Ibn al-Fāriḍ: Sufi Verse, Saintly Life*. The Classics of Western Spirituality. Edited by Bernard McGinn, et al. New York and Mahwah, NJ: Paulist Press, 2000.

Sibṭ Ibn al-Jawzī. *Mirʾāt al-zamān fī taʾrīkh al-aʿyān*. vol. 8, parts 1 and 2. Hyderabad: Osmania Oriental Publications Bureau, 1951–1952.

Simnānī, ʿAlāʾ al-Dawla. *Chihil majlis*. Edited by ʿAbd al-Rafīʿ Ḥaqīqat. Tehran: Asāṭīr, 1379 sh. [2000].

al-Subkī, Tāj al-Dīn. *Ṭabaqāt al-shāfiʿiyya al-kubrā*. 10 vols. Edited by Maḥmūd Muḥammad al-Tanāhī and ʿAbd al-Fattāḥ Muḥammad al-Ḥilw. Cairo: ʿĪsā al-Bābī al-Ḥalabī, 1964–1976.

al-Suhrawardī, Abū ʾl-Najīb ʿAbd al-Qāhir. *K. ādāb al-murīdīn*. Edited by Menahem Milson. Max Schloessinger Memorial Series, no. 2. Jerusalem: Institute of Asian and African Studies, Hebrew University of Jerusalem, 1977. Abridged translation by idem as *A Sufi Rule for Novices; Kitāb Ādāb al-Murīdīn of Abū al-Najīb al-Suhrawardī: An Abridged Translation and Introduction*. Cambridge, MA: Harvard University Press, 1975.

al-Suhrawardī, ʿImād al-Dīn Muḥammad. *K. zād al-musāfir wa-adab al-ḥāḍir*. MS. Köprülü 1603_2, fol. 11a–52b.

al-Suhrawardī, Shihāb al-Dīn Abū Ḥafṣ ʿUmar b. Muḥammad. *Ajwibat ʿan masāʾil baʿḍ aʾimmat Khurāsān*. Edited by Aḥmad Ṭāhirī ʿIrāqī as "Pāsukhhāʾi Shihāb al-Dīn ʿUmar-i Suhravardī." *Maqalāt u Barrasīhā* 49–50 (1369/1411/1991): 45–64.

——. *Aʿlām al-hudā wa-ʿaqīdat arbāb al-tuqā*. Edited by ʿAbd al-ʿAzīz al-Sayrawān. Damascus: Dār al-Anwār, 1996.

——. *ʿAwārif al-maʿārif*. 2 vols. Vol. 1 [= chs. 1–21] edited by ʿAbd al-Ḥalīm Maḥmūd and Maḥmūd b. al-Sharaf. Cairo: Maṭbaʿat al-Saʿāda & Dār al-Kutub al-Ḥadītha, 1971. Vol. 2 [= chs. 22–63], *Dhakhāʾir al-ʿarab*, no. 73, edited eadem. Cairo: Dār al-Maʿārif, 2000. German translation by Richard Gramlich as *Die Gaben der Erkenntnisse des ʿUmar as-Suhrawardī*. Freiburger Islamstudien, no. 6. Wiesbaden: Franz Steiner Verlag, 1978. Turkish translation by Hasan Kâmil Yılmaz and İrfan Gündüz as *Tasavvufun Esasları: Avarifu'l-Maarif Tercumesi*. Istanbul: Erkam Yayınları, 1989.

——. *Futūḥāt min kalāmihi*. I = MS. Süley., Şehid Ali Paşa 1393_8, fol. 69a–69b; II = MS. Tüb., Ma VI 90_{16}, fol. 85a–85b; III = MS. Köp., Fazıl Ahmed Paşa 1605_{14}, fol. 39a–40a; IV = MS. Süley., Şehid Ali Paşa 1393_{14}, fol. 71b–72a; V = MS. Süley., Şehid Ali Paşa 1393_9, fol. 69b; VI = MS. Süley., Şehid Ali Paşa 1393_{10}, fol. 69b–70a; VII = MS. Süley., Şehid Ali Paşa 1393_{11}, fol. 70a–70b; VIII = MS. Köp., Fazıl Ahmed Paşa 1605_{12}, fol. 38b–39a; IX = MS. Süley., Musalla Medresesi 20_6, fol. 292a–292b; XI = MS. Tüb., Ma VI 90_{27}, fol. 91b–92a; XIII, MS. Süley., Şehid Ali Paşa 1393_7, fol. 67b–69a; XIV = MS. Süley., Şehid Ali Paşa 1393_{15}, fol. 72a–72b; XV = MS. Süley., Şehid Ali Paşa 1393_{16}, fol. 72b; XVI = MS. Tüb. Ma VI 90_{34}, fol. 95b–96a; XVIII = MS. Tüb. Ma VI 90_{36}, fol. 96b–97a; XIX = MS. Tüb. Ma VI 90_{37}, fol. 97a–98b; XXI = MS. Süley., Musalla Medresesi 20_3, fol. 291b; XXVI = MS. Süley., Şehid Ali Paşa 1382_9, fol. 7b–8a; XXIX = trans. Amravhī in *Vaṣāyā*, 46 (*iqtibāsāt*, no. 4).

——. *Ḥilyat al-faqīr al-ṣādiq fī ʾl-taṣawwuf*. MS. Süley., Yazma Bağışlar 1971_3, fol. 114b–117b.

——. *Hudā al-ṭālibīn wa-miṣbāḥ al-sālikīn*. MS. Süley., İbrahim Ef. 870_{17}, fol. 88b–95a.

——. *Idālat al-ʿiyān ʿalā ʾl-burhān*. MS. Bursa, Ulu Cami 1597_4, fol. 82a–137b.

——. *Ijz. al-samāʿ li-ʿAwārif al-maʿārif*. MS. Süley., Lâlâ İsmail Ef. 180_4, fol. 234a.

——. *Ijz. li-ʿAlī b. Aḥmad al-Rāzī*. MS. Süley., Musalla Medresesi 20_{14}, fol. 295b.

——. *Ijz. li-Bahāʾ al-Dīn Zakariyyā Multānī*, MS. Tüb., Ma VI 90_4, fol. 71b–72a.

——. *Irshād al-murīdīn wa-injād al-ṭālibīn*. MS. Süley., Şehid Ali Paşa 1397_1, fol. 1a–47a; and, MS. Süley., Ayasofya 2117_5, fol. 130b–162b.

——. *Jadhdhāb al-qulūb ilā mawāṣilat al-maḥbūb*. MS. Süley., Reşit Ef. 247_1, fol. 1b–17a.
——. *K. fī 'l-futuwwa*. Edited by Morteza Sarraf in *Traites des compagnons-chevaliers, Rasa'il-e Javanmardan: recueil de sept Fotowwat-Nâmeh*. Bibliothèque iranienne, no. 20. Tehran & Paris: Departement d'Iranologie de l'Institut Franco-Iranien de Recherche & Librairie d'Amerique et d'Orient, 1973.
——. *Kashf al-faḍā'iḥ al-yūnāniyya wa-rashf al-naṣā'iḥ al-īmāniyya*. Edited by ʿĀ'isha Yūsuf al-Manāʿī. Cairo: Dār al-Salām, 1999.
——. *al-Lawāmiʿ al-ghaybiyya fī 'l-rūḥ*. MS. Süley., Bağdatlı Vehbi Ef. 2023_{38}, fol. 186a–187a.
——. *Mashyakhat al-Shaykh al-ʿālim al-qudrat Shihāb al-Dīn Abī Ḥafṣ ʿUmar b. Muḥammad ʿAbdullāh b. ʿAmmuya al-Suhrawardī ʿan shuyūkhihi*. MS. C.B., MS. Arab 495_9, fol. 84a–94b.
——. *Mukhtaṣar min kalām al-Suhrawardī*. MS. Süley., Ayasofya 4792_{46}, fol. 799a–801a (on the margins).
——. *Nughbat al-bayān fī tafsīr al-Qur'ān*. Partial edition (up through 9:128) by Yaşar Düzenli as "Şihâbuddin Sühreverdî ve Nuğbetü'l-Beyân fî Tefsîri'l-Kurân: Adlı Eserinin Tevbe Sûresine kadar Tahkîki." Ph.D. diss., Marmara Üniversitesi, Sosyal Bilimler Enstitütsü [Istanbul], 1994.
——. *R. dar kār-i murīd*. MS. Tüb. Ma VI 90_8, fol. 73b–74b.
——. *R. dar ṣifat-i khalvat va ādāb-i ān*. MS. Millet, Ali Emiri Ef. Farsca 1017_3, fol. 21b–23a.
——. *R. dar tawba*, MS. Tüb. Ma VI 90_9, fol. 74b.
——. *R. fī 'l-faqr*. MS. Süley., Esad Ef. 1761_5, fol. 52a–53b; Urdu translation by Amravhī as "Faqr o darveshī ke li'e bunyādī umūr: Vaṣiyyat bi-nām baʿḍ fuqarā' aur darvīsh", In *Vaṣāyā Shaykh Shihāb al-Dīn Suhravardī* (Lahore: al-Maʿārif, 1983), 39–40.
——. *R. fī 'l-faqr wa-l-ghinā*. MS. Süley., Reisülküttap 465_2, fol. 109b–111a.
——. *R. fī 'l-futuwwa*. Edited by Morteza Sarraf in *Traites des compagnons-chevaliers, Rasa'il-e Javanmardan: recueil de sept Fotowwat-Nâmeh*. Bibliothèque iranienne, no. 20. Tehran & Paris: Departement d'Iranologie de l'Institut Franco-Iranien de Recherche & Librairie d'Amerique et d'Orient, 1973.
——. *R. fī 'l-sayr wa-l-ṭayr*. MS. Süley., Bağdatlı Vehbi Ef. 2023_8, fol. 67b–69a.
——. *R. ilā Fakhr al-Dīn al-Rāzī*. MS. Süley., H. Hüsnü Paşa $585_{\text{mü/6}}$, fol. 220a.
——. *R. ilā ʿIzz al-Dīn Muḥammad b. Yaʿqūb*. MS. Tüb. Ma VI 90_{57}, fol. 123a–124a.
——. *R. ilā Kamāl al-Dīn al-Iṣfahānī*. MS. Tüb., Ma VI 90_{28}, fol. 92a–93a.
——. *Tarjama-yi al-lawāmiʿ al-ghaybiyya fī 'l-rūḥ*. MS. Tüb. Ma VI 90_{10}, fol. 74b–76b.
——. *Vaṣāyā Shaykh Shihāb al-Dīn Suhravardī*. Collected testaments and selections (*iqtisābāt*) from al-Suhrawardī's *Futūḥāt min kalāmihi* translated into Urdu by Nasīm Aḥmad Farīdī Amravhī. Lahore: al-Maʿārif, 1983.
——. *W.* III. Süley., İbrahim Ef. 870_9, fol. 81b–82b.
——. *W.* IV. MS. Tüb., Ma VI 90_{13}, fol. 80b–83a.
——. *W.* V (*R. fī 'l-istiqāma*). MS. Tüb., Ma VI 90_{15}, fol. 84b–85a.
——. *W.* VI. MS. Süley., Musalla Medresesi 20_{17}, fol. 296a.
——. *W. li-ʿAlī b. Aḥmad al-Rāzī*. MS. Süley., Musalla Medresesi 20_{15}, fol. 295b–296a.
——. *W. li-ʿAlī al Mawqānī*. MS. Tüb., Ma VI 90_{52}, fol. 116a–116b.
——. *W. li-baʿḍ aṣḥābihi*. Edited by Muḥammad Shīrvānī in "Vaṣiyyat-nāma-yi Shihāb al-Dīn Abū Ḥafṣ ʿUmar b. Muḥammad-i Suhravardī." *Sophia Perennis / Jāvidān-i khirād* 2.2 (1976): 31–32.
——. *W. li-baʿḍ al-murīdīn*. MS. Süley., İbrahim Ef. 870_{10}, fol. 82b–83a.
——. *W. li-ibnihi [ʿImād al-Dīn]*. Edited by Muḥammad Shīrvānī in "Vaṣiyyat-nāma-yi Shihāb al-Dīn Abū Ḥafṣ ʿUmar b. Muḥammad-i Suhravardī." *Sophia Perennis / Jāvidān-i khirād* 2.2 (1976): 33–35; and, MS. Süley., Nâfiz Paşa 428_4, fol. 190a–190b.
——. *W. li-Jamāl al-Dīn al-Iṣfahānī*. Edited by Angelika Hartmann in "Bemerkungen zu Handschriften ʿUmar as-Suhrawardīs, echten und vermeintlichen Autographen." *Der Islam* 60 (1983): 140–142.

——. *W. li-Najm al-Dīn al-Tiflīsī*. MS. Tüb., Ma VI 90_{14}, fol. 83a–84a.
——. *W. li-Naṣīr al-Dīn Baghdādī* (*R. fī 'l-irāda*). MS. Süley., Şehid Ali Paşa 1393_{6}, fol. 63a–67b.
——. *W. li-Rashīd al-Dīn Abī Bakr al-Ḥabash*. MS. Tüb., Ma VI 90_{53}, fol. 116b–118a.
——. *W. li-Rashīd al-Dīn al-Farghānī*. MS. Tüb., Ma VI 90_{30}, fol. 93a–94a.
al-Sulamī, Abū ʿAbd al-Raḥmān. *Bayān aḥwāl al-ṣūfiyya*. Edited by Süleyman Ateş in *Tisʿa kutub fī uṣūl al-taṣawwuf wa-l-zuhd*. Beirut: al-Nāshir li-Ṭibāʿa wa-l-Nashr al-Tawzīʿ wa-l-Iʿlān, 1993.
——. *Darajāt al-muʿāmalāt*. Edited by Aḥmad Ṭāhirī ʿIrāqī in *Majmūʿa-yi āthār-i Abū ʿAbd al-Raḥmān al-Sulamī*, vol. 1, edited by Nasrullāh Pūrjavādī. Tehran: Markaz-i Nashr-i Dānishgāh, 1369 sh. [1990].
——. *Jawāmiʿ ādāb al-ṣūfiyya*. Edited by Etan Kohlberg. Jerusalem: Maʿhad al-Dirāsāt al-Asiyawiyya wa-l-Ifrīqiyya, al-Jāmiʿa al-ʿIbriyya fī Urushsalīm, 1976. Reprinted in *Majmūʿa-yi āthār-i Abū ʿAbd al-Raḥmān al-Sulamī*, vol. 1, edited by Nasrullāh Pūrjavādī. Tehran: Markaz-i Nashr-i Dānishgāh, 1369 sh. [1990].
——. *K. ādāb al-ṣuḥba wa-ḥusn al-ʿishra*. Edited by M.J. Kister. Jerusalem: Israel Oriental Society, 1954. Reprinted in *Majmūʿa-yi āthār-i Abū ʿAbd al-Raḥmān al-Sulamī*, vol. 2, edited by Nasrullāh Pūrjavādī. Tehran: Markaz-i Nashr-i Dānishgāh, 1369 sh. [1990].
——. *K. al-arbaʿīn fī 'l-taṣawwuf*. Hyderabad: Dāʾirat al-Maʿārif al-ʿUthmāniyya, 1950.
——. *K. bayān zalal al-fuqarāʾ wa-l-ādābihim*. Edited by Süleyman Ateş in *Tisʿa kutub fī uṣūl al-taṣawwuf wa-l-zuhd*. Beirut: al-Nāshir li-Ṭibāʿa wa-l-Nashr al-Tawzīʿ wa-l-Iʿlān, 1993. Translated by Kenneth L. Honerkamp as "The Stumblings of Those Aspiring and the Conduct Required of Them." In *Three Early Sufi Texts*, edited and translated by idem. Louisville, KY: Fons Vitae, 2003.
——. *K. al-futuwwa*. Edited by Süleyman Ateş. Ankara: n.p. 1977. Reprinted in *Majmūʿa-yi āthār-i Abū ʿAbd al-Raḥmān al-Sulamī*, vol. 2, edited by Nasrullāh Pūrjavādī. Tehran: Markaz-i Nashr-i Dānishgāh, 1369 sh. [1990].
——. *K. nasīm al-arwāḥ*. Edited by Nasrullāh Pūrjavādī in "Dū risāla dar samāʿ." *Maʿārif* 5.3 (1367 sh. [1989]): 67–78. Reprinted in *Majmūʿa-yi āthār-i Abū ʿAbd al-Raḥmān al-Sulamī*, vol. 2, edited by idem. Tehran: Markaz-i Nashr-i Dānishgāh, 1369 sh. [1990].
——. *K. al-samāʿ*. Edited by Nasrullāh Pūrjavādī in *Majmūʿa-yi āthār-i Abū ʿAbd al-Raḥmān al-Sulamī*, vol. 2, edited by idem. Tehran: Markaz-i Nashr-i Dānishgāh, 1369 sh. [1990].
——. *K. sulūk al-ʿārifīn*. Edited by Süleyman Ateş in *Tisʿa kutub fī uṣūl al-taṣawwuf wa-l-zuhd*. Beirut: al-Nāshir li-Ṭibāʿa wa-l-Nashr al-Tawzīʿ wa-l-Iʿlān, 1993.
——. *Manāhij al-ʿārifīn*. Edited by Etan Kohlberg as "*Manāhij al-ʿĀrifīn*: A Treatise on Ṣūfism by Abū ʿAbd al-Raḥmān al-Sulamī." *Jerusalem Studies in Arabic and Islam* 1 (1979): 19–39.
——. *Masʾalat ṣifāt al-dhākirīn wa-l-mutaffakirīn*. Edited by Abū Maḥfūẓ al-Karīm Maʿṣūdī in *Majallat al-majmaʿ al-ʿilmī al-hindī* 7 (1982). Reprinted in *Majmūʿa-yi āthār-i Abū ʿAbd al-Raḥmān al-Sulamī*, vol. 2, edited by idem. Tehran: Markaz-i Nashr-i Dānishgāh, 1369 sh. [1990].
——. *al-Muqaddimat fī 'l-taṣawwuf*. Edited by Yūsuf Zaydān. Beirut: Dār al-Jīl, 1999.
——. *R. fī 'l-malāmatiyya*. Edited by Abū 'l-ʿAlāʾ ʿAfīfī in *al-Malāmatiyya wa-l-ṣūfiyya wa-ahl al-futuwwa*. Cairo: Dār Iḥyāʾ al-Kutub al-ʿArabiyya, 1945.
——. *Ṭabaqāt al-ṣūfiyya* [+*Dhikr al-niswat al-mutaʿabbidāt al-ṣūfiyyāt*]. Edited by Muṣṭafā ʿAbd al-Qādir ʿAṭāʾ. Beirut: Dār al-Kutub al-ʿIlmiyya, 1998. Updated edition of the Arabic text of *Dhikr al-niswa* and English translation by Rkia E. Cornell as *Early Sufi Women*. Louisville, KY: Fons Vitae, 1999.
——. *Uṣūl al-malāmatiyya wa-ghalaṭāt al-ṣūfiyya*. Edited by ʿAbd al-Fattāḥ Aḥmad al-Fāwī Maḥmūd. Cairo: Maṭbaʿat al-Irshād, 1975.

al-Tādifī, Yaḥyā. *Necklaces of Gems: A Biography of the Crown of the Saints, ʿAbd al-Qadir al-Jilani (Qalāʾid al-jawāhir fī manāqib ʿAbd al-Qādir)*. Translated by Muhtar Holland. Fort Lauderdale, FL: Al-Baz Publishing, 1998.

al-Tahānawī, Muḥammad. *Khashshāf al-iṣṭilāḥāt al-funūn* (*A Dictionary of Technical Terms used in the Sciences of the Musalmans*). 2 vols. Edited by Muḥammad Wajīh, ʿAbd al-Ḥaqq and Ghulām Qādir under the superintendence of A. Sprenger and W. Nassau Lees. Calcutta: Asiatic Society of Bengal, 1862; Reprint: Istanbul: n.p., 1984.

Tashköpruzāde. *Miftāḥ al-saʿāda wa-maṣābiḥ al-siyāda*. 4 vols. Edited by Kāmil Kāmil Bakrī and ʿAbd al-Wahhāb Abū ʾl-Nūr. Cairo: Dār al-Kutub al-Ḥadītha, 1968.

al-ʿUmarī, Shihāb al-Dīn. *Masālik al-abṣār fī mamālik al-amṣār*. Vol. 8, *al-Sifr al-thāmin fī tawāʾif al-fuqahāʾ wa-l-ṣūfiyya*. Edited by Basām Muḥammad Bārūd. Abu Dhabi: al-Majmaʿ al-Thaqāfī, 2001.

Wafāt al-Suhrawardī. MS. Süley., Fatih 2742_2, fol. 322a–322b.

al-Wāsiṭī, Taqī al-Dīn ʿAbd al-Raḥmān. *Tiryāq al-muḥibbīn fī ṭabaqāt khirqat al-mashāyikh al-ʿārifīn* (*K. ṭabaqāt khirqat al-ṣūfiyya*). Cairo: al-Maṭbaʿat al-Bahiyya al-Miṣriyya, 1304 [1887].

W. Abī Ḥanīfa. [s.v. Watt].

Watt, William Montgomery. *Islamic Creeds: A Selection*. Edinburgh: Edinburgh University Press, 1994.

al-Yāfiʿī, ʿAfīf al-Dīn Abū ʿAbdullāh b. Asʿad. *Mirʾāt al-jinān wa-ʿibrat al-yaqẓān*. 4 vols. Hyderabad: Dāʾirat al-Maʿārif al-Niẓāmiyya, 1918.

Yāqūt al-Rūmī, Abū ʿAbd Allāh. *Irshād al-arīb ilā maʿrifat al-adīb* (*Muʿjam al-udabāʾ*). Gibb Memorial Series, vol. 6.1–3/5–6. Edited by D.S. Margolioth. E.J. Brill: Leiden-London, 1907–1927.

——. *Muʿjam al-buldān* (*Jacut's Geographisches Wörterbuch*). 6 vols. Edited by Ferdinand Wüstenfeld. Leipzeig: In Commission bei F.A. Brockhaus, 1866–1873.

al-Yazdī, Muʿīn al-Dīn. *Rashf al-naṣāʾiḥ al-īmāniyya wa-kashf al-faḍāʾiḥ al-yūnāniyya*. Edited by Najīb Māyil Heravī. Tehran: Chap va Nashr-i Būnyād, 1365 sh. [1986].

Zarkūb-i Shīrāzī, Aḥmad. *Shīrāz-nāma*. Edited by Bahman-i Karīmī. Tehran: Intishārāt-i Būnyād-i Farhang-i Īrān, 1350 sh. [1972].

al-Zarnūjī, Burhān al-Dīn al-Ḥanafī. *Taʿlīm al-Mutaʿallim—Ṭarīq al-Taʿallum (Instruction of the Student: The Method of Learning)*. Translated by G.E. von Grunebaum and Theodora Abel. New York: King's Crown Press, 1947.

Secondary Sources

Addas, Claude. *Quest for the Red Sulphur: The Life of Ibn ʿArabī*. Translated by Peter Kingsley. Cambridge, UK: The Islamic Texts Society, 1993.

Ahmed, Shahab. "Review of *A Learned Society in a Period of Transition*, by Daphna Ephrat." *JAOS* 123.1 (2003): 179–182.

Anawati, Georges and Louis Gardet. *Mystique musulmane: aspects et tendences, expériences et techniques*. 4th revised edition. Etudes musulmanes, no. 8. Paris: J. Vrin, 1986.

Anṣārī, Qāsim. [s.v. Iṣfahānī, Ismāʿīl Māshāda].

Arberry, A.J. "The Teachers of Shihāb al-Dīn ʿUmar al-Suhrawardī." *BSOAS* 13 (1950): 339–356.

——. *Sufism: An Account of the Mystics of Islam*. London: George Allen & Unwin, Ltd., 1950.

Asad, Talal. *The Idea of an Anthropology of Islam*. Washington, D.C.: Center for Contemporary Arab Studies, Georgetown University, 1986.

Awn, Peter J. *Satan's Tragedy and Redemption: Iblīs in Sufi Psychology*. Studies in the History of Religions (Supplements to *Numen*), no. XLIV. Leiden: E.J. Brill, 1983.

Babayan, Kathryn. *Mystics, Monarchs, and Messiahs: Cultural Landscapes of Early Modern Iran*. Harvard Middle East Monographs, no. 35. Cambridge, MA: Harvard University Press, 2002.

Badeen, Edward. [s.v. al-Bidlīsī].
Baldick, Julian. *Mystical Islam: An Introduction to Sufism*. London: I.B. Tauris, 1989.
Bannerth, Ernest. "Dhikr et khalwa d'après Ibn ʿAṭāʾ Allāh." *MIDEO* 12 (1974): 65–90.
Barthold, W. (Vasilij Vladimorovič Bartol'd). *An Historical Geography of Iran*. Translated by Svat Soucek and edited with an introduction by C.E. Bosworth. Princeton: Princeton University Press, 1984.
——. *Four Studies on Central Asia*. Translated by V. Minorsky. Leyden: E.J. Brill, 1956.
Bayram, Mikâil. *Şeyh Evhadü'd-din Hâmid el-Kirmânî ve Evhadiyye Tarikatı*. Konya: Damla Matbaacılık ve Ticaret, 1993.
de Beaurecueil, S. de Laugier. "Le retour à Dieu (*tawba*): élément essential de la conversion, selon ʿAbdullāh Anṣārī." *MIDEO* 6 [1961]: 55–122.
Berkey, Jonathan. *The Transmission of Knowledge in Medieval Cairo: A Social History of Islamic Education*. Princeton: Princeton University Press, 1992.
Black, Anthony. *The History of Islamic Political Thought*. New York: Routledge, 2001.
Bonner, Michael. *Aristocratic Violence and Holy War*. New Haven, CT: American Oriental Society, 1996.
Bosworth, Clifford Edmund. *The New Islamic Dynasties: A Chronological and Genealogical Manual*. New York: Columbia University Press, 1996.
——. "The Rise of the Karrāmiyya in Khurāsān." *Muslim World* (1960): 5–14.
Boullata, Issa. "Toward a Biography of Ibn al-Fāriḍ." *Arabica* 38.1 (1981): 38–56.
Breebaart, Deodaat. "The Development and Structure of the Turkish Futūwah Guilds." Ph.D. diss., Princeton University, 1961.
Brockelmann, Carl. *Geschichte der arabischen Litteratur*. 2nd edition. 2 vols. Leiden: E.J. Brill, 1943–1949. Supplement. 3 vols. Leiden: E.J. Brill, 1937–1942.
Browne, Edward Granville. *A Literary History of Persia*. 4 vols. Cambridge: Cambridge University Press, 1902–1924.
Buehler, Arthur. *Sufi Heirs of the Prophet: The Indian Naqshbandiyya and the Rise of the Mediating Sufi Shaykh*. Columbia: University of South Carolina Press, 1998.
Bulliet, Richard. *The Patricians of Nishapur: A Study in Medieval Islamic Social History*. Cambridge, MA: Harvard University Press, 1972.
Cahen, Claude. *The Formation of Turkey: The Seljukid Sultanate of Rūm, Eleventh to Fourteenth Century*. Translated and Edited by P.M. Holt. London: Longman, 2001.
——. "Mouvements populaires et autonomisme urbain dans l'Asie musulmane du Moyen Âge." *Arabica* 5 (1958): 225–250; 6 (1959): 25–56, 233–265. Reprint, Leiden: E.J. Brill, 1959.
——. "Notes sur les débuts de la futuwwa d'al-Nāṣir." *Oriens* 6 (1953): 18–23.
——. "Sur les traces des premiers Akhis." In *Mélanges Fuad Köprülü*. Istanbul: Osman Yalçın Matbaası, 1953.
Çağatay, Neş'et. "Fütüvvet-Ahi Müessesesinin Menşi Meselesi." *Ankara Üniversitesi İlâhiyat Fakültesi Dergisi* 1 (1952): 59–84, 1.2–3 (1952): 61–84.
Carra de Vaux, Bernard. *Les penseurs de l'islam*. 5 vols. Paris: Librairie Paul Geuthner, 1923.
Chabbi, Jacqueline. "La fonction du ribat à Bagdad de Ve siècle au début du VIIe siècle." *REI* 42 (1974): 101–121.
——. "ʿAbd al-Ḳādir al-Djīlānī, personnage historique." *StI* 38 (1973): 61–74.
Chamberlain, Michael. *Knowledge and Social Practice in Medieval Damascus, 1190–1350*. Cambridge: Cambridge University Press, 1994.
Chittick, William. *The Self-Disclosure of God: Principles of Ibn al-ʿArabī's Cosmology*. Albany: State University of New York Press, 1988.
Cornell, Vincent. *Realm of the Saint: Power and Authority in Moroccan Sufism*. Austin: University of Texas Press, 1998.
Currie, P.M. *The Shrine and Cult of Muʿīn al-Dīn Chishtī of Ajmer*. Delhi: Oxford University Press, 1989.
Dabashi, Hamid. *Truth and Narrative: The Untimely Thoughts of ʿAyn al-Quḍāt al-Hamadhānī*. Surrey, Richmond: Curzon Press, 1999.

Dā'irat al-ma'ārif-i buzurg-i islāmī. 13 vols. to date. Edited by Kāẓim Mūsavī Bujnūrdī, et al. Tehran: Markaz-i Dā'irat al-Ma'ārif-i Buzurg-i Islāmī, 1367– sh. [1988–].

De Jong, Frederick. *Sufi Orders in Ottoman and post-Ottoman Egypt and the Middle East: Collected Studies.* Istanbul: Isis Press, 2000.

Demeerseman, André. *Nouveau regard sur la voie spirituelle d' 'Abd al-Qadir al-Jilani et sa tradition.* Études musulmanes, no. 30. Paris: J. Vrin, 1988.

Dozy, Reinhart Pieter Anne. *Dictionnaire détaillé des noms des vêtements chez les arabes.* Amsterdam: Jean Müller, 1845. Reprint, Beirut: Librairie du Liban, n.d.

During, Jean. *Musique et extase: l'audition spirituelle dans la tradition soufie.* Paris: Albin Michel, 1988.

Düzenli, Yaşar. [s.v. al-Suhrawardī, Abū Ḥafṣ 'Umar].

Ehrenkreutz, Andrew S. *Saladin.* Albany: State University of New York Press, 1972.

Elias, Jamal. "The Sufi Robe (Khirqa) as a Vehicle of Spiritual Authority." In Gordon Stewart, ed., *Robes of Honor: The Medieval World of Investiture.* New York: Palgrave, 2001.

——. *The Throne Carrier of God: The Life and Thought of 'Alā' ad-Dawla as-Simnānī.* Albany, NY: State University of New York Press, 1995.

Ellis, A.G. and E. Edwards. *A Descriptive List of the Arabic Manuscripts Acquired by the Trustees of the British Museum Since 1894.* London: The British Museum, 1912.

Encyclopaedia Iranica. 13 vols. to date. Edited by Ehsan Yarshater. London, Boston, Costa Mesa, CA, and New York: Routledge and Kegan Paul, Mazda, Encyclopaedia Iranica Foundation, 1982–.

The Encyclopaedia of Islam. 4 vols., incl. supp. Leiden and London: E.J. Brill, Ltd. and Luzac & Co., 1913–1938. Reprint as *E.J. Brill's First Encyclopaedia of Islam.* 9 vols. Leiden: E.J. Brill, 1993.

The Encyclopaedia of Islam, New Edition. 12 vols., incl. supp. Leiden: E.J. Brill, 1954–2004.

Ephrat, Daphna. *A Learned Society in a Period of Transition: The Sunni 'Ulama' of Eleventh Century Baghdad.* Albany, NY: State University of New York Press, 2000.

Ernst, Carl. *Eternal Garden: Mysticism, History, and Politics at a South Asian Sufi Center.* 2nd edition. New Delhi: Oxford University Press, 2004.

"Between Orientalism and Fundamentalism: Problematizing the Teaching of Sufism." In *Teaching Islam*, edited by Brannon Wheeler. New York: Oxford University Press, 2003.

——. *The Shambhala Guide to Sufism.* Boston & London: Shambhala, 1997.

——. *Words of Ecstasy in Sufism.* Albany, NY: State University of New York Press, 1985.

Ernst, Carl and Bruce Lawrence. *Sufi Martyrs of Love: The Chishti Order in South Asia and Beyond.* New York: Palgrave Macmillan, 2002.

van Ess, Joseph. *Theologie und Gesellschaft im 2. und 3. Jahrhundert Hidschra: Eine Geshichte des religiösen Denkens im frühen Islam.* 6 vols. Berlin: Walter de Gruyter, 1991–1997.

Fakhry, Majid. *A History of Islamic Philosophy.* 2nd edition. New York: Columbia University Press, 1983.

Fernandes, Leonor. *The Evolution of a Sufi Institution in Mamluk Egypt: The Khanqah.* Islamkundliche Untersuchungen, no. 134. Berlin: Klaus Schwarz Verlag, 1988.

Flügel, Gustav. *Die arabischen, persischen und türkischen Handschriften der Kaiserlich-Königlichen Hofbibliothek zu Wien.* 3 vols. Vienna: K.K. Hof- und Staatsdruckerei, 1865–1867.

Gardet, Louis. *Les Grandes problèmes de la théologie musulmane: Dieu et la destinée de l'homme.* Études musulmans, no. 9. Paris: J. Vrin, 1967.

Geoffroy, Eric. *Djihad et contemplation: vie et enseignement d'un soufi au temps des croisades.* Paris: Éditions Dervy, 1997.

——. *Le soufisme en Égypte et Syrie sous les derniers Mamlouks et les premiers Ottomans.* Damascus: Institut Français de Damas, 1995.

Gibb, H.A.R. *The Life of Saladin: From the Works of 'Imād ad-Dīn and Bahā' ad-Dīn*. Oxford: Oxford University Press, 1973.

——. *Studies on the Civilization of Islam*. Edited by S.J. Shaw and W.R. Polk. Boston: Beacon Press, 1962.

Goldziher, Ignaz. *Introduction to Islamic Theology and Law*. Translated by Andras and Ruth Hamori. Princeton: Princeton University Press, 1981.

Gottschalk, Hans L. *Al-Malik al-Kāmil von Egypten und seine Zeit; eine Studie zur Geschichte Vorderasiens und Egyptens in der ersten Hälfte des 7./13. Jahrhunderts*. Wiesbaden: Otto Harrassowitz, 1958.

Gramlich, Richard. *Alte Vorbilder des Sufitums*. 2 vols. Wiesbaden: Otto Harrassowitz, 1995–1996.

——. *Die Wunder der Freunde Gottes: Theologien und Erscheinungsformen des islamischen Heiligenwunders*. Freiburger Islamstudien, no. 11. Wiesbaden: Franz Steiner Verlag, 1987.

——. *Die schiitischen Derwischorden Persiens*. 3 vols. Abhandlungen für die Kunde des Morgenlandes, Bd. 36.1–2 and 45.2. Wiesbaden: Franz Steiner Verlag, 1965–1981.

——. "Vom islamischen Glauben an die 'gute alte Zeit'." In *Islamwissenschaftliche Abhandlungen Fritz Meier zum 60. Geburtstag*, edited by idem. Wiesbaden: Steinwi, 1974.

Gürer, Dilâver. *Abdülkâdir Geylânî: Hayatı, Eserleri, Görüşleri*. Istanbul: İnsan Yayınları, 1999.

Halm, Heinz. "Der Wesir al-Kunduri und die Fitna von Nishapur." *Welt des Orients* 6.2 (1971): 205–233.

Hartmann, Angelika. "Wollte der Kalif Ṣūfī werden? Amtstheorie und Abdankungspläne des Kalifen an-Nāṣir li-Dīn Allāh (reg. 1180–1225)." In *Egypt and Syria in the Fatimid, Ayyubid and Mamluk Eras*, Orientalia Lovaniensia analecta, no. 73. Edited by U. Vermeulen and D. de Smet. Leuven: Uitgeverij Peeters, 1995.

——. "Kosmogonie und Seelenlehre bei 'Umar as-Suhrawardi (st. 632/1234)." In *Gedenkschrift Wolfgang Reuschel: Akten des III. Arabistischen Kolloquiums, Leipzig 21.–22. November 1991*. Stuttgart: Franz Steiner Verlag, 1994.

——. "Cosmogonie et doctrine de l'âme dans l'oeuvre tardive de 'Umar as-Suhrawardi." *Quaderni di Studi Arabi* 11 (1993): 1–16.

——. "Sur l'édition d'un texte arabe médiéval: Le Rašf an-naṣā'iḥ al-īmānīya wa-kašf al-faḍā'iḥ al-yūnānīya de 'Umar as-Suhrawardī, composé à Baghdad en 621/1224." *Der Islam* 62 (1985): 71–97.

——. "Bemerkungen zu Handschriften 'Umar as-Suhrawardīs, echten und vermeintlichen Autographen." *Der Islam* 60 (1983): 112–142.

——. "Eine orthodoxe Polemik gegen Philosophen und Freidenker—ein zeitgenössiche Schrift gegen Ḥāfiẓ?" *Der Islam* 56.2 (1979): 274–293.

——. *An-Nāṣir li-Dīn Allāh (1180–1225). Politik, Religion, Kultur in der späten 'Abbāsidenzeit.* Studien zur Sprache, Geschichte und Kultur des islamischen Orients, n.F, Bd. 8. Berlin and New York: Walter de Gruyter, 1975.

——. "La conception governementale du calife an-Nāṣir li-Dīn Allāh." *Orientalia Suecana* 22 (1973): 52–61.

Heravī, Najīb Māyel. "Tarjama-yi 'Awārif al-ma'ārif." *Nashr-i Dānish* 6 (1364 sh. [1985–1986]): 114–120.

Hillenbrand, Carole. "Islamic Orthodoxy or Realpolitik? Al-Ghazālī's Views on Government." *Iran* 26 (1988): 81–94.

Hirtenstein, Stephen. *The Unlimited Mercifier: The Spiritual Life and Thought of Ibn 'Arabī*. Oxford: Anqa Publishing, 1999.

Herzfeld, Ernst. "Damascus: Studies in Architecture—I." *Ars Islamica* 9 (1942): 1–53.

Hodgson, Marshall G.S. *The Venture of Islam: Conscience and History in a World Civilization*. 3 vols. Chicago: University of Chicago Press, 1974.

Holt, P.M. *The Age of the Crusades: The Near East from the Eleventh Century to 1517*. London: Logman, 1986.

Homerin, Th. Emil. *From Arab Poet to Muslim Saint: Ibn al-Fāriḍ, His Verse and His Shrine.* Columbia, SC: University of South Carolina Press, 1994.

——. "ʿUmar ibn al-Fāriḍ, A Saint of Mamluk and Ottoman Egypt." In *Manifestations of Sainthood in Islam*, edited by Grace Martin Smith and Carl W. Ernst. Istanbul: The Isis Press, 1987.

Humāʾī, Jalāl al-Dīn. [s.v. Kāshānī].

Humphreys, R. Stephen. *From Saladin to the Mongols: The Ayyubids of Damascus, 1193–1260.* Albany: State University of New York Press, 1977.

Ibish, Yusuf. *The Political Doctrine of al-Baqillani.* Beirut: American University of Beirut Press, 1966.

ʿIrāqī, Aḥmad Ṭāhirī. [s.v., al-Suhrawardī, Abū Ḥafṣ ʿUmar].

Jawād, Muṣṭafā. "al-Rubuṭ al-baghdādiyya." *Sumer* 10 (1954): 218–249.

Kaḥḥāla, ʿUmar Riḍā. *Muʿjam al-muʾallifīn.* 15 vols. Damascus: al-Maktabat al-ʿArabiyya, 1957–1961.

Karamustafa, Ahmet. *God's Unruly Friends: Dervish Groups in the Islamic Later Middle Period, 1200–1550.* Salt Lake City: University of Utah Press, 1994.

Khouri, Raif. "Importance et authenticité des textes de Ḥilyat al-awliyāʾ wa-ṭabaqāt al-aṣfiyāʾ d'Abū Nuʿaym al-Iṣbahānī." *StI* 26 (1977):73–113.

King, Richard. *Orientalism and Religion: Postcolonial Theory, India and 'The Mystic East'.* London and New York: Routledge, 1999.

Kissling, Hans Joachim. "Aus der Geschichte des Chalvetijje-Ordens." *ZDMG* 103 (1953): 233–289.

Kiyānī, Muḥsin. *Tārīkh-i khānaqāh dar Īrān.* Tehran: Kitābkhāna-yi Ṭahūrī, 1369 sh. [1990].

Knysh, Alexander. *Islamic Mysticism: A Short History.* Themes in Islamic Studies, no. 1. Leiden: Brill, 2000.

——. *Ibn ʿArabi in the Later Islamic Tradition: The Making of a Polemical Image in Medieval Islam.* Albany, NY: State University of New York Press, 1999.

Lambton, A.K.S. *State and Government in Medieval Islam: An Introduction to the Study of Islamic Political Theory.* Oxford: Oxford University Press, 1981.

——. "Justice in the Medieval Persian Theory of Kingship." *StI* 17 (1962): 91–119.

——. "*Quis Custodiet Custodes*: Some Reflections on the Persian Theory of Government." *StI* 5 (1956): 125–148; 6 (1956): 125–146.

Laoust, Henri. "Le pensée et l'action politiques d'al-Māwardī (364–450/974–1058)." *REI* 36 (1968): 11–92.

——. *La profession de foi d'Ibn Baṭṭa.* Damascus: Institut Français de Damas, 1958.

Le Gall, Dina. *A Culture of Sufism: Naqshbandīs in the Ottoman World, 1450–1700.* Albany: State University of New York Press, 2005.

Le Strange, Guy. *The Lands of the Eastern Caliphate: Mesopotamia, Persia, and Central Asia from the Moslem Conquest to the Time of Timur.* 2nd edition. Cambridge: Cambridge University Press, 1930.

Leaman, Oliver. *An Introduction to Classical Islamic Philosophy.* 2nd edition. Cambridge: Cambridge University Press, 2002.

Lewis, Bernard and P.M. Holt, eds. *Historians of the Middle East.* London: Oxford University Press, 1962.

Lewis, Frank. *Rumi: Past and Present, East and West.* Oxford: Oneworld, 2000.

Lewisohn, Leonard, ed. *The Heritage of Sufism.* 3 vols. Oxford: Oneworld Publications, 1999.

Makdisi, George. *Ibn ʿAqīl: Religion and Culture in Classical Islam.* Edinburgh: Edinburgh University Press, 1997.

——. "Baghdad, Bologna, and Scholasticism." In *Centers of Learning: Learning and Location in pre-Modern Europe and the Near East*, edited by J.W. Drijvers and A.A. MacDonald. Leiden: Brill, 1995.

——. *The Rise of Humanism in Classical Islam and the Christian West, with Special Reference to Scholasticism.* Edinburgh: Edinburgh University Press, 1990.

——. *The Rise of Colleges: Institutions of Learning in Islam and the West*. Edinburgh: Edinburgh University Press, 1981.
——. "The Sunnī Revival." In *Islamic Civilisation, 950–1150: A Colloquium Published under the Auspices of the Near Eastern History Group, Oxford—The Near East Center, University of Pennsylvania*, Papers on Islamic History, no.3. Edited by D.S. Richards. Oxford: Bruno Cassirer Ltd., 1973.
——. "Muslim Institutions of Learning in Eleventh-century Baghdad." *BSOAS* 24 (1961): 1–56.
Makdisi, George, Dominique Sourdel, and Janine Sourdel-Thomine, eds. *La notion d'autorité au Moyen Age Islam, Byzance, Occident*. Paris: Presses Universitaires de France, 1982.
Malamud, Margaret Irene. "Sufi Organization and Structures of Authority in Medieval Nishapur." *IJMES* 26 (1994): 427–442.
——. "Sufism in Twelfth-Century Baghdad: The Sufi Practices of Abu Najib al-Suhrawardi." *Bulletin of the Henry Martyn Institute of Islamic Studies* 13 (1994): 6–18.
al-Manāʿī, ʿĀʾisha Yūsuf. *Abū Ḥafṣ ʿUmar al-Suhrawardī: ḥayātuhu wa-taṣawwufuhu*. Doha, Qatar: Dār al-Thaqāfa, 1991.
Mason, Herbert. *Two Statesmen of Mediaeval Islam: Vizir Ibn Hubayra (499–560 AH / 1105–1165 AD) and caliph an-Nâṣir lî Dîn Allâh (553–622 AH / 1158–1225 AD)*. The Hague: Mouton, 1972.
Massignon, Louis. *Essay on the Origins of the Technical Language of Islamic Mysticism*. Translated by B. Clark. South Bend, IN: University of Notre Dame Press, 1997.
——. "Le "jour du covenant" (*yawm al-mīthāq*)." *Oriens* 15 (1962): 86–92.
——. "Caliphs et naqībs bagdadiens." *WZKM* 51 (1948): 106–115.
Meier, Fritz. *Essays on Islamic Piety and Mysticism*. Edited and translated by John O'Kane. Leiden: Brill, 1999.
——. "Die Herzensbindung an den Meister." In *Zwei Abhandlungen über die Naqšbandiyya*, Beiruter Texte und Studien, bd. 58. Istanbul and Stuttgart: Im Kommission bei Franz Steiner Verlag, 1994.
——. *Abū Saʿīd b. Abīʾ l-Ḫayr (357–440/967–1049): Wirklichkeit und Legende*. Acta Iranica, no.11. Leiden-Tehran-Liège: E.J. Brill, 1976.
——. *Die Fawāʾiḥ al-Ǧalāl des Naǧm ad-Dīn al-Kubrā*. Wiesbaden: Franz Steiner Verlag, 1957.
Milson, Menahem. [s.v.: al-Suhrawardī, Abū ʾl-Najīb].
Mojaddedi, Jawid A. *The Biographical Tradition in Sufism: The Ṭabaqāt Genre from al-Sulamī to Jāmī*. Richmond, Surrey: Curzon Press, 2001.
Molé, Marjian. *Les mystiques musulmans*. Paris: Presses Universitaires de France, 1965.
——. "La danse extatique en Islam." In *Les danses sacrées*, Collection Sources orientales, 6. Paris: Éditions du Seuil, 1963.
Morris, James W. "Situating Islamic 'Mysticism': Between Written Traditions and Popular Spirituality." In *Mystics of the Book: Themes, Topics, and Typologies*, edited by Robert A. Herrera. New York: Peter Lang Publishing, Inc., 1993.
Mottahedeh, Roy. "The Transmission of Learning: The Role of the Islamic Northeast." In *Madrasa: la transmission du savoir dans le monde musulman*, edited by Nicole Grandin and Marc Gaborieau. Paris: Éditions Arguments, 1997.
Nicholson, R.A. *Studies in Islamic Mysticism*. Cambridge: Cambridge University Press, 1921.
Norris, H.T. "The *Mirʾāt al-Ṭālibīn*, by Zain al-Dīn al-Khawāfī of Khurāsān and Herat." *BSOAS* 53.1 (1990): 57–63.
O'Fahey, R.S. *Enigmatic Saint: Ahmad Ibn Idris and the Idrisi Tradition*. Evanston, IL: Northwestern University Press, 1990.
Ohlander, Erik S. "K̲erqa." In *Encyclopaedia Iranica*. New York: Encyclopaedia Iranica Foundation, forthcoming.
——. "Karāma." In *Encyclopaedia Iranica*. New York: Encyclopaedia Iranica Foundation, forthcoming.

——. "Abū Ṭālib al-Makkī." In *The Encyclopaedia of Islam Three*. Leiden: Brill, forthcoming.
——. "ʿAbd al-Razzāq b. ʿAbd al-Qādir al-Jīlānī." In *The Encyclopaedia of Islam Three*. Leiden: Brill, forthcoming.
——. "Altruism." In *The Encyclopaedia of Islam Three*. Leiden: Brill, forthcoming.
——. "Primary Schools, or Kuttab." In *Medieval Islamic Civilization: An Encyclopedia*, vol. 2, edited by Josef W. Meri. New York: Routledge, Taylor & Francis Group, 2006.
——. "Review of *Divine Love in Islamic Mysticism*, by Binyamin Abrahamov." *JRAS*, series 3 13.3 (2003): 383–385.
——. "Between Historiography, Hagiography and Polemic: The 'Relationship' between Abū Ḥafṣ ʿUmar al-Suhrawardī and Ibn ʿArabī." *JMIAS* 34 (Autumn, 2003): 59–82.
Popovic, Alexandre and Gilles Veinstein, eds. *Les voies d'Allah: Les ordres mystiques dans le monde musulman des origines à aujourd'hui*. Paris: Fayard, 1996.
——. *Les ordres mystiques dans l'islam: cheminements et situation actuelle*. Paris: Éditions de l'École des Hautes Études en Sciences Sociales, 1986.
Qazvīnī, Muḥammad. [s.v. Junayd-i Shīrāzī].
Rahman, Fazlur. *Islam*. 2nd edition. Chicago: The University of Chicago Press, 1979.
Richter-Bernburg, Lutz. *Der syrische Blitz: Saladins Sekretär zwischen Selbstdarstellung und Geschichtsschreibung*. Beiruter Texte und Studien, no. 52. Beirut and Stuttgart: Orient-Institut and Franz Steiner Verlag, 1998.
Ridgeon, Lloyd. *Persian Metaphysics and Mysticism: Selected Treatises of ʿAziz Nasafī*. Richmond, Surrey: Curzon Press, 2002.
Ritter, Helmut. "Philologika IX. Die vier Suhrawardī. Ihre Werke in Stambuler Handschriften." *Der Islam* 24 (1937): 270–286; 25 (1938): 35–86.
Rizvi, Athar Abbas. *A History of Sufism in India*. 2 vols. New Delhi: Munshiram Manoharlal Publishers Pvt. Ltd., 1978–1983.
Safi, Omid. *The Politics of Knowledge in Premodern Islam: Negotiating Ideology and Religious Inquiry*. Chapel Hill: The Unversity of North Carolina Press, 2006.
Schimmel, Annemarie. *Mystical Dimensions of Islam*. Chapel Hill, NC: University of North Carolina Press, 1975.
Shams, Muḥammad Javād. "ʿĀrifān-i suhravardiyya-yi buzghushiyya-yi Fārs." *Maʿārif* 17.2 (2000): 104–116.
Shīrvānī, Muḥammad. [s.v. al-Suhrawardī, Abū Ḥafṣ ʿUmar].
Siddiqi, A.H. "Caliphate and Kingship in Medieval Persia." *Islamic Culture* 9 (1935): 560–570; 10 (1936): 97–126; 11 (1937): 37–59.
Spies, Otto. *Muʾnīs al-ʿushshāq: The Lovers' Friend by Shihābuddīn Suhrawerdī Maqtūl*. Bonner Orientalistische Studien, no. 7. Stuttgart: Kohlhammer, 1935.
Steinfels, Amina M. "The Travels and Teachings of Sayyid Jalāl al-dīn Ḥusayn Bukhārī (1308–1384)." PhD diss., Yale University, 2003.
Sublet, Jacqueline. "Le modèle arabe: éléments de vocabulaire." In *Madrasa: la transmission du savior dans le monde musulman*, edited by Nicole Grandin and Marc Gaborieau. Paris: Éditions Arguments, 1997.
Taeschner, Franz, ed. and trans. *Zünfte und Bruderschaften im Islam: Texte zur Geschichte der Futuwwa*. Zurich: Artemis Verlag, 1979.
——. "Eine Schrift des Šihābaddīn Suhrawardī über die Futūwa." *Oriens* 15 (1962): 278–280.
——. "Futuwwa, eine gemeinschaftbildende Idee im mittelalterlicher Orient und ihre verschiedene Erscheinungsforme." *Schweizerisches Archiv für Volkskunde* 52.2–3 (1956): 122–158.
Trimingham, J. Spencer. *The Sufi Orders in Islam*. Oxford: Oxford University Press, 1971; Reprint with a new preface by John Voll. Oxford: Oxford University Press, 1998.

Türkiye Diyanet Vakfi İslâm Ansiklopedisi. 31 volumes to date. Üsküdar, Istanbul: Türkiye Diyanet Vakfi, İslâm Ansiklopedisi Genel Müdürlüğü, 1988–.
Turan, Osman. *Doğu Anadolu Türk devletleri tarihi.* 2nd edition. Istanbul: Turan Nakışlar Yayınevi, 1980.
ul-Huda, Qamar. *Striving for Divine Union: Spiritual Exercises for Suhrawardī Ṣūfīs.* London and New York: RoutledgeCurzon, 2003.
——. "The Remembrance of the Prophet in Suhrawardī's *ʿAwārif al-maʿārif.*" *JIS* 12.2 (2001): 129–150.
——. "The Ṣûfî Order of Shaikh ʿAbu Hafs ʿUmar al-Suhrawardî and the Transfer of Suhrawardîyya Religious Ideology to Multan." Ph.D. diss., University of California, Los Angeles, 1998.
Vadet, Jean-Claude. "La 'Futuwwa', morale professionnelle ou morale mystique?" *REI* 46:1 (1978) 57–90.
Vajda, Georges. "De la transmission du savior dans l'islam traditionnel." *L'Arabisant (Association Français des Arabisants, Paris)* 4 (1975): 1–9.
——. "Une liste d'autorités du Calife al-Nāṣir li-dīn Allāh." *Arabica* 6 (1959): 173–177.
Vikør, Knut. *Sufi and Scholar on the Desert Edge: Muhammad b. ʿAlî al-Sanûsî.* London: Hurst & Co., 1995.
Wensinck, A.J. *Concordance et indicies de la tradition musulmane.* 8 vols. Leiden: E.J. Brill, 1936–1971.
——. *The Muslim Creed: Its Genesis and Historical Development.* Cambridge: Cambridge University Press, 1932.
Wiet, Gaston. *Baghdad: Metropolis of the Abbasid caliphate.* Translated by Seymour Feiler. Norman, Oklahoma: University of Oklahoma Press, 1971.
Yahia, Osman. *Histoire et classification de l'œuvre d'Ibn ʿArabī.* 2 vols. Damascus: Institut Français de Damas, 1964.
Yılmaz, H. Kâmil. [s.v. al-Suhrawardī, Abū Ḥafṣ ʿUmar].
Zarrīnkūb, ʿAbd al-Ḥusayn. *Justujū dar taṣavvuf-i Īrān.* Tehran: Amīr Kabīr, 1357 sh. [1978].

INDEX OF PERSONS AND PLACES

INDEX OF BOOK TITLES

INDEX OF TERMS AND CONCEPTS